WILEY PLUS

www.wileyplus.com

With **WileyPLUS**:

- Students achieve concept mastery in a rich, structured environment that's available 24/7

- Instructors personalize and manage their course more effectively with assessment, assignments, grade tracking, and more

- manage time better
- study smarter
- save money

From multiple study paths, to self-assessment, to a wealth of interactive visual and audio resources, *WileyPLUS* gives you everything you need to personalize the teaching and learning experience.

»Find out how to MAKE IT YOURS»

www.wiley**plus**.com

This online teaching and learning environment
integrates the entire digital textbook with the

ALL THE HELP, RESOURCES, AND PERSONAL SUPPORT YOU AND YOUR STUDENTS NEED!

2-Minute Tutorials and all
of the resources you & your
students need to get started
www.wileyplus.com/firstday

Student support from an
experienced student user
Ask your local representative
for details!

Collaborate with your colleagues,
find a mentor, attend virtual and live
events, and view resources
www.WhereFacultyConnect.com

Pre-loaded, ready-to-use
assignments and presentations
www.wiley.com/college/quickstart

Technical Support 24/7
FAQs, online chat,
and phone support
www.wileyplus.com/support

Your WileyPLUS
Account Manager
Training and implementation support
www.wileyplus.com/accountmanager

www.wileyplus.com

MAKE IT YOURS!

11

th edition

Organizational
Behavior

11th edition

Organizational Behavior

International
Student
Version

John R. Schermerhorn, Jr.
Ohio University

James G. Hunt
Texas Tech University

Richard N. Osborn
Wayne State University

Mary Uhl-Bien
University of Nebraska–Lincoln

John Wiley & Sons, Inc.

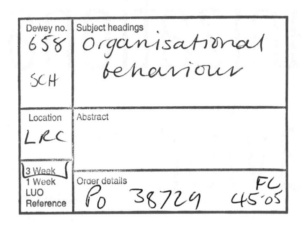
Copyright © 2011 John Wiley & Sons (Asia) Pte Ltd

Cover image from ©David S. Rose/Shutterstock

Contributing Subject Matter Expert: Sandi Dinger, Eastern University, Pennsylvania, USA

ISBN: 978-0-470-55311-4

Printed in Asia

10 9 8 7 6 5 4 3 2 1

Dr. John R. Schermerhorn, Jr. is the Charles G. O'Bleness Professor Emeritus of Management in the College of Business at Ohio University where he teaches undergraduate and MBA courses in management, organizational behavior, and Asian business. He also serves the university as Director of the Center for Southeast Asian Studies. He earned a Ph.D. in organizational behavior from Northwestern University, after receiving an M.B.A. (with distinction) in management and international business from New York University, and a B.S. in business administration from the State University of New York at Buffalo.

Dedicated to instructional excellence and serving the needs of practicing managers, Dr. Schermerhorn continually focuses on bridging the gap between the theory and practice of management in both the classroom and in his textbooks. He has won awards for teaching excellence at Tulane University, The University of Vermont, and Ohio University, where he was named a *University Professor*, the university's leading campus-wide award for undergraduate teaching. He also received the excellence in leadership award for his service as Chair of the Management Education and Development Division of the Academy of Management.

Dr. Schermerhorn's international experience adds a unique global dimension to his teaching and textbooks. He holds an honorary doctorate from the University of Pécs in Hungary, awarded for his international scholarly contributions to management research and education. He has also served as a Visiting Professor of Management at the Chinese University of Hong Kong, as on-site Coordinator of the Ohio University MBA and Executive MBA programs in Malaysia, and as Kohei Miura visiting professor at the Chubu University of Japan. Presently he is Adjunct Professor at the National University of Ireland at Galway, a member of the graduate faculty at Bangkok University in Thailand, Permanent Lecturer in the PhD program at the University of Pécs in Hungary, and advisor to the Lao-American College in Vientiane, Laos.

An enthusiastic scholar, Dr. Schermerhorn is a member of the Academy of Management, where he served as chairperson of the Management Education and Development Division. Educators and students alike know him as author of *Management 10e* (Wiley, 2010) and *Exploring Management 2e* (2010), and senior co-author of *Organizational Behavior 10/e* (Wiley, 2009). His many books are available in Chinese, Dutch, French, Indonesian, Portuguese, Russian, and Spanish language editions. Dr. Schermerhorn's published articles are found in the *Academy of Management Journal, Academy of Management Review Academy of Management Executive, Organizational Dynamics, Journal of Management Education*, and the *Journal of Management Development*.

Dr. Schermerhorn is a popular guest speaker at colleges and universities. His recent student and faculty workshop topics include innovations in business education, teaching the millennial generation, global perspectives in management education, and textbook writing and scholarly manuscript development.

Dr. John R. Schermerhorn, Jr.

Dr. James G. (Jerry) Hunt

The late ***Dr. James G. (Jerry) Hunt*** was the Paul Whitfield Horn Professor of Management, Professor of Health Organization Management, Former Director, Institute for Leadership Research, and former department chair of Management, Texas Tech University. He received his PhD and master's degrees from the University of Illinois after completing a BS (with honors) at Michigan Technological University. Dr. Hunt co-authored an organization theory text and *Core Concepts of Organizational Behavior* (Wiley, 2004) and authored or co-authored three leadership monographs. He founded the Leadership Symposia Series and co-edited the eight volumes based on the series. He was the former editor of the *Journal of Management* and *The Leadership Quarterly*. He presented or published some 200 articles, papers, and book chapters, and among his better-known books are *Leadership: A New Synthesis*, published by Sage, and *Out-of-the-Box Leadership*, published by JAI. The former was a finalist for the Academy of Management's 1993 Terry Distinguished Book Award. Dr. Hunt received the Distinguished Service Award from the Academy of Management, the Sustained Outstanding Service Award from the Southern Management Association, and the Barnie E. Rushing, Jr. Distinguished Researcher Award from Texas Tech University for his long-term contributions to management research and scholarship. He also lived and taught in England, Finland, and Thailand, and taught in China.

Dr. Richard N. Osborn

Dr. Richard N. Osborn is a Wayne State University Distinguished Professor, Professor of Management Emeritus, and former Board of Governors Faculty Fellow. He has received teaching awards at Southern Illinois University at Carbondale and Wayne State University, and he has also taught at Arizona State University, Monash University (Australia), Tulane University, University of Munich, and the University of Washington. He received a DBA from Kent State University after earning an MBA at Washington State University and a BS from Indiana University. With over 200 presentations and publications, he is a charter member of the Academy of Management Journals Hall of Fame. Dr. Osborn is a leading authority on international alliances in technology-intensive industries and is co-author of an organization theory text as well as *Basic Organizational Behavior* (John Wiley & Sons, 1995, 1998). He has served as editor of international strategy for the *Journal of World Business* and Special Issue Editor for *The Academy of Management Journal*. He serves or has served as a member of the editorial boards for *The Academy of Management Journal, The Academy of Management Review, Journal of High Technology Management, The Journal of Management, Leadership Quarterly*, and *Technology Studies*, among others. He is very active in the Academy of Management, having served as divisional program chair and president, as well as the Academy representative for the International Federation of Scholarly Associations of Management. Dr. Osborn's research has been sponsored by the Department of Defense, Ford Motor Company, National Science Foundation, Nissan, and the Nuclear Regulatory Commission, among others. In addition to teaching, Dr. Osborn spent a number of years in private industry, including a position as a senior research scientist with the Battelle Memorial Institute in Seattle, where he worked on improving the safety of commercial nuclear power.

Dr. Mary Uhl-Bien is the Howard Hawks Chair in Business Ethics and Leadership and associate Director of the Leadership Institute at the University of Nebraska-Lincoln. She earned her Ph.D. and MBA in organizational behavior at the University of Cincinnati after completing an undergraduate degree in International Business and Spanish. She teaches organizational behavior, leadership, and ethics courses at the undergraduate and graduate (MBA and doctoral) levels, and has been heavily involved in executive education, teaching to business executives and physicians in the United States, China, Europe, and Saudi Arabia and to the senior executive service of the U.S. government for The Brookings Institute in Washington, D.C. She has been a visiting professor/scholar at Pablo de Olavide University in Seville, Spain, the Universidade Nova de Lisboa/Catolica Portuguesa in Lisbon Portugal, and University Lund in Sweden.

Dr. Uhl-Bien's research interests are in leadership and followership. In addition to her conceptual work on complexity and relational leadership, some of the empirical projects she is currently involved in include investigations of "Leadership and Adaptability in the Healthcare Industry" (a $300,000 grant from Booz Allen Hamilton), "Adaptive Leadership and Innovation: A Focus on Idea Generation and Flow" (at a major financial institution in the U.S.), and "Social Constructions of Followership and Leading Up." She has published in such journals as *The Academy of Management Journal, the Journal of Applied Psychology, The Leadership Quarterly*, the *Journal of Management*, and *Human Relations*. She won the Best Paper Award in *The Leadership Quarterly* in 2001 for her co-authored article on Complex Leadership. She is on the editorial boards of *The Academy of Management Journal, The Academy of Management Review, The Leadership Quarterly, Leadership*, and *The International Journal of Complexity in Leadership and Management*, and is senior editor of the Leadership Horizons series (Information Age Publishers). Dr. Uhl-Bien has consulted with Disney, the U.S. Fish and Wildlife Service, British Petroleum, and the General Accounting Office, and served as the executive consultant for State Farm Insurance Co. from 1998–2004. She trained Russian business people for the American Russian Center at the University of Alaska Anchorage from 1993–1996, worked on a USAID grant at the Magadan Pedagogical Institute in Magadan, Russia from 1995–1996, and participated in a Fulbright-Hays grant to Mexico during the summer of 2003.

Dr. Mary Uhl-Bien

Global warming, economic turmoil, terrorism, ethnic conflict, poverty, discrimination, unemployment, illiteracy . . . these are among the many issues and problems we face as citizens today. But how often do we stop and recognize our responsibilities for problem solving and positive action in a global context? What we do today will have a lasting impact on future generations. And whether we are talking about families, communities, nations, or the organizations in which we work and volunteer, the core question remains: How can we join together to have a positive and lasting impact?

Yes, our students do have a lot to consider in the complex and ever-shifting world of today. But, we believe in them; we believe they are up to the challenge; and, we believe that courses in organizational behavior have strong roles to play in building their capabilities to make good judgments and move organizational performance forward in positive and responsible ways.

That message is a fitting place to begin *Organizational Behavior*, 11th Edition. Everyone wants to have a useful and satisfying job and career; everyone wants all the organizations of society—small and large businesses, hospitals, schools, governments, nonprofits, and more—to perform well; everyone seeks a healthy and sustainable environment. In this context the lessons of our discipline are strong and applicable. Armed with an understanding of organizational behavior, great things are possible as people work, pursue careers, and contribute to society through positive personal and organizational accomplishments.

Organizational behavior is a discipline rich with insights for career and life skills. As educators, our job is to bring to the classroom and to students the great power of knowledge, understanding, and inquiry that characterizes our discipline and its commitment to understanding human behavior in organizations. What our students do with their talents will not only shape how organizations of all types contribute to society, but also fundamentally alter lives around the globe. We must do our parts as educators to help them gain the understanding and confidence to become leaders of tomorrow's organizations.

John R. Schermerhorn Jr.
Ohio University

Richard N. Osborn
Wayne State University

Mary Uhl-Bien
University of Nebraska–Lincoln

about this book

Organizational Behavior, 11th Edition, brings to its readers the solid and complete content core of prior editions, an enriched and exciting "OB Skills Workbook," and many revisions, updates, and enhancements that reflect today's dynamic times.

Organization

The most significant change that past users will note is a rearrangement and shortening of the table of contents, as well as enhancement of online modular supplements. The book still covers the discipline in an orderly progression from individuals to groups to influence processes and leadership to organizations. But, it does so in an updated and more succinct fashion. Chapters are still written to be used out of sequence at the instructor's prerogative and to easily fit a variety of course designs.

Content

All chapters are updated to reflect new research findings and current applications and issues. For this edition, and in response to feedback, we have also rearranged chapters and adjusted both content and titles to best reflect developments and directions in the discipline as well as the realities of today's workplaces and career challenges. The major changes were made to strengthen the research component, expand and refocus the chapters dealing with individual behavior and performance, and more fully treat the emerging directions in leadership research and thinking. Look for these and other content changes to the 11th edition: Chapter 2 Individual Differences, Values, and Diversity; Chapter 9 Decision Making and Creativity; Chapter 11 Communication and Collaboration; Chapter 14 Leadership Challenges and Organizational Change; Chapter 15 Organizational Culture and Innovation; Chapter 17 Strategy, Technology, and Organizational Design. Note as well that Chapter 9 Decision Making and Creativity and Chapter 10 Conflict and Negotiation are now part of Part 3 on Teams and Teamwork. In addition to the text chapters, a module on Research Methods in OB has been placed online to offer easy ways to further enrich the course experience.

Ethics Focus

To help students anticipate, understand, and confront the ethical challenges of work and careers today we have continued our special feature in each chapter—*Ethics in OB*. This feature presents a situation or issue from an actual case or news report and asks a question of the student reader that requires personal reflection on the ethics and ethics implications. Examples include "Managers lose public trust," "Workers concerned about ethical workplace," and "MBA cheats."

Research Focus

To better communicate the timely research foundations of OB, new content has been added to the popular *Research Insights* found in each chapter. Each highlights an article from a respected journal such as the *Academy of Management Journal* and the *Journal of Applied Psychology*. Sample topics include interactional justice, racial bias, social loafing, demographic faultlines, and workplace identities. For those who want to give research a special focus in their course, we have provided an online module on Research Methods in Organizational Behavior.

Leadership Focus

To remind students that there are many positive leadership role models from alternative organizational contexts, the *Leaders on Leadership* feature offers short examples of real leaders, their experiences and perspectives. Examples include Rod Jones of Navitas, Indra Nooyi of PepsiCo, Haruka Nishimatsu of Japan Airlines, and Stelios Stavridis of Piscines Ideales.

Applications Focus

To help students apply the insights of OB to real situations and problems, *Mastering Management* boxes provide insights from real managers and organizations. Examples include "Managing emotions when times are tough," "Six points of human capital," and "How to become a networker." *OB Savvy* boxes are also interspersed to summarize major findings and applications. Examples include: "Seven steps to positive norms," "How to create a high-performing team," and "Developing your emotional intelligence."

Pedagogy

As always, our primary goal is to create a textbook that appeals to the student reader while still offering solid content. Through market research surveys and focus groups with students and professors, we continue to learn what features worked best from previous editions, what can be improved, and what can be added to accomplish this goal both effectively and efficiently. Our response is a pedagogical frame that combines popular elements from the last edition with new ones.

- **Chapter Opening**—a *Chapter at a Glance* section links *Study Topics/Learning Objectives* with an end-of-chapter Summary, and a *short opening vignette* leads the reader into chapter text.
- **Inside the Chapter**—a variety of thematic embedded boxes as previously noted—*Leaders on Leadership, Ethics in OB, Research Insight, OB Savvy,* and *Mastering Management*, highlight relevant, timely, and global themes and situations that reinforce chapter content. *Margin Photo Essays* provide further short examples highlighting events and issues. To assist with chapter study and test preparation, each chapter has a running *Margin Glossary* and *Margin List Identifiers*.
- **End of Chapter**—a *Study Guide* helps students review and test their mastery of chapter content. Key components are *Chapter Summary* (keyed to opening *Chapter at a Glance* topics). *Key Terms,* and a *Self-Test* (with multiple choice, short response, and essay questions).

The OB Skills Workbook

The end-of-text *OB Skills Workbook* has become a hallmark feature of the textbook, and it has been updated and expanded for the new edition. This edition features the Learning Style Inventory and Kouzes/Posner Student Leadership Practices Inventory. Both fit well in an OB course as opportunities for substantial student reflection and course enhancement. The five sections in the new updated workbook that offer many ways to extend the OB learning experience in creative and helpful ways are:

- Learning Style Inventory
- Student Leadership Practices Inventory
- Self-Assessment Portfolio
- Team and Experiential Exercises
- Cases for Critical Thinking

New Student and Instructor Support

Organizational Behavior, 11th Edition, is supported by a comprehensive learning package that assists the instructor in creating a motivating and enthusiastic environment.

Instructor's Resource Guide   The Instructor's Resource Guide written by Molly Pepper, Gonzaga University offers helpful teaching ideas, advice on course development, sample assignments, and chapter-by-chapter text highlights, learning objectives, lecture outlines, class exercises, lecture notes, answers to end-of-chapter material, and tips on using cases.

Test Bank   This comprehensive Test Bank written by Patricia Buhler, Goldey-Beacom College is available on the instructor portion of the Web site and consists of over 200 questions per chapter. Each chapter has true/false, multiple choice, and short answer questions. The questions are designed to vary in degree of difficulty to challenge your OB students.

The Computerized Test Bank is for use on a PC running Windows. It contains content from the Test Bank provided within a test-generating program that allows instructors to customize their exams.

PowerPoint   This robust set of lecture/interactive PowerPoints prepared by Victoria Weise, Lewis University is provided for each chapter to enhance your students' overall experience in the OB classroom. The PowerPoint slides can be accessed on the instructor portion of the Web site and include lecture notes to accompany each slide.

Web Quizzes   This online study guide with online quizzes varies in level of difficulty and is designed to help your students evaluate their individual progress through a chapter. Web quizzes are available on the student portion of the Web site. Here students will have the ability to test themselves with 15–25 questions per chapter and include true-false and multiple choice questions.

Pre- and Post-Lecture Quizzes   Included in WileyPLUS, the Pre- and Post-Lecture Quizzes written by Patricia Buhler, Goldey-Beacom College consist of 10–15 questions (multiple choice and true/false) per chapter. Varying in level of detail and difficulty, they focus on the key terms and concepts within each chapter so that professors can evaluate their students' progress from before the lecture to after it.

Companion Web Site   The text's Web site at http://www.wiley.com/go/global/schermerhorn contains myriad tools and links to aid both teaching and learning, including nearly all of the student and instructor resources.

Business Extra Select Online Courseware System   http://www.wiley.com/college/bxs. Wiley has launched this program that provides an instructor with millions of content resources from an extensive database of cases, journals, periodicals, newspapers, and supplemental readings. This courseware system lends itself extremely well to the integration of real-world content and allows instructors to convey the relevance of the course content to their students.

Videos

Lecture Launcher. Short video clips tied to the major topics in organizational behavior are available. These clips, available in WileyPLUS provide an excellent starting point for lectures or for general class discussion. Teaching notes for using the video clips written by Kasey Sheehan Madara are available on the Instructor's portion of the Web site.

WileyPLUS

WileyPLUS provides an integrated suite of teaching and learning resources, along with a complete online version of the text, in one easy-to-use Web site.

WileyPLUS will help you create class presentations, create assignments, and automate the assigning and grading of homework or quizzes, track your students' progress, and administer your course. Also includes mp3 downloads of the key chapter topics, providing students with audio module overviews, team evaluation tools, experiential exercises, student self-assessments, flashcards of key terms, and more! For more information, go to http://www.wiley.com/college/wileyplus.

Cases for Critical Thinking

Barry R. Armandi, *State University of New York*, David S. Chappell, *Ohio University*, Bernardo M. Ferdman, *Alliant International University*, Placido L. Gallegos, *Southwest Communications Resources, Inc.* and the *Kaleel Jamison Consulting Group. Inc.*, Carol Harvey, *Assumption College*, Ellen Ernst Kossek, *Michigan State University*, Barbara McCain, *Oklahoma City University*, Mary McGarry, *Empire State College*, Marc Osborn, *R&R Partners Phoenix, AZ*, Franklin Ramsoomair, *Wilfrid Laurier University*, Hal Babson and John Bowen of *Columbus State Community College*.

Experiential Exercises and Self-Assessment Inventories

Barry R. Armandi, *State University of New York, Old Westbury*, Ariel Fishman, *The Wharton School, University of Pennsylvania*, Barbara K. Goza, *University of California, Santa Cruz*, D.T. Hall, *Boston University*, F.S. Hall, *University of New Hampshire*, Lady Hanson, *California State Polytechnic University, Pomona*, Conrad N. Jackson, *MPC, Inc.*, Mary Khalili, *Oklahoma City University*, Robert Ledman, *Morehouse College*, Paul Lyons, *Frostburg State University*, J. Marcus Maier, *Chapman University*, Michael R. Manning, *New Mexico State University*, Barbara McCain, *Oklahoma City University*, Annie McKee, *The Wharton School, University of Pennsylvania*, Bonnie McNeely, *Murray State University*, W. Alan Randolph, *University of Baltimore*, Joseph Raelin, *Boston College*, Paula J. Schmidt, *New Mexico State University*, Susan Schor, *Pace University*, Timothy T. Serey, *Northern Kentucky University*, Barbara Walker, *Diversity Consultant*, Paula S. Weber, *New Mexico Highlands University*, Susan Rawson Zacur, *University of Baltimore*.

acknowledgments

Organizational Behavior, 11th Edition, benefits from insights provided by a dedicated group of management educators from around the globe who carefully read and critiqued draft chapters of this edition. We are pleased to express our appreciation to the following colleagues for their contributions to this new edition.

Richard Vaughn, *University of St. Francis*
Victoria Weise, *Lewis University*
Stacy Ball-Elias, *Southwest Minnesota State University*
Rita Bristol, *Midland Lutheran College*
Ed Tomlinson, *John Carroll University*
Larry McDaniel, *Alabama A & M University*
W. Randy Evans, *University of Arkansas, Little Rock*
Patricia M. Buhler, *Goldey-Beacom College*
Uzoamaka P. Anakwe, *Pace University*
Susan P. Eisner, *Ramapo College of New Jersey*
Gesilda R. Tolotta, *West Chester University*

We also thank those reviewers who contributed to the success of previous editions.

Merle Ace	Roosevelt Butler	Normandie Gaitley
Chi Anyansi-Archibong	Ken Butterfield	Daniel Ganster
Terry Armstrong	Joseph F. Byrnes	Joe Garcia
Leanne Atwater	Michal Cakrt	Virginia Geurin
Forrest Aven	Tom Callahan	Robert Giambatista
Steve Axley	Daniel R. Cillis	Manton Gibbs
Abdul Aziz	Nina Cole	Eugene Gomolka
Richard Babcock	Paul Collins	Barbara Goodman
David Baldridge	Ann Cowden	Stephen Gourlay
Michael Banutu-Gomez	Deborah Crown	Frederick Greene
Robert Barbato	Roger A. Dean	Richard Grover
Richard Barrett	Robert Delprino	Bengt Gustafsson
Nancy Bartell	Emmeline De Pillis	Peter Gustavson
Anna Bavetta	Pam Dobies	Lady Alice Hanson
Robb Bay	Delf Dodge	Don Hantula
Hrach Bedrosian	Dennis Duchon	Kristi Harrison
Bonnie Betters-Reed	Michael Dumler	William Hart
Gerald Biberman	Ken Eastman	Nell Hartley
Melinda Blackman	Norb Elbert	Neil J. Humphreys
Lisa Bleich	Theresa Feener	David Hunt
Mauritz Blonder	Janice M. Feldbauer	Eugene Hunt
Dale Blount	Claudia Ferrante	Howard Kahn
G. B. Bohn	Mark Fichman	Harriet Kandelman
William Bommer	Dalmar Fisher	Paul N. Keaton
H. Michal Boyd	J. Benjamin Forbes	Andrew Klein
Pat Buhler	Dean Frear	Leslie Korb
Gene E. Burton	Cynthia V. Fukami	Peter Kreiner

Eric Lamm	Edward B. Parks	Shanthi Srinivas
Donald Lantham	Robert F. Pearse	Paul L. Starkey
Jim Lessner	Lawrence Peters	Robert Steel
Les Lewchuk	Prudence Pollard	Ronni Stephens
Kristi M. Lewis	Joseph Porac	Ron Stone
Robert Liden	Samuel Rabinowitz	Tom Thompson
Beverly Linnell	Franklin Ramsoomair	Ed Tomlinson
Kathy Lippert	Clint Relyea	Sharon Tucker
Michael London	Bobby Remington	Nicholas Twigg
Michael Lounsbury	Charles L. Roegiers	Tony Urban
Carol Lucchesi	Steven Ross	Ted Valvoda
David Luther	Joel Rudin	Joyce Vincelette
Lorna Martin	Michael Rush	David Vollrath
Tom Mayes	Robert Salitore	Andy Wagstaff
Daniel McAllister	Terri Scandura	W. Fran Waller
Douglas McCabe	Mel Schnake	Charles Wankel
James McFillen	Holly Schroth	Edward Ward
Jeanne McNett	L. David Schuelke	Fred A. Ware, Jr.
Charles Milton	Richard J. Sebastian	Andrea F. Warfield
Herff L. Moore	Anson Seers	Harry Waters, Jr.
David Morand	William Sharbrough	Joseph W. Weiss
David Morean	R. Murray Sharp	Deborah Wells
Sandra Morgan	Ted Shore	Robert Whitcomb
Paula Morrow	Allen N. Shub	Donald White
Richard Mowday	Sidney Siegal	Bobbie Williams
Christopher Neck	Dayle Smith	Barry L. Wisdom
Linda Neider	Mary Alice Smith	Wayne Wormley
Judy C. Nixon	Walter W. Smock	Barry Wright
Regina O'Neill	Pat Sniderman	Kimberly Young
Dennis Pappas	Ritch L. Sorenson	Raymond Zammuto

We are grateful for all the hard work of the supplements authors, who worked to develop the comprehensive ancillary package described above. We thank Molly Pepper for preparing the Instructor's Resource Guide, Patricia Buhler for creating the Test Bank, Patricia Buhler for creating the web quizzes, Victoria Weise for developing the PowerPoint Presentations, Patricia Buhler for developing the Pre- and Post-Lecture quizzes, and Kasey Sheehan Madara for writing the scripts for the mp3 summaries. We'd also like to thank Robert (Lenie) Holbrook of Ohio University for his insightful creativity in putting together the *Art Imitates Life* guide.

As always, the support staff at John Wiley & Sons was most helpful in the various stages of developing and producing this edition. We would especially like to thank Lisé Johnson (Acquisitions Editor), George Hoffman (Publisher), Susan McLaughlin (Development Editor), Carissa Marker Doshi (Associate Editor), and Sarah Vernon (Senior Editorial Assistant) for their extraordinary efforts in support of this project. They took OB to heart and did their very best to build a high-performance team in support of this book. We thank everyone at Wiley for maintaining the quest for quality and timeliness in all aspects of the book's content and design. Special gratitude goes to Maddy Lesure as the creative force behind the new design. We also thank Sandra Dumas, and Ingrao Associates for their excellent production and design assistance, Allie Morris for overseeing the media development, and Amy Scholz for leading the marketing campaign. Thank you everyone!!

brief contents

contents

11th edition

Organizational Behavior

1

Introducing Organizational Behavior

chapter at a glance

People in all of their rich diversity are the basic build-ing blocks of organizations. The field of organizational behavior offers many insights on managing individuals and teams for high performance. Here's what to look for in Chapter 1. Don't forget to check your learning with the Summary Questions & Answers and Self-Test in the end-of-chapter Study Guide.

WHAT IS ORGANIZATIONAL BEHAVIOR AND WHY IS IT IMPORTANT?

Importance of Organizational Behavior

Scientific Foundations of Organizational Behavior

Shifting Paradigms of Organizational Behavior

WHAT ARE ORGANIZATIONS LIKE AS WORK SETTINGS?

Organizational Purpose, Mission, and Strategy

Organizational Environments and Stakeholders

Organizational Cultures

Diversity and Multiculturalism

WHAT IS THE NATURE OF MANAGERIAL WORK?

The Management Process

Managerial Activities, Roles, and Networks

Managerial Skills and Competencies

Moral Management

HOW DO WE LEARN ABOUT ORGANIZATIONAL BEHAVIOR?

Learning and Experience

Learning Styles

Learning Guide to *Organizational Behavior 11/E*

Organizational **Behavior**
OB

E

ach year the Great Place to Work Institute surveys companies from four major regions of the world. In Europe alone, approximately 1300 organizations in 16 European countries participated in the 2009 survey which equates to roughly 1.1 million employees.[1]

Companies are evaluated on numerous dimensions including credibility, respect, fairness, pride, and camaraderie. In essence, the Institute defines a great place to work as, "an organization whose employees trust the people they work for, have pride in what they do, and enjoy the people they work with."[1]

Microsoft won the Best Large Workplace in Europe 2009 Award which is the second year in running. Local offices in 16 countries also submitted applications for their nation's own top lists; impressively each office made the top 100 and six offices—Belgium, Ireland, Netherlands, Norway, Portugal and Spain—nabbed the top slot on their national list.

"People are at the heart of business, and a highly skilled, motivated, and passionate team is critical for success. Investing in people and creating a work environment that utilizes the latest technology has enabled staff to transform the way they work and interact with colleagues, delivering a strong work-life balance and a highly motivated and empowered team," **said Jean-Philippe Courtois, President, Microsoft International, senior vice president**.[1]

There is a pronounced human side to this technical company where employees are hired foremost for "foundational competencies" that consist of "confidence, cross-boundary collaboration, impact and influence, and interpersonal awareness." It's about hiring the right type of person from the start and then making them feel comfortable and valued.

Microsoft's training programs build knowledge and skills necessary for high performance on the job while numerous service programs encourage work-life balance and community involvement. This combined approach helps ensure each individual reaches their full potential—as an employee and as a human being.

microsoft europe: people first is winning formula

Introducing Organizational Behavior

As the opening case illustrates, companies that value individuals and teams experience success. Microsoft Europe's success translates into revenue, long-term sustainability as an organization, and satisfied, high performing employees and teams. As evidenced by the awards it has received, Microsoft Europe understands the importance of putting its employees first, providing them with the necessary tools and a healthy work environment that means success for employee and organization alike.

Whether your career unfolds in entrepreneurship, corporate enterprise, public service, or any other occupational setting, it is always worth remembering that people are the basic building blocks of organizational success. Organizations do well when the people in them work hard to achieve high performance as individuals and as members of teams. Creating success in and by organizations, therefore, requires respect for everyone's needs, talents, and aspirations, as well as an understanding of the dynamics of human behavior in organizational systems.

This book is about people, everyday people like you and like us, who work and pursue careers in today's new and highly demanding settings. It is about people who seek fulfillment in their lives and jobs in a variety of ways and in uncertain times. It is about the challenges of ethics, globalization, technology utilization, diversity, work-life balance, and other issues of the new workplace. And this book is also about how our complex environment requires people and organizations to learn and to continuously develop themselves in the quest for high performance and promising futures.

Importance of Organizational Behavior

• **Organizational behavior** is the study of individuals and groups in organizations.

In this challenging era of work and organizations, the body of knowledge we call "organizational behavior" offers many insights of great value. Called OB for short, **organizational behavior** is the study of human behavior in organizations. It is an academic discipline devoted to understanding individual and group behavior, interpersonal processes, and organizational dynamics with the goal of improving the performance of organizations and the people in them. Learning about OB can help you develop a better work-related understanding of yourself and others; it is a knowledge platform that can expand your potential for career success in the dynamic, shifting, and complex new workplaces of today—and tomorrow.

Scientific Foundations of Organizational Behavior

As far back as a century ago, consultants and scholars were giving increased attention to the systematic study of management. Although the early focus was initially on physical working conditions, principles of administration, and industrial engineering principles, interest soon broadened to include the human factor. This gave impetus to research dealing with individual attitudes, group dynamics, and the relationships between managers and workers. From this foundation, organizational behavior emerged as a scholarly discipline devoted to scientific understanding of individuals and groups in organizations and of the performance implications of organizational processes, systems, and structures.[2]

Interdisciplinary Body of Knowledge   Organizational behavior is an interdisciplinary body of knowledge with strong ties to the behavioral sciences—psychology, sociology, and anthropology—as well as to allied social sciences such as economics and political science. OB is unique, however, in its goals of integrating the diverse insights of these other disciplines and applying them to real-world problems and opportunities. The ultimate goal of OB is to improve the performance of people, groups, and organizations and to improve the quality of work life overall.

Use of Scientific Methods   The field of organizational behavior uses scientific methods to develop and empirically test generalizations about behavior in organizations. OB scholars often propose and test **models**—simplified views of reality that attempt to identify major factors and forces underlying real-world phenomena. These models link **independent variables**—presumed causes—with **dependent variables**—outcomes of practical value and interest. Here, for example, is a very basic model that describes one of the findings of OB research—job satisfaction (independent variable) influences absenteeism (dependent variable).

- **Models** are simplified views of reality that attempt to explain real-world phenomena.
- **Independent variables** are presumed causes that influence dependent variables.
- **Dependent variables** are outcomes of practical value and interest that are influenced by independent variables.

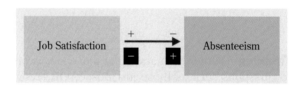

Notice that "+" and "−" signs in the above model also indicate that as job satisfaction increases, absenteeism tends to go down, and as job satisfaction decreases, absenteeism often goes up. As you look at this model you might ask what other dependent variables are important to study in OB—perhaps things like task performance, ethical behavior, work stress, and leadership effectiveness. In fact, job satisfaction can be a dependent variable in its own right. What independent variables do you believe might explain whether it will be high or low for someone doing a service job like an airline flight attendant or a managerial one like a school principal?

Figure 1.1 describes a set of research methods commonly used by OB researchers. They are based on scientific thinking, which means that (1) the process of data collection is controlled and systematic, (2) proposed explanations are carefully tested, and (3) only explanations that can be rigorously verified are accepted.

Focus on Application   As already suggested, the science of organizational behavior focuses on applications that can make a real difference in how organizations and people in them perform. Examples of the many practical questions addressed by the discipline of OB and reviewed in this book include: How should rewards such as merit pay raises be allocated? How can jobs be designed for both job satisfaction and high performance? What are the ingredients of successful teamwork? How can a manager deal with resistance to change? Should leaders make decisions by individual, consultative, or group methods? How can "win-win" outcomes be achieved in negotiations? What causes unethical and socially irresponsible behavior by people in organizations?

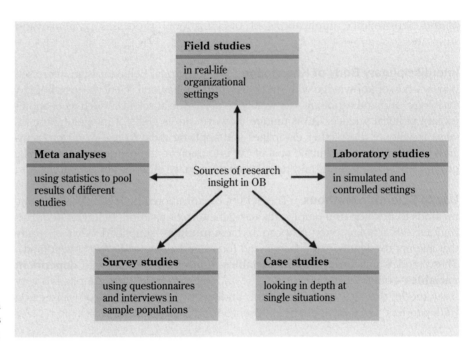

Figure 1.1 Common scientific research methods in organizational behavior.

- **Contingency thinking** seeks ways to meet the needs of different management situations.

Contingency Thinking   Rather than assuming that there is one "best" or universal answer to questions such as those just posed, OB recognizes that management practices must be tailored to fit the exact nature of each situation—this is called **contingency thinking**. In fact, one of the most accepted conclusions of scientific research to date is that there is no single best way to manage people and organizations. Said a bit differently, contingency thinking accepts that there are no cookie-cutter solutions that can be universally applied to common organizational problems. Managers must be able to understand the challenges and demands of different situations and craft responses to them that best fit the circumstances and people involved. And this is where solid scientific findings in organizational behavior become very helpful.

An essential responsibility of the science of organizational behavior, in fact, is to create and test models that offer *evidence-based foundations* for decision making and action. A book by scholars Jeffrey Pfeffer and Robert Sutton define the evidence-based approach as making decisions on "hard facts"—that is about what really works, rather than on "dangerous half-truths"—things that sound good but lack empirical substantiation.[3] One of the ways evidence-based thinking manifests itself in OB is through a contingency approach in which researchers identify how different situations can best be understood and handled.

In a time of complex globalization, for example, it's important for everyone from managers to government leaders to understand how OB theories and concepts apply in different countries.[4] Although it is relatively easy to conclude that what works in one culture may not work as well in another, it is far harder to describe how specific cultural differences can affect such things as motivation, job satisfaction, leadership style, negotiating tendencies, and ethical behavior. Fortunately, OB is now rich with empirically based insights into cross-cultural issues.

RESEARCH INSIGHT

Women Might Make Better Leaders

No one doubts there are good and bad leaders of both genders. But research by Alice Eagley and her colleagues at Northwestern University suggests that women may be more likely than men to use leadership styles that result in high performance by followers.

In a meta-analysis that statistically compared results of 45 research studies dealing with male and female leadership styles, Eagley and her team concluded that women are more likely than men to lead by inspiring, exciting, mentoring, and stimulating creativity. They point out these behaviors have "transformational" qualities that build stronger organizations through innovation and teamwork. Women also score higher on rewarding positive performance, while men score higher in punishing and correcting mistakes.

Eagley and her colleagues explain the findings in part by the fact that followers are more accepting

POSSIBLE LEADERSHIP STRENGTHS OF WOMEN

- "Transformational"
- Good at mentoring
- Very inspiring
- Encourage creativity
- Show excitement about goals
- Reward positive performance

of a transformational style when the leader is female, and that the style comes more naturally to women because of its emphasis on nurturing. They also suggest that because women may have to work harder than men to succeed, their leadership skills end up being better developed.

Do the Research

What do you think; is this study on track? Conduct an interview study of people working for female and male managers. Ask the question: Do women lead differently from men? Organize the responses and prepare an analysis in answer to your research question. Although not scientific, your study could prove quite insightful.

Reference: Alice H. Eagley, Mary C. Johannesen-Smith and Marloes L. Van Engen, "Transformational, Transactional and Laissez-Faire Leadership: A Meta-Analysis of Women and Men," *Psychological Bulletin,* Vol. 24 (4), 2003: 569–591.

Shifting Paradigms of Organizational Behavior

With the recent economic turmoil, financial crisis, and recession, there isn't any doubt that organizations and their members now face huge challenges. You'll notice organizations adopting new features, approaching work processes in new ways, and trying different strategies for serving customers and clients whose tastes, values, and needs are shifting as well.

Things have actually been changing for quite some time in our work environments, but recent events are especially dramatic in affecting both the nature and pace of change. The comments of consultant Tom Peters, while offered some time ago, seem even more relevant now. He called the changing environment of organizations a "revolution that feels something like this: scary, guilty, painful, liberating, disorienting, exhilarating, empowering, frustrating, fulfilling, confusing, and challenging. In other words, it feels very much like chaos."[5]

The environment of change in which we now live and work requires lots of learning and continuous attention. Among the trends affecting OB are these shifting paradigms in what many people expect and value in terms of human behavior in organizations.[6]

- *Commitment to ethical behavior:* Highly publicized scandals involving unethical and illegal business practices prompt concerns for ethical behavior in the workplace; there is growing intolerance for breaches of public faith by organizations and those who run them.

Global Forum for Responsible Management Education

The first global forum was recently held at United Nations headquarters. Secretary General Ban Ki-Moon called upon the 185 attending educators from 43 countries to work together and "ensure that management science is rooted in the concepts of sustainability and corporate citizenship."

Sustainability in respect to the environment, climate justice and preservation of resources is a growing theme in the dynamics of behavior in organizations.

- *Importance of human capital:* A dynamic and complex environment poses continuous human resource challenges; sustained success is earned through knowledge, experience, and commitments to people as valuable human assets of organizations.
- *Demise of command-and-control:* Traditional hierarchical structures are proving incapable of handling new environmental pressures and demands; they are being replaced by flexible structures and participatory work settings that fully value human capital.
- *Emphasis on teamwork:* Organizations today are designed to be less vertical and more horizontal in nature; driven by complex environments and customer demands, work is increasingly team based with a focus on peer contributions.
- *Pervasive influence of information technology:* As computers and communication technologies penetrate all aspects of the workplace, implications for workflows, work arrangements, and organizational systems and processes are far-reaching.
- *Respect for new workforce expectations:* The new generation of workers is less tolerant of hierarchy, more informal, and less concerned about status; organizations are paying more attention to helping members balance work responsibilities and personal affairs.
- *Changing concept of careers:* The new realities of a global economy find employers using more "offshoring" and "outsourcing" of jobs as well as cutting back their workforces and employee benefits; more people are now working as independent contractors who shift among employers rather than holding a traditional full-time jobs.
- *Concern for sustainability:* Rising quickly to the forefront of concerns in today's world, issues of sustainability are more and more on the minds of managers and organization members; decision making and goal setting in organizations increasingly gives attention to the environment, climate justice and preservation of resources for future generations.

Organizations as Work Settings

In order to understand the complex field of forces that relate to human behavior in organizations, we need to begin with the nature of the "organization" itself. Simply stated, an **organization** is a collection of people working together in a division of labor to achieve a common purpose. This definition describes everything from clubs, voluntary organizations, and religious bodies to entities such as small and large businesses, labor unions, schools, hospitals, and government agencies. All such organizations share a number of common features that can help us better understand and deal with them.

- **Organizations** are collections of people working together to achieve a common purpose.

Organizational Purpose, Mission, and Strategy

The core purpose of an organization may be stated as the creation of goods or services for customers. Nonprofit organizations produce services with public benefits, such as health care, education, judicial processing, and highway maintenance. Large and small for-profit businesses produce consumer goods and services such as automobiles, banking, travel, gourmet dining, and accommodations. Yet, as we all know, not all organizations of the same type pursue their purposes in the same ways or with equal success.

One way organizations differ is how their purposes are expressed with a sense of *mission*. Robert Reich, former U.S. Secretary of Labor, once said: "Talented people want to be part of something that they can believe in, something that confers meaning on their work, on their lives—something that involves a mission."[7] A **mission statement** describes and helps focus the attention of organizational members and external constituents on the organization's core purpose.[8] Ideally, it does so in a way that communicates to employees, customers, and the general public a sense of uniqueness for an organization and its products and services. And, it should provide a vision and sense of future aspiration.[9]

> • A **mission statement** describes the organization's purpose for stakeholders and the public.

Google's mission statement is simple, clear, and compelling: "to organize the world's information and make it universally accessible and useful." Compare that statement with those that follow. As you read, ask which, if any, communicates in a way that would make people want to join the organization and, as Reich says, "be part of something they can believe in."[10] Merck—"to discover, develop, manufacture and market a broad range of innovative products to improve human and animal health." AT&T—"to be the most admired and valuable company in the world." New Balance—"to build global brands that athletes are proud to wear, associates are proud to create and communities are proud to host." Amnesty International—"to undertake research and action focused on preventing and ending grave abuses of the rights to physical and mental integrity, freedom of conscience and expression, and freedom from discrimination . . ."

Given a sense of purpose and mission, organizations pursue strategies to accomplish them. A **strategy** is a comprehensive plan that guides an organization to operate in ways that allow it to outperform competitors. The variety of mergers, acquisitions, joint ventures, global alliances, and even restructurings and divestitures found in business today are examples of corporate strategies to achieve and sustain advantage in highly competitive environments.[11]

> • **Strategy** guides organizations to operate in ways that outperform competitors.

MASTERING MANAGEMENT

TEN GOLDEN RULES OF HIGH PERFORMANCE

Google isn't the only organization whose success rises and falls with how well it attracts and then manages a highly talented workforce. But it is consistently good at it. Here are Google's "Ten Golden Rules" of managing for high performance. Can you think of anything else to add to the list?

1. Hire by committee—make sure recruits talk to their future colleagues.
2. Cater to every need—make it easy, not hard, for people to perform.
3. Pack them in—put people to work close to one another.
4. Make coordination easy—use technology to keep people talking together.
5. Eat your own dog food—make use of company products.
6. Encourage creativity—allow freedom to come up with new ideas.
7. Strive for consensus—remember "many are better than the few."
8. Don't be evil—live tolerance and respect.
9. Data-driven decisions—do the analysis and stay on track.
10. Communicate effectively—hold many stay-in-touch meetings.

All organizations need good strategies; but strategy alone is no guarantee of success. Sustainable high performance is achieved only when strategies are both well chosen and well implemented. And it is in respect to implementation that understanding organizational behavior becomes especially important. After all, things happen in organizations because people working individually and in teams make them happen; as the chapter subtitle indicates, people really do make the difference. Armed with an understanding of the dynamics of human behavior in organizations, managers are well prepared to mobilize human capital and apply a great diversity of talents to best implement strategies to fulfill the organization's mission and purpose.

Organizational Environments and Stakeholders

The concept of strategy places great significance on the relationship between an organization and its external environment. As shown in Figure 1.2, organizations are dynamic **open systems** that obtain resource inputs from the environment and transform them into finished goods or services that are returned to the environment as product outputs.

If everything works right from an open systems perspective, suppliers value the organization as their customer and continue to provide needed resources, employees value their work opportunities and continue to infuse the transformation processes with their energies and intellects, and customers and clients value the organization's outputs and create a continuing demand for them. This is the concept of a **value chain**, or sequence of activities that results in the creation of goods and services of value to customers. It begins with the acquisition of inputs, continues through their transformation into product outputs, and ends when customers and clients are well served.

When the value chain is well managed, the organization as an open system is able to sustain operations and, hopefully, prosper over the long run. But if and when any aspect of this value chain breaks down due to input problems, transformation problems, or output problems, an organization's performance suffers and its

> • **Open systems** transform human and material resource inputs into finished goods and services.

> • The **value chain** is a sequence of activities that creates valued goods and services for customers.

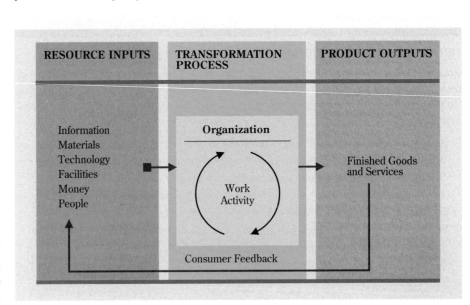

Figure 1.2 Organizations are open systems that create value while interacting with their environments.

livelihood may be threatened. In extreme cases such as those of General Motors and Chrysler in the recent economic downturn, the organization can be forced into bankruptcy or even go out of existence all together.

One way to describe and analyze the external environment of organizations is in terms of **stakeholders**—people, groups, and institutions that are affected by and thus have an interest or "stake" in an organization's performance. It is common in OB to recognize customers, owners, employees, suppliers, regulators, local communities, and future generations among the key stakeholders of organizations. And although an organization should ideally operate in ways that best serve all stakeholders, the realities are that conflicting interests can create challenges for decision makers. Consider, for example, the possibilities for conflict among these stakeholder interests—customers want value pricing and high-quality products, owners want profits and returns on investments, employees want secure jobs with good pay and benefits, suppliers want reliable contracts and on-time payments, regulators want compliance with all laws, local communities want good organizational citizenship and community support, and future generations want environmental protection and sustainability of natural resources.

> **Stakeholders** are people and groups with an interest or "stake" in the performance of the organization.

ETHICS IN OB

AMIDST ECONOMIC CRISIS AND SCANDALS MANAGERS LOSE PUBLIC TRUST

When the President of the United States forces the CEO of General Motors to resign, something is going on. And that's just what Barack Obama did to Rick Wagoner as GM struggled with the economic crisis. The move was politically controversial, but it was cheered by many frustrated American taxpayers.

As major banks and other firms perform poorly or fail altogether, many of their top executives still get rich salaries, bonuses, and severance packages. This is happening at the same time many workers are losing their jobs, taking pay cuts, or having their work hours reduced. And if that's not enough, there's the Bernard Madoff scandal. Sentenced to 150 years in prison, he lived lavishly while running an investment Ponzi scheme that bilked individuals, charitable foundations, colleges and universities, and other institutions of hundreds of millions of dollars.

Amid all this, the authors of a recent *Harvard Business Review* article point out that managers are now losing the public trust.[1] They call for business schools to address management as a profession governed by codes of conduct that "forge an implicit social contract with society." Indeed, we are now engaging a real debate about management ethics and corporate social responsibility. One model says managers should try to satisfy the interests of many stakeholders; an alternative says managers should act to maximize shareholder wealth.

> **Make Ethics Personal:** *What is your position on the shareholder wealth versus stakeholder interest debate? Do you agree with the movement to make management a profession? Would professionalizing management really make a difference in terms of performance accountability and everyday managerial behavior?*

Organizational Cultures

• **Organizational culture**
is a shared set of beliefs
and values within an
organization.

In the internal environment of organizations, the shared beliefs and values that influence the behavior of organizational members create what is called the **organizational culture**.[12] Former eBay CEO Meg Whitman calls it the "character" of the organization. She says organization culture "means the set of values and principles by which you run a company" and becomes the "moral center" that helps every member understand what is right and what is wrong in terms of personal behavior.[13]

If you're at all unsure about the importance of organizational culture, consider this example from Procter & Gamble. The firm gets some 400,000 applications for entry-management positions each year and hires about 4,000. P&G's CEO Robert McDonald points out that only applicants expected to be a good fit with the culture get hired; "We actually recruit for values," he says.[14] Organizations with "strong cultures" such as P&G operate with a clear vision of the future that is supported by well-developed and well-communicated beliefs and values, as well as a high-performance orientation. Even high-level managers at P&G can be found in people's homes learning how they live, clean, and cook with the firm's products. The program is called "live it, work it."[15]

Figure 1.3 shows an approach for mapping organizational cultures developed by Human Synergistics and using an instrument called the Organizational Culture Inventory, or OCI.[16] The OCI asks people to describe the behaviors and expectations that make up the prevailing cultures of their organizations, and the results are mapped into three culture types.[17] In a *constructive culture* members are encouraged to work together in ways that meet higher order human needs. In a *passive/defensive culture* members tend to act defensively in their working relationships, seeking to protect their security. In an *aggressive/defensive culture* members tend to act forcefully in their working relationships to protect their status and positions.

Among these three types of organizational cultures, the constructive culture would be most associated with high-performance organizations. In constructive cultures people tend to work with greater motivation, satisfaction, teamwork, and performance. In passive/defensive and aggressive/defensive cultures motivation tends to be lower and work attitudes less positive.[18] The expectation is that people prefer constructive cultures and behave within them in ways that fully tap the value of human capital, promoting both high-performance results and personal satisfaction.

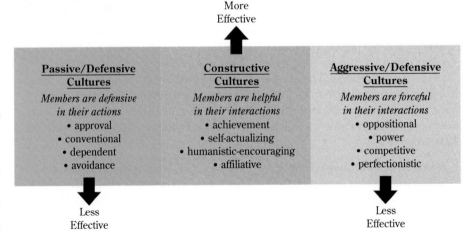

Figure 1.3 Insights on the performance implications of three types of organizational cultures. [*Source:* Developed with permission from "The Organizational Culture Inventory," published by Human Synergistics International, Plymouth, Michigan.]

Leaders on Leadership

ROD JONES GETS TOP GRADES FOR NAVITAS

For more than 30 years, Rod Jones has been a passionate advocate for education. Starting out in education administration, his role changed to that of entrepreneur in the mid-1990s with a vision to better prepare international students for college success. He co-founded what is now Navitas, an innovative global education company that seeks to positively impact the lives of those it serves.

"When we first began in Perth in the mid-1900s there was no one doing this in Australia. We saw a problem and an opportunity—about 70% of international students coming here to study were failing subjects, mostly due to transition issues, not because they weren't smart enough."

Its educational service has been dubbed "pathway education." This type of bridging program offers international students support in improving their English skills while assisting them in the transition to a new environment. They then have the tools necessary to gain admission into universities and achieve their goals of obtaining a college degree.

The business model is innovative in that Navitas establishes private colleges on university campuses; international students complete the first part of their degree programs in a supportive environment through the various services Navitas offers. Since its inception, the company has expanded from its Australian market and now operates on campuses in Britain, Canada, Sri Lanka, Kenya, Zambia and Indonesia offering bridging programs to over 20,000 students each year.

The company has seen tremendous success. "In Australia, about 90% of our university program students go on to study with our university partners and 95% will complete their degree." Mr. Jones has been recognized for his commitment to education; he was awarded an Honorary Doctor of Education degree from Edith Cowan University for his "contributions to increasing student participation in education." In addition, he was named the Ernst & Young Entrepreneur of the Year 2008 Award for Australia for his "entrepreneurial vision, persistence and financial discipline."

The innovation has not stopped there. His company has expanded into offering English language training for migrants and refugees and has undertaken workplace training to assist organizations with their training needs.

Diversity and Multiculturalism

Within the internal environments of organizations, **workforce diversity** describes the presence of individual differences based on gender, race and ethnicity, age, able-bodiedness, and sexual orientation.[19] As used in OB, the term **multiculturalism** refers to inclusion, pluralism, and genuine respect for diversity and individual differences.[20] And when it comes to people and their diversity, consultant R. Roosevelt Thomas makes the point that positive organizational cultures tap the talents, ideas, and creative potential of *all* members.[21] An extensive discussion of diversity and individual differences in the next chapter further addresses this theme.

The demographic trends driving workforce diversity in American society are well recognized. There are more women working than ever before in our history: They earn 60 percent of college degrees and fill a bit more than half of managerial jobs.[22] The proportion of African-Americans, Hispanics, and Asians in the

- **Workforce diversity** describes how people differ on attributes such as age, race, ethnicity, gender, physical ability, and sexual orientation.
- **Multiculturalism** refers to pluralism and respect for diversity in the workplace.

labor force is increasing. By the year 2060, people of color will constitute over 60 percent of the U.S. population; close to 30 percent of the population will be Hispanic.[23]

But trends alone are no guarantee that diversity will be fully valued and respected in the multicultural sense described by Thomas and others.[24] A key element in any organization that embraces multiculturalism is **inclusion**—the degree to which the culture values diversity and is open to anyone who can perform a job, regardless of their diversity attributes.[25] *Valuing diversity* is a core OB theme that is central to this book and the new workplace.[26] Yet in practice, valuing diversity must still be considered a work in progress. For example, data show women earning only about 76 cents per dollar earned by men. At *Fortune* 500 companies they hold only 12 CEO jobs and 6.2 percent of top-paying positions; women of color hold only 1.7 percent of corporate officer positions and 1 percent of top-paying jobs.[27] Indeed, when Ursula Burns was named CEO of Xerox in 2009, she became the first African-American woman to head a *Fortune* 500 firm.[28]

- **Inclusion** is the degree to which an organization's culture respects and values diversity.

Organizational Behavior and Management

Regardless of your career direction, the field of organizational behavior will some day be very important as you try to master the special challenges of serving as a **manager**, someone whose job it is to directly support the work efforts of others. The goal, of course, should be to become an **effective manager**—one whose team or work unit or total organization consistently achieves its performance goals while members remain capable, enthusiastic, and satisfied in their jobs.

This definition of an effective manager focuses attention on two key outcomes, or dependent variables, that are important in OB. The first outcome is **task performance**. You can think of it as the quality and quantity of the work produced or the services provided by an individual, team or work unit, or organization as a whole. The second outcome is **job satisfaction**. It indicates how people feel about their work and the work setting.

OB is quite clear in that managers should be held accountable for both results. The first, performance, pretty much speaks for itself; this is what we at the organization are supposed to accomplish. The second, satisfaction, however, might give you some pause for thought. But just as a valuable machine should not be allowed to break down for lack of proper maintenance, the talents and enthusiasm of an organization's workforce should never be lost or compromised for lack of proper care. In this sense, taking care of job satisfaction today can be considered an investment in tomorrow's performance potential.

- **Managers** are persons who support the work efforts of other people.

- An **effective manager** helps others achieve high levels of both performance and satisfaction.

- **Task performance** is the quantity and quality of work produced.

- **Job satisfaction** is a positive feeling about one's work and work setting.

The Management Process

Being a manager is a unique challenge with responsibilities that link closely with the field of organizational behavior. At the heart of the matter managers help other people get important things done in timely, high-quality, and personally satisfying ways. And in the workplaces of today this is accomplished more through "helping" and "supporting" than through traditional notions of "directing" and "controlling." Indeed, you'll find the word "manager" is increasingly being replaced by such terms as "coordinator," "coach," or "team leader."

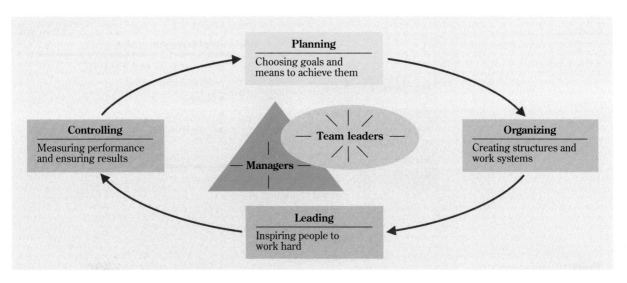

Figure 1.4 The management process of planning, organizing, leading, and controlling.

Among the ways that managerial work has been described and taught is through the four functions shown in Figure 1.4: planning, organizing, leading, and controlling. These functions describe what managers are supposed to do in respect to:[29]

- **Planning**—defining goals, setting specific performance objectives, and identifying the actions needed to achieve them
- **Organizing**—creating work structures and systems, and arranging resources to accomplish goals and objectives
- **Leading**—instilling enthusiasm by communicating with others, motivating them to work hard, and maintaining good interpersonal relations
- **Controlling**—ensuring that things go well by monitoring performance and taking corrective action as necessary

Managerial Activities, Roles, and Networks

Anyone serving as a manager or team leader faces a very demanding and complicated job that has been described by researchers in the following terms.[30] Managers work long hours; a work week of more than the standard 40 hours is typical. The length of the work week increases at higher managerial levels, and heads of organizations often work the longest hours. Managers are busy people. Their work is intense and involves doing many different things. The typical work day includes a shifting mix of incidents that demand immediate attention, with the number of incidents being greatest for lower-level managers. Managers are often interrupted; their work is fragmented and variable; many tasks must be completed quickly. Managers work mostly with other people and often spend little time working alone. They are communicators and spend a lot of time getting, giving, and processing information in face-to-face and electronic exchanges and in formal and informal meetings.

- **Planning** sets objectives and identifies the actions needed to achieve them.
- **Organizing** divides up tasks and arranges resources to accomplish them.
- **Leading** creates enthusiasm to work hard to accomplish tasks successfully.
- **Controlling** monitors performance and takes any needed corrective action.

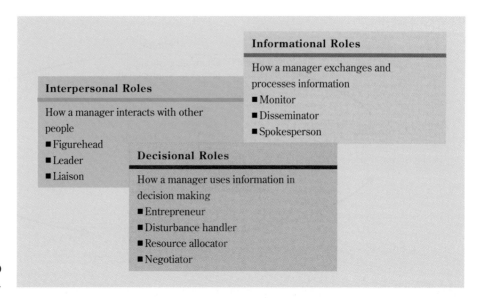

Figure 1.5 Mintzberg's 10 roles of effective managers.

In what has become a classic study, Henry Mintzberg described how managers perform a set of 10 managerial roles, falling into the three categories shown in Figure 1.5.[31] A manager's *interpersonal roles* involve working directly with other people, hosting and attending official ceremonies (figurehead), creating enthusiasm and serving people's needs (leader), and maintaining contacts with important people and groups (liaison). The *informational roles* involve managers exchanging information with other people, seeking relevant information (monitor), sharing it with insiders (disseminator), and sharing it with outsiders (spokesperson). A manager's *decisional roles* involve making decisions that affect other people, seeking problems to solve and opportunities to explore (entrepreneur), helping to resolve conflicts (disturbance handler), allocating resources to various uses (resource allocator), and negotiating with other parties (negotiator).

Good interpersonal relationships are essential to managerial success in each of these roles. Managers and team leaders need to develop, maintain, and work well in networks involving a wide variety of people, both inside and outside the organization.[32] These include *task networks* of specific job-related contacts, *career networks* of career guidance and opportunity resources, and *social networks* of trustworthy friends and peers.[33] It can be said in this sense that managers must develop and maintain **social capital** in the form of relationships and networks that they can call upon to get work done through other people.

• **Social capital** is a capacity to get things done due to relationships with other people.

Managerial Skills and Competencies

• A **skill** is an ability to turn knowledge into effective action.

A **skill** is an ability to translate knowledge into action that results in a desired performance. Robert Katz divides the essential managerial skills into three categories—technical, human, and conceptual.[34] He further suggests that the relative importance of these skills varies across the different levels of management. Technical skills are considered more important at entry levels of management, where supervisors and team leaders must deal with job-specific problems. Senior executives require more conceptual skills as they face sometimes ambiguous problems and deal with issues of organizational purpose, mission, and strategy.

Human skills, which are strongly grounded in the foundations of organizational behavior, are consistently important across all managerial levels.

Technical Skills   A **technical skill** is an ability to perform specialized tasks. Such ability derives from knowledge or expertise gained from education or experience. This skill involves proficiency at using select methods, processes, and expertise in one's job. Perhaps the best current example is skill in using the latest communication and information technologies. In the high-tech workplaces of today, technical proficiency in database management, spreadsheet analysis, presentation software, e-mail and electronic networks, and Internet searches is often a hiring prerequisite. Some technical skills require preparatory education, whereas others are acquired through specific training and on-the-job experience.

Human Skills   Central to all aspects of managerial work and team leadership are **human skills**, or the ability to work well with other people. They emerge as a spirit of trust, enthusiasm, and genuine involvement in interpersonal relationships. A person with good human skills will have a high degree of self-awareness and a capacity for understanding or empathizing with the feelings of others. People with this skill are able to interact well with others, engage in persuasive communications, and deal successfully with disagreements and conflicts.

An important emphasis in this area of human skills is **emotional intelligence**, or EI. As defined by Daniel Goleman, EI is the ability to understand and deal with emotions. With its focus on managing emotions both personally and in relationships with others, emotional intelligence is now considered an important leadership competency.[35] The core elements in emotional intelligence are:

- *Self-awareness*—ability to understand your own moods and emotions
- *Self-regulation*—ability to think before acting and to control disruptive impulses
- *Motivation*—ability to work hard and persevere
- *Empathy*—ability to understand the emotions of others
- *Social skill*—ability to gain rapport with others and build good relationships

Conceptual Skills   In addition to technical and human skills, managers should be able to view the organization or situation as a whole so that problems are always solved for the benefit of everyone concerned. This capacity to think analytically and solve complex and sometimes ambiguous problems is a **conceptual skill**. It involves the ability to see and understand how systems work and how their parts are interrelated, including human dynamics. Conceptual skill is used to identify problems and opportunities, gather and interpret relevant information, and make good problem-solving decisions.

Moral Management

Having the essential managerial skills is one thing; using them correctly to get things done in organizations is quite another. And when it comes to this issue of ethics and morality, scholar Archie B. Carroll draws a distinction between immoral managers, amoral managers, and moral managers.[36]

- **Technical skill** is an ability to perform specialized tasks.
- **Human skill** is the ability to work well with other people.
- **Emotional intelligence** is the ability to manage oneself and one's relationships effectively.
- **Conceptual skill** is the ability to analyze and solve complex problems.

Information overload and multitasking are a manager's nemesis, and we must work hard to increase brain capacity. So states Torkel Klingberg in his book *The Overflowing Brain*. "As advances in information technology and communication supply us with information at an ever accelerating rate," he says, "the limitations of our brains become all the more obvious."

Figure 1.6 Moral leadership, ethics mindfulness, and the virtuous shift. [*Source:* Developed from Terry Thomas, John R. Schermerhorn Jr., and John W. Dinehart, "Strategic Leadership of Ethical Behavior in Business," *Academy of Management Executive*, 18, May 2004, pp. 56–66.]

• An **immoral manager** chooses to behave unethically.

• An **amoral manager** fails to consider the ethics of a decision or behavior.

• A **moral manager** makes ethical behavior a personal goal.

• **Ethics mindfulness** is an enriched awareness that causes one to consistently behave with ethical consciousness.

The **immoral manager** doesn't subscribe to any ethical principles, making decisions and acting in any situation to simply gain best personal advantage. This manager essentially chooses to behave unethically. One might describe in this way disgraced executives like Bernard Madoff and others whose unethical acts make headlines. The **amoral manager**, by contrast, fails to consider the ethics of a decision or behavior. This manager acts unethically at times, but does so unintentionally. Common forms of unintentional ethics lapses that we all must guard against include prejudice that derives from unconscious stereotypes and attitudes, showing bias based on in-group favoritism, claiming too much personal credit for one's performance contributions, and giving preferential treatment to those who can benefit you.[37] Finally, the **moral manager** is one who incorporates ethics principles and goals into his or her personal behavior. For this manager, ethical behavior is a goal, a standard, and even a matter of routine; ethical reasoning is part of every decision, not just an occasional afterthought.

Carroll believes that the majority of managers tend to act amorally. They are well intentioned but often fail to take ethical considerations into account when taking action and making decisions. A review article by Terry Thomas and his colleagues suggests that this pattern may well fit the general membership of organizations.[38] They describe how the "ethics center of gravity" shown in Figure 1.6 can be moved positively through moral leadership or negatively through amoral leadership. In this view, a moral manager or moral leader always acts as an ethical role model, communicates ethics values and messages, and champions **ethics mindfulness**—an "enriched awareness" that causes one to behave with an ethical consciousness from one decision or behavioral event to another. This results in the "virtuous shift" shown in the figure and helps create an organizational culture in which people encourage one another to act ethically as a matter of routine.

Learning about Organizational Behavior

• **Learning** is an enduring change in behavior that results from experience.

Learning is an enduring change of behavior that results from experience. Our new and rapidly developing knowledge-based world places a great premium on learning by organizations as well as individuals. Only the learners, so to speak, will be able to maintain the pace and succeed in a high-tech, global, and constantly changing environment. At the individual level, the concept of **lifelong learning** is important. It involves learning continuously from day-to-day work experiences; conversations with colleagues and friends; counseling and advice provided by mentors, success models, training seminars, and workshops; and other daily opportunities. At the organizational level, consultants and scholars emphasize **organizational learning** as the process of acquiring knowledge and using information to adapt successfully to changing circumstances.[39] Just like individuals, organizations must be able to change continuously and positively while searching for new ideas and opportunities.

- **Lifelong learning** is continuous learning from everyday experiences.

- **Organizational learning** is the process of acquiring knowledge and using information to adapt to changing circumstances.

Learning and Experience

Figure 1.7 shows how the content and activities of the typical OB course can fit together in an experiential learning cycle.[40] The learning sequence begins with initial experience and subsequent reflection. It grows as theory building takes place to try to explain what has happened. Theory is then tested through future behavior. Textbooks, readings, class discussions, and other course assignments and activities should complement one another and help you move through the phases of the learning cycle. With practice, you can make experiential learning part of your commitment to continued personal and career development.

Learning Styles

Notice that Figure 1.7 assigns to you a substantial responsibility for learning. Along with your instructor, we can offer examples, cases, and exercises to provide you with initial experience. We can even stimulate your reflection and theory building by presenting concepts and discussing their research and practical implications. Sooner or later, however, you must become an active participant

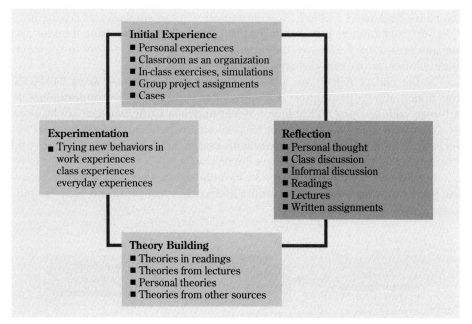

Figure 1.7 Experiential learning in an OB course.

Umsobomvu
Youth Fund

CEO Malose Kekana believes nonprofit work is special. "When people work at a nonprofit," he says, "they can't be thinking about themselves . . . the objective has to be the bigger goal." Umsobomvu's mission is large–to train South Africa's youth and help lift their generation out of poverty.

in the process; you and only you can do the work required to take full advantage of the learning cycle.

As you proceed with *Organizational Behavior* 11/E and your OB course, now is a good time to inquire further into your preferred learning style or tendencies. In the end-of-book OB Skills Workbook, we have included instructions for a *Learning Styles* self-assessment.[41] If you complete the recommended instrument it will provide feedback on how you like to learn through receiving, processing, and recalling new information. Armed with this understanding, you can take steps to maximize your learning and even course success by studying in ways that best fit your learning style. So, what type of learner are you? The seven learning styles from the assessment are:[42]

- *Visual learner*—learns by watching and viewing images and diagrams.
- *Print learner*—learns by reading and writing things down.
- *Auditory learner*—learns by listening and repeating verbal presentations.
- *Interactive learner*—learns through conversation and sharing information.
- *Haptic learner*—learns hands-on by drawing and putting things together.
- *Kinesthetic learner*—learns by doing and active involvement.
- *Olfactory learner*—learns through associative senses of smell and taste.

Learning Guide to *Organizational Behavior 11/E*

To facilitate your learning, the chapters in *Organizational Behavior 11/E* are presented in a logical building-block fashion. This first chapter constituting *Part 1* has introduced the discipline and context of OB, including its scientific foundations and link with the management process. *Part 2* focuses on individual behavior and performance. Key topics include diversity, values, personality, attitudes, emotions, perception, learning, and motivation. *Part 3* covers teams and teamwork, including the dynamics of decision making, conflict, and negotiation. *Part 4* examines leadership and influence processes, with an emphasis on communication and collaboration, power and politics, and important leadership theories and perspectives. *Part 5* discusses the organizational context in respect to organization cultures, structures, designs, and strategic capabilities.

At the end of Part 5 you will find the rich and useful *OB Skills Workbook* mentioned above. Its purpose is to provide a variety of active opportunities to advance your learning and help you better understand the practical applications of OB. In the workbook are cases for analysis, many team and experiential exercises, and a portfolio of self-assessments that includes the popular Kouzes and Posner "Student Leadership Practices Inventory."

Finally, and as you embark on your introductory study of organizational behavior, remember that OB and the learning it offers has real value and concrete purpose. Think about it this way.

These learning activities from *The OB Skills Workbook* are suggested for Chapter 1.

Cases for Critical Thinking	Team and Experiential Exercises	Self-Assessment Portfolio
• Trader Joe's • Management Training Dilemang	• My Best Manager • My Best Job • Graffiti Needs Assessment • Sweet Tooth: Pfeiffer Training Annual	• Student Leadership Practices Inventory • Learning Styles • Managerial Assumptions • 21st Century Manager

1 study guide

What is organizational behavior and why is it important?

- Organizational behavior is the study of individuals and groups in organizations.

- OB is an applied discipline based on scientific methods.

- OB uses a contingency approach, recognizing that management practices must fit the situation.

- Shifting paradigms of OB reflect a commitment to ethical behavior, the importance of human capital, an emphasis on teams, the growing influence of information technology, new workforce expectations, changing notions of careers, and concern for sustainability.

What are organizations like as work settings?

- An organization is a collection of people working together in a division of labor for a common purpose.

- Organizations are open systems that interact with their environments to obtain resources and transform them into outputs returned to the environment for consumption.

- Organizations pursue strategies that facilitate the accomplishment of purpose and mission; the field of OB is an important foundation for effective strategy implementation.

- Key stakeholders in the external environments of organizations include customers, owners, suppliers, regulators, local communities, employees, and future generations.

- The organizational culture is the internal "personality" of the organization, including the beliefs and values that are shared by members.

- Positive organizational cultures place a high value on workforce diversity and multi-culturalism, emphasizing respect and inclusiveness for all members.

What is the nature of managerial work?

- Managers directly support the work efforts of others; they are increasingly expected to act more like "coaches" and "facilitators" than like "bosses" and "controllers."
- An effective manager is one whose work unit, team, or group reaches high levels of performance and job satisfaction that are sustainable over the long term.
- The four functions of management are planning—to set directions; organizing—to assemble resources and systems; leading—to create workforce enthusiasm; and controlling—to ensure desired results.
- Managers fulfill a variety of interpersonal, informational, and decisional roles while working with networks of people both inside and outside of the organization.
- Managerial performance is based on a combination of essential technical, human, and conceptual skills; emotional intelligence is an important human skill.

How do we learn about organizational behavior?

- Learning is an enduring change in behavior that results from experience.
- True learning about organizational behavior involves a commitment to continuous lifelong learning from one's work and everyday experiences.
- Organizational learning is the process of organizations acquiring knowledge and utilizing information to adapt successfully to changing circumstances.
- Most organizational behavior courses use multiple methods and approaches that take advantage of the experiential learning cycle.
- People vary in their learning styles; an understanding of your style can help improve learning and course success.

Key Terms

Amoral manager (p. 18)
Conceptual skill (p. 17)
Contingency thinking (p. 6)
Controlling (p. 15)
Dependent variables (p. 5)
Effective manager (p. 14)
Emotional intelligence (p. 17)
Ethics mindfulness (p. 18)
Human skills (p. 17)
Immoral manager (p. 18)
Inclusion (p. 14)
Independent variables (p. 5)

Job satisfaction (p. 14)
Leading (p. 15)
Learning (p. 18)
Lifelong learning (p. 19)
Manager (p. 14)
Mission statement (p. 9)
Models (p. 5)
Moral manager (p. 18)
Multiculturalism (p. 13)
Open systems (p. 10)
Organization (p. 8)
Organizational behavior (p. 4)
Organizational culture (p. 12)

Organizational learning (p. 19)
Organizing (p. 15)
Planning (p. 15)
Skill (p. 16)
Social capital (p. 16)
Stakeholders (p. 11)
Strategy (p. 9)
Task performance (p. 14)
Technical skill (p. 17)
Value chain (p. 10)
Workforce diversity (p. 13)

Self-Test 1

Multiple Choice

1. Which of the following issues is most central to the field of organizational behavior? (a) ways to improve advertising for a new product (b) ways to increase job satisfaction and performance among employees (c) creation of new strategy for organizational growth (d) design of a new management information system

2. What is the best description of the setting facing organizational behavior today? (a) Command-and-control is in. (b) The new generation expects much the same as the old. (c) Empowerment is out. (d) Work–life balance concerns are in.

3. The term "workforce diversity" refers to differences in race, age, gender, ethnicity, and _____ among people at work. (a) social status (b) personal wealth (c) able-bodiedness (d) political preference

4. Which statement about OB is most correct? (a) OB seeks "one-best-way" solutions to management problems. (b) OB is a unique science that has little relationship to other scientific disciplines. (c) OB is focused on using knowledge for practical applications. (d) OB is so modern that it has no historical roots.

5. In the open-systems view of organizations, such things as technology, information, and money are considered _____. (a) transformation elements (b) feedback (c) inputs (d) outputs

6. In strategic management, the discipline of organizational behavior is most essential in terms of _____. (a) developing strategies (b) clarifying mission statements (c) implementing strategies (d) identifying organizational purpose

7. According to the Organizational Culture Inventory (OCI), an organization in which members are encouraged to work together in ways that meet higher-order human needs is classified as having a _____ culture. (a) constructive (b) motivational (c) passive (d) high-achievement

8. Which word best describes an organizational culture that embraces multiculturalism and in which workforce diversity is highly valued? (a) inclusion (b) effectiveness (c) dynamism (d) predictability

9. The management function of _____ is concerned with creating enthusiasm for hard work among organizational members. (a) planning (b) motivating (c) controlling (d) leading

10. In the management process, _____ is concerned with measuring performance results and taking action to improve future performance. (a) disciplining (b) organizing (c) leading (d) controlling

11. Among Mintzberg's 10 managerial roles, acting as a figurehead and liaison are examples of _____ roles. (a) interpersonal (b) informational (c) decisional (d) conceptual

12. According to current views of managerial work, it is highly unlikely that an effective manager will _____. (a) engage in extensive networking (b) have good interpersonal skills (c) spend a lot of time working alone (d) be good at solving problems

13. When a manager moves upward in responsibility, Katz suggests that _____ skills decrease in importance and _____ skills increase in importance. (a) human, conceptual (b) conceptual, emotional (c) technical, conceptual (d) emotional, human

14. A person with high emotional intelligence would be strong in _____, the ability to think before acting and to control disruptive impulses. (a) motivation (b) perseverance (c) self-regulation (d) empathy

15. Which statement about learning is *not* correct? (a) Learning is a change in behavior that results from experience. (b) People learn; organizations do not. (c) Experiential learning is common in OB courses. (d) Lifelong learning is an important personal responsibility for career development.

Short Response

16. What are the key characteristics of OB as a scientific discipline?

17. What does "valuing diversity" mean in the workplace?

18. What is an effective manager?

19. How would Henry Mintzberg describe a typical executive's workday?

Applications Essay

20. Carla, a college junior, is participating in a special "elementary education outreach" project in her local community. Along with other students from the business school, she is going to spend the day with fourth- and fifth-grade students and introduce them to the opportunities of going to college. One of her tasks is to lead a class discussion of the question: "How is the world of work changing today?" Help Carla out by creating an outline for her of the major points that she should try to develop with the students.

2

Individual Differences, Values, and Diversity

chapter at a glance

The recognition of individual differences is central to any discussion of organizational behavior. This chapter addresses the nature of individual differences and describes why understanding and valuing these differences is increasingly important in today's workplace. Here's what to look for in Chapter 2. When finished reading, check your learning with the Summary Questions & Answers and Self-Test in the end-of-chapter Study Guide.

ATP Denmark (Arbejdmarkedets TillaegsPension or Supplementary Pension Fund) was created in 1964 and is currently the largest pension fund in Denmark, covering all wage earners in the country. While it is respected for high efficiency and low costs, ATP Denmark stakes its pride on the work-life balance of its employees.

In 2009 it was recognized as a Work-Life Balance Champion by the European Region's Great Place to Work Institute. As ATP Denmark's Managing Director Lars Rohde describes, work-life balance is compatible with productivity, "Enjoying a balanced life isn't an obstacle to succeeding at work—it's a prerequisite! It's perfectly possible to be serious and ambitious at work and still take the day off on your children's birthdays."[1]

The company's ultimate objective is to provide Danish citizens with the best possible pension and Rohde believes this cannot be done without a workforce that is committed to the company, its mission and the impact employees have in each citizen's life. To ensure that employees understand their vital role, they are a visible part of the business strategy with the same priority as clients and investments.

Employee benefits are a serious matter and ATP Denmark has been creative in this area. "Benefits include home workstations, flexible working hours, take-home organic meals three times a week, dry cleaning service, sports during working hours and a playroom for children if employees need to take their child along to work for the day."[1]

Work-life balance is an important balance with high dividends. In one of the country's biggest disbursement projects, ATP Denmark found itself stretched between the resources needed and timeline involved. However, a highly satisfied, committed workforce easily rose to the challenge. "It's very impressive the way everyone in the organization has put in the extra effort to get us on target in a short space of time . . . And staff can only perform to their best ability if the employee welfare account is topped up, so to speak."[1]

work-life balance championed at ATP denmark

Individual Differences

Self-Awareness and Awareness of Others

People are complex. While you approach a situation one way, someone else may approach it quite differently. These differences among people can make the ability to predict and understand behavior in organizations challenging. They also contribute to what makes the study of organizational behavior so fascinating.

In OB, the term *individual differences* is used to refer to the ways in which people are similar and how they vary in their thinking, feeling, and behavior. Although no two people are completely alike, they are also not completely different. Therefore, the study of **individual differences** attempts to identify where behavioral tendencies are similar and where they are different. The idea is that if we can figure out how to categorize behavioral tendencies and identify which tendencies people have, we will be able to more accurately predict how and why people behave as they do.

Although individual differences can sometimes make working together effectively difficult, they can also offer great benefits. The best teams often result from combining people with different skills and approaches and who think in different ways—by putting the "whole brain" to work.[2] For people to capitalize on these differences requires understanding and valuing what differences are and what benefits they can offer.

In this chapter we examine factors that increase awareness of individual differences—our own and others—in the workplace. Two factors that are important for this are self-awareness and awareness of others. **Self-awareness** means being aware of our own behaviors, preferences, styles, biases, personalities, etc., and **awareness of others** means being aware of these same things in others. To help engage this awareness, we begin by understanding components of the self and how these components are developed. We then discuss what personality is and identify the personality characteristics and values that have the most relevance for OB. As you read these concepts, think about where you fall on them. Do they sound like you? Do they sound like people you know?

Components of Self

Collectively, the ways in which an individual integrates and organizes personality and the traits they contain make up the components of the self, or the self-concept. The **self-concept** is the view individuals have of themselves as physical, social, and spiritual or moral beings.[3] It is a way of recognizing oneself as a distinct human being.

A person's self-concept is greatly influenced by his or her culture. For example, Americans tend to disclose much more about themselves than do the English; that is, an American's self-concept is more assertive and talkative.[4]

Two related—and crucial—aspects of the self-concept are self-esteem and self-efficacy. **Self-esteem** is a belief about one's own worth based on an overall self-evaluation.[5] People high in self-esteem see themselves as capable, worthwhile, and acceptable and tend to have few doubts about themselves. The opposite is true of a person low in self-esteem. Some OB research suggests that whereas high self-esteem generally can boost performance and satisfaction outcomes, when under pressure, people with high self-esteem may become boastful

- **Individual differences** are the ways in which people are similar and how they vary in their thinking, feeling, and behavior.

- **Self-awareness** means being aware of one's own behaviors, preferences, styles, biases, personalities, etc.

- **Awareness of others** is being aware of behaviors, preferences, styles, biases, personalities, etc. of others.

- **Self-concept** is the view individuals have of themselves as physical, social, spiritual, or moral beings.

- **Self-esteem** is a belief about one's own worth based on an overall self-evaluation.

and act egotistically. They may also be overconfident at times and fail to obtain important information.[6]

Self-efficacy, sometimes called the "effectance motive," is a more specific version of self-esteem. It is an individual's belief about the likelihood of success-fully completing a specific task. You could have high self-esteem yet have a feel-ing of low self-efficacy about performing a certain task, such as public speaking.

- **Self-efficacy** is an individual's belief about the likelihood of successfully completing a specific task.

Development of Self

Just what determines the development of the self? Is our personality inherited or genetically determined, or is it formed by experience? You may have heard someone say something like, "She acts like her mother." Similarly, someone may argue that "Bobby is the way he is because of the way he was raised." These two arguments illustrate the nature/nurture controversy: Are we the way we are because of heredity—that is, genetic endowment—or because of the environ-ments in which we have been raised and live—cultural, social, situational? As shown, these two forces actually operate in combination. Heredity consists of those factors that are determined at conception, including physical characteris-tics, gender, and personality factors. Environment consists of cultural, social, and situational factors.

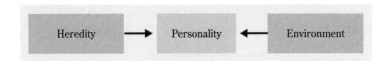

Heredity → Personality ← Environment

The impact of heredity on personality continues to be the source of consid-erable debate. Perhaps the most general conclusion we can draw is that hered-ity sets the limits on just how much personality characteristics can be developed; environment determines development within these limits. For instance, a person could be born with a tendency toward authoritarianism, and that tendency could be reinforced in an authoritarian work environment. These limits ap-pear to vary from one characteristic to the next, and across all characteris-tics there is about a 50–50 heredity-environment split.[7]

A person's development of the self is also related to his or her culture. As we show throughout this book, cultural values and norms play a sub-stantial role in the development of an individual's personality and behaviors. Contrast the individualism of U.S. culture with the collectivism of Mexican culture, for example.[8] Social factors reflect such things as family life, religion, and the many kinds of formal and informal groups in which people partic-ipate throughout their lives—friendship groups, athletic groups, and formal workgroups. Finally, the demands of differing *situational factors* emphasize or constrain different aspects of an individual's personality. For example, in class are you likely to rein in your high spirits and other related behaviors encour-aged by your personality? On the other hand, at a sporting event, do you jump up, cheer, and loudly criticize the referees?

The developmental approaches of Chris Argyris, Daniel Levinson, and Gail Sheehy systematically examine the ways personality develops across time. Argyris notes that people develop along a continuum of dimensions from immaturity to

The Whole Brain

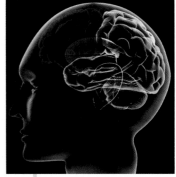

While the left brain is sequential, logical, and analytical, the right brain is nonlinear, intuitive, and holistic. In the Industrial Age the left brain ruled. In today's workplace, right brain and "whole brain" may be the keys to success.

RESEARCH INSIGHT

Twin Studies: Nature or Nurture?

A long-standing question in individual differences psychology is, how much of who we are is determined by nature and how much by nurture? Research findings are beginning to provide fascinating insights by investigating samples of twins. Before you read on, take a guess at the following: In thinking about leadership, how much of leadership capacity do you think is determined by nature and how much by nurture?

This question is being investigated in a research program by Rich Arvey and colleagues. In a recent study, they used a sample of 178 fraternal and 214 identical female twins to see if they could generalize their findings that 30 percent of the variance in leadership role occupancy among the male twins could be accounted for by genetic factors. Their sample came from the Minnesota Twin Registry—a registry of twins born in the state between 1936 and 1951 who had been reared together during childhood. Surveys were sent to the female twins with measures assessing their history of holding leadership roles (i.e., leadership role occupancy) and an assessment of developmental life experiences,

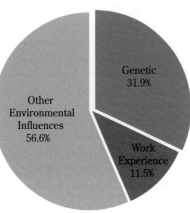

Nature v. Nurture on Leadership Role Occupancy Among Female Twins

Genetic 31.9%

Other Environmental Influences 56.6%

Work Experience 11.5%

including family and work experiences.

The results supported the pattern shown in the male sample—32 percent of the variance in leadership role occupancy of women was associated with hereditability. Family experience and work experience were also related to leadership role occupancy, though not surprisingly, experiences at work are more important than family experiences in shaping women's leadership development. The findings are important because they indicate that developmental experiences can help both men and women move into leadership roles.

Research Question

How close was your guess? Do these findings correspond with what you see in your own families (e.g., with brothers and sisters or with parents and children)? How would you test the question of nature versus nurture?

Source: Arvey, R., Zhang, Z., Avolio, B., and Krueger, R. (2007). Developmental and Genetic Determinants of Leadership Role Occupancy among Women. *Journal of Applied Psychology, 92*(3), 693–706.

maturity, as shown in Figure 2.1. He believes that many organizations treat mature adults as if they were still immature and that this creates many problems in terms of bringing out the best in employees. Levinson and Sheehy maintain that an individual's personality unfolds in a series of stages across time. Sheehy's model, for example, talks about three stages—ages 18–30, 30–45, and 45–85+. Each of these has a crucial impact on the worker's employment and career, as we will discuss in Chapter 3. The implications are that personalities develop over time and require different managerial responses. Thus, the needs and other personality aspects of people initially entering an organization change sharply as they move through different stages or toward increased maturity.[9]

From immaturity	**To maturity**
Passivity	Activity
Dependence	Independence
Limited behavior	Diverse behavior
Shallow interests	Deep interests
Short time perspective	Long time perspective
Subordinate position	Superordinate position
Little self-awareness	Much self-awareness

Figure 2.1 Argyris's maturity–immaturity continuum.

Personality

The term **personality** encompasses the overall combination of characteristics that capture the unique nature of a person as that person reacts to and interacts with others. As an example, think of a person who in his senior year in high school had turned selling newspapers into enough of a business to buy a BMW; who became a billionaire as the founder of a fast-growing, high-tech computer company by the time he was 30; who told his management team that his daughter's first words were "Daddy—kill-IBM, Gateway, Compaq"; who learned from production mistakes and brought in senior managers to help his firm; and who is so private he seldom talks about himself. In other words, you would be thinking of Michael Dell, the founder of Dell Computer, and of his personality.[10]

Personality combines a set of physical and mental characteristics that reflect how a person looks, thinks, acts, and feels. Sometimes attempts are made to measure personality with questionnaires or special tests. Frequently, personality can be inferred from behavior alone, such as by the actions of Michael Dell. Either way, personality is an important individual characteristic to understand—it helps us identify predictable interplays between people's personalities and their tendencies to behave in certain ways.

- **Personality** is the overall combination of characteristics that capture the unique nature of a person as that person reacts to and interacts with others.

Big Five Personality Traits

Numerous lists of **personality traits**—enduring characteristics describing an individual's behavior—have been developed, many of which have been used in OB research and can be looked at in different ways. A key starting point is to consider the personality dimensions that recent research has distilled from extensive lists into what is called the "Big Five":[11]

- *Extraversion*—outgoing, sociable, assertive
- *Agreeableness*—good-natured, trusting, cooperative
- *Conscientiousness*—responsible, dependable, persistent
- *Emotional stability*—unworried, secure, relaxed
- *Openness to experience*—imaginative, curious, broad-minded

- **Personality traits**—enduring characteristics describing an individual's behavior.

The Big Five personality dimensions

CHEATING ON COMPUTERIZED PERSONALITY TESTS

With the move to automation and the pervasiveness of the Internet, a new challenge has arisen for companies trying to rely on computerized personality testing: cheating. Job applicants are finding ways to use the Internet to "crib" answers to electronic personality tests. Answer keys are available on a wide variety of sites. For example, one question states: "You have to give up on some things before you start" and the direction from the online cheat sheet says "strongly disagree." The irony is, some of these tests are intended to judge applicants' integrity and temperament.

Since automated personality tests are often a critical determinant in who gets hired and who does not, the tests are raising other issues as well. Critics question whether such tests are fair, given that some workers are coached in the correct answers by friends or find answers on the Internet. They argue that these tests weed out honest applicants and select those who lie.

This problem seems to be accompanying a larger trend toward cheating in general. Recent studies found that nearly one in four workers lied about lateness and nearly one third of workers called in sick with fake excuses in the past year. These findings are consistent with studies that more than half of business school students report cheating, and more than 46 percent of respondents in a Gallup poll reported seeing some form of cheating in the workplace.

What do you think about this? Are we becoming a cheating society? How do you think companies should handle cheaters?[13]

Standardized personality tests determine how positively or negatively an individual scores on each of these dimensions. For instance, a person scoring high on openness to experience tends to ask lots of questions and to think in new and unusual ways. You can consider a person's individual personality profile across the five dimensions. In terms of job performance, research has shown that conscientiousness predicts job performance across five occupational groups of professions—engineers, police, managers, salespersons, and skilled and semi-skilled employees. Predictability of the other dimensions depends on the occupational group. For instance, not surprisingly, extraversion predicts performance for sales and managerial positions.

A second approach to looking at OB personality traits is to divide them into social traits, personal conception traits, and emotional adjustment traits, and then to consider how those categories come together dynamically.[12]

Social Traits

- **Social traits** are surface-level traits that reflect the way a person appears to others when interacting in social settings.
- **Problem-solving style** reflects the way a person gathers and evaluates information when solving problems and making decisions.

Social traits are surface-level traits that reflect the way a person appears to others when interacting in various social settings. The **problem-solving style**, based on the work of Carl Jung, a noted psychologist, is one measure representing social traits.[14] It reflects the way a person goes about gathering and evaluating information in solving problems and making decisions.

Information gathering involves getting and organizing data for use. Styles of information gathering vary from sensation to intuitive. *Sensation-type individuals* prefer routine and order and emphasize well-defined details in gathering information; they would rather work with known facts than look for possibilities. By contrast,

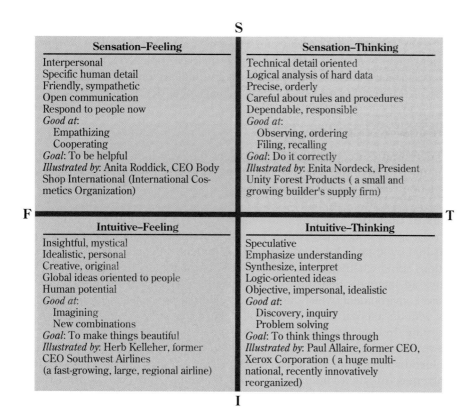

<table>
<tr><td colspan="2" align="center">S</td></tr>
</table>

S

Sensation–Feeling	Sensation–Thinking
Interpersonal	Technical detail oriented
Specific human detail	Logical analysis of hard data
Friendly, sympathetic	Precise, orderly
Open communication	Careful about rules and procedures
Respond to people now	Dependable, responsible
Good at:	*Good at*:
Empathizing	Observing, ordering
Cooperating	Filing, recalling
Goal: To be helpful	*Goal*: Do it correctly
Illustrated by: Anita Roddick, CEO Body Shop International (International Cosmetics Organization)	*Illustrated by*: Enita Nordeck, President Unity Forest Products (a small and growing builder's supply firm)

F _____ **T**

Intuitive–Feeling	Intuitive–Thinking
Insightful, mystical	Speculative
Idealistic, personal	Emphasize understanding
Creative, original	Synthesize, interpret
Global ideas oriented to people	Logic-oriented ideas
Human potential	Objective, impersonal, idealistic
Good at:	*Good at*:
Imagining	Discovery, inquiry
New combinations	Problem solving
Goal: To make things beautiful	*Goal*: To think things through
Illustrated by: Herb Kelleher, former CEO Southwest Airlines (a fast-growing, large, regional airline)	*Illustrated by*: Paul Allaire, former CEO, Xerox Corporation (a huge multinational, recently innovatively reorganized)

I

Figure 2.2 Four problem-solving style summaries.

intuitive-type individuals prefer the "big picture." They like solving new problems, dislike routine, and would rather look for possibilities than work with facts.

The second component of problem solving, *evaluation,* involves making judgments about how to deal with information once it has been collected. Styles of information evaluation vary from an emphasis on feeling to an emphasis on thinking. *Feeling-type individuals* are oriented toward conformity and try to accommodate themselves to other people. They try to avoid problems that may result in disagreements. *Thinking-type individuals* use reason and intellect to deal with problems and downplay emotions.

When these two dimensions (information gathering and evaluation) are combined, four basic problem-solving styles result: sensation–feeling (SF), intuitive–feeling (IF), sensation–thinking (ST), and intuitive–thinking (IT), together with summary descriptions as shown in Figure 2.2.

Research indicates that there is a fit between the styles of individuals and the kinds of decisions they prefer. For example, STs (sensation–thinkers) prefer analytical strategies—those that emphasize detail and method. IFs (intuitive–feelers) prefer intuitive strategies—those that emphasize an overall pattern and fit. Not surprisingly, mixed styles (sensation–feelers or intuitive–thinkers) select both analytical and intuitive strategies. Other findings also indicate that thinkers tend to have higher motivation than do feelers and that individuals who emphasize sensations tend to have higher job satisfaction than do intuitives. These and other findings suggest a number of basic differences among different problem-solving styles, emphasizing the importance of fitting such styles with a task's information processing and evaluation requirements.[15]

Problem-solving styles are most frequently measured by the typically 100-item *Myers-Briggs Type Indicator (MBTI),* which asks individuals how they usually act or feel in specific situations. Firms such as Apple, AT&T, and Exxon, as well as hospitals, educational institutions, and military organizations, have used the Myers-Briggs for various aspects of management development.[16]

Personal Conception Traits

The **personal conception traits** represent the way individuals tend to think about their social and physical setting as well as their major beliefs and personal orientation concerning a range of issues.

Locus of Control   The extent to which a person feels able to control his or her own life is concerned with a person's internal–external orientation and is measured by Rotter's **locus of control** instrument.[17] People have personal conceptions about whether events are controlled primarily by themselves, which indicates an internal orientation, or by outside forces, such as their social and physical environment, which indicates an external orientation. *Internals*, or persons with an internal locus of control, believe that they control their own fate or destiny. In contrast, *externals*, or persons with an external locus of control, believe that much of what happens to them is beyond their control and is determined by environmental forces (such as fate). In general, externals are more extraverted in their interpersonal relationships and are more oriented toward the world around them. Internals tend to be more introverted and are more oriented toward their own feelings and ideas. Figure 2.3 suggests that internals tend to do better on tasks requiring complex information processing and learning as well as initiative. Many managerial and professional jobs have these kinds of requirements.

Proactive Personality   Although some people in organizations are passive recipients when faced with constraints, others take direct and intentional action to change their circumstances. The disposition that identifies whether or not individuals act to influence their environments is known as **proactive personality**. Individuals with high proactive personality identify opportunities and act on them, show initiative, take action, and persevere until meaningful change occurs. In contrast, people who are not proactive fail to identify—let alone seize—opportunities to change things. Less proactive individuals are passive and reactive, preferring to adapt to circumstances rather than change them.[18]

Given the demanding nature of work environments today, many companies are seeking individuals with more proactive qualities—individuals who take initiative and engage in proactive problem solving. Research supports this, showing that proactive personality is positively related to job performance, creativity, leadership, and career success. Other studies have shown proactive personality related to team effectiveness and entrepreneurship. Moreover, when organizations try to make positive and innovative change, these changes have more positive effects for proactive individuals—they are more involved and more receptive to change.

Taken together, research is providing strong evidence that proactive personality is an important and desirable element in today's work environment.

• **Personal conception traits** represent individuals' major beliefs and personal orientation concerning a range of issues concerning social and physical setting.

• **Locus of control** is the extent a person feels able to control his or her own life and is concerned with a person's internal–external orientation.

• A **proactive personality** is the disposition that identifies whether or not individuals act to influence their environments.

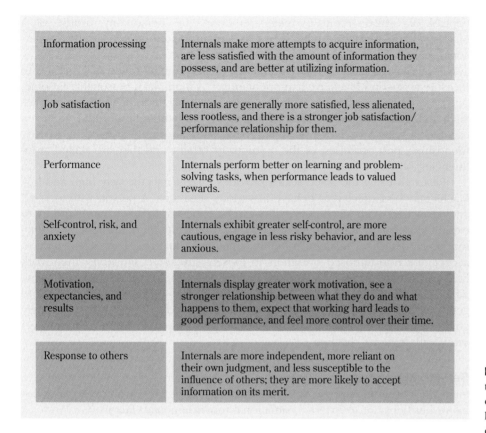

Information processing	Internals make more attempts to acquire information, are less satisfied with the amount of information they possess, and are better at utilizing information.
Job satisfaction	Internals are generally more satisfied, less alienated, less rootless, and there is a stronger job satisfaction/performance relationship for them.
Performance	Internals perform better on learning and problem-solving tasks, when performance leads to valued rewards.
Self-control, risk, and anxiety	Internals exhibit greater self-control, are more cautious, engage in less risky behavior, and are less anxious.
Motivation, expectancies, and results	Internals display greater work motivation, see a stronger relationship between what they do and what happens to them, expect that working hard leads to good performance, and feel more control over their time.
Response to others	Internals are more independent, more reliant on their own judgment, and less susceptible to the influence of others; they are more likely to accept information on its merit.

Figure 2.3 Ways in which those high in internal locus of control differ from those high in external locus of control.

Authoritarianism/Dogmatism   Both "authoritarianism" and "dogmatism" deal with the rigidity of a person's beliefs. A person high in **authoritarianism** tends to adhere rigidly to conventional values and to obey recognized authority. This person is concerned with toughness and power and opposes the use of subjective feelings. An individual high in **dogmatism** sees the world as a threatening place. This person regards legitimate authority as absolute, and accepts or rejects others according to how much they agree with accepted authority. Superiors who possess these latter traits tend to be rigid and closed. At the same time, dogmatic subordinates tend to want certainty imposed upon them.

From an ethical standpoint, we can expect highly authoritarian individuals to present a special problem because they are so susceptible to authority that in their eagerness to comply they may behave unethically.[19] For example, we might speculate that many of the Nazis who were involved in war crimes during World War II were high in authoritarianism or dogmatism; they believed so strongly in authority that they followed unethical orders without question.

Machiavellianism   A third personal conceptions dimension is **Machiavellianism**, which owes its origins to Niccolo Machiavelli. The very name of this sixteenth-century author evokes visions of a master of guile, deceit, and opportunism in interpersonal relations. Machiavelli earned his place in history by writing *The Prince,* a nobleman's guide to the acquisition and use of power.[20] The subject of Machiavelli's book is manipulation as the basic means of gaining and keeping

- **Authoritarianism** is a tendency to adhere rigidly to conventional values and to obey recognized authority.

- **Dogmatism** leads a person to see the world as a threatening place and to regard authority as absolute.

- **Machiavellianism** causes someone to view and manipulate others purely for personal gain.

control of others. From its pages emerges the personality profile of a Machiavellian—someone who views and manipulates others purely for personal gain.

Psychologists have developed a series of instruments called Mach scales to measure a person's Machiavellian orientation.[21] A high-Mach personality is someone who tends to behave in ways consistent with Machiavelli's basic principles. Such individuals approach situations logically and thoughtfully and are even capable of lying to achieve personal goals. They are rarely swayed by loyalty, friendships, past promises, or the opinions of others, and they are skilled at influencing others.

Research using the Mach scales provides insight into the way high and low Machs may be expected to behave in various situations. A person with a "cool" and "detached" high-Mach personality can be expected to take control and try to exploit loosely structured environmental situations but will perform in a perfunctory, even detached, manner in highly structured situations. Low Machs tend to accept direction imposed by others in loosely structured situations; they work hard to do well in highly structured ones. For example, we might expect that, where the situation permitted, a high Mach would do or say whatever it took to get his or her way. In contrast, a low Mach would tend to be much more strongly guided by ethical considerations and would be less likely to lie or cheat or to get away with lying or cheating.

Self-Monitoring A final personal conceptions trait of special importance to managers is self-monitoring. **Self-monitoring** reflects a person's ability to adjust his or her behavior to external, situational (environmental) factors.[22]

High self-monitoring individuals are sensitive to external cues and tend to behave differently in different situations. Like high Machs, high self-monitors can present a very different appearance from their true self. In contrast, low self-monitors, like their low-Mach counterparts, are not able to disguise their behaviors—"what you see is what you get." There is also evidence that high self-monitors are closely attuned to the behavior of others and conform more readily than do low self-monitors.[23] Thus, they appear flexible and may be especially good at responding to the kinds of situational contingencies emphasized throughout this book. For example, high self-monitors should be especially good at changing their leadership behavior to fit subordinates with more or less experience, tasks with more or less structure, and so on.

Emotional Adjustment Traits

The **emotional adjustment traits** measure how much an individual experiences emotional distress or displays unacceptable acts, such as impatience, irritability, or aggression. Often the person's health is affected if they are not able to effectively manage stress. Although numerous such traits are cited in the literature, a frequently encountered one especially important for OB is the Type A/Type B orientation.[24]

Individuals with a **Type A orientation** are characterized by impatience, desire for achievement, and perfectionism. In contrast, those with a **Type B orientation** are characterized as more easygoing and less competitive in relation to daily events.[25] Type A people tend to work fast and to be abrupt, uncomfortable, irritable, and aggressive. Such tendencies indicate "obsessive" behavior, a fairly

• **Self-monitoring** is a person's ability to adjust his or her behavior to external situational (environmental) factors.

• **Emotional adjustment traits** are traits related to how much an individual experiences emotional distress or displays unacceptable acts.

• **Type A orientations** are characterized by impatience, desire for achievement, and a more competitive nature than Type B.

• **Type B orientations** are characterized by an easygoing and less competitive nature than Type A.

widespread—but not always helpful—trait among managers. Many managers are hard-driving, detail-oriented people who have high performance standards and thrive on routine. But when such work obsessions are carried to the extreme, they may lead to greater concerns for details than for results, resistance to change, overzealous control of subordinates, and various kinds of interpersonal difficulties, which may even include threats and physical violence. In contrast, Type B managers tend to be much more laid back and patient in their dealings with co-workers and subordinates.

Personality and Stress

It is but a small step from a focus on the emotional adjustment traits of Type A/ Type B orientation to consideration of the relationship between personality and stress. We define **stress** as a state of tension experienced by individuals facing extraordinary demands, constraints, or opportunities. As we show, stress can be both positive and negative and is an important fact of life in our present work environment.[26]

An especially important set of stressors includes personal factors, such as individual needs, capabilities, and personality.[27] Stress can reach a destructive state more quickly, for example, when experienced by highly emotional people or by those with low self-esteem. People who perceive a good fit between job requirements and personal skills seem to have a higher tolerance for stress than do those who feel less competent as a result of a person-job mismatch.[28] Also, of course, basic aspects of personality are important. This is true not only for those with Type A orientation, but also for the Big Five dimensions of neuroticism or negative affectivity; extroversion or positive affectivity; and openness to experience, which suggests the degree to which employees are open to a wide range of experience likely to involve risk taking and making frequent changes.[29]

- **Stress** is tension from extraordinary demands, constraints, or opportunities.

Sources of Stress

Any look toward your career future in today's dynamic times must include an awareness that stress is something you, as well as others, are sure to encounter.[30] Stressors are the wide variety of things that cause stress for individuals. Some stressors can be traced directly to what people experience in the workplace, whereas others derive from nonwork and personal factors.

Work Stressors   Without doubt, work can be stressful, and job demands can disrupt one's work-life balance. A study of two-career couples, for example, found some 43 percent of men and 34 percent of women reporting that they worked more hours than they wanted to.[31] We know that work stressors can arise from many sources—from excessively high or low task demands, role conflicts or ambiguities, poor interpersonal relations, or career progress that is either too slow or too fast. A list of common stressors includes the following:

- *Task demands*—being asked to do too much or being asked to do too little
- *Role ambiguities*—not knowing what one is expected to do or how work performance is evaluated

Possible work-related stressors

Spillover Effect

American men spend four times as many hours in household and childcare responsibilities than Japanese men, and the number of hours they spend in childcare has doubled since 1965. When combined with the decreasing gap between American women and men in time spent on housework (from 7-1 to 2-1 since 1965), this means that spillover effects are a concern not only for women, but also for men.

- *Role conflicts*—feeling unable to satisfy multiple, possibly conflicting, performance expectations
- *Ethical dilemmas*—being asked to do things that violate the law or personal values
- *Interpersonal problems*—experiencing bad relationships or working with others with whom one does not get along
- *Career developments*—moving too fast and feeling stretched; moving too slowly and feeling stuck on a plateau
- *Physical setting*—being bothered by noise, lack of privacy, pollution, or other unpleasant working conditions

Life Stressors   A less obvious, though important, source of stress for people at work is the *spillover effect* that results when forces in their personal lives "spill over" to affect them at work. Such life stressors as family events (e.g., the birth of a new child), economic difficulties (e.g., the sudden loss of a big investment), and personal affairs (e.g., a separation or divorce) can all be extremely stressful. Since it is often difficult to completely separate work and nonwork lives, life stressors can affect the way people feel and behave on their jobs as well as in their personal lives.

Outcomes of Stress

- **Eustress** is a stress that has a positive impact on both attitudes and performance.
- **Distress** is a negative impact on both attitudes and performance.
- **Job burnout** is a loss of interest in or satisfaction with a job due to stressful working conditions.

Even though we tend to view and discuss stress from a negative perspective, it isn't always a negative influence on our lives. Indeed, there are two faces to stress—one positive and one negative.[32] Constructive stress, or **eustress**, acts in a positive way. It occurs at moderate stress levels by prompting increased work effort, stimulating creativity, and encouraging greater diligence. You may know such stress as the tension that causes you to study hard before exams, pay attention, and complete assignments on time in a difficult class. Destructive stress, or **distress**, is dysfunctional for both the individual and the organization. One form is the **job burnout** that shows itself as loss of interest in and satisfaction with a job due to stressful working conditions. When a person is "burned out," he or she feels exhausted, emotionally and physically, and thus unable to deal positively with work responsibilities and opportunities. Even more extreme reactions sometimes appear in news reports of persons who attack others and commit crimes in what is known as "desk rage" and "workplace rage."

Too much stress can overload and break down a person's physical and mental systems, resulting in absenteeism, turnover, errors, accidents, dissatisfaction, reduced performance, unethical behavior, and even illness. Stanford scholar and consultant Jeffrey Pfeffer calls those organizations that create excessive stress for their members "toxic workplaces." A toxic company implicitly says this to its employees: "We're going to put you in an environment where you have to work in a style and at a pace that is not sustainable. We want you to come in here and burn yourself out. Then you can leave."[33]

As is well known, stress can have a bad impact on a person's health. It is a potential source of both anxiety and frustration, which can harm the body's physiological and psychological well-being over time.[34] Health problems associated with distress include heart attacks, strokes, hypertension, migraine headache, ulcers, substance abuse, overeating, depression, and muscle aches. Managers and team leaders should be alert to signs of excessive distress in themselves and their co-workers. Key symptoms are changes from normal patterns—changes from regular attendance to absenteeism, from punctuality to tardiness, from diligent work to careless work, from a positive attitude to a negative attitude, from openness to change to resistance to change, or from cooperation to hostility.

Managing Stress

Coping Mechanisms   With rising awareness of stress in the workplace, interest is also growing in how to manage, or *cope,* with distress. **Coping** is a response or reaction to distress that has occurred or is threatened. It involves cognitive and behavioral efforts to master, reduce, or tolerate the demands that are created by the stressful situation.

Two major coping mechanisms are those which: (1) regulate emotions or distress (emotion-focused coping), and (2) manage the problem that is causing the distress (problem-focused coping). As described by Susan Folkman, **problem-focused coping** strategies include: "get the person responsible to change his or her mind," "make a plan of action and follow it," and "stand your ground and fight for what you want." **Emotion-focused coping** strategies include: "look for the silver lining, try to look on the bright side of things," "accept sympathy and understanding from someone," and "try to forget the whole thing."[35]

Individual differences are related to coping mechanisms. Not surprisingly, neuroticism has been found to be associated with increased use of hostile reaction, escapism/fantasy, self-blame, sedation, withdrawal, wishful thinking, passivity, and indecisiveness. On the other hand, people high in extraversion and optimism use rational action, positive thinking, substitution, and restraint. And individuals high in openness to experience are likely to use humor in dealing with stress. In other words, the more your personality allows you to approach the situation with positive affect the better off you will be.

Stress Prevention   Stress prevention is the best first-line strategy in the battle against stress. It involves taking action to keep stress from reaching destructive levels in the first place. Work and life stressors must be recognized before

- **Coping** is a response or reaction to distress that has occurred or is threatened.

- **Problem-focused coping** mechanisms manage the problem that is causing the distress.

- **Emotion-focused coping** mechanisms regulate emotions or distress.

MASTERING MANAGEMENT

MANAGING STRESS WITH A POSITIVE ATTITUDE

One of the ways to manage stress is to maintain a positive attitude. Some easy ways to develop a positive attitude include:

- *Be confident*—think: "I can do this"
- *Be positive*
- *Be punctual*—don't procrastinate
- *Be patient*—some things just take time to do
- *Believe in yourself*—you are unique in this world, and so are your talents
- *Set goals for yourself*—then work hard to achieve them
- *Get fun out of life*—don't take yourself too seriously[36]

Rising costs of healthcare are driving companies to focus on wellness. This translates into increased support for gym memberships and a focus on healthy eating, weight loss, and smoking cessation.

one can take action to prevent their occurrence or to minimize their adverse impacts. Persons with Type A personalities, for example, may exercise self-discipline; supervisors of Type A employees may try to model a lower-key, more relaxed approach to work. Family problems may be partially relieved by a change of work schedule; simply knowing that your supervisor understands your situation may also help to reduce the anxiety caused by pressing family concerns.

Personal Wellness   Once stress has reached a destructive point, special techniques of stress management can be implemented. This process begins with the recognition of stress symptoms and continues with actions to maintain a positive performance edge. The term "wellness" is increasingly used these days. **Personal wellness** involves the pursuit of one's job and career goals with the support of a personal health promotion program. The concept recognizes individual responsibility to enhance and maintain wellness through a disciplined approach to physical and mental health. It requires attention to such factors as smoking, weight, diet, alcohol use, and physical fitness. Organizations can benefit from commitments to support personal wellness. A University of Michigan study indicates that firms have saved up to $600 per year per employee by helping them to cut the risk of significant health problems.[37] Arnold Coleman, CEO of Healthy Outlook Worldwide, a health fitness consulting firm, states: "If I can save companies 5 to 20 percent a year in medical costs, they'll listen. In the end you have a well company and that's where the word 'wellness' comes from."[38]

- **Personal wellness** involves the pursuit of one's job and career goals with the support of a personal health promotion program.

Organizational Mechanisms   On the organizational side, there is an increased emphasis today on employee assistance programs designed to provide help for employees who are experiencing personal problems and the stress associated with them. Common examples include special referrals on situations involving spousal abuse, substance abuse, financial difficulties, and legal problems. In such cases, the employer is trying to at least make sure that the employee with a personal problem has access to information and advice on how to get the guidance and perhaps even treatment needed to best deal with it. Organizations that build positive work environments and make significant investments in their employees are best positioned to realize the benefits of their full talents and work potential. As Pfeffer says: "All that separates you from your competitors are the skills, knowledge, commitment, and abilities of the people who work for you. Organizations that treat people right will get high returns."[39] That, in essence, is what the study of organizational behavior is all about.

Values

- **Values** are broad preferences concerning appropriate courses of action or outcomes.

Values can be defined as broad preferences concerning appropriate courses of action or outcomes. As such, values reflect a person's sense of right and wrong or what "ought" to be.[40] "Equal rights for all" and "People should be treated with respect and dignity" are representative of values. Values tend to influence attitudes and behavior. For example, if you value equal rights for all and you go to work for an organization that treats its managers much better than it does its workers, you may form the attitude that the company is an unfair place to work; consequently, you may not produce well or may perhaps leave the company. It is likely that if the company had had a more egalitarian policy, your attitude and behaviors would have been more positive.

Sources of Values

Parents, friends, teachers, siblings, education, experience, and external reference groups are all value sources that can influence individual values. Indeed, peoples' values develop as a product of the learning and experience they encounter from various sources in the cultural setting in which they live. As learning and experiences differ from one person to another, value differences result. Such differences are likely to be deep seated and difficult (though not impossible) to change; many have their roots in early childhood and the way a person has been raised.[41]

Types of Values

The noted psychologist Milton Rokeach has developed a well-known set of values classified into two broad categories.[42] **Terminal values** reflect a person's preferences concerning the "ends" to be achieved; they are the goals an individual would like to achieve during his or her lifetime. Rokeach divides values into 18 terminal values and 18 instrumental values as summarized in Figure 2.4. **Instrumental values** reflect the "means" for achieving desired ends. They represent *how* you might go about achieving your important end states, depending on the relative importance you attached to the instrumental values.

- **Terminal values** reflect a person's preferences concerning the "ends" to be achieved.

- **Instrumental values** reflect a person's beliefs about the means to achieve desired ends.

Terminal Values	Instrumental Values
A comfortable life (and prosperous)	Ambitious (hardworking)
An exciting life (stimulating)	Broad-minded (open-minded)
A sense of accomplishment (lasting contibution)	Capable (competent, effective)
A world at peace (free of war and conflict)	Cheerful (lighthearted, joyful)
A world of beauty (beauty of nature and the arts)	Clean (neat, tidy)
Equality (brotherhood, equal opportunity)	Courageous (standing up for beliefs)
Family security (taking care of loved ones)	Forgiving (willing to pardon)
Freedom (independence, free choice)	Helpful (working for others' welfare)
Happiness (contentedness)	Honest (sincere, truthful)
Inner harmony (freedom from inner conflict)	Imaginative (creative, daring)
Mature love (sexual and spiritual intimacy)	Independent (self-sufficient, self-reliant)
National security (attack protection)	Intellectual (intelligent, reflective)
Pleasure (leisurely, enjoyable life)	Logical (rational, consistent)
Salvation (saved, eternal life)	Loving (affectionate, tender)
Self-respect (self-esteem)	Obedient (dutiful, respectful)
Social recognition (admiration, respect)	Polite (courteous, well mannered)
True friendship (close companionship)	Responsible (reliable, dependable)
Wisdom (mature understanding of life)	Self-controlled (self-disciplined)

Figure 2.4 Rokeach value survey.

Illustrative research shows, not surprisingly, that both terminal and instrumental values differ by group (for example, executives, activist workers, and union members).[43] These preference differences can encourage conflict or agreement when different groups have to deal with each other.

Another frequently used classification of human values has been developed by psychologist Gordon Allport and his associates. These values fall into six major types:[44]

Allport's six value categories

- *Theoretical*—interest in the discovery of truth through reasoning and systematic thinking
- *Economic*—interest in usefulness and practicality, including the accumulation of wealth
- *Aesthetic*—interest in beauty, form, and artistic harmony
- *Social*—interest in people and love as a human relationship
- *Political*—interest in gaining power and influencing other people
- *Religious*—interest in unity and in understanding the cosmos as a whole

Once again, groups differ in the way they rank order the importance of these values. Examples are: ministers—religious, social, aesthetic, political, theoretical, economic; purchasing executives—economic, theoretical, political, religious, aesthetic, social; industrial scientists—theoretical, political, economic, aesthetic, religious, social.[45]

The previous value classifications have had a major impact on the values literature, but they were not specifically designed for people in a work setting. A more recent values schema, developed by Bruce Meglino and associates, is aimed at people in the workplace:[46]

Meglino and associates' value categories

- *Achievement*—getting things done and working hard to accomplish difficult things in life
- *Helping and concern for others*—being concerned for other people and with helping others
- *Honesty*—telling the truth and doing what you feel is right
- *Fairness*—being impartial and doing what is fair for all concerned

These four values have been shown to be especially important in the workplace; thus, the framework should be particularly relevant for studying values in OB.

☞ **Value congruence** occurs when individuals express positive feelings upon encountering others who exhibit values similar to their own.

In particular, values can be influential through **value congruence**, which occurs when individuals express positive feelings upon encountering others who exhibit values similar to their own. When values differ, or are *incongruent*, conflicts over such things as goals and the means to achieve them may result. Meglino and colleagues' value schema was used to examine value congruence between leaders and followers. The researchers found greater follower satisfaction with the leader when there was such congruence in terms of achievement, helping, honesty, and fairness values.[47]

Patterns and Trends in Values   We should also be aware of applied research and insightful analyses of values trends over time. Daniel Yankelovich, for example, is known for his informative public opinion polls among North American workers, and William Fox has prepared a carefully reasoned book analyzing values trends.[48] Both Yankelovich and Fox note movements away from earlier values, with Fox emphasizing a decline in such shared values as duty, honesty, responsibility, and the like, while Yankelovich notes a movement away from valuing economic incentives, organizational loyalty, and work-related identity. The movement is toward valuing meaningful work, pursuit of leisure, and personal identity and self-fulfillment. Yankelovich believes that the modern manager must be able to recognize value differences and trends among people at work. For example, he reports finding higher productivity among younger workers who are employed in jobs that match their values and/or who are supervised by managers who share their values, reinforcing the concept of value congruence.

In a nationwide sample, managers and human resource professionals were asked to identify the work-related values they believed to be most important to individuals in the workforce, both now and in the near future.[49] The nine most popular values named were recognition for competence and accomplishments, respect and dignity, personal choice and freedom, involvement at work, pride in one's work, lifestyle quality, financial security, self-development, and health and wellness. These values are especially important for managers because they indicate some key concerns of the new workforce. Even though each individual worker places his or her own importance on these values, and even though the United States today has by far the most diverse workforce in its history, this overall characterization is a good place for managers to start when dealing with workers in the new workplace. It is important to remember, however, that although values are individual preferences, many tend to be shared within cultures and organizations.

At 83 million–the largest generation of all–Millenials are shaking up the workplace in unprecedented ways. They challenge their more senior colleagues with their techno savvy, multitasking, lower willingness to do "face time," and more casual dress and relaxed style.

Values across National Cultures

The word "culture" is frequently used in organizational behavior in connection with the concept of corporate culture, the growing interest in workforce diversity, and the broad differences among people around the world. Specialists tend to agree that **culture** is the learned, shared way of doing things in a particular society. It is the way, for example, in which its members eat, dress, greet and treat one another, teach their children, solve everyday problems, and so on.[50] Geert Hofstede, a Dutch scholar and consultant, refers to culture as the "software of the mind," making the analogy that the mind's "hardware" is universal among human beings.[51] But the software of culture takes many different forms. We are not born with a culture; we are born into a society that teaches us its culture. And because culture is shared among people, it helps to define the boundaries between different groups and affect how their members relate to one another.

Cultures vary in their underlying patterns of values and attitudes. The way people think about such matters as achievement, wealth and material gain, and risk and change may influence how they approach work and their relationships with organizations. A framework developed by Geert Hofstede offers one approach for understanding how value differences across national cultures can influence human behavior at work. The five dimensions of national culture in his framework can be described as follows:[52]

1. **Power distance** is the willingness of a culture to accept status and power differences among its members. It reflects the degree to which people are likely to respect hierarchy and rank in organizations. Indonesia is considered a high-power-distance culture, whereas Sweden is considered a relatively low-power-distance culture.

• **Culture** is the learned and shared way of thinking and acting among a group of people or society.

• **Power distance** is a culture's acceptance of the status and power differences among its members.

Hofstede's dimensions of national cultures

2. **Uncertainty avoidance** is a cultural tendency toward discomfort with risk and ambiguity. It reflects the degree to which people are likely to prefer structured versus unstructured organizational situations. France is considered a high uncertainty avoidance culture, whereas Hong Kong is considered a low uncertainty avoidance culture.

3. **Individualism–collectivism** is the tendency of a culture to emphasize either individual or group interests. It reflects the degree to which people are likely to prefer working as individuals or working together in groups. The United States is a highly individualistic culture, whereas Mexico is a more collectivist one.

4. **Masculinity–femininity** is the tendency of a culture to value stereotypical masculine or feminine traits. It reflects the degree to which organizations emphasize competition and assertiveness versus interpersonal sensitivity and concerns for relationships. Japan is considered a very masculine culture, whereas Thailand is considered a more feminine culture.

5. **Long-term/short-term orientation** is the tendency of a culture to emphasize values associated with the future, such as thrift and persistence, or values that focus largely on the present. It reflects the degree to which people and organizations adopt long-term or short-term performance horizons. South Korea is high on long-term orientation, whereas the United States is a more short-term-oriented country.

The first four dimensions in Hofstede's framework were identified in an extensive study of thousands of employees of a multinational corporation operating in more than 40 countries.[53] The fifth dimension of long-term/short-term orientation was added from research using the Chinese Values Survey conducted by cross-cultural psychologist Michael Bond and his colleagues.[54] Their research suggested the cultural importance of Confucian dynamism, with its emphasis on persistence, the ordering of relationships, thrift, sense of shame, personal steadiness, reciprocity, protection of "face," and respect for tradition.[55]

When using the Hofstede framework, it is important to remember that the five dimensions are interrelated, not independent.[56] National cultures may best be understood in terms of cluster maps or collages that combine multiple dimensions. For example, Figure 2.5 shows a sample grouping of countries based on individualism-collectivism and power distance. Note that high power distance and collectivism are often found together, as are low power distance and individualism. Whereas high collectivism may lead us to expect a work team in Indonesia to operate by consensus, the high power distance may cause the consensus to be heavily influenced by the desires of a formal leader. A similar team operating in more individualist and low-power-distance Great Britain or America might make decisions with more open debate, including expressions of disagreement with a leader's stated preferences.

At the national level, cultural value dimensions, such as those identified by Hofstede, tend to influence the previously discussed individual sources of values. The sources, in turn, tend to share individual values, which are then reflected in the recipients' value structures. For example, in the United States the sources would tend to be influenced by Hofstede's low-power-distance dimensions (along with his others, of course), and the recipients would tend to interpret their

		Collectivism	Colombia, Peru, Thailand, Singapore, Greece, Mexico, Turkey, Japan, Indonesia

Collectivism   **Countries**   Colombia, Peru, Thailand, Singapore, Greece, Mexico, Turkey, Japan, Indonesia

Individualism   Israel, Finland, Germany, Ireland, New Zealand, Canada, Great Britain, United States   Spain, South Africa, France, Italy, Belgium

Low Power Distance   **High Power Distance**

Figure 2.5 Sample country clusters on Hofstede's dimensions of individualism-collectivism and power distance.

own individual value structures through that low-power-distance lens. Similarly, people in other countries or societies would be influenced by their country's standing on such dimensions.

Diversity

We started this chapter by saying that individual differences are important because they can offer great benefits. The discussion now comes full circle with the topic of diversity.

Importance of Diversity

Interest in workplace diversity gained prominence years ago when it became clear that the demographic make-up of the workforce was going to experience dramatic changes. At that time the workforce was primarily white male. Since then workforce diversity has increased in both the United States and much of the rest of the world, and white males are no longer the majority in the labor force.

The focus on diversity is important, however, not just because of demographic trends but because of the *benefits* diverse backgrounds and perspectives can bring to the workplace. Rather than being something we have to "manage," current perspectives focus on diversity as a key element of the "Global War for Talent." As described by Rob McInness in *Diversity World:*

> It is clear that the greatest benefits of workforce diversity will be experienced not by the companies that have learned to employ people *in spite of* their differences, but by the companies that have learned to employ people *because of* them.[58]

From this perspective, **workforce diversity** refers to a mix of people within a workforce who are considered to be, in some way, different from those in the

Workforce diversity is a mix of people within a workforce who are considered to be, in some way, different from those in the prevailing constituency.

prevailing constituency. Seven important reasons for organizations to engage policies, practices, and perspectives to diversify their workforces are:[59]

1. *Resource Imperative:* Today's talent is overwhelmingly represented by people from a vast array of backgrounds and life experiences. Competitive companies cannot allow discriminatory preferences and practices to impede them from attracting the best available talent.

2. *Capacity-Building Strategy:* Tumultuous change is the norm. Companies that prosper have the capacity to effectively solve problems, rapidly adapt to new situations, readily identify new opportunities, and quickly capitalize on them. This capacity is only realized by a diverse range of talent, experience, knowledge, insight, and imagination in their workforces.

3. *Marketing Strategy:* To ensure that products and services are designed to appeal to the buying power of diverse customer bases, "smart" companies are hiring people from all walks of life for their specialized insights and knowledge; the makeup of their workforce reflects their customer base.

4. *Business Communications Strategy:* All organizations are seeing a growing diversity in the workforces around them—their vendors, partners, and customers. Those that choose to retain homogenous workforces will likely find themselves increasingly ineffective in their external interactions and communications.

5. *Economic Payback:* Many groups of people who have been excluded from workplaces are consequently reliant on tax-supported social service programs. Diversifying the workforce, particularly through initiatives like welfare-to-work, can effectively turn tax users into taxpayers.

6. *Social Responsibility:* By diversifying our workforces we can help people who are "disadvantaged" in our communities get opportunities to earn a living and achieve their dreams.

7. *Legal Requirement:* Many employers are under legislative mandates to be nondiscriminatory in their employment practices. Noncompliance with Equal Employment Opportunity or Affirmative Action legislation can result in fines and/or loss of contracts with government agencies.

Types of Diversity

Given that diversity addresses how people differ from one another in terms of physical or societal characteristics, it can be considered from many perspectives, including demographic (gender, race/ethnicity, age), disability, economic, religion, sexual orientation, marital status, parental status, and even others. Since we cannot address all of them here, this section focuses on several key topics.

Gender　Women now comprise 46.3 percent of U.S. business and 50 percent of management, professional, and related occupations. Even though this number has been increasing steadily over the last 60 years, women are still underrepresented at the highest levels of organizations.[60] Catalyst, a leading source of information on women in business (see Figure 2.7), tracks the number of women on Fortune 500 boards and in corporate officer positions (the highest-level executives who are often board-appointed or board approved).[61] Findings show

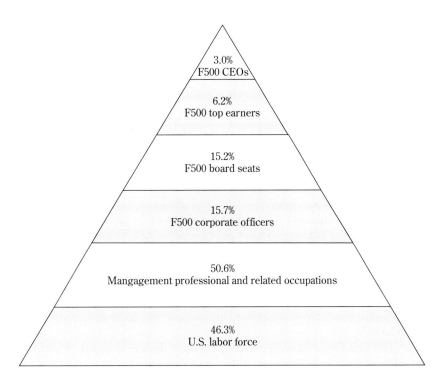

Figure 2.6 The Catalyst Pyramid of U.S. Women in Business.
[*Source:* Based on Catalyst.org/132/us-women-in-business (March, 2009). Used by permission].

that women have steadily gained access to the elite level of corporate leadership, but in the last two years this progress has stalled.[62] Women as top earners and CEOs lag far behind men, with women making up only 3 percent of Fortune 500 CEOs and 6.2 percent of Fortune 500 top earners (see Figure 2.6). As indicated in a Catalyst report,[63] the situation is even more difficult for women of color. In 2005, only 5 percent of all managers, professionals, and related occupations were African-American women; Latinas constituted 3.3 percent, and Asian women 2.6 percent. In Europe the numbers are slightly different, but show a similar pattern. In 2005, women (regardless of race/ethnicity) represented 44 percent of the workforce, 30 percent of managerial positions, and only 3 percent of company CEOs.[64]

Why should we care about this? Because research shows that companies with a higher percentage of female board directors and corporate officers, on average, financially outperform companies with the lowest percentages by significant margins.[65] Women leaders are also beneficial because they encourage more women in the pipeline and act as role models and mentors for younger women. Moreover, the presence of women leaders sends important signals that an organization has a broader and deeper talent pool, is an "employer of choice," and offers an inclusive workplace.

The Leaking Pipeline   Recognition that women have not penetrated the highest level, and even worse, that they are abandoning the corporate workforce just as they are positioned to attain these levels, has gained the attention of many organizations. The phrase **leaking pipeline** was coined to describe this phenomenon. The leaking pipeline theory gained credence with a study by Professor Lynda Gratton of the London Business School.[66] In her study she examined

Leaking pipeline is a phrase coined to describe how women have not reached the highest levels of organizations.

61 organizations operating in 12 European countries and found that the number of women decreases the more senior the roles become.

• **stereotyping** occurs when people make a generalization, usually exaggerated or oversimplified (and potentially offensive) that is used to describe or distinguish a group.

Although research is just beginning to examine what is behind the leaking pipeline, one reason being discussed is potential **stereotyping**. Catalyst research[67] finds that women consistently identify gender stereotypes as a significant barrier to advancement. They describe the stereotyping as the *"think-leader-think-male"* mindset: the idea that men are largely seen as the leaders by default. When probed further, both men and women saw women as better at stereotypically feminine "caretaking skills," such as supporting and encouraging others, and men as excelling at more conventionally masculine "taking charge" skills, such as influencing superiors and problem solving—characteristics previously shown to be essential to leadership. These perceptions are even more salient in traditionally male-dominated fields, such as engineering and law, where women are viewed as "out of place" and have to put considerable effort into proving otherwise.

This creates a problem in terms of a *double bind* for women, meaning that there is no easy choice. If they conform to the stereotype they are seen as weak; if they go against the stereotype they are going against norms of femininity. As some describe, it creates a situation of "damned if they do, doomed if they don't."[68]

The impact of stereotypic bias is often underestimated. Some believe that given the predominance of the stereotypes they must reflect real differences. However, research has shown they misrepresent reality: Gender is not a reliable predictor of how people will lead.[69] In fact, studies show that women outrank men on 42 of 52 executive competencies. Others believe that progress has been made so there is not a problem. As pointed out earlier, however, while progress has been made in management ranks, the same is not true at corporate officer levels. Given that approximately 50 percent of managerial positions have been occupied by women since 1990, we could expect current percentages of women at the highest levels to be higher than 2–3 percent.

As racial diversity is increasing in the workplace, attitudes toward diversity are changing as well. The younger generation, or "Millenials" (those born between 1981 and 2000), are infusing the workplace with an appreciation for differences. Young people want to join a diverse workforce because they feel they can learn from those of different backgrounds: "Once this generation is in management positions corporate diversity will really advance," says Ron Alsop, author of *The Trophy Kids Grow Up.*

What can companies do? One suggestion would be to address stereotypes and biases and consider the additional pressures placed on women as they work to meet the already challenging demands of executive environments. As Catalyst reports, "Ultimately, it is not women's leadership styles that need to change but the structures and perceptions that must keep up with today's changing times." Some things managers can do to change limiting structures and perceptions include:[70]

- Communicate leadership appointment opportunities and decision processes transparently (rather than based on who you know).
- Encourage females to communicate interest in, and apply for, leadership positions.
- Provide mentoring and development infrastructure for high potential female managers that are geared to their unique needs.
- Actively monitor and analyze satisfaction levels of the women managed/coached/mentored.
- Support career development through the family years—not seeing the woman as "not motivated" or the family as a delay in her career path.

- Emphasize personal and family goals, and more meaningful work that makes it worth staying in the workplace—stop the exodus of women poised to obtain top roles.
- Create organizational cultures that are more satisfying to women (e.g., less militaristic, less command-and-control, less status-based and more meaning-based).
- Measure performance through results—with less emphasis on "face-time."
- Value leadership styles that are more inclusive and collaborative and rely less on a high degree of hierarchy.

Race and Ethnicity   Racial and ethnic differences represent another prominent form of diversity in organizations. In the workplace, race and ethnicity are protected from discrimination by **Title VII of the Civil Rights Act of 1964**. This act protects individuals against employment discrimination on the basis of race and color, as well as national origin, sex, and religion. It applies to employers with 15 or more employees, including state and local governments.[71] It also applies to employment agencies and to labor organizations, as well as to the federal government. According to Title VII, equal employment opportunity cannot be denied any person because of his/her racial group or perceived racial group, his/her race-linked characteristics (e.g., hair texture, color, facial features), or because of his/her marriage to or association with someone of a particular race or color. It also prohibits employment decisions based on stereotypes and assumptions about abilities, traits, or the performance of individuals of certain racial groups.

Title VII's prohibitions apply regardless of whether the discrimination is directed at Whites, Blacks, Asians, Latinos, Arabs, Native Americans, Native Hawaiians and Pacific Islanders, multi-racial individuals, or persons of any other race, color, or ethnicity. It covers issues of recruiting, hiring and promotion, transfer, work assignments, performance measurements, the work environment, job training, discipline and discharge, wages and benefits, and any other term, condition, or privilege of employment.

A Focus on Inclusion   While in the past many organizations addressed the issue of racial and ethnic diversity from the standpoint of compliance (e.g., complying with the legal mandate by employing an Employment Equity and Affirmative Action Officer who kept track of and reported statistics), in recent years we have experienced a shift from a focus on diversity to a focus on **inclusion**. As described by Katharine Esty,[72] "This sea change has happened without fanfare and almost without notice. In most organizations, the word inclusion has been added to all the company's diversity materials with no explanation." As Esty explains, this change represents a shift from a numbers game to a focus on culture, and consideration of how organizations can create inclusive cultures for everyone.

The move from diversity to inclusion occurred primarily because employers began to learn that, although they were able to recruit diverse individuals, they were not able to retain them. In fact, some organizations found that after years of trying, they had *lower* representation among certain groups than they had earlier. They pieced together that this was related to the fact that the upper ranks of organizations continued to be primarily white male. In these environments awareness and diversity training was not enough—they needed to go more deeply. So, they asked different questions: Do employees in all groups and categories feel

Title VII of the Civil Rights Act of 1964 protects individuals against employment discrimination on the basis of race and color, national origin, sex, and religion.

Inclusion is the focus of an organization's culture on welcoming and supporting all types and groups of people.

comfortable and welcomed in the organization? Do they feel included, and do they experience the environment as inclusive?[73]

Social Identity Theory   As research shows, these questions are important because they relate to what social psychologists Henri Tajfel and John Turner termed **social identity theory**.[74] Social identity theory was developed to understand the psychological basis of discrimination. It describes individuals as having not one but multiple "personal selves" that correspond with membership in different social groups. For example, you have different "identities" depending on your group memberships: you may have an identity as a woman, a Latina, an "Alpha Delta Pi" sorority sister, etc. Social identity theory says that just the mere act of categorizing yourself as a member of a group will lead you to have favoritism toward that group. This favoritism will be displayed in the form of "in-group" enhancement at the expense of the out-group. In other words, by becoming a member of Alpha Delta Pi you enhance the status of that group and positively differentiate Alpha Delta Pi relative to the other sororities.

In terms of race and ethnicity, social identity theory suggests that simply by having racial or ethnic groups it becomes salient in people's minds; individuals will feel these identities and engage **in-group** and **out-group** categorizations. In organizational contexts these categorizations can be subtle but powerful—and primarily noticeable to those in the "out-group" category. Organizations may not intend to create discriminatory environments, but having only a few members of a group may evoke a strong out-group identity. This may make them feel uncomfortable and less a part of the organization.

Age   It is getting harder to have discussions with managers today without the issue of age differences arising. Age, or more appropriately *generational*, diversity is affecting the workplace like never before. And seemingly everyone has an opinion!

The controversy is being generated from Millenials, Gen Xers, and Baby Boomers mixing in the workplace—and trying to learn how to get along. Baby Boomers, the postwar generation born between 1946 and 1964, make up about 40 percent of today's workforce. Generation X, born between 1965 and 1980, make up about 36 percent of the workplace. Millenials, born between roughly 1981 and 2000, make up about 16 percent of the workforce (with the remaining 8 percent Matures, born between 1922 and 1945). The primary point of conflict: work ethic. Baby Boomers believe that Millenials are not hard working and are too "entitled." Baby Boomers value hard work, professional dress, long hours, and paying their dues—earning their stripes slowly.[75] Millenials believe Baby Boomers and Gen Xers are more concerned about the hours they work than what they produce. Millenials value flexibility, fun, the chance to do meaningful work right away, and "customized" careers that allow them the choice to go at the pace they want.

The generational mix provides an excellent example of diversity in action. Workforces that are more diverse have individuals with different backgrounds, values, perspectives, opinions, styles, etc. If the groups involved can learn to capitalize on these differences, they can create a work environment more beneficial for all. For example, one thing Millenials can bring to the workplace is their appreciation for gender equality and sexual, cultural, and racial diversity—Millenials embrace these concepts more than any previous generation. Millenials also have an appreciation for community and collaboration. They can help create a more

---

Social identity theory is a theory developed to understand the psychological basis of discrimination.

In-group occurs when individuals feel part of a group and experience favorable status and a sense of belonging.

Out-group occurs when one does not feel part of a group and experiences discomfort and low belongingness

relaxed workplace that reduces some of the problems that come from too much focus on status and hierarchy.[76] Boomers and Gen Xers bring a wealth of experience, dedication, and commitment that contribute to productivity, and a sense of professionalism that is benefiting their younger counterparts. Together, Millenials and Gen Xers may be able to satisfy the Gen X desire for work-life balance through greater demand for more flexible scheduling and virtual work. Accomplishing such changes will come when all the generations learn to understand, respect—and maybe even like—one another.

The concept of "universal design" means building so that the environment is aesthetic and usable to the greatest extent possible by everyone, regardless of age, ability, or status in life. One outcome being found from compliance with ADA and universal design is that not only people with disabilities, but *all* people, are benefiting from more careful and thoughtful attention to design.

Disability In recent years the "disability rights movement" has been working to bring attention and support to the needs of disabled workers.[77] The passage of the **Americans with Disabilities Act** (ADA) has been a significant catalyst in advancing their efforts. The ADA is a comprehensive federal civil-rights statute signed into law in 1990 to protect the rights of people with disabilities, and is parallel to acts previously established for women and racial, ethnic, and religious minorities. It prohibits discrimination and mandates that disabled Americans be accorded equality in pursuing jobs, goods, services, and other opportunities.

The focus of the ADA is to eliminate employers' practices that make people with disabilities unnecessarily different. **Disabilities** include any form of *impairment* (loss or abnormality of psychological or anatomical structure or function), *disability* (any restriction or lack of ability to perform an activity in the manner or within the range considered normal for a human being), or *handicap* (a disadvantage resulting from an impairment or disability that limits or prevents the fulfillment of a role that is normal, depending on age, sex, social, and cultural factors, for that individual).

The ADA has helped to generate a more inclusive climate where organizations are reaching out more to people with disabilities. The most visible changes from the ADA have been in issues of **universal design**—the practice of designing products, buildings, public spaces, and programs to be usable by the greatest number of people. You may see this in your own college or university's actions to make their campus and classrooms more accessible.[78]

The disability rights movement is working passionately to advance a redefinition of what it means to be disabled in American society. The goal is to overcome the "stigmas" attached to disability. A **stigma** is a phenomenon whereby an individual with an attribute, which is deeply discredited by his/her society, is rejected as a result of the attribute. Because of stigmas, many are reluctant to seek coverage under the ADA because they do not want to experience discrimination in the form of stigmas.

Estimates indicate that over 50 million Americans have one or more physical or mental disabilities. Even though recent studies report that disabled workers do their jobs as well as, or better than, nondisabled workers, nearly three-quarters of severely disabled persons are reported to be unemployed. Almost 80 percent of those with disabilities say they want to work.[79] Therefore, the need to address issues of stigmas and accessibility for disabled workers is not trivial.

As companies continue to appreciate the value of diversity and activists continue to work to "de-stigmatize" disabilities by working toward a society in which physical and mental differences are accepted as normal and expected—not abnormal or unusual—we can expect to see even greater numbers of disabled workers. This may be accelerated by the fact that the cost of accommodating these workers has been shown to be low.[80]

- The **Americans with Disabilities Act** is a federal civil-rights statute that protects the rights of people with disabilities.

- A **disability** is any form of impairment or handicap.

- **Universal design** is the practice of designing products, buildings, public spaces, and programs to be usable by the greatest number of people.

- **Stigma** is a phenomenon whereby an individual is rejected as a result of an attribute that is deeply discredited by his/her society, is rejected as a result of the attribute.

Leaders on Leadership

STEPHEN HAWKING SOARS DESPITE DISABILITY

Stephen Hawking cannot speak, and does not have use of his motor skills. But he doesn't let that stop him. Renowned for his work in theoretical physics, Hawking has been an influential voice in redefining the way we see black holes and the origin of the universe. He is perhaps most recognized outside academic circles for his book *A Brief History of Time,* in which he explains to laypeople the relationship

between Einstein's General Theory of Relativity and Quantum Theory. Hawking has maintained an extensive program of travel, public lectures, and television appearances—even defying gravity by experiencing weightlessness on a zero-gravity flight for two hours over the Atlantic.

Hawking was diagnosed with ALS, or Lou Gehrig's disease, a few years after his 21st birthday. Over time, ALS has gradually crippled his body, first making him dependent on a wheelchair and private nurse, and then requiring 24-hour nursing care. Unable to speak, he uses a voice synthesizer devised by a colleague that allows him to type rather than having to check letters off a card.

His accomplishments and ability to live a full life, with three children and three grandchildren, have inspired people around the world. As Hawking says, "I'm sure my disability has a bearing on why I'm well known. People are fascinated by the contrast between my very limited physical powers, and the vast nature of the universe I deal with. I'm the archetype of a disabled genius, or should I say a physically challenged genius, to be politically correct. At least I'm obviously physically challenged. Whether I'm a genius is more open to doubt."[81]

Genius or not, Hawking has shown that disability does not equate to inability.

Sexual Orientation   The issue of sexual orientation is also gaining attention in organizations. A December 2008 *Newsweek* poll shows that 87 percent of Americans believe that gays and lesbians should have equal rights in terms of job opportunities.[82] Moreover, many businesses are paying close attention to statistics showing that the gay market segment is one of the fastest growing segments in the United States. The buying power of the gay/lesbian market is set to exceed $835 billion by 2011.[83] Companies wanting to tap into this market will need employees who understand and represent it.

Although sexual orientation is not protected by the Equal Employment Opportunities Commission (EEOC), which addresses discrimination based on race, color, sex, religion, national origin, age, and disability,[84] some states have executive orders protecting the rights of gay and lesbian workers. The first state to pass a law against workplace discrimination based on sexual orientation was Wisconsin in 1982.[85] As of January 2008, thirteen states prohibited workplace discrimination against gay people, while seven more had extended such protections to LGB (lesbian, gay, bisexual) people.

Regardless of legislation, findings are beginning to show that the workplace is improving for gay Americans. Thirty years ago the first U.S. corporation added sexual orientation to its nondiscrimination policy. Can you guess who it was? The company was AT&T and its chairman John DeButts.[87] He made the statement that his company would "respect the human rights of our employees." This action opened the door for other companies, which then began adding same-sex domestic partners to health insurance benefits. In 2007, John Browne, CEO of oil and gas producer BP PLC, said: "If we want to be an employer of the most able people who happen to be gay or lesbian, we won't succeed unless we offer equal benefits for partners in same-sex relationships."

Browne reflects the attitude of a growing list of companies that are extending rights to gay and lesbian workers. In 2007, 4,463 companies offered health insurance benefits to employees' domestic partners, and 2,162 employers have nondiscrimination policies covering sexual orientation. The higher a company is on the Fortune 500 list, the more likely it is to have both domestic partner benefits and a written nondiscrimination policy covering sexual orientation.[88] Among the companies listed as most friendly to gays are Disney, Google, US Airways, the New York Times Co., Ford, Nike, and PepsiCo.

Human Rights Campaign As noted by the Human Rights Campaign president Joe Solmonese, "Each of these companies is working hard to transform their workplaces and make them safer for millions of employees around the country. We can now say that at least 10 million employees are protected on the basis of sexual orientation and gender identity on the job."[89]

While there is still a long way to go, as more gays and lesbians have become open about their sexuality at work and elsewhere, attitudes are changing. Companies are beginning to understand that respecting and recruiting gay employees is good for the employees—and good for the bottom line.

Valuing and Supporting Diversity

The concept of valuing diversity in organizations emphasizes appreciation of differences in creating a setting where everyone feels valued and accepted. Valuing diversity assumes that groups will retain their own characteristics and will shape the firm as well as be shaped by it, creating a common set of values that will strengthen ties with customers, enhance recruitment, and contribute to organizations and society. Sometimes diversity management is resisted because of fear of change and discomfort with differences. But as Dr. Santiago Rodriguez, Director of Diversity for Microsoft, says, true diversity is exemplified by companies that "hire people who are different— knowing and valuing that they will change the way you do business."

So how do managers and firms deal with all this? By committing to the creation of environments that welcome and embrace inclusion and working to promote a better understanding of factors that help support inclusion in organizations. The most prominent of these include:[90]

- Strong commitment to inclusion from the Board and Corporate Officers
- Influential mentors and sponsors who can help provide career guidance and navigate politics
- Opportunities for networking with influential colleagues
- Role models from same-gender, racial, or ethnic group
- Exposure through high visibility assignments

- An inclusive culture that values differences and does not require extensive adjustments to fit in
- Work to acknowledge and reduce subtle and subconscious stereotypes and stigmas

Resources in The OB Skills Workbook

These learning activities from *The OB Skills Workbook* are suggested for Chapter 2.

Case for Critical Thinking	Team and Experiential Exercises	Self-Assessment Portfolio
• Xerox	• What Do You Value in Work?	• Personal Values
	• Prejudice in Our Lives	• Personality Type
	• How We View Differences	
	• Alligator River Story	

2 studyguide

Summary Questions and Answers

What are individual differences and why are they important?

- The study of individual differences attempts to identify where behavioral tendencies are similar and where they are different to be able to more accurately predict how and why people behave as they do.

- For people to capitalize on individual differences they need to be aware of them. Self-awareness is being aware of our own behaviors, preferences, styles, biases, and personalities; awareness of others means being aware of these same things in others.

- Self-concept is the view individuals have of themselves as physical, social, and spiritual or moral beings. It is a way of recognizing oneself as a distinct human being.

- The nature/nurture controversy addresses whether we are the way we are because of heredity, or because of the environments in which we have been raised and live.

What is personality?

- Personality captures the overall profile, or combination of characteristics, that represents the unique nature of an individual as that individual interacts with others.

- Personality is determined by both heredity and environment; across all personality characteristics, the mix of heredity and environment is about 50–50. The Big Five personality traits consist of extraversion, agreeableness, conscientiousness, emotional stability, and openness to experience.

- A useful personality framework consists of social traits, personal conception traits, emotional adjustment traits, and personality dynamics, where each category represents one or more personality dimensions.

How are personality and stress related?

- Stress emerges when people experience tensions caused by extraordinary demands, constraints, or opportunities in their jobs.

- Personal stressors derive from personality type, needs, and values; they can influence how stressful different situations become for different people.

- Work stressors arise from such things as excessive task demands, interpersonal problems, unclear roles, ethical dilemmas, and career disappointments.

- Nonwork stress can spill over to affect people at work; nonwork stressors may be traced to family situations, economic difficulties, and personal problems.

- Stress can be managed by prevention—such as making adjustments in work and nonwork factors; it can also be dealt with through coping mechanisms and personal wellness—taking steps to maintain a healthy body and mind capable of better withstanding stressful situations.

What are value differences and how do they vary across cultures?

- Values are broad preferences concerning courses of action or outcomes.

- Rokeach identifies terminal values (preferences concerning ends) and instrumental values (preferences concerning means); Allport and his associates identify six value categories, ranging from theoretical to religious; Meglino and his associates classify values into achievement, helping and concern for others, honesty, and fairness.

- Hofstede's five national culture values dimensions are power distance, individualism–collectivism, uncertainty avoidance, masculinity–femininity, and long-term/short-term orientation.

- Culture is the learned and shared way of doing things in a society; it represents deeply ingrained influences on the way people from different societies think, behave, and solve problems.

What is diversity and why is it important in the workplace?

- Workforce diversity is increasing in the United States and other countries. It is important because of the benefits diverse backgrounds and perspectives can bring to the workplace.

- Rather than being something we have to "manage," diversity should be something we value. There are many reasons to value diversity, from resource and capacity-building perspectives to social and legal responsibilities.

- There are many types of diversity, but the most commonly discussed in the workplace are gender, racial/ethnic, age, disability, and sexual orientation.

- In recent years there has been a shift from a focus on diversity to a focus on inclusion. This represents a need to emphasize not only recruitment but retention.

- Social identity theory suggests that many forms of discrimination are subtle but powerful, and may occur in subconscious psychological processes that individuals of out-groups perceive in the workplace.

- Companies can value diversity by promoting cultures of inclusion that implement policies and practices to help create a more equitable and opportunity-based environment for all.

Key Terms

Americans with Disabilities
   Act (p. 51)
Authoritarianism (p. 35)
Awareness of others
   (p. 28)
Coping (p. 39)
Culture (p. 43)
Disability (p. 51)
Distress (p. 38)
Dogmatism (p. 35)
Emotion-focused coping
   (p. 39)
Emotional adjustment traits
   (p. 36)
Eustress (p. 38)
Inclusion (p. 49)
Individual differences
   (p. 28)
Individualism-collectivism
   (p. 44)
In-group (p. 50)
Instrumental values (p. 41)

Job burnout (p. 38)
Leaking pipeline (p. 47)
Locus of control (p. 34)
Long-term/short-term
   orientation (p. 44)
Machiavellianism (p. 35)
Masculinity-femininity
   (p. 44)
Out-group (p. 50)
Personal conception traits
   (p. 34)
Personal wellness (p. 40)
Personality (p. 31)
Personality traits (p. 31)
Power distance (p. 43)
Proactive personality
   (p. 34)
Problem-focused coping
   (p. 39)
Problem-solving style
   (p. 32)
Self-awareness (p. 28)

Self-concept (p. 28)
Self-esteem (p. 28)
Self-efficacy (p. 29)
Self-monitoring (p. 36)
Social identity theory
   (p. 50)
Social traits (p. 32)
Stereotyping (p. 48)
Stigma (p. 51)
Stress (p. 37)
Terminal values (p. 41)
Title VII of the Civil Rights
   Act of 1964 (p. 49)
Type A orientation (p. 36)
Type B orientation (p. 36)
Uncertainty avoidance
   (p. 44)
Universal design (p. 51)
Value congruence (p. 42)
Values (p. 40)
Workforce diversity (p. 45)

Self-Test 2

Multiple Choice

1. Values in the United States _____. (a) are largely unchanged across time (b) have moved away from earlier values (c) are virtually the same as attitudes (d) tend not to be shared within cultures and organizations

2. Values are _____. (a) similar to personality variables (b) used in place of abilities (c) related to aptitudes (d) similar to attitudes

3. _____ is the study of how people in different cultures use persistence, the ordering of relationships, thrift, sense of shame, personal steadiness, reciprocity, protection of "face," and respect for tradition to communicate. (a) Confucian dynamism (b) The Whorfian hypothesis (c) Proxemics (d) Domestic multiculturalism

4. One would expect to find respect for authority and acceptance of status differences in cultures with high _____. (a) power distance (b) individualism (c) uncertainty avoidance (d) aggressiveness

5. Asian countries such as Japan and China are described on Hofstede's dimensions of national culture as generally high in _____. (a) uncertainty avoidance (b) short-term orientation (c) long-term orientation (d) individualism

6. The Big Five framework consists of _____. (a) five aptitudes and abilities (b) five demographic characteristics (c) extraversion, agreeableness, strength, emotional stability, and openness to experience (d) extraversion, agreeableness, conscientiousness, emotional stability, and openness to experience

7. Personality dynamics is represented by _____. (a) self-esteem and self-efficacy (b) Type A/Type B orientation (c) self-monitoring (d) Machiavellianism

8. Task demands and ethical dilemmas are examples of _____ stressors, while a Type A personality is a _____ stressor. (a) work-related; personal (b) work-related; nonwork (c) nonpersonal; personal (d) real; imagined

9. Stress that comes from not knowing or understanding what you are expected to do is caused by the stressor of _____. (a) role conflict (b) task demands (c) interpersonal problems (d) role ambiguity

10. Which is an example of stress management by using the personal wellness strategy? (a) role negotiation (b) empowerment (c) regular physical exercise (d) flexible hours

11. In the United States, Canada, the European Union, and much of the rest of the world, the workforce is _____. (a) becoming more homogeneous (b) more highly motivated than before (c) becoming more diverse (d) less motivated than before

12. Stereotyping occurs when one thinks of an individual _____. (a) as different from others in a given group (b) as possessing characteristics commonly associated with members of a given group (c) as like some members of a given group but different from others (d) as basically not very competent

13. Managing diversity and affirmative action are _____. (a) similar terms for the same thing (b) both mandated by law (c) different but complementary (d) becoming less and less important

14. Demographic differences _____. (a) are especially valuable in selecting workers (b) are based on aptitudes and abilities (c) are the background variables that help shape who a person becomes over time (d) are important personality aspects

Short Response

15. Why is the individualism-collectivism dimension of national culture important in OB?

16. How do power-distance values affect management practices across cultures?

17. In what ways are demographic characteristics important in the workplace?

18. How might stress influence individual performance?

Applications Essay

19. Your boss is trying to figure out how to get the kinds of people she needs for her organization to do well, while at the same time dealing appropriately with an increasing number of nonwhite workers. She has asked you to respond to this concern. Prepare a short report with specific suggestions for your boss.

3

Emotions, Attitudes, and Job Satisfaction

chapter at a glance

When we're feeling good there's hardly anything better. But when we're feeling down, it takes a toll on us and possibly others. OB scholars are very interested in emotions, attitudes, and job satisfaction. Here's what to look for in Chapter 3. Don't forget to check your learning with the Summary Questions & Answers and Self-Test in the end-of-chapter Study Guide.

WHAT ARE EMOTIONS AND MOODS?

Emotions
Emotional Intelligence
Types of Emotions
Moods

HOW DO EMOTIONS AND MOODS INFLUENCE BEHAVIOR IN ORGANIZATIONS?

Emotion and Mood Contagion
Emotional Labor
Emotions and Moods across Cultures
Emotions and Moods as Affective Events
Functions of Emotions and Moods

WHAT ARE ATTITUDES?

Components of Attitudes
Attitudes and Behavior
Attitudes and Cognitive Consistency
Types of Job Attitudes

WHAT IS JOB SATISFACTION AND WHAT ARE ITS IMPLICATIONS?

Components of Job Satisfaction
Job Satisfaction Findings
Job Satisfaction and Behavior
Job Satisfaction and Performance

Ibukun Awosika is a force for change in Nigeria. Recognized as a successful entrepreneur, her lasting legacy will undoubtedly be her commitment to integrating values in business.

After receiving degrees in Chemistry and Business in Nigeria, she received a Global Executive MBA from IESE Business School in Barcelona, Spain. An ordained minister with her own television program, she is active in various organizations that support women in business and workplace training and development programs for Nigerians.

Her company, The Chair Centre Ltd, became a market leader in the office furniture industry. Overcoming infrastructure issues in Nigeria, she designed the components herself and arranged for them to be manufactured abroad then shipped back to Nigeria for assembly. Her ingenuity was in taking the few imported components and creating a variety of product designs. She was the first to introduce ergonomic chairs in Nigeria and expanded her business operations beyond furniture to introduce the first bank security doors to the Nigerian market as well.

Her business was threatened in 2004 when the Nigerian government banned importation of furniture as a means to develop the local industry. "This could have been the end for us in business. Conversely, we had a choice to either resort to smuggling or find a more acceptable way of remaining in business. We settled for the latter." She entered a joint venture with Sokoa SA of France and successfully opened a local manufacturing plant that created more jobs for Nigerians. An ordained minister, Awosika believes that values play a critical role in business and that those in business must serve as role models in integrating faith-based principles in their business practices.

Her recent entrepreneurial ventures have been social in nature such as the AfterSchool Graduate Development Center. It is an effort to counsel individuals about careers and increase their employability.

When asked about her future goals she says, "Only God can tell exactly. But I see me becoming a better person in all counts and more accomplished in my set dreams to make a difference in society." Her strong work ethic, positive attitude, persistence and faith are key ingredients in her success, the success of her businesses, and her efforts to help others improve their own lives.

ibukun awosika and values in business

Foundations of Emotions and Moods

How do you feel when you are driving a car and halted by a police officer? You are in class and find out you received a poor grade on an exam? A favorite pet passes away? You check your e-mail and discover that you are being offered a job interview? A good friend walks right by without speaking? A parent or sibling or child loses their job? Or, you get this SMS from a new acquaintance: "Ur gr8 ☺!"?

• **Affect** is the range of feelings in the forms of emotions and moods that people experience in their life context.

These examples show how what happens to us draws out "feelings" of many forms, such as happy or sad, angry or pleased. These feelings constitute what scholars call **affect**, the range of feelings in the forms of emotions and moods that people experience in their life context.[1] Affects have important implications not only for our lives in general but also our behavior at work.[2] Don Johnson, featured in the opening example, might have allowed his "frustration" at slow career progress to turn into negative affect toward McDonald's. Fortunately for him and the company it didn't. With the help of a career mentor, his willingness to work hard was supported by positive affects that surely contributed to his rise to senior management.

Emotions

• **Emotions** are strong positive or negative feelings directed toward someone or something.

Anger, excitement, apprehension, attraction, sadness, elation, grief . . . An **emotion** is a strong positive or negative feeling directed toward someone or something.[3] Emotions are usually intense, not long-lasting, and always associated with a source—someone or something that makes us feel the way we do. For example, you might feel positive emotion of elation when an instructor congratulates you on a fine class presentation; you might feel negative emotion of anger when an instructor criticizes you in front of the class. In both situations the object of your emotion is the instructor, but the impact of the instructor's behavior on your feelings is quite different in each case. And your behavior in response to the aroused emotions is likely to differ as well—perhaps breaking into a wide smile after the compliment, or making a nasty side comment or withdrawing from further participation after the criticism.

Emotional Intelligence

• **Emotional intelligence** is an ability to understand emotions and manage relationships effectively.

All of us are familiar with the notions of cognitive ability and intelligence, or IQ, which have been measured for many years. A more recent concept is **emotional intelligence**, or EI. First introduced in Chapter 1 as a component of a manager's essential human skills, it is defined by scholar Daniel Goleman as an ability to understand emotions in ourselves and others and to use that understanding to manage relationships effectively.[4] EI is demonstrated in the ways in which we deal with affect, for example, by knowing when a negative emotion is about to cause problems and being able to control that emotion so that it doesn't become disruptive.

Goleman's point with the concept of emotional intelligence is that we perform better when we are good at recognizing and dealing with emotions in ourselves and others. When we are high in EI, we are more likely to behave in ways that avoid having our emotions "get the better of us." Knowing that an instructor's criticism causes us to feel anger, for example, we might be better able to control that anger when being criticized, maintain a positive face, and perhaps earn the instructor's praise when we make future class contributions. If the unchecked anger caused us to act in a verbally aggressive way—creating a negative impression in the instructor's eyes—or to withdraw from all class participation—causing the instructor to believe we have no interest in the course, our course experience would likely suffer.

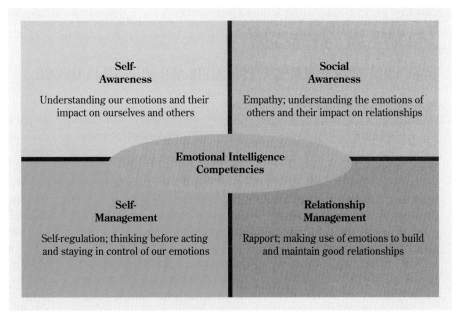

Figure 3.1 Four key emotional intelligence competencies for leadership success.

The essential argument is that if you are good at knowing and managing your emotions and are good at reading others' emotions, you may perform better while interacting with other people. This applies to work and life in general, and to leadership situations in particular.[5] Figure 3.1 identifies four essential emotional intelligence competencies that can and should be developed for leadership success and, we can say, success more generally in all types of interpersonal situations.[6] The competencies are self-awareness, social awareness, self-management, and relationship management.

Self-awareness is the ability to understand our emotions and their impact on our work and on others. You can think of this as a continuing appraisal of your emotions that results in a good understanding of them and the capacity to express them naturally. **Social awareness** is the ability to empathize, to understand the emotions of others, and to use this understanding to better relate to them. It involves continuous appraisal and recognition of others' emotions, resulting in better perception and understanding of them.

Self-management in emotional intelligence is the ability to think before acting and to be in control of otherwise disruptive impulses. It is a form of *self-regulation* in which we stay in control of our emotions and avoid letting them take over. **Relationship management** is an ability to establish rapport with others in ways that build good relationships and influence their emotions in positive ways. It shows up as the capacity to make good use of emotions by directing them toward constructive activities and improved relationships.

- **Self-awareness** is the ability to understand our emotions and their impact on us and others.
- **Social awareness** is the ability to empathize and understand the emotions of others.
- **Self-management** is the ability to think before acting and control disruptive impulses.
- **Relationship management** is the ability to establish rapport with others to build good relationships.

Types of Emotions

When it comes to emotions and emotional intelligence, researchers have identified six major types of emotions: anger, fear, joy, love, sadness, and surprise. The key question from an emotional intelligence perspective is: Do we recognize these emotions in ourselves and others, and can we manage them well? Anger, for example, may involve disgust and envy, both of which can have

Leaders on Leadership

MARGARITA BARNEY ALMEIDA: EDUCATION AND ACTIVISM IN MEXICO

Margarita Barney, a native of Chihuahua, Mexico was brought up in a wealthy, conservative family. She attributes her strong work ethic and respect for others and nature to her experience as a student in the Montessori system in Mexico. Her interest in the environment, cultivated at a young age, took a more focused turn when she moved with her husband to Mexico City.

Witnessing first hand extensive pollution and confronted with an apathetic attitude from the majority of city residents, she felt the need to make a difference. At first, Margarita approached the problem by organizing community initiatives to clean up dumps and plant trees. While successful with these efforts, she soon realized she needed to become more educated herself on how to make a more lasting impact.

Ms. Almeida sought to learn more about environmental topics and thus began her personal journey in strengthening her own knowledge and skills. She took a variety of courses and seminars educating herself about the environment and ecotechnologies that can improve the relationship between humans and their particular local environment.

Her most significant achievement has been in successfully changing the perceptions among her fellow citizens on how they view and interact with the environment. She has been able to do so through programs offered by her organization, Grupo ara Promover la Educacion y el Dessarrollo Sustentable, A.C. (GRUPEDSAC) or the Group to Promote Education and Sustainable Development.

Her organization operates two demonstration centers, one in Estado de Mexico and one in Oaxaca which were built using the same self-sufficient ecological technologies taught to local residents. Construction materials consist of local resources such as packed earth, straw, and cob; one center uses solar energy for lighting and rainwater is collected and used.

Her passion for protecting the environment is evident through the many educational programs her organization offers to community members, state governments, and corporations. While the overall focus is on self-sufficiency and sustainability, her youth programs focus on making young people protectors of the environment and allows her to pass her passion for the environment on to future generations.

Margarita's efforts have been widely recognized with various accolades and awards. Her work has been praised by the Ashoka organization and the World Economic Forum. A Kellogg Foundation grant has allowed her to expand beyond Mexico and offer programs in approximately 18 Latin American countries.

very negative consequences. Fear may contain alarm and anxiety; joy may contain cheerfulness and contentment; love may contain affection, longing, and lust; sadness may contain disappointment, neglect, and shame.

- **Self-conscious emotions** arise from internal sources, and **social emotions** derive from external sources.

It is also common to differentiate between **self-conscious emotions** that arise from internal sources and **social emotions** that are stimulated by external sources.[7] Shame, guilt, embarrassment, and pride are examples of internal emotions. Understanding self-conscious emotions helps individuals regulate their relationships with others. Social emotions like pity, envy, and jealousy derive from external cues and information. An example is feeling envious or jealous upon learning that a co-worker received a promotion or job assignment that you were hoping to get.

Moods

Whereas emotions tend to be short-term and clearly targeted at someone or something, **moods** are more generalized positive and negative feelings or states of mind that may persist for some time. Everyone seems to have occasional moods, and we each know the full range of possibilities they represent. How often do you wake up in the morning and feel excited and refreshed and just happy, or wake up feeling grouchy and depressed and generally unhappy? And what are the consequences of these different moods for your behavior with friends and family, and at work or school?

In respect to OB a key question relating to moods is how do they affect someone's likeability and performance at work? When it comes to CEOs, for example, a *Business Week* article claims that it pays to be likable; "harsh is out, caring is in."[8] Some CEOs are even hiring executive coaches to help them manage their affects to come across as more personable and friendly in relationships with others. If a CEO goes to a meeting in a good mood and gets described as "cheerful," "charming," "humorous," "friendly," and "candid," she or he may be viewed as on the upswing. But if the CEO goes into a meeting in a bad mood and is perceived as "prickly," "impatient," "remote," "tough," "acrimonious," or even "ruthless," the view will more likely be of a CEO on the downslide.

Figure 3.2 offers a brief comparison of emotions and moods. In general, emotions are intense feelings directed at someone or something; they always have rather specific triggers; and they come in many types—anger, fear, happiness, and the like. Moods tend to be more generalized positive or negative feelings. They are less intense than emotions and most often seem to lack a clear source; it's often hard to identify how or why we end up in a particular mood.[9] But moods tend to be more long-lasting than emotions. When someone says or does something that causes a quick and intense positive or negative reaction from you, that emotion will probably quickly pass. However, a bad or good mood is likely to linger for hours or even days, is generally displayed in a wide range of behaviors, and is less likely to be linked with a specific person or event.

> **Moods** are generalized positive and negative feelings or states of mind.

Emotions and Moods in Organizations

Not too long ago, CEO Mark V. Hurd of Hewlett-Packard found himself dealing with a corporate scandal. It seems that the firm had hired "consultants" to track down what were considered to be confidential leaks by members of HP's Board

Emotions	Moods
"I was really angry when Prof. Nitpicker criticized my presentation."	*"Oh, I just don't have the energy to do much today; I've felt down all week."*
• identified with a source, cause	• hard to identify source, cause
• tend to be brief, episodic	• can be long lasting
• many forms and types	• either "positive" or "negative"
• action-oriented; link with behavior	• more cerebral; less action oriented
• can turn into a mood	• can influence emotions

Figure 3.2 Emotions and moods are different, but can also influence one another.

of Directors. When meeting the press and trying to explain the situation and resignation of Board Chair Patricia C. Dunn, Hurd called the actions "very disturbing" and *The Wall Street Journal* described him as speaking with "his voice shaking."[10]

Looking back on this situation, we can say that Hurd was emotional and angry that the incident was causing public humiliation for him and the company. Chances are the whole episode resulted in him being in a bad mood for a while. In the end both he and the company came out of the scandal fine, but in the short run, at least, Hurd's emotions and mood probably had consequences for those working directly with him and for HP's workforce as a whole.

Emotion and Mood Contagion

Although emotions and moods are influenced by different events and situations, each of us may be prone to displaying some relatively stable tendencies.[11] Some people seem most always positive and upbeat about things. For these optimists we might say the glass is nearly always half full. Others, by contrast, seem to be often negative or downbeat. They tend to be pessimists viewing the glass as half empty. Such tendencies toward optimism and pessimism not only influence the individual's behavior, they can also influence other people he or she interacts with—co-workers, friends, and family members.

- **Emotion and mood contagion** is the spillover of one's emotions and mood onto others.

- **Emotional labor** is a situation where a person displays organizationally desired emotions in a job.

Researchers are increasingly interested in **emotion and mood contagion**—the spillover effects of one's emotions and mood onto others.[12] You might think of emotion and mood contagion as a bit like catching a cold from someone. Evidence shows that positive and negative emotions are "contagious" in much the same ways, even though the tendency may be underrecognized in work settings. In one study team members were found to share good and bad moods within two hours of being together; bad moods, interestingly, traveled person-to-person faster than good moods.[13] Other research found that when mood contagion is positive followers report being more attracted to their leaders and rate the leaders more highly. Mood contagion can also have inflationary and deflationary effects on the moods of co-workers and teammates, as well as family and friends.[14]

Daniel Goleman and his colleagues studying emotional intelligence consider emotion and mood contagion an important leadership issue that should be managed with care. "Moods that start at the top tend to move the fastest," they say, "because everyone watches the boss."[15] This was very evident as CEOs in all industries—business and nonprofit alike, struggled to deal with the impact of economic crisis on their organizations and workforces. "Moaning is not a management task," said Rupert Stadler of Audi: "We can all join in the moaning, or we can make a virtue of the plight. I am rather doing the latter."[16]

Emotional Labor

The concept of **emotional labor** relates to the need to show certain emotions in order to do a job well. It is a form of self-regulation to display organizationally desired emotions in one's job. Good examples come from service settings such as airline check-in personnel or flight attendants. They are supposed to appear approachable, receptive, and friendly while taking care of the things you require as a customer. Some airlines like Southwest go even

Life is Good

Bert and John Jacobs began selling tee shirts on Boston streets and now run an $80 million company–Life is Good. John says: "Life is good . . . Don't determine that you're going to be happy when you get the new car or the big promotion or meet that special person. You can decide that you're going to be happy today."

further in asking service employees to be "funny" and "caring" and "cheerful" while doing their jobs.

Emotional labor isn't always easy; it can be hard to be consistently "on," projecting the desired emotions associated with one's work. If you're having a bad mood day or just experienced an emotional run-in with a neighbor, for example, being "happy" and "helpful" with a demanding customer might seem a little much to ask. Such situations can cause **emotional dissonance** where the emotions we actually feel are inconsistent with the emotions we try to project.[18] That is, we are expected to act with one emotion while we actually feel quite another.

Using the service setting as an example again, imagine how often service workers struggling with personal emotions and moods experience dissonance when having to display very different ones toward customers.[19] Scholars point out that *deep acting* occurs when someone tries to modify their feelings to better fit the situation—such as putting yourself in the position of the air travelers whose luggage went missing and feeling the same sense of loss. *Surface acting* is a case of hiding true feelings while displaying very different ones—such as smiling at a customer even though they just offended you.

> • **Emotional dissonance** is inconsistency between emotions we feel and those we try to project.

WELL-TREATED STAFF DELIVERS CONSISTENT RESULTS

Have you had a Chick-fil-A sandwich lately? Don't plan on stopping in on a Sunday; the chain's stores are all closed. It is a tradition started by 85-year-old founder Truett Cathy, who believes that employees deserve a day of rest. As someone who believes in "people before profits," Truett has built a successful, fast-growing, fast-food franchise known for consistent quality and great customer service. He says: "It's important to keep people happy."

The president of the national Restaurant Association Educational Foundation says: "I don't think there's any chain that creates such a wonderful culture around the way they treat their people and the respect they have for their employees."

Current President Dan T. Cathy, the founder's son, believes the Sunday day of rest is a statement about Chick-fil-A's culture. "If we take care of our team members and operators behind the counter," he says, "then they are going to do a better job on Monday. In fact I say our food tastes better on Monday because we are closed on Sunday."

Another statement of the family values behind the firm is the Leadership Scholarship program for employees. When the 20,000th education scholarship was awarded, Truett said: "It has long been my goal to encourage our restaurant employees to strive for excellence . . . so they will have the tools necessary to secure a bright future for themselves and our nation."

> **Ethics Question:** *There seems to be something ethical, almost spiritual about Truett's notion of "people before profits." How about it? Can ethics in leadership result in positive emotion and mood contagion among members of a workforce? And when Dan Cathy says "our food tastes better on Monday because we are closed Sunday," what does this suggest about how emotions, attitudes, and job satisfaction influence work performance?*

Emotions and Moods across Cultures

Issues of emotional intelligence, emotion and mood contagion, and emotional labor, become even more complicated in cross-cultural situations. The frequency and intensity of emotions has been shown to vary among cultures. In mainland China, for example, research suggests that people report fewer positive and negative emotions as well as less intense emotions than in other cultures.[20] Yet people's interpretations of emotions and moods appear similar across cultures, with the major emotions of happiness, joy, and love all valued positively.[21]

Norms for emotional expression can vary across cultures. In collectivist cultures that emphasize group relationships, individual emotional displays are less likely to occur and less likely to be accepted than in individualistic cultures.[22] Informal cultural standards called **display rules** govern the degree to which it is appropriate to display emotions. For example, British culture tends to encourage downplaying emotions, while Mexican culture is much more demonstrative in public. When Wal-Mart first went to Germany, its executives found that an emphasis on friendliness embedded in its U.S. Roots, didn't work as well in the local culture. The more "serious" German shoppers did not respond well to Wal-Mart's friendly greeters and helpful personnel. And along the same lines, Israeli shoppers equate smiling cashiers with inexperience; cashiers are encouraged to look somber while performing their jobs.[23] Overall, the lesson is that we should be sensitive to the way emotions are displayed in other cultures; often they may not mean what they do at home.

• **Display rules** govern the degree to which it is appropriate to display emotions.

Emotions and Moods as Affective Events

Figure 3.3 summarizes the Affective Events Theory as a way of summarizing and integrating this discussion of emotions, moods, and human behavior in organizations.[24] The basic notion of the theory is that our emotions and moods are influenced by events involving other people and situations, and these emotions and moods, in turn, influence the work performance and satisfaction of us and others.

The left-hand side of Figure 3.3 indicates how the work environment, including emotional labor requirements, and work events like hassles and uplifts create emotional reactions. These, in turn, influence satisfaction and performance.[25]

We have all experienced hassles and uplifts on the job, sometimes many of these during a work day. People respond to these experiences through positive and negative emotional reactions. Personality may influence positive and negative reactions, as can moods. Your mood at a given time can exaggerate the nature of the emotions you experience as a result of an event. For example, if you have just been laid off, you are likely to feel worse than you would otherwise when a colleague says something to you that was meant as a neutral comment.

Functions of Emotions and Moods

In the final analysis, we should remember that emotions and moods can be functional as well as dysfunctional. The important thing is to manage them well—the

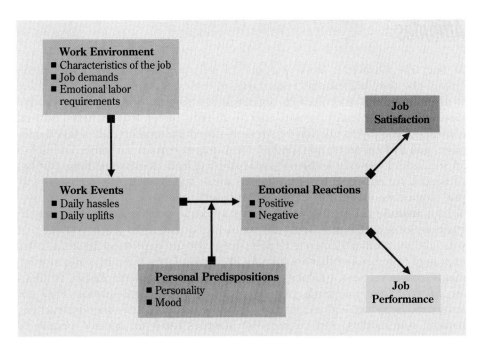

Figure 3.3 Figurative summary of affective events theory.

essence of emotional intelligence. Emotions and moods communicate; they are messages to us that can be valuable if heard and understood.[26] Some, such as Charles Darwin, have argued that emotions are useful in a person's survival process. For instance, the emotion of excitement may encourage you to deal with situations requiring high levels of energy, such as special school and job assignments. Although the emotion of anger is often bad, when channeled correctly it might stop someone from taking advantage of you.

MASTERING MANAGEMENT

MANAGING EMOTIONS WHEN TIMES ARE TOUGH

Especially when times are bad, the ways managers deal with emotions and moods might be as important as the actual decisions they make. So says executive coach Catherine Sandler. Her advice to leaders struggling to deal with the economic crisis was to contain anxieties and help others feel safe while following these guidelines.

- *Take quick and considered action*—make clear the problems are a top priority even though time might be required to fix them.
- *Communicate honestly and consistently*—stay calm, don't get cross, repeat the message even when asked the same questions over and over.
- *Make an emotional connection with everyone*—bad news is shocking and makes people unsettled; avoid being remote or aloof; show regret and understanding.
- *Be sure to inspire*—make and keep a positive connection with everyone; make temperament and character part of your confidence-boosting contributions.

Attitudes

At one time Challis M. Lowe was one of only two African-American women among the five highest-paid executives in U.S. companies surveyed by the woman's advocacy and research organization Catalyst.[27] She became executive vice president at Ryder System after a 25-year career that included several changes of employers and lots of stressors—working-mother guilt, a failed marriage, gender bias on the job, and an MBA degree earned part-time. Through it all she says: "I've never let being scared stop me from doing something. Just because you haven't done it before doesn't mean you shouldn't try." That, simply put, is what we would call a can-do "attitude!"

• An **attitude** is a predisposition to respond positively or negatively to someone or something.

An **attitude** is a predisposition to respond in a positive or negative way to someone or something in one's environment. For example, when you say that you "like" or "dislike" someone or something, you are expressing an attitude. It's important to remember that an attitude, like a value, is a hypothetical construct; that is, one never sees, touches, or actually isolates an attitude. Rather, attitudes are *inferred* from the things people say or through their behavior. They are influenced by values and are acquired from the same sources—friends, teachers, parents, role models, and culture. But attitudes focus on specific people or objects. The notion that shareholders should have a voice in setting CEO pay is a value; your positive or negative feeling about a specific company due to the presence or absence of shareholder inputs on CEO pay is an attitude toward it.

Components of Attitudes

The three basic components of an attitude are shown in Figure 3.4—cognitive, affective, and behavioral.[28] The *cognitive component* of an attitude reflects underlying beliefs, opinions, knowledge, or information a person possesses. It represents a person's ideas about someone or something and the conclusions drawn about them. The statement "My job lacks responsibility" is a belief shown in the figure. The statement "Job responsibility is important to me" reflects an underlying value. Together they comprise the cognitive component of an attitude toward one's work or workplace.

The *affective component* of an attitude is a specific feeling regarding the personal impact of the antecedent conditions evidenced in the cognitive component.

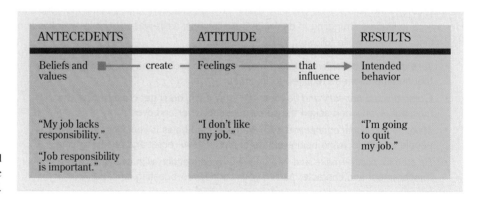

Figure 3.4 A work-related example of the three components of attitudes.

In essence this becomes the actual attitude, such as the feeling "I don't like my job." Notice that the affect in this statement displays the negative attitude; "I don't like my job" is a very different condition than "I do like my job."

The *behavioral component* is an intention to behave in a certain way based on the affect in one's attitude. It is a predisposition to act, but one that may or may not be implemented. The example in the figure shows behavioral intent expressed as "I'm going to quit my job." Yet even with such intent, whether or not the person really quits is quite another story indeed.

Attitudes and Behavior

As just discussed, the link between attitudes and behavior is tentative. An attitude expresses an intended behavior that may or may not be carried out. In general we can say that the more specific attitudes are, the stronger the relationship with eventual behavior. A person who feels "I don't like my job" may be less likely to actually quit than someone who feels "I can't stand another day with Alex harassing me at work." It's also necessary to have the opportunity or freedom to behave in the intended way. In today's recessionary economy there are most likely many persons who stick with their jobs while still holding negative job attitudes. The fact is they may not have any other choice.[29]

Attitudes and Cognitive Consistency

An important issue in the attitude-behavior linkage is consistency. Leon Festinger, a noted social psychologist, uses the term **cognitive dissonance** to describe a state of inconsistency between an individual's attitudes and/or between attitudes and behavior.[30] Let's assume that you have the attitude that recycling is good for the economy; you also realize you aren't always recycling everything you can while traveling on vacation. Festinger points out that such cognitive inconsistency is uncomfortable and results in attempts to reduce or eliminate the dissonance. This can be done in one of three ways: (1) changing the underlying attitude, (2) changing future behavior, or (3) developing new ways of explaining or rationalizing the inconsistency.

The way we respond to cognitive dissonance is influenced by the degree of control we seem to have over the situation and the rewards involved. In the case of recycling dissonance, for example, the lack of convenient recycling containers would make rationalizing easier and changing the positive attitude less likely. A reaffirmation of intention to recycle in the future can also reduce the dissonance.

Types of Job Attitudes

Even though attitudes do not always predict behavior, the link between attitudes and potential or intended behavior is important for managers to understand. Think about your work experiences or conversations with other people about their work. It isn't uncommon to hear concerns expressed about someone's "bad attitude" or another's "good attitude." Such attitudes appear in different forms, including job satisfaction, job involvement, organizational commitment, and employee engagement.

Employee Morale Varies Around the World

FDS International surveyed the morale of workers in 23 countries. Those with the highest worker morale were in the Netherlands, Ireland and Thailand (tie), and Switzerland. The U.S. ranked 10th in the sample and Japan came in last.

Cognitive dissonance is experienced inconsistency between one's attitudes and or between attitudes and behavior.

Job satisfaction is the degree to which an individual feels positive or negative about a job.

You often hear the term "morale" used when describing the feelings of a workforce toward their employer. It relates to the more specific notion of **job satisfaction**, an attitude reflecting a person's positive and negative feelings toward a job, co-workers, and the work environment. Indeed, you should remember that helping others achieve job satisfaction is considered as a key result that effective managers accomplish. That is, they create a work environment in which people achieve both high performance and high job satisfaction. This concept of job satisfaction is very important in OB and receives special attention in the following section.

Job involvement is the extent to which an individual is dedicated to a job.

In addition to job satisfaction there are other attitudes that OB scholars and researchers study and measure. One is **job involvement**, which is defined as the extent to which an individual is dedicated to a job. Someone with high job involvement psychologically identifies with her or his job, and, for example, would be expected to work beyond expectations to complete a special project.

Organizational commitment is the loyalty of an individual to the organization.

Another work attitude is **organizational commitment**, or the degree of loyalty an individual feels toward the organization. Individuals with a high organizational commitment identify strongly with the organization and take pride in considering themselves members. Researchers recognize two primary dimensions to organizational commitment. *Rational commitment* reflects feelings that the job serves one's financial, developmental, professional interests. *Emotional commitment* reflects feelings that what one does is important, valuable, and of real benefit to others. Evidence is that strong emotional commitments to the organization, based on values and interests of others, are as much as four times more powerful in positively influencing performance than are rational commitments, based primarily on pay and self-interests.[31]

Employee engagement is a positive feeling or strong sense of connection with the organization.

A survey of 55,000 American workers by the Gallup Organization suggests that profits for employers rise when workers' attitudes reflect high job involvement and organizational commitment. This combination creates a high sense of **employee engagement**—a positive work attitude that Gallup defines as working with "passion" and feeling "a profound connection" with one's employer.[32] Active employee engagement shows up as a willingness to help others, to always try to do something extra to improve performance, and to speak positively about the organization. Things that counted most toward high engagement in the Gallup research were believing one has the opportunity to do one's best every day, believing one's opinions count, believing fellow workers are committed to quality, and believing there is a direct connection between one's work and the company's mission.[33]

Job Satisfaction

There is no doubt that one of the most talked about of all job attitudes is job satisfaction, defined earlier as an attitude reflecting a person's evaluation of his or her job or job experiences at a particular point in time.[34] And when it comes to job satisfaction there are several good questions that we should answer. What are the major components of job satisfaction? What are the main job satisfaction findings? What is the relationship between job satisfaction and job performance?

Components of Job Satisfaction

Managers can infer the job satisfaction of others by careful observation and interpretation of what people say and do while going about their jobs. Interviews and questionnaires can also be used to more formally examine levels of job satisfaction.[35] Two of the more popular job satisfaction questionnaires used over the years are the Minnesota Satisfaction Questionnaire (MSQ) and the Job Descriptive Index (JDI).[36] Both address components of job satisfaction with which all good managers should be concerned. The MSQ measures satisfaction with working conditions, chances for advancement, freedom to use one's own judgment, praise for doing a good job, and feelings of accomplishment, among others. The five facets of job satisfaction measured by the JDI are

- *The work itself*—responsibility, interest, and growth
- *Quality of supervision*—technical help and social support
- *Relationships with co-workers*—social harmony and respect
- *Promotion opportunities*—chances for further advancement
- *Pay*—adequacy of pay and perceived equity vis-à-vis others

Job Satisfaction Findings

If you watch or read the news, you'll regularly find reports on the job satisfaction of workers. You'll also find lots of job satisfaction studies in the academic literature. The results don't always agree, but they usually fall within a common range. We can generally conclude that the majority of American workers are at least somewhat satisfied with their jobs, with a recent survey placing this figure at about 65 percent even during a time of economic downturn.[37] But job satisfaction has been declining for a dozen years or more. It also tends to be higher in small firms and lower in large ones; it tends to be lower among the youngest workers. And, job satisfaction and overall life satisfaction tend to run together.[38] When workers in a global study were asked to report on common job satisfaction or "morale" problems, they identified pay dissatisfaction, number of hours worked, not getting enough holiday or personal time off, lack of flexibility in working hours, and time spent commuting to and from work.[39]

Job Satisfaction and Behavior

Surely you can agree that job satisfaction is important on quality-of-work-life grounds alone. Don't people deserve to have satisfying work experiences? But is job satisfaction important in other than a "feel good" sense? How does it impact job behaviors and performance?

Withdrawal Behaviors   There is a strong relationship between job satisfaction and physical withdrawal behaviors like *absenteeism* and *turnover*. Workers who are more satisfied with their jobs are absent less often than those who are dissatisfied. And satisfied workers are more likely to remain with their present employers, while dissatisfied workers are more likely to quit or at least be on the lookout for other jobs.[40] Withdrawal through absenteeism and turnover can be very costly in terms of lost experience, and the expenses for recruiting and training of replacements. In fact, one study found that up or down changes in retention rates result in magnified changes to corporate earnings.[41]

On this issue of turnover and retention, a survey by Salary.com showed not only that employers tend to overestimate the job satisfactions of their employees, they underestimate the amount of job seeking they were doing. Whereas employers estimated that 37 percent of employees were on the lookout for new jobs, 65 percent of the employees said they were actively or passively job seeking by networking, Web surfing, posting resumes, or checking new job possibilities. Millennials in their 20's and early 30's were most likely to engage in these "just-in-case" job seeking activities. The report concluded that "most employers have not placed enough emphasis on important retention strategies.[42]

There is also a relationship between job satisfaction and psychological withdrawal behaviors. These show up in such things as daydreaming, cyber loafing by Internet surfing or personal electronic communications, excessive socializing, and even just giving the appearance of being busy when you're not. Such psychological withdrawal behaviors are forms of work disengagement, something that Gallup researchers say as many as 71 percent of workers report feeling at times.[43]

* **Organizational citizenship behaviors** are the extras people do to go the extra mile in their work.

* **Counterproductive work behaviors** intentionally disrupt relationships or performance at work.

Organizational Citizenship   Job satisfaction is also linked with **organizational citizenship behaviors**.[44] These are discretionary behaviors, sometimes called "OCBs," that represent a willingness to "go beyond the call of duty" or "go the extra mile" in one's work.[45] A person who is a good organizational citizen does things that although not required of them help others—*interpersonal OCBs*, or advance the performance of the organization as a whole—*organizational OCBs*.[46] You might observe interpersonal OCBs in a service worker who is extraordinarily courteous while taking care of an upset customer or a team member who is altruistic in taking on extra tasks when a co-worker is ill or absent. Examples of organizational OCBs are evident as co-workers who are always willing volunteers for special committee or task force assignments, and those who whose voices are always positive when commenting publicly on their employer.

The flip-side of organizational citizenship shows up in a variety of possible **counterproductive work behaviors** shown in OB Savvy.[47] Often associated with some form of job dissatisfaction, they purposely disrupt relationships, organizational culture or performance in the workplace.[48] Counterproductive workplace behaviors cover a wide range from things like work avoidance to physical and verbal aggression of others to bad mouthing to outright work sabotage to theft.

At Home Affect   When OB scholars talk about "spillover" effects, they are often referring to how what happens to us at home can affect our work attitudes

---

OB SAVVY

Spotting Counterproductive or Deviant Workplace Behaviors

Whereas organizational citizenship behaviors help make the organization a better and more pleasant place, counterproductive or deviant behaviors do just the opposite. They harm the work, the people, and the organizational culture. You can spot them in forms such as these.

* *Personal aggression*—sexual harassment, verbal abuse, physical abuse, intimidation, humiliation
* *Production deviance*—wasting resources, avoiding work, disrupting workflow, making deliberate work errors
* *Political deviance*—spreading harmful rumors, gossiping, using bad language, lacking civility in relationships
* *Property deviance*—destroying or sabotaging facilities and equipment, stealing money and other resources

Job Satisfaction Spillover onto Family Lives

The spillover of job satisfaction onto workers' family lives is the subject of a study published in the *Academy of Management Journal* by Remus Ilies, Kelly Schwind Wilson, and David T. Wagner. Noting that communication technologies and flexibility in work schedules have narrowed the gap between work and home, the researchers asked the question: how does daily job satisfaction spill over to affect a person's feelings and attitudes in the family role?

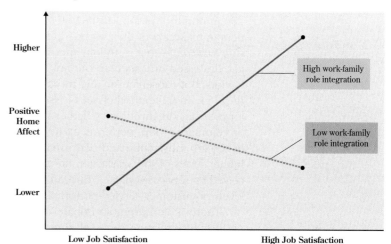

Citing inconsistent findings from previous studies, Ilies et al. surmised that work-family role integration would influence the possible spillover. High work-family role integration was defined as making "little distinction between their work and family roles," while low work-family role integration meant that work and family were quite segmented from one another. A key hypothesis in the research was that job satisfaction spillover from work to home on any given day would be higher for the high work-family role integration employees.

The research was conducted by survey and telephone interviews with 101 university employees and their spouses or significant others over a two-week period. Results showed that workers displayed higher positive affect at home on days when they also reported higher job satisfaction. As shown in the figure, workers with high work-family role integration showed a stronger relationship between daily job satisfaction and positive

affect at home versus those with low work-family role integration. In fact, workers with low work-family integration, those that tended to segment work and family roles, positive home affect actually declined as job satisfaction increased.

Do the Research

How can the findings for the low-work family integration group be explained? What research questions does this study raise in your mind that might become the topics for further study in this area? Would you hypothesize that the job satisfaction–home spillover effects would vary by type of occupation, age of worker, family responsibilities such as number of at-home children, or other factors?

Source: Remus Ilies, Kelly Schwind Wilson, and David T. Wagner, "The Spillover of Daily Job Satisfaction onto Employees' Family Lives: The Facilitating Role of Work-Family Integration," *Academy of Management Journal*, Vol. 52, No. 1 (2009), pp. 87–102.

and behaviors, and how the same holds true as work experiences influence how we feel and behave at home. Research finds that people with higher daily job satisfaction show more positive after-work home affect.[49] In a study that measured spouse or significant other evaluations, more positive at-home affect scores were reported on days when workers experienced higher job satisfaction.[50] Issues of the job satisfaction and at-home affect link are especially significant as workers in today's high-tech and always-connected world strug-gle with work-life balance.

Job Satisfaction and Performance

The importance of job satisfaction can be viewed in the context of two decisions people make about their work—belonging and performing. The first is the *decision to belong*—that is, to join and remain a member of an organization. This was just discussed in respect to the link between job satisfaction and withdrawal be-haviors, both absenteeism and turnover. The second decision, the *decision to perform*, raises quite another set of issues. We all know that not everyone who be-longs to an organization, whether it's a classroom or workplace or sports team or voluntary group, performs up to expectations. So, what is the relationship be-tween job satisfaction and performance?[51] A recent study, for example, finds that higher levels of job satisfaction are related to higher levels of customer ratings re-ceived by service workers.[52] But can it be said that high job satisfaction causes high levels of customer service performance?

There is considerable debate on the issue of causality in the satisfaction–performance relationship, with three different positions being advanced. The first is that job satisfaction causes performance; "a happy worker is a productive worker." The second is that performance causes job satisfaction. The third is that job satisfaction and performance are intertwined, influencing one another, and mutually affected by other factors such as the availability of rewards. Perhaps you can make a case for one or more of these positions based on your work experiences.

Satisfaction Causes Performance   If job satisfaction causes high levels of performance, the message to managers is: to increase employees' work perform-ance, make them happy. Research, however, finds no simple and direct link between individual job satisfaction at one point in time and later work perform-ance. A sign once posted in a tavern near one of Ford's Michigan plants helps tell the story: "I spend 40 hours a week here, am I supposed to work too?" Even though some evidence exists for the satisfaction → performance relation-ship among professional or higher-level employees, the best conclusion is that job satisfaction alone is not a consistent predictor of individual work performance.

Performance Causes Satisfaction   If high levels of performance cause job satisfaction, the message to managers is quite different. Rather than focusing on job satisfaction as the pathway to performance, attention shifts to creating high performance as a precursor to job satisfaction, that is performance → satisfaction. It generally makes sense that people should feel good about their job when they perform well. And indeed, research does find a link between individual performance measured at one time and later job satisfaction.

Figure 3.5 shows a basic model explaining this relationship as based on the work of Edward E. Lawler and Lyman Porter. It suggests that performance leads to rewards that, in turn, lead to satisfaction.[53] Rewards are intervening variables that, when valued by the recipient, link performance with later satisfaction. The model also includes a moderator variable—perceived equity of rewards. This

*Millennials Need
Special Handling*

Also called "Gen Ys" or "Echo Boomers" or the "Net Generation," *The Wall Street Journal* says Millennials want "a good work environment . . . meaningful responsibility, continuous feedback from managers and peers, an active say in what goes on, and a good work-life-balance."

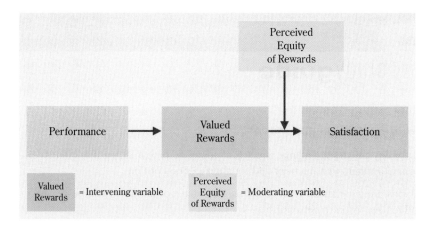

Figure 3.5 Simplified Porter-Lawler model of the performance → satisfaction relationship.

indicates that high performance leads to satisfaction only if rewards are perceived as fair and equitable. Although this model is a good starting point, and one that we will use again in discussing motivation and rewards in Chapter 6, we also know from personal experience that some people may perform great but still not like the jobs that they have to do.

Rewards Cause Both Satisfaction and Performance   The final position in the job satisfaction–performance discussion builds from and somewhat combines the prior two. It suggests that the right rewards allocated in the right ways will positively influence both performance and satisfaction, which also influence one another. The key issue in respect to the allocation of rewards is *performance contingency*, or varying the size of the reward in proportion to the level of performance.

Research generally finds that rewards influence satisfaction while performance-contingent rewards influence performance.[54] Thus the management advice is to use performance-contingent rewards well in the attempt to create both. Although giving a low performer a small reward may lead to dissatisfaction at first, the expectation is that he or she will make efforts to improve performance in order to obtain higher rewards in the future.[55]

Resources in The OB Skills Workbook

These learning activities from *The OB Skills Workbook* are suggested for Chapter 3.

Cases for Critical Thinking	Team and Experiential Exercises	Self-Assessment Portfolio
• Management Training Dilemma	• Interrogatories • My Asset Base • Prejudice in Our Lives • What Do You Value in Your Work?	• Learning Style Inventory • Student Leadership Practices Inventory • 21st Century Manager • Global Readiness Index

studyguide

Summary Questions and Answers

What are emotions and moods?

- Emotions are strong feelings directed at someone or something that influence behavior, often with intensity and for short periods of time.

- Moods are generalized positive or negative states of mind that can be persistent influences on one's behavior.

- Affect is a generic term that covers a broad range of feelings that individuals experience as emotions and moods.

- Emotional Intelligence is the ability to detect and manage emotional cues and information. Four emotional intelligence skills or competencies are self-awareness, self-management, social awareness, and relationship management.

- Social emotions refer to individuals' feelings based on information external to them and include pity, envy, scorn, and jealousy; self-conscious emotions include shame, guilt, embarrassment, and pride.

How do emotions and moods influence behavior in organizations?

- Emotional contagion involves the spillover effects onto others of one's emotions and moods; in other words emotions and moods can spread from person to person.

- Emotional labor is a situation where a person displays organizationally desired emotions while performing their jobs.

- Emotional dissonance is the discrepancy between true feelings and organizationally desired emotions; it is linked with deep acting to try to modify true inner feelings, and surface acting to hide one's true inner feelings.

- Display rules govern the degree to which it is appropriate for people from different cultures to display their emotions similarly.

- Affective Events Theory (AET) relates characteristics of the work environment and daily hassles and uplifts to positive and negative emotional reactions and, ultimately, job satisfaction.

What are attitudes?

- An attitude is a predisposition to respond in a certain way to people and things.

- Attitudes have three components—affective, cognitive, and behavioral.

- Although attitudes predispose individuals toward certain behaviors they do not guarantee that such behaviors will take place.

- Individuals desire consistency between their attitudes and their behaviors, and cognitive dissonance occurs when a person's attitude and behavior are inconsistent.

- Job satisfaction is an attitude toward one's job, co-workers, and workplace.

- Job involvement is a positive attitude that shows up in the extent to which an individual is dedicated to a job.

- Organizational commitment is a positive attitude that shows up in the loyalty of an individual to the organization.

What is job satisfaction and what are its implications?

- Five components of job satisfaction are the work itself, quality of supervision, relationships with co-workers, promotion opportunities, and pay.

- Job satisfaction influences withdrawal behaviors such as absenteeism, turnover, day dreaming and cyber loafing.

- Job satisfaction is linked with organizational citizenship behaviors that are both interpersonal—such as doing extra work for a sick team mate—and organizational—such as always speaking positively about the organization.

- Job dissatisfaction may be reflected in counterproductive work behaviors such as purposely performing with low quality, avoiding work, acting violent at work, or even engaging in workplace theft.

- Three possibilities in the job satisfaction and performance relationship are: satisfaction causes performance, performance causes satisfaction, and rewards cause both performance and satisfaction.

Key Terms

Affect (p. 62)
Attitude (p. 70)
Cognitive dissonance (p. 71)
Counterproductive work behaviors (p. 74)
Display rules (p. 68)
Emotions (p. 62)
Emotional dissonance (p. 67)
Employee engagement (p. 72)

Emotional intelligence (p. 62)
Emotion and mood contagion (p. 66)
Emotional labor (p. 66)
Job involvement (p. 72)
Job satisfaction (p. 72)
Moods (p. 65)
Organizational citizenship behaviors (p. 74)

Organizational commitment (p. 72)
Relationship management (p. 63)
Self-awareness (p. 63)
Self-conscious emotions (p. 64)
Self-management (p. 63)
Social awareness (p. 63)
Social emotions (p. 64)

Self-Test 3

Multiple Choice

1. In terms of individual psychology, a/an _____ represents a rather intense but short-lived feeling about a person or a situation, while a/an _____ describes a more generalized positive or negative state of mind. (a) stressor, role ambiguity (b) external locus of control, internal locus of control (c) self-serving bias, halo effect (d) emotion, mood

2. When someone is feeling anger toward something that a co-worker did she is experiencing a/an _____, but when someone is just "having a bad day overall" he is experiencing a/an _____. (a) mood, emotion (b) emotion, mood (c) affect, effect (d) dissonance, consonance

3. Emotions and moods as personal affects are known to influence _____. (a) attitudes (b) ability (c) aptitude (d) intelligence

4. In contrast to self-conscious emotions, social emotions such as pity or envy are based on _____. (a) information from external sources (b) feelings of guilt or pride (c) information from internal sources (d) feelings of shame or embarrassment

5. The _____ component of an attitude is what indicates a person's belief about something, while the _____ component indicates a specific positive or negative feeling about it. (a) cognitive, affective (b) emotional, affective (c) cognitive, mood (d) behavioral, mood

6. The term used to describe the discomfort someone feels when his or her behavior is inconsistent with an expressed attitude is _____. (a) alienation (b) cognitive dissonance (c) job dissatisfaction (d) person-job imbalance

7. Affective Events Theory shows how one's emotional reactions to work events, environment, and personal predispositions can influence _____. (a) job satisfaction and performance (b) emotional labor (c) emotional intelligence (d) emotional contagion

8. Deep acting involves _____ and is linked with the concept of emotional labor. (a) trying to modify your true inner feelings based on display rules (b) appraisal and recognition of emotions in others (c) creation of cognitive dissonance (d) avoidance of emotional contagion

9. When an airline flight attendant engages in self-regulation to display organizationally desired emotions during his interactions with passengers, this is an example of _____. (a) emotional labor (b) emotional contagion (c) rational commitment (d) negative affect

10. A person who is always willing to volunteer for extra work or to help someone else with their work or to contribute personal time to support an organizational social event can be said to be high in _____. (a) job performance (b) self-serving bias (c) emotional intelligence (d) organizational commitment

11. Job satisfaction is known from research to be a reasonable predictor of _____. (a) Type A personality (b) emotional intelligence (c) cognitive dissonance (d) absenteeism

12. Which statement about employee engagement is most correct? (a) OB researchers are showing little interest in the topic. (b) It can be increased by letting workers know their opinions count. (c) Only persons paid very well show high employee engagement. (d) On any given day as much as 70 percent of workers may be at least somewhat disengaged.

13. When employers are asked to describe the job satisfactions of their employees and the implications, they often _____. (a) overestimate job satisfaction (b) underestimate job satisfaction (c) overestimate inclinations to job search (d) underestimate intentions to stay on the job

14. The best conclusion about job satisfaction in today's workforce is probably that _____. (a) It isn't an important issue for managers to consider. (b) The only

real concern is pay. (c) Most people are not satisfied with their jobs most of the time. (d) Most people are at least somewhat satisfied with their jobs most of the time.

15. Which statement about the job satisfaction–job performance relationship is most true based on research? (a) A happy worker will be a productive worker. (b) A productive worker will be a happy worker. (c) A productive worker well rewarded for performance will be a happy worker. (d) There is no relationship between being happy and being productive in a job.

Short Response

16. What are the major differences between emotions and moods as personal affects?

17. Compare and contrast the positive and negative aspects of both anger and empathy as common emotions that people may display at work.

18. List five components of job satisfaction and briefly discuss their importance.

19. Why is cognitive dissonance an important concept for managers to understand?

Applications Essay

20. Your boss has a sign posted in her office: "A satisfied worker is a productive worker." In a half-joking and half-serious way she points to it and says, "You are fresh out of college, am I right or wrong?" What is your response?

4

Perception, Attribution, and Learning

Called "a recognized force for women's rights and self-sufficiency" and "a lifeline for women in war-torn countries," Zainab Salbi grew up in the tyranny of Saddam Hussein's Iraq. It is a long journey from those days of war and strife to Davos, Switzerland, where she was honored as Young Global Leader by the World Economic Forum.

What has she done to earn the praise? Lots. Salbi founded Women for Women International with the mission of "changing the world one woman at a time." The nonprofit organization's Web site says, "Women for Women International provides women survivors of war, civil strife and other conflicts with the tools and resources to move from crisis and poverty to stability and self-sufficiency, thereby promoting viable civil societies." The goal is to provide women with training, financial aid, and rights awareness that can help them move from despair and poverty to independence and economic security.

Zainab Salbi founded Women for Women International with the mission of "changing the world one woman at a time."

Salbi says, "Women who survive war are strong, resilient and courageous—they just need some support dealing with the aftermath of conflict." Violette of Rwanda is one such survivor. She joined a "women's circle" set up by Women for Women International to link women in need with sponsors from other countries. With the encouragement of a sponsor from Boston, Violette built a business of sorghum-based drinks from her experience in sorghum harvesting. She became a community leader and was able to send her children to school.

Elsewhere Salbi's organization has made $4 million in micro-credit loans to help women in Afghanistan start small businesses, organized "Action Agenda for Women" in Kosovo, and ran a Men's Leadership Program in Kenya to help men learn how they can work in their communities to change male attitudes and perceptions that foster violence against women. In just one year alone Women for Women International touched the lives of almost 70,000 women worldwide.

it's in the eye of the beholder

The Perception Process

Suppose you had the same early life experiences as Zainab Salwi from the chapter openers, is it likely that you would have ended up making similar accomplishments? Doesn't a lot depend on how we perceive people and events, and learn from what happens to us? And when it comes to things like male attitudes and stereotypes toward women, can organizations like Women for Women International really make a difference?

• **Perception** is the process through which people receive and interpret information from the environment.

Such questions in many ways raise the issue of **perception**, the process by which people select, organize, interpret, retrieve, and respond to information from the world around them.[1] Perception is a way of forming impressions about oneself, other people, and daily life experiences. It also serves as a screen or filter through which information passes before it has an effect on people. Because perceptions are influenced by many factors, different people may perceive the same situation quite differently. And since people behave according to their perceptions, the consequences of these differences can be quite substantial in terms of what happens next.

Consider the example shown in Figure 4.1. It shows rather substantial differences in how a performance appraisal discussion is perceived by managers and their subordinates. The managers in this case may end up not giving much attention to things like career development, performance goals, and supervisory support since they perceive these were adequately addressed at performance appraisal time. But the subordinates may end up frustrated and unsatisfied because they perceive less attention is being given to these issues.

Factors Influencing Perception

We can think of perception as a bubble that surrounds us and influences significantly the way we receive, interpret, and process information received from our environments. The many factors influencing perception are shown

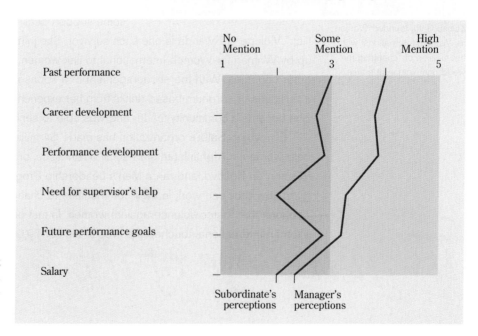

Figure 4.1 Contrasting perceptions between managers and subordinates regarding performance appraisal interviews.

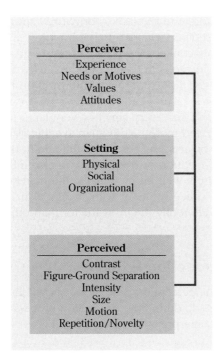

Figure 4.2 Factors influencing the perception process.

in Figure 4.2 and include characteristics of the *perceiver*, the *setting*, and the *perceived*.

The Perceiver   A person's past experiences, needs or motives, personality, values, and attitudes may all influence the perceptual process. Someone with a strong achievement need tends to perceive a situation in terms of that need. If doing well in class is perceived as a way to help meet your achievement need, for example, you will tend to emphasize that aspect when choosing classes to take. In the same way, a person with a negative attitude toward younger workers may react antagonistically when asked to work for a young, newly-hired team leader.

The Setting   The physical, social, and organizational context of the setting also can influence the perceptual process. When Kim Jeffrey was promoted to CEO of Nestlés Perrier, he was perceived by subordinates as a frightening figure because he gave vent to his temper and had occasional confrontations with them. Before the promotion Jeffrey's flare-ups had been tolerable; in the new setting as CEO they caused intimidation. The problem was resolved after he received feedback and learned of his subordinates' perceptions.[2]

The Perceived   Characteristics of the perceived person, object, or event—such as contrast, intensity, figure-ground separation, size, motion, and repetition or novelty—are also important in the perceptual process. For example, one MacIntosh computer among six HPs, or one man among six women will be perceived differently than one of six MacIntosh computers or one of six men because there is less contrast. Intensity can vary in terms of brightness,

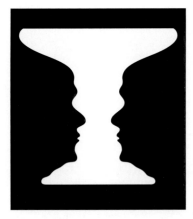

Figure 4.3 Figure and ground illustration.

color, depth, sound, and the like. A bright red sports car stands out from a group of gray sedans; whispering or shouting stands out from ordinary conversation. This concept is known as figure-ground separation: it depends on which image is perceived as the background and which as the figure. Look, for example, at the small illustration in Figure 4.3. What do you see, faces or a vase?

In the matter of size, very small or very large people tend to be perceived differently and more readily than average-sized people. In terms of motion, moving objects are perceived differently than stationary objects. And, of course, repetition or frequency can also influence perceptions, as television advertisers well know. Finally, the novelty of a situation affects its perception. A college student with streaks of hair dyed purple may be perceived quite differently by an instructor than others wearing more natural hair colors.

Stages of the Perception Process

The various stages of the perception process are shown in Figure 4.4. They show that information processing during the perception process involves attention and selection, organization, interpretation, and retrieval.

Attention and Selection   Our senses are constantly bombarded with so much information that if we don't screen it, we quickly become incapacitated with information overload. *Selective screening* lets in only a tiny proportion of all the information available. Some of the selectivity comes from controlled processing—consciously deciding what information to pay attention to and what to ignore. Think for example, about the last time you were at a noisy restaurant and screened out all the sounds but those of the person with whom you were talking. Screening can also take place without the perceiver's conscious awareness. We

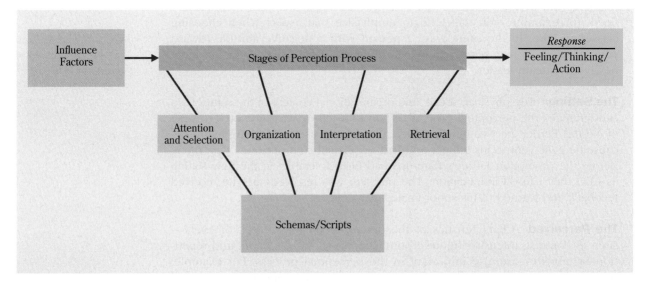

Figure 4.4 Stages of information processing during the perception process.

drive cars often without consciously thinking about the process of driving; we're aware of things like traffic lights and other cars but don't pay conscious attention to them. Such selectivity of attention and automatic information processing works well most of the time. But if a nonroutine event occurs, such as an animal darting onto the road, you may have an accident unless you quickly shift to controlled processing.

Organization   Even though selective screening takes place in the attention stage, it is still necessary to find ways to organize the information efficiently. **Schemas** help us do this. They are cognitive frameworks that represent organized knowledge developed through experience about a given concept or stimulus.[3]

A *script schema* is defined as a knowledge framework that describes the appropriate sequence of events in a given situation.[4] For example, an experienced manager would use a script schema to think about the appropriate steps involved in running a meeting. A *self schema* contains information about a person's own appearance, behavior, and personality. For instance, people with decisiveness schemas tend to perceive themselves in terms of that aspect, especially in circumstances calling for leadership.

Person schemas refer to the way individuals sort others into categories, such as types or groups, in terms of similar perceived features. The terms prototype and stereotype are often used in this regard. They are abstract sets of features commonly associated with members of a category. Once the prototype is formed, it is stored in long-term memory and retrieved only when needed for a comparison of how well a person matches the prototype's features. For instance, you may have a "good worker" prototype that includes hard work, intelligence, punctuality, articulateness, and decisiveness. This prototype is used as a measure against which to compare people at work. Stereotypes can be considered as prototypes based on such demographic characteristics as gender, age, physical ability, and racial and ethnic groups.

Finally, *person-in-situation schemas* combine schemas built around persons (self and person schemas) and events (script schemas).[5] A manager might organize his or her perceived information in a meeting around a decisiveness schema for both himself or herself and a key participant in the meeting. Here, a script schema would provide the steps and their sequence in the meeting; the manager would push through the steps decisively and would call on the selected participants periodically throughout the meeting to respond decisively. Note that although this approach might facilitate organization of important information, the perceptions of those attending might not be completely accurate because the decisiveness element of the person-in-situation schema did not allow them enough time for open discussion.

Interpretation   Once your attention has been drawn to certain stimuli and you have grouped or organized this information, the next step is to uncover the reasons behind the actions. That is, even if your attention is called to the same information and you organize it in the same way your friend does, you may interpret it differently or make different attributions about the reasons behind what you have perceived. For example, as a team leader, you might attribute

• **Schemas** are cognitive frameworks that represent organized knowledge developed through experience about people, objects, or events.

Interactional Justice Perceptions Affect Intent to Leave

Research reported by Merideth Ferguson, Neta Moye, and Ray Friedman links perceptions of interactional justice during recruitment interviews with effects on long term employment relationships. Focusing on issues of fairness in the workplace, a substantial literature on organizational justice shows that people respond to perceived fair and unfair treatments in positive and negative ways, with the links between perceived injustice and negative behaviors being particularly strong.

This research examined fairness perceptions regarding negotiations taking place during the recruitment process and how these perceptions affected later intentions to leave. Two hypotheses were tested. First, it was hypothesized that perceived use of negotiation pressure by recruiters would have a negative impact on perceived interactional justice by job applicants. Second, it was hypothesized that perceived interactional injustice during recruiting negotiations would have a positive long-term impact on later intentions to leave by the newly hired employees.

Two studies were conducted. The first study asked a sample of 68 university alumni of a busi-

ness program about their retrospective perceptions of interactional justice during job negotiations and their current intentions to leave. The second study asked a sample of recent MBA graduates to report perceptions of interactional justice during their job negotiations; they were asked six months later to report on their intentions to leave the new employer. Results from both studies offered confirmation for the two hypotheses.

In conclusion, Ferguson et al. state: "the sense of injustice one feels during a negotiation affects an employee's turnover intentions with the hiring organization . . . negotiations in the recruitment process can set the tone for the future employment relationship." They recommend future research to examine how negotiating tactics like slow responses, dishonesty, disrespect, and lack of concessions influence justice perceptions and later intent to leave. They also suggest that perceived injustice in recruiting when jobs are plentiful may lead to applicants making alternative job choices, while such injustice when jobs are scarce may result in employees accepting the jobs but harboring intent to leave when the opportunity permits.

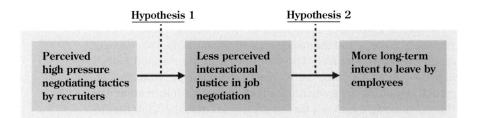

Do the Research

What is your experience with interactional justice in the recruiting process? Can you design a study to gather the experiences of your cohorts, friends, and others on campus? How can your study pin-

point the impact of tactics such as setting a tight time limit on a job offer?

Source: Merideth Ferguson, Neta Moye, and Ray Friedman, "The Lingering Effects of the Recruitment Experience on the Long-Term Employment Relationship," *Negotiation and Conflict Management Research*, Vol. 1 (2008), pp. 246–262.

compliments from a team member to his being an eager worker, whereas your friend might interpret the behavior as insincere flattery.

Retrieval   So far, we have discussed the stages of the perception process as if they all occurred at the same time. However, to do so ignores the important component of memory. Each of the previous stages forms part of that memory and contributes to the stimuli or information stored there. The information stored in our memory must be retrieved if it is to be used.

All of us at times have trouble retrieving information stored in our memories. More commonly, memory decays, so that only some of the information is retrieved. Schemas play an important role in this area, and make it difficult for people to remember things not included in them. For example, given the prototype of a "good worker" as someone showing lots of effort, punctuality, intelligence, articulateness, and decisiveness, you may emphasize these traits and overlook others when evaluating the performance of a team member whom you generally consider good. Something like decisiveness gets overestimated because it is part of your high-performance prototype.

- **Impression management** is the systematic attempt to influence how others perceive us.

Perception and Impression Management

Richard Branson, CEO of the Virgin Group, may be one of the richest and most famous executives in the world. One of his early business accomplishments was the successful startup of Virgin Airlines, now a major competitor of British Airways (BA). In a memoir, the former head of BA, Lord King, said: "If Richard Branson had worn a shirt and tie instead of a goatee and jumper, I would not have underestimated him."[6] This is an example of how much our impressions count—both positive and negative. Knowing this, scholars today emphasize the importance of **impression management**, the systematic attempt to behave in ways that will create and maintain desired impressions in the eyes of others.[7]

Donna Byrd, publisher of TheRoot.com

Using the right social networks can create the right impression. Donna Byrd, publisher at TheRoot.com, uses LinkedIn and Twitter to voice expert opinions and publicize her company. "If you do it consistently," she says, "you can become a trusted voice in your particular area of expertise."

Social Networks

Most of us have heard the advice: "Don't forget to make a good first impression." And, no doubt, first impressions do count in how others perceive us. In fact, we practice a lot of impression management as a matter of routine in everyday life. We dress, talk, act, and surround ourselves with things that reinforce a desirable self-image and help to convey that same image to other persons. When well done, impression management can help us to advance in jobs and careers, form relationships with people we admire, and even create pathways to group memberships. It involves such activities as associating with the "right people," "dressing up" and "dressing down" at the right times, making eye contact when introduced to someone, doing favors to gain approval, flattering others to favorably impress them, taking credit for a favorable event, apologizing for a negative event while seeking a pardon, agreeing with the opinions of others, and downplaying the severity of a negative event.[8]

MASTERING MANAGEMENT

NETWORKING SKILLS FOR IMPRESSION MANAGEMENT

Consultant William C. Byham, CEO of Development Dimensions International, says that it's important to build networks within the first 30–60 days of a new job or promotion. That's when impressions are being formed and you have the best chances of influencing how others think about you. His advice includes these tips.

1. *Map your ideal network.*
   - Ask: Who can help me?
   - Ask: Who knows what's going on?
   - Ask: Who can get around roadblocks?
   - Ask: Who's critical in the workflow?
2. *Take action to build the network.*
   - Don't be shy; chances are the other persons will be receptive.
   - Start conversations with: "I'm new in my job, and I'm trying to get to know people who . . . "
3. *Reciprocate and invest in your network.*
   - Share information useful to others.
   - Take the time to stay in touch with network members; invest at least an hour a week and probably more.
   - Update the network as structures and people change.

Common Perceptual Distortions

A variety of common distortions can cause inaccuracies in our impressions and in the perception process more generally. These are stereotypes and prototypes, halo effects, selective perception, projection, contrast effects, and the self-fulfilling prophecy.

Stereotypes

Given the complexity of the information streaming toward us from the environments, we use various means of simplifying and organizing our perceptions. One of the most common is the **stereotype**. It occurs when we identify someone with a group or category, and then use the attributes perceived to be associated with the group or category to describe the individual. Although this makes things easier for us by reducing the need to deal with unique individual characteristics, it is an oversimplification. Because stereotypes obscure individual differences, we can easily end up missing the real individual. For managers this means not accurately understanding the needs, preferences, and abilities of others in the workplace.

Some of the most common stereotypes, at work and in life in general, relate to such factors as gender, age, race, and physical ability. Why are so few top executives in industry African-Americans or Hispanics? Legitimate questions can be asked about *racial and ethnic stereotypes* and about the slow progress of minority managers into America's corporate mainstream.[9] Why is

*A **stereotype** assigns attributes commonly associated with a group to an individual.*

it that women constitute only a small percentage of American managers sent abroad to work on international business assignments? A Catalyst study of opportunities for women in global business points to *gender stereotypes* that place women at a disadvantage compared to men for these types of opportunities. The tendency is to assume women lack the ability and/or willingness to work abroad.[10] Gender stereotypes may cause even everyday behavior to be misconstrued, for example: "He's talking with co-workers." (Interpretation: He's discussing a new deal); "She's talking with co-workers." (Interpretation: She's gossiping).[11]

Ability stereotypes and *age stereotypes* also exist in the workplace. A physically or mentally challenged candidate may be overlooked by a recruiter even though possessing skills that are perfect for the job. A talented older worker may not be promoted because a manager assumes older workers are cautious and tend to avoid risk.[12] Yet a Conference Board survey of workers 50 and older reports that 72 percent felt they could take on additional responsibilities, and two-thirds were interested in further training and development.[13] And then there's the flip side; can a young person be a real leader, even a CEO? Facebook's founder and CEO Mark Zuckerberg is only in his mid-20s, and when current CEO Sheryl Sandberg was being recruited from Google she admits to this thought: "Wow, I'm going to work for a CEO who is quite young." After working for him she now says: "Mark is a great leader . . . Mark has a real purity of vision . . . He brings people along with him."[14]

Halo Effects

A **halo effect** occurs when one attribute of a person or situation is used to develop an overall impression of the individual or situation. Like stereotypes, these distortions are more likely to occur in the organization stage of perception. Halo effects are common in our everyday lives. When meeting a new person, for example, a pleasant smile can lead to a positive first impression of an overall "warm" and "honest" person. The result of a halo effect is the same as that associated with a stereotype, however, in that individual differences are obscured.

Halo effects are particularly important in the performance appraisal process because they can influence a manager's evaluations of subordinates' work performance. For example, people with good attendance records tend to be viewed as intelligent and responsible; those with poor attendance records are considered poor performers. Such conclusions may or may not be valid. It is the manager's job to try to get true impressions rather than allowing halo effects to result in biased and erroneous evaluations.

Selective Perception

Selective perception is the tendency to single out those aspects of a situation, person, or object that are consistent with one's needs, values, or attitudes. Its strongest impact occurs in the attention stage of the perceptual process. This perceptual distortion was identified in a classic research study involving executives in a manufacturing company.[15] When asked to identify the key problem in a comprehensive business policy case, each executive selected a problem consistent with his or her functional area work assignments.

- A **halo effect** uses one attribute to develop an overall impression of a person or situation.

- **Selective perception** is the tendency to define problems from one's own point of view.

Google and Procter & Gamble

Selective perception is an enemy of innovation, one that the two firms are tackling head-on through job swaps. "Proctoids" from P&G's rigid culture and "Googlers" from a fashion-forward flexible culture are spending time in each other's firms. And they end up talking about how much they learned.

They're hi-tech young professionals called the Elsewhere Class and they struggle to balance work and leisure. "Elsewhere" is the place you are thinking about even though physically not there; technology is an enabler. You may be at home or out shopping, but you're thinking it's time to check work messages.

• **Projection** assigns personal attributes to other individuals.

• A **contrast effect** occurs when the meaning of something that takes place is based on a contrast with another recent event or situation.

• A **self-fulfilling prophecy** is creating or finding in a situation that which you expected to find in the first place.

Most marketing executives viewed the key problem area as sales, whereas production people tended to see the problem as one of production and organization. These differing viewpoints would likely affect how each executive would approach the problem; they might also create difficulties as the executives tried to work together to improve things.

Projection

Projection is the assignment of one's personal attributes to other individuals; it is especially likely to occur in the interpretation stage of perception. A classic projection error is illustrated by managers who assume that the needs of their subordinates and their own coincide. Suppose, for example, that you enjoy responsibility and achievement in your work. Suppose, too, that you are the newly appointed manager of a team whose jobs seem dull and routine. You may move quickly to expand these jobs to help the workers achieve increased satisfaction from more challenging tasks because you want them to experience things that you, personally, value in work. But this may not be a good decision. If you project your needs onto the subordinates, individual differences are lost. Instead of designing the subordinates' jobs to best fit their needs, you have designed their jobs to best fit your needs. The problem is that the subordinates may be quite satisfied and productive doing jobs that seem dull and routine to you. Projection can be controlled through a high degree of self-awareness and empathy—the ability to view a situation as others see it.

Contrast Effects

We mentioned earlier how a bright red sports car would stand out from a group of gray sedans because of its contrast. This shows a **contrast effect** in which the meaning or interpretation of something is arrived at by contrasting it with a recently occurring event or situation. This form of perceptual distortion can occur say, when a person gives a talk following a strong speaker or is interviewed for a job following a series of mediocre applicants. A contrast effect occurs when an individual's characteristics are contrasted with those of others recently encountered and who rank higher or lower on the same characteristics.

Self-Fulfilling Prophecies

A final perceptual distortion is the **self-fulfilling prophecy**—the tendency to create or find in another situation or individual that which you expected to find in the first place. A self-fulfilling prophecy is sometimes referred to as the "Pygmalion effect," named for a mythical Greek sculptor who created a statue of his ideal mate and then made her come to life.[16]

Managers will find that self-fulfilling prophecies can have both positive and negative outcomes. In effect, they may create in work situations that which we expect to find. Suppose you assume that team members prefer to satisfy most of their needs outside the work setting and want only minimal involvement with their jobs. Consequently, you provide them with simple, highly structured jobs

WORKERS REPORT VIEWS ON ETHICAL WORKPLACE CONDUCT

These data on ethical workplace conduct are from a survey conducted for Deloitte & Touche USA.

- 42 percent of workers say the behavior of their managers is a major influence on an ethical workplace.
- Most common unethical acts by managers and supervisors include verbal, sexual and racial harassment, misuse of company property, and giving preferential treatment.
- Most workers consider it unacceptable to steal from an employer, cheat on expense reports, take credit for another's accomplishments, and lie on time sheets.
- Most workers consider it acceptable to ask a work colleague for a personal favor, take sick days when not ill, use company technology for personal affairs.
- Top reasons for unethical behavior are lack of personal integrity (80%) and lack of job satisfaction (60%).
- 91 percent of workers are more likely to behave ethically when they have work-life balance; 30 percent say they suffer from poor work-life balance.

Whose Ethics Count? *Shouldn't an individual be accountable for her or his own ethical reasoning and analysis? How and why is it that the ethics practices of others, including managers, influence our ethics behaviors? What can be done to strengthen people's confidence in their own ethical frameworks so that even bad management won't result in unethical practices?*

designed to require little involvement. Can you predict what response they will have to this situation? In fact, they may show the very same lack of commitment you assumed they would have in the first place; your initial expectations get confirmed as a negative self-fulfilling prophecy.

Self-fulfilling prophecies can also have a positive side. We know that students introduced to their teachers as "intellectual bloomers" often do better on achievement tests than do their counterparts who lack such a positive introduction. But why? In a study of army tank crews, one set of tank commanders was told that some members of their assigned crews had exceptional abilities while others were only average. In reality, the crew members had been assigned randomly so that the two test groups were equal in ability. The commanders later reported that the so-called "exceptional" crew members performed better than the "average" ones. The study also revealed the commanders had given more attention and praise to the crew members for whom they had the higher expectations.[17] The self-fulfilling effects in these cases argue strongly for managers to adopt positive and optimistic approaches toward others at work.

Perception and Attribution

One of the ways in which perception exerts its influence on behavior is through **attribution**. This is the process of developing explanations or assigning perceived causes for events. It is natural for people to try to explain what they observe and

- **Attribution** is the process of creating explanations for events.

the things that happen to them. And one of the most significant places for this is the workplace. What happens when you perceive that someone else in a job or student group isn't performing up to expectations? How do you explain this? And, depending on the explanation, what do you do to try and correct things?

Importance of Attributions

Attributions play roles in perception, and attribution theory helps us to understand this process. It focuses on how people attempt to understand the causes of an event, assess responsibility for the outcomes, and evaluate the personal qualities of the people involved in it.[18] Attribution theory is especially concerned with whether the assumption is that an individual's behavior has been internally or externally caused. Internal causes are believed to be under an individual's control—you believe Jake's performance is poor because he is lazy. External causes are seen as coming from outside a person—you believe Kellie's performance is poor because the software she's using is out of date.

According to attribution theory three factors influence this internal or external determination of causality: distinctiveness, consensus, and consistency. *Distinctiveness* considers how consistent a person's behavior is across different situations. If Jake's performance is typically low, regardless of the technology with which he is working, we tend to assign the poor performance to an internal attribution—there's something wrong with Jake. If the poor performance is unusual, we tend to assign an external cause to explain it—there's something happening in the work context.

Consensus takes into account how likely all those facing a similar situation are to respond in the same way. If all the people using the same technology as Jake perform poorly, we tend to assign his performance problem to an external attribution. If others do not perform poorly, we attribute the poor performance to internal causation. *Consistency* concerns whether an individual responds the same way across time. If Jake performs poorly over a sustained period of time, we tend to give the poor performance an internal attribution. If his low performance is an isolated incident, we may well attribute it to an external cause.

Attribution Errors

* **Fundamental attribution error** overestimates internal factors and underestimates external factors as influences on someone's behavior.

* **Self-serving bias** underestimates internal factors and overestimates external factors as influences on someone's behavior.

Two perception errors are associated with the assignment of internal versus external causation—*fundamental attribution error* and *self-serving bias*.[19] Look at the data reported in Figure 4.5. When managers were asked to identify, or attribute, causes of poor performance among their subordinates, they most often blamed internal deficiencies of the individual—lack of ability and effort, rather than external deficiencies in the situation—lack of support. This demonstrates **fundamental attribution error**—the tendency to underestimate the influence of situational factors and to overestimate the influence of personal factors in evaluating someone else's behavior. When asked to identify causes of their own poor performance, however, the managers mostly cited lack of support—an external, or situational, deficiency. This indicates **self-serving bias**—the tendency to deny personal responsibility for performance problems but to accept personal responsibility for performance success.

Cause of Poor Performance by Their Subordinates	Most Frequent Attribution	Cause of Poor Performance by Themselves
7	Lack of *ability*	1
12	Lack of *effort*	1
5	Lack of *support*	23

Figure 4.5 Health care managers' attributions of causes for poor performance.

The managerial implications of attribution theory can be traced back to the fact that perceptions influence behavior.[20] For example, a manager who believes that subordinates are not performing well and perceives the reason to be an internal lack of effort is likely to respond with attempts to "motivate" the subordinates to work harder; the possibility of changing external, situational factors that may remove job constraints and provide better organizational support may be largely ignored. This oversight could sacrifice major performance gains. Interestingly, when supervisors in the study evaluated their own behavior, they indicated their performance would benefit from having better support. Because of self-serving bias, the supervisors' own abilities or willingness to work hard were not believed to be at issue.

Attributions across Cultures

In cross-cultural comparisons of attribution tendencies, the highly individualistic American culture tends to overemphasize internal causes and underemphasize external ones when explaining events. This can result in negative attributions toward other persons experiencing performance problems, such as one's team mates or direct reports. Such negative attributions, in turn, tend to generate actions designed to improve performance by correcting individual deficiencies—by negative performance evaluations and more training, for example, rather than those designed to increase external support for work performance.[21] By contrast, research from Korea shows tendencies toward negative self-serving bias; that is, Korean managers are more prone to attribute work group failure to themselves—"I was not a capable leader," than to external causes.[22] In India the fundamental attribution error overemphasizes external rather than internal causes for failure. Why these various differences occurred is not clear, but differing cultural values appear to play a role.

Attribution and Social Learning

Perception and attribution are important components in **social learning theory**, which describes how learning takes place through the reciprocal interactions among people, behavior, and environment. Figure 4.6 illustrates this model as drawn from the work of Albert Bandura.[23] According to the figure, the individual uses modeling or vicarious learning to acquire behavior by observing and imitating others. The person then attempts to acquire these behaviors by modeling

- **Social learning theory** describes how learning occurs through interactions among people, behavior, and environment.

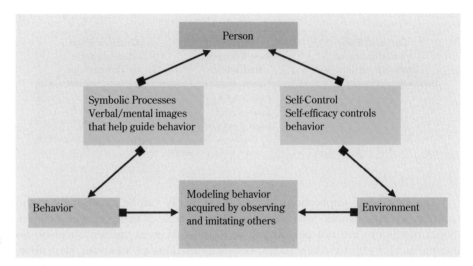

Figure 4.6 Simplified model of social learning.

them through practice. In a work situation, the model may be a manager or co-worker who demonstrates desired behaviors. Mentors or senior workers who befriend younger and more inexperienced protégés can also be important models. Indeed, some have argued that a shortage of mentors for women in senior management has been a major constraint to their progression up the career ladder.[24]

The symbolic processes shown in Figure 4.6 are important in social learning. Words and symbols used by managers and others in the workplace can help communicate values, beliefs, and goals and thus serve as guides to an individual's behavior. For example, a "thumbs up" or other signal from the boss lets you know your behavior is appropriate. At the same time, the person's self-control is important in influencing his or her own behavior. And **self-efficacy**—the person's belief that he or she can perform adequately in a situation, is an important part of such self-control. Closely associated with the concept of self-efficacy are such terms as confidence, competence, and ability.[25]

People with high self-efficacy believe that they have the necessary abilities for a given job, that they are capable of the effort required, and that no outside events will hinder them from attaining their desired performance level.[26] In contrast, people with low self-efficacy believe that no matter how hard they try, they cannot manage their environment well enough to be successful. For example, if you feel self-efficacy as a student, a low grade on one test is likely to encourage you to study harder, talk to the instructor, or do other things to enable you to do well the next time. In contrast, a person low in self-efficacy would probably drop the course or give up studying. Of course, even people who are high in self-efficacy do not control their environment entirely. Some ideas on how to build or enhance self-efficacy are listed in OB Savvy 4.1.

> • **Self-efficacy** is a person's belief that she or he is capable of performing a task.

OB SAVVY 4.1

Four Ways of Building or Enhancing Self-Efficacy

1. *Enactive mastery*–gaining confidence through positive experience. The more you work at a task, so to speak, the more your experience builds and the more confident you become at doing it.

2. *Vicarious modeling*–gaining confidence by observing others. When someone else is good at a task and we are able to observe how they do it, we gain confidence in being able to do it ourselves.

3. *Verbal persuasion*–gaining confidence from someone telling us or encouraging us that we can perform the task. Hearing others praise our efforts and link those efforts with performance successes is often very motivational.

4. *Emotional arousal*–gaining confidence when we are highly stimulated or energized to perform well in a situation. A good analogy for arousal is how athletes get "psyched up" and highly motivated to perform in key competitions.

Leaders on Leadership

RICHARD BRANSON LEADS WITH PERSONALITY AND FLAMBOYANCE

Sir Richard Branson, well-known founder of Virgin Group, is a believer in positive reinforcement. "For the people who work for you or with you, you must lavish praise on them at all times," he says. "If a flower is watered, it flourishes. If not it shrivels up and dies." And besides, he goes on to add: "Its much more fun looking for the best in people."

Virgin Group is a business conglomerate employing some

25,000 people around the globe. It holds over 200 companies, including Virgin Mobile, Virgin Records, and even a space venture—Virgin Galactic. It's all very creative and ambitious—but that's Branson. "I love to learn things I know little about," he says.

But if you bump into Branson on the street you might be surprised. He's casual, he's smiling, and he's fun; he's also brilliant when it comes to business and leadership. He's been listed among the 25 most influential business leaders. His goal is to build Virgin into "the most respected brand in the world." And as the man behind the brand he's described as "flamboyant," something that he doesn't deny and also considers a major business advantage that keeps him and his ventures in the public eye.

About leadership Branson says: "Having a personality of caring about people is important . . . You can't be a good

leader unless you generally like people. That is how you bring out the best in them." He claims his own style was shaped by his family and childhood. At age 10 his mother put him on a 300-mile bike ride to build character and endurance. At 16 he started a student magazine. By the age of 22 he was launching Virgin record stores. And by the time he was 30 Virgin Group was running at high speed.

As for himself, Branson says he'll probably never retire. Now known as Sir Richard after being knighted, he enjoys Virgin today "as a way of life" that he greatly enjoys. But he also says that "In the next stage of my life I want to use our business skills to tackle social issues around the world . . . Malaria in Africa kills four million people a year. AIDS kills even more . . . I don't want to waste this fabulous situation in which I've found myself."

Learning by Reinforcement

When it comes to learning, the concept of "reinforcement" is very important in OB. It has a very specific meaning that has its origin in some classic studies in psychology.[27] **Reinforcement** is the administration of a consequence as a result of a behavior. Managing reinforcement properly can change the direction, level, and persistence of an individual's behavior. To understand this idea, we need to review some of the concepts of conditioning and reinforcement you may have already learned in a basic psychology course.

• **Reinforcement** is the delivery of a consequence as a result of behavior.

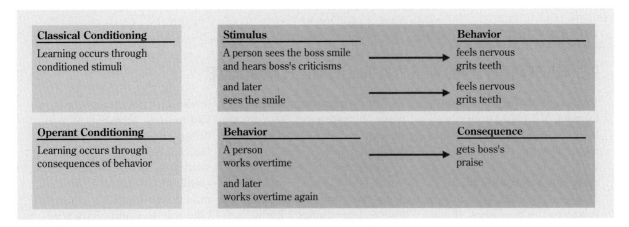

Figure 4.7 Differences between classical and operant conditioning approaches for a boss and subordinate.

Classical and Operant Conditioning

Classical conditioning, studied by Ivan Pavlov, is a form of learning through association that involves the manipulation of stimuli to influence behavior. The Russian psychologist "taught" dogs to salivate at the sound of a bell by ringing the bell when feeding the dogs. The sight of the food naturally caused the dogs to salivate. The dogs "learned" to associate the bell ringing with the presentation of meat and to salivate at the ringing of the bell alone. Such learning through association is so common in organizations that it is often ignored until it causes considerable confusion.

The key here is to understand stimulus and conditioned stimulus. A stimulus is something that incites action and draws forth a response, such as food for the dogs. The trick is to associate one neutral potential stimulus—the bell ringing, with another initial stimulus that already affects behavior—the food. The once-neutral stimulus is called a conditioned stimulus when it affects behavior in the same way as the initial stimulus. Take a look at Figure 4.7 for a work example. Here, the boss's smiling becomes a conditioned stimulus because of its linkage to his criticisms.

The reinforcement approach popularized by B. F. Skinner extends reinforcement to applications that include more than just stimulus and response behavior.[28] It involves **operant conditioning** as the process of controlling behavior by manipulating its consequences. You may think of operant conditioning as learning by reinforcement. In management the goal is to use reinforcement principles to systematically reinforce desirable work behavior and discourage undesirable work behavior.[29]

- **Operant conditioning** is the control of behavior by manipulating its consequences.

Classical and operant conditioning differ in two important ways. First, control in operant conditioning is via manipulation of consequences. Second, operant conditioning calls for examining antecedents, behavior, and consequences. The *antecedent* is the condition leading up to or "cueing" behavior. Figure 4.7 gives the example of an agreement with the boss to work overtime as needed. If the employee actually does work overtime, this is the *behavior*. The *consequence* would be the boss's praise. In operant conditioning, the behavior based in the antecedent is drawn forth by the manipulation of consequences.

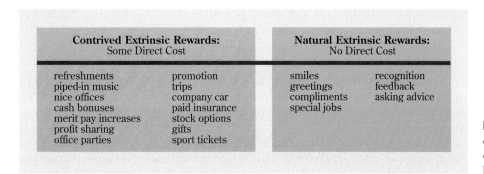

Contrived Extrinsic Rewards: Some Direct Cost		Natural Extrinsic Rewards: No Direct Cost	
refreshments	promotion	smiles	recognition
piped-in music	trips	greetings	feedback
nice offices	company car	compliments	asking advice
cash bonuses	paid insurance	special jobs	
merit pay increases	stock options		
profit sharing	gifts		
office parties	sport tickets		

Figure 4.8 A sample of contrived and natural extrinsic rewards that can be allocated by managers.

Law of Effect

The basis for operant conditioning rests in E. L. Thorndike's **law of effect**.[30] It is simple but powerful: behavior that results in a pleasant outcome is likely to be repeated, whereas behavior that results in an unpleasant outcome is not likely to be repeated. The implications of this law are rather straightforward. If, as a supervisor, you want more of a behavior, you must make the consequences for the individual positive.

Note that the emphasis is on consequences that can be manipulated rather than on consequences inherent in the behavior itself. OB research often emphasizes specific types of rewards that are considered from the reinforcement perspective to influence individual behavior. **Extrinsic rewards**, such as pay and praise, are positively valued work outcomes that are given to the individual by some other person. They become external reinforcers or environmental consequences that can substantially influence a person's work behaviors through the law of effect.

Figure 4.8 presents a sample of extrinsic rewards that can be allocated by managers in using the law of effect in the workplace.[31] Some of these rewards are *contrived rewards* that are planned, and have direct costs and budgetary implications. Examples are pay increases and cash bonuses. A second category includes *natural rewards* that have no cost other than the manager's personal time and efforts. Examples are verbal praise and recognition in the workplace. The use of such rewards to systematically reinforce desirable work behavior and to discourage unwanted work behavior is known as **organizational behavior modification**, or OB Mod for short. It involves the use of four basic reinforcement strategies: positive reinforcement, negative reinforcement (or avoidance), punishment, and extinction.[32]

Positive Reinforcement

B. F. Skinner and his followers advocate **positive reinforcement**—the administration of positive consequences that tend to increase the likelihood of repeating the desirable behavior in similar settings. For example, a team leader nods to a team member to express approval after she makes a useful comment during a sales meeting. This increases the likelihood of future useful comments from the team member, just as the leader would hope.

To begin using a strategy of positive reinforcement, we need to be aware that positive reinforcers and rewards are not necessarily the same. Recognition,

- The **law of effect** is that behavior followed by pleasant consequences is likely to be repeated; behavior followed by unpleasant consequences is not.

- **Organizational behavior modification** is the use of extrinsic rewards to systematically reinforce desirable work behavior and discourage undesirable behavior.

- **Positive reinforcement** strengthens a behavior by making a desirable consequence contingent on its occurrence.

for example, is both a reward and a potential positive reinforcer. But it becomes a positive reinforcer only if a person's performance later improves. Sometimes, a "reward" doesn't work as intended. For example, a team leader might praise a team member in front of others for finding errors in a report that the group had prepared. If the members then give their teammate the silent treatment, however, the worker is less likely to report such errors in the future. In this case, the "reward" fails to serve as a positive reinforcer of the desired work behavior.

To have maximum reinforcement value, a reward must be delivered only if the desired behavior is exhibited. That is, the reward must be contingent on the desired behavior. This principle is known as the law of contingent reinforcement. For example, a supervisor's praise should be contingent on the subordinate's doing something identifiably well, such as giving a constructive suggestion in a meeting. Also, the reward must be given as soon as possible after the desired behavior. This is known as the law of immediate reinforcement.[33] If the supervisor waits for the annual performance review to praise the subordinate for providing constructive comments, the law of immediate reinforcement would be violated.

Shaping   The power of positive reinforcement can be mobilized through a process known as **shaping**. This is the creation of a new behavior by the positive reinforcement of successive approximations to it. For example, new machine operators in the Ford Motor casting operation in Ohio must learn a complex series of tasks in pouring molten metal into castings in order to avoid gaps, overfills, or cracks.[34] The molds are filled in a three-step process, with each step progressively more difficult than its predecessor. Astute master craftspersons first show newcomers how to pour as the first step and give praise based on what they did right. As the apprentices gain experience, they are given praise only when all of the elements of the first step are completed successfully. Once the apprentices have mastered the first step, they move to the second. Reinforcement is given only when the entire first step and an aspect of the second step are completed successfully. Over time, apprentices learn all three steps and are given contingent positive rewards immediately upon completing a casting that has no cracks or gaps. In this way behavior is shaped gradually rather than changed all at once.

- **Shaping** is positive reinforcement of successive approximations to the desired behavior.

Scheduling Positive Reinforcement   Positive reinforcement can be given according to either continuous or intermittent schedules. **Continuous reinforcement** administers a reward each time a desired behavior occurs, whereas **intermittent reinforcement** rewards behavior only periodically. In general, continuous reinforcement draws forth a desired behavior more quickly than does intermittent reinforcement. But it is costly in the consumption of rewards and the behavior is more easily extinguished when reinforcement is no longer present. Behavior acquired under intermittent reinforcement lasts longer upon the discontinuance of reinforcement, and thus is more resistant to extinction. This is why shaping typically begins with a continuous reinforcement schedule and then gradually shifts to an intermittent one.

- **Continuous reinforcement** administers a reward each time a desired behavior occurs.

- **Intermittent reinforcement** rewards behavior only periodically.

As shown in Figure 4.9, intermittent reinforcement can be given according to fixed or variable schedules. *Variable schedules* typically result in more consistent patterns of desired behavior than do fixed reinforcement schedules.

	Interval	Ratio

Fixed	**Fixed interval**
	
	Reinforcer given after a given
	    time
	Weekly or monthly paychecks
	Regularly scheduled exams
		Fixed ratio
		
		Reinforcer given after a given
		    number of behavior
		    occurrences
		Piece-rate pay
		Commissioned salespeople:
		    certain amount is given for
		    each dollar of sales

Variable	**Variable interval**
	
	Reinforcer given at random times
	Occasional praise by boss on
	    unscheduled visits
	Unspecified number of pop
	    quizzes to students
		Variable ratio
		
		Reinforcer given after a random
		    number of behavior
		    occurrences
		Random quality checks with
		    praise for zero defects
		Commissioned salespeople:
		    a varying number of calls are
		    required to obtain a given sale

	Time-based	**Behavior occurrence–based**

Figure 4.9 Alternative schedules of reinforcement in OB Mod.

Fixed-interval schedules provide rewards at the first appearance of a behavior after a given time has elapsed. *Fixed-ratio schedules* result in a reward each time a certain number of the behaviors have occurred. A *variable-interval schedule* rewards behavior at random times, while a *variable-ratio schedule* rewards behavior after a random number of occurrences.

Negative Reinforcement

A second reinforcement strategy used in OB Mod is **negative reinforcement** or avoidance learning. It uses the withdrawal of negative consequences to increase the likelihood of repeating the desirable behavior in similar settings. For example, a manager at McDonald's regularly nags a worker about being late for work and then doesn't nag when the worker next shows up on time. The term "negative reinforcement" comes from this withdrawal of the negative consequences. The strategy is also sometimes called *avoidance* because its intent is for the person to avoid the negative consequence by performing the desired behavior. For instance, we stop at a red light to avoid a traffic ticket, or a worker who prefers the day shift is allowed to return to that shift if she performs well on the night shift.

- **Negative reinforcement** strengthens a behavior by making the avoidance of an undesirable consequence contingent on its occurrence.

Punishment

A third reinforcement strategy is punishment. Unlike positive reinforcement and negative reinforcement, it is intended not to encourage positive behavior but to discourage negative behavior. Formally defined, **punishment** is the administration of negative consequences or the withdrawal of positive consequences that tend to reduce the likelihood of repeating the behavior in similar settings.

- **Punishment** discourages a behavior by making an unpleasant consequence contingent on its occurrence.

OB SAVVY 4.2

Guidelines for Positive Reinforcement and Punishment

Positive Reinforcement:
- Clearly identify desired work behaviors.
- Maintain a diverse inventory of rewards.
- Inform everyone what must be done to get rewards.
- Recognize individual differences when allocating rewards.
- Follow the laws of immediate and contingent reinforcement.

Punishment:
- Tell the person what is being done wrong.
- Tell the person what is being done right.
- Make sure the punishment matches the behavior.
- Administer the punishment in private.
- Follow the laws of immediate and contingent reinforcement.

There is evidence that punishment administered for poor performance can lead to better performance without a significant effect on satisfaction. But punishment seen by workers as arbitrary and capricious leads to low satisfaction as well as low performance.[35] The point is that punishment can be handled poorly, or it can be handled well as suggested in OB Savvy 4.2.

Finally, punishment may be offset by positive reinforcement received from another source. It is possible for a worker to be reinforced by peers at the same time that the worker is receiving punishment from the manager. Sometimes the positive value of such peer support is so great that the individual chooses to put up with the punishment. Thus, the undesirable behavior continues. As many times as an experienced worker may be verbally reprimanded by a supervisor for playing jokes on new employees, for example, the "grins" offered by other workers may well justify continuation of the jokes in the future.

Extinction

Extinction discourages a behavior by making the removal of a desirable consequence contingent on its occurrence.

The final reinforcement strategy in OB Mod is **extinction**—the withdrawal of the reinforcing consequences for a given behavior. For example, Enya is often late for work and co-workers cover for her (positive reinforcement). The manager instructs Enya's co-workers to stop covering, thus withdrawing the positive consequences. This is a use of extinction to try and get rid of an undesirable behavior.

This extinction strategy decreases the frequency of or weakens behavior. But the behavior is not "unlearned"; it simply is not exhibited. Since the behavior is no longer reinforced, it will reappear if reinforced again. Whereas positive reinforcement seeks to establish and maintain desirable work behavior, extinction is intended to weaken and eliminate undesirable behavior.

Reinforcement Pros and Cons

Figure 4.10 summarizes and illustrates the use of each reinforcement strategy in OB Mod. They are all designed to direct work behavior toward practices desired by management. Both positive and negative reinforcement are used to strengthen the desirable behavior of improving work quality when it occurs. Punishment is used to weaken the undesirable behavior of high error rates and involves either administering negative consequences or withdrawing positive consequences. Similarly, extinction is used deliberately to weaken the undesirable behavior of high error rates when it occurs. Note also that these strategies may be used in combination as well as independently.

The effective use of the four reinforcement strategies can help manage human behavior at work. Testimony to this effect is found in the wide application of

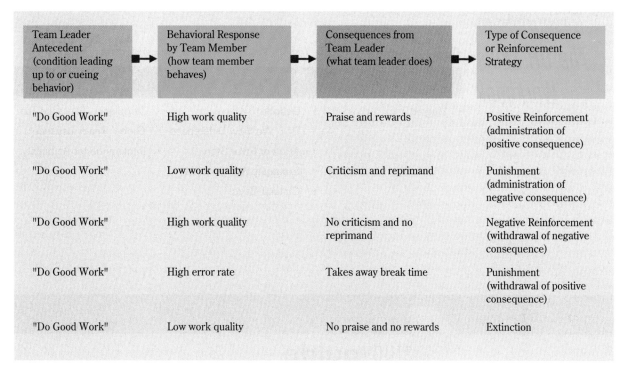

Team Leader Antecedent (condition leading up to or cueing behavior)	Behavioral Response by Team Member (how team member behaves)	Consequences from Team Leader (what team leader does)	Type of Consequence or Reinforcement Strategy
"Do Good Work"	High work quality	Praise and rewards	Positive Reinforcement (administration of positive consequence)
"Do Good Work"	Low work quality	Criticism and reprimand	Punishment (administration of negative consequence)
"Do Good Work"	High work quality	No criticism and no reprimand	Negative Reinforcement (withdrawal of negative consequence)
"Do Good Work"	High error rate	Takes away break time	Punishment (withdrawal of positive consequence)
"Do Good Work"	Low work quality	No praise and no rewards	Extinction

Figure 4.10 Examples of comprehensive managerial use of reinforcement strategies.

these strategies in all sorts of work settings, and by the growing number of consulting firms that specialize in reinforcement techniques. But use of these approaches is not without criticism.

Some critics of the reinforcement approach claim that the success of specific programs involves isolated cases that have been analyzed without the benefit of scientific research designs; it is hard to conclude definitively whether the observed results were caused by reinforcement dynamics. In fact, one critic argues that the improved performance may well have occurred only because of the goal setting involved—that is, because specific performance goals were clarified, and workers were individually held accountable for their accomplishment.[36] Another major criticism rests with potential value dilemmas associated with using reinforcement to influence human behavior at work. For example, some maintain that the systematic use of reinforcement strategies leads to a demeaning and dehumanizing view of people that stunts human growth and development.[37] Others believe managers abuse the power of their position and knowledge by exerting external control over individual behavior.

Advocates of the reinforcement approach attack its critics head on. They agree that behavior modification involves the control of behavior, but they also argue that behavior control is an irrevocable part of every manager's job. The real question, they say, is how to ensure that any manipulation is done in a positive and constructive fashion.[38]

Resources in The OB Skills Workbook

These learning activities from *The OB Skills Workbook* are suggested for Chapter 4.

Cases for Critical Thinking	Team and Experiential Exercises	Self-Assessment Portfolio
• Magrec, Inc.	• Decode	• Turbulence Tolerance Test
	• How We View Differences	• Global Readiness Index
	• Alligator River Story	• Intolerance for Ambiguity
	• Expatriate Assignments	
	• Cultural Cues	

4 study guide

Summary Questions and Answers

What is perception?

- Individuals use the perception process to select, organize, interpret, and retrieve information from the world around them.

- Perception acts as a filter through which all communication passes as it travels from one person to the next.

- Because people tend to perceive things differently, the same situation may be interpreted and responded to differently by different people.

- Factors influencing perceptions include characteristics of the perceiver, the setting, and the perceived.

What are common perceptual distortions?

- Stereotypes occur when a person is identified with a category and is assumed to display characteristics otherwise associated with members of that category.

- Halo effects occur when one attribute of a person or situation is used to develop an overall impression of the person or situation.

- Selective perception is the tendency to single out for attention those aspects of a situation or person that reinforce or emerge and are consistent with existing beliefs, values, and needs.

- Projection involves the assignment of personal attributes to other individuals.

- Contrast effects occur when an individual's characteristics are contrasted with those of others recently encountered who rank higher or lower on the same characteristics.

What is the link between perception and attribution?

- Attribution theory addresses the interpretation stage of the perception process where tendencies are to view events or behaviors as primarily the results of external causes or internal causes.

- Three factors that influence the attribution of external or internal causation are distinctiveness, consensus, and consistency.

- Fundamental attribution error occurs when we blame others for performance problems while excluding possible external causes.

- Self-serving bias occurs when, in judging our own performance, we take personal credit for successes and blame failures on external factors.

- Social learning theory links perception and attribution by recognizing how learning is achieved through the reciprocal interactions among people, behavior, and environment.

What is involved in learning by reinforcement?

- Reinforcement theory recognizes that human behavior is influenced by environmental consequences.

- The law of effect states that behavior followed by a pleasant consequence is likely to be repeated; behavior followed by an unpleasant consequence is unlikely to be repeated.

- Reinforcement strategies used by managers include positive reinforcement, negative reinforcement, punishment, and extinction.

- Positive reinforcement is the administration of positive consequences that tend to increase the likelihood of a person's repeating a behavior in similar settings.

- Positive reinforcement should be contingent and immediate, and it can be scheduled continuously or intermittently depending on resources and desired outcomes.

- Negative reinforcement, avoidance learning, is used to encourage desirable behavior through the withdrawal of negative consequences for previously undesirable behavior.

- Punishment is the administration of negative consequences or the withdrawal of positive consequences, both of which tend to reduce the likelihood of repeating an undesirable behavior in similar settings.

- Extinction is the withdrawal of reinforcing consequences for a given behavior.

Key Terms

Attribution (p. 93)
Contrast effect (p. 92)
Continuous reinforcement (p. 100)
Extinction (p. 102)
Fundamental attribution error (p. 94)
Halo effect (p. 91)
Impression management (p. 89)
Intermittent reinforcement (p. 100)

Law of effect (p. 99)
Negative reinforcement (p. 101)
Operant conditioning (p. 98)
Organizational behavior modification (p. 99)
Perception (p. 84)
Positive reinforcement (p. 99)
Projection (p. 92)
Punishment (p. 101)

Reinforcement (p. 97)
Schemas (p. 87)
Selective perception (p. 91)
Self-efficacy (p. 96)
Self-fulfilling prophecy (p. 92)
Self-serving bias (p. 94)
Shaping (p. 100)
Social learning theory (p. 95)
Stereotype (p. 90)

Self-Test 4

Multiple Choice

1. Perception is the process by which people _____ information. (a) generate (b) retrieve (c) transmit (d) verify

2. Which is not a stage in the perceptual process? (a) attention/selection (b) interpretation (c) follow-through (d) retrieval

3. Self-serving bias is a form of attribution error that involves _____. (a) blaming yourself for problems caused by others (b) blaming the environment for problems you caused (c) poor emotional intelligence (d) authoritarianism

4. In the fundamental attribution error, the influence of _____ as causes of a problem are _____. (a) situational factors, overestimated (b) personal factors, underestimated (c) personal factors, overestimated (d) situational factors, underestimated

5. If a new team leader changes job designs for persons on her work team mainly "because I would prefer to work the new way rather than the old," the chances are that she is committing a perceptual error known as _____. (a) halo effect (b) stereotype (c) selective perception (d) projection

6. Use of special dress, manners, gestures, and vocabulary words when meeting a prospective employer in a job interview are all examples of how people use _____ in daily life. (a) projection (b) selective perception (c) impression management (d) self-serving bias

7. Which of the following is not a common perceptual distortion? (a) prototype (b) social learning (c) the halo effect (d) the contrast effect

8. If a manager allows one characteristic of person, say a pleasant personality, to bias performance ratings of that individual overall, the manager is falling prey to a perceptual distortion known as _____. (a) halo effect (b) stereotype (c) selective perception (d) projection

9. The underlying premise of reinforcement theory is that _____. (a) behavior is a function of environment (b) motivation comes from positive expectancy (c) higher order needs stimulate hard work (d) rewards considered unfair are de-motivators

10. The law of _____ states that behavior followed by a positive consequence is likely to be repeated, whereas behavior followed by an undesirable consequence is not likely to be repeated. (a) reinforcement (b) contingency (c) goal setting (d) effect

11. _____ is a positive reinforcement strategy that rewards successive approximations to a desirable behavior. (a) Extinction (b) Negative reinforcement (c) Shaping (d) Merit pay

12. B. F. Skinner would argue that "getting a paycheck on Friday" reinforces a person for coming to work on Friday but would not reinforce the person for doing an extraordinary job on Tuesday. This is because the Friday paycheck fails the law of _____ reinforcement. (a) negative (b) continuous (c) immediate (d) intermittent

13. The purpose of negative reinforcement as an operant conditioning technique is to _____. (a) punish bad behavior (b) discourage bad behavior (c) encourage desirable behavior (d) offset the effects of shaping

14. Punishment _____. (a) may be offset by positive reinforcement from another source (b) generally is the most effective kind of reinforcement (c) is especially important in today's workplace (d) emphasizes the withdrawal of reinforcing consequences for a given behavior.

15. A major difference between reinforcement and social learning theory is _____. (a) reinforcement recognizes the existence of vicarious learning, and social learning does not (b) reinforcement recognizes objective consequences while social learning theory emphasizes how individuals perceive and define consequences (c) reinforcement emphasizes modeling behavior while social learning theory does not (d) there is no major difference between reinforcement and social learning theory

Short Response

16. Draw and briefly discuss a model showing the important stages of the perception process.

17. Select two perceptual distortions, briefly define them, and show how they can lead to poor decisions by managers.

18. Briefly compare and contrast classical conditioning and operant conditioning.

19. Explain how the reinforcement learning and social learning approaches are similar and dissimilar to one another.

Applications Essay

20. One of your friends has just been appointed as leader of a work team. This is her first leadership assignment and she has recently heard a little about attribution theory. She has asked you to explain it to her in more detail, focusing on its possible usefulness in managing the team. What will you tell her?

5

Motivation Theories

chapter at a glance

Even with great talents many people fail to achieve great things. A good part of the reason lies with unwillingness to work hard enough to achieve high performance. Here's what to look for in Chapter 5. Don't forget to check your learning with the Summary Questions & Answers and Self-Test in the end-of-chapter Study Guide.

_W_all _Street Journal_ columnist Carol Hymowitz opened an article written about successful female executives with this sentence: "Reach for the top—and don't eliminate choices too soon or worry about the myth of balance."

One of the first leaders mentioned in her article is Carol Bartz, former executive chairman of the board of the noted software firm Autodesk and the new CEO of Yahoo. In her interview with Hymowitz, Bartz points out that women often suffer from guilt, inappropriately she believes, as they pursue career tracks. In her own case she has both a demanding career and a family. And in both respects she says that she's found happiness.

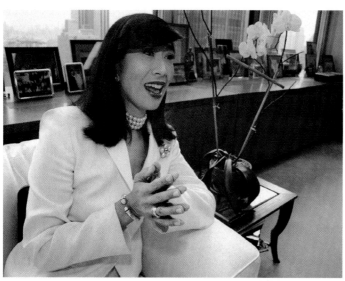

"If you are comfortable with your choices, that's the definition of peace."

Andrea Jung, both chair and CEO of Avon products, agrees with Bartz that women have to work long hours and meet the challenges of multiple demands as they work their way to the top. For Jung this includes lots of international travel, overnight flights, and jet lag. She makes no bones about the fact that sacrifices are real: missed family gatherings, children's school functions, and more. But she also considers the trade-offs worthwhile, saying: "If you're comfortable with your choices, that's the definition of peace."

Nancy Peretsman is managing director and executive vice president of the investment bank Allen & Company. She laments that many young women believe they have to trade career advancement for fulfillment in their personal lives. Not so, says Peretsman, who has a top job and a family that includes teenage daughters. She says: "No one will die if you don't show up at every business meeting or every school play."

As for Hymowitz's conclusions, one stands out clearly. She finds that the lessons from women at the top of the corporate ladder come down to these: setting goals, persevering, accepting stretch assignments, obtaining broad experiences, focusing on strengths not weaknesses, and being willing to take charge of one's own career. That advice seems well voiced. It also seems appropriate for anyone, be they man or woman, seeking career and personal success in today's corporate world.

achievement requires effort

What Is Motivation?

The opening voices from women at the top of the corporate ladder raise interesting issues. Among them is "motivation." The featured corporate leaders all work very hard, have high goals, and are realistic about the trade-offs between career and family. It's easy and accurate to say that they are highly motivated. But how much do we really know about motivation and the conditions under which people, ourselves included, become highly motivated to work hard . . . at school, in our jobs, and in our leisure and personal pursuits?

- **Motivation** refers to forces within an individual that account for the level, direction, and persistence of effort expended at work.

- **Content theories** profile different needs that may motivate individual behavior.

- **Process theories** examine the thought processes that motivate individual behavior.

Motivation Defined

By definition, **motivation** refers to the individual forces that account for the direction, level, and persistence of a person's effort expended at work. *Direction* refers to an individual's choice when presented with a number of possible alternatives (e.g., whether to pursue quality, quantity, or both in one's work). *Level* refers to the amount of effort a person puts forth (e.g., to put forth a lot or very little). *Persistence* refers to the length of time a person sticks with a given action (e.g., to keep trying or to give up when something proves difficult to attain).

Types of Motivation Theories

There are many available theories of motivation, and they can be divided into two broad categories: content theories and process theories.[1] Theories of both types contribute to our understanding of motivation to work, but none offers a complete explanation. In studying a variety of theories, our goal is to gather useful insights that can be integrated into motivational approaches that are appropriate for different situations.

Content theories of motivation focus primarily on individual needs—that is, physiological or psychological deficiencies that we feel a compulsion to reduce or eliminate. The content theories try to explain work behaviors based on pathways to need satisfaction and the influence of blocked needs. This chapter discusses Maslow's hierarchy of needs theory, Alderfer's ERG theory, McClelland's acquired needs theory, and Herzberg's two-factor theory.

Process theories of motivation focus on the thought or cognitive processes that take place within the minds of people and that influence their behavior. Whereas a content approach may identify job security as an important individual need, a process approach would probe further to identify why the person decides to behave in certain ways relative to available rewards and work opportunities. Three process theories discussed in this chapter are equity theory, expectancy theory, and goal-setting theory.

Working Mother
Media

Working Mother magazine covers issues from kids to health to personal motivation and more. Its goal is to help women "integrate their professional lives, their family lives and their inner lives." Each year it publishes a list of the "100 Best Companies for Working Mothers."

Motivation across Cultures

An important caveat should be noted before examining specific motivation theories. Although motivation is a key concern in organizations everywhere, the theories are largely developed from a North American perspective. As a result, they are subject to cultural limitations and contingencies.[2] Indeed, the determinants of motivation and the best ways to deal with it are likely to vary considerably across the cultures of Asia, South America, Eastern Europe, and Africa, as well as North America. For example, an individual financial bonus might prove "motivational" as a reward in one culture, but not in another. In researching, studying, and using motivation theories we should be sensitive to cross-cultural issues. We must avoid being parochial or ethnocentric by assuming that people in all cultures are motivated by the same things in the same ways.[3]

Needs Theories of Motivation

Content theories, as noted earlier, suggest that motivation results from our attempts to satisfy important needs. They suggest that managers should be able to understand individual needs and to create work environments that respond positively to them. Each of the following theories takes a slightly different approach in addressing this challenge.

Hierarchy of Needs Theory

Abraham Maslow's **hierarchy of needs theory**, depicted in Figure 5.1, identifies five levels of individual needs. They range from self-actualization and esteem needs at the top, to social, safety, and physiological needs at the bottom.[4] The concept of a needs "hierarchy" assumes that some needs are more important than others and must be satisfied before the other needs can serve as motivators. For example, physiological needs must be satisfied before safety needs are activated; safety needs must be satisfied before social needs are activated; and so on.

• Maslow's **hierarchy of needs theory** offers a pyramid of physiological, safety, social, esteem, and self-actualization needs.

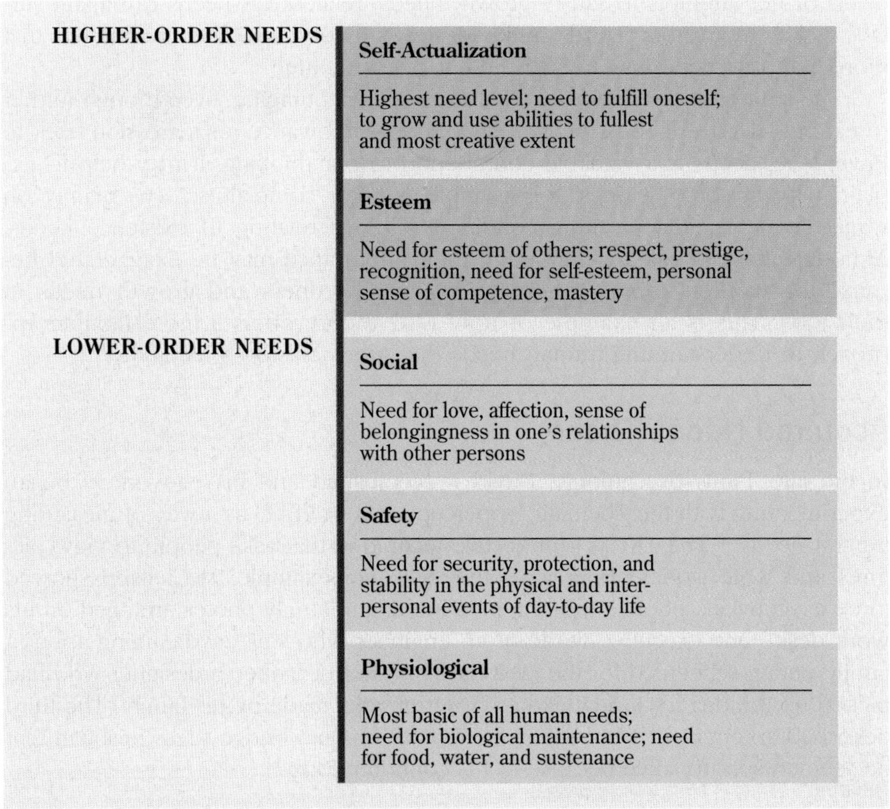

HIGHER-ORDER NEEDS

Self-Actualization

Highest need level; need to fulfill oneself; to grow and use abilities to fullest and most creative extent

Esteem

Need for esteem of others; respect, prestige, recognition, need for self-esteem, personal sense of competence, mastery

LOWER-ORDER NEEDS

Social

Need for love, affection, sense of belongingness in one's relationships with other persons

Safety

Need for security, protection, and stability in the physical and interpersonal events of day-to-day life

Physiological

Most basic of all human needs; need for biological maintenance; need for food, water, and sustenance

Figure 5.1 Higher-order and lower-order needs in Maslow's hierarchy of needs.

- **Higher-order needs** in Maslow's hierarchy are esteem and self-actualization.
- **Lower-order needs** in Maslow's hierarchy are physiological, safety, and social.
- Alderfer's **ERG theory** identifies existence, relatedness, and growth needs.
- **Existence needs** are desires for physiological and material well-being.
- **Relatedness needs** are desires for satisfying interpersonal relationships.
- **Growth needs** are desires for continued personal growth and development.

Maslow's model is easy to understand and quite popular. But research evidence fails to support the existence of a precise five-step hierarchy of needs. If anything, the needs are more likely to operate in a flexible rather than in a strict, step-by-step sequence. Some research suggests that **higher-order needs** (esteem and self-actualization) tend to become more important than **lower-order needs** (psychological, safety, and social) as individuals move up the corporate ladder.[5] Studies also report that needs vary according to a person's career stage, the size of the organization, and even geographic location.[6] There is also no consistent evidence that the satisfaction of a need at one level decreases its importance and increases the importance of the next-higher need.[7] And findings regarding the hierarchy of needs vary when this theory is examined across cultures. For instance, social needs tend to take on higher importance in more collectivist societies, such as Mexico and Pakistan, than in individualistic ones like the United States.[8]

ERG Theory

Clayton Alderfer's **ERG theory** is also based on needs, but it differs from Maslow's theory in three main respects.[9] First, ERG theory collapses Maslow's five needs categories into three: **existence needs**, desires for physiological and material well-being; **relatedness needs**, desires for satisfying interpersonal relationships; and **growth needs**, desires for continued personal growth and development. Second, ERG theory emphasizes a unique *frustration-regression* component. An already satisfied lower-level need can become activated when a higher-level need cannot be satisfied. Thus, if a person is continually frustrated in his or her attempts to satisfy growth needs, relatedness needs can again surface as key motivators. Third, unlike Maslow's theory, ERG theory contends that more than one need may be activated at the same time.

The supporting evidence for ERG theory is encouraging, even though further research is needed.[10] In particular, ERG theory's allowance for regression back to lower-level needs is a valuable contribution to our thinking. It may help to explain why in some settings, for example, worker complaints focus mainly on wages, benefits, and working conditions—things relating to existence needs. Although these needs are important, their importance may be exaggerated because the workers cannot otherwise satisfy relatedness and growth needs in their jobs. This is an example of how ERG theory offers a more flexible approach to understanding human needs than does Maslow's hierarchy.

Acquired Needs Theory

In the late 1940s psychologist David I. McClelland and his co-workers began experimenting with the Thematic Apperception Test (TAT) as a way of measuring human needs.[11] The TAT is a projective technique that asks people to view pictures and write stories about what they see. For example, McClelland showed three executives a photograph of a man looking at family photos arranged on his work desk. One executive wrote of an engineer who was daydreaming about a family outing scheduled for the next day. Another described a designer who had picked up an idea for a new gadget from remarks made by his family. The third described an engineer who was intently working on a bridge stress problem that he seemed sure to solve because of his confident look.[12]

Leaders on Leadership

LEADERSHIP AT PISCINES IDEALES: IT'S ALL ABOUT FAMILY

Founded in 1991, Piscines Ideales is the largest manufacturer of private and professional swimming pools in Europe. Unique in its franchise-based operation, the company has been praised by numerous organizations for its business excellence.

Among its most recent accolades was being named Greece's Best Place to Work 2009 and one of the top 10 Best Places to Work in Europe in the same year. It's been especially recognized for its sound ecological products, superior service, ethics and fostering a workplace of respect.

Piscines Ideales CEO, Stelios Stavridis, is a man who values personal connections with his employees and building a world-class organization that can serve as a model to other corporations.

When asked about the secrets to his success, he describes the essence of what he calls Piscines Ideales' water world: "We created an environment of continuous learning that brings out and develops the leader and entrepreneur in each individual. We developed a culture of openness, candor, free expression and equality."

As a leader he strives to "inspire and motivate people to give each other equal opportunities, believe in their unlimited capabilities, and develop a winner's mentality. When they fail, I want them to persist, to stand up, and fight. They should always be optimistic and understand that behind every drawback lies a great opportunity."

Investing in employees is one of Mr. Stavridis' main goals as a leader. Training for skills is important, but he emphasizes the need to "develop our people and teach them— especially the younger ones—to take pleasure and pride in their growth and achievements." As a CEO committed to his employees, he feels a responsibility to "take all necessary action in order not to be obliged to lay off people" in tough economic times.

Known for its family atmosphere, the company takes family spirit seriously. The annual company meeting is referred to as the "family gathering" and this translates to a strong team spirit that keeps employees motivated to help each other reach their full potential, and the company at the top of its industry.

McClelland identified themes in the TAT stories that he believed correspond to needs that are acquired over time as a result of our life experiences. **Need for achievement** (nAch) is the desire to do something better or more efficiently, to solve problems, or to master complex tasks. **Need for affiliation** (nAff) is the desire to establish and maintain friendly and warm relations with others. **Need for power** (nPower) is the desire to control others, to influence their behavior, or to be responsible for others.

Because each need can be linked with a set of work preferences, McClelland encouraged managers to learn how to identify the presence of nAch, nAff, and nPower in themselves and in others. Someone with a high need for achievement will prefer individual responsibilities, challenging goals, and performance feedback. Someone with a high need affiliation is drawn to interpersonal relationships and opportunities for communication. Someone with a high need for power seeks influence over others and likes attention and recognition.

- **Need for achievement (nAch)** is the desire to do better, solve problems, or master complex tasks.
- **Need for affiliation (nAff)** is the desire for friendly and warm relations with others.
- **Need for power (nPower)** is the desire to control others and influence their behavior.

Since these three needs are acquired, McClelland also believed it may be possible to teach people to develop need profiles required for success in various types of jobs. His research indicated, for example, that a moderate to high need for power that is stronger than a need for affiliation is linked with success as a senior executive. The high nPower creates the willingness to exercise influence and control over others; the lower nAff allows the executive to make difficult decisions without undue worry over being disliked.[13]

Research lends considerable insight into the need for achievement in particular, and it includes some interesting applications in developing nations. For example, McClelland trained businesspeople in Kakinda, India to think, talk, and act like high achievers by having them write stories about achievement and participate in a business game that encouraged achievement. The businesspeople also met with successful entrepreneurs and learned how to set challenging goals for their own businesses. Over a two-year period following these activities, the participants from the Kakinda study engaged in activities that created twice as many new jobs as those who hadn't received the training.[14]

Two-Factor Theory

Frederick Herzberg took yet another approach to examining the link between individual needs and motivation. He began by asking workers to report the times they felt exceptionally good about their jobs and the times they felt exceptionally bad about them.[15] The researchers noticed that people talked about very different things when they reported feeling good or bad about their jobs. Herzberg explained these results using the **two-factor theory**, also known as the motivator-hygiene theory, because this theory identifies two different factors as primary causes of job satisfaction and job dissatisfaction.

Hygiene factors are sources of job dissatisfaction, and they are associated with the job context or work setting. That is, they relate more to the environment in which people work than to the nature of the work itself. The two-factor theory suggests that job dissatisfaction results when hygiene factors are poor. But it also suggests that improving the hygiene factors will only decrease job dissatisfaction; it will not increase job satisfaction. Among the hygiene factors shown on the left in Figure 5.2, perhaps the most surprising is salary. Herzberg found

- Herzberg's **two-factor theory** identifies job context as the source of job dissatisfaction and job content as the source of job satisfaction.

- **Hygiene factors** in the job context are sources of job dissatisfaction.

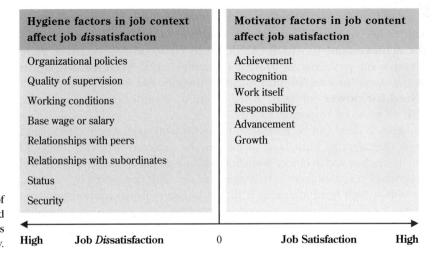

Hygiene factors in job context affect job *dis*satisfaction	Motivator factors in job content affect job satisfaction
Organizational policies	Achievement
Quality of supervision	Recognition
Working conditions	Work itself
Base wage or salary	Responsibility
Relationships with peers	Advancement
Relationships with subordinates	Growth
Status	
Security	

High   Job *Dis*satisfaction   0   Job Satisfaction   High

Figure 5.2 Sources of dissatisfaction and satisfaction in Herzberg's two-factor theory.

that a low base salary or wage makes people dissatisfied, but that paying more does not necessarily satisfy or motivate them.

Motivator factors, shown on the right in Figure 5.2, are sources of job satisfaction. These factors are related to job content—what people actually do in their work. They include such things as a sense of achievement, opportunities for personal growth, recognition, and responsibility. According to the two-factor theory, the presence or absence of satisfiers or motivators in people's jobs is the key link to satisfaction, motivation, and performance. When motivator factors are minimal, low job satisfaction decreases motivation and performance; when motivator factors are substantial, high job satisfaction raises motivation and performance.

Job satisfaction and job dissatisfaction are separate dimensions in the two-factor theory. Taking action to improve a hygiene factor, such as by giving pay raises or creating better physical working conditions, will not make people satisfied with their work; it will only prevent them from being dissatisfied on these matters. To improve job satisfaction, Herzberg suggests the technique of *job enrichment* as a way of building satisfiers into job content. This technique is given special attention in the next chapter as a job design alternative. For now, the implication is well summarized in this statement by Herzberg: "If you want people to do a good job, give them a good job to do."[16]

OB scholars have long debated the merits of the two-factor theory, with special concerns being directed at failures to confirm the theory through additional research.[17] It is criticized as being method bound, or only replicable when Herzberg's original methods are used. This is a serious criticism, since the scientific approach valued in OB requires that theories be verifiable under different research methods.[18] Yet, the distinction between hygiene and motivator factors has been a useful contribution to OB. As will be apparent in the discussions of job designs and alternative work schedules in the next chapter, the notion of two factors—job content and job context—has a practical validity that adds useful discipline to management thinking.

Equity Theory of Motivation

What happens when you get a grade back on a written assignment or test? How do you interpret your results, and what happens to your future motivation in the course? Such questions fall in the domain of the first process theory of motivation to be discussed here—**equity theory**. As applied to the workplace through the writing of J. Stacy Adams, equity theory argues that any perceived inequity becomes a motivating state of mind; in other words, people are motivated to behave in ways that restore or maintain equity in situations.[19]

Equity and Social Comparisons

The basic foundation of equity theory is social comparison. Think back to the earlier questions. When you receive a grade, do you try to find out what others received as well? And when you do, does the interpretation of your grade depend, in part, on how well your grade compared to those of others? Equity theory would predict that your response upon receiving a grade will be based on whether or not you perceive it as fair and equitable. Furthermore, that determination is only made after you compare your results with those received by others.

AJ's Music Cafe

AJ's hosted a 10-day live music Assembly Line Concert to praise Detroit's auto workers. One attendee said: "Detroit is a city that makes things. I wish people would attempt to understand the kind of person who has worked on the line, and whose father worked on the line, and whose grandfather worked on the line."

• **Motivator factors** in the job content are sources of job satisfaction.

• Adams's **equity theory** posits that people will act to eliminate any felt inequity in the rewards received for their work in comparison with others.

Adams argues that this logic applies equally well to the motivational consequences of any rewards that one might receive at work. Adams believes that motivation is a function of how one evaluates rewards received relative to efforts made, and as compared to the rewards received by others relative to their efforts made. A key word in this comparison is "fairness," and as you might expect, any feelings of unfairness or perceived inequity are uncomfortable. They create a state of mind we are motivated to eliminate.

Equity Theory Predictions

Perceived inequity occurs when someone believes that the rewards received for his or her work contributions compare unfavorably to the rewards other people appear to have received for their work. The basic equity comparison can be summarized as follows:

$$\frac{\text{Individual Outcomes}}{\text{Individual Efforts}} \quad \genfrac{}{}{0pt}{}{>}{<} \quad \frac{\text{Others' Outcomes}}{\text{Others' Efforts}}$$

Felt negative inequity in this equation exists when an individual feels that he or she has received relatively less than others have in proportion to work inputs. *Felt positive inequity* exists when an individual feels that he or she has received relatively more than others have. When either feeling exists, the theory states that people will be motivated to act in ways that remove the discomfort and restore a sense of felt equity. In the case of perceived negative inequity, for example, people are likely to respond by engaging in one or more of the following behaviors:

- Change work inputs (e.g., reduce performance efforts).
- Change the outcomes (rewards) received (e.g., ask for a raise).
- Leave the situation (e.g., quit).
- Change the comparison points (e.g., compare self to a different co-worker).
- Psychologically distort the comparisons (e.g., rationalize that the inequity is only temporary and will be resolved in the future).
- Take actions to change the inputs or outputs of the comparison person (e.g., get a co-worker to accept more work).

Research on equity theory indicates that people who feel they are overpaid (perceived positive inequity) are likely to try to increase the quantity or quality of their work, whereas those who feel they are underpaid (perceived negative inequity) are likely to try to decrease the quantity or quality of their work.[20] The research is most conclusive with respect to felt negative inequity. It appears that people are less comfortable when they are under-rewarded than when they are over-rewarded.

You can view the equity comparison as intervening between the allocation of rewards and the ultimate motivational impact for the recipient. That is:

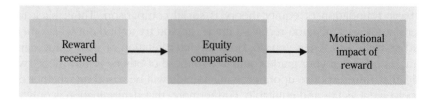

A reward given by a team leader and expected to be highly motivational to a team member, for example, may or may not work as intended. Unless the reward is perceived as fair and equitable in comparison with the results for other teammates, the reward may create negative equity dynamics and work just the opposite of what the team leader expected. Equity theory reminds us that the motivational value of rewards is determined by the individual's interpretation in the context of social comparison. It is not the reward-giver's intentions that count; it is how the recipient perceives the reward that will determine actual motivational outcomes. OB Savvy 5.1 offers ideas on how people cope with such equity dynamics.

> **OB SAVVY 5.1**
>
> ## Steps for Managing Equity Dynamics
>
> - Recognize that equity comparisons are inevitable in the workplace.
> - Anticipate felt negative inequities when rewards are given.
> - Communicate clear evaluations of any rewards given.
> - Communicate the performance reason for the reward.
> - Communicate comparison points appropriate in the situation.

The processes associated with equity theory and its predictions about motivation are subject to cultural contingencies. The findings and predictions reported here are particularly tied to individualistic cultures in which self-interest tends to govern social comparisons. In more collectivist cultures, such as those of many Asian countries, the concern often runs more for equality than equity. This allows for solidarity with the group and helps to maintain harmony in social relationships.[21]

Equity Theory and Organizational Justice

One of the basic elements of equity theory is the fairness with which people perceive they are being treated. This raises an issue in organizational behavior known as **organizational justice**—how fair and equitable people view the practices of their workplace. In ethics, the justice view of moral reasoning considers behavior to be ethical when it is fair and impartial in the treatment of people. Organizational justice notions are important in OB, and in respect to equity theory, they emerge along three dimensions.[22]

Procedural justice is the degree to which the rules and procedures specified by policies are properly followed in all cases to which they are applied. In a sexual harassment case, for example, this may mean that required formal hearings are held for every case submitted for administrative review. **Distributive justice** is the degree to which all people are treated the same under a policy, regardless of race, ethnicity, gender, age, or any other demographic characteristic. In a sexual harassment case, this might mean that a complaint filed by a man against a woman would receive the same consideration as one filed by a woman against a man. **Interactional justice** is the degree to which the people affected by a decision are treated with dignity and respect.[23] Interactional justice in a sexual harassment case, for example, may mean that both the accused and accusing parties believe they have received a complete explanation of any decision made.

Among the many implications of equity theory, those dealing with organizational justice also must be considered. The ways in which people perceive they are being treated at work with respect to procedural, distributive, and interactional justice are likely to affect their motivation. And it is their perceptions of these justice types, often made in a context of social comparison, that create the ultimate motivational influence.

- **Organizational justice** is an issue of how fair and equitable people view workplace practices.

- **Procedural justice** is the degree to which rules are always properly followed to implement policies.

- **Distributive justice** is the degree to which all people are treated the same under a policy.

- **Interactional justice** is the degree to which the people are treated with dignity and respect in decisions affecting them.

Expectancy Theory of Motivation

Vroom's **expectancy theory** argues that work motivation is determined by individual beliefs regarding effort/performance relationships and work outcomes.

Another of the process theories of motivation is Victor Vroom's **expectancy theory**.[24] It posits that motivation is a result of a rational calculation—people will do what they can do when they want to do it.

Expectancy Terms and Concepts

In expectancy theory, and as summarized in Figure 5.3, a person is motivated to the degree that he or she believes that: (1) effort will yield acceptable performance (expectancy), (2) performance will be rewarded (instrumentality), and (3) the value of the rewards is highly positive (valence). Each of the key underlying concepts or terms is defined as follows.

Expectancy is the probability that work effort will be followed by performance accomplishment.

- **Expectancy** is the probability assigned by an individual that work effort will be followed by a given level of achieved task performance. Expectancy would equal zero if the person felt it were impossible to achieve the given performance level; it would equal one if a person were 100 percent certain that the performance could be achieved.

Instrumentality is the probability that performance will lead to various work outcomes.

- **Instrumentality** is the probability assigned by the individual that a given level of achieved task performance will lead to various work outcomes. Instrumentality also varies from 0 to 1. Strictly speaking, Vroom's treatment of instrumentality would allow it to vary from −1 to +1. We use the probability definition here and the 0 to +1 range for pedagogical purposes; it is consistent with the instrumentality notion.

Valence is the value to the individual of various work outcomes.

- **Valence** is the value attached by the individual to various work outcomes. Valences form a scale from −1 (very undesirable outcome) to +1 (very desirable outcome).

Vroom posits that motivation, expectancy, instrumentality, and valence are related to one another by this equation.

$$\text{Motivation} = \text{Expectancy} \times \text{Instrumentality} \times \text{Valence}$$

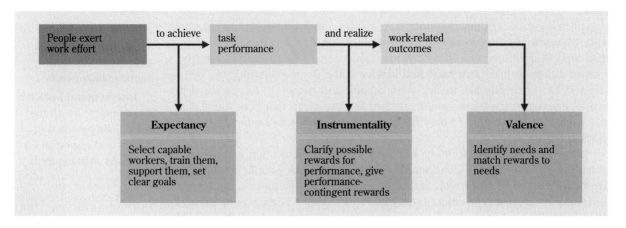

Figure 5.3 Key terms and managerial implications of Vroom's expectancy theory.

SOCIAL ENTREPRENEUR TACKLES ILLITERACY, TURNS DREAM INTO PROGRESS

There was a time when John Wood was just another, albeit up-and-coming, Microsoft executive. Now he's a social entrepreneur fighting the scourge of illiteracy through a nonprofit called Room to Read. What began as a dream of making a contribution to the fight against illiteracy has become a reality, one that grows stronger each day.

During a successful career as a Microsoft executive, his life changed on a vacation to the Himalayas of Nepal. Wood was shocked at the lack of schools. He discovered a passion that determines what he calls the "second chapter" in his life: to provide the lifelong benefits of education to poor children. He quit his Microsoft job and started Room to Read. So far, the organization has built over 100 schools and 1,000 libraries in Cambodia, India, Nepal, Vietnam, and Laos.

Noting that one-seventh of the global population can't read or write, Wood says: "I don't see how we are going to solve the world's problems without literacy." The Room to Read model is so efficient that it can build schools for as little as $6,000. *Time* magazine has honored Wood and his team as "Asian Heroes," and *Fast Company* magazine tapped his organization for a Social Capitalist Award.

Could You Do It? *What social problems do you see in your community, and which of them seems most pressing in terms of negative consequences? Who seems to be stepping forward in the attempt to solve the problems in innovative ways? Where and how might you engage in social entrepreneurship and make a very personal contribution to what is taking place? What, if anything, is holding you back?*

You can remember this equation simply as M = E × I × V, and the multiplier effect described by the "×" signs is significant. It means that the motivational appeal of a given work path is sharply reduced whenever any one or more of these factors approaches the value of zero. Conversely, for a given reward to have a high and positive motivational impact as a work outcome, the expectancy, instrumentality, and valence associated with the reward all must be high and positive.

Expectancy Theory Predictions

Suppose that a manager is wondering whether or not the prospect of earning a merit pay raise will be motivational to an employee. Expectancy theory predicts that motivation to work hard to earn the merit pay will be low if *expectancy* is low—a person feels that he or she cannot achieve the necessary performance level. Motivation will also be low if *instrumentality* is low—the person is not confident a high level of task performance will result in a high merit pay raise. Motivation will also be low if *valence* is low—the person places little value on a merit pay increase. Finally, motivation will be low if any combination of these exists. Thus, the multiplier effect advises managers to act to maximize expectancy, instrumentality, and valence when seeking to create high levels of work motivation. A zero at any location on the right side of the expectancy equation will result in zero motivation.

Expectancy Implications and Research

Expectancy logic argues that managers should always try to intervene actively in work situations to maximize work expectancies, instrumentalities, and valences that support organizational objectives.[25] To influence expectancies, the advice is to select people with proper abilities, train them well, support them with needed resources, and identify clear performance goals. To influence instrumentality, the advice is to clarify performance-reward relationships, and then to confirm or live up to them when rewards are actually given for performance accomplishments. To influence valences, the advice is to identify the needs that are important to each individual and then try to adjust available rewards to match these needs.

A great deal of research on expectancy theory has been conducted.[26] Even though the theory has received substantial support, specific details, such as the operation of the multiplier effect, remain subject to some question. In addition, expectancy theory has proven interesting in terms of helping to explain some apparently counterintuitive findings in cross-cultural management situations. For example, a pay raise motivated one group of Mexican workers to work fewer hours. They wanted a certain amount of money in order to enjoy things other than work, rather than just getting more money in general. A Japanese sales representative's promotion to manager of a U.S. company adversely affected his performance. His superiors did not realize that the promotion embarrassed him and distanced him from his colleagues.[27]

MASTERING MANAGEMENT

SIX POINTS OF HUMAN CAPITAL

Competency is a performance driver. Knowing that one has or is developing the right competencies to do well in a job and career can be a powerful motivator. How are you doing at building a strong portfolio of these human capital competencies?

- *Psychological Capital*—build a positive state of mind that includes a personal sense of self-efficacy, optimism, hope, and resiliency.
- *Management Capital*—build skills and competencies in resource acquisition, cultivation, and allocation, including human resource management.
- *Strategic Capital*—build expertise dealing with strategic situations such as cutting costs, driving growth, and dealing with cyclical markets.
- *Relationship Capital*—build capabilities to act based on networking with others with whom you have strong working relationships.
- *Industry Capital*—build familiarity with technologies, customers, regulations, suppliers, and competition specific to an industry.
- *Organizational Capital*—build knowledge about internal workings of the organization, its policies, practices, and culture.

Goal-Setting Theory of Motivation

Some years ago a Minnesota Vikings defensive end gathered up an opponent's fumble. Then, with obvious effort and delight, he ran the ball into the wrong end zone. Clearly, the athlete did not lack motivation. Unfortunately, however, he failed to channel his energies toward the right goal. Similar problems in goal direction are found in many work settings. Goals are important aspects of motivation, and yet they often go unaddressed. Without clear goals, employees may suffer direction problems; when goals are both clear and properly set, employees may be highly motivated to move in the direction of goal accomplishment.

Motivational Properties of Goals

Goal setting is the process of developing, negotiating, and formalizing the targets or objectives that a person is responsible for accomplishing.[28] Over a number of years Edwin Locke, Gary Latham, and their associates have developed a comprehensive framework linking goals to performance. About the importance of goals and goal setting, Locke and Latham say: "Purposeful activity is the essence of living action. If the purpose is neither clear nor challenging, very little gets accomplished."[29] Research on goal setting is now quite extensive. Indeed, more research has been done on goal setting than on any other theory related to work motivation.[30] Nearly 400 studies have been conducted in several countries, including Australia, England, Germany, Japan, and the United States.[31] Although the theory has its critics, the basic precepts of goal-setting theory remain an important source of advice for managing human behavior in the work setting.[32]

"Public firms focus on maximizing shareholder value; the American Red Cross in Greater New York focuses on maximizing community value," says CEO Theresa Bischoff. She heads a staff of 200 paid and 4,000 volunteer workers who draw motivation from the nonprofit's goals and first responder mission.

Goal-Setting Guidelines

Managerially speaking, the implications of research on goal setting can be summarized in the following guidelines.[33]

- *Difficult goals are more likely to lead to higher performance than are less difficult ones.* If the goals are seen as too difficult or impossible, however, the relationship with performance no longer holds. For example, you will likely perform better as a financial services agent if you have a goal of selling 6 annuities a week than if you have a goal of selling 3. But if your goal is selling 15 annuities a week, you may consider that impossible to achieve, and your performance may well be lower than what it would be with a more realistic goal.

- *Specific goals are more likely to lead to higher performance than are no goals or vague or very general ones.* All too often people work with very general goals such as the encouragement to "do your best." Research indicates that more specific goals, such as selling six computers a day, are much more motivational than a simple "do your best" goal.

- *Task feedback, or knowledge of results, is likely to motivate people toward higher performance by encouraging the setting of higher performance goals.* Feedback lets people know where they stand and whether they are on course or off course in their efforts. For example, think about how eager you are to find out how well you did on an examination.

RESEARCH INSIGHT

Conscious and Subconscious Goals Interact for Motivational Impact

Writing in the *Journal of Applied Psychology*, Alexander D. Stajkovic, Edwin A. Locke, and Eden S. Blair note that the literature on goal-setting theory and motivation is well established, but they point out that it deals only with conscious motivation. In two empirical studies they attempt to link this set of findings with a body of literature in social psychology concerned with subconscious goal motivation.

One of the key findings of research on goal-setting theory is that difficult goals lead to higher performance than do general "do your best" or easy goals when performance feedback, goal commitment, and task knowledge are present. A research stream of social psychology literature deals with the subconscious activation of goals by primers found in environments in which goals are regularly pursued. Using this background, the researchers' stated purpose "was to link subconscious and conscious goals by empirically examining the interaction between the two."

A pilot study and a main study were conducted with samples of undergraduate and graduate students at a university in the Midwest. Study participants were divided into two groups, with one group receiving a "priming" treatment where subjects did setup work involving identification

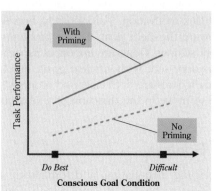

or use of achievement-related words before they completed a performance task. In the second, or "no prime" group, only achievement-neutral words were identified or used in the setup work prior to the performance task.

In both studies the results confirmed predictions from goal-setting theory by showing that "difficult" conscious goals increased performance relative to "easy" and "do your best" goal-setting conditions. Additionally, the researchers found that subjects in primed subconscious conditions performed better than did those in unprimed subconscious conditions on both "difficult" and "do your best" goals. In other words, primed subconscious goals had positive interactions with conscious goals for both difficult and do your best goals.

The overall conclusions from these studies show that more research is needed on the links between conscious and subconscious goals with task performance. But the initial findings are favorable in suggesting that when both types of goals are used together, their motivational impact is increased.

Reference: Alexander D. Stajkovic, Edwin A. Locke, and Eden S. Blair, "A First Examination of the Relationships Between Primed Subconscious Goals, Assigned Conscious Goals, and Task Performance," *Journal of Applied Psychology*, Vol. 91 (2006), pp. 1172–1180.

- *Goals are most likely to lead to higher performance when people have the abilities and the feelings of self-efficacy required to accomplish them.* The individual must be able to accomplish the goals and feel confident in those abilities. To take the financial services example again, you may be able to do what is required to sell 6 annuities a week and feel confident that you can. If your goal is to sell 15, however, you may believe that your abilities are insufficient to the task, and thus you may lack the confidence to work hard enough to accomplish it.

- *Goals are most likely to motivate people toward higher performance when they are accepted and there is commitment to them.* Participating in the goal-setting process helps build acceptance and commitment; it creates a sense of "ownership" of the goals. But goals assigned by someone else can be equally effective when the assigners are authority figures that can have an impact, and when the subordinate can actually reach the goal. According to research, assigned goals most often lead to poor performance when they are curtly or inadequately explained.

Goal Setting and the Management Process

When we speak of goal setting and its motivational potential, the entire management process comes into play. Goals launch the process during planning, provide critical focal points for organizing and leading, and then facilitate controlling to make sure the desired outcomes are achieved. One approach that integrates goals across these management functions is known as **management by objectives**, or **MBO**, for short. MBO is essentially a process of joint goal setting between managers and those who report to them.[34] The process involves managers working with team members to establish performance goals and to make plans that are consistent with higher-level work unit and organizational objectives. This unlocks the motivational power of goal setting as just discussed. And when done throughout an organization, MBO also helps clarify the hierarchy of objectives as a series of well-defined means-ends chains.

- **Management by objectives**, or **MBO** is a process of joint goal setting between a supervisor and a subordinate.

Figure 5.4 shows how the process allows managers to make use of goal-setting principles. The joint manager and team member discussions are designed to extend participation from the point of establishing initial goals to the point of evaluating results in terms of goal attainment. But the approach requires careful implementation. Not only must workers have the freedom to carry out the required tasks, managers should also be prepared to actively support workers' efforts to achieve the agreed-upon goals.

Although a fair amount of research based on case studies of MBO success is available, reports from scientifically rigorous studies have shown mixed results.[35]

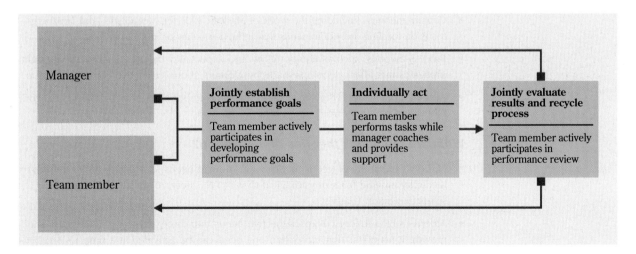

Figure 5.4 How a management by objectives process works.

Some reported difficulties with the process include too much paperwork required to document goals and accomplishments, too much emphasis on goal-oriented rewards and punishments, as well as too much focus on top-down goals, goals that are easily stated and achieved, and individual instead of team goals. When these issues are resolved, the MBO approach has much to offer, both as a general management practice and as an application of goal-setting theory.

Resources in The OB Skills Workbook

These learning activities from *The OB Skills Workbook* are suggested for Chapter 5.

Case for Critical Thinking	Team and Experiential Exercises	Self-Assessment Portfolio
• It Isn't Fair	• What Do You Value in Work?	• Managerial Assumptions
	• Teamwork and Motivation	• Two-Factor Profile
	• Downside of Punishment	
	• Annual Pay Raises	

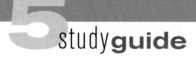

5 studyguide

Summary Questions and Answers

What is motivation?

• Motivation is an internal force that accounts for the level, direction, and persistence of effort expended at work.

• Content theories—including the work of Maslow, Alderfer, McClelland, and Herzberg—focus on locating individual needs that influence behavior in the workplace.

• Process theories, such as equity theory and expectancy theory, examine the thought processes that affect decisions made by workers about alternative courses of action.

• Although motivation is of universal interest and importance, specific aspects of work motivation may vary from one culture to the next.

What are the needs theories of motivation?

• Maslow's hierarchy of needs theory views human needs as activated in a five-step hierarchy ranging from physiological (lowest) to safety, to social, to esteem, to self-actualization (highest).

• Alderfer's ERG theory collapses the five needs into three: existence, relatedness, and growth; it maintains that more than one need can be activated at a time.

• McClelland's acquired needs theory focuses on the needs for achievement, affiliation, and power, and it views needs as developed over time through experience and training.

- Herzberg's two-factor theory links job satisfaction to motivator factors, such as responsibility and challenge, associated with job content; it links job dissatisfaction to hygiene factors, such as pay and working conditions, associated with job context.

What is the equity theory of motivation?

- Equity theory points out that social comparison takes place when people receive rewards.

- Any felt inequity in social comparison will motivate people to behave in ways that restore a sense of perceived equity to the situation.

- When felt inequity is negative—that is, when the individual feels unfairly treated—he or she may decide to work less hard in the future or to quit a job for other, more attractive opportunities.

- Organizational justice is an issue of how fair and equitable people view workplace practices; it is described in respect to distributive, procedural, and interactive justice.

What is the expectancy theory of motivation?

- Vroom's expectancy theory describes motivation as a function of an individual's beliefs concerning effort-performance relationships (expectancy), work-outcome relationships (instrumentality), and the desirability of various work outcomes (valence).

- Expectancy theory states that Motivation = Expectancy $\times$ Instrumentality $\times$ Valence, and argues that managers should make each factor positive in order to ensure high levels of motivation.

What is the goal-setting theory of motivation?

- Goal setting is the process of developing, negotiating, and formalizing performance targets or objectives.

- Research supports predictions that the most motivational goals are challenging and specific, allow for feedback on results, and create commitment and acceptance.

- The motivational impact of goals may be affected by individual difference moderators such as ability and self-efficacy.

- Management by objectives is a process of joint goal setting between a supervisor and worker; it is an action framework for applying goal-setting theory in day-to-day management practice and on an organization-wide basis.

Key Terms

Content theories (p. 110)
Distributive justice (p. 117)
Equity theory (p. 115)
ERG theory (p. 112)
Existence needs (p. 112)
Expectancy (p. 118)
Expectancy theory (p. 118)
Growth needs (p. 112)
Hierarchy of needs theory (p. 111)
Higher-order needs (p. 112)

Hygiene factors (p. 114)
Instrumentality (p. 118)
Interactional justice (p. 117)
Lower-order needs (p. 112)
Management by objectives, or MBO (p. 123)
Motivation (p. 110)
Motivator factors (p. 115)
Need for achievement (nAch) (p. 113)

Need for affiliation (nAff) (p. 113)
Need for power (nPower) (p. 113)
Organizational justice (p. 117)
Procedural justice (p. 117)
Process theories (p. 110)
Relatedness needs (p. 112)
Two-factor theory (p. 114)
Valence (p. 118)

Self-Test 5

Multiple Choice

1. Motivation is defined as the level and persistence of _____. (a) effort (b) performance (c) need satisfaction (d) performance instrumentalities

2. A content theory of motivation is most likely to focus on _____. (a) organizational justice (b) instrumentalities (c) equities (d) individual needs

3. A process theory of motivation is most likely to focus on _____. (a) frustration-regression (b) expectancies regarding work outcomes (c) lower-order needs (d) higher-order needs

4. According to McClelland, a person high in need achievement will be _____. (a) guaranteed success in top management (b) motivated to control and influence other people (c) motivated by teamwork and collective responsibility (d) motivated by challenging but achievable goals

5. In Alderfer's ERG theory, the _____ needs best correspond with Maslow's higher-order needs of esteem and self-actualization. (a) existence (b) relatedness (c) recognition (d) growth

6. Improvements in job satisfaction are most likely under Herzberg's two-factor theory when _____ are improved. (a) working conditions (b) base salary (c) co-worker relationships (d) opportunities for responsibility

7. In Herzberg's two-factor theory _____ factors are found in job context. (a) motivator (b) satisfier (c) hygiene (d) enrichment

8. In equity theory, the _____ is a key issue. (a) social comparison of rewards and efforts (b) equality of rewards (c) equality of efforts (d) absolute value of rewards

9. In equity motivation theory, felt negative inequity _____. (a) is not a motivating state (b) is a stronger motivating state than felt positive inequity (c) can be as strong a motivating state as felt positive inequity (d) does not operate as a motivating state

10. A manager's failure to enforce a late-to-work policy the same way for all employees is a violation of _____ justice. (a) interactional (b) moral (c) distributive (d) procedural

11. In expectancy theory, _____ is the probability that a given level of performance will lead to a particular work outcome. (a) expectancy (b) instrumentality (c) motivation (d) valence

12. In expectancy theory, _____ is the perceived value of a reward. (a) expectancy (b) instrumentality (c) motivation (d) valence

13. Expectancy theory posits that _____. (a) motivation is a result of rational calculation (b) work expectancies are irrelevant (c) need satisfaction is critical (d) valence is the probability that a given level of task performance will lead to various work outcomes.

14. Which goals tend to be more motivating? (a) challenging goals (b) easy goals (c) general goals (d) no goals

15. The MBO process emphasizes _____ as a way of building worker commitment to goal accomplishment. (a) authority (b) joint goal setting (c) infrequent feedback (d) rewards

Short Response

16. What is the frustration-regression component in Alderfer's ERG theory?

17. What does job enrichment mean in Herzberg's two-factor theory?

18. What is the difference between distributive and procedural justice?

19. What is the multiplier effect in expectancy theory?

Applications Essay

20. While attending a business luncheon, you overhear the following conversation at a nearby table. Person A: "I'll tell you this: if you satisfy your workers' needs, they'll be productive." Person B: "I'm not so sure; if I satisfy their needs, maybe they'll be real good about coming to work but not very good about working really hard while they are there." Which person do you agree with and why?

6

Motivation and Performance

chapter at a glance

In our busy multi-tasking world where work, family, and leisure are often intertwined, there's much to consider when trying to build high-performance work settings that also fit well with individual needs and goals. Here's what to look for in Chapter 6. Don't forget to check your learning with the Summary Questions & Answers and Self-Test in the end-of-chapter Study Guide.

WHAT IS THE LINK BETWEEN MOTIVATION, PERFORMANCE, AND REWARDS?

Integrated Model of Motivation

Intrinsic and Extrinsic Rewards

Pay for Performance

Pay for Skills

WHAT ARE THE ESSENTIALS OF PERFORMANCE MANAGEMENT?

Performance Management Process

Performance Appraisal Methods

Performance Appraisal Errors

HOW DO JOB DESIGNS INFLUENCE MOTIVATION AND PERFORMANCE?

Scientific Management

Job Enlargement and Job Rotation

Job Enrichment

Job Characteristics Model

WHAT ARE THE MOTIVATIONAL OPPORTUNITIES OF ALTERNATIVE WORK ARRANGEMENTS?

Compressed Work Weeks

Flexible Working Hours

Job Sharing

Telecommuting

Part-Time Work

nimerco's CEO, Kenneth Iverson, grew up in a Danish fishing village where crews of fishing boats would routinely split their catch. Half of the yield went toward expenses while the remaining half was divided equally among the crews. This experience influenced the egalitarian business model that is used at Unimerco today.

Founded in 1964 by Hans Foxby, the Lind, Denmark company is a world-class customs tool service and manufacturer operating in Denmark, Sweden, UK, Germany, USA, Czech Republic, Poland and China. What started out as a trading company gradually expanded into new markets and products through strategic partnerships to address the needs of clients and as a response to changes in the building industry.

Today, Unimerco is especially noted for its extensive employee ownership program. The new ownership structure was introduced back in 1977 when all employees were offered to buy shares. By 1995, Unimerco became wholly owned by management and employees. Today, the 440-employee Danish facility has 96% of employees co-owners.

While impressive, this is just one component of the company's formula for success. "Good working conditions combined with co-ownership, job security, profit sharing and influence" increases "the sense of responsibility, adaptability and flexibility among everyone in the company."

Employees report high levels of satisfaction and a sense of camaraderie in the workplace. That hasn't happened by accident. In fact the Danish headquarters was designed specifically to encourage a collaborative, boundaryless culture. Called the "roofed village," the 22,000 square meter building is one open space where managers and employees work side by side. Even Mr. Iverson has a desk among the rest which helps to break down the traditional walls–quite literally–of status and authority that can hinder effective teamwork in organizations.

What results is an open communication culture where each member of the organization is highly engaged. Receiving real-time updates about the company's performance and revenues serves to motivate employees. When the company succeeds and profits are high, employees succeed as well; a share of those profits gets distributed to employees on top of their regular salaries.

unimerco's work environment and employee ownership program are strong motivators

Motivation and Rewards

Wouldn't it be nice if we could all connect with our jobs and organizations the way those at Unimerco seem to do? In fact there are lots of great workplaces out there, and they become great because the managers at all levels of responsibility do things that end up turning people on to their work rather than off of it. This book is full of insights and ideas in this regard, and the motivation theories discussed in the last chapter are an important part of the story. In many ways the link between theory and application rests with a manager's abilities to activate rewards so that the work environment offers motivational opportunities to people in all the rich diversity of their individual differences.

Integrated Model of Motivation

Figure 6.1 outlines an integrated model of motivation, one that ties together much of the previous discussion regarding the basic effort → performance → rewards relationship. Note that the figure shows job performance and satisfaction as separate but potentially interdependent work results. Performance is influenced most directly by *individual attributes* such as ability and experience; *organizational support* such as resources and technology; and *effort*, or the willingness of someone to work hard at what they are doing. Satisfaction results when rewards received for work accomplishments are performance contingent and perceived as equitable.

● **Motivation** accounts for the level and persistence of a person's effort expended at work.

It is in respect to effort that an individual's level of motivation is of key importance. In the last chapter **motivation** was defined as forces that account for the level and persistence of an individual's effort expended at work. In other words and as shown in the figure, motivation predicts effort. But since motivation is a property of the individual, all that managers can do is try to create work environments within which someone finds sources of motivation. As the theories in the last chapter suggest, a major key to achieving this is to build into the job and work setting a set of rewards that match well with individual needs and goals.

Double check Figure 6.1 and locate where various motivation theories come into play. Reinforcement theory is found in the importance of performance contingency and immediacy in determining how rewards affect future performance. Equity theory is an issue in the perceived fairness of rewards. The content theories are useful guides to understanding individual needs that give motivational value to the possible rewards. And expectancy theory is central to the effort → performance → reward linkage.

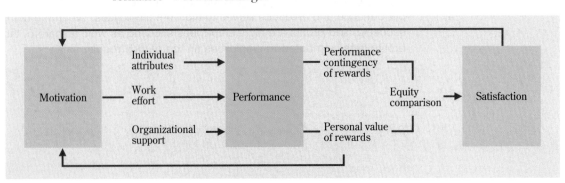

Figure 6.1 An integrated model of individual motivation to work.

Leaders on Leadership

HARUKA NISHIMATSU: THE CEO WHO CUT HIS OWN PAY

Haruka Nishimatsu is definitely not your typical CEO. The top executive at Japan Airlines rides the city bus to work; at lunch, he waits patiently in the cafeteria line like every other employee. And in a time of economic trouble for most of the world, he voluntarily reduced his own salary to a level where he is making less than his company's pilots.

Reflecting the humbleness of his character, what Mr. Nishimatsu finds interesting is why so many find his decision to cut his own pay strange or shocking. He considers it a natural response to the airline's move to eliminate jobs and ask older employees to retire early. His first move was to cut each of his executive perks and for the past three years has reduced his own salary.

He doesn't consider it a big deal. "The employees who took early retirement are the same generation and age as me. I thought I should share the pain with them, so I changed my salary."

This is in stark contrast to top executives elsewhere in the world. In USA executives are answering to government inquiries as to why they appear to be emptying the corporate coffers during an economic downturn, paying out substantial bonuses when employee jobs are being eliminated and debts cannot be paid.

This comparison might be a stretch since the gap between what the top and bottom is paid in USA and Japan differ drastically. In the United States, CEOs typically earn approximately 300 times more than the average worker while in Japan the gap is much lower.

According to Mr. Nishimatsu, "We in Japan learned during the bubble economy that businesses who pursue money first fail. The business world has lost sight of this basic tenet of business ethics."

Intrinsic and Extrinsic Rewards

The typical reward systems of organizations emphasize a mix of intrinsic and extrinsic rewards. **Intrinsic rewards** are positively valued work outcomes that the individual receives directly as a result of task performance; they do not require the participation of another person or source. It was intrinsic rewards that were largely behind Herzberg's concept of job enrichment discussed in the last chapter. He believes that people are turned on and motivated by high content jobs that are rich in intrinsic rewards. A feeling of achievement after completing a particularly challenging task in a job designed with a good person-job fit is an example.

- **Intrinsic rewards** are valued outcomes received directly through task performance.

Extrinsic rewards are positively valued work outcomes that are given to an individual or group by some other person or source in the work setting. They might include things like sincere praise for a job well done or symbolic tokens of accomplishment such as "employee-of-the-month" awards. Importantly too, anything dealing with compensation, or the pay and benefits one receives at work, is an extrinsic reward. And, like all extrinsic rewards, pay and benefits have to be well managed in all aspects of the integrated model for their motivational value to prove positive in terms of performance impact.

- **Extrinsic rewards** are valued outcomes given by some other person.

Pay for Performance

Pay is the most obvious and perhaps most talked about extrinsic reward for many of us. And it is not only an important extrinsic reward; it is an especially complex one. When pay functions well in the context of the integrated model of motivation, it can help an organization attract and retain highly capable workers. It can also help satisfy and motivate these workers to work hard to achieve high performance. But when something goes wrong with pay, the results may well be negative effects on satisfaction and performance. Pay dissatisfaction is often reflected in bad attitudes, increased absenteeism, intentions to leave and actual turnover, poor organizational citizenship, and even adverse impacts on employees' physical and mental health.

- The essence of **performance-contingent pay** is that you earn more when you produce more and earn less when you produce less.

The research of scholar and consultant Edward Lawler generally concludes that for pay to serve as a motivator, high levels of job performance must be viewed as the path through which high pay can be achieved.[1] This is the essence of **performance-contingent pay** or pay for performance. It basically means that you earn more when you produce more and earn less when you produce less. Although the concept is compelling, a survey by the Hudson Institute demonstrates that it is more easily said than done. When asked if employees who do perform better really get paid more, a sample of managers responded with 48 percent agreement while only 31 percent of nonmanagers indicated agreement. And when asked if their last pay raise had been based on performance, 46 percent of managers and just 29 percent of nonmanagers said yes.[2]

- **Merit pay** links an individual's salary or wage increase directly to measures of performance accomplishment.

Merit Pay   It is most common to talk about pay for performance in respect to **merit pay**, a compensation system that directly ties an individual's salary or

---

ETHICS IN OB

PRESENTEEISM: HOW COMING IN SICK AFFECTS BUSINESS

You wake up and you're feeling even worse than the day before. Sniffling, sneezing, coughing, you make your way to work, hoping to get through the day as best as you can. Fine, but what about everyone that you'll come into contact with that day, and what about the impact your *presenteeism*—basically meaning that you go to work sick—can have on office productivity and your co-workers' and customers' lives in general?

Brett Gorovsky of CCH, a business information resource, says that when people come to work sick it "can take a very real hit on the bottom line." His firm reports that 56 percent of executives in one poll considered this a problem; that figure is up some 17 percent in a two-year period. Estimates are that the cost of lost productivity is as much as $180 billion annually. Just think of the costs of Swine Flu season.

WebMD reports a study claiming that the cost of lost productivity could be higher than what might be paid out in authorized sick days. But the fact remains: many of us work sick because we have to if we want to be paid.

You Tell Us: What are the ethics of coming to work sick and sharing our illnesses with others? And from the management side of things, what are the ethics of not providing benefits sufficient to allow employees to stay home from work when they aren't feeling well?

wage increase to measures of performance accomplishments during a specified time period. Although research supports the logic and theoretical benefits of merit pay, it also indicates that the implementation of merit pay plans is not as universal or as easy as might be expected. In fact, surveys over the past 30 or so years have found that as many as 80 percent of respondents felt that they were not rewarded for a job well done.[3]

To work well, a merit pay plan should create a belief among employees that the way to achieve high pay is to perform at high levels. This means that the merit system should be based on realistic and accurate measures of individual work performance. It also means that the merit system is able to clearly discriminate between high and low performers in the amount of pay increases awarded. Finally, it is also important that any "merit" aspects of a pay increase are not confused with across-the-board "cost-of-living" adjustments.

Merit pay is also subject to criticisms. For example, merit pay plans may cause problems when they emphasize individual achievements and fail to recognize the high degree of task interdependence that is common in many organizations today. Also, merit pay systems must be consistent with overall organization strategies and environmental challenges if they are to be effective. For example, a firm facing a tight labor market with a limited supply of highly skilled individuals might benefit more from a pay system that emphasizes employee retention rather than strict performance results.[4] With these points in mind, it is appropriate to examine a variety of additional and creative pay practices.[5]

Bonuses The awarding of cash bonuses, or extra pay for performance that meets certain benchmarks or is above expectations, has been a common practice for many employers. It is especially common in the higher executive ranks. Top managers in some industries earn annual bonuses of 50 percent or more of their base salaries. One of the trends now emerging is the attempt to extend such opportunities to employees at lower levels in organizations, and in both managerial and nonmanagerial jobs. Employees at Applebee's, for example, may earn "Applebucks"—small cash bonuses that are given to reward performance and increase loyalty to the firm.[6]

Gain Sharing and Profit Sharing Another way to link pay with performance accomplishments is through **gain sharing**. Such a plan gives workers the opportunity to earn more by receiving shares of any productivity gains that they help to create. The Scanlon Plan is probably the oldest and best-known gain-sharing plan. It gives workers monetary rewards tied directly to specific measures of increased organizational productivity. Participation in gain sharing is supposed to create a greater sense of personal responsibility for organizational performance improvements and increase motivation to work hard. They are also supposed to encourage cooperation and teamwork in the workplace.[7]

Profit sharing is somewhat similar to gain sharing, but instead of rewarding employees for specific productivity gains they are rewarded for increased organizational profits; the more profits made, the more money that is available for distribution to employees through profit sharing.[8] Of course when profits are lower, individuals earn less due to reduced profit-sharing returns. And indeed, one of the criticisms of the approach is that profit increases and

Amazon.com

Amazon's founder and CEO Jeff Bezos once sent this note to two top executives. "In recognition and appreciation of your contributions Amazon.com will pay you a special bonus in the amount of $1,000,000."

• **Gain sharing** rewards employees in some proportion to productivity gains.

• **Profit sharing** rewards employees in some proportion to changes in organizational profits.

decreases are not always a direct result of employees' efforts; many other factors, including the bad global economy recently experienced, can come into play. In such cases the question becomes whether it is right or wrong for workers to earn less because of things over which they have no control.

Stock Options and Employee Ownership Another way to link pay and performance is for a company to offer its employees **stock options** linked to their base pay.[9] Such options give the owner the right to buy shares of stock at a future date at a fixed or "strike" price. This means that they gain financially the more the stock price rises above the original option price. The expectation is that employees with stock options will be highly motivated to do their best so that the firm performs well; they gain financially as the stock price increases. However, as the recent economic downturn reminded us, the value of the options an employee holds can decline or zero out when the stock price falls.

In **employee stock ownership plans**, or ESOPs, companies may give stock to employees or allow stock to be purchased by them at a price below market value. The incentive value of the stock awards or purchases is like the stock options; "employee owners" will be motivated to work hard so that the organization will perform well, its stock price will rise, and as owners they will benefit from the gains. Of course, the company's stock prices can fall as well as rise.[10] During the economic crisis many people who had invested heavily in their employer's stock were hurt substantially. Such risk must be considered in respect to the motivational value of stock options and employee ownership plans.

Pay for Skills

An alternative to pay for performance is to pay people according to the skills they possess and continue to develop. **Skill-based pay** rewards people for acquiring and developing job-relevant skills. Pay systems of this sort pay people for the mix and depth of skills they possess, not for the particular job assignment they hold. An example is the cross-functional team approach at Monsanto-Benevia, where each team member has developed quality, safety, administrative, maintenance, coaching, and team leadership skills. In most cases, these skills involve the use of high-tech, automated equipment. Workers are paid for this "breadth" of capability as well as for their willingness to use any of the skills needed by the company.

Skill-based pay is one of the fastest-growing pay innovations in the United States. Besides flexibility, some advantages of skill-based pay are employee cross-training—workers learn to do one another's jobs; fewer supervisors—workers can provide more of these functions themselves; and more individual control over compensation—workers know in advance what is required to receive a pay raise. One disadvantage is possible higher pay and training costs that are not offset by greater productivity. Another is the possible difficulty of deciding on appropriate monetary values for each skill.[11]

Performance Management

If you want to get hired by Procter & Gamble and make it to the upper management levels you better be good. Not only is the company highly selective in hiring, it also carefully tracks the performance of every manager in every job they are asked

• **Stock options** give the right to purchase shares at a fixed price in the future.

• **Employee stock ownership plans** give stock to employees or allow them to purchase stock at special prices.

• **Skill-based pay** rewards people for acquiring and developing job-relevant skills.

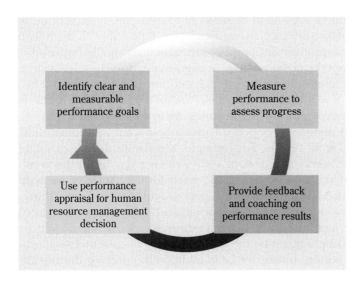

Figure 6.2 Four steps in the performance management process.

to do. The firm always has at least three performance-proven replacements ready to fill any vacancy that occurs. And by linking performance to career advancement, motivation to work hard is built into the P&G management model.[12]

The effort → performance → reward relationship is evident in the P&G management approach. However, we shouldn't underestimate the challenge of managing any such performance-based reward system. It entails responsibility for accurately measuring performance and then correctly using those measurements in making pay and other human resource management decisions. Performance must be measured in ways that are accurate and respected by everyone involved. When the performance measurement fails, the motivational value of any pay or reward systems will fail as well.

As described in Figure 6.2, performance management involves this sequence of steps: (1) identify and set clear and measurable performance goals, (2) take performance measurements to monitor goal progress, (3) provide feedback and coaching on performance results, and (4) use performance assessment for human resource management decisions such as pay, promotions, transfers, terminations, training, and career development.

Essentials of Performance Management

The foundation for any performance management system is performance measurement. And if performance measurement is to be done well, managers must have good answers to both the "Why?" and the "What?" questions.

The "Why?" question in performance management addresses purpose, which is two-fold. Performance management serves an *evaluation purpose* when it lets people know where their actual performance stands relative to objectives and standards. Such an evaluation also becomes a key input to decisions that allocate rewards and otherwise administer the organization's human resource management systems. Performance management serves a *developmental purpose* when it provides insights into individual strengths and weaknesses that can be used to plan helpful training and career development activities.

The "What?" question in performance management takes us back to the old adage "what gets measured happens." It basically argues that people will do what they know is going to be measured. Given this, managers are well advised to always make sure they are measuring the right things in the right ways in the performance management process. Measurements should be based on clear job performance criteria, be accurate in assessing performance, provide a defensible basis for differentiating between high and low performance, and be an insightful source of feedback that can help improve performance in the future. Both output measures and activity measures are in common use.

Output measures of performance assess what is accomplished in respect to concrete work results. For example, a software developer might be measured on the number of lines of code written a day or on the number of lines written that require no corrections upon testing. **Activity measures** of performance assess work inputs in respect to activities tried and efforts expended. These are often used when output measures are difficult and in cases where certain activities are known to be good predictors of eventual performance success. An example might be the use of number of customer visits made per day by a sales person, instead of or in addition to counting the number of actual sales made.

- **Output measures** of performance assess achievements in terms of actual work results.

- **Activity measures** of performance assess inputs in terms of work efforts.

Performance Appraisal Methods

The formal procedure for measuring and documenting a person's work performance is called *performance appraisal*. As might be expected, there are a variety of alternative performance appraisal methods, and they each have strengths and weaknesses that make them more appropriate for use in some situations than others.[13]

Comparative Methods Comparative methods of performance appraisal seek to identify one worker's standing relative to others. **Ranking** is the simplest approach and is done by rank ordering each individual from best to worst on overall performance or on specific performance dimensions. Although relatively simple to use, this method can become burdensome when there are many people to consider. An alternative is the **paired comparison** in which each person is directly compared with every other person being rated. Each person's final ranking is determined by the number of pairs for which they emerged the "winner." As you might expect, this method gets quite complicated when there are many people to compare.

- **Ranking** in performance appraisal orders each person from best to worst.

- **Paired comparison** in performance appraisal compares each person with every other.

Another alternative is **forced distribution**. This method forces a set percentage of all persons being evaluated into pre-determined performance categories such as outstanding, good, average, and poor. For example, it might be that a team leader must assign 10 percent of members to "outstanding," another 10 percent to "poor," and another 40 percent each to "good" and "average." This forces the rater to use all the categories and avoid tendencies to rate everyone about the same. But it can be a problem if most of the people being rated are truly about the same.

- **Forced distribution** in performance appraisal forces a set percentage of persons into pre-determined rating categories.

Rating Scales Graphic rating scales list a variety of dimensions that are thought to be related to high-performance outcomes for a given job that the individual is accordingly expected to exhibit, including cooperation, initiative, and attendance. The scales allow the manager to assign the individual scores on each

- **Graphic rating scales** in performance appraisal assigns scores to specific performance dimensions.

Employee: Jayne Burroughs **Supervisor:** Dr. Cutter
Department: Pathology **Date:** 11-28

Work Quantity		Work Quality		Cooperation	
1. Far below average	___	1. Far below average	___	1. Far below average	___
2. Below average	✓	2. Below average	___	2. Below average	✓
3. Average	___	3. Average	✓	3. Average	___
4. Above average	___	4. Above average	___	4. Above average	___
5. Far above average	___	5. Far above average	___	5. Far above average	___

Figure 6.3 Sample six-month performance reviews using graphic rating scale.

dimension. An example is shown in Figure 6.3. These ratings are sometimes given point values and combined into numerical ratings of performance.

The primary appeal of graphic rating scales is their ease of use. They are efficient in the use of time and other resources, and they can be applied to a wide range of jobs. Unfortunately, because of generality, they may not be linked to job analysis or to other specific aspects of a given job. This difficulty can be dealt with by ensuring that only relevant dimensions of work based on sound job analysis procedures are rated. However, there is a trade-off: the more the scales are linked to job analyses, the less general they are when comparing people on different jobs.

The **behaviorally anchored rating scale** (BARS) adds more sophistication by linking ratings to specific and observable job-relevant behaviors. These are typically provided by managers and personnel specialists and include descriptions of superior and inferior performance. Once a large sample of behavioral descriptions has been collected, each behavior is evaluated to determine the extent to which it describes good versus bad performance. The final step is to develop a rating scale in which the anchors are specific critical behaviors, each reflecting a different degree of performance effectiveness.

• The **behaviorally anchored rating scale** links performance ratings to specific and observable job-relevant behaviors.

A sample BARS for a retail department manager is shown in Figure 6.4. Note the specificity of the behaviors and the scale values for each. Similar behaviorally anchored scales would be developed for other dimensions of the job. The BARS approach is detailed and complex, and requires time to develop. But it can provide specific behavioral information that is useful for counseling and feedback, especially when combined with comparative methods just discussed and other methods described next.[14]

Critical Incident Diary **Critical incident diaries** are written records that give examples of a person's work behavior that leads to either unusual performance success or failure. The incidents are typically recorded in a diary-type log that is kept daily or weekly under predetermined dimensions. In a sales job, for example, following up sales calls and communicating necessary customer information might be two of the dimensions recorded in a critical incident diary. Descriptive paragraphs can then be used to summarize each salesperson's performance for

• **Critical incident diaries** record actual examples of positive and negative work behaviors and results.

Coaching Sales Personnel

Gives sales personnel a clear idea of their job duties and responsibilities; exercises tact and consideration in working with subordinates; handles work scheduling efficiently and equitably; supplements formal training with his or her own "coaching"; keeps informed of what the salespeople are doing on the job; and follows company policy in agreements with subordinates.

Effective   9   Could be expected to conduct full day's sales clinic with two new sales personnel and thereby develop them into top salespeople in the department.

8   Could be expected to give his or her sales personnel confidence and strong sense of responsibility by delegating many important tasks.

7   Could be expected never to fail to conduct weekly training meetings with his or her people at a scheduled hour and to convey to them exactly what is expected.

6   Could be expected to exhibit courtesy and respect toward his or her sales personnel.

5   Could be expected to remind sales personnel to wait on customers instead of conversing with one another.

4   Could be expected to be rather critical of store standards in front of his or her own people, thereby risking their development of poor attitudes.

3   Could be expected to tell an individual to come in anyway even though he or she called in to say he or she was ill.

2   Could be expected to go back on a promise to an individual who he or she had told could transfer back into previous department if he or she did not like the new one.

Ineffective   1   Could be expected to make promises to an individual about his or her salary being based on department sales even when he or she knew such a practice was against company policy.

Figure 6.4 Sample performance appraisal dimension from the behaviorally anchored rating scale for a department store manager.

each dimension as activities are observed. This approach is excellent for employee development and feedback. But because the method consists of qualitative statements rather than quantitative ratings, it is more debatable in terms of summative evaluations. This is why we often find the critical incident technique used in combination with one of the other methods.

360° Evaluation   To obtain as much appraisal information as possible, many organizations now use a combination of evaluations from a person's bosses, peers, and subordinates, as well as internal and external customers and self-ratings. Such a comprehensive approach is called a **360° evaluation** and it is very common now in horizontal and team-oriented organization structures.[15] The 360° evaluation has also moved online with software that both collects and organizes the results of ratings from multiple sources. A typical approach asks the jobholder to do a self rating and then discuss with the boss and perhaps a sample of the 360° participants the implications from both evaluation and counseling perspectives.

• A **360° evaluation** gathers evaluations from a jobholder's bosses, peers, and subordinates, as well as internal and external customers and self-ratings.

Performance Appraisal Errors

Regardless of the method being employed, any performance appraisal system should meet two criteria: **reliability**—providing consistent results each time it is used for the same person and situation, and **validity**—actually measuring people on dimensions with direct relevance to job performance. In addition to the strengths and weaknesses of the methods just discussed, there are a number of measurement errors that can reduce the reliability or validity of performance appraisals.[16]

- *Halo error*—results when one person rates another person on several different dimensions and gives a similar rating for each dimension.
- *Leniency error*—just as some professors are known as "easy A's," some managers tend to give relatively high ratings to virtually everyone under their supervision; the opposite is *strictness error*—giving everyone a low rating.
- *Central tendency error*—occurs when managers lump everyone together around the average, or middle, category; this gives the impression that there are no very good or very poor performers on the dimensions being rated.
- *Recency error*—occurs when a rater allows recent events to influence a performance rating over earlier events; an example is being critical of an employee who is usually on time but shows up one hour late for work the day before his or her performance rating.
- *Personal bias error*—displays expectations and prejudices that fail to give the jobholder complete respect, such as showing racial bias in ratings.

> **OB SAVVY 6.1**
>
> ### How to Reduce Performance Appraisal Errors
>
> 1. Train raters to understand the evaluation process rationale and recognize sources of measurement error.
> 2. Make sure raters observe ratees on an ongoing, regular basis, and that they do not try to limit evaluations to designated evaluation periods.
> 3. Do not have one rater rate too many ratees; ability to identify performance differences drops and fatigue sets in when large numbers are involved.
> 4. Make sure performance dimensions and standards are stated clearly; avoid terms such as "average" because different raters react differently to such terms.

- **Reliability** means a performance measure gives consistent results.
- **Validity** means a performance measure addresses job-relevant dimensions.

Job-Design Alternatives

When it comes to motivation we might say that nothing beats a good person-job fit. This means that the job requirements fit well with individual abilities and needs, and that the experience of performing the job under these conditions is likely to be high in intrinsic rewards. By contrast, a poor person-job fit is likely to cause performance problems and be somewhat demotivating for the worker. You might think of the goal this way: Person + Good Job Fit = Intrinsic Motivation.

Job design is the process through which managers plan and specify job tasks and the work arrangements that allow them to be accomplished. Figure 6.5 shows three major alternative job design approaches, and it also indicates how they differ in the way required tasks are defined and in the motivation provided for the worker. In this sense, the "best" job design is always one that meets organizational requirements for high performance, offers a good fit with individual skills and needs, and provides valued opportunities for job satisfaction.

- **Job design** is the process of specifying job tasks and work arrangements.

RESEARCH INSIGHT

Racial Bias May Exist in Supervisor Ratings of Workers

That is a conclusion of a research study by Joseph M. Stauffer and M. Ronald Buckley reported in a recent *Journal of Applied Psychology*. The authors point out that it is important to have performance criteria and supervisory ratings that are free of bias. They cite a meta-analysis by Kraiger and Ford (1985) that showed White raters tended to rate White employees more favorably than Black employees, while Black raters rated Blacks more favorably than Whites. They also cite a later study by Sackett and DuBois (1991) that disputed the finding that raters tended to favor members of their own racial groups.

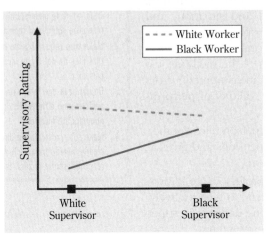

In their study, Stauffer and Buckley reanalyzed the Sackett and DuBois data to pursue in more depth the possible interactions between rater and ratee race. The data included samples of military and civilian workers, each of whom was rated by Black and White supervisors. Their findings are that in both samples White supervisors gave significantly higher ratings to White workers than they did to Black workers, while Black supervisors also tended to favor White workers in their ratings.

Stauffer and Buckley advise caution in interpreting these results as meaning that the rating differences are the result of racial prejudice, saying the data aren't sufficient to address this issue. The researchers call for additional studies designed to further examine both the existence of bias in supervisory ratings and the causes of such bias. In terms of workplace implications, however, the authors are quite definitive: "If you are a White ratee then it doesn't matter if your supervisor is Black or White. If you are a Black ratee, then it is important whether your supervisor is Black or White."

Do the Research

These findings raise questions that certainly deserve answering. Can you design a research study that could discover whether or not racial bias affects instructor ratings of students? Also, when you bring this issue up with family and friends do their experiences seem to support or deny the findings reported here?

Source: Joseph M. Stauffer and M. Ronald Buckley, "The Existence and Nature of Racial Bias in Supervisory Ratings," *Journal of Applied Psychology* 90 (2005), pp. 586–591. Also cited: K. Kraiger and J. K. Ford, "A Meta-analysis of Ratee Race Effects in Performance Ratings," *Journal of Applied Psychology* 70 (1985), pp. 56–65; and, P. R. Sackett and C. L. Z. DuBois, "Rater-Ratee Race Effects on Performance Evaluations: Challenging Meta-Analytic Conclusions," *Journal of Applied Psychology* 76 (1991), pp. 873–877.

• Taylor's **scientific management** used systematic study of job components to develop practices to increase people's efficiency at work.

Scientific Management

The history of scholarly interest in job design can be traced in part to Frederick Taylor's work with **scientific management** in the early 1900s.[17] Taylor and his contemporaries wanted to create management and organizational practices that would increase people's efficiency at work. Their approach was to study a job carefully, break it into its smallest components, establish exact time and motion requirements for each task to be done, and then train workers to do these tasks

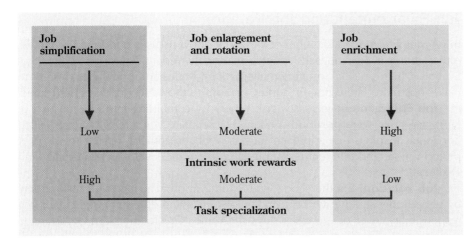

Figure 6.5 A continuum of job design strategies.

in the same way over and over again. Taylor's principles of scientific management can be summarized as follows:

1. Develop a "science" for each job that covers rules of motion, standard work tools, and supportive work conditions.
2. Hire workers with the right abilities for the job.
3. Train and motivate workers to do their jobs according to the science.
4. Support workers by planning and assisting their work using the job science.

These early efforts were forerunners of current industrial engineering approaches to job design that emphasize efficiency. Such approaches attempt to determine the best processes, methods, workflow layouts, output standards, and person-machine interfaces for various jobs. A good example is found at United Parcel Service (UPS), where calibrated productivity standards carefully guide workers. At regional centers, sorters must load vans at a set number of packages per hour. After analyzing delivery stops on regular van routes, supervisors generally know within a few minutes how long a driver's pickups and deliveries will take. Engineers devise precise routines for drivers, who save time by knocking on customers' doors rather than looking for doorbells. Handheld computers further enhance delivery efficiencies.

Today, the term **job simplification** is used to describe a scientific management approach to job design that standardizes work procedures and employs people in clearly defined and highly specialized tasks. The machine-paced automobile assembly line is a classic example. Why is it used? Typically, the answer is to increase operating efficiency by reducing the number of skills required to do a job, by being able to hire low-cost labor, by keeping the needs for job training to a minimum, and by emphasizing the accomplishment of repetitive tasks. However, the very nature of such jobs creates potential disadvantages as well. These include loss of efficiency in the face of lower quality, high rates of absenteeism and turnover, and demand for higher wages to compensate for unappealing jobs. One response to such problems is through advanced applications of new technology. In automobile manufacturing, for example, robots now do many different kinds of work previously accomplished with human labor.

Job simplification standardizes work to create clearly defined and highly specialized tasks.

In-N-Out Burger

The work is typical fast-food routine, but the California-based hamburger chain pays employees above average, gives part-timers paid vacation, and gives full-timers 401(K) and health insurance plans. Most managers come from the ranks and the firm has one of the lowest turnover rates in the industry.

Job Enlargement and Job Rotation

In job simplification the number or variety of different tasks performed is limited. Although this makes the tasks easier to master, the repetitiveness can reduce motivation. This result has prompted alternative job design approaches that try to make jobs more interesting by adding breadth to the variety of tasks performed.

Job enlargement increases task variety by combining into one job two or more tasks that were previously assigned to separate workers. Sometimes called horizontal loading, this approach increases job breadth by having the worker perform more and different tasks, but all at the same level of responsibility and challenge.

Job rotation, another horizontal-loading approach, increases task variety by periodically shifting workers among jobs involving different tasks. Again, the responsibility level of the tasks stays the same. The rotation can be arranged according to almost any time schedule, such as hourly, daily, or weekly schedules. An important benefit of job rotation is training. It allows workers to become more familiar with different tasks and increases the flexibility with which they can be moved from one job to another.

- **Job enlargement** increases task variety by combining into one job two or more tasks that were previously assigned to separate workers.
- **Job rotation** increases task variety by periodically shifting workers among jobs involving different tasks.

Job Enrichment

A third job design alternative traces back to Frederick Herzberg's two-factor theory of motivation described in Chapter 5. This theory suggests that jobs designed on the basis of simplification, enlargement, or rotation shouldn't be expected to deliver high levels of motivation.[18] "Why," asks Herzberg, "should a worker become motivated when one or more 'meaningless' tasks are added to previously existing ones or when work assignments are rotated among equally 'meaningless' tasks?" He recommends using **job enrichment** to build high-content jobs full of motivating factors such as responsibility, achievement, recognition, and personal growth. Such jobs include planning and evaluating duties that would otherwise be reserved for managers.

- **Job enrichment** builds high-content jobs that involve planning and evaluating duties normally done by supervisors.

The content changes made possible by job enrichment (see OB Savvy 6.2) involve what Herzberg calls *vertical loading* to increase job depth. This essentially means that tasks normally performed by supervisors are pulled down into the job to make it bigger. Such enriched jobs, he believes, satisfy higher-order needs and increase motivation to achieve high levels of job performance.

Job Characteristics Model

OB scholars have been reluctant to recommend job enrichment as a universal solution to all job performance and satisfaction problems, particularly given the many individual differences that characterize people at work. Their answer to the question "Is job enrichment for everyone?" is a clear "No." Present thinking focuses more on a diagnostic approach to job design developed by Richard Hackman and Greg Oldham.[19] Their job characteristics model provides a

---

OB SAVVY 6.2

Job Enrichment Advice from Frederick Herzberg

Frederick Herzberg argues in favor of job enrichment to give workers access to motivating factors in job content. His recommendations on building such enriched jobs through vertical loading are quite straightforward.

- Allow workers to plan.
- Allow workers to control.
- Maximize job freedom.
- Increase task difficulty.
- Help workers become task experts.
- Provide performance feedback.
- Increase performance accountability.
- Provide complete units of work.

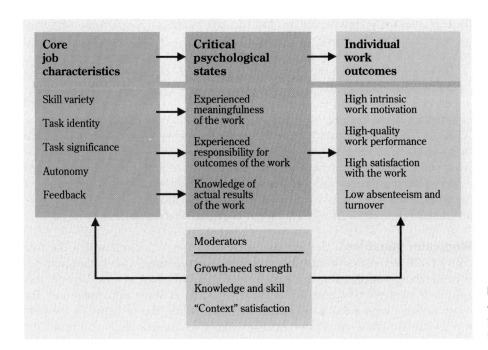

Figure 6.6 Job design considerations according to the job characteristics theory.

data-based approach for creating job designs with good person-job fit that maximize the potential for motivation and performance.

Figure 6.6 shows how five core job characteristics activate the model and inform the process of job design. The higher a job scores on each core characteristic, the more it is considered to be enriched.

- *Skill variety*—the degree to which a job includes a variety of different activities and involves the use of a number of different skills and talents
- *Task identity*—the degree to which the job requires completion of a "whole" and identifiable piece of work, one that involves doing a job from beginning to end with a visible outcome
- *Task significance*—the degree to which the job is important and involves a meaningful contribution to the organization or society in general
- *Autonomy*—the degree to which the job gives the employee substantial freedom, independence, and discretion in scheduling the work and determining the procedures used in carrying it out
- *Job feedback*—the degree to which carrying out the work activities provides direct and clear information to the employee regarding how well the job has been done

Job Diagnostic Survey   Hackman and Oldham recommend measuring the current status of a job based on each core characteristic.[20] These characteristics can then be changed systematically to enrich the job and increase its motivational potential. This assessment can be accomplished using an instrument called the Job Diagnostic Survey (JDS), which is included in the OB Skills Workbook as part of the team and experiential exercise "Job Design." Scores on the JDS are combined to create a motivating potential score, or MPS, which indicates the degree to which the job is capable of motivating people.

A job's MPS can be raised by combining tasks to create larger jobs, opening feedback channels to enable workers to know how well they are doing, establishing client relationships to experience such feedback directly from customers, and employing vertical loading to create more planning and controlling responsibilities. When the core characteristics are enriched in these ways to raise the MPS as high as possible, the redesigned job can be expected to positively influence three critical psychological states: (1) experienced meaningfulness of the work, (2) experienced responsibility for the outcomes of the work, and (3) knowledge of actual results of the work. These positive psychological states, in turn, are supposed to have a positive impact on individual motivation, performance, and satisfaction.

Moderator Variables   The job characteristics model recognizes that the five core job characteristics do not affect all people in the same way. Rather than accept Herzberg's implication that enriched jobs should be good for everyone, this approach suggests that enriched jobs will lead to positive outcomes only for those persons who are a good match for them. When the fit between the person and an enriched job is poor, positive outcomes are less likely and problems may well result. "Fit" in the job characteristics model is viewed from the perspective of three moderator variables shown in Figure 6.6 and briefly summarized again here.

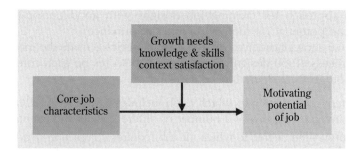

The first moderator is *growth-need strength*, or the degree to which a person desires the opportunity for self-direction, learning, and personal accomplishment at work. It is similar to Abraham Maslow's esteem and self-actualization needs and Alderfer's growth needs, as discussed in Chapter 5. When applied here, the expectation is that people high in growth-need strengths at work will respond positively to enriched jobs, whereas people low in growth-need strengths will find enriched jobs to be sources of anxiety.

The second moderator is *knowledge and skill*. People whose capabilities fit the demands of enriched jobs are predicted to feel good about them and perform well. Those who are inadequate or who feel inadequate in this regard are likely to experience difficulties.

The third moderator is *context satisfaction*, or the extent to which an employee is satisfied with aspects of the work setting such as salary levels, quality of supervision, relationships with co-workers, and working conditions. In general, people who are satisfied with job context are more likely to do well with job enrichment.

Research Considerable research has been done on the job characteristics model in a variety of work settings, including banks, correctional institutions, telephone companies, and manufacturing firms, as well as in government agencies. Experts generally agree that the model and its diagnostic approach are useful, but not yet perfect, guides to job design.[21] On average, job characteristics do affect performance but not nearly as much as they do satisfaction. The research also emphasizes the importance of growth-needs strength as a moderator of the job design–job performance–job satisfaction relationships. Positive job characteristics affect performance more strongly for high-growth-need than for low-growth-need individuals. The relationship is about the same with job satisfaction. It is also clear that job enrichment can fail when job requirements are increased beyond the level of individual capabilities or interests.

One note of caution is raised by Gerald Salancik and Jeffrey Pfeffer, who question whether jobs have stable and objective characteristics to which individuals respond predictably and consistently.[22] Instead, they view job design from the perspective of social information processing theory. This theory argues that individual needs, task perceptions, and reactions are a result of socially constructed realities. Social information in organizations influences the way people perceive their jobs and respond to them. The same holds true, for example, in the classroom. Suppose that several of your friends tell you that the instructor for a course is bad, the content is boring, and the requirements involve too much work. You may then think that the critical characteristics of the class are the instructor, the content, and the workload, and that they are all bad. All of this may substantially influence the way you perceive your instructor and the course, and the way you deal with the class—regardless of the actual characteristics.

Finally, research suggests the following answers to common questions about job enrichment and its applications. *Should everyone's job be enriched?* The answer is clearly no. The logic of individual differences suggests that not everyone will want an enriched job. Individuals most likely to have positive reactions to job enrichment are those who need achievement, who exhibit a strong work ethic, or who are seeking higher-order growth-need satisfaction at work. Job enrichment also appears to be most advantageous when the job context is positive and when workers have the abilities needed to do the enriched job. Furthermore, costs, technological constraints, and workgroup or union opposition may make it difficult to enrich some jobs. *Can job enrichment apply to groups?* The answer is yes. The application of job-design strategies at the group level is growing in many types of settings. Part 3 discusses creative workgroup designs, including cross-functional work teams and self-managing teams.

Phoenix Bats

Charlie Trudeau used to make baseball bats for himself and his friends. Now major leaguers are his customers. Each bat is made by hand out of carefully selected wood and designed to the player's needs. Says Charlie, "it's got to have the right feel, it's got to have the right center of balance, and . . . there is no perfect design."

Alternative Work Schedules

New work arrangements are reshaping the traditional 40-hour week, with its 9-to-5 schedules and work done at the company or place of business. Virtually all such plans are designed to influence employee satisfaction and to help employees balance the demands of their work and nonwork lives.[23] They are becoming more and more important in fast-changing societies where demands for "work-life balance" and more "family-friendly" employers are growing ever more apparent. If you have any doubts at all regarding the importance of work-life issues, consider these facts: 78 percent of American couples are dual wage earners; 63 percent believe they don't have enough time for spouses and partners; 74 percent believe they don't have enough time for their children; 35 percent are spending time caring for elderly relatives.[24] And, both baby boomers (87 percent) and Gen Ys (89 percent) rate flexible work as important; they also want opportunities to work remotely at least part of the time—Boomers (63 percent) and Gen Ys (69 percent).[25]

Compressed Work Weeks

• A **compressed work week** allows a full-time job to be completed in fewer than the standard five days.

A **compressed work week** is any scheduling of work that allows a full-time job to be completed in fewer than the standard five days. The most common form of compressed work week is the "4/40," or 40 hours of work accomplished in four 10-hour days.

This approach has many possible benefits. For the worker, additional time off is a major feature of this schedule. The individual often appreciates increased leisure time, three-day weekends, free weekdays to pursue personal business, and lower commuting costs. The organization can benefit, too, in terms of lower employee absenteeism and improved recruiting of new employees. But there are also potential disadvantages. Individuals can experience increased fatigue from the extended workday and family adjustment problems.

The organization can experience work scheduling problems and customer complaints because of breaks in work coverage. Some organizations may face occasional union opposition and laws requiring payment of overtime for work exceeding eight hours of individual labor in any one day. Overall reactions to compressed work weeks are likely to be most favorable among employees who are allowed to participate in the decision to adopt the new work week, who have their jobs enriched as a result of the new schedule, and who have the strong higher-order needs identified in Maslow's hierarchy.[26]

Flexible Working Hours

• **Flexible working hours** gives individuals some amount of choice in scheduling their daily work hours.

Another innovative work schedule, **flexible working hours** or *flextime* gives individuals a daily choice in the timing of their work commitments. One such schedule requires employees to work four hours of "core" time but leaves them free to choose their remaining four hours of work from among flexible time blocks. One person, for example, may start early and leave early, whereas another may start later and leave later. This flexible work schedule is becoming increasingly popular and is a valuable alternative for structuring work to accommodate individual interests and needs. All top 100 companies in *Working Mother* magazine's list of best employers for working moms offer flexible scheduling. Reports indicate that flexibility in dealing with nonwork obligations reduces stress and unwanted job turnover.[27]

The individual autonomy in work scheduling allowed by flextime can help reduce absenteeism, tardiness, and turnover for the organization, and also contribute to higher levels of organizational commitment and performance by workers. On the individual side it brings potential advantages in terms of commuting times and opportunities to meet personal responsibilities during the work week.

MASTERING MANAGEMENT

HOW TO BEAT THE MOMMY DRAIN

It's no secret that more and more employers are turning to flexibility in work schedules to better accommodate today's workers. Among them, Accenture and Booz Allen Hamilton are taking special steps to make sure they can attract and retain talented working mothers. Here is a selection of ways top employers are counteracting the "Mommy drain," and responding to Daddy's needs as well.

- Offer increased pay and extended time for maternity leave.
- Offer increased pay and extended time for parental leave.
- Allow employee pay set-asides to buy more time for maternal and parental leave.
- Create alternative and challenging jobs that require less travel.
- Make sure pay for performance plans do not discriminate against those on maternal or parental leave.
- Set up mentoring and networking systems to support working parents.
- Make sure new mothers feel they are wanted back at work.
- Keep in contact with employees on maternity and parental leaves.

It is a way for dual-career couples to handle children's schedules as well as their own; it is a way to meet the demands of caring for elderly parents or ill family members; it is even a way to better attend to such personal affairs as medical and dental appointments, home emergencies, banking needs, and so on. Proponents of this scheduling strategy argue that the discretion it allows workers in scheduling their own hours of work encourages them to develop positive attitudes and to increase commitment to the organization.

Job Sharing

In **job sharing**, one full-time job is assigned to two or more persons who then divide the work according to agreed-upon hours. Often, each person works half a day, but job sharing can also be done on a weekly or monthly basis. Organizations benefit from job sharing when they can attract talented people who would otherwise be unable to work. An example is the qualified teacher who also is a parent. This person may be able to work only half a day. Through job sharing, two such persons can be employed to teach one class. Some job sharers report less burnout and claim that they feel recharged each time they report for work. The tricky part of this arrangement is finding two people who will work well with each other.

Job sharing should not be confused with something called **work sharing**. This occurs when workers agree to cut back on the number of hours they work in order to protect against layoffs. In the recent economic crisis, for example, workers in some organizations agreed to voluntarily reduce their paid hours worked so that others would not lose their jobs. Many employers tried to manage the crisis with an involuntary form of work sharing. An example is Pella Windows which went to a four-day workweek for some 3,900 workers to avoid layoffs.[28]

• In **job sharing** one full-time job is split between two or more persons who divide the work according to agreed-upon hours.

• **Work sharing** is when employees agree to work fewer hours to avoid layoffs.

Jelly Columbus

A "jelly" is a co-worker community, people who meet together to do individual work in public places like libraries or coffee shops rather than at home. Jody Dzuranin of the Columbus, Ohio, Jelly says: "I call it study hall for adults . . . a nice mix of interacting in person and getting your work done silently."

• **Telecommuting** is work done at home or from a remote location using computers and advanced telecommunications.

Telecommuting

Technology has enabled yet another alternative work arrangement that is now highly visible in many employment sectors ranging from higher education to government, and from manufacturing to services. **Telecommuting** is work done at home or in a remote location via the use of computers and advanced telecommunications linkages with a central office or other employment locations. And, it's popular; the number of workers who are telecommuting is growing daily, with corporate telecommuters now numbering at least 9 million.[29]

When asked what they like, telecommuters report increased productivity, fewer distractions, the freedom to be their own boss, and the benefit of having more time for themselves. Potential advantages also include more flexibility, the comforts of home, and the choice of locations consistent with the individual's lifestyle. But there are potential negatives as well. Some telecommuters report working too much while having less time to themselves, difficulty separating work and personal life, and less time for family.[30] Other complaints include not being considered important, isolation from co-workers, decreased identification with the work team, and even the interruptions of everyday family affairs. One telecommuter says: "You have to have self-discipline and pride in what you do, but you also have to have a boss that trusts you enough to get out of the way."[31]

A recent development is the *co-working center*, essentially a place where telecommuters go to share an office environment outside of the home and join the company of others. One marketing agency telecommuter says: "we have two kids, so the ability to work from home—it just got worse and worse. I found myself saying, 'If daddy could just have two hours. . . .'" Now he has started his own co-working center to cater to his needs and those of others. One of those using his center says: "What you're paying for is not the desk, it's access to networking, creativity and community."[32]

Part-Time Work

Part-time work has become an increasingly prominent and controversial work arrangement. In *temporary part-time work* an employee works only when needed and for less than the standard 40-hour work week. Some choose this part-time schedule because they like it. But others are *involuntary part-timers* that would prefer a full-time work schedule but do not have access to one. Someone doing *permanent part-time* work is considered a "permanent" member of the workforce although still working fewer hours than the standard 40-hour week. Called *permatemps*, these workers are regularly employed but not given access to health insurance, pension, and other fringe benefits. Their situations fall into a murky area under the law and is attracting more public attention, including that of labor unions.

A part-time work schedule can be a benefit to people who want to supplement other jobs or who want something less than a full work week for a variety of personal reasons. But there are downsides. When a person holds multiple part-time jobs, the work burdens can be stressful; performance may suffer on the job, and spillover effects to family and leisure time can be negative. Also, part-timers often fail to qualify for fringe benefits such as health care insurance and retirement plans. And they may be paid less than their full-time counterparts.

Many employers use part-time work to hold down labor costs and to help smooth out peaks and valleys in the business cycle. Temporary part-timers are easily released and hired as needs dictate; during difficult business times they will most likely be laid off before full-timers. In today's economy the use of part-timers is growing as employers try to cut back labor costs; in just one year the number of involuntary part-time workers grew from 4.5 million to 9 million.[33]

Resources in The OB Skills Workbook

These learning activities from *The OB Skills Workbook* are suggested for Chapter 6.

Cases for Critical Thinking	Team and Experiential Exercises	Self-Assessment Portfolio
• Perfect Pizzeria • Hovey and Beard	• My Best Job • Tinkertoys • Job Design Preferences • My Fantasy Job	• Personal Values • Two-Factor Profile • Are You Cosmopolitan?

6 studyguide

Summary Questions and Answers

What is the link between motivation, performance, and rewards?

- The integrated model of motivation brings together insights from content, process, and learning theories around the basic effort → performance → reward linkage.

- Reward systems emphasize a mix of intrinsic rewards—such as a sense of achievement from completing a challenging task, and extrinsic rewards—such as receiving a pay increase.

- Pay for performance systems take a variety of forms, including merit pay, gain-sharing and profit-sharing plans, lump-sum increases, and employee stock ownership.

- Pay for skills is an increasingly common practice; flexible benefits plans are also increasingly common as the role of benefits as part of an employee's total compensation package gains in motivational importance.

What are the essentials of performance management?

- Performance management is the process of managing performance measurement and the variety of human resource decisions associated with such measurement.

- Performance measurement serves both an evaluative purpose for reward allocation and a development purpose for future performance improvement.

- Performance measurement can be done using output measures of performance accomplishment or activity measures of performance efforts.

- The ranking, paired comparison, and forced-distribution approaches are examples of comparative performance appraisal methods.

- The graphic rating scale and behaviorally anchored rating scale use individual ratings on personal and performance characteristics to appraise performance.

- 360° appraisals involve the full circle of contacts a person may have in job performance—from bosses, to peers, to subordinates, to internal and external customers.

- Common measurement errors in performance appraisal include halo errors, central tendency errors, recency errors, personal bias errors, and cultural bias errors.

How do job designs influence motivation?

- Job design by scientific management or job simplification standardizes work and employs people in clearly defined and specialized tasks.

- Job enlargement increases task variety by combining two or more tasks previously assigned to separate workers; job rotation increases task variety by periodically rotating workers among jobs involving different tasks; job enrichment builds bigger and more responsible jobs by adding planning and evaluating duties.

- Job characteristics theory offers a diagnostic approach to job enrichment based on analysis of five core job characteristics: skill variety, task identity, task significance, autonomy, and feedback.

- Job characteristics theory does not assume that everyone wants an enriched job; it indicates that job enrichment will be more successful for persons with high growth needs, requisite job skills, and context satisfaction.

What are the motivational opportunities of alternative work schedules?

- Today's complex society is giving rise to a number of alternative work arrangements designed to balance the personal demands on workers with job responsibilities and opportunities.

- The compressed work week allows a full-time work week to be completed in fewer than five days, typically offering four 10-hour days of work and three days free.

- Flexible working hours allow employees some daily choice in timing between work and nonwork activities.

- Job sharing occurs when two or more people divide one full-time job according to agreements among themselves and the employer.

- Telecommuting involves work at home or at a remote location while communicating with the home office as needed via computer and related technologies.

- Part-time work requires less than a 40-hour work week and can be done on a schedule classifying the worker as temporary or permanent.

Key Terms

Activity measures (p. 136)
Behaviorally anchored
  rating scale (p. 137)
Compressed work week
  (p. 146)
Critical incident diaries
  (p. 137)
Employee stock ownership
  plans (p. 134)
Extrinsic rewards (p. 131)
Flexible working hours
  (p. 146)
Forced distribution (p. 136)
Gain sharing (p. 133)

Graphic rating scales
  (p. 136)
Intrinsic rewards (p. 131)
Job design (p. 139)
Job enlargement (p. 142)
Job enrichment (p. 142)
Job rotation (p. 142)
Job sharing (p. 147)
Job simplification (p. 141)
Merit pay (p. 133)
Motivation (p. 130)
Output measures (p. 136)
Paired comparison (p. 136)

Performance-contingent
  pay (p. 132)
Profit sharing (p. 133)
Ranking (p. 136)
Reliability (p. 139)
Scientific management
  (p. 140)
Skill-based pay (p. 134)
Stock options (p. 134)
Telecommuting (p. 148)
360° evaluation (p. 138)
Validity (p. 139)
Work sharing (p. 147)

Self-Test 6

Multiple Choice

1. In the integrated model of motivation, what predicts effort? (a) rewards (b) organizational support (c) ability (d) motivation

2. Pay is generally considered a/an _____ reward, while a sense of personal growth experienced from working at a task is an example of a/an _____ reward. (a) extrinsic, skill-based (b) skill-based, intrinsic (c) extrinsic, intrinsic (d) absolute, comparative

3. If someone improves productivity by developing a new work process and receives a portion of the productivity savings as a monetary reward, this is an example of a/an _____ plan. (a) cost sharing (b) gain sharing (c) ESOP (d) pay-for-skills

4. Performance measurement serves two broad purposes: evaluation and _____. (a) reward allocation (b) counseling (c) discipline (d) benefits calculations

5. Which form of performance appraisal is an example of the comparative approach? (a) forced distribution (b) graphic rating scale (c) BARS (d) critical incident diary

6. If a performance appraisal method fails to accurately measure a person's performance on actual job content, it lacks _____. (a) performance contingency (b) leniency (c) validity (d) strictness

7. A written record that describes in detail various examples of a person's positive and negative work behaviors is most likely part of which performance appraisal method? (a) forced distribution (b) critical incident diary (c) paired comparison (d) graphic rating scale

8. When a team leader evaluates the performance of all team members as "average," the possibility for _____ error in the performance appraisal is quite high. (a) personal bias (b) recency (c) halo (d) central tendency

9. Job simplification is closely associated with _____ as originally developed by Frederick Taylor. (a) vertical loading (b) horizontal loading (c) scientific management (d) self-efficacy

10. Job _____ increases job _____ by combining into one job several tasks of similar difficulty. (a) rotation, depth (b) enlargement, depth (c) rotation, breadth (d) enlargement, breadth

11. If a manager redesigns a job through vertical loading, she would most likely _____. (a) bring tasks from earlier in the workflow into the job (b) bring tasks from later in the workflow into the job (c) bring higher level or managerial responsibilities into the job (d) raise the standards for high performance

12. In the job characteristics model, a person will be most likely to find an enriched job motivating if they _____. (a) receive stock options (b) have ability and support (c) are unhappy with job context (d) have strong growth needs

13. In the job characteristics model, _____ indicates the degree to which an individual is able to make decisions affecting his or her work. (a) task variety (b) task identity (c) task significance (d) autonomy

14. When a job allows a person to do a complete unit of work, for example, process an insurance claim from point of receipt from the customer to the point of final resolution with the customer, it would be considered high on which core characteristic? (a) task identity (b) task significance (c) task autonomy (d) feedback

15. The "4/40" is a type of _____ work arrangement. (a) compressed workweek (b) "allow workers to change machine configurations to make different products" (c) job-sharing (d) permanent part-time

Short Response

16. Explain how a 360° evaluation works as a performance appraisal approach.

17. Explain the difference between halo errors and recency errors in performance appraisal.

18. What role does growth-need strength play in the job characteristics model?

19. What are the potential advantages and disadvantages of a compressed work week?

Applications Essay

20. Assume you belong to a student organization on campus. Discuss in detail how the concepts and ideas in this chapter could be applied in various ways to improve motivation and performance among members.

7

Teams in Organizations

chapter at a glance

Organizations today run on the foundation of teams and teamwork. Teams that achieve synergy bring out the best in their members in respect to performance, creativity, and enthusiasm. Here's what to look for in Chapter 7. Don't forget to check your learning with the Summary Questions & Answers and Self-Test in the end-of-chapter Study Guide.

WHY ARE TEAMS IMPORTANT IN ORGANIZATIONS?

Teams and Teamwork
What Teams Do
Organizations as Networks of Teams
Cross-Functional and Problem-Solving Teams
Virtual Teams
Self-Managing Teams

WHEN IS A TEAM EFFECTIVE?

Criteria of an Effective Team
Synergy and Team Benefits
Social Loafing and Team Problems

WHAT ARE THE STAGES OF TEAM DEVELOPMENT?

Forming Stage
Storming Stage
Norming Stage
Performing Stage
Adjourning Stage

HOW CAN WE UNDERSTAND TEAMS AT WORK?

Team Inputs
Diversity and Team Performance
Team Processes

Tandberg is a Norway-based technology company that builds and introduces innovative video conferencing tools to a wide variety of users. With over 41% of the world market, it is one of the fastest growing companies in the video conferencing industry.

The key to Tandberg's success is teamwork. It's quite fitting, actually, for a company that creates and sells collaborative technology tools that help clients improve their own work teams.

Its mission is simple: change the way people communicate. By making that communication unencumbered by technology people can bridge the physical distances that separate us. Communicating over video becomes as natural as speaking to someone right in front of us. An important tool for organizations spread across countries and continents, video conferencing is a practical technology for saving travel time and money which helps the environment as well.

With 1,500 employees working in 45 countries, CEO Fredrik Halvorsen is quick to describe Tandberg as a "we" company, not an "I" company. Seeing himself as more of a facilitator than manager, Mr. Halvorsen describes how the company's collaborative culture and flat structure contribute to high performance results. "Ultimately, high-tech companies do not have time for hierarchies. A clear sense of direction that allows for maximum empowerment and on-the-spot decision making by the team member closest to the issue or opportunity is paramount."

With regard to effective team work, Halverson comments, "We have many strong leaders in this company and a culture that encourages open and honest communication. Our 1,500 people make in excess of 100,000 video calls per month. People look each other in the eyes, whether it is for small trivial matters or huge issues that need immediate attention."

Trust and one-on-one interaction helps clear up misunderstandings while allowing team members to provide each other with honest feedback. It's this strong feedback culture, "where people are expected to address issues they/we may have to whoever can do something about it. As a team rule, no one sends flame-emails or voice mails. If you have an issue, go see the person or address it over video in real-time."

tandberg: using teams to create team-based solutions

Teams in Organizations

The fact is that there is a lot more to teamwork than simply assigning members to the same group, calling it a "team," appointing someone as "team leader," and then expecting them all to do a great job.[1] That's part of the lesson in the opening example. And it is a good introduction to the four chapters in this part of the book that are devoted to an understanding of teams and team processes. As the discussion begins, it helps to remember that the responsibilities for building high-performance, teams rest not only with the manager, coach, or team leader, but also with the team members themselves. If you look now at OB Savvy 7.1, you'll find a checklist of several must-have team contributions, the types of things that team members and leaders can do to help their teams achieve high performance.[2]

Teams and Teamwork

When we think of the word "team," a variety of popular sporting teams might first come to mind, perhaps a college favorite like the University of Maryland "Terps," or professionals like the Cleveland Cavaliers or the St. Louis Cardinals. Just pick your sport.

> *Scene—NBA Basketball*: Scholars find that both good and bad basketball teams win more games the longer the players have been together. Why? They claim it's a "teamwork effect" that creates wins because players know each other's moves and playing tendencies.[3]

But let's not forget that teams are important in work settings as well. And whether or not a team lives up to expectations can have a major impact on how well its customers and clients are served.

> *Scene—Hospital Operating Room*: Scholars notice that the same heart surgeons have lower death rates for similar procedures when performed in hospitals where they do more operations. Why? They claim it's because the doctors spend more time working together with members of these surgery teams. The scholars argue it's not only the surgeon's skills that count: "the skills of the team, and of the organization, matter."[4]

What is going on in these examples? Whereas a group of people milling around a coffee shop counter is just that—a "group" of people—teams like those in the examples are supposed to be something more: "groups+" if you will. That is what distinguishes the successful NBA basketball teams from the also-rans and the best surgery teams from all the others. In OB we define a **team** as a group of people brought together to use their complementary skills to achieve a common purpose for which they are collectively accountable.[5] Real **teamwork** occurs when team members accept and live up to their collective

---

OB SAVVY 7.1

"Must Have" Contributions by Team Members

- Putting personal talents to work.
- Encouraging and motivating others.
- Accepting suggestions.
- Listening to different points of view.
- Communicating information and ideas.
- Persuading others to cooperate.
- Resolving and negotiating conflict.
- Building consensus.
- Fulfilling commitments.
- Avoiding disruptive acts and words.

accountability by actively working together so that all their respective skills are best used to achieve important goals.[6]

What Teams Do

When we talk about teams in organizations, one of the first things to recognize is that they do many things and make many types of performance contributions. In general we can describe them as teams that recommend things, run things, and make or do things.[7]

First, there are *teams that recommend things*. Established to study specific problems and recommend solutions for them, these teams typically work with a target completion date and often disband once the purpose has been fulfilled. These teams include task forces, ad hoc committees, special project teams, and the like. Members of these teams must be able to learn quickly how to work well together, accomplish the assigned task, and make good action recommendations for follow-up work by other people.

Second, there are *teams that run things*. Such management teams consist of people with the formal responsibility for leading other groups. These teams may exist at all levels of responsibility, from the individual work unit composed of a team leader and team members to the top-management team composed of a CEO and other senior executives. Key issues addressed by top-management teams include, for example, identifying overall organizational purposes, goals, and values, as well as crafting strategies and persuading others to support them.[8]

Third, there are *teams that make or do things*. These are teams and work units that perform ongoing tasks such as marketing, sales, systems analysis, or manufacturing. Members of these teams must have effective long-term working relationships with one another, solid operating systems, and the external support needed to achieve effectiveness over a sustained period of time. They also need energy to keep up the pace and meet the day-to-day challenges of sustained high performance.

Organizations as Networks of Teams

When it was time to reengineer its order-to-delivery process to streamline a noncompetitive and costly cycle time, Hewlett-Packard turned to a team. In just nine months, they had slashed the time, improved service, and cut costs. How did they do it? Team leader Julie Anderson said: "We took things away: no supervisors, no hierarchy, no titles, no job descriptions . . . the idea was to create a sense of personal ownership." One team member said, "No individual is going

> • A **team** is a group of people holding themselves collectively accountable for using complimentary skills to achieve a common purpose.

> • **Teamwork** occurs when team members live up to their collective accountability for goal accomplishment.

Microsoft

A Microsoft survey of 38,000 workers worldwide addressed teamwork and productivity. Results showed that the average worker spends 5.6 hours per week in meetings and that 69 percent of meetings were considered ineffective. The major problems were unclear goals, poor communication, and procrastination.

to have the best idea, that's not the way it works—the best ideas come from the collective intelligence of the team." [9] This isn't an isolated example. Organizations everywhere are using teams and teamwork to improve performance. The catchwords of these new approaches are empowerment, participation, and involvement.

The many **formal teams** found in organizations are created and officially designated to serve specific organizational purposes. Some are permanent and ongoing. They appear on organization charts as departments (e.g., market research department), divisions (e.g., consumer products division), or teams (e.g., product-assembly team). Such teams can vary in size from very small departments or teams of just a few people to large divisions employing a hundred or more people. Other formal teams are temporary and short lived. They are created to solve specific problems or perform defined tasks and are then disbanded once the purpose has been accomplished. Examples include the many temporary committees and task forces that are important components of any organization. [10]

One way to view organizations is as interlocking networks of permanent and temporary teams. On the vertical dimension the manager is a linchpin serving as a team leader at one level and a team member at the next higher level. [11] On the horizontal dimension, for example, a customer service team member may also serve on a special task force for new product development and head a committee set up to examine a sexual harassment case.

In addition to their networks of formal teams, Figure 7.1 also shows that organizations have vast networks of **informal groups** that emerge and co-exist as a shadow to the formal structure and without any formal purpose or official endorsement. These informal groups form spontaneously through personal relationships or special interests and create their own interlocking networks of relationships within the organization. *Friendship groups*, for example, consist of persons with natural affinities for one another. They tend to work together, sit together, take breaks together, and even do things together outside of the workplace. *Interest groups* consist of persons who share common interests. These may be job-related interests, such as an intense desire to learn more about computers, or nonwork interests, such as community service, sports, or religion.

Although informal groups can be places where people join to complain, spread rumors, and disagree with what is happening in the organization, they can be quite functional as well. Informal networks can speed up workflows as

• Formal teams are official and designated to serve a specific purpose.

• Informal groups are unofficial and emerge to serve special interests.

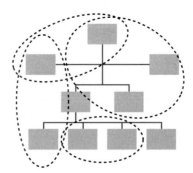

Figure 7.1 The organization as an interlocking network of informal groups.

people assist each other in ways that cut across the formal structures. They can also help satisfy needs, for example by providing social companionship or a sense of personal importance that is otherwise missing in someone's formal team assignments.

A tool known as **social network analysis** is used to identify the informal groups and networks of relationships that are active in an organization. Such an analysis typically asks people to identify co-workers who help them most often, who communicate with them regularly, and who energize and de-energize them. When results are analyzed, social networks are drawn with lines running from person to person according to frequency and type of relationship maintained. This map shows how a lot of work really gets done in organizations, in contrast to the formal arrangements depicted on organization charts. Managers use such information to redesign the formal team structure for better performance and also to legitimate informal networks as pathways to high performance for people in their daily work.

- **Social network analysis** identifies the informal structures and their embedded social relationships that are active in an organization.

Cross-Functional and Problem-Solving Teams

Management scholar Jay Conger calls the organization built around teams and teamwork the management system of the future and the best response to the needs for speed and adaptability in an ever-more-competitive environment.[12] He cites the example of an American jet engine manufacturer that changed from a traditional structure of functional work units to one in which people from different functions worked together in teams. The new approach cut the time required to design and produce new engines by 50 percent. Conger calls such "cross-functional" teams "speed machines."[13]

A **cross-functional team** consists of members assigned from different functional departments or work units. It plays an important role in efforts to achieve more horizontal integration and better lateral relations. Members of cross-functional teams are expected to work together with a positive combination of functional expertise and integrative or total systems thinking. The expected result is higher performance driven by the advantages of better information and faster decision making.

- A **cross-functional team** has members from different functions or work units.

Cross-functional teams are a way of trying to beat the **functional silos problem**, also called the *functional chimneys problem*. It occurs when members of functional units stay focused on matters internal to their function and minimize their interactions with members dealing with other functions. In this sense, the functional departments or work teams create artificial boundaries, or "silos," that discourage rather than encourage interaction with other units. The result is poor integration and poor coordination with other parts of the organization. The use of cross-functional teams is a way to break down the barriers among functional units by creating a forum in which members from different functions work together as one team with a common purpose.[14]

- The **functional silos problem** occurs when members of one functional team fail to interact with others from other functional teams.

Organizations also use any number of **problem-solving teams**, which are created temporarily to serve a specific purpose by dealing with a specific problem or opportunity. They exist as the many committees, task forces, and special project teams that are common facts of working life. The president of a company, for example, might convene a task force to examine the possibility of

- A **problem-solving team** is set up to deal with a specific problem or opportunity.

implementing flexible work hours for employees; a human resource director might bring together a committee to advise her on changes in employee benefit policies; a project team might be formed to plan and implement a new organization-wide information system. Temporary teams like these are usually headed by chairpersons or team leaders who are held accountable for meeting the task force goal or fulfilling the committee's purpose, much as is the manager of a formal work unit.

• An **employee involvement team** meets regularly to address workplace issues.

The term **employee involvement team** applies to a wide variety of teams whose members meet regularly to collectively examine important workplace issues. They might discuss, for example, ways to enhance quality, better satisfy customers, raise productivity, and improve the quality of work life. In this way, employee involvement teams mobilize the full extent of workers' know-how and gain the commitment needed to fully implement solutions. An example is what some organizations call a **quality circle**—a small team of persons who meet periodically to discuss and develop solutions for problems relating to quality and productivity.[15]

• A **quality circle** team meets regularly to address quality issues.

Virtual Teams

• Members of **virtual teams** work together through computer mediation.

Information technology has brought a new type of group into the workplace. This is the **virtual team**, whose members convene and work together electronically via computers.[16] It used to be that teamwork was confined in concept and practice to those circumstances in which members could meet face to face. The advent of new technologies and computer programs have changed all that. Working in electronic space and free from the constraints of geographical distance, members of virtual teams can do the same things in computer networks as do members of face-to-face groups: share information, make decisions, and complete tasks.

In terms of potential advantages, virtual teams bring together people who may be located at great distances from one another.[17] This offers obvious cost and time efficiencies. The electronic rather than face-to-face environment of the virtual team can help focus interaction and decision making on objective information rather than emotional considerations and distracting interpersonal problems.

Texas Instruments

On any given day you can find talented engineers in Bangalore, India, laboring on complex chip designs with their counterparts in Texas. Virtual teammates are in constant contact, sending work back and forth while taking advantage of the near half-day time difference.

In addition, discussions and information shared among team members can also be electronically stored for continuous access and historical record keeping.

Many of the downsides to virtual teams occur for the same reasons they do in other groups. Members of virtual teams can have difficulties establishing good working relationships. When the computer is the go-between, relationships and interactions among virtual team members are different from those of face-to-face settings. The lack of face-to-face interaction limits the role of emotions and nonverbal cues in the communication process, perhaps depersonalizing relations among team members.

Some steps to successful teams are summarized in Mastering Management, and in many ways they mirror in electronic space the essentials of good team leadership in face-to-face teams.[18] Managers and team leaders should also understand that the computer technology should be appropriate to the task, and that team members should be well trained in using it. Finally, researchers note that virtual teams may work best when the tasks are more structured and the work is less interdependent.

MASTERING MANAGEMENT

STEPS TO SUCCESSFUL VIRTUAL TEAMS

- Select team members high in initiative and capable of self-starting.
- Select members who will join and engage the team with positive attitudes.
- Select members known for working hard to meet team goals.
- Begin with social messaging that allows members to exchange information about each other to personalize the process.
- Assign clear goals and roles so that members can focus while working alone and also know what others are doing.
- Gather regular feedback from members about how they think the team is doing and how it might do better.
- Provide regular feedback to team members about team accomplishments.

Self-Managing Teams

In the last chapter we discussed job enrichment and its implications for individual motivation and performance. Now we can talk about a form of job enrichment for teams. A high-involvement work-group design that is becoming increasingly well established is known as the **self-managing team**. Sometimes called *self-directed work teams*, these are small groups empowered to make the decisions needed to manage themselves on a day-to-day basis.[19]

Self-managing teams basically replace traditional work units with teams whose members assume duties otherwise performed by a manager or first-line supervisor. Figure 7.2 shows that members of true self-managing teams make their own decisions about scheduling work, allocating tasks, training for job skills, evaluating performance, selecting new team members, and controlling the quality of work.

A self-managing team should probably include between 5 and 15 members. The teams need to be large enough to provide a good mix of skills and resources but small enough to function efficiently. Because team members have a lot of discretion in determining work pace and in distributing tasks, **multiskilling** is important. This means that team members are expected to perform many different jobs—even all of the team's jobs—as needed. Ideally, the more skills someone masters, the higher his or her base pay. Team members should also be responsible for conducting training and certifying one another as having mastered various skills.

The expected benefits of self-managing teams include productivity and quality improvements, production flexibility and faster response to technological change, reduced absenteeism and turnover, and improved work attitudes and quality of work life. But just as with all organizational changes, the shift from traditional work units to self-managing teams may have its difficulties. It may be hard for some team members to adjust to the "self-managing" responsibilities. And higher-level managers may have problems dealing with the loss of the first-line supervisor positions; they must learn to deal with teams instead of the individual supervisors as direct reporters. Given all this, self-managing teams are probably not right for all organizations, work situations, and people. They have great potential, but they also require a proper setting and a great deal of management support. At a

- **Self-managing teams** are empowered to make decisions to manage themselves in day-to-day work.

- **Multiskilling** is where team members are each capable of performing many different jobs.

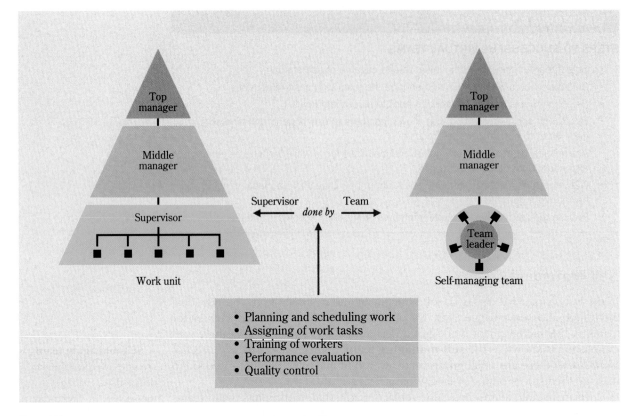

Figure 7.2 Organizational and management implications of self-managing teams.

minimum, the essence of any self-managing team—high involvement, participation, and empowerment—must be consistent with the values and culture of the organization.

Team Effectiveness

There is no doubt that teams are pervasive and important in organizations; they accomplish important tasks and help members achieve satisfaction in their work. But we also know from personal experiences that teams and teamwork have their difficulties; not all teams perform well, and not all team members are always satisfied. Surely you've heard the sayings "a camel is a horse put together by a committee" and "too many cooks spoil the broth." They raise an important question: Just what are the foundations of team effectiveness?

Criteria of an Effective Team

Teams, just like individuals, should be held accountable for their performance. And to do this we need to have some understanding of team effectiveness. In

OB we define an **effective team** as one that achieves high levels of task performance, member satisfaction, and team viability.

| An effective team achieves high performance | → | An effective team generates high member satisfaction | → | An effective team stays viable for long-term action |

With regard to *task performance*, an effective team achieves its performance goals in the standard sense of quantity, quality, and timeliness of work results. For a formal work unit such as a manufacturing team this may mean meeting daily production targets. For a temporary team such as a new policy task force this may involve meeting a deadline for submitting a new organizational policy to the company president.

With regard to *member satisfaction*, an effective team is one whose members believe that their participation and experiences are positive and meet important personal needs. They are satisfied with their tasks, accomplishments, and interpersonal relationships. With regard to *team viability*, the members of an effective team are sufficiently satisfied to continue working well together on an ongoing basis and/or to look forward to working together again at some future point in time. Such a group has all-important long-term performance potential.

Synergy and Team Benefits

When teams are effective, they offer the potential for **synergy**—the creation of a whole that is greater than the sum of its parts. Synergy works within a team and it works across teams as their collective efforts are harnessed to serve the organization as a whole. As noted in the chapter subtitle, synergy is the goal, and it always should be. It creates the great beauty of teams: people working together and accomplishing more through teamwork than they ever could by working alone. In general we can say that:

- Teams are good for people.
- Teams can improve creativity.
- Teams can make better decisions.
- Teams can increase commitments to action.
- Teams help control their members.
- Teams help offset large organization size.

The performance advantages of teams over individuals acting alone are most evident in three situations.[20] First, when there is no clear "expert" for a particular task or problem, teams seem to make better judgments than does the average individual alone. Second, teams are typically more successful than individuals when problems are complex, requiring a division of labor and the sharing of information. Third, because of their tendencies to make riskier decisions, teams can be more creative and innovative than individuals.

Teams are beneficial as settings where people learn from one another and share job skills and knowledge. The learning environment and the pool of

> **Synergy** is the creation of a whole greater than the sum of its parts.

Cleveland Clinic

Teamwork between physicians and nonphysicians is one of the keys to success at the Cleveland Clinic. Dr. Bruce Lytle says there is no room for inflated egos. "We're not built around the notion of one superstar surrounded by supporting role players," he says.

experience within a team can be used to solve difficult and unique problems. This is especially helpful to newcomers, who often need help in their jobs. When team members support and help each other in acquiring and improving job competencies, they may even make up for deficiencies in organizational training systems.

Teams are also important sources of need satisfaction for their members. Opportunities for social interaction within a team can provide individuals with a sense of security through work assistance and technical advice. Team members can also provide emotional support for one another in times of special crisis or pressure. And the many contributions individuals make to teams can help members experience self-esteem and personal involvement.

Social Loafing and Team Problems

* **Social loafing** occurs when people work less hard in groups than they would individually.

Although teams have enormous performance potential, they can also have problems. One concern is **social loafing**, also known as the *Ringlemann effect*. It is the tendency of people to work less hard in a group than they would individually.[21] Max Ringlemann, a German psychologist, pinpointed the phenomenon by asking people to pull on a rope as hard as they could, first alone and then as part of a team.[22] He found that average productivity dropped as more people joined the rope-pulling task. He suggested that people may not work as hard in groups because their individual contributions are less noticeable in the group context and because they prefer to see others carry the workload.

You may have encountered social loafing in your work and study teams, and been perplexed in terms of how to best handle it. Perhaps you have even been surprised at your own social loafing in some performance situations. Rather than give in to the phenomenon and its potential performance losses, social loafing can often be reversed or prevented. Steps that team leaders can take include keeping group size small and redefining roles so that free-riders are more visible and peer pressures to perform are more likely, increasing accountability by making individual performance expectations clear and specific, and making rewards directly contingent on an individual's performance contributions.[23]

* **Social facilitation** is the tendency for one's behavior to be influenced by the presence of others in a group.

This discussion moves us to another concept known as **social facilitation**—the tendency for one's behavior to be influenced by the presence of others in a group or social setting.[24] In a team context social facilitation can be a boost or a detriment to an individual member's performance contributions. Social facilitation theory suggests that working in the presence of others creates an emotional arousal or excitement that stimulates behavior and therefore affects performance. The effect works to the positive and stimulates extra effort when one is proficient with the task at hand. An example is the team member who enthusiastically responds when asked to do something she is really good at, such as making Power Point slides for a team presentation. But the effect of social facilitation can be negative when the task is unfamiliar or a person lacks the necessary skills. A team member might withdraw or even tend toward social loafing, for example, when asked to do something he isn't very good at, such as being included among those delivering the team's final presentation in front of a class or larger audience.

Other common problems of teams include personality conflicts and differences in work styles that antagonize others and disrupt relationships and accomplishments. Sometimes team members withdraw from active participation due to uncertainty over tasks or battles about goals or competing visions. Ambiguous agendas or ill-defined problems can also cause fatigue and loss of motivation when teams work too long on the wrong things with little to show for it. And

RESEARCH INSIGHT

Membership, Interactions, and Evaluation Influence Social Loafing in Groups

"Why do individuals reduce their efforts or withhold inputs when in team contexts?" This question, asked by researchers Kenneth H. Price, David A. Harrison, and Joanne H. Gavin, leads one into the area of social loafing theory. The authors designed a study of natural teams consisting of students working together in course study groups for a semester. They posed hypotheses linking the presence of individual evaluation, perceived dispensability, and perceived fairness of group processes with the presence or absence of social loafing.

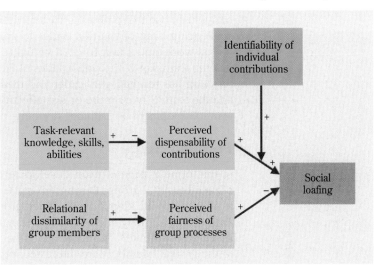

Price and colleagues studied 144 groups with a total of 515 students in 13 undergraduate and graduate university courses. Participants completed a questionnaire before group work started and again at the end. The final questionnaire included a section asking respondents to rate the extent to which each other group member "loafed by not doing his or her share of the tasks, by leaving work for others to do, by goofing off, and by having other things to do when asked to help out"—in other words, the extent to which each group member engaged in social loafing.

Findings showed that social loafing was negatively related to perceived fairness of group processes, and was positively related to perceived dispensability of one's contributions. In addition, the relationship between social loafing and perceived dispensability strengthened when individual contributions were more identifiable. Task-relevant ability was negatively associated with perceived dispensability; the presence of relational differences among members was negatively associated with perceived fairness of group processes.

The researchers suggest that this is the first study to show a link between decision making, organizational justice, and social loafing in groups. They also point out that the link found between relational differences and both perceived dispensability and fairness have implications regarding diversity management within groups.

Further Research

Build a model that explains social loafing in the teams you often work with. What are the major hypotheses? How might you test them in an actual research study?

Source: Kenneth H. Price, David A. Harrison, and Joanne H. Gavin, "Withholding Inputs in Team Contexts: Member Composition, Interaction Processes, Evaluation Structure, and Social Loafing," *Journal of Applied Psychology,* 91.6 (2006), pp. 1375–1384.

finally, not everyone is always ready to do group work. This might be due to lack of motivation, but it may also stem from conflicts with other work deadlines and priorities. Low enthusiasm may also result from perceptions of poor team organization or progress, as well as from meetings that seem to lack purpose. These and other difficulties can easily turn the great potential of teams into frustration and failure.

Stages of Team Development

There is no doubt that groups can be great resources for organizations, creating synergies and helping to accomplish things that are far beyond the efforts of any individual. But the pathways to team effectiveness are often complicated and challenging. One of the first things to consider, whether we are talking about a formal work unit, a task force, a virtual team, or a self-managing team, is the fact that the team passes through a series of life cycle stages.[25] Depending on the stage the team has reached, the leader and members can face very different challenges and the team may be more or less effective. Figure 7.3 describes the five stages of team development as forming, storming, norming, performing, and adjourning.[26]

Forming Stage

In the forming stage of team development, a primary concern is the initial entry of members to a group. During this stage, individuals ask a number of questions as they begin to identify with other group members and with the team itself. Their concerns may include "What can the group offer me?" "What will I be asked to contribute?" "Can my needs be met at the same time that I contribute to the group?" Members are interested in getting to know each other and discovering what is considered acceptable behavior, in determining the real task of the team, and in defining group rules.

Storming Stage

The storming stage of team development is a period of high emotionality and tension among the group members. During this stage, hostility and infighting may occur, and the team typically experiences many changes. Coalitions or cliques may form as individuals compete to impose their preferences on the group and to achieve a desired status position. Outside demands such as premature perform-ance expectations may create uncomfortable pressures. In the process, member-ship expectations tend to be clarified, and attention shifts toward obstacles standing in the way of team goals. Individuals begin to understand one another's interpersonal styles, and efforts are made to find ways to accomplish team goals while also satisfying individual needs.

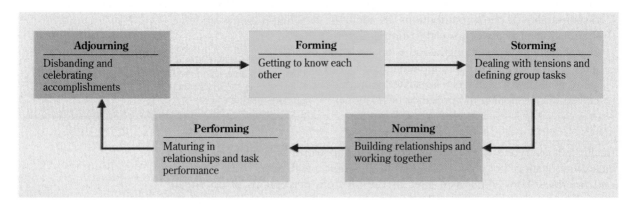

Figure 7.3 Five stages of team development.

Norming Stage

The norming stage of team development, sometimes called initial integration, is the point at which the members really start to come together as a coordinated unit. The turmoil of the storming stage gives way to a precarious balancing of forces. With the pleasures of a new sense of harmony, team members will strive to maintain positive balance. Holding the team together may become more important to some than successfully working on the team tasks. Minority viewpoints, deviations from team directions, and criticisms may be discouraged as members experience a preliminary sense of closeness. Some members may mistakenly perceive this stage as one of ultimate maturity. In fact, a premature sense of accomplishment at this point needs to be carefully managed as a stepping stone to the next level of team development—performing.

Performing Stage

The performing stage of team development, sometimes called total integration, marks the emergence of a mature, organized, and well-functioning team. Team members are now able to deal with complex tasks and handle internal disagreements in creative ways. The structure is stable, and members are motivated by team goals and are generally satisfied. The primary challenges are continued efforts to improve relationships and performance. Team members should be able to adapt successfully as opportunities and demands change over time. A team that has achieved the level of total integration typically scores high on the criteria of team maturity as shown in Figure 7.4.

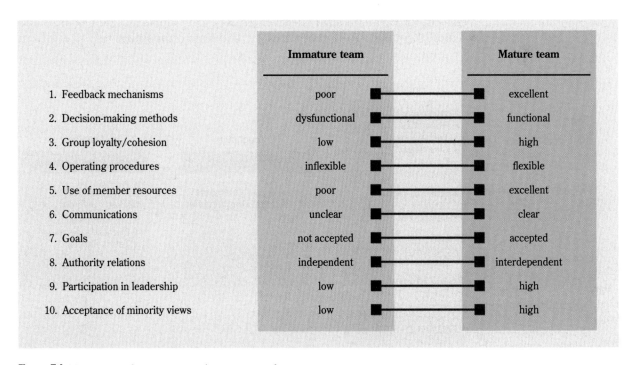

Figure 7.4 Ten criteria for measuring the maturity of a team.

Adjourning Stage

A well-integrated team is able to disband, if required, when its work is accomplished. The adjourning stage of team development is especially important for the many temporary teams such as task forces, committees, project teams, and the like. Their members must be able to convene quickly, do their jobs on a tight schedule, and then adjourn—often to reconvene later if needed. Their willingness to disband when the job is done and to work well together in future responsibilities, team or otherwise, is an important long-term test of team success.

Foundations of Team Performance

Procter & Gamble's former CEO A. G. Lafley says that team effectiveness comes together when you have "the right players in the right seats on the same bus, headed in the same direction."[27] This wisdom is quite consistent with the findings of OB scholars. The open systems model in Figure 7.5 shows team effectiveness being influenced by both inputs—"right players in the right seats," and by processes—"on the same bus, headed in the same direction."[28] You can remember the implications of this figure by this equation:

Team effectiveness = Quality of inputs + (Process gains − Process losses)

Team Inputs

The inputs to a team are the initial "givens" in the situation. They set the foundations for all subsequent action; the stronger the input foundations, the better the chances for long-term team effectiveness. Key team inputs include resources and setting, the nature of the task, team size, and team composition.

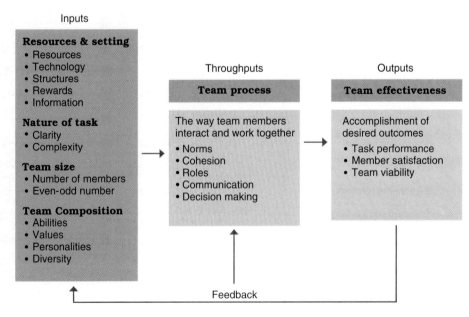

Figure 7.5 An open-systems model of team effectiveness. [*Source:* John R. Schermerhorn, Jr., *Management*, Tenth Edition (Hoboken, NJ: John Wiley & Sons, 2009), used by permission].

Resources and setting   Appropriate goals, well-designed reward systems, adequate resources, and appropriate technology are all essential to support the work of teams. Just as an individual's performance, team performance can suffer when goals are unclear, insufficiently challenging, or arbitrarily imposed. It can also suffer if goals and rewards are focused too much on individual-level instead of group-level accomplishments. In addition, it can suffer when resources—information, budgets, work space, deadlines, rules and procedures, technologies, and the like— are insufficient to accomplish the task. By contrast, having a supportive organizational setting within which to work can be a strong launching pad for team success.

The importance of setting and support in the new, team-based organization designs is evident in the attention now being given to things like office architecture and how well it supports teamwork. At SEI Investments, for example, employees work in a large, open space without cubicles or dividers. Each person has a private set of office furniture and fixtures, but all on wheels. Technology easily plugs and unplugs from suspended power beams that run overhead. This makes it easy for project teams to convene and disband as needed and for people to meet and converse intensely within the ebb and flow of daily work.[29]

Nature of the Task   The tasks they are asked to perform can place different demands on teams, with varying implications for group effectiveness. When tasks are clear and well defined, it is easier for members to both know what they are trying to accomplish and to work together while doing it. But team effectiveness is harder to achieve when the task is highly complex.[30] Complex tasks require lots of information exchange and intense interaction, and this all takes place under conditions of some uncertainty. To deal well with complexity, team members have to fully mobilize their talents and use the available resources well if they are to achieve desired results. Success at complex tasks, however, is a source of high satisfaction for team members.

One way to analyze the nature of the team task is in terms of its technical and social demands. The *technical demands* of a group's task include the degree to which it is routine or not, the level of difficulty involved, and the information requirements. The *social demands* of a task involve the degree to which issues of interpersonal relationships, egos, controversies over ends and means, and the like come into play. Tasks that are complex in technical demands require unique solutions and more information processing; those that are complex in social demands involve difficulties reaching agreement on goals or methods for accomplishing them.

Team Size   The size of a team, as measured by the number of its members, can have an impact on team effectiveness. As a team becomes larger, more people are available to divide up the work and accomplish needed tasks. This can boost performance and member satisfaction, but only up to a point. As teams grow in size, communication and coordination problems often set in due to the sheer number of linkages that must be maintained. Satisfaction may dip, and turnover, absenteeism, and social loafing may increase. Even logistical matters, such as finding time and locations for meetings, become more difficult for larger groups and can hurt performance.[31] Amazon.com's founder and CEO, Jeff Bezos, is a great fan of teams. But he also has a simple rule when it comes to the size of product development teams: No team should be larger than two pizzas can feed.[32]

Teams sometimes use voting as a way to make decisions and avoid discussion of member disagreements, but "winners" and "losers" may have trouble working together.

Leaders on Leadership

INDRA NOOYI BRINGS STYLE AND A SHARP EYE TO PEPSI

When Indra Nooyi became Chair and CEO of PepsiCo, only the 12th woman to head a Fortune 500 firm, Shirley Myrick of the American Business Women's Association called her appointment a significant step for diversity. "If the largest portion of our workface is a minority population," she says, "it [Nooyi's promotion] demonstrates fairness and competition in our workplace."

The best advice she ever got, says Nooyi, came from her father. Calling him "an

absolutely wonderful human being," she says: "From him I learned to always assume positive intent. Whatever anybody says or does, assume positive intent. You will be amazed at how your whole approach to a person or problem becomes very different . . . You are trying to understand and listen because at your basic core you are saying, 'Maybe they are saying something to me that I am not hearing.'"

That advice has carried Nooyi to the top ranks of global business. She grew up in Chennai, India, and earned her first university degree in chemistry. After a Master's in Management from Yale, she joined the Boston Consulting Group and eventually joined PepsiCo where she moved through a variety of management positions to become CEO.

Business Week described her "prescient business sense" as behind the firm's moves to spin off its fast food businesses Taco Bell, Pizza Hut, and KFC, a merger with Quaker Oats, and the purchase of Tropicana—all decisions that proved successful for the firm.

Throughout her rise to the top Nooyi kept to a personal style that has allowed her personality to shine. Former CEO Roger Enrico says "Indra can drive as deep and hard as anyone I've ever met, but she can do it with a sense of heart and fun." On occasion Nooyi can be seen walking barefoot in the office and even singing in the halls; she was a member of a teen-age rock band in Chennai. ABC news described her as a blend of "Indian culture mixed in with the traditional American working mom."

A good size for problem-solving teams is between five and seven members. Chances are that fewer than five may be too small to adequately share all the team responsibilities. With more than seven, however, individuals may find it harder to join in the discussions, contribute their talents, and offer ideas. Larger teams are also more prone to possible domination by aggressive members and have tendencies to split into coalitions or subgroups.[33] When voting is required, odd-numbered teams are preferred to help rule out tie votes. But when careful deliberations are required and the emphasis is more on consensus, such as in jury duty or very complex problem solving, even-numbered teams may be more effective because members are forced to confront disagreements and deadlocks rather than simply resolve them by majority voting.[34]

Team Composition   "If you want a team to perform well, you've got to put the right members on the team to begin with." Does that advice sound useful? It's something we hear a lot in training programs with executives. There is no doubt that one of the most important input factors is the *team composition*. You can think of this as the mix of abilities, skills, backgrounds, and experiences that the members bring to the team.

The basic rule of thumb for team composition is to choose members whose talents and interests fit well with the tasks to be accomplished and whose personal characteristics increase the likelihood of being able to work well with others. In this sense ability counts; it's probably the first thing to consider in selecting members for a team. The team is more likely to perform better when its members have skills and competencies that best fit task demands. Although talents alone cannot guarantee desired results, they establish an important baseline of high performance potential.

Surely you've been on teams or observed teams where there was lots of talent but very little teamwork. A likely cause is that the blend of members caused relationship problems over everything from needs to personality to experience to age and other background characteristics. In this respect, the **FIRO-B theory** (with FIRO standing for "fundamental interpersonal orientation") identifies differences in how people relate to one another in groups based on their needs to express and receive feelings of inclusion, control, and affection.[35] Developed by William Schultz, the theory suggests that teams whose members have compatible needs are likely to be more effective than teams whose members are more incompatible. Symptoms of incompatibilities include withdrawn members, open hostilities, struggles over control, and domination by a few members. Schultz states the management implications of the FIRO-B theory this way: "If at the outset we can choose a group of people who can work together harmoniously, we shall go far toward avoiding situations where a group's efforts are wasted in interpersonal conflicts."[36]

In **homogeneous teams** where members are very similar to one another, teamwork usually isn't much of a problem. The members typically find it quite easy to work together and enjoy the team experience. But researchers warn about the risks of homogeneity. When team members are too similar in background, training, and experience, they tend to underperform even though the members may feel very comfortable with one another.[37]

In **heterogeneous teams** where members are very dissimilar, teamwork problems are more likely. The mix of diverse personalities, experiences, backgrounds, ages, and other personal characteristics may create difficulties as members try to define problems, share information, mobilize talents, and deal with obstacles or opportunities. Nevertheless, if, and this is a big "if," members can work well together, the diversity can be a source of advantage and enhanced performance potential.[38]

Another issue in team composition is *status*—a person's relative rank, prestige, or social standing. Status within a team can be based on any number of factors, including age, work seniority, occupation, education, performance, or reputation for performance on other teams. **Status congruence** occurs when a person's position within the team is equivalent in status to positions the individual holds outside of it. Any status incongruence can create problems for teams. In high-power-distance cultures such as Malaysia, for example, the chair of a committee is expected to be the highest-ranking member of the group. When this is the case the status congruity helps members feel comfortable in proceeding with their work. But if the senior member is not appointed to head the committee, perhaps because an expatriate manager from another culture selected the chair on some other criterion, members are likely to feel uncomfortable and have difficulty

FIRO-B theory examines differences in how people relate to one another based on their needs to express and receive feelings of inclusion, control, and affection.

In **homogeneous teams** members share many similar characteristics.

In **heterogeneous teams** members differ on many characteristics.

Status congruence involves consistency between a person's status within and outside a group.

working. Similar problems might occur, for example, when a young college graduate in his or her first job is appointed to chair a project team composed of senior and more experienced workers.

Diversity and Team Performance

As discussed in respect to team composition, *team diversity* in the form of different values, personalities, experiences, demographics, and cultures among the members, is an important team input. And it can pose both opportunities and problems.[39] We have already noted that when teams are relatively homogeneous, displaying little or no diversity, it is probably easier for members to quickly build social relationships and engage in the interactions needed for teamwork. But the lack of diversity may foster narrow viewpoints and otherwise limit the team in terms of ideas, perspectives, and creativity. When teams are more heterogeneous, having a diverse membership, they gain potential advantages in these latter respects; there are more resources and viewpoints available to engage in problem solving, especially when tasks are complex and demanding. Yet these advantages are not automatic; the diversity must be tapped if the team is to realize the performance benefits.[40]

• **Diversity–consensus dilemma** is the tendency for diversity in groups to create process difficulties even as it offers improved potential for problem solving.

Performance difficulties due to diversity issues are especially likely in the initial stages of team development. What is called the **diversity–consensus dilemma** is the tendency for the existence of diversity among group members to make it harder for them to work together, even though the diversity itself expands the skills and perspectives available for problem solving.[41] These dilemmas may be most pronounced in the critical zone of the storming and norming stages of development as described in Figure 7.6. Problems may occur in this zone as interpersonal stresses and conflicts emerge from the heterogeneity. The challenge to effectiveness in a multinational team, for example, is to take advantage of the diversity without suffering process disadvantages.[42]

Working through the diversity–consensus dilemma can slow team development and impede relationship building, information sharing, and problem solving. But if and when such difficulties are resolved, diverse teams can emerge from the

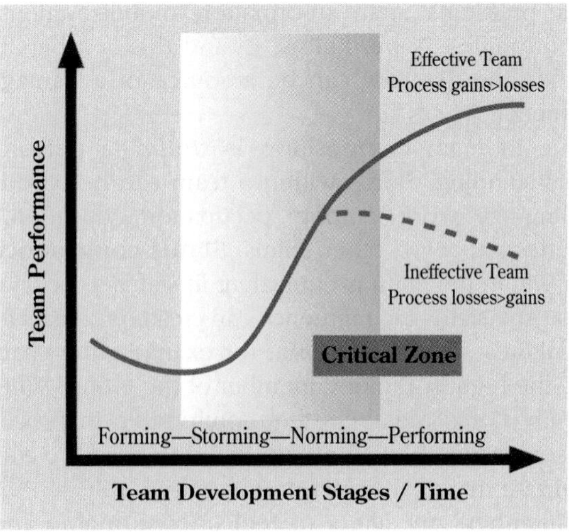

Figure 7.6 Member diversity, stages of team development, and team performance.

critical zone shown in the figure to achieve effectiveness and often outperform less diverse ones. In this regard Scholar Brian Uzzi reminds us to take a broad view; diversity in team dynamics means more than gender, race, and ethnicity. He points out that when teams lack diversity of backgrounds, training, and experiences, members tend to feel comfortable with one another, but their teams tend to underperform.[43] For example, research shows that the most creative teams include a mix of experienced people and others whom they haven't worked with before.[44] The "old timers" have the experience and connections; the newcomers bring in new talents and fresh thinking.

Team Processes

Casey Stengel, a famous baseball manager, once said: "Getting good players is easy. Getting them to play together is the hard part." His comment certainly rings true in respect to the discussion we just had on diversity and team performance. There is no doubt that the effectiveness of any team requires more than having the right inputs. To achieve effectiveness, team members must work well together to turn the available inputs into the desired outputs. Here again, it's helpful to remember the equation: Team Effectiveness = Quality of inputs + (Process gains − Process losses).

When it comes to analyzing how well people "work together" in teams and whether or not process gains exceed process losses, the focus is on critical **group dynamics**—the forces operating in teams that affect the way members relate to and work with one another. George Homans described group dynamics in terms of *required behaviors*—those formally defined and expected by the team—and *emergent behaviors*—those that team members display in addition to any requirements.[45]

You can think of required behaviors as things like punctuality, respect for customers, and assistance to co-workers. An example of emergent behaviors might

Group dynamics are the forces operating in teams that affect the ways members work together.

ETHICS IN OB

MBA CHEATS

Tough headline and scary message, but all true. A study reported by Rutgers University professor Donald McCabe found that 56 percent of MBA students reported cheating by plagiarizing, downloading essays from the Web, and more. He believes the actual figure may be higher and that some respondents held back confessions for fear of losing their anonymity.

Another study, by University of Arkansas professor Tim West and colleagues, surveyed students who had cheated on an accounting test by finding answers online. When asked why, student responses ranged from being unsure that what they did was cheating, to blaming West for giving a test that had answers available on the Web, to rationalizing that "everyone cheats" and "this is how business operates."

What's Your Position? Is this the way business operates? And just because "everyone" may be doing something, does that make it okay for us to do it as well? Berkshire Hathaway chairman Warren Buffett says: "The five most dangerous words in the English language are 'Everyone else is doing it.'" Professor Alma Acevedo of the University of Puerto Rico Rio Piedras calls this the fallacy of the "assumed authority of the majority." How often does it creep into your thinking?

be someone taking the time to send an e-mail message to an absent member to keep her informed about what happened during a group meeting. Such helpful emergent behaviors are often essential in moving teams toward effectiveness. But emergent behaviors can be disruptive and harmful as well. A common example is when some team members spend more time discussing and laughing about personal issues than they do working on the team tasks. Another disturbing example involves unethical practices such as the "cheating" discussed in the Ethics in OB box.

Resources in The OB Skills Workbook

These learning activities from *The OB Skills Workbook* are suggested for Chapter 7.

Case for Critical Thinking	Team and Experiential Exercises	Self-Assessment Portfolio
• The Forgotten Team Member	• Sweet Tooth	• Team Effectiveness
	• Interrogatories	• Decision-Making Biases
	• Teamwork and Motivation	
	• Serving on the Boundary	
	• *Eggs*periential Exercise	

7 studyguide

Summary Questions and Answers

What do teams do in organizations?

- A team is a group of people working together to achieve a common purpose for which they hold themselves collectively accountable.

- Teams help organizations by improving task performance; teams help members experience satisfaction from their work.

- Teams in organizations serve different purposes—some teams run things, some teams recommend things, and some teams make or do things.

- Organizations consist of formal teams that are designated by the organization to serve an official purpose and informal groups that emerge from special interests and relationships but are not part of an organization's formal structure.

- Organizations can be viewed as interlocking networks of permanent teams such as project teams and cross-functional teams, as well as temporary teams such as committees and task forces.

- Virtual teams, whose members meet and work together through computer mediation, are increasingly common and pose special management challenges.

- Members of self-managing teams typically plan, complete, and evaluate their own work, train and evaluate one another in job tasks, and share tasks and responsibilities.

When is a team effective?

- An effective team achieves high levels of task accomplishment, member satisfaction, and viability to perform successfully over the long term.

- Teams help organizations through synergy in task performance, the creation of a whole that is greater than the sum of its parts.

- Teams help satisfy important needs for their members by providing them with things like job support and social interactions.

- Team performance can suffer from social loafing when a member slacks off and lets others do the work.

- Social facilitation occurs when the behavior of individuals is influenced positively or negatively by the presence of others in a team.

What are the stages of team development?

- Teams pass through various stages of development during their life cycles, and each stage poses somewhat distinct management problems.

- In the forming stage, team members first come together and form initial impressions; it is a time of task orientation and interpersonal testing.

- In the storming stage, team members struggle to deal with expectations and status; it is a time when conflicts over tasks and how the team works are likely.

- In the norming or initial integration stage, team members start to come together around rules of behavior and what needs to be accomplished; it is a time of growing cooperation.

- In the performing or total integration stage, team members are well-organized and well-functioning; it is a time of team maturity when performance of even complex tasks becomes possible.

- In the adjourning stage, team members achieve closure on task performance and their personal relationships; it is a time of managing task completion and the process of disbanding.

How do teams work?

- Teams are open systems that interact with their environments to obtain resources that are transformed into outputs.

- The equation summarizing the implications of the open systems model for team performance is: Team Effectiveness = Quality of Inputs $\times$ (Process Gains $-$ Process Losses).

- Input factors such as resources and organizational setting, the nature of the task, team size, and team composition, establish the core performance foundations of a team.

- Team processes include basic group dynamics, the way members work together to use inputs and complete tasks.

- Important team processes include member entry, task and maintenance leadership, roles and role dynamics, norms, cohesiveness, communications, decision making, conflict, and negotiation.

Key Terms

Cross-functional team (p. 159)
Diversity–consensus dilemma (p. 172)
Effective team (p. 163)
Employee involvement team (p. 160)
FIRO-B theory (p. 171)
Formal teams (p. 158)
Functional silos problem (p. 159)

Group dynamics (p. 173)
Heterogeneous teams (p. 171)
Homogeneous teams (p. 171)
Informal groups (p. 158)
Multiskilling (p. 161)
Problem-solving team (p. 159)
Quality circle (p. 160)
Self-managing team (p. 161)
Social facilitation (p. 164)

Social loafing (p. 164)
Social network analysis (p. 159)
Status congruence (p. 171)
Synergy (p. 163)
Team (p. 156)
Teamwork (p. 156)
Virtual team (p. 160)

Self-Test 7

Multiple Choice

1. The FIRO-B theory deals with _____ in teams. (a) membership compatibilities (b) social loafing (c) dominating members (d) conformity

2. It is during the _____ stage of team development that members begin to come together as a coordinated unit. (a) storming (b) norming (c) performing (d) total integration

3. An effective team is defined as one that achieves high levels of task performance, member satisfaction, and _____. (a) coordination (b) harmony (c) creativity (d) team viability

4. Task characteristics, reward systems, and team size are all _____ that can make a difference in group effectiveness. (a) group processes (b) group dynamics (c) group inputs (d) human resource maintenance factors

5. The best size for a problem-solving team is usually _____ members. (a) no more than 3 or 4 (b) 5 to 7 (c) 8 to 10 (d) around 12 to 13

6. When a new team member is anxious about questions such as "Will I be able to influence what takes place?" the underlying issue is one of _____. (a) relationships (b) goals (c) processes (d) control

7. Self-managing teams _____. (a) reduce the number of different job tasks members need to master (b) largely eliminate the need for a traditional supervisor (c) rely heavily on outside training to maintain job skills (d) add another management layer to overhead costs

8. Which statement about self-managing teams is correct? (a) They can improve perform-ance but not satisfaction. (b) They should have limited decision-making authority.

(c) They should operate without any team leaders. (d) They should let members plan their own work schedules.

9. When a team of people is able to achieve more than what its members could by working individually, this is called _____. (a) distributed leadership (b) consensus (c) team viability (d) synergy

10. Members of a team tend to become more motivated and better able to deal with conflict during the _____ stage of team development. (a) forming (b) norming (c) performing (d) adjourning

11. The Ringlemann effect describes _____. (a) the tendency of groups to make risky decisions (b) social loafing (c) social facilitation (d) the satisfaction of members' social needs

12. Members of a multinational task force in a large international business should probably be aware that _____ might initially slow the progress of the team in meeting its task objectives. (a) synergy (b) groupthink (c) the diversity-consensus dilemma (d) intergroup dynamics

13. When a team member engages in social loafing, one of the recommended strategies for dealing with this situation is to _____. (a) forget about it (b) ask another member to force this person to work harder (c) give the person extra rewards and hope he or she will feel guilty (d) better define member roles to improve individual accountability

14. When a person holds a prestigious position as a vice president in a top management team, but is considered just another member of an employee involvement team that a lower-level supervisor heads, the person might experience _____. (a) role underload (b) role overload (c) status incongruence (d) the diversity–consensus dilemma

15. The team effectiveness equation states: team effectiveness = _____ + (process gains − process losses). (a) nature of setting (b) nature of task (c) quality of inputs (d) available rewards.

Short Response

16. In what ways are teams good for organizations?
17. What types of formal teams are found in organizations today?
18. What is the difference between required and emergent behaviors in group dynamics?
19. What are members of self-managing teams typically expected to do?

Applications Essay

20. One of your Facebook friends has posted this note. "Help! I have just been assigned to head a new product design team at my company. The division manager has high expectations for the team and me, but I have been a technical design engineer for four years since graduating from college. I have never 'managed' anyone, let alone led a team. The manager keeps talking about her confidence that I will be very good at creating lots of teamwork. Does anyone out there have any tips to help me master this challenge? Help!" You smile while reading the message and start immediately to formulate your recommendations. Exactly what message will you send?

8

Teamwork and Team Performance

chapter at a glance

To get the best teamwork you have to build teams with strong team processes. Here's what to look for in Chapter 8. Don't forget to check your learning with the Summary Questions & Answers and Self-Test in the end-of-chapter Study Guide.

HOW CAN WE CREATE HIGH-PERFORMANCE TEAMS?

Characteristics of High-Performance Teams

The Team-Building Process

Team-Building Alternatives

HOW CAN TEAM PROCESSES BE IMPROVED?

Entry of New Members

Task and Maintenance Leadership

Roles and Role Dynamics

Team Norms

Team Cohesiveness

Inter-Team Dynamics

HOW CAN TEAM COMMUNICATIONS BE IMPROVED?

Communication Networks

Proxemics and Use of Space

Communication Technologies

HOW CAN TEAM DECISIONS BE IMPROVED?

Ways Teams Make Decisions

Assets and Liabilities of Team Decisions

Groupthink Symptoms and Remedies

Team Decision Techniques

When you hear the name Toyota you might automatically think of cars, but manufacturing and selling high quality vehicles is just one part of what Toyota Industries Corporation does.

Established in 1926 to manufacture and market an automatic loom, the company gradually expanded to other products and markets. Today, it is involved in the manufacture and sales of textile machinery, automobiles, materials handling equipment, electronics, and logistics.

Toyota is an established name when it comes to teamwork. Organizations throughout the world have studied and incorporated the lessons from Toyota's successful implementation of the Kaizen philosophy.

A cornerstone of the Total Quality Management movement, Kaizen derives from the Japanese words Kai "*change*" and zen "*[good] improvement*". Essentially the Kaizen philosophy involves managers facilitating groups of employees to address quality issues.

Another important concept for Toyota is Jishuken (pronounced jee-shoe-ken), a lesser known quality tool. Here the focus is on autonomous self-study groups driven by teams of managers. The term Jishuken is translated as "*self-study*" groups.

Jishuken "is a highly collaborative enterprise. Its success rests on your willingness, energy and drive to do your own homework so that you are pushed to the edge of your ability and are therefore receptive and positioned to benefit from feedback, critique and coaching."

That's because teams within a particular department or division first rigorously analyze the issue at hand. When a particularly difficult and complex problem cannot be solved, a team from across the organization is assembled and visits the location. The host team debriefs the visitors on the issue and their problem-solving approach. The visiting team then reviews the information (including the process used) and offers its expertise.

This approach to teamwork has been quite successful for Toyota and is a model for other organizations interested in collaborative techniques to increase team performance.

teams make the difference at toyota industries

High-Performance Teams

Are you an iPod, iPhone, iTouch, or iMac user? Have you ever wondered who and what launched Apple, Inc. on the pathway to giving us a stream of innovative and trendsetting products? We might say that the story started with Apple's co-founder Steve Jobs, the first Macintosh computer, and a very special team. The "Mac" was Jobs's brainchild; and to create it he put together a team of high-achievers who were excited and turned on to a highly challenging task. They worked all hours and at an unrelenting pace, while housed in a separate building flying the Jolly Roger. To display their independence from Apple's normal bureaucracy, the MacIntosh team combined youthful enthusiasm with great expertise and commitment to an exciting goal. In the process they set a new benchmark for product innovation as well as new standards for what makes for a high-performance team.[1]

The Apple story and the opening vignette on Toyota's team-building are interesting examples of how teams and teamwork can be harnessed to stimulate innovations. But let's not forget that there are a lot of solid contributions made by good, old-fashioned, everyday teams in organizations as well—the cross-functional, problem-solving, virtual, and self-managing teams introduced in the last chapter. We also need to remember, as scholar J. Richard Hackman points out, that many teams underperform and fail to live up to their potential; they simply, as Hackman says, "don't work."[2] The question becomes: What differentiates high performing teams from the also-rans?

Characteristics of High-Performance Teams

Some "must have" team leadership skills are described in OB Savvy 8.1. And it's appropriate that "setting a clear and challenging direction" is at the top of the list.[3] Whatever the purpose or tasks, the foundation for any high performing team is a set of members who believe in team goals and are motivated to work hard to accomplish them. Indeed, an essential criterion of a high-performance team is that the members feel "collectively accountable" for moving together in what Hackman calls "a compelling direction" toward a goal. Yet, he points out that in "most" teams, members don't agree on the goal and don't share an understanding of what the team is supposed to accomplish.[4]

High-performance teams also are able to turn a general sense of purpose into specific performance objectives. Whereas a shared sense of purpose gives general direction to a team, commitment to targeted performance results makes this purpose truly meaningful. Specific objectives provide a clear focus for solving problems and resolving conflicts. They also set standards for measuring results and obtaining performance feedback. And they help group members understand the need for collective versus purely individual efforts. Again, the Macintosh story sets an example. In November, 1983, *Wired* magazine's correspondent Steven Levy was given a sneak look at what he had been told was the "machine that was

---

OB SAVVY 8.1

"Must Have" Contributions by Team Leaders

- Setting a clear and challenging direction
- Keeping goals and expectations clear
- Communicating high standards
- Creating a sense of urgency
- Ensuring members have the right skills
- Establishing rules for behavior
- Modeling expected behaviors
- Creating early "successes"
- Introducing useful information
- Helping members spend time together
- Giving positive feedback

supposed to change the world." He says: "I also met the people who cre-ated that machine. They were groggy and almost giddy from three years of creation. Their eyes blazed with Visine and fire. They told me that with Macintosh, they were going to "put a dent in the Universe." Their leader, Steven P. Jobs, told them so. They also told me how Jobs referred to this new computer: 'Insanely Great.'" [5]

Members of high-performance teams have the right mix of skills, in-cluding technical, problem-solving, decision-making, and interpersonal skills. A high-performance team has strong core values that help guide team members' attitudes and behaviors in directions consistent with the team's pur-pose. Such values act as an internal control system for a group or team that can substitute for outside direction and supervisory attention.

Team Composition

Members of high performing teams have skill sets–technical, problem-solving, and interpersonal–that match well with task demands.

The Team-Building Process

In order to create and maintain high-performance teams, all elements of the open systems model of team effectiveness discussed in the last chapter must be ad-dressed and successfully managed. Teamwork doesn't always happen naturally when a group of people comes together to work on a task; it is something that team members and leaders must work hard to achieve.

In the sports world coaches and managers spend a lot of time at the start of each season to join new members with old ones and form a strong team. Yet we all know that even the most experienced teams can run into problems as a season progresses. Members slack off or become disgruntled with one another; some have performance "slumps" and others criticize them for it; some are traded gladly or unhappily to other teams. Even world-champion teams have losing streaks, and the most talented players can lose motivation at times, quibble among themselves, and end up contributing little to team success. When these things happen, concerned owners, managers, and players are apt to examine their problems, take corrective action to rebuild the team, and restore the teamwork needed to achieve high-performance results.[6]

Workgroups and teams face similar challenges. When newly formed, they must master many challenges as members learn how to work together while passing through the stages of team development. Even when mature, most work teams encounter problems of insufficient teamwork at different points in time. At the very least we can say that teams sometimes need help to perform well and that teamwork always needs to be nurtured. This is why a process known as **team-building** is so important. It is a sequence of planned activities designed to gather and analyze data on the functioning of a team and to initiate changes de-signed to improve teamwork and increase team effectiveness.[7] When done well and at the right times, team-building is an effective way to deal with teamwork problems or to help prevent them from occurring in the first place.

• **Team-building** is a collaborative way to gather and analyze data to improve teamwork.

The action steps for team-building are highlighted in Figure 8.1. Although it is tempting to view the process as something that consultants or outside experts are hired to do, the fact is that it can and should be part of any team leader and man-ager's action repertoire. Team-building begins when someone notices an actual or a potential problem with team effectiveness. Data is gathered to examine the prob-lem. This can be done by questionnaire, interview, nominal group meeting, or other creative methods. The goal is to get good answers to such questions as: "How well are we doing in terms of task accomplishment?" "How satisfied are we

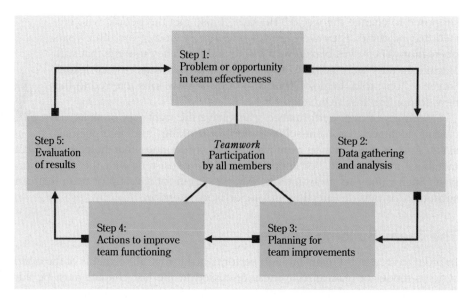

Figure 8.1 Steps in the team-building process.

as individuals with the group and the way it operates?" Members then work together to analyze the data, plan for improvements, and implement the action plans.

Note that the entire team-building process is highly collaborative. Everyone is expected to participate actively as team functioning is assessed and decisions are made on what needs to be done to improve team performance in the future.

Seagate Technologies

CEO Bill Watkins takes team-building to the extreme. At Eco Seagate in New Zealand employees engage in kayaking, cycling, swimming, and cliff rappelling. They also join in a haka dance with everyone chanting "Seagate is powerful" in the Maori language.

Team-Building Alternatives

Team-building can be accomplished in a wide variety of ways. In the *formal retreat approach*, team-building takes place during an off-site "retreat." The agenda, which may cover from one to several days, is designed to engage team members in a variety of assessment and planning tasks. These are initiated by a review of team functioning using data gathered through survey, interviews, or other means. Formal retreats are often held with the assistance of a consultant, who is either hired from the outside or made available from in-house staff. Team-building retreats offer opportunities for intense and concentrated efforts to examine group accomplishments and operations.

The *outdoor experience approach* is an increasingly popular team-building activity that may be done on its own or in combination with other approaches. It places group members in a variety of physically challenging situations that must be mastered through teamwork, not through individual work. By having to work together in the face of difficult obstacles, team members are supposed to experience increased self-confidence, more respect for others' capabilities, and a greater commitment to teamwork. On one fall day, for example, a team of employees from American Electric Power (AEP) went to an outdoor camp for a day of team-building activities. They worked on problems like how to get six members through a spider-web maze of bungee cords strung 2 feet above the ground. When her colleagues lifted Judy Gallo into their hands to pass her over the obstacle, she was nervous. But a trainer told the team this was just like solving a problem together at the office. The spider Web was just another performance constraint, like the difficult policy issues or financial limits they might face at work. After "high-fives" for making it through the Web, Judy's team jumped tree stumps together, passed hula hoops while holding hands, and more. Says one team trainer, "We throw clients into situations to try and bring out the traits of a good team."[8]

Not all team-building is done at a formal retreat or with the assistance of outside consultants. In a *continuous improvement approach*, the manager, team leader, or group members themselves take responsibility for regularly engaging in the team-building process. This method can be as simple as periodic meetings that implement the team-building steps; it can also include self-managed formal retreats. In all cases, the team members commit themselves to continuously monitoring group development and accomplishments and making the day-to-day changes needed to ensure team effectiveness. Such continuous improvement of teamwork is essential to the themes of total quality and total service management so important to organizations today.

Improving Team Processes

As more and more jobs are turned over to teams, and as more and more traditional supervisors are asked to function as team leaders, special problems relating to team processes may arise. Team leaders and members alike must be prepared to deal positively with such issues as introducing new members, handling disagreements on goals and responsibilities, resolving delays and disputes when making decisions, reducing friction, and dealing with interpersonal conflicts. These are all targets for team-building. And given the complex nature of group dynamics, team-building is, in a sense, never finished. Something is always happening that creates the need for further leadership efforts to help improve team processes.

Entry of New Members

Special difficulties are likely to occur when members first get together in a new group or team, or when new members join an existing team. Problems arise as new members try to understand what is expected of them while dealing with the anxiety and discomfort of a new social setting. New members, for example, may worry about the following issues.

- *Participation*—"Will I be allowed to participate?"
- *Goals*—"Do I share the same goals as others?"
- *Control*—"Will I be able to influence what takes place?"
- *Relationships*—"How close do people get?"
- *Processes*—"Are conflicts likely to be upsetting?"

Edgar Schein points out that people may try to cope with individual entry problems in self-serving ways that may hinder team development and performance.[9] He identifies three behavior profiles that are common in such situations.

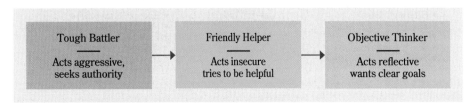

The *tough battler* is frustrated by a lack of identity in the new group and may act aggressively or reject authority. This person wants answers to this question: "Who am I in this group?" The best team response may be to allow the new member to share his or her skills and interests, and then have a discussion about how they can best be used to help the team. The *friendly helper* is insecure, suffering uncertainties of intimacy and control. This person may show extraordinary support for others, behave in a dependent way, and seek alliances in subgroups or cliques. The friendly helper needs to know whether he or she will be liked. The best team response may be to offer support and encouragement while encouraging the new member to be more confident in joining team activities and discussions. The *objective thinker* is anxious about how personal needs will be met in the group. This person may act in a passive, reflective, and even single-minded manner while struggling with the fit between individual goals and group directions. The best team response may be to engage in a discussion to clarify team goals and expectations, and to clarify member roles in meeting them.

Task and Maintenance Leadership

Research in social psychology suggests that teams have both "task needs" and "maintenance needs," and that both must be met for teams to be successful.[10] Even though a team leader should be able to meet these needs at the appropriate times, each team member is responsible as well. This sharing of responsibilities for making task and maintenance contributions that move a group forward is called **distributed leadership**, and it is usually well evidenced in high-performance teams.

Figure 8.2 describes **task activities** as the various things team members and leaders do that directly contribute to the performance of important group tasks. They include initiating discussion, sharing information, asking information of others, clarifying something that has been said, and summarizing the status of a deliberation.[11] A team will have difficulty accomplishing its objectives when task activities are not well performed. In an effective team, by contrast, members pitch in to contribute important task leadership as needed.

The figure also shows that **maintenance activities** support the social and interpersonal relationships among team members. They help a team stay intact and healthy as an ongoing and well-functioning social system. A team member or leader can contribute maintenance leadership by encouraging the participation of others, trying to harmonize differences of opinion, praising the contributions of others, and agreeing to go along with a popular course of action. When maintenance leadership is poor, members become dissatisfied with one another, the value of their group membership diminishes, and emotional conflicts may drain energies otherwise needed for task performance. In an effective team, by

- **Distributed leadership** is the sharing of responsibility for meeting group task and maintenance needs.
- **Task activities** directly contribute to the performance of important tasks.
- **Maintenance activities** support the emotional life of the team as an ongoing social system.

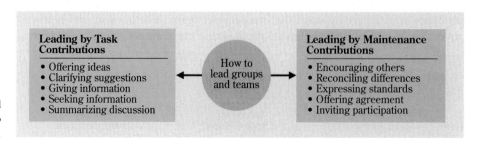

Figure 8.2 Task and Maintenance Leadership in Team Dynamics.

contrast, maintenance activities support the relationships needed for team members to work well together over time.

In addition to helping meet a group's task and maintenance needs, team members share additional responsibility for avoiding and eliminating any **disruptive behaviors** that harm the group process. These dysfunctional activities include bullying and being overly aggressive toward other members, withdrawing and refusing to cooperate with others, horsing around when there is work to be done, using the group as a forum for self-confession, talking too much about irrelevant matters, and trying to compete for attention and recognition. *Incivility* or *antisocial behavior* by members can be especially disruptive of team dynamics and performance. Research shows that persons who are targets of harsh leadership, social exclusion, and harmful rumors often end up working less hard, performing less well, being late and absent more, and reducing their commitment.[12]

Roles and Role Dynamics

In groups and teams, new and old members alike need to know what others expect of them and what they can expect from others. A **role** is a set of expectations associated with a job or position on a team. When team members are unclear about their roles or experience conflicting role demands, performance problems can occur. Although this is a common problem, it can be managed through awareness of role dynamics and their causes. Simply put, teams tend to perform better when their members have clear and realistic expectations regarding their tasks and responsibilities.

Role ambiguity occurs when a person is uncertain about his or her role in a job or on a team. In new group or team situations, role ambiguities may create problems as members find that their work efforts are wasted or unappreciated by others. Even in mature groups and teams, the failure of members to share expectations and listen to one another may, at times, create a similar lack of understanding.

Being asked to do too much or too little as a team member can also create problems. **Role overload** occurs when too much is expected and someone feels overwhelmed. **Role underload** is just the opposite; it occurs when too little is expected and the individual feels underused. Both role overload and role underload can cause stress, dissatisfaction, and performance problems.

Role conflict occurs when a person is unable to meet the expectations of others. The individual understands what needs to be done but for some reason cannot comply. The resulting tension is stressful, and can reduce satisfaction; it can affect an individual's performance and relationships with other group members. There are four common forms of role conflict that people at work and in teams can experience.

1. *Intrasender role conflict* occurs when the same person sends conflicting expectations. Example: Team leader—"You need to get the report written right away, but I need you to help me with the Power Point presentation."
2. *Intersender role conflict* occurs when different people signal conflicting and mutually exclusive expectations. Example: Team leader (to you)—"Your job is to criticize our decisions so that we don't make mistakes." Team member (to you)—"You always seem so negative, can't you be more positive for a change?"
3. *Person-role conflict* occurs when a person's values and needs come into conflict with role expectations. Example: Other team members (showing

- **Disruptive behaviors** in teams harm the group process and limit team effectiveness.

- A **role** is a set of expectations for a team member or person in a job.

- **Role ambiguity** occurs when someone is uncertain about what is expected of him or her.

- **Role overload** occurs when too much work is expected of the individual.

- **Role underload** occurs when too little work is expected of the individual.

- **Role conflict** occurs when someone is unable to respond to role expectations that conflict with one another.

American Psychological Association

An APA survey finds that 35 percent of employed Americans experience stress because work interferes with family responsibilities or personal time. Only 28 percent say they are managing stress "extremely well" and 54 percent say stress causes them to fight with people close to them.

agreement with each other)—"We didn't get enough questionnaires back, so quickly everyone just make up two additional ones." You (to yourself)—"Mmm, I don't think this is right."

4. *Inter-role conflict* occurs when the expectations of two or more roles held by the same individual become incompatible, such as the conflict between work and family demands. Example: Team leader—"Don't forget the big meeting we have scheduled for Thursday evening." You (to yourself)—"But my daughter is playing in her first little-league soccer game at that same time."

• **Role negotiation** is a process for discussing and agreeing upon what team members expect of one another.

A technique known as **role negotiation** is a helpful team-building activity for managing role dynamics. This is a process in which team members meet to discuss, clarify, and agree upon the role expectations each holds for the other. Such a negotiation might begin, for example, with one member writing down this request of another: "If you were to do the following, it would help me to improve my performance on the team." Her list of requests might include such things as: "respect it when I say that I can't meet some evenings because I have family obligations to fulfill"—indicating role conflict; "stop asking for so much detail when we are working hard with tight deadlines"—indicating role overload; and "try to make yourself available when I need to speak with you to clarify goals and expectations"—indicating role ambiguity.

Team Norms

The role dynamics we have just discussed develop in large part from conflicts and concerns regarding what team members expect of one another and of themselves. This brings up the issue of team **norms**—the ideas or beliefs about how members are expected to behave. They can be considered as rules or standards of conduct that are supposed to guide team members.[13] Norms help members to guide their own behavior and predict what others will do. When someone violates a team norm, other members typically respond in ways that are aimed at enforcing it and bringing behavior back into alignment with the norm. These responses may include subtle hints, direct criticisms, or reprimands; at the extreme someone violating team norms may be ostracized or even be expelled.

• **Norms** are rules or standards for the behavior of group members.

Deadly Meetings

Sins of deadly meetings: meeting scheduled in the wrong place; meeting scheduled at a bad time; people arrive late; meeting is too long; people go off topic; discussion lacks candor; right information not available; no follow-through when meeting is over.

Types of Team Norms   A key norm in any team setting is the *performance norm* that conveys expectations about how hard team members should work and what the team should accomplish. In some teams the performance norm is strong; there is no doubt that all members are expected to work very hard, that high performance is the goal, and if someone slacks off they get reminded to work hard or end up removed from the team. In other teams the performance norm is weak; members are left to work hard or not as they like, with little concern expressed by the other members.

The best case for any manager is to be leading work teams with high performance norms. But many other norms also influence the day-to-day functioning of teams. In order for a task force or a committee to operate effectively, for example, norms regarding attendance at meetings, punctuality, preparedness, criticism, and social behavior are needed. Teams also commonly have norms regarding how to deal with supervisors, colleagues, and customers, as well as norms establishing guidelines for honesty and ethical behaviors. You can often find norms being expressed in everyday conversations. The following examples show the types of norms that operate with positive and negative implications for teams and organizations.[14]

COACH PUTS PLAYERS IN CHARGE OF BEHAVIOR PROBLEMS

Don't take those high steps in the end zone if you want to play football at Ohio State University. That's the message of head coach Jim Tressel. Doing a great job on the field is one thing, and celebrating accomplishments as a team is fine as well. But step out too high, as Antonio Smith did in a game against Penn State, and you will feel the coach's wrath. Says Tressel: "We talk a lot about handing the ball to the official and find the other 10 guys that made it possible and celebrate with them."

Misbehavior by college athletes, on and off the field, is a much discussed topic. Tressel believes it's a problem that is best tackled within the team and by team leadership. His coaching model is to call the senior players together and give them the task of making sure teammates act properly at all times, in other words set and enforce the right norms. The school's athletic director says this approach works by "putting the accountability in the locker room . . . so players police themselves." It's also classic Tressel: creating a team that he describes as caring "for one another from top to bottom, side to side and all be pulling the oars in the same direction."

From the Sidelines *When there's bad behavior by members of a team or organization, who is responsible—the individuals involved, the team members, or the manager? Does Tressel's approach to self-policing on the football team have carry-over lessons for the world of work? Can managers do more to harness the power of team norms to support ethics and ethical behavior at work?*

- *Ethics norms*—"We try to make ethical decisions, and we expect others to do the same" (positive); "Don't worry about inflating your expense account; everyone does it here" (negative).
- *Organizational and personal pride norms*—"It's a tradition around here for people to stand up for the company when others criticize it unfairly" (positive); "In our company, they are always trying to take advantage of us" (negative).
- *High-achievement norms*—"On our team, people always try to work hard" (positive); "There's no point in trying harder on our team; nobody else does" (negative).
- *Support and helpfulness norms*—"People on this committee are good listeners and actively seek out the ideas and opinions of others" (positive); "On this committee it's dog-eat-dog and save your own skin" (negative).
- *Improvement and change norms*—"In our department people are always looking for better ways of doing things" (positive); "Around here, people hang on to the old ways even after they have outlived their usefulness" (negative).

How to Influence Team Norms   There are several things managers and team leaders can do to help their teams develop and operate with positive norms, ones that foster high performance as well as membership satisfaction. The first thing is to always *act as a positive role model*. In other words, the team leader should be the exemplar of the norm; always demonstrating it in his or her everyday behavior as part of the team. It is helpful to hold meetings where time is set aside for members to *discuss team goals* and also *discuss team norms* that can best contribute to their achievement. Norms are too important to be left to chance; the more directly they are discussed and confronted in the early stages of team development the better.

Team leaders should always try to *select members who can and will live up to the desired norms*; they should *provide training and support* so that members are able to live up to them; and they should *reward and positively reinforce desired behaviors*. This is a full-cycle approach to team norm development— select the right people, give them training and support, and then make sure that rewards and positive reinforcements are contingent on doing the right things while on the team. Finally, team leaders should *hold regular meetings to discuss team performance and plan how to improve it* in the future.

Team Cohesiveness

• **Cohesiveness** is the degree to which members are attracted to a group and motivated to remain a part of it.

The **cohesiveness** of a group or team is the degree to which members are attracted to and motivated to remain part of it.[15] We might think of it as the "feel good" factor that causes people to value their membership on a team, positively identify with it, and strive to maintain positive relationships with other members. Because cohesive teams are such a source of personal satisfaction, their members tend to display fairly predictable behaviors that differentiate them from members of less cohesive teams—they are more energetic when working on team activities, less likely to be absent, less likely to quit the team, and more likely to be happy about performance success and sad about failures. Cohesive teams are able to satisfy a broad range of individual needs, often providing a source of loyalty, security, and esteem for their members.

• **Rule of conformity** is the greater the cohesiveness the greater the conformity of members to team norms.

Team Cohesiveness and Conformity to Norms Even though cohesive groups are good for their members, they may or may not be good for the organization. The issue is performance: will the cohesive team also be a high-performance team? The answer to this question depends on the match of cohesiveness with performance norms. And the guiding **rule of conformity** in team dynamics is: The greater the cohesiveness of a team, the greater the conformity of members to team norms. You can remember it this way:

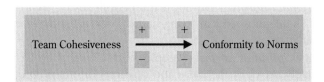

Figure 8.3 shows the performance implications of this rule of conformity. When the performance norms are positive in a highly cohesive work group or team, the resulting conformity to the norm should have a positive effect on both team performance and member satisfaction. This is a best-case situation for team members, the team leader, and the organization. When the performance norms are negative in a highly cohesive group, however, the same power of conformity creates a worst-case situation for the team leader and the organization. Although the high cohesiveness leaves the team members feeling loyal and satisfied, they are also highly motivated to conform to the negative performance norm. In this situation the team is good for the members but performs poorly. In between these two extremes are two mixed-case situations for teams low in cohesion. Because there is little conformity to either the positive or negative norm, member behaviors will vary and team performance will most likely fall on the moderate or low side.

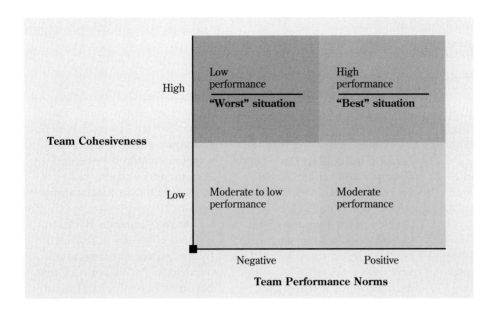

Figure 8.3 How cohesiveness and conformity to norms influence team performance.

How to Influence Team Cohesiveness   What can a manager or team leader do to tackle the worst-case and mixed-case scenarios just described? The answer rests with some basic understandings about the factors influencing team cohesiveness. Cohesiveness tends to be high when teams are more homogeneous in make-up, that is, when members are similar in age, attitudes, needs, and backgrounds. Cohesiveness also tends to be high in teams of small size, where members respect one another's competencies, agree on common goals, and work together rather than alone on team tasks. And cohesiveness tends to increase when groups are physically isolated from others and when they experience performance success or crisis.

Figure 8.4 shows how team cohesiveness can be increased or decreased by making changes in such things as goals, membership composition, interactions,

How to Decrease Cohesion	TARGETS	How to Increase Cohesion
Create disagreement	Goals	Get agreement
Increase heterogeneity	Membership	Increase homogeneity
Restrict within team	Interactions	Enhance within team
Make team bigger	Size	Make team smaller
Focus within team	Competition	Focus on other teams
Reward individual results	Rewards	Reward team results
Open up to other teams	Location	Isolate from other teams
Disband the team	Duration	Keep team together

Figure 8.4 Ways to increase and decrease team cohesiveness.

Leaders on Leadership

GRAMEEN BANK THRIVES ON POWER OF TEAMS

A world without poverty is a dream that Muhammad Yunus, Nobel Prize winner and noted social entrepreneur from Bangladesh, has long been pursuing. He's CEO of Grameen Bank, an innovator in microfinance that provides loans to poor people with no collateral. A large part of the global population, at least a billion people, lives chronically hungry and in poverty on less than one dollar per day. And two-thirds of the world's population has no access to banks.

Yunus says: "The way the banking institutions have been designed and built is based on certain criteria which poor people don't fulfill." He developed the Grameen Bank to help poor people start small businesses and try to work their way out of poverty. Recognizing that many poor people couldn't get regular bank loans because they didn't have sufficient collateral, Yunus

came up with the "micro credit" idea to lend small amounts of money at very low interest rates with the goal of promoting self-sufficiency through operating small enterprises.

By design the vast majority of loan recipients, 97 percent, are women. Yunus says: ". . . we saw real benefits of money going straight to women—children benefited directly and women had long-term vision for escaping poverty."

At the Grameen Bank, traditional collateral is replaced by the power of teams and teamwork. Each loan recipient becomes part of a local team of similar borrowers who agree to support and encourage one another. Loans are paid off in weekly installments, and a borrower only gets another loan when the first is paid off successfully. The team tries to make sure that everyone does just that. And, the system works. Grameen Bank has loaned over $7.5 billion to date, and the repayment rate is 98 percent.

size, rewards, competition, location, and duration. When the team norms are positive but cohesiveness is lacking, the goal is to take actions to increase cohesion and gain more conformity to the positive norms. But when team norms are negative and cohesiveness is high, just the opposite may have to be done. The goal in this situation is to reduce cohesiveness and thus reduce conformity to the negative norms. Finally, it should be remembered that team norms can be positively influenced to harness the power of conformity in teams that are already cohesive or in those where cohesion is being rebuilt or strengthened.

Inter-Team Dynamics

• **Inter-team dynamics** are relationships between groups cooperating and competing with one another.

In the prior discussion it was pointed out that the presence of competition with other teams tends to create more cohesiveness within a team. This raises the issue of what happens between, not just within, teams. The term **inter-team dynamics** refers to the dynamics that take place between two or more teams in these and other similar situations. Organizations ideally operate as cooperative

RESEARCH INSIGHT

Demographic Faultlines Pose Implications for Managing Teams in Organizations

According to researchers Dora Lau and Keith Murnighan, strong "fault-lines" occur in groups when demographic diversity results in the formation of two or more subgroups whose members are similar to and strongly identify with one another. Examples include teams with subgroups forming around age, gender, race, ethnic, occupational, or tenure differences. When strong faultlines are present, members are expected to identify more strongly with their subgroups than with the team as a whole. Lau and Murnighan predict that this will affect what happens with the team in terms of conflict, politics, and performance.

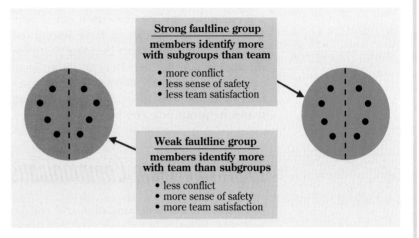

Strong faultline group
members identify more with subgroups than team
- more conflict
- less sense of safety
- less team satisfaction

Weak faultline group
members identify more with team than subgroups
- less conflict
- more sense of safety
- more team satisfaction

Using subjects from 10 organizational behavior classes at a university, the researchers randomly assigned students to case-work groups based on sex and ethnicity. After working on their cases, group members completed questionnaires about group processes and outcomes. Results showed, as predicted, that members in strong faultline groups evaluated those in their subgroups more favorably than did members of weak faultline groups. Members of weak faultline groups also experienced less conflict, more psychological safety, and more satisfaction than did those in strong faultline groups. More communication across faultlines had a positive effect on outcomes for weak fault-line groups but not for strong faultline groups.

Check the Research

See if you can verify these findings. Be a "participant observer" in your work teams. Focus on faultlines and their effects. Keep a diary, make notes, and compare your experiences with this study in mind.

Source: Dora C. Lau and J. Keith Murnighan, "Interactions within Groups and Subgroups: The Effects of Demographic Faultlines," *Academy of Management Journal*, Vol. 48 (2005), pp. 645–659; and "Demographic Diversity and Faultlines: The Compositional Dynamics of Organizational Groups," *Academy of Management Review* 23 (1998), pp. 325–340.

systems in which the various components support one another. In the real world, however, competition and inter-team problems often develop within an organization and with mixed consequences.

On the negative side, such as when manufacturing and sales units don't get along, between-team dynamics may drain and divert energies because members spend too much time focusing on their animosities or conflicts with another team than on the performance of their own.[16] On the positive side, competition among teams can stimulate them to become more cohesive, work harder, become more focused on key tasks, develop more internal loyalty and satisfaction, or achieve a higher level of creativity in problem solving. This effect is demonstrated at virtually any intercollegiate athletic event, and it is common in work settings as well. Sony, for example, once rallied its workers around the slogan: "Beat Matsushita whatsoever."[17]

A variety of steps can be taken to avoid negative and achieve positive effects from inter-team dynamics. Teams engaged in destructive competition, for example, can be refocused on a common enemy or a common goal. Direct negotiations can be held among the teams. Members can also be engaged in intergroup team-building that brings about positive interactions and through which the members of different teams learn how to work more cooperatively together. Reward systems can also be refocused to emphasize team contributions to overall organizational performance and on how much teams help out one another.

Improving Team Communications

In Chapter 11 on communication and collaboration we provide extensive coverage of basic issues in interpersonal and organizational communication. The focus there is on such things as communication effectiveness, techniques for overcoming barriers and improving communication, information flows within organizations, and the use of collaborative communication technologies. And in teams, it is important to make sure that every member is strong and capable in basic communication and collaboration skills as discussed in Chapter 11. When the focus is on communication as a team process, the team-building questions are: What communication networks are being used by the team and why? How does space affect communication among team members? Is the team making good use of the available communication technologies?

Communication Networks

Three patterns typically emerge when team members interact with one another while working on team tasks—the interacting team, the co-acting team, and the counteracting team. Each is associated with a different communication network as shown in Figure 8.5.[18]

In order for a team to be effective and high-performing, the interaction pattern and communication network should fit well with the task at hand, ideally with the patterns and networks shifting as task demands develop and change over time. In fact, one of the most common mistakes discovered during team-building is that teams are not using the right interaction patterns and communication networks as they try to accomplish various tasks. An example might be a student project team whose members believe every member must always be present when any work gets done on the project; in other words, no one works on their own and everything is done together.

When task demands require intense interaction, this is best done with a **decentralized communication network**. Also called the *star network* or *all-channel network*, the basic characteristic is that everyone communicates as needed with everyone else; information flows back and forth constantly, with no one person serving as the center point.[19] This creates an interacting team in

• In **decentralized communication networks** members communicate directly with one another.

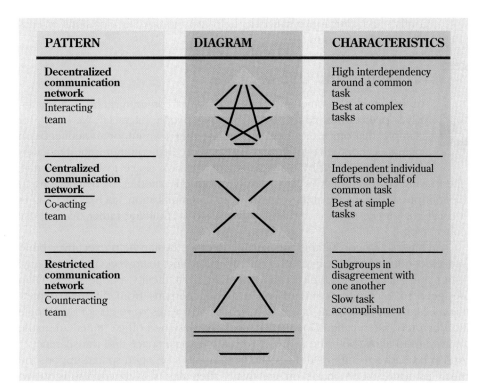

PATTERN	DIAGRAM	CHARACTERISTICS
Decentralized communication network Interacting team		High interdependency around a common task Best at complex tasks
Centralized communication network Co-acting team		Independent individual efforts on behalf of common task Best at simple tasks
Restricted communication network Counteracting team		Subgroups in disagreement with one another Slow task accomplishment

Figure 8.5 Communication networks and interaction patterns found in teams.

which all members communicate directly and share information with one another. Figure 8.5 indicates that decentralized communication networks work best when team tasks are complex and nonroutine, perhaps ones that involve uncertainty and require creativity. With success, member satisfaction on interacting teams is usually high.

When task demands allow for more independent work by team members, a **centralized communication network** is the best option. Also called the *wheel network* or *chain network*, its basic characteristic is the existence of a central "hub" through which one member, often the team leader, collects and distributes information among the other members. Members of such coaching teams work on assigned tasks independently while the hub keeps everyone linked together through some form of central coordination. Teams operating in this fashion divide up the work among members, who then work independently to complete their assigned tasks; results are passed to the hub member and pooled to create the finished product. The centralized network works best when team tasks are routine and easily subdivided. It is usually the hub member who experiences the most satisfaction on successful coaching teams.

Counteracting teams form when subgroups emerge within a team due to issue-specific disagreements, such as a temporary debate over the best means to achieve a goal, or emotional disagreements, such as personality clashes. In both cases a **restricted communication network** forms in which the subgroups contest each other's positions and restrict interactions with one another. The poor communication characteristic of such situations often creates problems, although there are times when counteracting teams might be set up to provide

• **Centralized communication networks** link group members through a central control point.

• **Restricted communication networks** link subgroups that disagree with one another's positions.

Space Counts

Organizations are making use of architects to create space designs and office layouts that facilitate rather then hinder teamwork.

- **Proxemics** involves the use of space as people interact.

- **Virtual communication networks** link team members through electronic communication.

conflict and critical evaluation to help test out specific decisions or chosen courses of action.

Proxemics and Use of Space

An important but sometimes neglected part of communication in teams involves **proxemics**, or the use of space as people interact.[20] We know, for example, that office or workspace architecture is an important influence on communication behavior. It only makes sense that communication in teams might be improved by either arranging physical space to best support it, like moving chairs and tables into proximity with one another, or by choosing to meet in physical spaces that are conducive to communication, such as meeting in a small conference room in the library or classroom building rather than a busy coffee shop.

Architects and consultants specializing in office design help executives build spaces conducive to the intense communication and teamwork needed today. When Sun Microsystems built its San Jose, California, facility, public spaces were designed to encourage communication among persons from different departments. Many meeting areas had no walls, and most walls were glass.[21] At Google headquarters, often called Googleplex, specially designed office "tents" are made of acrylics to allow both the sense of private personal space and transparency.[22] And at b&a advertising in Dublin, Ohio, an emphasis on open space supports the small ad agency's emphasis on creativity; after all, its Web address is www.babrain.com. Face-to-face communication is the rule at b&a to the point where internal e-mail among employees is banned. There are no offices or cubicles, and all office equipment is portable. Desks have wheels so that informal meetings can happen by people repositioning themselves for spontaneous collaboration. Even the formal meetings are held standing up in the company kitchen.[23]

Communication Technologies

It hardly seems necessary in the age of Facebook, Twitter, and YouTube to mention that teams now have access to many useful technologies that can facilitate communication and break down the need to be face-to-face all or most of the time. We live and work in an age of instant messaging, individual–individual and group chats, e-mail and voice-mail, tweets and texting, wikis, online discussions, videoconferencing, and more. We are networked socially 24-7 to the extent we want, and there's no reason the members of a team can't utilize the same technologies to good advantage.

In effect we can think of technology as allowing and empowering teams to use **virtual communication networks** in which team members can always be in electronic communication with one another as well as with a central database. In effect the team works in both physical space and in virtual space, with the results achieved in each contributing to overall team performance. Technology, such as an online discussion forum, acts as the "hub member" in the centralized communication network; simultaneously, through chats and tweets and more, it acts as an ever-present "electronic router" that links members of decentralized networks on an as-needed and always-ready basis. General Electric, for example, started a "Tweet Squad" to advise employees how social networking could be used to improve internal collaboration; the insurer MetLife has its own social network, connect.MetLife, which facilitates collaboration through a Facebook-like setting.[24]

Of course, and as mentioned in the last chapter, there are certain steps that need to be taken to make sure that virtual teams and communication technologies are as successful as possible—things like doing online team-building so that members get to know one another, learn about and identify team goals, and otherwise develop a sense of cohesiveness.[25] And we shouldn't forget the protocols and just everyday "manners" of using technology as part of teamwork. For example, Richard Anderson, CEO of Delta Airlines, says: "I don't think it's appropriate to use Blackberrys in meetings. You might as well have a newspaper and open the newspaper up in the middle of the meeting."[26] Might we say the same for the classroom?

Improving Team Decisions

One of the most important activities for any team is **decision making**, the process of choosing among alternative courses of action. The topic is so important that the entire next chapter is devoted to it. There is no doubt that the quality and timeliness of decisions made and the processes through which they are arrived at can have an important impact on team effectiveness. One of the issues addressed in team-building is how a team goes about making decisions and whether or not these choices are good or bad for team performance.

> **Decision making** is the process of choosing among alternative courses of action.

Ways Teams Make Decisions

Consider the many teams of which you have been and are a part. Just how do major decisions get made? Most often there's a lot more going on than meets the eye. Edgar Schein, a noted scholar and consultant, has worked extensively with teams to identify, analyze, and improve their decision processes.[27] He observes that teams may make decisions through any of the six methods shown in Figure 8.6—lack of response, authority rule, minority rule, majority rule, consensus, or unanimity.

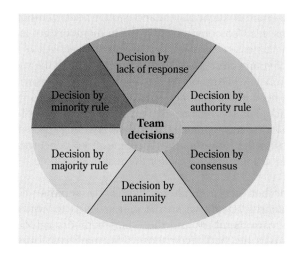

Figure 8.6 Alternative ways that teams make decisions.

Schein doesn't rule out any method, but he does point out the disadvantages that teams suffer when decisions are made without high levels of member involvement.

Lack of Response   In *decision by lack of response*, one idea after another is suggested without any discussion taking place. When the team finally accepts an idea, all others have been bypassed and discarded by simple lack of response rather than by critical evaluation. This may be most common early in a team's development when new members are struggling to find their identities and confidence in team deliberations; it's also common in teams with low-performance norms and when members just don't care enough to get involved in what is taking place. But whenever lack of response drives decisions, it's relatively easy for a team to move off in the wrong, or at least not the best, direction.

Authority Rule   In *decision by authority rule*, the chairperson, manager, or leader makes a decision for the team. This can be done with or without discussion and contributions by other members and is very time efficient. Whether the decision is a good one or a bad one depends on whether the authority figure has the necessary information and on how well other group members accept this approach. When the authority is also an expert, this decision approach can work well, assuming other members are willing to commit to the direction being set. But when an authority decision is made without expertise or member commitment, problems are likely.

Minority Rule   In *decision by minority rule*, two or three people are able to dominate, or "railroad," the group into making a decision with which they agree. This is often done by providing a suggestion and then forcing quick agreement by challenging the group with such statements as: "Does anyone object? . . . No? Well, let's go ahead then." While such forcing and bullying may get the team moving in a certain direction, the likelihood is that member commitment to making the decision successful will be low; "kickback" and "resistance," especially when things get difficult, aren't unusual in these situations.

Majority Rule   One of the most common ways that groups make decisions is *decision by majority rule*. This usually takes place as a formal vote with members being polled publicly or confidentially to find the majority viewpoint. This method parallels the democratic political system and is often used without awareness of its potential problems. It's also common when team members get into disagreements that seem irreconcilable; voting is seen to be an easy way out of the situation. But the very process of voting creates coalitions, especially when the voting is close. That is, some team members will turn out to be "winners" and others will be "losers" after votes are tallied. Those in the minority—the "losers"—may feel left out or discarded without having had a fair say. As a result, they may be less enthusiastic about implementing the decision of the "winners." And their lingering resentments may impair team effectiveness in the future as they become more concerned about winning the next vote than doing what is best for the team as a whole.

Consensus is a group decision that has the expressed support of most members.

Consensus   Another decision alternative is **consensus**. Formally defined, decision by consensus occurs when discussion leads to one alternative being favored by most team members and the other members agreeing to support it. When a consensus is reached, even those who may have opposed the chosen

MASTERING MANAGEMENT

SEVEN STEPS FOR ACHIEVING CONSENSUS

It's easy to say that consensus is good; it's a lot harder to strive for consensus as part of a group; it can be even harder to try to manage a group so that consensus is possible when tough decisions are needed. Here are some tips for personal behavior in consensus-seeking teams. These ideas will be of equal value to you as a leader with team members whom you hope to move toward consensus decisions.

1. Don't argue blindly; consider others' reactions to your points.
2. Be open and flexible, but don't change your mind just to reach quick agreement.
3. Avoid voting, coin tossing, and bargaining to avoid or reduce conflict.
4. Act in ways that encourage everyone's involvement in the decision process.
5. Allow disagreements to surface so that information and opinions can be deliberated.
6. Don't focus on winning versus losing; seek alternatives acceptable to all.
7. Discuss assumptions, listen carefully, and encourage participation by everyone.

course of action know that they have been listened to and have had a fair chance to influence the outcome. Consensus does not require unanimity. What it does require, as pointed out in Mastering Management, is the opportunity for any dissenting members to feel that they have been able to speak and that their voices have been heard.[28] Because of the extensive process involved in reaching a consensus decision, it may be inefficient from a time perspective, but it is very powerful in terms of generating commitments among members to making the final decision work best for the team.

Unanimity   A *decision by unanimity* may be the ideal state of affairs. Here, all team members agree totally on the course of action to be taken. This is a "logically perfect" decision situation that is extremely difficult to attain in actual practice. One reason that teams sometimes turn to authority decisions, majority voting, or even minority decisions, in fact, is the difficulty of managing the team process to achieve decisions by consensus or unanimity.

Assets and Liabilities of Team Decisions

Just as with communication networks, the best teams don't limit themselves to any one of the decision methods just described. More likely, they move back and forth among them but somehow tend to use each in circumstances that are most appropriate. In our cases for example, we never complain when a department head makes an authority decision to have a welcome reception for new majors at the start of the academic year or to call for a faculty vote on a proposed new travel policy—things we are content to "leave to the boss" so to speak. Yet, we are quick to disapprove when a department head makes an authority decision to hire a new faculty member—something we believe should be made by consensus.

The key for our department head and any team leader is to use and support decision methods that best fit the problems and situations at hand. Achieving the goal of making timely and quality decisions to which the members are highly committed,

Groupthink

There are times when otherwise well-intended team members place loyalty to the team above being critical when bad decisions are about to be made.

however, always requires a good understanding of the potential assets and liabilities of decision making.[29] On the positive side, the more team-oriented decision methods, such as consensus and unanimity, offer the advantages of bringing more information, knowledge, and expertise to bear on a problem. The discussion tends to create broader understanding of the final decision; this, in turn, increases acceptance and strengthens the commitments of members to follow through and support the decision. But on the negative side, the "team" aspect of such decisions can be imperfect. Social pressures to conform might make some members unwilling to go against or criticize what appears to be the will of the majority. In the guise of a team decision, furthermore, a team leader or a few members might "railroad" or "force" other members to accept their preferred decision. And there is a time cost to the more deliberative team decision methods. Simply put, it usually takes a team longer to make a decision than it does an individual.

Groupthink Symptoms and Remedies

- **Groupthink** is the tendency of cohesive group members to lose their critical evaluative capabilities.

An important potential problem that arises when teams try to make decisions is **groupthink**—the tendency of members in highly cohesive groups to lose their critical evaluative capabilities.[30] As identified by social psychologist Irving Janis, groupthink is a property of highly cohesive teams, and it occurs because team members seek conformity and become unwilling to criticize each other's ideas and suggestions. Desires to hold the team together, feel good, and avoid unpleasant disagreements bring about an overemphasis on agreement and an underemphasis on critical discussion. According to Janis, the result often is a poor decision.

By way of historical examples Janis suggests that groupthink played a role in the lack of preparedness by U.S. forces at Pearl Harbor before the United States' entry into World War II. It has also been linked to flawed U.S. decision making during the Vietnam War, to events leading up to the space shuttle disasters, and, most recently, to failures of American intelligence agencies regarding the status of weapons of mass destruction in Iraq. Against this context, the following symptoms of teams displaying groupthink should be well within the sights of any team leader and member.[31]

- *Illusions of invulnerability*—Members assume that the team is too good for criticism or beyond attack.
- *Rationalizing unpleasant and disconfirming data*—Members refuse to accept contradictory data or to thoroughly consider alternatives.
- *Belief in inherent group morality*—Members act as though the group is inherently right and above reproach.
- *Stereotyping competitors as weak, evil, and stupid*—Members refuse to look realistically at other groups.
- *Applying direct pressure to deviants to conform to group wishes*—Members refuse to tolerate anyone who suggests the team may be wrong.
- *Self-censorship by members*—Members refuse to communicate personal concerns to the whole team.
- *Illusions of unanimity*—Members accept consensus prematurely, without testing its completeness.
- *Mind guarding*—Members protect the team from hearing disturbing ideas or outside viewpoints.

There is no doubt that groupthink is a serious threat to the quality of decision making in teams at all levels and in all types of organizations. Team leaders and members alike should be alert to its symptoms and be quick to take any necessary action to prevent its occurrence.[32] For example, President Kennedy chose to absent himself from certain strategy discussions by his cabinet during the Cuban Missile Crisis. This reportedly facilitated critical discussion and avoided tendencies for members to try to figure out what the president wanted and then give it to him. As a result the decision-making process was open and expansive, and the crisis was successfully resolved. Richard Anderson, Delta's CEO, follows a similar strategy to try to avoid groupthink in his executive team. Although he attends the meetings, he takes care to avoid groupthink. "I tend to be a stoic going into the meeting," he says. "I want the debate. I want to hear everybody's perspective, so you try to ask more questions than make statements."[33] OB Savvy 8.2 identifies a number of steps that teams and their leaders can take to avoid groupthink or at least minimize its occurrence.

> **OB SAVVY 8.2**
>
> ## What Team Leaders Can Do to Avoid Groupthink
>
> - Assign the role of critical evaluator to each team member.
> - Have the leader avoid seeming partial to one course of action.
> - Create subgroups that each work on the same problem.
> - Have team members discuss issues with outsiders and report back.
> - Invite outside experts to observe and react to team processes.
> - Assign someone to be a "devil's advocate" at each team meeting.
> - Hold "second-chance" meetings after consensus is apparently achieved.

Team Decision Techniques

In order to take full advantage of the team as a decision-making resource, care should be exercised to avoid groupthink and otherwise manage problems in team dynamics.[34] Team process losses often occur, for example, when meetings are poorly structured or poorly led as members try to work together. When tasks are complex, information is uncertain, creativity is needed, time is short, "strong" voices are dominant, and debates turn emotional and personal, decisions can easily get bogged down or go awry. Fortunately, there are some team decision techniques that can be helpful in such situations.[35]

Brainstorming   In **brainstorming**, team members actively generate as many ideas and alternatives as possible, and they do so relatively quickly and without inhibitions. IBM, for example, uses online brainstorming as part of a program called Innovation Jam. It links IBM employees, customers, and consultants in an "open source" approach. Says CEO Samuel J. Palmisano: "A technology company takes its most valued secrets, opens them up to the world and says, O.K., world, you tell us what to do with them."[36]

- **Brainstorming** involves generating ideas through "freewheeling" and without criticism.

You are probably familiar with the rules that typically govern the brainstorming process. First, all criticism is ruled out. No one is allowed to judge or evaluate any ideas until the idea generation process has been completed. Second, "freewheeling" is welcomed. The emphasis is on creativity and imagination; the wilder or more radical the ideas, the better. Third, quantity is wanted. The emphasis is also on the number of ideas; the greater the number, the more likely a superior idea will appear. Fourth, "piggy-backing" is good. Everyone is encouraged to suggest how others' ideas can be turned into new ideas or how two or more ideas can be joined into still another new idea.

Nominal Group Technique   In any team there will be times when the opinions of members differ so much that antagonistic arguments will develop during discussions. At other times the team is so large that open discussion and brainstorming are awkward to manage. In such cases a structured approach called the **nominal group technique** may be helpful, and it can be done face-to-face or in a computer-mediated meeting.[37]

- The **nominal group technique** involves structured rules for generating and prioritizing ideas.

The technique begins by asking team members to respond individually and in writing to a *nominal question*, such as: "What should be done to improve the effectiveness of this work team?" Everyone is encouraged to list as many alternatives or ideas as they can. Next, participants in round-robin fashion are asked to read aloud their responses to the nominal question. A recorder writes each response on large newsprint or in a computer database as it is offered. No criticism is allowed. The recorder asks in round-robin fashion for any questions that may clarify specific items on the list, but no evaluation is allowed; the goal is simply to make sure that everyone present fully understands each response. A structured voting procedure is then used to prioritize responses to the nominal question and arrive at the choice or choices with the most support. This nominal group procedure allows ideas to be evaluated without risking the inhibitions, hostilities, and distortions that may occur in an open and unstructured team meeting.

Delphi Technique   The Rand Corporation developed a third group-decision approach, the **Delphi Technique**, for situations when group members are unable to meet face-to-face. In this procedure, questionnaires are distributed online or in hard copy to a panel of decision makers, who submit initial responses to a decision coordinator. The coordinator summarizes the solutions and sends the summary back to the panel members, along with a follow-up questionnaire. Panel members again send in their responses, and the process is repeated until a consensus is reached and a clear decision emerges.

- The **Delphi technique** involves generating decision-making alternatives through a series of survey questionnaires.

Resources in The OB Skills Workbook

These learning activities from *The OB Skills Workbook* are suggested for Chapter 8.

Case for Critical Thinking	Team and Experiential Exercises	Self-Assessment Portfolio
• NASCAR's Racing Teams	• Scavenger Hunt Team-Building	• Team Effectiveness
	• Work Team Dynamics	• Empowering Others
	• Identifying Team Norms	
	• Work Team Culture	
	• The Hot Seat	

8 studyguide

How can we create high-performance teams?

- Team-building is a collaborative approach to improving group process and performance.

- High-performance teams have core values, clear performance objectives, the right mix of skills, and creativity.

- Team-building is a data-based approach to analyzing group performance and taking steps to improve performance in the future.

- Team-building is participative and engages all group members in collaborative problem solving and action.

How can team processes be improved?

- Individual entry problems are common when new teams are formed and when new members join existing teams.

- Task leadership involves initiating, summarizing, and making direct contributions to the group's task agenda; maintenance leadership involves gate-keeping, encouraging, and supporting the social fabric of the group over time.

- Distributed leadership occurs when team members step in to provide helpful task and maintenance activities and discourage disruptive activities.

- Role difficulties occur when expectations for group members are unclear, overwhelming, underwhelming, or conflicting.

- Norms are the standards or rules of conduct that influence the behavior of team members; cohesiveness is the attractiveness of the team to its members.

- Members of highly cohesive groups value their membership and are very loyal to the group; they also tend to conform to group norms.

- The best situation is a team with positive performance norms and high cohesiveness.

- Intergroup dynamics are the forces that operate between two or more groups.

How can team communications be improved?

- Effective teams use alternative communication networks and decision-making methods to best complete tasks.

- Interacting groups with decentralized networks tend to perform well on complex tasks; co-acting groups with centralized networks may do well at simple tasks.

- Restricted communication networks are common in counteracting groups with subgroup disagreements.

- Wise choices on proxemics, or the use of space, can help teams improve communication among members.

- Information technology ranging from e-mail to instant messaging, tweets, and discussion groups can improve communication in teams, but it must be well used.

How can team decisions be improved?

- Teams can make decisions by lack of response, authority rule, minority rule, majority rule, consensus, and unanimity.

- Although team decisions often make more information available for problem solving and generate more understanding and commitment, the potential liabilities of group decision making include social pressures to conform and greater time requirements.

- Groupthink is a tendency of members of highly cohesive teams to lose their critical evaluative capabilities and make poor decisions.

- Techniques for improving creativity in teams include brainstorming and the nominal group technique.

Key Terms

Brainstorming (p. 199)
Centralized communication
  network (p. 193)
Cohesiveness (p. 188)
Consensus (p. 196)
Decentralized communica-
  tion network (p. 192)
Decision making (p. 195)
Delphi technique (p. 200)
Disruptive behavior
  (p. 185)
Distributed leadership
  (p. 184)

Groupthink (p. 198)
Inter-team dynamics
  (p. 190)
Maintenance activities
  (p. 184)
Nominal group technique
  (p. 200)
Norms (p. 186)
Proxemics (p. 194)
Restricted communication
  network (p. 193)
Role (p. 185)
Role ambiguity (p. 185)

Role conflict (p. 185)
Role negotiation (p. 186)
Role overload (p. 185)
Role underload (p. 185)
Rule of conformity
  (p. 188)
Task activities (p. 184)
Team-building (p. 181)
Virtual communication
  networks (p. 194)

Self-Test 8

Multiple Choice

1. One of the essential criteria of a true team is _____. (a) large size (b) homogeneous membership (c) isolation from outsiders (d) collective accountability

2. The team-building process can best be described as participative, data-based, and _____. (a) action-oriented (b) leader-centered (c) ineffective (d) short-term

3. A person facing an ethical dilemma involving differences between personal values and the expectations of the team is experiencing _____ conflict. (a) person-role (b) intrasender role (c) intersender role (d) interrole

4. The statement "On our team, people always try to do their best" is an example of a(n) _____ norm. (a) support and helpfulness (b) high-achievement (c) organizational pride (d) organizational improvement

5. Highly cohesive teams tend to be _____. (a) bad for organizations (b) good for members (c) good for social loafing (d) bad for norm conformity

6. To increase team cohesiveness, one would _____. (a) make the group bigger (b) increase membership diversity (c) isolate the group from others (d) relax performance pressures

7. A team member who does a good job at summarizing discussion, offering new ideas, and clarifying points made by others is providing leadership by contributing _____ activities to the group process. (a) required (b) disruptive (c) task (d) maintenance

8. When someone is being aggressive, makes inappropriate jokes, or talks about irrelevant matters in a group meeting, these are all examples of _____. (a) dysfunctional behaviors (b) maintenance activities (c) task activities (d) role dynamics

9. If you heard from an employee of a local bank that "it's a tradition here for us to stand up and defend the bank when someone criticizes it," you could assume that the bank employees had strong _____ norms. (a) support and helpfulness (b) organizational and personal pride (c) ethical and social responsibility (d) improvement and change

10. What can be predicted when you know that a work team is highly cohesive? (a) high-performance results (b) high member satisfaction (c) positive performance norms (d) status congruity

11. When two groups are in competition with one another, _____ may be expected within each group. (a) more in-group loyalty (b) less reliance on the leader (c) poor task focus (d) more conflict

12. A co-acting group is most likely to use a(n) _____ communication network. (a) interacting (b) decentralized (c) centralized (d) restricted

13. A complex problem is best dealt with by a team using a(n) _____ communication network. (a) all-channel (b) wheel (c) chain (d) linear

14. The tendency of teams to lose their critical evaluative capabilities during decision making is a phenomenon called _____. (a) groupthink (b) the slippage effect (c) decision congruence (d) group consensus

15. When a team decision requires a high degree of commitment for its implementation, a(n) _____ decision is generally preferred. (a) authority (b) majority-vote (c) consensus (d) railroading

Short Response

16. Describe the steps in a typical team-building process.

17. How can a team leader build positive group norms?

18. How do cohesiveness and conformity to norms influence group performance?

19. How can inter-team competition be bad and good for organizations?

Applications Essay

20. Alejandro Puron recently encountered a dilemma in working with his employer's diversity task force. One of the team members claimed that a task force must always be unanimous in its recommendations. "Otherwise," she said, "we will not have a true consensus." Alejandro, the current task force leader, disagrees. He believes that unanimity is desirable but not always necessary to achieve consensus. You are a management consultant specializing in using groups in organizations. Alejandro calls you for advice. What would you tell him and why?

9

Decision Making and Creativity

Google's mission is "to organize the world's information and make it universally accessible and useful."[1] In a world of massive information overload, this may seem a tall order to fill. But its persistent pursuit of innovation keeps the company focused in its drive to deliver information effectively and efficiently to users across the globe.

Innovation is key for any organization competing in a rapidly changing, high-tech world and Google has a way of making it look easy. Consistently coming up with new and revolutionary products that change the way we experience the internet, this global search and on-line software company relies heavily on the creativity of its workers.

Employees, affectionately referred to as Googlers, enjoy a work environment that allows them to express themselves and pursue their own interests which translates into higher creativity and productivity levels. It nurtures that creativity by "encouraging and empowering its people to think freely in all areas of their lives."[1]

While global offices are designed to express local culture, a few basic elements permeate the typical Google workplace. These include providing employees with a budget to decorate their workspace, bicycles or scooters, lava lamps, massage chairs, pianos, gyms, video games, pool tables, and a variety of cafes that offer health lunches and dinners.

There is no dress code, employees are free to bring their children or pets to work, and one of the few rules caps how much vacation time employees can roll over from year to year since the idea is to make sure employees take time off to recharge.

The work environment itself is designed to encourage the free flow of ideas. Many meeting rooms are equipped with bean bags instead of chairs and white boards are mounted around the office to help record creative ideas when they come to mind.

"The Zurich engineering division has even gone to the extreme of designing meeting rooms to look like a Swiss chalet, an old library, and an aquarium in which employees can lie on red foam and stare at fish."[1]

Google's culture makes it a fun, relaxing place to work, encourages employees to be free thinkers, and has led to some of the company's most innovative products.

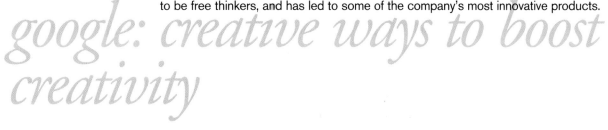

google: creative ways to boost creativity

The Decision-Making Process

A cornerstone of good decision-making is the information we use to make the myriad decisions required of individuals and groups each day, both personally and professionally. Google's goal "to organize the world's information and make it universally accessible and useful" can greatly impact the quality of the decisions we make. In an age of information overload our ability to access useful information and our willingness to then use that information effectively in making decisions is paramount.

In our personal lives, at work, within teams, and in management in general, a continuing stream of information, data, problems, and opportunities fuel decision making. It's a lot to sort through, and not all teams end up with the right results. In the last chapter we learned that teams make decisions in different ways, team decisions have assets and liabilities, and techniques such as brainstorming and the nominal group can help improve team decisions. Now, it's time to examine the decision-making process more thoroughly and become better prepared as leaders and members to assist teams in making high-performance decisions.

Steps in Decision Making

• **Decision making** is the process of choosing a course of action to deal with a problem or opportunity.

A common definition of **decision making** is the process of choosing a course of action for dealing with a problem or opportunity.[2] The process is usually described in five steps for both individuals and teams. Together they are often called the *rational decision model*.

| Define Problem | Analyze Alternatives | Make a Choice | Take Action | Evaluate Result |

1. *Recognize and define the problem or opportunity*—a stage of information gathering, and deliberation to specify exactly why a decision is needed and what it should accomplish. Three mistakes are common in this critical first step in decision making. First, teams may define the problem too broadly or too narrowly. Second, teams may focus on problem symptoms instead of causes. Third, teams may choose the wrong problem to deal with.

2. *Identify and analyze alternative courses of action*—a stage where possible alternative courses of action and their anticipated consequences are evaluated for costs and benefits. Teams at this stage must be clear on exactly what they know and what they need to know. They should identify key stakeholders and consider the effects of each possible course of action on them.

3. *Choose a preferred course of action*—a stage where a choice is made to pursue one course of action rather than others. Criteria used in making the choice typically involve costs and benefits, timeliness of results, impact on stakeholders, and ethical soundness. Another issue for the team at this stage is who makes the decision: team leader, team members, or some combination?

4. *Implement the preferred course of action*—a stage where actions are taken to put the preferred course of action into practice. This is a point where teams may suffer from **lack-of-participation error** because they haven't included in the decision-making process those persons whose support is necessary for its eventual implementation. Teams that use participation and involvement well gain not only inputs and insights, they also gain commitments to support implementation of the decision.

> **Lack-of-participation error** occurs when important people are excluded from the decision-making process.

5. *Evaluate the results and follow up as necessary*—a stage that measures performance results against initial goals and examines both anticipated and unanticipated outcomes. This is where teams exercise control over their actions, being careful to ensure that the desired results are achieved and undesired side effects are avoided. It is a stage that many teams often neglect, with negative implications for their performance effectiveness.

Ethical Reasoning and Decision Making

Decision making means making choices, and these choices, made at each step in the decision-making process just described, usually have a moral dimension that might easily be overlooked. Would you agree, for example, that there is a moral side to decisions such as these? Choosing to allow social loafing by a team member rather than confronting it; choosing to pursue a course of action that causes a teammate some difficulties at home; choosing to compromise on quality in order to speed up teamwork to meet deadlines; or, choosing not to ask really hard questions about whether or not a team's course of action is the correct one?

Figure 9.1 links the steps in the decision-making process with corresponding issues of ethical reasoning.[3] As suggested in the figure we are advocating that an

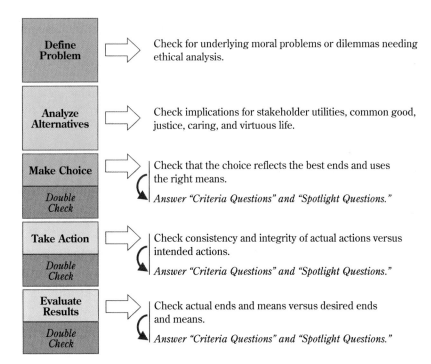

Figure 9.1 The decision-making process with embedded ethical reasoning model.

In the rush to make decisions it is far too common for moral problems and dilemmas to be downplayed, handled poorly, and even overlooked.

ethical reasoning approach be followed when decisions are made, and that this approach be linked with each step in the decision-making process. In other words, decision making is incomplete without ethical analysis.

Moral Problems and Dilemmas   **Ethics** is the philosophical study of morality or standards regarding good character and conduct.[4] When we apply ethical reasoning to decisions made by individuals and teams in organizations, the focus is on moral problems and dilemmas that are associated with the decision-making process. A **moral problem** is one that poses major ethical consequences for the decision maker or for others. Importantly, it is possible to address a personal, management, or business problem and not properly consider any moral problems that might be associated with it. A preferred approach is to carefully examine the consequences of each alternative for all decision stakeholders, and make choices that minimize negative impact and maximize respect for everyone's rights.

We hear almost every day, for example, about job layoffs in a bad economy. For the manager or executive teams involved, layoffs may seem straightforward and necessary solutions to a business problem—there are insufficient sales to justify the payroll and some jobs must be cut. But this business situation also involves a moral problem: persons losing their jobs have families, debts, and perhaps limited job options; they will be hurt even if the business benefits from lowering its costs. Although addressing the moral problem might not change the business decision, it might change how the business decision is reached and implemented. This includes addressing whether or not better alternatives to job eliminations exist and what support is offered to those who do lose jobs.

Sometimes problems create **moral dilemmas** in which the decision maker faces two or more ethically uncomfortable alternatives. An example might be deciding on an opportunity to make an outsourcing contract with a supplier in a country where employment discrimination exists, but also where the country is poor and new jobs are important for economic development. Such situations involve the uncomfortable position of choosing between alternatives that have both potential benefits and harm. Although such moral dilemmas are difficult to resolve, ethical reasoning helps insure the decisions will be made with rigor and thoughtful consideration. Indeed, a willingness to pause to examine the ethics of a proposed decision may well result in a better decision, preservation of respect and reputation for one's self and the organization, and the prevention of costly litigation and even jail.

Ethics Double Checks   If you look back at Figure 9.1, you will see that "ethics double checks" are built into the ethical reasoning framework. This is a way of testing to make sure our decisions at least meet personal moral standards. The recommended ethics double checks are accomplished by asking and answering two sets of questions—criteria questions and spotlight questions. Ethicist Gerald Cavanagh and his associates, identify these four **criteria questions** for assessing ethics in decision making.[5]

1. *Utility*—Does the decision satisfy all constituents or stakeholders?
2. *Rights*—Does the decision respect the rights and duties of everyone?
3. *Justice*—Is the decision consistent with the canons of justice?
4. *Caring*—Is the decision consistent with my responsibilities to care?

• **Ethics** is the philosophical study of morality.

• A **moral problem** poses major ethical consequences for the decision maker or others.

• A **moral dilemma** involves a choice between two or more ethically uncomfortable alternatives.

• **Criteria questions** assess a decision in terms of utility, rights, justice, and caring.

ETHICS IN OB

DISCRIMINATION EVIDENT IN EMPLOYERS' RECRUITMENT DECISIONS

The newspaper headline read: "Racism rife as Irish twice as likely to be given job."
The report was on a study conducted in Ireland by the Economic and Social Research Institute, which found high levels of discrimination in recruitment decisions by Irish employers. Researchers distributed pairs of resumes identical in all respects expect for the job applicant's name, which looked and sounded Irish, African, Asian, or German. Results showed:

- Overall: 78 Irish and 38 minority applicants were called to interview.
- Irish vs. African: 18 Irish and 5 African applicants were called.
- Irish vs. Asian: 19 Irish and 7 Asian applicants were called.
- Irish vs. German: 18 Irish and 3 German applicants were called.

In one case an Irish applicant received a telephone call to discuss her resume, and an African applicant received an e-mail stating that the job had already been filled. Researchers concluded that the pattern of discrimination in the data was so strong it was only "a one in a million chance" that the preferences shown Irish applicants were accidental.

> ***Is It Racism?*** *What explains this pattern of decision making among the Irish recruiters? The newspaper headline suggests racism, but is this going too far? When does a preference for "local" job candidates over "foreign" ones become discrimination? Can you design a study that might be done in your community to check on local recruitment practices?*

The **spotlight questions** basically expose a decision to public scrutiny and forces us to consider it in the context of full transparency.[6] They are especially powerful when a person comes from a morally scrupulous family background or social structure and prospects for shame would be very upsetting.

- **Spotlight questions** expose a decision to public scrutiny and full transparency.

1. "How would I feel if my family found out about this decision?"
2. "How would I feel if this decision were published in the local newspaper or posted on the Internet?"
3. "What would the person you know or know of who has the strongest character and best ethical judgment do in this situation?"

In the earlier example of job layoffs, business executives who have been criticized in the local news for making the cuts might scramble to provide counseling and job-hunting assistance to the affected employees. But this is after the fact, and moral conduct does not arise from after-the-fact embarrassment. As Stephen Fineman suggests: "If people are unable to anticipate shame or guilt before they act in particular ways, then moral codes are invalid. . . . Decisions may involve lying, deceit, fraud, evasion of negligence—disapproved of in many cultures. But ethical monitoring and control go beyond just the pragmatics of harm."[7] In other words, when you are the decision maker, decision making is not just a process followed for the good of the organization; it involves your values and your morality. The results should not only solve a problem or capitalize on choices, they should also match your values and help others. It is little wonder, then, that decision making is one of our biggest challenges. So, why not engage the ethical reasoning framework and ethics double-checks suggested in Figure 9.1 as a way of strengthening the process?[8]

Types of Decisions

Decisions made by teams and individuals are basically attempts to deal with a specific task, resolve a performance deficiency, or take advantage of a performance opportunity. They fall into two major types called programmed and nonprogrammed decisions.

• **Programmed decisions** simply implement solutions that have already been determined by past experience as appropriate for the problem at hand.

Programmed decisions are made as standardized responses to recurring situations and routine problems, things that the team already has experience dealing with. Basically, they implement alternatives that are known to be appropriate for situations that occur somewhat frequently. Examples might include teams that review compensation or human resource policies for equity and justice, or those that manage recurring projects.

• **Nonprogrammed decisions** are created to deal specifically with a problem at hand.

Teams often face the unexpected problem that demands a unique response, one for which a standard response from a decision inventory is not available. These **nonprogrammed decisions** are specifically crafted or tailored to the situation at hand. Higher-level management teams generally spend a greater proportion of their decision-making time on nonroutine problems, but teams at all levels face them as well. An example is a marketing team that has to respond to the introduction of a new product by a foreign competitor. Although past experience may help deal with this competitive threat, the immediate decision requires a creative solution based on the unique characteristics of the present market situation.

• A **crisis decision** occurs when an unexpected problem can lead to disaster if not resolved quickly and appropriately.

An extreme type of nonprogrammed decision is the **crisis decision** where an unexpected problem threatens major harm and disaster if not resolved quickly and appropriately.[9] Acts of terrorism, workplace violence, IT failures and security breaches, ethical scandals, and environmental catastrophes are all examples. And the ability to handle crises could well be the ultimate decision-making test. Unfortunately, research indicates that we sometimes react to crises by doing exactly the wrong things. Managers err in crisis situations when they isolate themselves and try to solve the problem alone or in a small, closed group. Teams do the same when they withdraw into the isolation of groupthink. In both instances the decision makers cut themselves off from access to crucial information at the very time that they need it the most. This not only sets them up for poor decisions, it may create even more problems.

Especially in our post–9/11 and economic-recession world, many organizations, perhaps all really strong ones, are developing formal crisis management programs. They train managers in crisis decision making along lines suggested in Mastering Management, assign people ahead of time to crisis management teams, and develop crisis management plans to deal with various contingencies. Just as fire and police departments, the Red Cross and community groups plan ahead and train people to best handle civil and natural disasters, and airline crews train for flight emergencies. So, too, can managers and work teams plan ahead and train to best deal with organizational crises.[10]

MASTERING MANAGEMENT

SIX RULES FOR CRISIS MANAGEMENT

1. *Figure out what is going on*—Take the time to understand what's happening and the conditions under which the crisis must be resolved.
2. *Remember that speed matters*—Attack the crisis as quickly as possible, trying to catch it when it is as small as possible.
3. *Remember that slow counts, too*—Know when to back off and wait for a better opportunity to make progress with the crisis.
4. *Respect the danger of the unfamiliar*—Understand the danger of all-new territory where you and others have never been before.
5. *Value the skeptic*—Don't look for and get too comfortable with agreement; appreciate skeptics and let them help you see things differently.
6. *Be ready to "fight fire with fire"*—When things are going wrong and no one seems to care, you may have to start a crisis to get their attention.

Decision Environments

Decisions in organizations are typically made under the three conditions or environments shown in Figure 9.2—certainty, risk, and uncertainty.[11] The levels of risk and uncertainty in the decision environment tends to increase the higher one moves in management ranks. Think about this, for example, the next time you hear about Coca-Cola or Pepsi launching a new flavor or product. Is the executive team making these decisions *certain* that the results will be successful; or, is it taking *risks* in market situations that are *uncertain* as to whether the new flavor or product will be positively received by customers?

Certain environments exist when information is sufficient to predict the results of each alternative in advance of implementation. When a person invests

> **Certain environments** provide full information on the expected results for decision-making alternatives.

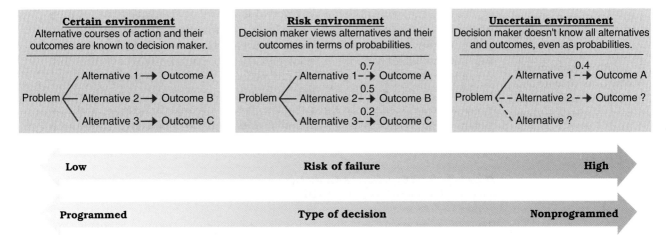

Figure 9.2 Certainty, risk, and uncertainty in organizational decision environments.
[*Source:* John R. Schermerhorn, Jr., *Management* 10th Edition (Hoboken, NJ: John Wiley & Sons, 2010). Used by permission.]

Ford

Talk about taking risk: have you heard about Ford's online gamble? The company gave Fiesta subcompacts to 100 young drivers for six months. All it asked in return was that they post their impressions on YouTube, Flickr, and Twitter. It's an interesting online campaign, but it carries a fair amount of risk–the drivers will be posting both the "goods" and the "bads."

money in a savings account, for example, absolute certainty exists about the interest that will be earned on that money in a given period of time. Certainty is an ideal condition for managerial problem solving and decision making. The challenge is simply to locate the alternative that offers the best or ideal solution. Unfortunately, certainty is the exception instead of the rule in decision environments.

Risk environments exist when decision makers lack complete certainty regarding the outcomes of various courses of action but are aware of the probabilities associated with their occurrence. A probability, in turn, is the degree of likelihood of an event's occurrence. Probabilities can be assigned through objective statistical procedures or through personal intuition. For instance, managers can make statistical estimates of quality rejects in production runs, or a senior production manager can make similar estimates based on past experience. Risk is a common decision environment in today's organizations.

Uncertain environments exist when managers have so little information on hand that they cannot even assign probabilities to various alternatives and their possible outcomes. This is the most difficult of the three decision environments. Uncertainty forces decision makers to rely heavily on individual and group creativity to succeed in problem solving. It requires unique, novel, and often totally innovative alternatives to existing patterns of behavior. Responses to uncertainty are often heavily influenced by intuition, educated guesses, and hunches.

Risk Management in Decision Making

- **Risk environments** provide probabilities regarding expected results for decision-making alternatives.

- **Uncertain environments** provide no information to predict expected results for decision-making alternatives.

- **Risk management** involves anticipating risks and factoring them into decision making.

The recent financial crisis has shown once again the fact that many decisions are made in risk and uncertain environments. It has also prompted renewed interest in **risk management**, something often associated with insurance and finance. We use the term in general management as well, focusing on anticipating risk in situations and factoring risk alternatives into the decision-making process.[12] Risk management involves identifying critical risks and then developing strategies and assigning responsibilities for dealing with them.

KPMG, one of the world's largest consulting firms, has a large practice in enterprise risk management that is designed to help executives identify risks to their firms and manage them.[13] KPMG consultants systematically ask managers to separately identify *strategic risks*—threats to overall business success; *operational risks*—threats inherent in the technologies used to reach business success; and, *reputation risks*—threats to a brand or to the firm's reputation. Although they also note the importance of threats from regulatory sources, KPMG consultants pay special attention to financial threats, challenges to information systems, and new initiatives from competitors, in addition to change in the competitive setting such as recession or disasters.

Decision-Making Models

The field of organizational behavior has historically emphasized two alternative approaches to decision making as shown in Figure 9.3—classical and behavioral.[14] The classical decision model views people acting in a world of complete certainty, while the behavioral decision model accepts the notion of bounded rationality and suggests that people act only in terms of what they perceive about a given situation.

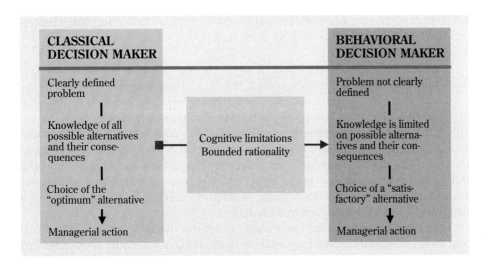

Figure 9.3 Decision making viewed from the classical and behavioral perspectives.

Classical Decision Model

The **classical decision model** views the manager or team as acting rationally and in a fully informed manner. The problem is clearly defined, all possible action alternatives are known, and their consequences are clear. This allows for an **optimizing decision** that gives the absolute best solution to the problem. This model fits the five-step decision-making process described earlier. It is an ideal situation of complete information where the decision maker moves through the steps one-by-one in a logical fashion. And, it nicely lends itself to various forms of quantitative decision analysis as well as to computer-based applications.

In the 1960s Nobel laureate and decision scientist Herbert Simon was convinced that computers would someday be more intelligent than humans. Today we study *artificial intelligence*, or AI, to determine how computers can be programmed to think like the human brain and basically act as decision makers. The applications of AI to organizational decision making are already significant. Most of us have access to decision-making support from *expert systems* that reason like human experts and follow "either–or" rules to make deductions. For example, if you call an advertised 800 number to apply for a home equity loan, you will not get a human, but a computer program that will take all the necessary information and provide confirmation of a loan. *Fuzzy logic* that reasons beyond either–or and neural networks that reason inductively by simulating the brain's parallel processing capabilities are becoming operational realities that will move beyond simple programmed decisions. Uses for such systems may be found everywhere from hospitals, where they check on medical diagnoses, to investment houses, where they will analyze potential investment portfolios, to a wide and growing variety of other settings.[15]

Behavioral Decision Model

As appealing as the classical model and its rational approach may be, the reality is that decision situations faced by individuals and teams in organizations are often much more complicated than the assumptions of the model fit. Recognizing this, the premise of the **behavioral decision model** is that people act only in terms of their perceptions, which are frequently imperfect. Furthermore, this makes it

- **Classical decision model** views decision makers as acting in a world of complete certainty.

- **Optimizing decisions** give the absolute best solution to a problem.

- **Behavioral decision model** views decision makers as acting only in terms of what they perceive about a given situation.

difficult to realize the ideal of classical decision making. As a result, the classical model does not give a full and accurate description of how most decisions are made in organizations.[16]

Behavioral scientists recognize that the human mind is a wonderful creation, capable of infinite achievements. But they also recognize that human beings have *cognitive limitations*, literally limits on what we are able to know at any point in time, that restrict our information-processing capabilities. The result is that information deficiencies and overloads compromise the ability of decision makers to achieve complete certainty and otherwise operate according to the classical model. They end up acting with *bounded rationality* in which things are interpreted and made sense of as perceptions and only within the context of the situation. They engage in decision making "within the box" of a simplified view of a more complex reality.

Armed with only partial knowledge about the available action alternatives and their consequences, decision makers in the behavioral model are considered likely to choose the first alternative that appears satisfactory to them. Herbert Simon calls this the tendency to make **satisficing decisions**. He states: "Most human decision making, whether individual or organizational, is concerned with the discovery and selection of satisfactory alternatives; only in exceptional cases is it concerned with the discovery and selection of optimal decisions."[17]

> • **Satisficing decisions** choose the first alternative that appears to give an acceptable or satisfactory resolution of the problem.

Garbage Can Decision Model

A third view of decision making stems from the so-called **garbage can model**.[18] In this view, the main components of the choice process—problems, solutions, participants, and situations—are all mixed up together in the "garbage can" of the organization. In many organizations where the setting is stable and the technology is well known and fixed, tradition, strategy, and the administrative structure help order the contents of the garbage can. Specific problems can be matched to specific solutions, an orderly process can be maintained, and the behavioral view of decision making may be appropriate. But when the setting is dynamic, the technology is changing, demands are conflicting, or the goals are unclear, things can get mixed up. More action than thinking can take place. Solutions emerge as "potential capabilities"—capabilities independent of problems or opportunities. Solutions emerge not so much in relationship with specific problems but as lessons learned from the experiences of others. Many solutions get implemented without being tied to a specific problem; they are just done for the sake of doing something. Although such actions may change things in some ways, they are unlikely to solve persistent problems.

> • The **garbage can model** views problems, solutions, participants, and choice situations as all mixed together in a dynamic field of organizational forces.

The garbage can model highlights an important feature of decision making in many large organizations. Often the jobs of individuals and teams are to do things that make decisions already made by senior managers' work. This means they must interpret the intentions of their bosses as well as address local problems. Lots of agendas operate at once. Also, many problems go unsolved and organizations end up with chronic, persistent deficiencies that never seem to get much better. In a garbage can view, this is because decision makers cannot agree to match chronic problems with solutions, make choices, and implement them in a timely and consistent manner. Something happens, in a sense, only when a problem and a solution "bump into one another."

Google

Avichal Garg started PrepMe.com with financial backing from Xooglers, ex-Google employees known for using their wealth and experience to do great things. One of Google's top decision-making lessons is "Fact-based decision-making–always rely on data. Never make an emotional decision."

Intuitive Decision Model

Like individuals, teams may be described as using both "systematic" and "intuitive" thinking. **Systematic thinking** is consistent with the rational model where a decision is approached in step-by-step and analytical fashion. You might recognize this when a team member tries to break a complex problem into smaller components that can be addressed one by one. We expect teams engaged in systematic thinking to make a plan before taking action, and to search for information and proceed with problem solving in a fact-based and step-by-step fashion.

Individuals and teams using **intuitive thinking** are more flexible and spontaneous in decision making.[19] You might observe this pattern as someone who always seems to come up with an imaginative response to a problem, often based on a quick and broad evaluation of the situation. In what is called the intuitive decision model, decision makers tend to deal with many aspects of a problem at once, jump quickly from one issue to another, and act on hunches from experience or on spontaneous ideas. This approach is common under conditions of risk and uncertainty.

We think of *intuition* as the ability to know or recognize quickly and readily the possibilities of a given situation.[20] Its presence adds personality and spontaneity to decision making and, as a result, also offers the potential for creativity and innovation. Especially in conditions of risk and uncertainty, decisions in organizations rely on impressions; people involved in them are more likely to synthesize than to analyze data as they search for the "big picture" in order to redefine problems and link problems with a variety of solutions. Things have to be done fast, a variety of things have to be done, and the people doing all this are frequently interrupted. When there isn't a lot of time to think, plan, or make decisions systematically, we should be confident in tapping our or a team's intuitive skills.

But does this mean that we should always favor the more intuitive and less systematic approach? Most likely not—teams, like individuals, should combine analytical and intuitive approaches to create new and novel solutions to complex problems. Amazon.com's Jeff Bezos says that when it's not possible for the firm's top managers to make systematic fact-based decisions, "you have to rely on experienced executives who've honed their instincts" and are able to make good judgments.[21] In other words, there's a place for both systematic and intuitive decision making in management.

- **Systematic thinking** approaches problems in a rational and analytical fashion.

- **Intuitive thinking** approaches problems in a flexible and spontaneous fashion.

Decision-Making Traps and Issues

The pathways to good decisions can seem like a minefield of challenging issues and troublesome traps. Whether working individually or as part of a team, it is important to understand the influence of judgmental heuristics and other potential decision biases, as well as be capable in making critical choices regarding if, when, and how decisions get made.

Judgmental Heuristics

Judgment, or the use of intellect, is important in all aspects of decision making. When we question the ethics of a decision, for example, we are questioning the judgment of the person making it. Research shows that people who are prone to

Intuitive Thinkers

Intuitive thinkers take a flexible and spontaneous approach to decision making. Their presence on a team adds potential for creative problem solving and innovation.

mistakes use biases that often interfere with the quality of decision making.[22] These can be traced to the use of **heuristics**, which are simplifying strategies or "rules of thumb" used to make decisions. Heuristics serve a useful purpose in making it easier to deal with uncertainty and the limited information common to problem situations. But they can also lead to systematic errors that affect the quality, and perhaps the ethical implications, of any decisions made. It is helpful to understand the common judgmental heuristics of availability, representativeness, and anchoring and adjustment.[23]

• **Heuristics** are simplifying strategies or "rules of thumb" used to make decisions.

Availability Heuristic The **availability heuristic** involves assessing a current event based on past occurrences that are easily available in one's memory. An example is the product development specialist who bases a decision not to launch a new product on her recent failure with another product offering. In this case, the existence of a past product failure has negatively, and perhaps inappropriately, biased her judgment regarding how best to handle the new product.

• The **availability heuristic** bases a decision on recent events relating to the situation at hand.

Representativeness Heuristic The **representativeness heuristic** involves assessing the likelihood that an event will occur based on its similarity to one's stereotypes of similar occurrences. An example is the team leader who selects a new member, not because of any special qualities of the person, but only because the individual comes from a department known to have produced high performers in the past. In this case, the individual's current place of employment—not his or her job qualifications—is the basis for the selection decision.

• The **representativeness heuristic** bases a decision on similarities between the situation at hand and stereotypes of similar occurrences.

Anchoring and Adjustment Heuristic The **anchoring and adjustment heuristic** involves assessing an event by taking an initial value from historical precedent or an outside source and then incrementally adjusting this value to make a current assessment. An example is the executive who makes salary increase recommendations for key personnel by simply adjusting their current base salaries by a percentage amount. In this case, the existing base salary becomes an "anchor" that drives subsequent salary increases. In some situations this anchor may be inappropriate, such as in the case of an individual whose market value has become substantially higher than is reflected by the base salary plus increment approach.

• The **anchoring and adjustment heuristic** bases a decision on incremental adjustments to an initial value determined by historical precedent or some reference point.

Decision Biases

In addition to using the common judgmental heuristics, decision makers are also prone to more general biases in decision making. One bias is the **confirmation error**, whereby the decision maker seeks confirmation for what is already thought to be true and neglects opportunities to acknowledge or find disconfirming information. A form of selective perception, this bias involves seeking only those cues in a situation that support a preexisting opinion.

• The **confirmation trap** is the tendency to seek confirmation for what is already thought to be true and not search for disconfirming information.

A second bias is the **hindsight trap**, whereby the decision maker overestimates the degree to which he or she could have predicted an event that has already taken place. One risk of hindsight is that it may foster feelings of inadequacy or insecurity in dealing with future decision situations.

• The **hindsight trap** is a tendency to overestimate the degree to which an event that has already taken place could have been predicted.

Also in this context we can talk about **framing error**. It occurs when managers and teams evaluate and resolve a problem in the context in which they perceive it—either positive or negative. Suppose that research data show that a

• **Framing error** is solving a problem in the context perceived.

new product has a 40 percent market share. What does this really mean to the marketing team? A negative frame views the product as deficient because it is missing 60 percent of the market. Discussion and problem solving within this frame would likely focus on: "What are we doing wrong?" If the marketing team used a positive frame and considered a 40 percent share as a success, the conversation might have been quite different: "How can we do even better?" And by the way, we are constantly exposed to framing in the world of politics; the word used to describe it is *spin*.

Knowing When to Decide

Not only do decision makers have to be on guard against errors caused by heuristics and biases, they also have to manage the decision-making process itself by making the right decisions in the right way at the right time.[24] One of the first issues is whether to actually address a decision situation. Most people are too busy and have too many valuable things to do with their time to personally make decisions on every problem or opportunity that comes their way. The effective manager and team leader knows when to delegate decisions to others, how to set priorities, and when to abstain from acting altogether. When faced with the dilemma of whether or not to deal with a specific problem, asking and answering the following questions can sometimes help.

- *What really matters?* Small and less-significant problems should not get the same time and attention as bigger ones. Even if a mistake is made, the cost of a decision error on a small problem is also small.

- *Might the problem resolve itself?* Putting problems in rank order leaves the less significant for last. Surprisingly, many of these less important problems resolve themselves or are solved by others before you get to them. One less problem to solve leaves decision-making time and energy for other uses.

- *Is this my or our problem?* Many problems can be handled by other people. These should be delegated to people who are best prepared to deal with them; ideally, they should be delegated to people whose work they most affect.

- *Will time spent make a difference?* A really effective decision maker recognizes the difference between problems that realistically can be solved and those that are simply not solvable for all practical purposes.

Knowing Who to Involve

You've most likely heard of this case, and the video is available on YouTube. US Airways flight 1549 hit a flock of birds on take off from LaGuardia Airport, lost engine power, and was headed for a crash. Pilot Chesley Sullenberger III made the decision to land in the Hudson River. The landing was successful and no lives were lost. Called a "hero" for his efforts, Sullenberger described his thinking this way.[25]

> I needed to touch down with the wings exactly level. I needed to touch down with the nose slightly up. I needed to touch down at . . . a descent rate that was survivable. And I needed to touch down just above our minimum flying speed but not below it. And I needed to make all these things happen simultaneously.

McDonald's

When McDonald's launched its new line of specialty drinks not made with coffee–smoothies and sweet frappes–there was a lot of research behind the decision. Focus groups were used to test hot and cold drinks with various combinations of chocolate, caramel, and mint flavors.

Sullenberger obviously did the right thing—he made the decision himself betting on his training and experience and, literally, standing behind it with his own life on the line. But we have to be careful with the lesson from this type of case. Many new managers and team leaders make mistakes in presuming that they must solve every problem by making every decision themselves or that they must allow them to be made by the team itself.[26] In practice, good organizational decisions are made by individuals acting alone, by individuals consulting with others, and by people working together in teams. In true contingency fashion no one option is always superior to the others; who participates and how decisions are to be made should reflect the issues at hand.[27]

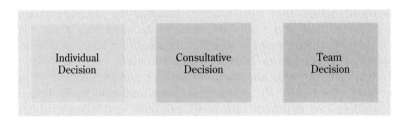

Individual decisions, or authority decisions, are made by one person on behalf of the team.

Consultative decisions are made by one individual after seeking input from or consulting with members of a group.

Team decisions are made by all members of the team.

When **individual decisions**, also called *authority decisions*, are made, the manager or team leader uses information that he or she possesses and decides what to do without involving others. This decision method basically reflects the prerogatives of the persons in authority. In deciding a rotation for lunch hours in a retail store for instance, the team leader may post a schedule for others to follow. In **consultative decisions**, by contrast, inputs are gathered from other persons, and based on this information, the decision maker arrives at a final choice. To continue the example, the team leader may tell members individually that a lunch schedule is needed and ask each for their lunch time preferences before making the decision. In other cases **team decisions** allow group members to make the final choice together. To complete the example, the team leader may facilitate a meeting so that team members collectively reach agreement on a lunch schedule.

Victor Vroom, Phillip Yetton, and Arthur Jago developed the framework shown in Figure 9.4 for helping managers choose the decision-making methods most appropriate for various problem situations to insure both better choices and implementation.[28] They identify these variants on the individual, consultative, and team decision options just described.

- *AI (first variant on the authority decision):* The manager solves the problem or makes the decision alone, using information available at that time.
- *AII (second variant on the authority decision):* The manager obtains the necessary information from team members and then decides on the problem's solution. The team members provide the necessary information but do not generate or evaluate alternatives.
- *CI (first variant on the consultative decision):* The manager shares the problem with team members individually, getting their ideas and suggestions without bringing them all together. The manager then makes a decision.

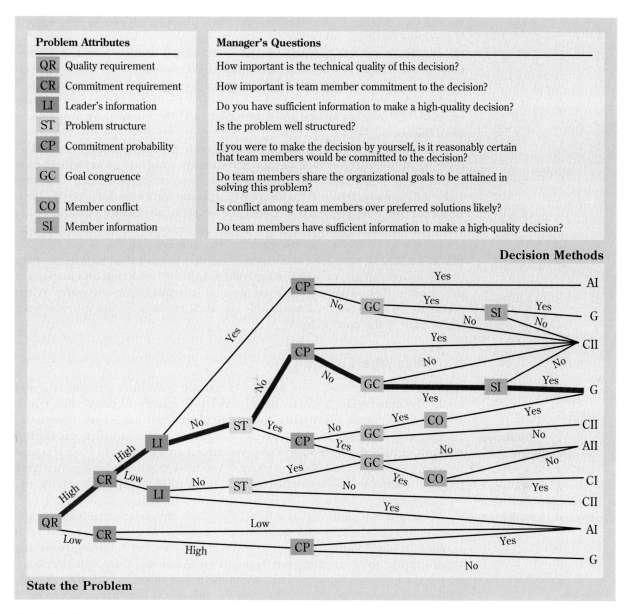

Figure 9.4 The Vroom-Jago model for a manager's use of alternative decision-making methods.

- *CII (second variant on the consultative decision):* The manager shares the problem with team members, collectively obtaining their ideas and suggestions. The manager then makes a decision.
- *G (the team or consensus decision):* The manager shares the problem with team members as a total group and engages them in consensus seeking to arrive at a final decision.

   Figure 9.4 is a decision tree developed from the research of Vroom and his colleagues. Although complex, it helps to illustrate how decision makers can choose among the individual, consultative, and team decision options by considering key decision attributes and criteria. In a team situation, for example, these include: (1) required quality of the decision, (2) commitment needed from team members to implement the decision, (3) amount of information available to team leader, (4) problem structure, (5) chances team members will be committed if leader makes the decision, (6) degree to which team leader and members agree on goals, (7) conflict among team members, and (8) information available to team members.

The key to effectively managing participation in decision making is first knowing when to use each decision method and then knowing how to implement each of them well. Consultative and team decisions are recommended when the leader lacks sufficient expertise and information to solve this problem alone, the problem is unclear and help is needed to clarify the situation, acceptance of the decision and commitment by others are necessary for implementation, and adequate time is available to allow for true participation. By contrast, authority decisions work best when team leaders have the expertise needed to solve the problem, they are confident and capable of acting alone, others are likely to accept and implement the decision they make, and little or no time is available for discussion. When problems must be resolved immediately, the authority decision made by the team leader may be the only option.[29]

Knowing When to Quit

• **Escalating commitment** is the tendency to continue a previously chosen course of action even when feedback suggests that it is failing.

After the sometimes agonizing process of making a decision is completed and implementation begins, it can be hard for decision makers to change their minds and admit a mistake even when things are clearly not going well. Instead of backing off, the tendency is to press on to victory. This is called **escalating commitment**—continuation and renewed efforts on a previously chosen course of action, even though it is not working.[30] The tendency toward escalating commitment is reflected in the popular adage: "If at first you don't succeed, try, try, and try again."

Escalating commitments are a form of decision entrapment that leads people to do things that the facts of a situation do not justify. We should be proactive in spotting "failures" and more open to reversing decisions or dropping plans that do not appear to be working. But again, this is easier said than done. In beginning finance courses, students learn about the fallacy of sunk costs: money committed and spent is gone. The decision to continue is just that—a decision. It needs to be based on what investment is needed and the returns on that investment. This is one of the most difficult aspects of decision making to convey to executives simply because so many of these executives rose to their positions by turning apparently losing courses of action into winners.[31]

The tendency to escalate commitments often outweighs the willingness to disengage from them. Decision makers may rationalize negative feedback as a temporary condition, protect their egos by not admitting that the original decision was a mistake, or characterize any negative results as a "learning experience" that can be overcome with added future effort.

Perhaps you have experienced an inability to call it quits or been on teams with similar reluctances. It's hard to admit to a mistake, especially when a lot of thought and energy went into the decision in the first place; it can be even

Escalation of Commitment by Bank Loan Officers and College Students

Study 1—Bank Loan Officers

Some individuals escalate commitment to a losing course of action when it is clear to others they should quit. McNamara, Moon, and Bromiley asked whether monitoring by more senior management would help stop escalating commitment in a group of bank loan officers.

At first glance their data seem to suggest that monitoring worked. When individual clients were put in higher-risk categories, the loan officers on these accounts were monitored more closely. Undue overcommitment to these higher-risk individuals was apparently reduced. But on closer examination the researchers found that loan officers showed "intervention avoidance" and were reluctant to place clients with deteriorating credit into a higher-risk category which would subject the officers to greater monitoring. For this group of clients, there was overcommitment by the loan officers.

McNamara et al. use their data to argue that the question of escalation is more complex than traditionally recognized and may involve a host of organizational factors that indirectly influence the tendencies of individuals to make undesirable decision commitments.

Study 2—College Students

Escalating commitments breed unethical behavior. That's the conclusion reached in an empirical

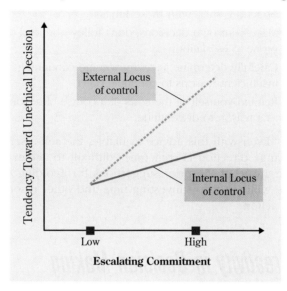

study by Marc and Vera L. Street. They conducted an experiment with 155 undergraduate students working on a computerized investment task. Results showed that exposure to escalation situations increases tendencies toward unethical acts, and that the tendencies further increase with the magnitude of the escalation. Street and Street explain this link between escalation and poor ethics as driven by desires to get out of and avoid the increasing stress of painful situations.

Additional findings from the study showed that students with an external locus of control had a higher propensity to choose an unethical decision alternative than their counterparts with an internal locus of control.

Research Question

What role does escalating commitment play in the day-to-day performance of your work and class teams? Design a study that might identify when and why escalation is likely.

Source: Study 1—Gerry McNamara, Henry Moon, and Philip Bromiley, "Banking on Commitment: Intended and Unintended Consequences of Organizations' Attempt to Attenuate Escalation of Commitment," *Academy of Management Journal* 45 (2002), pp. 443–452. Study 2—Marc Street and Vera L. Street, "The Effects of Escalating Commitment on Ethical Decision Making," *Journal of Business Ethics*, Vol. 64 (2006), pp. 343–356.

harder when one's ego and reputation are tied up with the decision. Fortunately, researchers have provided these ideas on how to avoid getting trapped in escalating commitments.

- Set advance limits on your involvement and commitment to a particular course of action; stick with these limits.
- Make your own decisions; don't follow the lead of others, because they are also prone to escalation.
- Carefully determine just why you are continuing a course of action; if there are insufficient reasons to continue, don't.
- Remind yourself of the costs of a course of action; consider saving these costs as a reason to discontinue.

Even with this advice available, the self-discipline to admit a mistake and change direction is sometimes difficult to achieve. But good decision makers are aware of the prior suggestions for avoiding decision escalation, and they are willing to stop investing time and other resources in unsuccessful courses of action.

Creativity in Decision Making

The last chapter ended with a discussion of brainstorming and the nominal group technique as ways of improving decision making in teams. One of the things often at issue when such techniques are used is **creativity**—the generation of a novel idea or unique approach to solving performance problems or exploiting performance opportunities.[32] In a dynamic environment full of nonroutine problems and vague opportunities, creativity in crafting decisions often determines how well people, teams, and organizations do in response to complex challenges.[33] Just imagine what we can accomplish with all the creative potential that exists within a team and in an organization's workforce. But how do you turn that potential into performance? Part of the answer to this question rests with the individual team members; part also rests with the team and organizational context in which they are asked to perform.

> • **Creativity** generates unique and novel responses to problems.

Stages of Creative Thinking

Creative thinking may unfold in a series of stages as shown in Figure 9.5. First is *preparation*.[34] Here people engage in the active learning and day-to-day sensing required to deal successfully with complex environments. The second stage is *concentration*, whereby actual problems are defined and framed so that

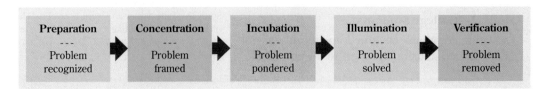

Figure 9.5 Five stages of creative thinking.

alternatives can be considered for dealing with them. In the third stage, *incubation*, people look at the problems in diverse ways that permit the consideration of unusual alternatives, avoiding tendencies toward purely linear and systematic problem solving. The fourth stage is *illumination*, where people respond to flashes of insight and recognize when all pieces to the puzzle suddenly fit into place. The fifth and final stage is *verification*, which proceeds with logical analysis to confirm that good problem-solving decisions have really been made.[35]

Personal Creativity Drivers

Creativity is one of our greatest personal assets, even though it is sometimes untapped. One source of insight into personal creativity drivers is the three-component model of task expertise, task motivation, and creativity skills shown in Figure 9.6.[36] From a management standpoint the model is helpful because it points us in the direction of actions that can be taken to build creativity drivers into a team or work setting.

Creative decisions are more likely to occur when a person has a lot of *task expertise*. Creativity is an outgrowth of skill and typically extends in new directions something one is already good at or knows about. Creative decisions are also more likely when the people making them are high in *task motivation*. Creativity happens in part because people work exceptionally hard to resolve a problem or exploit an opportunity. And creative decisions are more likely when the people involved have stronger *creativity skills* sets. In popular conversations you might refer to this as the contrast between "right brain" thinking—imagination, intuition, spontaneity, and emotion; and "left brain" thinking—logic, order, method,

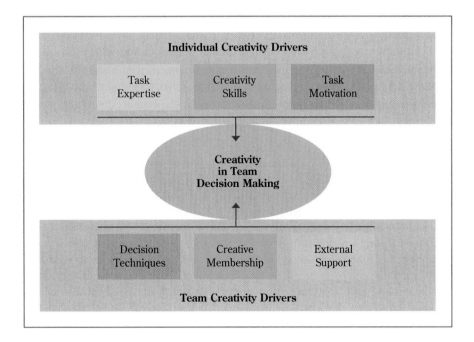

Figure 9.6 Individual and team creativity drivers.

and analysis. Overall, researchers tend to agree that most of us can develop creativity skill sets that involve abilities to:[37]

- work with high energy
- hold ground in face of criticism
- accept responsibility for what happens
- be resourceful even in difficult situations
- be both systematic and intuitive
- be objective—step back and question assumptions
- use divergent thinking—think outside of the box
- use convergent thinking—synthesize and find correct answers
- use lateral thinking—look at diverse ways to solve problems
- transfer learning from one setting to others

Team Creativity Drivers

If you mix creative people together on a team will you get creative results? Not necessarily. It takes more than individual creativity alone to bring creativity to bear on the full multitude of team decisions that are made every day. The team creativity drivers shown in Figure 9.6 are also important. Creativity in teams is enhanced when the situation offers opportunities for creativity, eliminates as many constraints as possible, and provides rewards for creative effort.[38]

The basic building block of team creativity is membership composition. If we want teams to be creative they should be staffed with a *creative membership*. The use of special *decision techniques* such as brainstorming and the nominal group technique can also be helpful, especially when a team encounters process problems.[39] Many other techniques for moving teams toward more creativity in decision making are available, including:

- *Associative play*—making up and telling stories, engaging in art projects, and building toy models that come to mind when dealing with a problem.
- *Cross pollination*—switching members among teams to gain insights from diverse interests, backgrounds, and experiences when working on problems.
- *Analogies and metaphors*—using analogies and metaphors to describe a problem and open pathways to creative thinking.

Even with the right members and decision techniques available, the full creative potential of a team can only be unlocked when the necessary *external support* is added to the mix. At one level this involves making creativity a strategic priority in the broader organizational context. But it also involves smaller, more everyday things that are easily missed. Team creativity is enhanced by team leaders who have the patience to allow for creative processes to work themselves through a decision situation and by top management that is willing to provide the resources—time, technology, and space, for example, that are helpful to the creative processes. Think creatively, for example, the next time you see a young child playing with a really neat toy. It may be from *Fisher-Price Toys*, part of Mattel, Inc. In the firm's headquarters you'll find a special place

Leaders on Leadership

EVAN WILLIAMS AND BIZ STONE HAVE US ALL A TWITTER

"My Siamese cat Skimbleshanks is up a tree . . . At Wilco concert—Jeff Tweedy is so cool . . . Home alone ☹ with Willie Nelson ☺ . . . . Flying to Ireland, wish me luck driving . . . Just saw Todd with Stephanie!"

So who cares? Well it turns out that almost everyone cares. That's the genius of Evan Williams and Biz Stone, cofounders of Twitter, the microblog Web site. Twitter moved texting into the upper limits and was a rush from the get go. Sending 140 character or less "tweets" by mobile text, instant messaging, or Web quickly hit the mark with traffic rising to over 6 million users in a year's time.

Surprisingly though, Stone says that Twitter was a "side project," and that "It took us a while to figure out it was really a big deal." Now Williams says, "We want to have as large an impact as possible."

And the impact is already there. Twitter is quick, easy, and ever-present as a social networking tool. But it isn't just for friends and family—companies are using it, radio and television shows are using it, and, of course, celebrities are using it.

Williams and Stone are thinking millions too—dollars, that is. Expectations are that the firm will be sold and that the bidding will be high. But a rumored $500 million offer from Facebook was turned down. "I guess we have a lot of things we think we can prove," Stone says, "to provide the infrastructure for a new kind of communication, and then support the creativity that emerges." For his part, Williams points out "we're totally focused on making the best user experience possible and building a defensible communications network."

Both Stone and Williams have been part of the Internet business community through many past ventures, including Blogger, which was purchased by Google. Williams is credited with coining the word "blog," and Stone has published two books on blogging. No wonder that Williams, self-described as "An American entrepreneur, originally a farm boy from Nebraska, who's been very lucky in business and life" has this to say: "We really believe Twitter is potentially massive in terms of its impact on millions and millions of people." How else can you so easily find out where people are and what they are doing right now?

Hiring like crazy. . . . Growing faster than Google, eBay, and Amazon at its young age of three, Twitter has transformed from something that Stone calls "the side project that took," into something of transformative proportions.

called the "Cave," and it's not your typical office space. Picture bean-bag chairs, soft lighting, casual chairs, and couches. It's a place for brainstorming, where designers, marketers, engineers, and others can meet and join in freewheeling to come up with the next great toy for preschoolers. Consultants recommend that such innovation spaces be separated from the normal workplace and be large enough for no more than 15 to 20 people.[40]

Resources in The OB Skills Workbook

These learning activities from *The OB Skills Workbook* are suggested for Chapter 9.

Case for Critical Thinking	Team and Experiential Exercises	Self-Assessment Portfolio
• Decisions, Decisions	• Decode	• Intuitive Ability
	• Lost at Sea	• Decision-Making Biases
	• Entering the Unknown	
	• Fostering the Creative Spirit	

study guide

Summary Questions and Answers

What is involved in the decision-making process?

- Decision making is a process of identifying problems and opportunities and choosing among alternative courses of action for dealing successfully with them.

- The steps in the decision-making process, viewed as a rational model, are (1) find and define the problem, (2) generate and evaluate alternatives, (3) decide on the preferred course of action, (4) implement the decision, and (5) evaluate the results.

- Ethical reasoning should be applied in each stage of the decision-making process to ensure that all possible moral problems and dilemmas are dealt with properly.

- Use of recommended "criteria questions" and "spotlight questions" is a way of double checking the ethical soundness of decision making.

- Decisions in organizations are made under conditions of certainty, risk, and uncertainly; the challenges to the decision maker are higher in risk and uncertain environments.

- Routine problems can be dealt with through programmed decisions; nonroutine or novel problems require nonprogrammed decisions that are crafted to fit the situation at hand; crisis problems occur unexpectedly and can lead to disaster if managers fail to handle them quickly and properly.

What are the alternative decision-making models?

- In the classical decision model, optimum decisions identifying the absolute best alternative are made in conditions where full information is available and after fully analyzing all possible alternatives and their known consequences.

- In the behavioral decision model, satisficing decisions that choose the first acceptable alternative are made in conditions of limited information and bounded rationality.

- In the garbage can model of decision-making, problems, solutions, participants, and choice situations are all mixed up in dynamic interactions within an ever changing field of organizational forces.

- In the intuitive model, decision makers tend to deal with many aspects of a problem at once, jump quickly from one issue to another, and act on hunches from experience or on spontaneous ideas.

What decision-making traps and issues are common?

- The use of judgmental heuristics, or simplifying rules of thumb, can lead to biased results in decision making; such heuristics include availability decisions based on recent events, representativeness decisions based on similar events, and anchoring and adjustment decisions based on historical precedents.

- Other sources of bias in individual and team decisions are confirmation error, seeking information to justify a decision already made; hindsight trap, overestimating the extent to which current events could have been predicted; and framing error, viewing a problem in a limited context.

- Individuals and teams must know when to make decisions, realizing that not every problem requires an immediate decision.

- Individuals and teams must know who should be involved in making decisions, making use of individual, consultative, and team decisions as needed to best fit the problems and opportunities being faced.

- Individuals and teams must know when to decide to quit and abandon a course of action; they are aware of and able to counteract tendencies toward escalating commitment to previously chosen courses of action that are not working.

What can be done to stimulate creativity in decision making?

- Creativity is the generation of a novel idea or unique approach to solving performance problems or exploiting performance opportunities.

- The process of creative thinking can be described in the five steps of preparation, concentration, incubation, illumination, and verification.

- Creativity in decision making can be enhanced by personal creativity drivers that include task expertise, motivation, and individual creativity skills.

- Creativity in decision making can be enhanced by situational creativity drivers that include a composition of creative members, use of helpful decision techniques, and external support for creativity.

Key Terms

Anchoring and adjustment heuristic (p. 216)
Availability heuristic (p. 216)
Behavioral decision model (p. 213)

Certain environments (p. 211)
Classical decision model (p. 213)
Confirmation trap (p. 216)

Consultative decisions (p. 218)
Creativity (p. 222)
Crisis decision (p. 210)
Criteria questions (p. 208)

Self-Test 9

Multiple Choice

1. After a preferred course of action has been implemented, the next step in the decision-making process is to _____. (a) recycle the process (b) look for additional problems or opportunities (c) evaluate results (d) document the reasons for the decision

2. In which environment does the decision maker deal with probabilities regarding possible courses of action and their consequences? (a) certain (b) risk (c) organized anarchy (d) uncertain

3. If a team approaches problems in a rational and analytical way, with members trying to solve them in step-by-step fashion, it is well described as a team using _____. (a) systematic thinking (b) intuitive thinking (c) escalating thinking (d) associative thinking

4. An individual or team that must deal with limited information and substantial risk is most likely to make decisions based on _____. (a) optimizing (b) classical decision theory (c) behavioral decision theory (d) escalation

5. A team leader who makes a decision not to launch a new product because the last new product launch failed is falling prey to the _____ heuristic. (a) anchoring (b) availability (c) adjustment (d) representativeness

6. The five steps in the creativity process are preparation, _____, illumination, _____, and verification. (a) extension, evaluation (b) reduction, concentration (c) adaptation, extension (d) concentration, incubation

7. In Vroom's decision-making model, the choice among individual and team decision approaches is based on criteria that include quality requirements, availability of information, and _____. (a) need for implementation commitments (b) size of the organization (c) number of people involved (d) position power of the leader

8. The saying "If at first you don't succeed, try, try again" is most associated with a decision-making tendency called _____. (a) groupthink (b) the confirmation trap (c) escalating commitment (d) associative choice

9. The _____ decision model views individuals as making optimizing decisions, whereas the _____ decision model views them as making satisficing decisions. (a) behavioral/judgmental heuristics (b) classical/behavioral (c) judgmental heuristics/ethical (d) crisis/routine

10. A common mistake by managers facing crisis situations is _____. (a) trying to get too much information before responding (b) relying too much on team decision making (c) isolating themselves to make the decision alone (d) forgetting to use their crisis management plan

11. Which model views the main components of the choice process—problems, solutions, participants, and choice situations—as all mixed up together in a dynamic and shifting field of organizational forces? (a) the garbage can model (b) the behavioral model (c) the turbulence model (d) the classical model

12. The _____ bases a decision on similarities between the situation at hand and stereotypes of similar occurrences. (a) representativeness heuristic (b) anchoring and adjustment heuristic (c) confirmation trap (d) hindsight trap

13. The _____ bases a decision on incremental adjustments to an initial value determined by historical precedent or some reference point. (a) representativeness heuristic (b) anchoring and adjustment heuristic (c) confirmation trap (d) hindsight trap

14. The _____ is the tendency to seek confirmation for what is already thought to be true and not to search for disconfirming information. (a) representativeness heuristic (b) anchoring and adjustment heuristic (c) confirmation trap (d) hindsight trap

15. Team creativity drivers include creative members, decision techniques, and _____. (a) task motivation (b) task expertise (c) long-term goals (d) external support

Short Response

16. What are heuristics, and how can they affect individual decision making?

17. What are the main differences among individual, consultative, and team decisions?

18. What is escalating commitment, and why is it important to recognize it in decision making?

19. What questions might a manager or team leader ask to help determine which problems to deal with and in which priority?

Applications Essay

20. As a participant in a new mentoring program between your university and a local high school, you have volunteered to give a presentation to a class of sophomores on the challenges of achieving creativity in teams. The goal is to motivate them to think creatively as individuals and to help make sure that their course teams achieve creativity as well when assignments call for it. What will you tell them?

10

Conflict and Negotiation

chapter at a glance

Managerial work is interpersonal work, and the word "yes" can often open doors, particularly in situations prone to conflict or involving negotiations. Here's what to look for in Chapter 10. Don't forget to check your learning with the Summary Questions & Answers and Self-Test in the end-of-chapter Study Guide.

WHAT IS THE NATURE OF CONFLICT IN ORGANIZATIONS?

Types of Conflict

Levels of Conflict

Functional and Dysfunctional Conflict

Culture and Conflict

HOW CAN CONFLICT BE MANAGED?

Stages of Conflict

Causes of Conflict

Indirect Conflict Management Strategies

Direct Conflict Management Strategies

WHAT IS THE NATURE OF NEGOTIATION IN ORGANIZATIONS?

Negotiation Goals and Outcomes

Ethical Aspects of Negotiation

Organizational Settings for Negotiation

Culture and Negotiation

WHAT ARE ALTERNATIVE STRATEGIES FOR NEGOTIATION?

Distributive Negotiation

Integrative Negotiation

How to Gain Integrative Agreements

Common Negotiation Pitfalls

Third-Party Roles in Negotiation

Why is it that a CEO brought in from outside the industry fared the best as the big three automakers went into crisis mode during the economic downturn? That's a question that Ford Motor Company's chairman, William Clay Ford Jr., is happy to answer. The person he's talking about is Alan Mulally, a former Boeing executive hired to retool the automaker and put it back on a competitive track.

Bill Ford says: "Alan was the right choice and it gets more right every day."

Many wondered at the time if an "airplane guy" could run an auto company. But Mulally's management experience and insights are proving well up to the task. One consultant remarked: "The speed with which Mulally has transformed Ford into a more nimble and healthy operation has been one of the more impressive jobs I've seen." He went on to say that without Mulally's impact Ford might well have gone out of business. One of his senior managers says: "I'm going into my fourth year on the job. I've never had such consistency of purpose before."

In addition to many changes to modernize plants and streamline operations, Mulally tackled the problems dealing with functional chimneys and a lack of open communication. William Ford says that the firm had a culture that "loved to meet" and in which managers got together to discuss the message they wanted to communicate to the top executives: all agreement, no conflict. Mulally changed that with a focus on transparency, data-based decision making, and cooperation between divisions. When some of the senior executives balked and

Alan Mulally makes mark by restructuring Ford.

tried to complain to Ford, he refused to listen and reinforced Mulally's authority to run the firm his way. And when executives were reluctant to resolve conflicts among themselves, Mulally remained tough: "They can either work together or they can come see me," he says. And he hasn't shied away from the United Auto Workers Union either. He negotiated new agreements that brought labor costs down to be more competitive with arch-rival Toyota.

don't underestimate the power of "yes"

Conflict in Organizations

The daily work of organizations revolves around people and the interpersonal dynamics involved in getting them engaged in goal accomplishment. And just as in the case of Alan Mulally at Ford, we all need skills to work well with others who don't always agree with us and in team situations that are often complicated and stressful.[1] **Conflict** occurs whenever disagreements exist in a social situation over issues of substance, or whenever emotional antagonisms create frictions between individuals or groups.[2] Team leaders and members can spend considerable time dealing with conflicts; sometimes they are directly involved, and other times they act as mediators or neutral third parties to help resolve conflicts between other people.[3] Managers have to be comfortable with conflict dynamics in the workplace and know how to best deal with them. This includes being able to recognize situations that have the potential for conflict and address them in ways that will best serve the needs of both the organization and the people involved.[4]

> • **Conflict** occurs when parties disagree over substantive issues or when emotional antagonisms create friction between them.

Types of Conflict

Conflicts in teams, at work, and in our personal lives occur in at least two basic forms—substantive and emotional. Both types are common, ever present, and challenging. The question is: How well prepared are you to deal successfully with them?

Substantive conflict is a fundamental disagreement over ends or goals to be pursued and the means for their accomplishment.[5] A dispute with one's boss or other team members over a plan of action to be followed, such as the marketing strategy for a new product, is an example of substantive conflict. When people work together every day, it is only normal that different viewpoints on a variety of substantive workplace issues will arise. At times people will disagree over such things as team and organizational goals, the allocation of resources, the distribution of rewards, policies and procedures, and task assignments.

> • **Substantive conflict** involves fundamental disagreement over ends or goals to be pursued and the means for their accomplishment.

In contrast, **emotional conflict** involves interpersonal difficulties that arise over feelings of anger, mistrust, dislike, fear, resentment, and the like.[6] This conflict is commonly known as a "clash of personalities." How many times, for example, have you heard comments such as "I can't stand working with him" or "She always rubs me the wrong way" or "I wouldn't do what he asked if you begged me"? When emotional conflicts creep into work situations, they can drain energies and distract people from task priorities and goals. They can emerge in a wide variety of settings and are common in teams, among co-workers, and in superior–subordinate relationships.

> • **Emotional conflict** involves interpersonal difficulties that arise over feelings of anger, mistrust, dislike, fear, resentment, and the like.

Levels of Conflict

Our first tendency may be to think of conflict as something that happens between people, and that is certainly a valid example of what we can call "interpersonal conflict." But scholars point out that conflicts in teams and organizations need to be recognized and understood on other levels as well. The full range of conflicts that we experience at work includes those emerging from the interpersonal, intrapersonal, intergroup, and interorganizational levels.

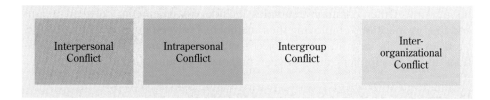

Interpersonal conflict occurs between two or more individuals who are in opposition to one another. It may be substantive, emotional, or both. Two persons debating each other aggressively on the merits of hiring a specific job applicant is an example of a substantive interpersonal conflict. Two persons continually in disagreement over each other's choice of work attire is an example of an emotional interpersonal conflict. Interpersonal conflict often arises in the performance evaluation process. When P. J. Smoot became learning and development leader at International Paper's Memphis, Tennessee, office, for example, she recognized that the traditional concept of the boss passing judgment often fails in motivating subordinates and improving their performance. So she started a new program that began the reviews from the bottom up—with the employee's self-evaluation and a focus on the manager's job as a coach and facilitator. Her advice is to "Listen for understanding and then react honestly and constructively. Focus on the business goals, not the personality."[7]

Intrapersonal conflict is tension experienced within the individual due to actual or perceived pressures from incompatible goals or expectations. *Approach–approach conflict* occurs when a person must choose between two positive and equally attractive alternatives. An example is when someone has to choose between a valued promotion in the organization or a desirable new job with another firm. *Avoidance–avoidance conflict* occurs when a person must choose between two negative and equally unattractive alternatives. An example is being asked either to accept a job transfer to another town in an undesirable location or to have one's employment with an organization terminated. *Approach–avoidance conflict* occurs when a person must decide to do something that has both positive and negative consequences. An example is being offered a higher-paying job with responsibilities that make unwanted demands on one's personal time.

Intergroup conflict occurs between teams, perhaps ones competing for scarce resources or rewards, and perhaps ones whose members have emotional problems with one another. The classic example is conflict among functional groups or departments, such as marketing and manufacturing, within organizations. Sometimes such conflicts have substantive roots, such as marketing focusing on sales revenue goals and manufacturing focusing on cost efficiency goals. Other times such conflicts have emotional roots as "egos" in the respective departments cause each to want to look better than the other in a certain situation. Intergroup conflict is quite common in organizations, and it can make the coordination and integration of task activities very difficult.[8] The growing use of cross-functional teams and task forces is one way of trying to minimize such conflicts by improving horizontal communication.

Interorganizational conflict is most commonly thought of in terms of the competition and rivalry that characterizes firms operating in the same markets.

- **Interpersonal conflict** occurs between two or more individuals in opposition to each other.

- **Intrapersonal conflict** occurs within the individual because of actual or perceived pressures from incompatible goals or expectations.

- **Intergroup conflict** occurs among groups in an organization.

- **Interorganizational conflict** occurs between organizations.

Twitter

Employers are finding that all that Twitters is not gold. Problems and conflicts arise when employee "Tweets" cross the line in discussing customers, new hires, and even co-workers. Two rules of thumb are finding their way into Twitter Codes of Conduct: 1–Don't be stupid. 2–Don't post anything you don't want your mom to read.

A good example is the continuing battle between U.S. businesses and their global rivals: Ford vs. Toyota, or Nokia vs. Motorola, for example. But interorganizational conflict is a much broader issue than that represented by market competition alone. Other common examples include disagreements between unions and the organizations employing their members, between government regulatory agencies and the organizations subject to their surveillance, between organizations and their suppliers, and between organizations and outside activist groups.

Functional and Dysfunctional Conflict

There is no doubt that conflict in organizations can be upsetting both to the individuals directly involved and to others affected by its occurrence. It can be quite uncomfortable, for example, to work in an environment in which two co-workers are continually hostile toward each other or two teams are always battling for top management attention. In OB, and as shown in Figure 10.1, however, we recognize that conflict can have both a functional or constructive side and a dysfunctional or destructive side.

• **Functional conflict** results in positive benefits to the group.

Functional conflict, also called *constructive conflict*, results in benefits to individuals, the team, or the organization. On the positive side, conflict can bring important problems to the surface so they can be addressed. It can cause decisions to be considered carefully and perhaps reconsidered to ensure that the right path of action is being followed. It can increase the amount of information used for decision making. And it can offer opportunities for creativity that can improve individual, team, or organizational performance. Indeed, an effective manager or team leader is able to stimulate constructive conflict in situations in which satisfaction with the status quo inhibits needed change and development.

• **Dysfunctional conflict** works to the group's or organization's disadvantage.

Dysfunctional conflict, or *destructive conflict*, works to the disadvantage of an individual or team. It diverts energies, hurts group cohesion, promotes interpersonal hostilities, and overall creates a negative environment for workers. This type of conflict occurs, for example, when two team members are unable to work together because of interpersonal differences—a destructive emotional conflict, or when the members of a work unit fail to act because they cannot agree on task goals—a destructive substantive conflict. Destructive conflicts of

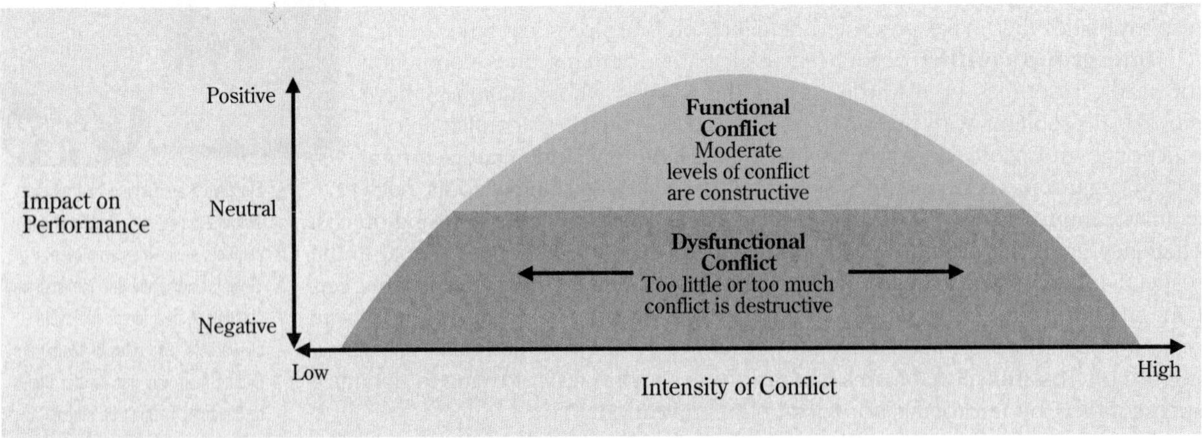

Figure 10.1 The two faces of conflict: functional conflict and dysfunctional conflict.

AGE BECOMES AN ISSUE IN JOB LAYOFFS

Picture the manager—well meaning, an overall good person, but facing a real dilemma. Job cuts need to be made in a bad economy. Who gets laid off? Sarah is young, single, and years out of college; she is very hard working, topped the performance ratings this year, and always steps forward when volunteers are needed for evening work or travel. Mary is mid-40s, has two children, and her husband is a pediatrician; her performance is good, always at or above average during performance reviews, but she has limited time available for evening work and out-of-town travel.

Who gets picked for the layoff, Sarah or Mary? Chances are it's going to be Sarah. *The Wall Street Journal* reports that younger workers are at greater risk of layoffs because many employers use a "last in/first out" rule when cutting back staff. This is true even though the younger workers tend to earn less than their older counterparts and may even be outper-forming them. One reason is conflict avoidance; who wants to face an age discrimination lawsuit? Another is the emotional toll that making layoff decisions places on managers; it just seems easier to let go the younger person, who has few complicating personal and family situations.

David Schauer, a school superintendent in Phoenix, says he sent layoff notices to 68 teachers all in their first year of employment. But he also says "My worst fear is that really good people will leave teaching." Nicole Ryan, a teacher in New York, received just such a notice. She says: "I knew it was coming because, based on seniority, I was lower on the totem pole." But, she adds: "It didn't make it any easier."

> **What's Right?** Are managers doing the right things when they lay off younger workers first, even when they are high performers? Is it correct to take "personal and family" factors into account when making decisions on who gets to keep their jobs and who doesn't? Is it fair that younger workers have more to fear about keeping their jobs because some managers are unwilling to face possible age discrimination claims from older workers?

these types can decrease performance and job satisfaction as well as contribute to absenteeism and job turnover. Managers and team leaders should be alert to destructive conflicts and be quick to take action to prevent or eliminate them—or at least minimize their disadvantages.

Culture and Conflict

Society today shows many signs of wear and tear in social relationships. We experience difficulties born of racial tensions, homophobia, gender gaps, and more. All trace their roots to tensions among people who are different from one another in some way. They are also a reminder that culture and cultural differences must be considered for their conflict potential. Among the dimensions of national culture, for example, substantial differences may be noted in time orientation. When persons from short-term cultures such as the United States try to work with persons from long-term cultures such as Japan, the likelihood of conflict developing is high. The same holds true when individualists work with collectivists and when persons from high-power-distance cultures work with those from low-power-distance cultures.[9]

People who are not able or willing to recognize and respect cultural differences can contribute to the emergence of dysfunctional situations in multicultural teams. On the other hand, sensitivity and respect when working across cultures can often tap the performance advantages of both diversity and constructive conflict. Consider these comments from members of a joint European and American project team at Corning. "Something magical happens," says engineer John Thomas. "Europeans are very creative thinkers; they take time to really reflect on a problem to come up with the very best theoretical solution, Americans are more tactical and practical—we want to get down to developing a working solution as soon as possible." His partner at Fontainebleau in France says: "The French are more focused on ideas and concepts. If we get blocked in the execution of those ideas, we give up. Not the Americans. They pay more attention to details, processes, and time schedules. They make sure they are prepared and have involved everyone in the planning process so that they won't get blocked. But it's best if you mix the two approaches. In the end, you will achieve the best results."[10]

Conflict Management

Conflict can be addressed in many ways, but the important goal is to achieve or set the stage for true **conflict resolution**—a situation in which the underlying reasons for dysfunctional conflict are eliminated. When conflicts go unresolved the stage is often set for future conflicts of the same or related sort. Rather than trying to deny the existence of conflict or settle on a temporary resolution, it is always best to deal with important conflicts in such ways that they are completely resolved.[11] This requires a good understanding of the stages of conflict, the potential causes of conflict, and indirect and direct approaches to conflict management.

* **Conflict resolution** occurs when the reasons for a conflict are eliminated.

Stages of Conflict

Most conflicts develop in stages, as shown in Figure 10.2. *Conflict antecedents* establish the conditions from which conflicts are likely to develop. When the antecedent conditions become the basis for substantive or emotional differences between people or groups, the stage of *perceived conflict* exists. Of course, this perception may be held by only one of the conflicting parties. It is important to distinguish between perceived and *felt conflict*. When conflict is felt, it is experienced as tension that motivates the person to take action to reduce feelings of discomfort. For conflict to be resolved, all parties should perceive the conflict and feel the need to do something about it.

Manifest conflict is expressed openly in behavior. It is followed by *conflict aftermath*. At this stage removing or correcting the antecedents results in *conflict resolution* while failing to do so results in *conflict suppression*. With suppression, no change in antecedent conditions occurs even though the manifest conflict behaviors may be temporarily controlled. This occurs, for example, when one or both parties choose to ignore conflict in their dealings with one another. Conflict suppression is a superficial and often temporary state that leaves the situation open to future conflicts over similar issues. Although it is perhaps useful in the short run, only true conflict resolution establishes conditions that eliminate an existing conflict and reduce the potential for it to recur in the future.

Manifest conflict can be addressed through true conflict resolution or merely suppressed, a condition leaving the situation prone to future conflicts of a similar nature.

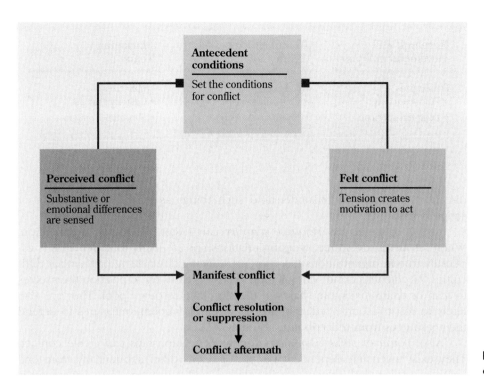

Figure 10.2 The stages of conflict.

Causes of Conflict

The very nature of organizations as hierarchical systems provides a basis for conflict as individuals and teams work within the authority structure. *Vertical conflict* occurs between levels and commonly involves supervisor–subordinate and team leader–team member disagreements over resources, goals, deadlines, or performance results. *Horizontal conflict* occurs between persons or groups working at the same hierarchical level. These disputes commonly involve goal incompatibilities, resource scarcities, or purely interpersonal factors. And, *line–staff conflict* involves disagreements between line and staff personnel over who has authority and control over decisions on matters such as budgets, technology, and human resource practices. Also common are *role ambiguity conflicts* that occur when the communication of task expectations is unclear or upsetting in some way, such as a team member receiving different expectations from different sources. Conflict is likely when individuals or teams are placed in ambiguous situations where it is difficult for them to understand just who is responsible for what, and why.

Task and workflow interdependencies are breeding grounds for conflicts. Disputes and open disagreements may erupt among people and teams that are required to cooperate to meet challenging goals.[12] When interdependence is high—that is, when a person or group must rely on or ask for contributions from one or more others to achieve its goals—conflicts often occur. You will notice this, for example, in a fast-food restaurant, when the people serving the food have to wait too long for it to be delivered from the cooks. Conflict escalates with *structural differentiation* where different teams and work units pursue different goals with different time horizons as shown in Figure 10.3. Conflict also develops out of *domain ambiguities* when individuals or teams lack adequate task

Research & Development Team	Manufacturing Team	Marketing Team
Emphasizes • Product quality • Long time horizon	Emphasizes • Cost efficiency • Short time horizon	Emphasizes • Customer needs • Short time horizon

Figure 10.3 Structural differentiation as a potential source of conflict among functional teams.

direction or goals and misunderstand such things as customer jurisdiction or scope of authority.

Actual or perceived *resource scarcity* can foster destructive competition. When resources are scarce, working relationships are likely to suffer. This is especially true in organizations that are experiencing downsizing or financial difficulties. As cutbacks occur, various individuals or teams try to position themselves to gain or retain maximum shares of the shrinking resource pool. They are also likely to resist resource redistribution or to employ countermeasures to defend their resources from redistribution to others.

Also, *power or value asymmetries* in work relationships can create conflict. They exist when interdependent people or teams differ substantially from one another in status and influence or in values. Conflict resulting from asymmetry is prone to occur, for example, when a low-power person needs the help of a high-power person who does not respond, when people who hold dramatically different values are forced to work together on a task, or when a high-status person is required to interact with and perhaps be dependent on someone of lower status.

OB SAVVY 10.1
Common Causes of Conflicts in Organizations

- *Unresolved prior conflicts*—When conflicts go unresolved, they remain latent and often reemerge in the future as the basis for conflicts over the same or related matters.
- *Role ambiguities*—When people aren't sure what they are supposed to do, conflict with others is likely; task uncertainties increase the odds of working at cross-purposes at least some of the time.
- *Resource scarcities*—When people have to share resources with one another and/or when they have to compete with one another for resources, the conditions are ripe for conflict.
- *Task interdependencies*—When people must depend on others doing things first before they can do their own jobs, conflicts often occur; dependency on others creates anxieties and other pressures.
- *Domain ambiguities*—When people are unclear about how their objectives or those of their teams fit with those being pursued by others, or when their objectives directly compete in win-lose fashion, conflict is likely to occur.
- *Structural differentiation*—When people work in parts of the organization where structures, goals, time horizons, and even staff compositions are very different, conflict is likely with other units.

Indirect Conflict Management Strategies

Most managers will tell you that not all conflict management in teams and organizations can be resolved by getting the people involved to adopt new attitudes, behaviors, and stances toward one another. Think about it. Aren't there likely to be times when personalities and emotions prove irreconcilable? In such cases a more indirect or structural approach to conflict management can often help. It uses such strategies as reduced interdependence, appeals to common goals, hierarchical referral, and alterations in the use of mythology and scripts to deal with the conflict situation.

Reduced Interdependence   When workflow conflicts exist, managers can adjust the level of interdependency among teams or individuals.[13] One simple option is *decoupling*, or taking action to eliminate or reduce the required contact between conflicting parties. In some cases team tasks can be adjusted to reduce the number of required points of coordination. The conflicting units can then be separated from one another, and each can be provided separate access to valued resources. Although decoupling may reduce conflict, it may also result in duplication and a poor allocation of valued resources.

Buffering is another approach that can be used when the inputs of one team are the outputs of another. The classic buffering technique is to build an inventory, or buffer, between the teams so that any output slowdown or excess is absorbed by the inventory and does not directly pressure the target group. Although it reduces conflict, this technique is increasingly out of favor because it increases inventory costs. This consequence is contrary to the elements of just-in-time delivery, which is now valued in operations management.

Conflict management can sometimes be facilitated by assigning people to serve as formal linking pins between groups that are prone to conflict.[14] Persons in *linking-pin roles*, such as project liaisons, are expected to understand the operations, members, needs, and norms of their host teams. They are supposed to use this knowledge to help the team work better with others in order to accomplish mutual tasks. Although expensive, this technique is often used when different specialized groups, such as engineering and sales, must closely coordinate their efforts on complex and long-term projects.

Appeals to Common Goals   An *appeal to common goals* can focus the attention of potentially conflicting individuals and teams on one mutually desirable conclusion. By elevating the potential dispute to a common framework wherein the parties recognize their mutual interdependence in achieving common goals, petty disputes can be put in perspective. In a course team where members are arguing over content choices for a PowerPoint presentation, for example, it might help to remind everyone that the goal is to impress the instructor and get an "A" for the presentation and that this is only possible if everyone contributes their best. An appeal to higher goals offers a common frame of reference that can be very helpful for analyzing differences and reconciling disagreements.

Hierarchical Referral   *Hierarchical referral* uses the chain of command for conflict resolution.[15] Here, problems are moved from the level of conflicting individuals or teams and referred up the hierarchy for more senior managers to address. Whereas hierarchical referral can be definitive in a given case, it also has limitations. If conflict is severe and recurring, the continual use of hierarchical referral may not result in true conflict resolution. Managers removed from day-to-day affairs may fail to diagnose the real causes of a conflict, and conflict resolution may be superficial. Busy managers may tend to consider most conflicts as results of poor interpersonal relations and may act quickly to replace a person with a perceived "personality" problem.

Altering Scripts and Myths   In some situations, conflict is superficially managed by scripts, or behavioral routines, that become part of the organization's culture.[16] The scripts become rituals that allow the conflicting parties to vent their frustrations and to recognize that they are mutually dependent on one another via the larger corporation. An example is a monthly meeting of "department heads," which is held presumably for purposes of coordination and problem solving but

Workplace Bullying Institute

Have you been bullied at work, perhaps in conflict situations? About 37 percent of workers say they have been exposed to such bullying tactics as being glared at with hostility, given the silent treatment, or treated rudely and disrespectfully, as well as having false rumors spread about them.

actually becomes just a polite forum for superficial agreement.[17] Managers in such cases know their scripts and accept the difficulty of truly resolving any major conflicts. By sticking with the script, expressing only low-key disagreement, and then quickly acting as if everything has been resolved, for instance, the managers publicly act as if problems are being addressed. Such scripts can be altered to allow and encourage active confrontation of issues and disagreements.

Direct Conflict Management Strategies

In addition to the indirect conflict management strategies just discussed, it is also very important for everyone to understand how conflict management plays out in face-to-face fashion. Figure 10.4 shows five direct conflict management strategies that vary in their emphasis on cooperativeness and assertiveness in the interpersonal dynamics of the situation. Consultants and academics generally agree that true conflict resolution can occur only when the underlying substantive and emotional reasons for the conflict are identified and dealt with through a solution that allows all conflicting parties to "win." However, the reality is that direct conflict management may pursue lose-lose and win-lose as well as win-win outcomes.[18]

Lose-Lose Strategies   *Lose-lose conflict* occurs when nobody really gets what he or she wants in a conflict situation. The underlying reasons for the conflict remain unaffected, and a similar conflict is likely to occur in the future. Lose-lose

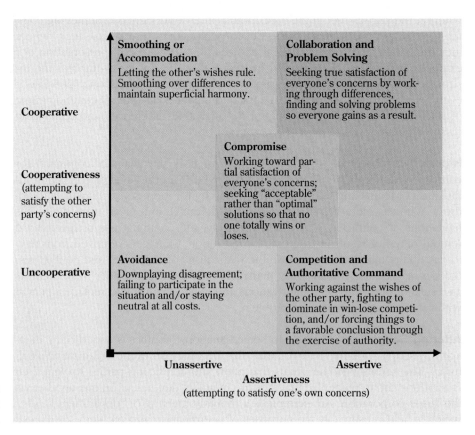

Figure 10.4 Five direct conflict management strategies.

outcomes are likely when the conflict management strategies involve little or no assertiveness.

Avoidance is an extreme form that basically displays no attention toward a conflict. No one acts assertively or cooperatively; everyone simply pretends the conflict does not really exist and hopes it will go away. **Accommodation**, or **smoothing** as it is sometimes called, involves playing down differences among the conflicting parties and highlighting similarities and areas of agreement. This peaceful coexistence ignores the real essence of a given conflict and often creates frustration and resentment. **Compromise** occurs when each party shows moderate assertiveness and cooperation and is ultimately willing to give up something of value to the other. As a result of no one getting their full desires, the antecedent conditions for future conflicts are established. See OB Savvy 15.1 for tips on when to use this and other conflict management styles.

Win-Lose Strategies   In *win-lose conflict*, one party achieves its desires at the expense and to the exclusion of the other party's desires. This is a high-assertiveness and low-cooperativeness situation. It may result from outright **competition** in which one party achieves a victory through force, superior skill, or domination. It may also occur as a result of **authoritative command**, whereby a formal authority such as manager or team leader simply dictates a solution and specifies what is gained and what is lost by whom. Win-lose strategies of these types fail to address the root causes of the conflict and tend to suppress the desires of at least one of the conflicting parties. As a result, future conflicts over the same issues are likely to occur.

Win-Win Strategies   *Win-win conflict* is achieved by a blend of both high cooperativeness and high assertiveness.[19] **Collaboration**, or *problem solving*, involves recognition by all conflicting parties that something is wrong and needs attention. It stresses gathering and evaluating information in solving disputes and making choices. Win-win outcomes eliminate the reasons for continuing or resurrecting the conflict because nothing has been avoided or suppressed. All relevant issues are raised and openly discussed.

The ultimate test for collaboration and a win-win solution is whether or not the conflicting parties see that the solution to the conflict (1) achieves each party's goals, (2) is acceptable to both parties, and (3) establishes a process whereby all parties involved see a responsibility to be open and honest about facts and feelings. When success in each of these areas is achieved, the likelihood of true conflict resolution is greatly increased. However, it is also important to recognize that collaboration and problem solving often take time and consume lots of energy; something to which the parties must be willing to commit. Collaboration and problem solving may not be feasible if the firm's dominant culture rewards competition too highly and fails to place a value on cooperation.[20] And finally, OB Savvy 10.2 points out that each of the conflict management strategies has advantages under certain conditions.

- **Avoidance** involves pretending a conflict does not really exist.
- **Accommodation**, or **smoothing**, involves playing down differences and finding areas of agreement.
- **Compromise** occurs when each party gives up something of value to the other.
- **Competition** seeks victory by force, superior skill, or domination.
- **Authoritative command** uses formal authority to end conflict.
- **Collaboration** involves recognition that something is wrong and needs attention through problem solving.

OB SAVVY 10.2

When Alternative Conflict Management Strategies May Be Useful

- *Avoidance* may be used when an issue is trivial, when more important issues are pressing, or when people need to cool down temporarily and regain perspective.
- *Accommodation* may be used when issues are more important to others than to yourself or when you want to build "credits" for use in later disagreements.
- *Compromise* may be used to arrive at temporary settlements of complex issues or to arrive at expedient solutions when time is limited.
- *Authoritative command* may be used when quick and decisive action is vital or when unpopular actions must be taken.
- *Collaboration and problem solving* are used to gain true conflict resolution when time and cost permit.

Negotiation

Picture yourself trying to make a decision in the following situation: You are about to order a new state-of-the-art notebook computer for a team member in your department. Then another team member submits a request for one of a different brand. Your boss says that only one brand can be ordered. Or consider this one: You have been offered a new job in another city and want to take it, but are disappointed with the salary. You've heard friends talk of how they "negotiated" better offers when taking jobs. You are concerned about the costs of relocating and would like a signing bonus as well as a guarantee of an early salary review.

The preceding examples are just two of the many situations that involve **negotiation**—the process of making joint decisions when the parties involved have different preferences.[21] Negotiation has special significance in teams and work settings, where disagreements are likely to arise over such diverse matters as wage rates, task objectives, performance evaluations, job assignments, work schedules, work locations, and more.

• **Negotiation** is the process of making joint decisions when the parties involved have different preferences.

Negotiation Goals and Outcomes

Two important goals must be considered in any negotiation: substance goals and relationship goals. *Substance goals* deal with outcomes that relate to the "content" issues under negotiation. The dollar amount of a wage agreement in a collective-bargaining situation is one example. Relationship goals deal with outcomes that relate to how well people involved in the negotiation and any constituencies they may represent are able to work with one another once the process is concluded. An example is the ability of union members and management representatives to work together effectively after a contract dispute has been settled.

Unfortunately, many negotiations result in damaged relationships because the negotiating parties become preoccupied with substance goals and self-interests. In contrast, **effective negotiation** occurs when substance issues are resolved and working relationships are maintained or even improved. Three criteria for effective negotiation are:

• **Effective negotiation** occurs when substance issues are resolved and working relationships are maintained or improved.

- *Quality*—The negotiation results offer a "quality" agreement that is wise and satisfactory to all sides.
- *Harmony*—The negotiation is "harmonious" and fosters rather than inhibits good interpersonal relations.
- *Efficiency*—The negotiation is "efficient" and no more time consuming or costly than absolutely necessary.

Ethical Aspects of Negotiation

Managers and others involved in negotiations should strive for high ethical standards of conduct, but this goal can get sidetracked by an overemphasis on self-interests. The motivation to behave ethically in negotiations is put to the test by each party's desire to "get more" than the other from the negotiation and/or by a belief that there are insufficient resources to satisfy all parties.[22] After the heat of negotiations dies down, the parties involved often try to rationalize or explain

Leaders on Leadership

UN SECRETARY GENERAL BAN KI-MOON PURSUES WORLD PEACE

Talk about conflict and negotiation! Whose job could be more intense in this regard than Ban Ki-Moon, the 37th secretary general of the United Nations? On any given day he could be getting off the plane in some far part of the world to meet with heads of state, dealing with problems in Somalia, marshalling aid for relief in some natural disaster, or handling delicate disagreements with and among the UN's member nations.

But Mr. Ban is well prepared, having come to his post

with 37 years experience in public and government service. Prior to becoming secretary general he served as the Republic of Korea's minister of foreign affairs and trade, and was well traveled and highly respected in global leadership circles. Mr. Ban speaks Korean, English, and French, and his principles for world peace and prosperity are reflected in his priorities as found on the United Nations Web site. They include:

Peace and security—"By enhancing our capacity for preventive diplomacy and supporting sustainable peace processes, we will build long-term solutions and respond more effectively to conflict."

Climate change—"If we care about our legacy for succeeding generations, this is the time for decisive global action. The UN is the natural forum for building consensus and negoti-

ating future global action—all nations can take firm steps towards being carbon-neutral."

Development—"While threats to peace must be addressed, my concern lies equally with those men, women and children of the world struggling to make ends meet—it is intolerable that almost 1 billion people still live on less than $1 a day . . . I will mobilize political will and hold leaders to their commitment to allocate adequate resources and development aid."

UN Reform—"Global problems demand global solutions—and going it alone is not a viable option . . . I do have faith in human decency, diligence and incremental progress. Above all, I believe in results, not rhetoric. The fundamental purposes and principles of this Organization are inspiring and enduring—we need to renew our pledge to live up to them."

away questionable ethics as unavoidable, harmless, or justified. Such after-the-fact rationalizations may be offset by long-run negative consequences, such as not being able to achieve one's wishes again the next time. At the very least the unethical party may be the target of revenge tactics by those who were disadvantaged. Furthermore, once some people have behaved unethically in one situation, they may become entrapped by such behavior and prone to display it again in the future.[23]

Organizational Settings for Negotiation

Managers and team leaders should be prepared to participate in at least four major action settings for negotiations. In *two-party negotiation* the manager negotiates directly with one other person. In a *group negotiation* the manager is

Laid-off workers in Caterpillar's French plant took five managers hostage for 24 hours. The bosses were released after the company agreed to renegotiate compensation for workers losing their jobs. A poll showed some 45 percent of French people approved of such "bossnapping."

part of a team or group whose members are negotiating to arrive at a common decision. In an *intergroup negotiation* the manager is part of a group that is negotiating with another group to arrive at a decision regarding a problem or situation affecting both. And in a *constituency negotiation* each party represents a broader constituency, for example, representatives of management and labor negotiating a collective bargaining agreement.

Culture and Negotiation

The existence of cultural differences in time orientation, individualism, collectivism, and power distance can have a substantial impact on negotiation.

For example, when American business executives try to negotiate quickly with their Chinese counterparts, culture is not always on their side. A typical Chinese approach to negotiation might move much more slowly, require the development of good interpersonal relationships prior to reaching any agreement, display reluctance to commit everything to writing, and anticipate that any agreement reached will be subject to modification as future circumstances may require.[24] All this is quite the opposite of the typical expectations of negotiators used to the individualist and short-term American culture.

Negotiation Strategies

When we think about negotiating for something, perhaps cars and salaries are the first things that pop into mind. But in organizations, managers and workers alike are constantly negotiating over not only just pay and raises, but also such things as work goals or preferences and access to any variety of scarce resources. These resources may be money, time, people, facilities, equipment, and so on. In all such cases the general approach to, or strategy for, the negotiation can have a major influence on its outcomes. In OB we generally talk about two broad approaches—distributive and integrative.

In **distributive negotiation** the focus is on "positions" staked out or declared by conflicting parties. Each party is trying to claim certain portions of the available "pie" whose overall size is considered fixed. In **integrative negotiation**, sometimes called *principled negotiation*, the focus is on the "merits" of the issues. Everyone involved tries to enlarge the available pie and find mutually agreed-upon ways of distributing it, rather than stake claims to certain portions of it.[25] Think of the conversations you overhear and are part of in team situations. The notion of "my way or the highway" is analogous to distribution negotiation; "let's find a way to make this work for both of us" is more akin to integrative negotiation.

- **Distributive negotiation** focuses on positions staked out or declared by the parties involved, each of whom is trying to claim certain portions of the available pie.
- **Integrative negotiation** focuses on the merits of the issues, and the parties involved try to enlarge the available pie rather than stake claims to certain portions of it.

Distributive Negotiation

In distributive bargaining approaches, the participants would each ask this question: "Who is going to get this resource?" This question frames the negotiation as a "win-lose" episode that will have a major impact on how parties approach the negotiation process and the outcomes that may be achieved. A case of distributive negotiation usually unfolds in one of two directions, with neither one nor the other yielding optimal results.

MASTERING MANAGEMENT

IT'S POSSIBLE TO GET A BETTER RAISE

We all do it—wish we'd asked for more when negotiating a starting salary or a pay raise. Why didn't we? And, even if we did, would it have made a difference? Chances are you'll go into a salary negotiation unprepared. And you may pay a price for that. There's quite a bit of advice around for how to negotiate pay raises. A compilation of thoughts and tips follows.

- *Prepare, prepare, prepare*—do the research and find out what others make for a similar position inside and outside the organization, including everything from salary to benefits, bonuses, incentives, and job perks.
- *Document and communicate*—identify and communicate your value; put forth a set of accomplishments that show how you have saved or made money and created value for an employer, or how your skills and attributes will do so for a prospective one.
- *Advocate and ask*—be your own best advocate; in salary negotiation the rule is "Don't ask, don't get." But don't ask too soon; your boss or interviewer should be the first to bring up salary.
- *Stay focused on the goal*—the goal is to satisfy your interests to the maximum extent possible; this means everything from getting immediate satisfaction to being better positioned for future satisfaction.
- *View things from the other side*—test your requests against the employer's point of view; ask if you are being reasonable, convincing, and fair; ask how the boss could explain to higher levels and to your peers a decision to grant your request.
- *Don't overreact to bad news*—never "quit on the spot" if you don't get what you want; be willing to search for and consider alternative job offers.

"Hard" distributive negotiation takes place when each party holds out to get its own way. This leads to competition, whereby each party seeks dominance over the other and tries to maximize self-interests. The hard approach may lead to a win-lose outcome in which one party dominates and gains. Or it can lead to an impasse.

"Soft" distributive negotiation, in contrast, takes place when one party is willing to make concessions to the other to get things over with. In this case one party tries to find ways to meet the other's desires. A soft approach leads to accommodation, in which one party gives in to the other, or to compromise, in which each party gives up something of value in order to reach agreement. In either case at least some latent dissatisfaction is likely to develop. Even when the soft approach results in compromise (e.g., splitting the difference between the initial positions equally), dissatisfaction may exist since each party is still deprived of what it originally wanted.

Figure 10.5 illustrates the basic elements of classic two-party negotiation by the example of the graduating senior negotiating a job offer with a corporate recruiter.[26] Look at the situation first from the graduate's perspective. She has told the recruiter that she would like a salary of $55,000; this is her initial offer. But she also has in mind a minimum reservation point of $50,000—the lowest salary that she will accept for this job. Thus she communicates a salary request of $55,000 but is willing to accept one as low as $50,000. The situation is somewhat the reverse from the recruiter's perspective. His initial offer to the graduate is $45,000, and his maximum reservation point is $55,000; this is the most he is prepared to pay.

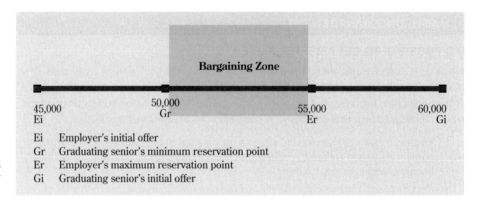

Figure 10.5 The bargaining zone in classic two-party negotiation.

> The **bargaining zone** is the range between one party's minimum reservation point and the other party's maximum.

The **bargaining zone** is defined as the range between one party's minimum reservation point and the other party's maximum reservation point. In Figure 10.5, the bargaining zone is $50,000–$55,000. This is a positive bargaining zone since the reservation points of the two parties overlap. Whenever a positive bargaining zone exists, bargaining has room to unfold. Had the graduate's minimum reservation point been greater than the recruiter's maximum reservation point (for example, $57,000), no room would have existed for bargaining. Classic two-party bargaining always involves the delicate tasks of first discovering the respective reservation points (one's own and the other's), and then working toward an agreement that lies somewhere within the resulting bargaining zone and is acceptable to each party.

Integrative Negotiation

In the integrative approach to negotiation, participants begin by asking not "Who's going to get this resource?" but "How can the resource best be used?" The latter question is much less confrontational than the former, and it permits a broader range of alternatives to be considered in the negotiation process. From the outset there is much more of a "win-win" orientation.

At one extreme, integrative negotiation may involve selective avoidance, in which both parties realize that there are more important things on which to focus their time and attention. The time, energy, and effort needed to negotiate may not be worth the rewards. Compromise can also play a role in the integrative approach, but it must have an enduring basis. This is most likely to occur when the compromise involves each party giving up something of perceived lesser personal value to gain something of greater value. For instance, in the classic two-party bargaining case over salary, both the graduate and the recruiter could expand the negotiation to include the starting date of the job. Because it will be a year before the candidate's first vacation, she may be willing to take a little less money if she can start a few weeks later. Finally, integrative negotiation may involve true collaboration. In this case, the negotiating parties engage in problem solving to arrive at a mutual agreement that maximizes benefits to each.

How to Gain Integrative Agreements

Underlying the integrative or principled approach is a willingness to negotiate based on the merits of the situation. The foundations for gaining truly integrative agreements can be described as supportive attitudes, constructive behaviors, and good information.[27]

Attitudinal Foundations   There are three attitudinal foundations of integrative agreements. First, each party must approach the negotiation with a *willingness to trust* the other party. This is a reason why ethics and maintaining relationships are so important in negotiations. Second, each party must convey a *willingness to share* information with the other party. Without shared information, effective problem solving is unlikely to occur. Third, each party must show a *willingness to ask concrete questions* of the other party. This further facilitates information sharing.

Behavioral Foundations   During a negotiation all behavior is important for both its actual impact and the impressions it leaves behind. Accordingly, the following behavioral foundations of integrative agreements must be carefully considered and included in any negotiator's repertoire of skills and capabilities:

- Separate people from the problem.
- Don't allow emotional considerations to affect the negotiation.
- Focus on interests rather than positions.
- Avoid premature judgments.
- Keep the identification of alternatives separate from their evaluation.
- Judge possible agreements by set criteria or standards.

Information Foundations   The information foundations of integrative agreements are substantial. They involve each party becoming familiar with the BATNA, or "best alternative to a negotiated agreement." That is, each party must know what he or she will do if an agreement cannot be reached. This requires that both negotiating parties identify and understand their personal interests in the situation. They must know what is really important to them in the case at hand, and they must come to understand the relative importance of the other party's interests. As difficult as it may seem, each party must achieve an understanding of what the other party values, even to the point of determining its BATNA.

Common Negotiation Pitfalls

The negotiation process is admittedly complex on ethical, cultural, and many other grounds. It is further characterized by all the possible confusions of complex, and sometimes even volatile interpersonal and team dynamics. Accordingly, negotiators need to guard against some common negotiation pitfalls when acting individually and in teams.[28]

The first pitfall is the tendency in negotiation to stake out your position based on the assumption that in order to gain your way, something must be

Words Affect Outcomes in Online Dispute Resolution

A study of dispute resolution among eBay buyers and sellers finds that using words that give "face" were more likely than words that attack "face" to result in the settlement of online disputes. Jeanne Brett, Marla Olekans, Ray Friedman, Nathan Goates, Cameron Anderson, and Cara Cherry Lisco studied real disputes being addressed through Square Trade, an online dispute resolution service to which eBay refers unhappy customers. The researchers note that a study by the National Consumer League reported that 41 percent of participants in online trading had problems, often associated with late deliveries. For purposes of the study, a "dispute" was defined as a form of conflict in which one party to a transaction made a claim that the other party rejected.

The researchers point out that most past research on dispute resolution has focused on situational and participant characteristics. In this case they adopted what they call a "language-based" approach based on the perspectives of face theory, essentially arguing that how participants use language to give and attack the face of the other party will have a major impact on results. For example, in filing a claim an unhappy buyer might use polite words that preserve the positive self-image or face of the seller, or they might use negative words that attack this sense of face. Examples of negative words are "*agitated, angry, apprehensive, despise, disgusted, frustrated, furious, and hate.*"

Dispute resolution less likely when	Dispute resolution more likely when
• Negative emotions are expressed	• Causal explanation given
	• Suggestion are offered
• Commands are issued	• Communications are firm

This study examined 386 eBay-generated disputes processed through Square Trade. Words used in the first social interchange between parties were analyzed. Results showed that expressing negative emotions and giving commands to the other party inhibited dispute resolution, whereas providing a causal explanation, offering suggestions, and communicating firmness all made dispute resolution more likely. A hypothesis that expressing positive emotions would increase the likelihood of dispute resolution was not supported. The study also showed that the longer a dispute played out, the less likely it was to be resolved.

In terms of practical implications the researchers specifically state: "Watch your language; avoid attacking the other's face either by showing your anger toward them, or expressing contempt; avoid signaling weakness; be firm in your claim. Provide causal accounts that take responsibility and give face." Finally, they note that these basic principles apply in other dispute resolution contexts, not just online.

You Be the Researcher

Consider the suggestions for successful online dispute resolution. Can you design a study to test how well they apply to disputes that may occur in virtual teamwork?

Source: Jeanne Brett, Marla Olekans, Ray Friedman, Nathan Goates, Cameron Anderson, and Cara Cherry Lisco, "Sticks and Stones: Language and On-Line Dispute Resolution," *Academy of Management Journal* 50 (February 2007).

subtracted from the gains of the other party. This *myth of the fixed pie* is a purely distributive approach to negotiation. The whole concept of integrative negotiation is based on the premise that the pie can sometimes be expanded or used to the maximum advantage of all parties, not just one.

Second, because parties to negotiations often begin by stating extreme demands, the possibility of *escalating commitment* is high. That is, once demands have been stated, people become committed to them and are reluctant to back down. Concerns for protecting one's ego and saving face may lead to the irrational escalation of a conflict. Self-discipline is needed to spot this tendency in one's own behavior as well as in the behavior of others.

Third, negotiators often develop *overconfidence* that their positions are the only correct ones. This can lead them to ignore the other party's needs. In some cases negotiators completely fail to see merits in the other party's position—merits that an outside observer would be sure to spot. Such overconfidence makes it harder to reach a positive common agreement.

Fourth, communication problems can cause difficulties during a negotiation. It has been said that "negotiation is the process of communicating back and forth for the purpose of reaching a joint decision."[29] This process can break down because of a *telling problem*—the parties don't really talk to each other, at least not in the sense of making themselves truly understood. It can also be damaged by a *hearing problem*—the parties are unable or unwilling to listen well enough to understand what the other is saying. Indeed, positive negotiation is most likely when each party engages in active listening and frequently asks questions to clarify what the other is saying. Each party occasionally needs to "stand in the other party's shoes" and to view the situation from the other's perspective.[30]

Third-Party Roles in Negotiation

Negotiation may sometimes be accomplished through the intervention of third parties, such as when stalemates occur and matters appear not resolvable under current circumstances. In a process called *alternative dispute resolution*, a neutral third party works with persons involved in a negotiation to help them resolve impasses and settle disputes. There are two primary forms through which ADR is implemented.

In **arbitration**, such as the salary arbitration now common in professional sports, the neutral third party acts as a "judge" and has the power to issue a decision that is binding on all parties. This ruling takes place after the arbitrator listens to the positions advanced by the parties involved in a dispute. In **mediation**, the neutral third party tries to engage the parties in a negotiated solution through persuasion and rational argument. This is a common approach in labor–management negotiations, where trained mediators acceptable to both sides are called in to help resolve bargaining impasses. Unlike an arbitrator, the mediator is not able to dictate a solution.

* In **arbitration** a neutral third party acts as judge with the power to issue a decision binding for all parties.
* In **mediation** a neutral third party tries to engage the parties in a negotiated solution through persuasion and rational argument.

Resources in The OB Skills Workbook

These learning activities from *The OB Skills Workbook* are suggested for Chapter 10.

Case for Critical Thinking	Team and Experiential Exercises	Self-Assessment Portfolio
• The Case of the Missing Raise	• Choices • The Ugli Orange • Vacation Puzzle • Conflict Dialogues	• Conflict Management Strategies

10 studyguide

Summary Questions and Answers

What is the nature of conflict in organizations?

- Conflict appears as a disagreement over issues of substance or emotional antagonisms that create friction between individuals or teams.

- Conflict situations in organizations occur at intrapersonal, interpersonal, intergroup, and interorganizational levels.

- When kept within tolerable limits, conflict can be a source of creativity and performance enhancement; it becomes destructive when these limits are exceeded.

- Moderate levels of conflict can be functional for performance, stimulating effort and creativity.

- Too little conflict is dysfunctional when it leads to complacency; too much conflict is dysfunctional when it overwhelms us.

How can conflict be managed?

- Most typically, conflict develops through a series of stages, beginning with antecedent conditions and progressing into manifest conflict.

- Unresolved prior conflicts set the stage for future conflicts of a similar nature.

- Indirect conflict management strategies include appeals to common goals, hierarchical referral, organizational redesign, and the use of mythology and scripts.

- Direct conflict management strategies engage different tendencies toward cooperativeness and assertiveness to styles of avoidance, accommodation, compromise, competition, and collaboration.

- Win-win conflict is achieved through collaboration and problem solving.

- Win-lose conflict is associated with competition and authoritative command.

- Lose-lose conflict results from avoidance, smoothing or accommodation, and compromise.

What is the nature of negotiation in organizations?

- Negotiation is the process of making decisions and reaching agreement in situations in which the participants have different preferences.

- Managers may find themselves involved in various types of negotiation situations, including two-party, group, intergroup, and constituency negotiation.

- Effective negotiation occurs when both substance goals (dealing with outcomes) and relationship goals (dealing with processes) are achieved.

- Ethical problems in negotiation can arise when people become manipulative and dishonest in trying to satisfy their self-interests at any cost.

What are the different strategies for negotiation?

- The distributive approach to negotiation emphasizes win-lose outcomes; the integrative or principled approach to negotiation emphasizes win-win outcomes.

- In distributive negotiation the focus of each party is on staking out positions in the attempt to claim desired portions of a "fixed pie."

- In integrative negotiation, sometimes called principled negotiation, the focus is on determining the merits of the issues and finding ways to satisfy one another's needs.

- The success of negotiations often depends on avoiding common pitfalls such as the myth of the fixed pie, escalating commitment, overconfidence, and both the telling and hearing problems.

- When negotiations are at an impasse, third-party approaches such as mediation and arbitration offer alternative and structured ways for dispute resolution.

Key Terms

Accommodation
  (smoothing) (p. 241)
Arbitration (p. 249)
Authoritative command
  (p. 241)
Avoidance (p. 241)
Bargaining zone
  (p. 246)
Collaboration (p. 241)
Competition (p. 241)
Compromise (p. 241)
Conflict (p. 232)

Conflict resolution
  (p. 236)
Distributive negotiation
  (p. 244)
Dysfunctional conflict
  (p. 234)
Effective negotiation
  (p. 242)
Emotional conflict (p. 232)
Functional conflict (p. 234)
Integrative negotiation
  (p. 244)

Intergroup conflict
  (p. 233)
Interorganizational conflict
  (p. 233)
Interpersonal conflict
  (p. 233)
Intrapersonal conflict
  (p. 233)
Mediation (p. 249)
Negotiation (p. 242)
Substantive conflict
  (p. 232)

Self-Test 10

Multiple Choice

1. A/an _____ conflict occurs in the form of a fundamental disagreement over ends or goals and the means for accomplishment. (a) relationship (b) emotional (c) substantive (d) procedural

2. The indirect conflict management approach that uses chain of command for conflict resolution is known as _____. (a) hierarchical referral (b) avoidance (c) smoothing (d) appeal to common goals

3. Conflict that ends up being "functional" for the people and organization involved would most likely be _____. (a) of high intensity (b) of moderate intensity (c) of low intensity (d) nonexistent

4. One of the problems with the suppression of conflicts is that it _____. (a) creates winners and losers (b) is often a temporary solution that sets the stage for future conflict (c) works only with emotional conflicts (d) works only with substantive conflicts

5. When a manager asks people in conflict to remember the mission and purpose of the organization and to try to reconcile their differences in that context, she is using a conflict management approach known as _____. (a) reduced interdependence (b) buffering (c) resource expansion (d) appeal to common goals

6. The best time to use accommodation in conflict management is _____. (a) when quick and decisive action is vital (b) when you want to build "credit" for use in later disagreements (c) when people need to cool down and gain perspective (d) when temporary settlement of complex issues is needed

7. Which is an indirect approach to managing conflict? (a) buffering (b) win-lose (c) workflow interdependency (d) power asymmetry

8. A lose-lose conflict is likely when the conflict management approach focuses on _____. (a) linking pin roles (b) altering scripts (c) accommodation (d) problem-solving

9. Which approach to conflict management can be best described as both highly cooperative and highly assertive? (a) competition (b) compromise (c) accommodation (d) collaboration

10. Both _____ goals should be considered in any negotiation. (a) performance and evaluation (b) task and substance (c) substance and relationship (d) task and performance

11. The three criteria for effective negotiation are _____. (a) harmony, efficiency, and quality (b) quality, efficiency, and effectiveness (c) ethical behavior, practicality, and cost-effectiveness (d) quality, practicality, and productivity

12. Which statement is true? (a) Principled negotiation leads to accommodation. (b) Hard distributive negotiation leads to collaboration. (c) Soft distributive negotiation leads to accommodation or compromise. (d) Hard distributive negotiation leads to win-win conflicts.

13. Another name for integrative negotiation is _____. (a) arbitration (b) mediation (c) principled negotiation (d) smoothing

14. When a person approaches a negotiation with the assumption that in order for him to gain his way, the other party must lose or give up something, which negotiation pitfall is being exhibited? (a) myth of the fixed pie (b) escalating commitment (c) overconfidence (d) hearing problem

15. In the process of alternative dispute resolution known as _____, a neutral third party acts as a "judge" to determine how a conflict will be resolved. (a) mediation (b) arbitration (c) conciliation (d) collaboration

Short Response

16. List and discuss three conflict situations faced by managers.

17. List and discuss the major indirect conflict management approaches.

18. Under what conditions might a manager use avoidance or accommodation?

19. Compare and contrast distributive and integrative negotiation. Which is more desirable? Why?

Applications Essay

20. Discuss the common pitfalls you would expect to encounter in negotiating your salary for your first job, and explain how you would best try to deal with them.

11

Communication and Collaboration

f any organization recognizes the importance of communication and collaboration, it is IDEO. At IDEO, collaborative interaction is a core competitive advantage.

Founded in 1991, the global design and innovation firm uses a human-centered, design-based approach to help organizations in the business, government, education, healthcare, and social sectors innovate and grow. IDEO is organized and managed to foster *design thinking*, a collaborative approach that engages people from different disciplines in dynamic dialogue to generate breakthrough ideas and creative solutions. When hiring, IDEO looks for what it calls "T-shaped people," those who have depth in a specific discipline (the vertical stroke) and a breadth of interests and passions (the horizontal stroke). A key characteristic of IDEO designers is their willingness to engage in collaborative work. "We see ourselves as a mosaic of individuals, where the big picture is beautiful but each individual is different. Your passions, your enthusiasm, your ability to collaborate . . . We ask ourselves . . . What will this person be like at dinner, or during a brainstorm, or during a conflict? We are eclectic, diverse, and there is always room for another angle."

At IDEO, collaborative interaction is a core competitive advantage.

Brainstorming is a fundamental element of design thinking, and failure is an accepted part of the culture. To succeed at IDEO, you have to be able to function with "confusion, incomplete information, paradox, irony, and fun for its own sake." Once ideas are developed, the key becomes telling the story. Approaches such as videos, immersive environments, narratives, animations, and even story boards are used to help embrace, adopt, and elaborate ideas faster and more efficiently.

To accomplish this, IDEO promotes a "democracy of ideas." It discourages formal titles, does not have a dress code, and encourages employees to move around, especially during mental blocks. Stimulating interactions are encouraged by creating open work spaces and many opportunities for collaboration in the office. Designers are encouraged to talk to one another in whatever forum possible, and experts co-mingle in offices that look like "cacophonous kindergarten classrooms." As described by Tom Peters, "Walk into the offices of IDEO design in Palo Alto, California, immediately you'll be caught up in the energy, buzz, creative disarray and sheer lunacy of it all." For IDEO, creative interaction and collaborative communication are keys to success. •

communicating in a collaborative world

The Wiki Workplace

At Google, collaborative interaction means a different kind of control over the way in which decisions are made. CEO Eric Schmidt says "You talk about the strategy, you get people excited, you tell people what the company's priorities are, and somehow it works out."

The Nature of Communication

Workplaces are becoming increasingly collaborative, making communication more important than ever. New technologies, trends toward global real-time work, and a younger generation more comfortable with social connectivity are dramatically reshaping how companies and employees function. Social tools such as wikis and blogs are putting more communication power in the hands of employees and customers. Do companies worry that this will lead to confusion and loss of control? Not at Google, IBM, and Xerox, where collaborative communication processes are breaking down traditional corporate barriers and allowing self-organization and peer production to emerge as new organizing principles for the workplace.

Collaboration requires effective communication. Communication is the glue that holds organizations together. It is the way we share information, ideas, goals, directions, expectations, feelings, and emotions in the context of coordinated action. As the opening suggests, and we will see below, successful organizations value and promote effective communication both at the interpersonal level and across organizational boundaries.

The Communication Process

It is useful to describe **communication** as a process of sending and receiving messages with attached meanings. The key elements in the communication process are illustrated in Figure 11.1. They include a source, which encodes an intended meaning into a message, and a receiver, which decodes the message into a perceived meaning. The receiver may or may not give feedback to the source. Although this process may appear to be elementary, it is not quite as simple as it

- **Communication** is the process of sending and receiving symbols with attached meanings.

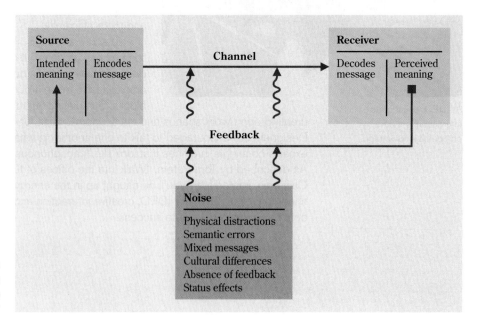

Figure 11.1 The communication process and possible sources of "noise."

looks. **Noise** is the term used to describe any disturbance that disrupts communication effectiveness and interferes with the transference of messages within the communication process. For example, if your stomach is growling because your class is right before lunch, or if you are worried about an exam later in the day, these can interfere with your ability to pay attention to what your professor and classmates are saying. In effect they are *noise* in the communication process.

> **Noise** is anything that interferes with the effectiveness of communication.

The information source, or **sender**, is a person or group trying to communicate with someone else. The source seeks to communicate, in part, to change the attitudes, knowledge, or behavior of the receiver. A team leader, for example, may want to communicate with a division manager in order to explain why the team needs more time or resources to finish an assigned project. This involves **encoding**—the process of translating an idea or thought into a message consisting of verbal, written, or nonverbal symbols (such as gestures), or some combination of them. Messages are transmitted through various **communication channels**, such as face-to-face meetings, e-mail and online discussions, written letters or memoranda, and telephone communications or voice mail, among others. The choice of channel can have an important impact on the communication process. Some people are better at using certain channels over others, and specific channels are better able to handle some types of messages. In the case of the team leader communicating with the division manager, for example, it can make quite a difference whether the message is sent face to face, in a written memo, by voice mail, or by e-mail.

> **The sender** is a person or group trying to communicate with someone else.

> **Encoding** is the process of translating an idea or thought into a message consisting of verbal, written, or nonverbal symbols (such as gestures), or some combination of them.

> **Communication channels** are the pathways through which messages are communicated.

The communication process is not completed even though a message is sent. The **receiver** is the individual or group of individuals to whom a message is directed. In order for meaning to be assigned to any received message, its contents must be interpreted through decoding. This process of translation is complicated by many factors, including the knowledge and experience of the receiver and his or her relationship with the sender. A message may also be interpreted with the added influence of other points of view, such as those offered by friends, co-workers, or organizational superiors. Ultimately, the decoding may result in the receiver interpreting a message in a way that is different from that originally intended by the source.

> **The receiver** is the individual or group of individuals to whom a message is directed.

Feedback and Communication

Most receivers are well aware of the potential gap between the intended message of the source and the perceived meaning assigned to it by the recipient. As discussed in Chapter 4 on perception, learning, and attribution, this often occurs because individuals misinterpret the message by attributing motives or meanings the sender did not intend. When there are gaps in messages (and even when there aren't) receivers will often "fill in the blanks," resulting in large potential for miscommunication in the workplace.

One way these gaps are identified and corrected is **feedback**, the process through which the receiver communicates with the sender by returning another message. Feedback represents two-way communication, going from sender to receiver and back again. Compared to one-way communication, which flows from sender to receiver only, two-way communication is more accurate and

> **Feedback** communicates how one feels about something another person has done or said.

effective, although it may also be more costly and time consuming. Because of their efficiency, one-way forms of communication—memos, letters, e-mail, reports, and the like—are frequently used in work settings. One-way messages are easy for the sender but often frustrating for the receiver, who may be left unsure of just what the sender means or wants done.

In most workplaces, there is too little feedback rather than too much. This is particularly true when the feedback is negative in nature because people are afraid of how the feedback will be received or of raising emotions they are not prepared to handle. Words that are intended to be polite and helpful can easily end up being perceived as unpleasant and even hostile. This risk is particularly evident in the performance appraisal process. A manager or team leader must be able to do more than just complete a written appraisal to document another person's performance for the record. To serve the person's developmental needs, feedback regarding the results of the appraisal—both the praise and the criticism—must be well communicated. As pointed out in OB Savvy 11.1, there is an art to giving feedback so that the receiver accepts it and uses it constructively.

Nonverbal Communication

• **Nonverbal communication** occurs through facial expressions, body motions, eye contact, and other physical gestures.

We all know that people communicate in ways other than the spoken or written word. Indeed, the **nonverbal communication** that takes place through facial expressions, body position, eye contact, and other physical gestures is important both to understand and to master. It is the act of speaking without using words. *Kinesics*, the study of gestures and body postures, has achieved a rightful place in communication theory and research.[1]

The nonverbal side to communication can often hold the key to what someone is really thinking or meaning. When verbal and nonverbal do not match, research has shown that receivers will pay more attention to the nonverbal. Nonverbal can also affect the impressions we make on others. Interviewers, for example, tend to respond more favorably to job candidates whose nonverbal cues, such as eye contact and erect posture, are positive than to those displaying negative nonverbal cues, such as looking down or slouching. The art of impression management during interviews and in other situations requires careful attention to both verbal and nonverbal aspects of communication, including one's dress, timeliness, and demeanor.

Nonverbal communication can also take place through the physical arrangement of space or workspace designs, such as that found in various office layouts. *Proxemics*, the study of the way space is used, is important to communication.[2] Figure 11.2 shows three different office arrangements and the messages they may communicate to visitors. Check the diagrams against the furniture arrangement in your office or that of your instructor or a person with whom you are familiar. What are you or they saying to visitors by the choice of furniture placement?[3]

Conflict avoidance is a major problem in the workplace. To foster healthy dialogue, people need to recognize the importance of being willing to give and receive feedback.

"I am the boss!"   "I am the boss, but let's talk."   "Forget I'm the boss, let's talk."

Figure 11.2 Furniture placement and nonverbal communication in the office.

Interpersonal Communication

Our organizations are information rich and increasingly high tech. But even with the support provided by continuing developments in information technology, it is important to remember that people still drive organizational systems and performance. People who are willing and able to collaborate and commit their mutual talents and energies to the tasks at hand are the foundations of any high performance organization. And to create this foundation, people must excel in interpersonal communication and not succumb to the barriers that can detract from it.

Communication Barriers

In interpersonal communication, it is important to understand the barriers that can easily create communication problems. The most common barriers in the workplace include interpersonal issues, physical distractions, and meaning, or *semantic*, barriers.

Interpersonal barriers are reflected in a quote from Ralph Waldo Emerson: "I can't hear what you say because who you are speaks so loudly."[4] Interpersonal barriers occur when individuals are not able to objectively listen to the sender due to things such as lack of trust, personality clashes, a bad reputation, stereotypes/prejudices, etc. In such cases, receivers and senders may distort communication by evaluating and judging a message or failing to communicate it effectively. Think of someone you don't like or a co-worker or a classmate who rubs you the wrong way. Now think about how you communicate with that person. Do you listen effectively, or do you turn him or her off? Do you share information with him or her, or do you keep your interactions short and curt, or potentially even evasive?

Such problems are indicative of selective listening and filtering. In **selective listening**, individuals block out information or only hear things that match preconceived notions. Someone who does not trust another will assume the other is not telling the truth, or may "hear" things in the communication that are not

- **Interpersonal barriers** occur when individuals are not able to objectively listen to the sender due to things such as lack of trust, personality clashes, a bad reputation, stereotypes/prejudices, etc.

- In **selective listening**, individuals block out information or only hear things that match preconceived notions.

In **filtering**, senders convey only certain parts of relevant information.

accurate. An employee who believes a co-worker is incompetent may disregard important information if it comes from that person. In **filtering**, senders convey only certain parts of relevant information. If we don't like a co-worker we may decide to leave out critical details or pointers that would help him or her be more successful in getting things done.

Interpersonal barriers may also occur due to ego problems or poor communication skills. Individuals with ego problems may twist what someone says to serve their own purpose, or overly emphasize their own contributions while failing to acknowledge others. Poor communication skills involve failing to effectively listen, rambling on in conversations or meetings rather than presenting a concise and coherent message, or inability to frame messages appropriate to the audience.

Physical distractions include interruptions from noises, visitors, etc., that interfere with communication.

Physical distractions are another barrier that can interfere with the effectiveness of a communication attempt. Some of these distractions are evident in the following conversation between an employee, George, and his manager.[5]

> Okay, George, let's hear your problem (phone rings, boss picks it up, promises to deliver the report "just as soon as I can get it done"). Uh, now, where were we—oh, you're having a problem with marketing. So, (the manager's secretary brings in some papers that need immediate signatures; he scribbles his name and the secretary leaves) . . . you say they're not cooperative? I tell you what, George why don't you (phone rings again, lunch partner drops by) . . . uh, take a stab at handling it yourself. I've got to go now.

Besides what may have been poor intentions in the first place, George's manager allowed physical distractions to create information overload. As a result, the communication with George suffered. Setting priorities and planning can eliminate this mistake. If George has something to say, his manager should set aside adequate time for the meeting. In addition, interruptions such as telephone calls, drop-in visitors, and the like should be prevented. At a minimum, George's manager could start by closing the door to the office and instructing his secretary to not disturb them.

Semantic barriers involve a poor choice or use of words and mixed messages.

Semantic barriers involve a poor choice or use of words and mixed messages. When in doubt regarding the clarity of your written or spoken messages, the popular KISS principle of communication is always worth remembering: "Keep it short and simple." Of course, that is often easier said than done. The following illustrations of the "bafflegab" that once tried to pass as actual "executive communication" are a case in point.[6]

> A. "We solicit any recommendations that you wish to make, and you may be assured that any such recommendations will be given our careful consideration."
>
> B. "Consumer elements are continuing to stress the fundamental necessity of a stabilization of the price structure at a lower level than exists at the present time."

One has to wonder why these messages weren't stated more understandably: (A) "Send us your recommendations; they will be carefully considered." (B) "Consumers want lower prices."

Active Listening

"We have two ears and one mouth so we should listen twice as much as we speak."[7] This quote, a variation on that of the Greek philosopher Epictetus,

Leaders on Leadership

DAME ANITA RODDICK: SPREAD THE ENTHUSIASM

Known as the Queen of Green, the late Anita Roddick was never shy about sharing her views on a variety of social and business issues. Passing away in 2007 from a brain hemorrhage at the age of 64, she left a strong legacy that lives on through her company and the many individuals whom she inspired.

She started The Body Shop in 1976 more as a way to earn a living for her family than as a statement for social activism. As the company grew, however, so did her passion for making a difference in the world around her. She saw her growing cosmetics company and the profits it generated as powerful means for influence.

Her own personal values and interests in social responsibility are reflected clearly in The Body Shop's values: no animal testing; support community trade; activate self-esteem; defend human rights; and protect our planet.

A noted international speaker admired for her convictions and ability to inspire, she used her role as successful entrepreneur to speak to other business leaders and government officials about the importance of social responsibility. One of her famous speeches was to the 1999 International Forum on Globalization's Tech-In in Seattle, Washington.

Regarding globalization and human rights, she said, "It's difficult for all of us. But if we are going to change the world then nobody—not governments, not the media, not individuals—are going to get a free ride. And certainly not business, because business is now faster, more creative and far wealthier than governments ever were. Business has to be a force for social change. It is not enough to avoid hideous evil—it must, we must, actively do good. If business stays parochial, without moral energy or codes of behavior, claiming there are no such things as values, then God help us all. If you think morality is a luxury business can't afford, try living in a world without it."

Her vision was, and still is, compelling but, according to Ms. Roddick, "vision has to be communicated clearly and persuasively, and always, always with passion."

She leaves us with an important task, but speaks of its rewards, "Quite apart from anything else, my experience is trying to change things for the better makes you feel better, healthier. Humans are communicative animals: when you do good in a community, the benefits eventually get back to you."

indicates another common interpersonal communication pitfall: the failure to effectively listen. The ability to listen well is a distinct asset to anyone whose job success depends on communicating with other people. After all, there are always two sides to the communication process: (1) sending a message, or "telling," and (2) receiving a message, or "listening." And as the quote indicates, the emphasis should be more on the listening and less on the telling.[8]

Everyone in the new workplace should develop good skills in **active listening**— the ability to help the source of a message say what he or she really means. The concept comes from the work of counselors and therapists, who are trained to help people express themselves and talk about things that are important to them.[9] Take a moment to review the guidelines for active listening shown in OB Savvy 11.2. Then read the following conversations. How would you feel as the group leader in each case?[10]

- **Active listening** encourages people to say what they really mean.

OB SAVVY 11.2

Guidelines for Active Listening

1. Listen for content–try to hear exactly what is being said.
2. Listen for feelings–try to identify how the source feels about things.
3. Respond to feelings–let the source know that his or her feelings are recognized.
4. Note all cues–be sensitive to both verbal and nonverbal expressions.
5. Reflect back–repeat in your own words what you think you are hearing.

Conversation 1

- *Group leader:* Hey, Sal, I don't get this work order. We can't handle this today. What do they think we are?
- *Branch manager:* But that's the order. So get it out as soon as you can. We're under terrific pressure this week.
- *Group leader:* Don't they know we're behind schedule already because of that software problem?
- *Branch manager:* Look, I don't decide what goes on upstairs. I just have to see that the work gets out, and that's what I'm going to do.
- *Group leader:* The team won't like this.
- *Branch manager:* That's something you'll have to work out with them, not me.

Conversation 2

- *Group leader:* Hey, Kelley, I don't get this work order. We can't handle this today. What do they think we are?
- *Branch manager:* Sounds like you're pretty upset about it.
- *Group leader:* I sure am. We're just about getting back to schedule while fighting that software breakdown. Now this comes along.
- *Branch manager:* As if you didn't have enough work to do?
- *Group leader:* Right, I don't know how to tell the team about this. They're under a real strain today. Seems like everything we do around here is rush, rush, rush.
- *Branch manager:* I guess you feel like it's unfair to load anything more on them.
- *Group leader:* Well, yes. But I know there must be plenty of pressure on everybody up the line. If that's the way it is, I'll get the word to them.
- *Branch manager:* Thanks. If you'll give it a try, I'll do my best to keep to the schedule in the future.

The second example shows active listening skills on the part of the branch manager. She responded to the group leader's communication in a way that increased the flow of information. The manager learned more about the situation, while the group leader most likely felt better after having been able to really say what she thought—after being heard. Compare, by contrast, these outcomes with those in the first example where the manager lacked active listening skills.

Cross-Cultural Communication

We all know that globalization is here to stay. What we might not realize is that the success of international business often rests with the quality of cross-cultural communication. And all is not well. A recent study of large firms by Accenture reports that 92 percent find that the biggest challenge in working with outsourcing providers is communication.[11] People must always exercise caution when they are involved in cross-cultural communication—whether between persons of different geographic or ethnic groupings within one country, or between persons of different national cultures.

A common problem in cross-cultural communication is **ethnocentrism**, the tendency to believe one's culture and its values are superior to those of others. It is often accompanied by an unwillingness to try to understand alternative points of view and to take the values they represent seriously. Another problem in cross-cultural communication arises from **parochialism**—assuming that the ways of your culture are the only ways of doing things. It is parochial for traveling American businesspeople to insist that all of their business contacts speak English, whereas it is ethnocentric for them to think that anyone who dines with a spoon rather than a knife and fork lacks proper table manners.

The difficulties with cross-cultural communication are perhaps most obvious in respect to language differences. Advertising messages, for example, may work well in one country but encounter difficulty when translated into the language of another. Problems accompanied the introduction of Ford's European model, the "Ka," into Japan. (In Japanese, *ka* means "mosquito.") Gestures may also be used quite differently in the various cultures of the world. For example, crossed legs are quite acceptable in the United Kingdom but are rude in Saudi Arabia if the sole of the foot is directed toward someone. Pointing at someone to get his or her attention may be acceptable in Canada, but in Asia it is considered inappropriate and even offensive.[12]

The role of language in cross-cultural communication has additional and sometimes even more subtle sides. The anthropologist Edward T. Hall notes important differences in the ways different cultures use language, and he suggests that misunderstood communications are often caused by them.[13] Members of **low-context cultures** are very explicit in using the spoken and written word. In these cultures, such as those of Australia, Canada, and the United States, the message is largely conveyed by the words someone uses, and not particularly by the "context" in which they are spoken. In contrast, members of **high-context cultures** use words to convey only a limited part of the message. The rest must be inferred or interpreted from the context, which includes body language, the physical setting, and past relationships—all of which add meaning to what is being said. Many Asian and Middle Eastern cultures are considered high context, according to Hall, whereas most Western cultures are low context.

International business experts advise that one of the best ways to gain understanding of cultural differences is to learn at least some of the language of the country that one is dealing with. Says one global manager: "Speaking and understanding the local language gives you more insight; you can avoid misunderstandings." A former American member of the board of a German multinational says: "Language proficiency gives a [nonGerman] board member a better grasp of what is going on . . . not just the facts and figures but also texture and nuance."[14] Although the prospect of learning another language may sound daunting, there is little doubt that it can be well worth the effort.[15]

Not only does language differ across cultures, so does the nature of nonverbal communication. While Americans are used to wider personal space and less physical touch, persons from Asian and Hispanic cultures are much more comfortable with close contact.

- **Ethnocentrism** is the tendency to believe one's culture and its values are superior to those of others.

- **Parochialism** assumes the ways of your culture are the only ways of doing things.

- In **low-context cultures**, messages are expressed mainly by the spoken and written word.

- In **high-context cultures**, words convey only part of a message, while the rest of the message must be inferred from body language and additional contextual cues.

PRIVACY IN THE AGE OF SOCIAL NETWORKING

Is there a clear line between your personal and professional life? In the age of social networking, the answer to this question is becoming less clear. Today many companies are using the Internet to evaluate employees—both current and prospective—and if you fail to maintain a "professional" demeanor, you could find yourself at a loss. There are stories of college athletes who are disciplined because of something they posted on their Web site, employees who are fired for things they say online about the company or their co-workers, or individuals who aren't hired because of a photo on their Facebook page.

To make matters more complicated, employment law in many states is still quite unclear, and in most cases, provides little protection to workers who are punished for their online postings. Take the case of Stacy Snyder, 25, a senior at Millersville University in Millersville, PA, who was dismissed from the student teaching program at a high school and denied her teaching credential after the school staff came across a photograph on her MySpace profile showing a pirate's hat perched atop her head while she was sipping from a large plastic cup whose contents cannot be seen. The caption on the photo: "drunken pirate."

Ms. Snyder filed a lawsuit in federal court in Philadelphia contending that her rights to free expression under the First Amendment had been violated. Millersville University, in a motion asking the court to dismiss the case, countered that Ms. Snyder's student teaching had been unsatisfactory—although they acknowledged that she was dismissed based on her MySpace photograph. The university backed the school authorities' contentions that her posting was "unprofessional" and might "promote under-age drinking." It also cited a passage in the teacher's handbook that said staff members are "to be well-groomed and appropriately dressed."

> **What Do You Think?** *The case of Stacy Snyder and others raises interesting questions. Is what an employee does after hours, as long as no laws are broken, any of the organization's business? Does a line need to be drawn that demarcates the boundary between an employee's work and his or her private life?*

Organizational Communication

One of the greatest changes in organizations and in everyday life in recent years has been the explosion in new communication technologies. We have moved from the world of the telephone, mail, photocopying, and face-to-face meetings into one of voice mail, e-mail, texting, twittering, blogs, wikis, video conferencing, net meetings, and more. These changes are creating more collaborative environments and challenging traditional notions of hierarchy and structure in organizations.

Communication Channels

Organizations are designed based on bureaucratic organizing principles, meaning that jobs are arranged in hierarchical fashion with specified job descriptions and formal reporting relationships. However, much information in organizations is also passed along more fluidly, through informal communication networks. These illustrate two types of information flows in organizations: formal and informal communication channels.

Formal channels follow the chain of command established by an organization's hierarchy of authority. For example, an organization chart indicates the proper routing for official messages passing from one level or part of the hierarchy to another. Because formal channels are recognized as authoritative, it is typical for communication of policies, procedures, and other official announcements to adhere to them. On the other hand, much "networking" takes place through the use of **informal channels** that do not adhere to the organization's hierarchy of authority.[16] They coexist with the formal channels but frequently diverge from them by skipping levels in the hierarchy or cutting across divisional lines. Informal channels help to create open communications in organizations and ensure that the right people are in contact with one another.[17]

A common informal communication channel is the **grapevine**, or network of friendships and acquaintances through which rumors and other unofficial information are passed from person to person. Grapevines have the advantage of being able to transmit information quickly and efficiently. Grapevines also help fulfill the needs of people involved in them. Being part of a grapevine can provide a sense of security that comes from "being in the know" when important things are going on. It also provides social satisfaction as information is exchanged interpersonally. The primary disadvantage of grapevines occurs when they transmit incorrect or untimely information. Rumors can be very dysfunctional, both to people and to organizations. One of the best ways to avoid rumors is to make sure that key persons in a grapevine get the right information to begin with.

Today, the traditional communication grapevine in organizations is often technology assisted. The most common form is probably the e-mail message, but as text messaging and social networking technologies continue to evolve, so, too, do informal communication channels. In more and more organizations people are communicating officially and unofficially by blogs and wikis. As evidence of the power of technology in this regard, the U.S. military set strict regulations on blogs after becoming concerned about the messages from a proliferation of bloggers stationed in Iraq. On the other hand, reports indicate that, by 2009, wikis were used by at least 50 percent of organizations world-wide as a communications improvement tool.[18]

Channel richness indicates the capacity of a channel to convey information. And as indicated in Figure 11.3, the richest channels are face to face. Next are telephone, video conferences, and instant messaging, followed by e-mail, written memos, and letters. The leanest channels are posted notices and bulletins. When messages get more complex and open ended, richer channels are necessary to achieve effective communication. Leaner channels work well for more routine and straightforward messages, such as announcing the location of a previously scheduled meeting.

- **Formal channels** follow the official chain of command.

- **Informal channels** do not follow the chain of command.

- A **grapevine** transfers information through networks of friendships and acquaintances.

- **Channel richness** indicates the capacity of a channel to convey information.

Figure 11.3 Richness of communication channels.

Communication Flows

- **Downward communication** follows the chain of command from top to bottom.

Within organizations, information flows through both the formal and informal channels just described as well as downward, upward, and laterally. **Downward communication** follows the chain of command from top to bottom. One of its major functions is to achieve influence through information. Lower-level personnel need to know what those in higher levels are doing and to be regularly reminded of key policies, strategies, objectives, and technical developments. Of special importance is feedback and information on performance results. Sharing such information helps minimize the spread of rumors and inaccuracies regarding higher-level intentions. It also helps create a sense of security and involvement among receivers who believe they know the whole story. Unfortunately, a lack of adequate downward communication is often cited as a management failure. On the issue of corporate downsizing, for example, one sample showed that 64 percent of employees did not believe what management said, 61 percent felt uninformed about company plans, and 54 percent complained that decisions were not well explained.

- **Upward communication** is the flow of messages from lower to higher organizational levels.

The flow of messages from lower to higher organizational levels is **upward communication**. As shown in Figure 11.4, it serves several purposes. Upward communication keeps higher levels informed about what lower-level workers are doing, what their problems are, what suggestions they have for improvements, and how they feel about the organization and their jobs. Upward communication has historically been a problem in organizations due to lower-level employees filtering information that goes up, leaving many higher-level organizational managers in the dark about what is really happening in the organization.

- **Lateral communication** is the flow of messages at the same levels across organizations.

The importance of **lateral communication** for promotion of collaborative environments in the new workplace has been a recurrent theme in this book. Today's customer-sensitive organizations need timely and accurate feedback and product information. To serve customer needs they must get the right information—and get it fast enough—into the hands of workers. Furthermore, inside the organization,

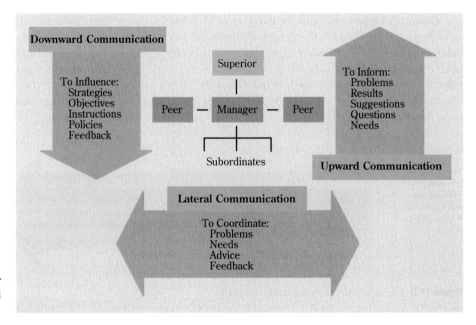

Figure 11.4 Directions for information flows in and around organizations.

RESEARCH INSIGHT

Leadership Behavior and Employee Voice: Is the Door Really Open?

In today's environment, the willingness of all members to provide thoughts and ideas about critical work processes characterizes successful learning in various types of teams. Yet, despite this "learning imperative," many individuals do not work in environments where they perceive it as safe to speak up. To address these issues, James Detert and Ethan Burris engaged in a study of employee *voice*, which they define as "the discretionary provision of information intended to improve organizational functioning to someone inside an organization with the perceived authority to act, even though such information may challenge and upset the status quo of the organization and its powerholders."

In their study of leadership behaviors and employee voice, Detert and Burris found that leader positivity or personalized behavior is not enough to generate employee voice. Instead, if leaders are going to overcome employee restraint

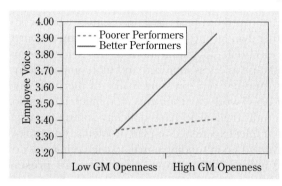

in speaking up, they need to indicate openness to change and willingness to act on input from below. Although transformational leader behaviors are positively related to voice, openness behaviors clearly send the stronger signal that voice is welcome.

Openness behaviors are important because they provide a "safe" environment for employees to voice their opinions. The authors concluded that the signals leaders send are key inputs to employees in assessing the potential costs and benefits of speaking up.

Do the Research

Do you think the findings are applicable to your work situation? How would you conduct a study in your workplace to find out? What other variables would you include?

Source: J. Detert and E. Burris, "Leadership Behavior and Employee Voice: Is the Door Really Open?" *Academy of Management Journal* 50(4) 2007, pp. 869–884.

people must be willing and able to communicate across departmental or functional boundaries and to listen to one another's needs as "internal customers."

Collaborative organization designs emphasize lateral communication in the form of cross-departmental committees, teams, or task forces as well as matrix structures. There is also growing attention to organizational ecology—the study of how building design may influence communication and productivity by improving lateral communications—as illustrated in the opening case on IDEO. Information technology is allowing organizations to (1) distribute information more instantaneously, (2) make more information available than ever before, (3) allow broader and more immediate access to this information, (4) encourage participation in the sharing and use of information, and (5) integrate systems and functions as well as use information to link with other environments in unprecedented ways.

These new forms of communication also have potential downsides. When they are largely impersonal or mostly one-way, such as e-mail, they remove nonverbal communications from the situation and thereby lose aspects that may otherwise add important context to an interaction. Studies show that recipients of e-mail are accurate less than 50 percent of the time in identifying the tone or intent of the message.[19] They may also create difficulties with understanding the emotional aspects of communication. In this respect, little smiley or frowning faces and other symbols often do not carry the message. Another problem is a failure in the electronic medium to control one's emotions, a skill considered essential in interpersonal communications.[20] Some argue, for example, that it is far easier to be blunt, overly critical, and insensitive when conveying messages electronically rather than face-to-face. The term **flaming** is sometimes used to describe rudeness in electronic communication. In this sense, the use of computer mediation may make people less inhibited and more impatient in what they say.

• **Flaming** is expressing rudeness when using e-mail or other forms of electronic communication.

Another very pressing reality of the new workplace is information overload and 24-7 work environments. Too much information may create stressful situations for individuals who have difficulty sorting the useful from the trivial. Even the IT giant Intel experiences e-mail problems. An employee once commented: "We're so wrapped up in sending e-mail to each other, we don't have time to be dealing with the outside."[21] The growing trend toward **presence-aware tools** that allow for real-time collaboration create difficulties for employees trying to determine when they get to finish working. As described by Kevin Angley of SAS, there are "a lot of people who find it to be an intrusion and invasion of privacy, because they walk away from their desk for five minutes and their machine declares that they're idle, or they're reading a document on paper at their desk and all of a sudden their computer claims that they're idle." At Procter & Gamble, director of computers and communications services Laurie Heltsley says they are telling employees it's acceptable for people to turn their presence status to off or unavailable.[22]

• **Presence-aware tools** are software that allow a user to view others' real-time availability status and readiness to communicate.

Status Effects

Another key element of organizational communication associated with hierarchical organizing principles is status differences. **Status differences** create potential communication barriers between persons of higher and lower ranks. On the one hand, given the authority of their positions, managers may be inclined to do a lot of "telling" but not much "listening." As mentioned earlier, we know that communication is frequently biased when flowing upward in organizational hierarchies.[23] Subordinates may filter information and tell their superiors only what they think the bosses want to hear. Whether the reason is a fear of retribution for bringing bad news, an unwillingness to identify personal mistakes, or just a general desire to please, the result is the same: the higher-level decision maker may end up taking the wrong actions because of biased and inaccurate information supplied from below. This is sometimes called the **mum effect**, in reference to tendencies to sometimes keep "mum" from a desire to be polite and a reluctance to transmit bad news.[24]

• **Status differences** are differences between persons of higher and lower ranks.

• The **mum effect** occurs when people are reluctant to communicate bad news.

Collaborative Work Environments

As we proceed deeper into the Internet age, collaborative communication is becoming less a choice and more a reality—and it is changing the face of the work environment. Collaborative environments are characterized by boundaryless information flows, more open and transparent communication, and more supportive communication dynamics.

MASTERING MANAGEMENT

DON'T LET YOUR BLACKBERRY GET YOU DOWN

Look around as you go through an airport, sit in a meeting, take a train, or walk down the street: Blackberrys are everywhere and are taking up our time. And the sad fact is that it isn't just the amount of time spent dealing with that never-sleeping e-mail carrier that's the problem; the quality of the time is often in question. It's time to get better at managing your e-mail and, by default, managing your time. Here are some tips gleaned from corporate training.

- Read e-mail items once, only once.
- Take action immediately to answer, move to folders, or delete.
- Regularly purge folders of outdated messages.
- Send group mail and use "reply to all" only when really necessary.
- Get off distribution lists that don't offer value to your work.
- Send short messages in the subject line, avoiding a full-text message.
- Put large files on Web sites, instead of sending as attachments.
- Don't send confidential, personal, or embarrassing messages by e-mail.
- Turn off the sound indicating arrival of a new e-mail.

Collaboration Technologies

In hierarchical organizing, information can often become a source of power that employees hold and use for their own advantage. With the rise of social networking tools, such as Facebook, Twitter, and YouTube, and video technologies, such as camera phones and videography, the withholding of information is becoming more and more difficult. Customers now have more information power than ever due to the power of emerging collaboration technologies.

Instead of fighting these trends, organizations are identifying ways to capitalize on emerging technologies. At Xerox, rather than leaving the design of high-level strategy documents to a handful of people at the top of the corporate hierarchy, they set up a wiki that allows researchers in the R&R group to collaboratively generate the company's technology strategy. Chief Technology Officer Sophie VanDebroek says that with the wiki, "we'll get more content and knowledge in all of our areas of expertise . . . including everything from material science to the latest document services and solutions." At IBM, up to $100 million have been committed to sessions such as the *Innovation Jam*, where employees in more than 160 countries and their clients, business partners—and even family members— engage in online moderated discussions to glean insights that will transform industries, improve human health, and help protect the environment over the course of the coming decades.[25]

The result is a reduction of status differentials and breaking down of corporate silos. At Mars Inc., the President's Challenge brings together thought leaders in the company with the most senior people in Mars to explore new enabling strategies for business. As part of this exploration, team members work together to challenge and engage in "fierce debate" of proposed strategies. As a result, Mars has broken down silos and developed leaders throughout the organization. The collaborative communication has resulted in a ferment of innovation with many new best practices being driven throughout the business.[26]

Although many interactions are now occurring through technology, face-to-face interaction is still the richest means of communication. For difficult conversations, supportive communication principles can be instrumental in helping avoid problems that can lead to communication breakdowns.

Interactional Transparency

In the financial world, "transparency" means opening the books. In the context of management, it is increasingly being used to symbolize more open and honest sharing of information. Interest in transparency concepts has been on the rise since the passage of the Sarbanes-Oxley Act, which, to guard against corporate fraud, requires public organizations to disclose information concerning financial transactions.

Interactional transparency has been conceptualized in the OB literature as the ability for both leaders and followers to be open, accountable, and honest with each other.[27] It comprises multiple components. First, transparent communication involves sharing relevant information. For example, contrary to information power games of the past, transparent communication means that individuals work together to share all pertinent information and not withhold important information from one another. Second, transparent communication involves being forthcoming regarding motives and the reasoning behind decisions. Such transparency about motives helps avoid the problem of faulty attributions that can often break down communication processes. Third, transparent communication involves proactively seeking and giving feedback. Transparent communication is two-way and collaborative, involving a free and open exchange of information.

Supportive Communication Principles

To achieve transparency requires that individuals are comfortable communicating openly and honestly. However, we know that is not always the case. Avoidance continues to be a major issue in interpersonal communication. If a problem arises between employees or work groups, many individuals are much more likely to avoid than address it. Why is this?

A major reason is fear the conversation will be uncomfortable or worry that trying to talk about the problem will only make it worse. This fear often comes with a lack of understanding about how to approach difficult conversations. However, a set of tools known as **supportive communication principles** can help focus the conversation on joint problem solving to address communication breakdowns and change problematic behaviors before they lead to larger relational problems.[28]

The primary emphasis of supportive communication is to avoid defensiveness and disconfirmation. **Defensiveness** occurs when individuals feel they are being attacked and they need to protect themselves. If you are communicating with someone who begins to get angry and becomes aggressive, that person is likely feeling defensive. **Disconfirmation** occurs when an individual feels his self-worth is being questioned. A person shows he is feeling disconfirmed when he withdraws from the conversation or starts engaging in show-off behaviors to try to make himself look good. In either case, the communicator needs to stop the conversation and work to reduce the defensiveness and disconfirmation by refocusing the conversation and building the other person up before continuing.

This can be accomplished using several techniques (see OB Savvy 11.3). First, focus on the problem and not the person. This helps keep the communication problem-oriented and not person-oriented. For example, instead of saying "you are bad," you would say "you are behaving badly." By focusing on behavior you are addressing something the individual can do something about—he

* **Interactional transparency** is the open and honest sharing of information.

* **Supportive communication principles** are a set of tools focused on joint problem solving.

* **Defensiveness** occurs when individuals feel they are being attacked and they need to protect themselves.

* **Disconfirmation** occurs when an individual feels his or her self-worth is being questioned.

can change his *behavior* but he can't change who he is as a person.

Second, be specific and descriptive, not global or evaluative. In the prior example, once you target the behavior, you then have to be specific about which behavior is the problem. Do not focus on too many behaviors at one time. Pick a couple examples that illustrate the problem behavior and identify them as specifically (and preferably as recently) as you can. Instead of saying "you never listen to me," you can say "the other day in the meeting you interrupted me three times and that made it impossible for me to get my point across to the group."

Third, own the communication. As a manager, instead of saying "Corporate tells us we need to better document our work hours," you would say "I believe that better documenting our work hours will help us be more effective in running our business."

Finally, be congruent—make sure your message is consistent with your body language. If your words say "No, I'm not mad," but your body language conveys anger, you are being dishonest in the communication and only provoking less open and collaborative communication.

By learning to use the supportive communication principles as shown in OB Savvy 11.3, you can enhance not only your ability to communicate effectively in your workplace but also in your life.

OB SAVVY 11.3
Supportive Communication Principles

1. Focus on the problem and not the person.
   . . . Not "You are bad!" but rather "You are behaving badly."
2. Be specific and descriptive, not global or evaluative.
   . . . Avoid using never or always, as in "you *never* listen to me."
3. Own, rather than disown, the communication.
   . . . "I believe we need to change" rather than "Management tells us we have to change."
4. Be congruent—match the words with the body language.
   . . . Don't say "No I'm not angry!" if your body language says you are.

Resources in The OB Skills Workbook

These learning activities from *The OB Skills Workbook* are suggested for Chapter 11.

Case for Critical Thinking	Team and Experiential Exercises	Self-Assessment Portfolio
• The Poorly Informed Walrus	• Active Listening • Upward Appraisal • 360° Feedback	• "TT" Leadership Style • Empowering Others

11 study guide

Summary Questions and Answers

What is communication?

- Collaborative communication is becoming more important as technology changes the way we work.
- Communication is the process of sending and receiving messages with attached meanings.

- The communication process involves encoding an intended meaning into a message, sending the message through a channel, and receiving and decoding the message into perceived meaning.

- Noise is anything that interferes with the communication process.

- Feedback is a return message from the original recipient back to the sender.

- To be constructive, feedback must be direct, specific, and given at an appropriate time.

- Nonverbal communication involves communication other than through the spoken word (e.g., facial expressions, body position, eye contact, and other physical gestures).

- When verbal and nonverbal do not match, research has shown that receivers will pay more attention to the nonverbal.

What are the issues in interpersonal communication?

- To create collaborative communication, people must not succumb to communication barriers.

- Interpersonal barriers detract from communication because individuals are not able to objectively listen to the sender due to personal biases; they include selective listening and filtering.

- Physical distractions are barriers due to interruptions from noises, visitors, etc.

- Semantic barriers involve a poor choice or use of words and mixed messages.

- Active listening encourages a free and complete flow of communication from the sender to the receiver; it is nonjudgmental and encouraging.

- Parochialism and ethnocentrism contribute to the difficulties of experiencing truly effectual cross-cultural communication.

What is the nature of communication in organizations?

- Organizational communication is the specific process through which information moves and is exchanged within an organization.

- Technologies continue to change the workplace, challenging traditional notions of hierarchy and structure in organizations.

- Communication in organizations uses a variety of formal and informal channels; the richness of the channel, or its capacity to convey information, must be adequate for the message.

- Information flows upward, downward, and laterally in organizations.

- Status effects in organizations may result in restricted and filtered information exchanges between subordinates and their superiors.

How can we build more collaborative work environments?

- With the rise of social networking tools, the restriction of information is becoming more and more difficult.

- Instead of fighting these trends, organizations are identifying ways to capitalize on emerging technologies that are resulting in a reduction of status differentials and breaking down of corporate silos.

- More companies are valuing transparency in communication.

- Transparency is enhanced through the use of supportive communication principles.

Key Terms

Active listening (p. 261)
Channel richness (p. 265)
Communication (p. 256)
Communication channels (p. 257)
Defensiveness (p. 270)
Disconfirmation (p. 270)
Downward communication (p. 266)
Encoding (p. 257)
Ethnocentrism (p. 263)
Feedback (p. 257)
Filtering (p. 260)
Flaming (p. 268)
Formal channels (p. 265)

Grapevine (p. 265)
High-context cultures (p. 263)
Informal channels (p. 265)
Interactional Transparency (p. 270)
Interpersonal barriers (p. 259)
Lateral communication (p. 266)
Low-context cultures (p. 263)
Mum effect (p. 268)
Noise (p. 257)
Nonverbal communication (p. 258)

Parochialism (p. 263)
Physical distractions (p. 260)
Presence-aware tools (p. 268)
Receiver (p. 257)
Selective listening (p. 259)
Semantic barriers (p. 260)
Sender (p. 257)
Status differences (p. 268)
Supportive communication principles (p. 270)
Upward communication (p. 266)

Self-Test 11

Multiple Choice

1. In communication, _____ is anything that interferes with the transference of the message. (a) channel (b) sender (c) receiver (d) noise

2. When you give criticism to someone, the communication will be most effective when the criticism is _____. (a) general and nonspecific (b) given when the sender feels the need (c) tied to things the recipient can do something about (d) given all at once to get everything over with

3. Which communication is the best choice for sending a complex message? (a) face to face (b) written memorandum (c) e-mail (d) telephone call

4. When someone's words convey one meaning but body posture conveys something else, a(n) _____ is occurring. (a) ethnocentric message (b) lack of congruence (c) semantic problem (d) status effect

5. Personal bias is an example of _____ in the communication process. (a) an interpersonal barrier (b) a semantic barrier (c) physical distractions (d) proxemics

6. Which communication method has the most two-way characteristics? (a) e-mail (b) blog (c) voice mail (d) instant messaging

7. _____ is an example of an informal channel through which information flows in an organization. (a) The grapevine (b) Top-down communication (c) The mum effect (d) Transparency

8. New electronic communication technologies have the advantage of handling large amounts of information, but they may also make communication among organizational members _____. (a) less accessible (b) less immediate (c) more informal (d) less private

9. The study of gestures and body postures for their impact on communication is an issue of _____. (a) kinesics (b) proxemics (c) semantics (d) informal channels

10. In _____ communication the sender is likely to be most comfortable, whereas in _____ communication the receiver is likely to feel most informed. (a) one-way; two-way (b) top-down; bottom-up (c) bottom-up; top-down (d) two-way; one-way

11. A manager who spends a lot of time explaining his or her motives and engaging in frank and open dialogue could be described as using _____. (a) the KISS principle (b) transparency (c) MBO (d) the grapevine

12. _____ interfere(s) with open communication in most workplaces. (a) Status effects (b) The mum effect (c) Organizational ecology (d) Nonverbal communication

13. If someone is interested in proxemics as a means of improving communication with others, that person would likely pay a lot of attention to his or her _____. (a) office layout (b) status (c) active listening skills (d) 360-degree feedback

14. Among the rules for active listening is _____. (a) remain silent and communicate only nonverbally (b) confront emotions (c) don't let feelings become part of the process (d) reflect back what you think you are hearing

15. The use of supportive communication principles is helpful for _____. (a) reducing defensiveness and disconfirmation (b) the use of computer technology (c) privacy and electronic performance monitoring (d) improving the correctness of one's vocabulary

Short Response

16. Why is channel richness a useful concept for managers?

17. What place do informal communication channels have in organizations today?

18. Why is communication between lower and higher levels sometimes filtered?

Applications Essay

19. "People in this organization don't talk to one another anymore. Everything is e-mail, e-mail, e-mail. If you are mad at someone, you can just say it and then hide behind your computer." With these words, Wesley expressed his frustrations with Delta General's operations. Xiaomei echoed his concerns, responding, "I agree, but surely the managing director should be able to improve organizational communication without losing the advantages of e-mail." As a consultant overhearing this conversation, how do you suggest the managing director respond to Xiaomei's challenge?

12

Power and Politics

chapter at a glance

Because individuals join organizations for their own reasons and goals, power and politics are inevitable and must be understood. Here's what to look for in Chapter 12. Don't forget to check your learning with the Summary Questions & Answers and Self-Test in the end-of-chapter Study Guide.

WHAT ARE POWER AND INFLUENCE?

Interdependence, Legitimacy, and Power

Obedience

Acceptance of Authority and the Zone of Indifference

WHAT ARE THE KEY SOURCES OF POWER AND INFLUENCE?

Position Power

Personal Power

Power and Influence Capacity

Relational Influence

WHAT IS EMPOWERMENT?

Keys to Empowerment

Power as an Expanding Pie

From Empowerment to Valuing People

WHAT IS ORGANIZATIONAL POLITICS?

Traditions of Organizational Politics

Politics of Self-Protection

Politics and Governance

An encyclopedia was once written by "experts" and carefully edited. The person in charge had a formal title, and the authors of each entry worked for the publisher. This encyclopedia was expensive to buy and tightly controlled by the publisher. Wikipedia has not only changed this scene, it has represented a new power dynamic. Not only was it free and open for use by all, it was at first totally open to online editing by its users.

The controversial guru of this new wave offering, Jimmy Wales, does not have a formal title such as CEO or president even though he is on the board of directors of the Wikimedia Foundation that runs the Web site. He is the driving force behind an idea he attributes to libertarian economist F. A. Hayek. The idea: When information is dispersed, decisions should be left to those with the most local knowledge. Thus, hundreds of individuals edited Wikipedia entries every day to provide corrections and update the material. They collectively interacted to update Wikipedia in real time. But not all entries were accurate, and this created controversy. According to Wales, "Errors are human . . . Openness is the solution not the problem."

Wikipedia's tremendous growth and popularity, as well as even a few hoaxes, have lead Sue Gardner, Wikipedia Foundations' executive director, to institute a number of editorial controls. She also enforces the rule to take "a neutral point of

"Errors are human . . . Openness is the solution not the problem."

view." Now there are some 1,000 official editors, and it is more difficult to provide a change to existing material. If you want to modify an entry on a current business CEO, for instance, it will be reviewed by a Wikipedia administrator. Wales's original notion of total user control is fading. Wikipedia's current challenge is to keep the excitement of contributions and openness while exerting some power to protect its integrity.

getting things done while you help yourself

Power and Influence

What do power and politics have to do with the interaction among individuals, inside or outside of organizations? Plenty. The basis for both power and politics is the degree of interconnectness among individuals.[1] As individuals pursue their own goals within an organization, they must also deal with the interests of other individuals and their desires.[2] There are never enough resources—money, people, time, or authority—to meet everyone's needs. Managers may see a power gap as they constantly face too many competing demands to satisfy. They must choose to favor some interests over others.[3] For example, you may want a flexible schedule in order to achieve a balance between work and home demands but the organization requires you to be present on a regular basis. Your interests and those of the organization do not appear to be consistent. And your manager may not even have the authority to offer you the flexible schedule you need. The managers see a power gap as they recognize that giving you a flexible schedule means others might also ask for one.

The power gap and its associated political dynamics have at least two sides. On the one hand, power and politics can represent the unpleasant side of organizational life. Organizations are not democracies composed of individuals with equal influence. Some people have a lot more power than others. There are winners and losers in the battles for resources and rewards. On the other hand, power and politics are important organizational tools that managers must use to get the job done. More organizational members can "win" when managers identify areas where individual and organizational interests are compatible.

• **Power** is the ability to get someone else to do something you want done or the ability to make things happen or get things done the way you want.

• **Influence** is a behavioral response to the exercise of power.

In organizational behavior, **power** is defined as the ability to get someone to do something you want done or the ability to make things happen in the way you want them to. The essence of power is control over the behavior of others.[4] Without a direct or indirect connection it is not possible to alter the behavior of others.

While power is the force used to make things happen in an intended way, **influence** is what an individual has when he or she exercises power, and it is expressed by others' behavioral response to the exercise of power. In Chapters 13 and 14 we will examine leadership as a key power mechanism to make things happen. This chapter will discuss other ways that power and politics form the context for leadership influence.

Interdependence, Legitimacy, and Power

It is important to remember that the foundation for power rests in interdependence. Each member of an organization's fate is, in part, determined by the actions of all other members. All members of an organization are interdependent. It is apparent that employees are closely connected with the individuals in their work group, those in other departments they work with, and, of course, their supervisors. In today's modern organization the pattern of interdependence and, therefore the base for power and politics, rests on a system of authority and control.[5] Additionally, organizations have societal backing to seek reasonable goals in legitimate ways.

Leaders on Leadership

JOSE MOURINHO, "THE SPECIAL ONE"

Jose Mourinho has a commanding presence in the world of European football. This native of Portugal is described as handsome, supremely self-confident, passionate about the game and undeniably one of the sport's top coaches.

The media takes its fair share of jabs at Mourinho but recognizes unequivocally his talent to lead his teams to championship level play. His "meteoric rise" from "mere translator" for coaching legend Bobby Robson to dominating the European soccer scene has been remarkable. He's drawn considerable attention and criticism for his abrasive confrontations with referees and coaches alike.

Admitting his lack of ability as a footballer himself, he set his sights on coaching and waited his turn on the sidelines. Serving as Robson's translator, he proved himself a valuable asset when he prepared an impressive dossier for the coach. From then on his reputation increased as an astute analyst of the game and greatly enhanced his power as an expert in the game.

Among his players he is respected for his knowledge, experience, motivational abilities and the genuine interest he takes in their careers and development as professionals. His often brazen, critical comments are reserved for referees, other coaches, other clubs and his favorite target—the media. This adds to Mourinho's charisma in addition to other bases of power which he yields quite skillfully in maneuvering through a highly political sport.

Love him or hate him, his power ultimately reflects his ability to influence others and underlies the confidence he has to proclaim himself to be "The Special One." So far his coaching talent and personal flare haven't contradicted him.

The unstated foundation of legitimacy in most organizations is an understood technical and moral order. From infancy to retirement, individuals in our society are taught to obey "higher authority." In societies, "higher authority" does not always have a bureaucratic or organizational reference but consists of those with moral authority such as tribal chiefs and religious leaders. In most organizations, "higher authority" means those close to the top of the corporate pyramid. The legitimacy of those at the top derives from their positions as representatives for various constituencies. This is a technical or instrumental role. For instance, senior managers may justify their lofty positions by suggesting they represent stockholders. The importance of stockholders is, in turn, a foundation for our capitalistic economic system.

Some senior executives evoke ethics and social causes in their role as authority figures because ethics and social contributions are important foundations for the power of these institutions. For instance, take a look at Leaders on Leadership and Edward J. Zore, President of Northwestern Mutual. Yet, just talking about the ethical and social foundations for power would not be enough to ensure that individuals comply with their supervisor's orders if they were not prone to obedience.

The tendency to obey today is a powerful force. Will you be prepared to say "no" the next time someone asks you to do something of questionable virtue?

Obedience

The mythology of American independence and unbridled individualism is so strong we need to spend some time explaining how most of us are really quite obedient. So we turn to the seminal studies of Stanley Milgram on obedience from the early 1960s.[6]

Milgram designed experiments to determine the extent to which people would obey the commands of an authority figure, even if they believed they were endangering the life of another person. Subjects from a wide variety of occupations and ranging in age from 20 to 50 were paid a nominal fee for participation in the project. The subjects were told that the purpose of the study was to determine the effects of punishment on learning. The subjects were to be the "teachers." The "learner," a partner of Milgram's, was strapped to a chair in an adjoining room with an electrode attached to his wrist. The "experimenter," another partner of Milgram's, was dressed in a laboratory coat. Appearing impassive and somewhat stern, the "experimenter" instructed the "teacher" to read a series of word pairs to the learner and then to reread the first word along with four other terms. The learner was supposed to indicate which of the four terms was in the original pair by pressing a switch that caused a light to flash on a response panel in front of the "teacher."

The "teacher" was instructed to administer a shock to the learner each time an incorrect answer was given. This shock was to be increased one level of intensity each time the learner made a mistake. The "teacher" controlled switches that supposedly administered the electric shocks. In reality, there was no electric current in the apparatus. And the "learners" purposely made mistakes often and responded to each shock level in progressively distressing ways. If a "teacher" proved unwilling to administer a shock, the experimenter used the following sequential prods to get him or her to perform as requested. (1) "Please continue"; (2) "The experiment requires that you continue"; (3) "It is absolutely essential that you continue"; and (4) "You have no choice; you must go on." Only when the teacher refused to go on after the fourth prod would the experiment be stopped.

So what happened? Some 65 percent of the "teachers" actually administered an almost lethal shock to the "learners." Shocked at the results, Milgram tried a wide variety of variations (e.g., different commands to continue, a bigger gap between the teacher and the experimenter) with similar if less severe shocks. He concluded that there is a tendency for individuals to comply and be obedient—to switch off their emotions and merely do exactly what they are told to do.

The tendency to obey is powerful and it is a major problem in the corporate boardroom where the lack of dissent due to extreme obedience to authority has been associated with the lack of rationality and questionable ethics.[7]

Acceptance of Authority and the Zone of Indifference

Obedience is not the only reason for compliance in organizations. The author of groundbreaking research in management theory and organizational studies, Chester Barnard, suggested that it also stemmed from the "consent of the governed."[8] From this notion, Barnard developed the concept of the acceptance of authority—the idea that some directives would naturally be followed while others would not. The basis of this acceptance view was the notion of an implicit contract between the individual and the firm, known as a psychological contract. These two ideas led Barnard to outline the notion of the "zone of indifference" where individuals would comply without much thought.

Acceptance of Authority   In everyday organizational life Barnard argued that subordinates accepted or followed a managerial directive only if four circumstances were met.

- The subordinate can and must understand the directive.
- The subordinate must feel mentally and physically capable of carrying out the directive.
- The subordinate must believe that the directive is not inconsistent with the purpose of the organization.
- The subordinate must believe that the directive is not inconsistent with his or her personal interests.

Note the way in which the organizational purpose and personal interest requirements are stated. The subordinate does not need to understand how the proposed action will help the organization. He or she only needs to believe that the requested action is not inconsistent with the purpose of the firm. Barnard found the issue of personal interest to be more complicated and he built his analysis on the notion of a psychological contract between the individual and the firm.

Zone of Indifference   Most people seek a balance between what they put into an organization (contributions) and what they get from an organization in return (inducements). Within the boundaries of this **psychological contract**, therefore, employees will agree to do many things in and for the organization because they think they should. In exchange for the inducements, they recognize the authority of the organization and its managers to direct their behavior in certain ways. Outside of the psychological contract's boundaries, however, things become much less clear.

> The **psychological contract** is an unwritten set of expectations about a person's exchange of inducements and contributions with an organization.

The notion of the psychological contract turns out to be a powerful concept, particularly in the "breach" where an individual feels the contract has been violated. When employees believe the organization has not delivered on its implicit promises, in addition to disobedience, there is less loyalty, higher turnover intentions, and less job satisfaction.[9]

Based on his acceptance view of authority, Chester Barnard calls the area in which authoritative directions are obeyed the **zone of indifference**. It describes the range of requests to which a person is willing to respond without subjecting the directives to critical evaluation or judgment. Directives falling within the zone are obeyed routinely. Requests or orders falling outside the zone of indifference are not considered legitimate under terms of the psychological contract. Such "extraordinary" directives may or may not be obeyed. This link between the zone of indifference and the psychological contract is shown in Figure 12.1.

> **Zone of indifference** is the range of authoritative requests to which a subordinate is willing to respond without subjecting the directives to critical evaluation or judgment.

The zone of indifference is not fixed. There may be times when a boss would like a subordinate to do things that fall outside of the zone. In this case, the manager must enlarge the zone to accommodate additional behaviors. We have chosen to highlight a number of ethical issues that are within, or may be beyond, the

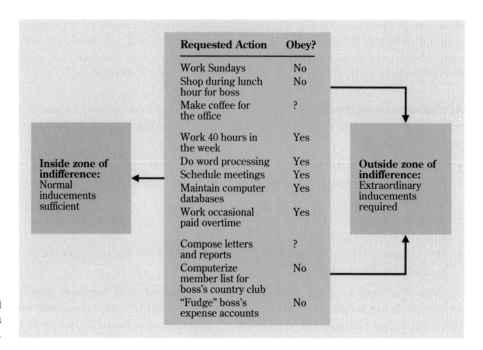

Requested Action	Obey?
Work Sundays	No
Shop during lunch hour for boss	No
Make coffee for the office	?
Work 40 hours in the week	Yes
Do word processing	Yes
Schedule meetings	Yes
Maintain computer databases	Yes
Work occasional paid overtime	Yes
Compose letters and reports	?
Computerize member list for boss's country club	No
"Fudge" boss's expense accounts	No

Inside zone of indifference: Normal inducements sufficient

Outside zone of indifference: Extraordinary inducements required

Figure 12.1 Hypothetical psychological contract for a secretary.

typical zone of indifference. Research on ethical managerial behavior shows that supervisors can become sources of pressure for subordinates to do such things as support incorrect viewpoints, sign false documents, overlook the supervisor's wrongdoing, and conduct business with the supervisor's friends.[11]

Most of us will face such ethical dilemmas during our careers. There are no firm answers to these issues as they are cases of individual judgment. We realize that saying "No" or "refusing to keep quiet" can be difficult and potentially costly. We also realize that you might be willing to do some things for one boss but not another. In different terms, the boss has two sources of power: power position derived from his or her position in the firm, and personal power derived from the individual actions of the manager.[12]

Sources of Power and Influence

Within each organization a manager's power is determined by his or her position and personal power, his or her individual actions, and the ability to build upon combinations of these sources.

Position Power

- **Legitimate power** or formal authority is the extent to which a manager can use the "right of command" to control other people.

One important source of power available to a manager stems solely from his or her position in the organization. Specifically, position power stems from the formal hierarchy or authority vested in a particular role. There are six important aspects of position power: legitimate, reward, coercive, process, information, and representative power.[13]

Based on our discussion of obedience and the acceptance theory of authority it is easy to understand **legitimate power**, or formal hierarchical authority. It

ETHICS OF INCENTIVE SYSTEMS

Incentives are a major way of influencing employees. From a purely economic standpoint the ethical issue is the degree of choice the individual has over the ramifications of his or her behavior. Or in simple terms, do you choose to go after the incentive offered? For instance, telemarketers are often required to read a script that includes less than honest statements. If they read the script, they are given a bonus. If they depart from the script no bonus is given, thereby encouraging the employee to act in a way that may be considered unethical.

Incentives can also be seen in political terms as a use of reward power. Some suggest that in addition to voluntarism, incentives are ethical only when their purpose is legitimate and when they do not affect the character of the individual being offered the incentive. For example, a CEO's bonus may depend upon a short-term increase in the firm's stock price. That sounds fine until you recognize that the bonus may be in the ten of millions of dollars and that the CEO is tempted to trade short-term gains (e.g., reductions in R&D) for longer-term benefits?

What Would You Do? What would you do if you were offered a bonus for each mortgage you closed with or without a verification of the applicant's financial qualifications? Would you be tempted to "believe" the applicant in order to speed up the process and increase the number of mortgages closed?

stems from the extent to which a manager can use subordinates' internalized values or beliefs that the "boss" has a "right of command" to control their behavior. For example, the boss may have the formal authority to approve or deny such employee requests as job transfers, equipment purchases, personal time off, or overtime work. Legitimate power represents the unique power a manager has because subordinates believe it is legitimate for a person occupying the managerial position to have the right to command. If this legitimacy is lost, authority will not be accepted by subordinates.

Reward power is the extent to which a manager can use extrinsic and intrinsic rewards to control other people. Examples of such rewards include money, promotions, compliments, or enriched jobs. Although all managers have some access to rewards, success in accessing and utilizing rewards to achieve influence varies according to the skills of the manager. While giving rewards may appear ethical, it is not always the case. The use of incentives by unscrupulous managers can be unethical. Check the Ethics in OB for some guidelines.

- **Reward power** is the extent to which a manager can use extrinsic and intrinsic rewards to control other people.

Power can also be based on punishment instead of reward. For example, a manager may threaten to withhold a pay raise or to transfer, demote, or even recommend the firing of a subordinate who does not act as desired. Such **coercive power** is the extent to which a manager can deny desired rewards or administer punishments to control other people. The availability of coercive power also varies from one organization and manager to another. The presence of unions and organizational policies on employee treatment can weaken this power base considerably.

- **Coercive power** is the extent to which a manager can deny desired rewards or administer punishment to control other people.

- **Process power** is the control over methods of production and analysis.

- **Information power** is the access to and/or the control of information.
- **Representative power** is the formal right conferred by the firm to speak for and to a potentially important group.

Mellody Hobson, Ariel Investments

Mellody Hobson is president of the money-management firm Ariel Investments, one of the few such firms that is minority owned. But Hobson is concerned that minority advancement will slow down. She admits "There are lots of conversations about the pipeline of people" but wonders why there aren't more "ready to go."

Process power is the control over methods of production and analysis. The source of this power is the placing of the individual in a position to influence how inputs are transformed into outputs for the firm, a department in the firm, or even a small group. Firms often establish process specialists who work with managers to ensure that production is accomplished efficiently and effectively. Closely related to this is control of the analytical processes used to make choices. For example, many organizations have individuals with specialties in financial analysis. They may review proposals from other parts of the firm for investments. Their power derives not from the calculation itself, but from the assignment to determine the analytical procedures used to judge the proposals.

Process power may be separated from legitimate hierarchical power simply because of the complexity of the firm's operations. A manager may have the formal hierarchical authority to make a decision but may be required to use the analytical schemes of others or to consult on effective implementation with process specialists. The issue of position power can get quite complex very quickly in sophisticated operations. This leads us to another related aspect of position power—the role of access to and control of information.

Information power is the access information or the control of it. It is one of the most important aspects of legitimacy. The "right to know" and use information can be, and often is, conferred on a position holder. Thus, information power may complement legitimate hierarchical power. Information power may also be granted to specialists and managers who are in the middle of the information systems in the firm.

For example, the chief information officer of the firm may not only control all the computers, but may also have access to any and all information desired. Managers jealously guard the formal "right to know," because it means they are in a position to influence events, not merely react to them. Most chief executive officers believe they have the right to know about everything in "their" firm. Deeper in the organization, managers often protect information from others based on the notion that outsiders would not understand it. Engineering drawings, for example, are not typically allowed outside of the engineering department. In other instances, information is to be protected from outsiders. Marketing and advertising plans may be labeled "top secret." In most cases the nominal reason for controlling information is to protect the firm. The real reason is often to allow information holders the opportunity to increase their power.

Representative power is the formal right conferred to an individual by the firm enabling him or her to speak as a representative for a group comprised of individuals from across departments or outside the firm. In most complex organizations there is a wide variety of different constituencies that may have an important impact on the firm's operations and its success. They include such groups as investors, customers, alliance partners, and, of course, unions.

Astute executives often hire individuals to act as representatives to ensure that their influence is felt but does not dominate. An example would be an investor relations manager who is expected to deal with the mundane inquiries of small investors, anticipate the questions of financial analysts, and represent the sentiment of investors to senior management. The investor relations manager may be asked to anticipate investors' questions and guide senior managers' responses. The influence of the investor relations manager is, in part, based on the assignment to represent the interests of this particular group.

Personal Power

Personal power resides in the individual and is independent of that individual's position within an organization. Personal power is important in many well-managed firms, as managers need to supplement the power of their formal positions. Four bases of personal power are expertise, rational persuasion, reference, and coalitions.[14]

Expert power is the ability to control another person's behavior through the possession of knowledge, experience, or judgment that the other person does not have but needs. A subordinate obeys a supervisor possessing expert power because the latter usually knows more about what is to be done or how it is to be done than does the subordinate. Expert power is relative, not absolute. So if you are the best cook in the kitchen, you have expert power until a real chef enters. Then the chef has the expert power.

Rational persuasion is the ability to control another's behavior because, through the individual's efforts, the person accepts the desirability of an offered goal and a reasonable way of achieving it. Much of what a supervisor does on a day-to-day basis involves rational persuasion up, down, and across the organization. Rational persuasion involves both explaining the desirability of expected outcomes and showing how specific actions will achieve these outcomes. Relational persuasion relies on trust. OB Savvy 12.1 provides tips to building trust, the key to developing personal power.

Referent power is the ability to control another's behavior because the person wants to identify with the power source. In this case, a subordinate obeys the manager because he or she wants to behave, perceive, or believe as the manager does. This obedience may occur, for example, because the subordinate likes the boss personally and therefore tries to do things the way the boss wants them done. In a sense, the subordinate attempts to avoid doing anything that would interfere with the boss–subordinate relationship.

A person's referent power can be enhanced when the individual taps into the morals held by another or shows a clearer long-term path to a morally desirable end. Individuals with the ability to tap into these more esoteric aspects of corporate life have "charisma" and "vision." Followership is not based on what the subordinate will get for specific actions or specific levels of performance, but on what the individual represents—a role model and a path to a morally desired future. For example, an employee can increase his or her referent power by showing subordinates how they can develop better relations with each other and how they can serve the greater good.

Coalition power is the ability to control another's behavior indirectly because the individual has an obligation to someone as part of a larger collective

- **Expert power** is the ability to control another's behavior because of the possession of knowledge, experience, or judgment that the other person does not have but needs.

- **Rational persuasion** is the ability to control another's behavior because, through the individual's efforts, the person accepts the desirability of an offered goal and a reasonable way of achieving it.

- **Referent power** is the ability to control another's behavior because of the individual's desire to identify with the power source.

- **Coalition power** is the ability to control another's behavior indirectly because the individual owes an obligation to you or another as part of a larger collective interest.

OB SAVVY 12.1

Developing Trust to Build Personal Power

The key to ethically developing power is to build trust. To build trust, you should, at a minimum:

- Always honor implied and explicit social contracts.
- Seek to prevent, avoid, and rectify harm to others.
- Respect the unique needs of others.

interest. Coalitions are often built around issues of common interest.[15] To build a coalition, individuals negotiate trade-offs in order to arrive at a common position. Individuals may also trade across issues in granting support for one another. These trade-offs and trades represent informational obligations of support. To maintain the coalition, individuals may be asked to support a position on an issue and act in accordance with the desires of the supervisor. When they do, there is a reciprocal obligation to support them on their issues. For example, members of a department should support a budget increase.

These reciprocal obligations can extend to a network of individuals as well. A network of mutual support provides a powerful collective front to protect members and to accomplish shared interests. Think about all of the required courses you must take to graduate; the list was probably developed by a coalition of professors led by their department chairs. Faculty members who support a required course from another department expect help from the supported department in getting their course on the list.

Power and Influence Capacity

• **Power-oriented behavior** is action directed primarily at developing or using relationships in which other people are willing to defer to one's wishes.

A considerable portion of any manager's time is directed toward what is called **power-oriented behavior**. Power-oriented behavior is action directed primarily at developing or using relationships in which other people are willing to defer to one's wishes.[16] Figure 12.2 shows three basic dimensions of power and influence affecting a manager and include downward, upward, and lateral dimensions. Also shown in the figure are the uses of personal and position power. The effective manager is one who succeeds in building and maintaining high levels of both position and personal power over time. Only then is sufficient power of the right types available when the manager needs to exercise influence on downward, lateral, and upward dimensions.

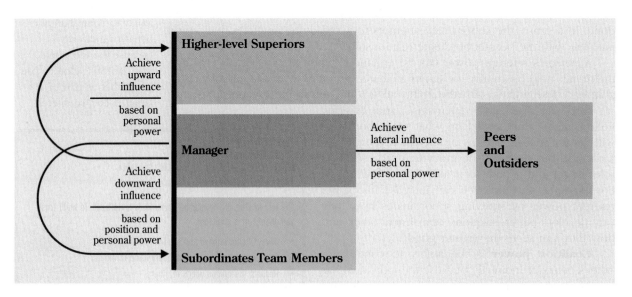

Figure 12.2 Three dimensions of managerial power and influence.

Building Position Power   Position power can be enhanced when a manager is able to demonstrate to others that their work unit is highly relevant to organizational goals, called centrality, and is able to respond to urgent organizational need, called criticality. Managers may seek to acquire a more central role in the workflow by having information filtered through them, making at least part of their job responsibilities unique, and expanding their network of communication contacts.

A manager may also attempt to increase task relevance to add criticality. There are many ways to do this. The manager may try to become an internal coordinator within the firm or an external representative. When the firm is in a dynamic setting of changing technology, the executive may also move to provide unique services and information to other units. A manager may shift the emphasis on his or her group's activities toward emerging issues central to the organization's top priorities. To effectively initiate new ideas and new projects may not be possible unless a manager also delegates more routine activities and expands both the task variety and task novelty for subordinates. Of course, not all attempts to build influence may be positive. Some managers are known to have defined tasks so they are difficult to evaluate by creating an ambiguous job description or developing a unique language for their work.

Building Personal Power   Personal power arises from the individual characteristics of the manager. Three personal characteristics—expertise, political savvy, and likeability—have potential for enhancing personal power in an organization. The most obvious is *building expertise*. Additional expertise may be gained by advanced training and education, participation in professional associations, and involvement in the early stages of projects.

A somewhat less obvious way to increase personal power is to learn **political savvy**—better ways to negotiate, persuade individuals, and understand the goals and means they are most willing to accept. The novice believes that most individuals are very much the same: they acknowledge the same goals, and will accept similar paths toward these goals. The more astute individual recognizes important individual differences among coworkers. The most experienced managers are adept at building coalitions and developing a network of reciprocal obligations.

Finally, a manager's personal power is increased by characteristics that enhance his or her *likeability* and create personal appeal in relationships with other people. These include pleasant personality traits, agreeable behavior patterns, and attractive appearance. See Mastering Management for tips on how to bring these factors together.

• **Political savvy** is knowing how to negotiate, persuade, and deal with people regarding goals they will accept.

Building Influence Capacity   One of the ways people build influence capacity is by taking steps to increase their visibilities in the organization. This is done by (1) expanding the number of contacts they have with senior people, (2) making oral presentations of written work, (3) participating in problem-solving task forces, (4) sending out notices of accomplishments, and (5) seeking additional opportunities to increase personal name recognition.[17] Most managers also recognize that, between superiors and subordinates, access to or control over information is an important element.

Another way of building influence capacity is by controlling access to information. A manager may appear to expand his or her expert power over a

THE RIGHT SKILLS CAN BUILD ORGANIZATIONAL POLITICAL SAVVY

To develop political savvy, Gerald Ferris, Sherry Davidson, and Pamela Perrewé suggest cultivating your political skills. How? For starters, focus on developing four key skills:

1. Become more aware of others' concerns and improve your understanding of why they act the way they do.
2. Work on communication skills and develop friendly relationships.
3. Sharpen your ability to network by finding others inside and outside the firm who have shared interests.
4. Perfect your approach to become viewed as a person who genuinely cares for others.

subordinate by not allowing the individual access to critical information. Although the denial may appear to enhance the boss's expert power, it may reduce the subordinate's effectiveness. In a similar manner, a supervisor may also control access to key organizational decision makers. An individual's ability to contact key persons informally can offset some of this disadvantage. Furthermore, astute senior executives routinely develop "back channels" to lower-level individuals deep within the firm to offset the tendency of bosses to control information and access.

Expert power is often relational and embedded within the organizational context. Many important decisions are made outside formal channels and are substantially influenced by key individuals with the requisite knowledge. By developing and using coalitions and networks, an individual may build on his or her expert power. And through coalitions and networks, an individual may alter the flow of information and the context for analysis. By developing coalitions and networks, executives also expand their access to information and their opportunities for participation.

Managers can also build influence capacity by controlling, or at least attempting to control, decision premises. A decision premise is a basis for defining the problem and selecting among alternatives. By defining a problem in a manner that fits the executive's expertise, it is natural for that executive to be in charge of solving it. Thus, the executive subtly shifts his or her position power. Executives who want to increase their power often make their goals and needs clear and bargain effectively to show that their preferred goals and needs are best. They do not show their power base directly but instead provide clear "rational persuasion" for their preferences. So the astute executive does not threaten or attempt to invoke sanctions to build power. Instead, he or she combines personal power with the position of the unit to enhance total power. As the organizational context changes, different personal sources of power may become more important alone and in combination with the individual's position power. There is an art to building power.

Relational Influence

Using position and personal power successfully to achieve the desired influence over other people is a challenge for most managers. Practically speaking, there are many useful ways of exercising relational influence. The most common techniques involve the following:[18]

Reason: Using facts and data to support a logical argument.

Friendliness: Using flattery, goodwill, and favorable impressions.

Coalition: Using relationships with other people for support.

Bargaining: Using the exchange of benefits as a basis for negotiation.

Assertiveness: Using a direct and forceful personal approach.

Higher authority: Gaining higher-level support for one's requests.

Sanctions: Using organizationally derived rewards and punishments.

Research on these strategies suggests that reason is the most popular technique overall.[19] Friendliness, assertiveness, bargaining, and higher authority are used more frequently to influence subordinates than to influence supervisors. This pattern of attempted influence is consistent with our earlier contention that downward influence generally includes mobilization of both position and personal power sources, whereas upward influence is more likely to draw on personal power.

Truly effective managers, as suggested earlier in Figure 12.2, are able to influence their bosses as well as their subordinates. One study reports that both supervisors and subordinates view reason, or the logical presentation of ideas, as the most frequently used strategy of upward influence.[20] When queried on reasons for success and failure, however, the two groups show similarities and differences in their viewpoints. The perceived causes of success in upward influence are very similar for both supervisors and subordinates and involve the favorable content of the influence attempt, a favorable manner of its presentation, and the competence of the subordinate.[21]

There is, however, some disagreement between the two groups on the causes of failure. Subordinates attribute failure in upward influence to the closed-mindedness of the supervisor, and unfavorable and difficult relationship with the supervisor, as well as the content of the influence attempt. Supervisors also attribute failure to the unfavorable content of the attempt, but report additional causes of failure as the unfavorable manner in which it was presented, and the subordinate's lack of competence.

Empowerment

Empowerment is the process by which managers help others to acquire and use the power needed to make decisions affecting themselves and their work. More than ever before, managers in progressive organizations are expected to be good at and comfortable with empowering the people with whom they work. Rather than considering power to be something to be held only at higher levels in the traditional "pyramid" of organizations, this view considers power to be something that can be shared by everyone working in flatter and more collegial structures.[22]

• **Empowerment** is the process by which managers help others to acquire and use the power needed to make decisions affecting themselves and their work.

The concept of empowerment is part of the sweeping change taking place in today's corporations. Corporate staff is being cut back; layers of management are being eliminated; and the number of employees is being reduced as the volume of work increases. What is left is a leaner and trimmer organization staffed by fewer managers who must share more power as they go about their daily tasks. Indeed, empowerment is a key foundation of the increasingly popular self-managing work teams and other creative worker involvement groups. While empowerment has been popular and successfully implemented in the United States and Europe for over a decade, new evidence suggests it can boost performance and commitment in firms worldwide, as well.[23]

Keys to Empowerment

One of the bases for empowerment is a radically different view of power itself. So far, our discussion has focused on power that is exerted over other individuals. In this traditional view, power is relational in terms of individuals. In contrast, the concept of empowerment emphasizes the ability to make things happen. Power is still relational, but in terms of problems and opportunities, not just individuals. Cutting through all of the corporate rhetoric on empowerment is quite difficult, because the term has become quite fashionable in management circles. Each individual empowerment attempt needs to be examined in light of how power in the organization will be changed.

Changing Position Power   When an organization attempts to move power down the hierarchy, it must also alter the existing pattern of position power. Changing this pattern raises some important questions. Can "empowered" individuals give rewards and sanctions based on task accomplishment? Has their new right to act been legitimized with formal authority? All too often, attempts at empowerment disrupt well-established patterns of position power and threaten middle- and lower-level managers. As one supervisor said, "All this empowerment stuff sounds great for top management. They don't have to run around trying to get the necessary clearances to implement the suggestions from my group. They never gave me the authority to make the changes, only the new job of asking for permission."

Expanding the Zone of Indifference   When embarking on an empowerment program, management needs to recognize the current zone of indifference and systematically move to expand it. All too often, management assumes that its directive for empowerment will be followed because management sees empowerment as a better way to manage. Management needs to show precisely how empowerment will benefit the individuals involved and provide the inducement needed to expand the zone of indifference.

Power as an Expanding Pie

Along with empowerment, employees need to be trained to expand their power and their new influence potential. This is the most difficult task for managers and a challenge for employees, for it often changes the dynamic between supervisors and subordinates. The key is to change the concept of power within the organization from a view that stresses power over others to one that emphasizes the use of power to get things done. Under the new definition of power, all employees can be more powerful and the chances of success can be enhanced.

A clearer definition of roles and responsibilities may help managers to empower others. For instance, senior managers may choose to concentrate on long-term, large-scale adjustments to a variety of challenging and strategic forces in the external environment. If top management tends to concentrate on the long term and downplay quarterly mileposts, others throughout the organization must be ready and willing to make critical operating decisions to maintain current profitability. By providing opportunities for creative problem solving coupled with the discretion to act, real empowerment increases the total power available in an organization. In other words, the top levels don't have to give up power in order for the lower levels to gain it. Note that senior managers must give up the illusion of control—the false belief that they can direct the actions of employees even when the latter are five or six levels of management below them.

Johnson County, Iowa

The concept of empowerment applies not just within firms but also in communities. In Johnson County, Iowa, the goal of community empowerment is to "empower individuals and their communities to achieve desired results for improving the quality of life for children 0–5 and their families."

The same basic arguments hold true in any manager–subordinate relationship. Empowerment means that all managers need to emphasize different ways of exercising influence. Appeals to higher authority and sanctions need to be replaced by appeals to reason. Friendliness must replace coercion, and bargaining must replace orders for compliance. Given the all too familiar history of an emphasis on coercion and compliance within firms, special support may be needed for individuals so that they become comfortable in developing their own power over events and activities. For instance, one recent study found that management's efforts at increasing empowerment in order to boost performance was successful only when directly supported by individual supervision. Without leader support there is no increase in empowerment and, therefore, less improvement in performance.[24]

What executives fear, and all too often find, is that employees passively resist empowerment by seeking directives they can obey or reject. The fault lies with the executives and the middle managers who need to rethink their definition of power and reconsider the use of traditional position and personal power sources. The key is to lead, not push; reward, not sanction; build, not destroy; and expand, not shrink. To expand the zone of indifference also calls for expanding the inducements for thinking and acting, not just for obeying.

From Empowerment to Valuing People

Beyond empowering employees, a number of organizational behavior scholars argue that U.S. firms need to change how they view employees in order to sustain a competitive advantage in an increasingly global economy.[25] While no one firm may have all of the necessary characteristics, Jeffrey Pfeffer suggests that the goals of the firm should include placing employees at the center of their strategy. To do so they need to:

- develop employment security for a selectively recruited workforce;
- pay high wages with incentive pay and provide potential for employee ownership;
- encourage information sharing and participation with an emphasis on self-managed teams;
- emphasize training and skill development by utilizing talent and cross-training; and
- pursue egalitarianism (at least symbolically) with little pay compression across units and enable extensive internal promotion.

*Cisco Systems—
Getting Back
to the Basics*

John Chambers, President and CEO of Cisco Systems, is "getting back to the basics in terms of focusing on the areas that a company can influence and control: cash generation, available market share gains, productivity increases, profitability and technology innovation ..." Chambers suggests an emphasis on interactions that will favor those people who can add value and content to networks.

Of course, this also calls for taking a long-term view coupled with a systematic emphasis on measuring what works and what does not, as well as a supporting managerial philosophy. This is a long list. However, it appears consistent with sentiments of John Chambers, CEO of Cisco, and his emphasis on people and interconnections.

Organizational Politics

Any study of power and influence inevitably leads to the subject of "politics." For many, this word may conjure up thoughts of illicit deals, favors, and advantageous personal relationships. Perhaps this image of shrewd, often dishonest, practices of obtaining one's way is reinforced by Machiavelli's classic fifteenth-century work, *The Prince*, which outlines how to obtain and hold power by way of political action. For Machiavelli, the ends justified the means. It is important, however, to understand the importance of organizational politics and adopt a perspective that allows work place politics to function in a much broader capacity.[26]

Traditions of Organizational Politics

There are two different traditions in the analysis of organizational politics. One tradition builds on Machiavelli's philosophy and defines *politics in terms of self-interest* and the use of nonsanctioned means. In this tradition, **organizational politics** may be formally defined as the management of influence to obtain ends not sanctioned by the organization or to obtain sanctioned ends by way of nonsanctioned influence.[27] Managers are often considered political when they seek their own goals, use means that are not currently authorized by the organization or those that push legal limits. Where there is uncertainty or ambiguity, it is often extremely difficult to tell whether or not a manager is being political in this self-serving sense.[28] For example, to earn a bonus, some mortgage brokers often neglected to verify the income of mortgage applicants. It was not illegal but it certainly was self-serving and could be labeled political.

The second tradition treats politics as a necessary function resulting from differences in the self-interests of individuals. Here, **organizational politics** is viewed as the art of creative compromise among competing interests. Under this view, the firm is more than just an instrument for accomplishing a task or a mere collection of individuals with a common goal. It acknowledges that the interests of individuals, stakeholders, and society must also be considered.

In a heterogeneous society, individuals will disagree as to whose self-interests are most valuable and whose concerns should therefore be bounded by collective interests. Politics arise because individuals need to develop compromises, avoid confrontation, and live and work together. This is especially true in organizations, where individuals join, work, and stay together because their self-interests are served. Furthermore, it is important to remember that the goals of the organization and the acceptable means of achieving them are established by powerful individuals in the organization in their negotiation with others. Thus, organizational politics is also the use of power to develop socially acceptable ends and means that balance individual and collective interests.

• **Organizational politics** is the management of influence to obtain ends not sanctioned by the organization or to obtain sanctioned ends through nonsanctioned means and the art of creative compromise among competing interests.

Political Interpretation   The two different traditions of organizational politics are reflected in the ways executives describe the effects on managers and their organizations. In one survey, some 53 percent of those interviewed indicated that organizational politics enhanced the achievement of organizational goals and survival. Yet some 44 percent also suggested that politics distracted individuals from organizational goals.[29]

Organizational politics is not inherently good or bad. It can serve a number of important functions, including overcoming personnel inadequacies, coping with change, and substituting for formal authority. Even in the best-managed firms, mismatches arise among managers who are learning, are burned out, lack necessary training and skills, are overqualified, or are lacking the resources needed to accomplish their assigned duties. Organizational politics provides a mechanism for circumventing these inadequacies and getting the job done. It can also facilitate adaptation to changes in the environment and technology of an organization.

Organizational politics can also help identify problems and move ambitious, problem-solving managers into action. It is quicker than restructuring and allows the firm to meet unanticipated problems with people and resources quickly, before small headaches become major problems. Finally, when a person's formal authority breaks down or fails to apply to a particular situation, political actions can be used to prevent a loss of influence. Managers may use political behavior to maintain operations and to achieve task continuity in circumstances where the failure of formal authority may otherwise cause problems. And as shown in OB Savvy 12.2, political skill has even been linked to lowering executive stress.

Political Forecasting   Managers may gain a better understanding of political behavior in order to forecast future actions by placing themselves in the positions of other persons involved in critical decisions or events. Each action and decision can be seen as having benefits for and costs to all parties concerned. Where the costs exceed the benefits, the manager may act to protect his or her position. Figure 12.3 shows a sample payoff table for two managers, Lee and Leslie, in a problem situation involving a decision as to whether or not they should allocate resources to a special project.

If both managers authorize the resources, the project gets completed on time and their company keeps a valuable client. Unfortunately, if they do this, both Lee and Leslie spend more than they have in their budgets. Taken on its own, a budget overrun would be bad for the managers' performance records. Assume that the overruns are acceptable only if the client is kept. Thus, if both managers act, both they and the company win, as depicted in the upper-left block of the figure. Obviously, this is the most desirable outcome for all parties concerned.

Assume that Leslie acts, but Lee does not. In this case, the company loses the client, Leslie overspends the budget in a futile effort, but Lee ends up within budget. While the company and Leslie lose, Lee wins. This scenario is illustrated in the lower-left block of

> **OB SAVVY 12.2**
>
> ## Political Skills as an Antidote for Stress
>
> Ever wonder why executives who deal with a tremendous amount of daily stress do not burn out? Some argue that their political skills save them. Which specific skills are most useful? They include:
>
> - Using practical intelligence as opposed to analytical or creative intelligence
> - Being calculating and shrewd about social connections
> - Inspiring trust and confidence
> - Dealing with individuals who have a wide variety of backgrounds, styles, and personalities

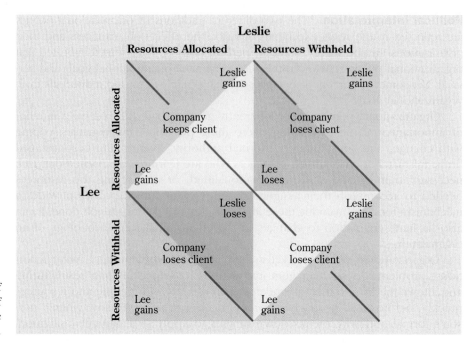

Figure 12.3 Political payoff matrix for the allocation of resources on a sample project.

the figure. The upper-right block shows the reverse situation, where Lee acts but Leslie does not. In this case, Leslie wins, while the company and Lee lose. Finally, if both Lee and Leslie fail to act, each stays within the budget and therefore gains, but the company loses the client.

The company clearly wants both Lee and Leslie to act. But will they? Would you take the risk of overspending the budget, knowing that your colleague may refuse to do the same? The question of trust is critical here, but building trust among co-managers and other workers can be difficult and takes time. The involvement of higher-level managers may be needed to set the stage. Yet in many organizations both Lee and Leslie would fail to act because the "climate" or "culture" too often encourages people to maximize their self-interest at minimal risk.

Subunit Power To be effective in political action, managers should also understand the politics of subunit relations.[30] Units that directly contribute to organizational goals are typically more powerful than units that provide advice or assistance. Units toward the top of the hierarchy are often more powerful than are those toward the bottom. More subtle power relationships are found among units at or near the same level in a firm. Political action links managers more formally to one another as representatives of their work units.

Five of the more typical lateral, intergroup relations a manager may engage with are workflow, service, advisory, auditing, and approval.[31] Workflow linkages involve contacts with units that precede or follow in a sequential production chain. Service ties involve contacts with units established to help with problems. For instance, an assembly-line manager may develop a service link by asking the maintenance manager to fix an important piece of equipment on a priority basis. In contrast, advisory connections involve formal staff units having special expertise, such as a manager seeking the advice of the personnel department on evaluating subordinates.

Auditing linkages involve units that have the right to evaluate the actions of others after action has been taken, whereas approval linkages involve units whose approval must be obtained before action may be taken. In general, units gain power as more of their relations with others are of the approval and auditing types. Workflow relations are more powerful than are advisory associations, and both are more powerful than service relations.

Politics of Self-Protection

While organizational politics may be helpful to the organization as a whole, it is more commonly known and better understood in terms of self-protection.[32] Whether or not management likes it, all employees recognize that in any organization they must first watch out for themselves. In too many organizations, if the employee doesn't protect himself or herself, no one else will. Individuals can employ three common strategies to protect themselves. They can (1) avoid action and risk taking, (2) redirect accountability and responsibility, or (3) defend their turf.

Avoidance   Avoidance is quite common in controversial areas where the employee must risk being wrong or where actions may yield a sanction. Perhaps the most common reaction is to "work to the rules." That is, employees are protected when they adhere strictly to all the rules, policies, and procedures and do not allow deviations or exceptions. Perhaps one of the most frustrating but effective techniques is to "play dumb." We all do this at some time or another. When was the last time you said, "Officer, I didn't know the speed limit was 35. I couldn't have been going 52 miles an hour."

Although working to the rules and playing dumb are common techniques, experienced employees often practice somewhat more subtle techniques of self-protection. These include depersonalization and stalling. Depersonalization involves treating individuals, such as customers, clients, or subordinates, as numbers, things, or objects. Senior managers don't fire long-term employees; the organization is merely "downsized" or "delayered." Routine stalling involves slowing down the pace of work to expand the task so that the individuals look as if they are working hard. With creative stalling, the employees may spend the time supporting the organization's ideology, position, or program and delaying implementation of changes they consider undesirable.

Redirecting Responsibility   Politically sensitive individuals will always protect themselves from accepting blame for the negative consequences of their actions. Again, a variety of well-worn techniques may be used for redirecting responsibility. "Passing the buck" is a common method employees and managers use. The trick here is to define the task in such a way that it becomes someone else's formal responsibility. The ingenious ways in which individuals can redefine an issue to avoid action and transfer responsibility are often amazing.

Both employees and managers may avoid responsibility by bluffing or rigorous documentation. Here, individuals take action only when all the paperwork is in place and it is clear that they are merely following procedure. Closely related to rigorous documentation is the "blind memo," or blind e-mail, which explains an objection to an action implemented by the individual. Here, the required action is taken, but the

Smuckers

Timothy P. Smucker and Richard K. Smucker solved the problem of who should run the business named after their grandfather–they would. Timothy is Chairman and CO-CEO while Richard is President and CO-CEO of this producer of jams, ice cream toppings, peanut butter, and shortening. They believe this arrangement minimizes the organizational politics so typical of family run businesses.

Defending "Turf" in Organizations

Just like sports teams, work units and teams in organizations often spend lots of time defending "turf" in relationships with one another. Rather than cooperating, they end up competing, and organizational accomplishments may be compromised in the process.

blind memo or e-mail is prepared should the action come into question. Politicians are particularly good at this technique. They will meet with a lobbyist and then send a memo to the files confirming the meeting. Any relationship between what was discussed in the meeting and the memo is "accidental."

As the last example suggests, a convenient method some managers use to avoid responsibility is merely to rewrite history. If a program is successful, the manager claims to have been an early supporter. If a program fails, the manager was the one who expressed serious reservations in the first place. Whereas a memo in the files is often nice to have in order to show one's early support or objections, some executives don't bother with such niceties. They merely start a meeting by recapping what has happened in such a way that makes them look good.

For the truly devious, there are three other techniques for redirecting responsibility. One technique is to blame the problem on someone or some group that has difficulty defending itself. Fired employees, outsiders, and opponents are often targets of such scapegoating. Closely related to scapegoating is blaming the problem on uncontrollable events.[33] The astute manager goes far beyond this natural tendency to place the blame on events that are out of their control. A perennial favorite is, "Given the unexpected severe decline in the overall economy, firm profitability was only somewhat below reasonable expectations." Meaning, the firm lost a bundle of money.

Should these techniques fail, there is always another possibility: facing apparent defeat, the manager can escalate commitment to a losing cause of action. That is, when all appears lost, assert your confidence in the original action, blame the problems on not spending enough money to implement the plan fully, and embark on actions that call for increased effort. The hope is that you will be promoted, have a new job with another firm, or be retired by the time the negative consequences are recognized. It is called "skating fast over thin ice."[34]

Defending Turf Defending turf is a time-honored tradition in most large organizations. As noted earlier in the chapter, managers seeking to improve their power attempt to expand the jobs their groups perform. Defending turf also results from the coalitional nature of organizations. That is, the organization may be seen as a collection of competing interests held by various departments and groups. As each group attempts to expand its influence, it starts to encroach on the activities of other groups. Turf protection is common in organizations and runs from the very lowest position to the executive suite.

When you see these actions by others, the question of ethical behavior should immediately come to mind. Check the Ethics in OB to make sure you are not using organizational politics to justify unethical behavior.

Politics and Governance

From the time of the robber barons such as Jay Gould in the 1890s, Americans have been fascinated with the politics of the chief executive suite. Recent accounts of alleged and proven criminal actions emanating from the executive suites of Washington Mutual, Bear Stearns, WorldCom, Enron, Global Crossings, and Tyco have caused the media spotlight to penetrate the mysterious veil shrouding politics at the top of organizations.[35] An analytical view of executive suite dynamics may lift some of the mystery.

ETHICS IN OB

AVOIDING COMMON RATIONALIZATIONS FOR UNETHICAL BEHAVIOR

Choosing to be ethical often involves considerable personal sacrifice, and it involves avoiding common rationalizations. When confronting potentially unethical actions, make sure you are not justifying your actions by suggesting that:

1. the behavior is not really illegal and so it could be morally acceptable;
2. the action appears to be in the firm's best interests even though it hurts others;
3. the action is unlikely ever to be detected; and
4. it appears that the action demonstrates loyalty to the boss, the firm, or short-term stockholder interests.

> **Would You Stand Up to Your Boss?** *What would you do if your boss asked you to put a penalty on credit card payers when their charges exceeded their limits on the same day their check arrived to pay their account in full? You will not be held personally accountable and to challenge the practice is to challenge your boss and your firm. Would you stand up to your boss and refuse to add the penalty?*

Agency Theory An essential power problem in today's modern corporation arises from the separation of owners and managers. A body of work called **agency theory** suggests that public corporations can function effectively even though their managers are self-interested and do not automatically bear the full consequences of their managerial actions. The theory argues that (1) all the interests of society are served by protecting stockholder interests, (2) stockholders have a clear interest in greater returns, and (3) managers are self-interested and unwilling to sacrifice these self-interests for others (particularly stockholders) and thus must be controlled. The term *agency theory* stems from the notion that managers are "agents" of the owners.[36]

So what types of controls should be instituted? There are several. One type of control involves making sure that what is good for stockholders is good for management. Incentives in the pay plan for executives may be adjusted to align with the interests of management and stockholders. For example, executives may get most of their pay based on the stock price of the firm via stock options. A second type of control involves the establishment of a strong, independent board of directors, since the board is to represent the stockholders. While this may sound unusual, it is not uncommon for a CEO to pick a majority of the board members and to place many top managers on the board. A third way is for stockholders with a large stake in the firm to take an active role on the board. For instance, mutual fund managers have been encouraged to become more active in monitoring management. And there is, of course, the so-called market for corporate control. For instance, poorly performing executives can be replaced by outsiders.[37]

The problem with the simple application of all of these control mechanisms is that they do not appear to work very well even for the stockholders and clearly, some suggest, not for others either. For example, the recent challenges faced by General Motors were met by a very passive Board of Directors. The compensation of the CEO increased even when the market share of the firm

> • **Agency theory** suggests that public corporations can function effectively even though their managers are self-interested and do not automatically bear the full consequences of their managerial actions.

declined. Many board members were appointed at the suggestion of the old CEO and only a few board members held large amounts of GM stock.

Recent studies strongly suggest that agency-based controls backfire when applied to CEOs. One study found that when options were used extensively to reward CEOs for short-term increases in the stock price, it prompted executives to make risky bets. The results were extreme with big winners and big losers. In a related investigation the extensive use of stock options was associated with manipulation of earnings when these options were not going to give the CEOs a big bonus. These researchers concluded that "stock-based managerial incentives lead to incentive misalignment."[38]

The recent storm of controversy over CEO pay and the studies cited above illustrate questions for using a simple application of agency theory to control executives. Until the turn of the century, U.S. CEOs made about 25 to 30 times the pay of the average worker. This was similar to CEO pay scales in Europe and Japan. Today, however, many U.S. CEOs are paid 300 times the average salary of workers.[39] Why are they paid so much? It is executive compensation specialists who suggest these levels to the board of directors. The compensation specialists list the salaries of the top paid, most successful executives as the basis for suggesting a plan for a client CEO. The board or the compensation committee of the board, selected by the current CEO and consisting mainly of other CEOs, then must decide if the firm's CEO is one of the best. If not one of the best then why should they continue the tenure of the CEO? Of course, if the candidate CEO gets a big package it also means that the base for subsequent comparison is increased. And round it goes.

It is little wonder that there is renewed interest in how U.S. firms are governed. Rather than proposing some quick fix based on a limited theory of the firm, it is important to come to a better understanding of different views on the politics of the executive suite. By taking a broader view, you can better understand politics in the modern corporation.

Resource Dependencies   Executive behavior can sometimes be explained in terms of resource dependencies—the firm's need for resources that are controlled by others.[40] Essentially, the resource dependence of an organization increases as (1) needed resources become more scarce, (2) outsiders have more control over needed resources, and (3) there are fewer substitutes for a particular type of resource controlled by a limited number of outsiders. Thus, one political role of the chief executive is to develop workable compromises among the competing resource dependencies facing the organization—compromises that enhance the executive's power.

To create executive-enhancing compromises, managers need to diagnose the relative power of outsiders and to craft strategies that respond differently to various external resource suppliers. For larger organizations, many strategies may center on altering the firm's degree of resource dependence. Through mergers and acquisitions, a firm may bring key resources within its control. By changing the "rules of the game," a firm may also find protection from particularly powerful outsiders. For instance, before being absorbed by another firm, Netscape sought relief from the onslaught of Microsoft by appealing to the U.S. government. Markets may also be protected by trade barriers, or labor unions may be put in check by "right to work" laws. Yet there are limits on the ability of even our largest and most powerful organizations to control all important external contingencies.

International competition has narrowed the range of options for chief executives and they can no longer ignore the rest of the world. For instance, once

RESEARCH INSIGHT

Female Members on Corporate Boards of Directors

While the number of women on corporate boards of directors is increasing, there is still a lack of representation across the board. Less than 16 percent of board members in major U.S. corporations are female. Amy Hillman, Christine Shropshire, and Albert Cannalla used a resource-dependence perspective to identify potentially important factors leading to greater participation by women on the boards of the top 1,000 U.S. firms with headquarters in the United States from 1990 to 2003. What did they find?

- Larger firms were more likely to have female board members than smaller corporations.
- Firms with more female employees were more likely to have a female board member.
- Firms with less diversification and more closely related products and services were more likely to have a female board member.
- Firms doing a lot of business with organizations that also had a female board member were more likely to have female board members.

Do the Research

What do you think the proportion of females on a board of directors is in your area? Find a list of the largest private employers in your state. Check each web site and count the number of female directors. What do you think the proportion should be? If the board was all female would this be a problem? If it were all male, would this be a problem?

Source: Amy J. Hillman, Christine Shropshire, and Albert Cannella, "Organizational Predictors of Women on Corporate Boards," *Academy of Management Journal* 5 (2007), pp. 941–968; http://www.catalyst.org/file/241/08_Census_COTE_JAN.pdf.

U.S. firms could go it alone without the assistance of foreign corporations. Now, chief executives are increasingly leading companies in the direction of more joint ventures and strategic alliances with foreign partners from around the globe. Such "combinations" provide access to scarce resources and technologies among partners, as well as new markets and shared production costs.[41]

Organizational Governance   With some knowledge of agency theory and resource dependencies it is much easier to understand the notion of organizational governance. **Organizational governance** refers to the pattern of authority, influence, and acceptable managerial behavior established at the top of the organization. This system establishes what is important, how issues will be defined, who should and should not be involved in key choices, and the boundaries for acceptable implementation. Students of organizational governance suggest that a "dominant coalition" comprised of powerful organizational actors is a key to understanding a firm's governance.[42]

Although one expects many top officers within the organization to be members of this coalition, the dominant coalition occasionally includes outsiders with access to key resources. Thus, analysis of organizational governance builds on the resource dependence perspective by highlighting the effective control of key resources by members of a dominant coalition. It also recognizes the relative power of key constituencies, such as the power of stockholders stressed in agency theory. Recent research suggests that some U.S. corporations are responding to stakeholder and agency pressures in the composition of their boards of directors.[43]

This dependence view of the executive suite recognizes that the daily practice of organizational governance is the development and resolution of issues. Through the governance system, the dominant coalition attempts to define reality. By accepting or rejecting proposals from subordinates, by directing questions toward

• **Organizational governance** is the pattern of authority, influence, and acceptable managerial behavior established at the top of the organization.

the interests of powerful outsiders, and by selecting individuals who appear to espouse particular values and qualities, the pattern of governance is slowly established within the organization. Furthermore, this pattern rests, at least in part, on political foundations.

While organizational governance was an internal and a rather private matter in the past, it is now becoming more public and controversial. Some argue that senior managers don't represent shareholder interests well enough, as we noted in the discussion of agency theory. Others are concerned that managers give too little attention to broader constituencies. We think managers should recognize the basis for their power and legitimacy and become leaders. The next two chapters are devoted to the crucial topic of leadership.

Resources in The OB Skills Workbook

These learning activities from *The OB Skills Workbook* are suggested for Chapter 12.

Case for Critical Thinking	Team and Experiential Exercises	Self-Assessment Portfolio
• Faculty Empowerment	• Interview a Leader • My Best Manager: Revisited • Power Circles	• Managerial Assumptions • Empowering Others • Machiavellianism • Personal Power Profile

12 study guide

Summary Questions and Answers

What are power and influence?

- Power is the ability to get someone else to do what you want him or her to do.
- Power vested in managerial positions derives from three sources: rewards, punishments, and legitimacy or formal authority.
- Influence is what you have when you exercise power.
- Position power is formal authority based on the manager's position in the hierarchy.
- Personal power is based on one's expertise and referent capabilities.
- Managers can pursue various ways of acquiring both position and personal power.
- Managers can also become skilled at using various techniques—such as reason, friendliness, and bargaining—to influence superiors, peers, and subordinates.

What are the key sources of power and influence?

- Individuals are socialized to accept power, the potential to control the behavior of others, and formal authority, the potential to exert such control through the legitimacy of a managerial position.
- The Milgram experiments illustrate that people have a tendency to obey directives that come from others who appear powerful and authoritative.
- Power and authority work only if the individual "accepts" them as legitimate.
- The zone of indifference defines the boundaries within which people in organizations let others influence their behavior.

What is empowerment?

- Empowerment is the process through which managers help others acquire and use the power needed to make decisions that affect themselves and their work.
- Clear delegation of authority, integrated planning, and the involvement of senior management are all important to implementing empowerment.
- Empowerment emphasizes power as the ability to get things done rather than the ability to get others to do what you want.

What is organizational politics?

- Politics involves the use of power to obtain ends not officially sanctioned as well as the use of power to find ways of balancing individual and collective interests in otherwise difficult circumstances.
- For the manager, politics often occurs in decision situations where the interests of another manager or individual must be reconciled with one's own.
- For managers, politics also involves subunits that jockey for power and advantageous positions vis-à-vis one another.
- The politics of self-protection involves efforts to avoid accountability, redirect responsibility, and defend one's turf.
- While some suggest that executives are agents of the owners, politics also comes into play as resource dependencies with external environmental elements that must be strategically managed.
- Organizational governance is the pattern of authority, influence, and acceptable managerial behavior established at the top of the organization.
- CEOs and managers can develop an ethical organizational governance system that is free from rationalizations.

Key Terms

Agency theory (p. 297)
Coalition power (p. 285)
Coercive power (p. 283)
Empowerment (p. 289)
Expert power (p. 285)
Influence (p. 278)
Information power (p. 284)
Legitimate power (p. 282)

Organizational governance (p. 299)
Organizational politics (p. 292)
Political savvy (p. 287)
Power (p. 278)
Power-oriented behavior (p. 286)
Process power (p. 284)

Psychological contract (p. 281)
Reward power (p. 283)
Rational persuasion (p. 285)
Referent power (p. 285)
Representative power (p. 284)
Zone of indifference (p. 281)

Self-Test 12

Multiple Choice

1. Three bases of position power are _____. (a) reward, expertise, and coercive power (b) legitimate, experience, and judgment power (c) knowledge, experience, and judgment power (d) reward, coercive, and knowledge power

2. _____ is the ability to control another's behavior because, through the individual's efforts, the person accepts the desirability of an offered goal and a reasonable way of achieving it. (a) Rational persuasion (b) Legitimate power (c) Coercive power (d) Charismatic power

3. A worker who behaves in a certain manner to ensure an effective boss–subordinate relationship shows _____ power. (a) expert (b) reward (c) approval (d) referent

4. One guideline for implementing a successful empowerment strategy is that _____. (a) delegation of authority should be left ambiguous and open to individual interpretation (b) planning should be separated according to the level of empowerment (c) it can be assumed that any empowering directives from management will be automatically followed (d) the authority delegated to lower levels should be clear and precise

5. The major lesson of the Milgram experiments is that _____. (a) Americans are very independent and unwilling to obey (b) individuals are willing to obey as long as it does not hurt another person (c) individuals will obey an authority figure even if it does appear to hurt someone else (d) individuals will always obey an authority figure

6. The range of authoritative requests to which a subordinate is willing to respond without subjecting the directives to critical evaluation or judgment is called the _____. (a) psychological contract (b) zone of indifference (c) Milgram experiments (d) functional level of organizational politics

7. The three basic power relationships to ensure success are _____. (a) upward, downward, and lateral (b) upward, downward, and oblique (c) downward, lateral, and oblique (d) downward, lateral, and external

8. In which dimension of power and influence would a manager find the use of both position power and personal power most advantageous? (a) upward (b) lateral (c) downward (d) workflow

9. Reason, coalition, bargaining, and assertiveness are strategies for _____. (a) enhancing personal power (b) enhancing position power (c) exercising referent power (d) exercising influence

10. Negotiating the interpretation of a union contract is an example of _____. (a) organizational politics (b) lateral relations (c) an approval relationship (d) an auditing linkage

11. _____ is the ability to control another's behavior because of the possession of knowledge, experience, or judgment that the other person does not have but needs. (a) Coercive power (b) Expert power (c) Information power (d) Representative power

12. A _____ is the range of authoritative requests to which a subordinate is willing to respond without subjecting the directives to critical evaluation or judgment. (a) A zone of indifference (b) Legitimate authority (c) Power (d) Politics

13. The process by which managers help others to acquire and use the power needed to make decisions affecting themselves and their work is called _____. (a) politics (b) managerial philosophy (c) authority (d) empowerment

14. The pattern of authority, influence, and acceptable managerial behavior established at the top of the organization is called _____. (a) organizational governance (b) agency linkage (c) power (d) politics

15. _____ suggests that public corporations can function effectively even though their managers are self-interested and do not automatically bear the full consequences of their managerial actions. (a) Power theory (b) Managerial philosophy (c) Virtual theory (d) Agency theory

Short Response

16. Explain how the various bases of position and personal power do or do not apply to the classroom relationship between instructor and student. What sources of power do students have over their instructors?

17. Identify and explain at least three guidelines for the acquisition of (a) position power and (b) personal power by managers.

18. Identify and explain at least four strategies of managerial influence. Give examples of how each strategy may or may not work when exercising influence (a) downward and (b) upward in organizations.

19. Define *organizational politics* and give an example of how it operates in both functional and dysfunctional ways.

Applications Essay

20. Some argue that mergers and acquisitions rarely produce positive financial gains for the shareholders. What explanations could you offer to explain why mergers and acquisitions continue?

13

Leadership Essentials

chapter at a glance

One of the major challenges faced by all aspiring managers is to become an effective leader. Here's what to look for in Chapter 13. Don't forget to check your learning with the Summary Questions & Answers and Self-Test in the end-of-chapter Study Guide.

WHAT IS LEADERSHIP?

Managers versus Leaders

Trait Leadership Perspectives

Behavioral Leadership Perspectives

WHAT IS SITUATIONAL CONTINGENCY LEADERSHIP?

Fiedler's Leadership Contingency View

House's Path-Goal View of Leadership

Hersey and Blanchard Situational Leadership Model

Graen's Leader-Member Exchange Theory

Substitutes for Leadership

WHAT IS IMPLICIT LEADERSHIP?

Leadership as Attribution

Leadership Prototypes

WHAT ARE INSPIRATIONAL LEADERSHIP PERSPECTIVES?

Charismatic Leadership

Transactional and Transformational Leadership

Transformational Leadership Dimensions

Issues in Charismatic and Transformational Leadership

Even in a bad economy it is possible for an outstanding CEO to lead a company to profitability. If often takes, however, a unique individual. Avon has one in Andrea Jung. The firm bills itself as the company for women, and it is a leading global beauty firm with over $10 billion in annual revenue. As the world's largest direct seller, Avon markets to women in more than 100 countries through 5.8 million independent Avon Sales Representatives. Avon's product line includes beauty products, as well as fashion and home products.

Jung is responsible for developing and executing all of the company's long-term growth strategies, launching new brand initiatives, developing earnings opportunities for women worldwide, and defining Avon as the premier direct seller of beauty products.

Avon CEO Andrea Jung feels ". . . there is a big difference between being a leader and being a manager."

Commenting on the recent performance of Avon, she stated, "Our bold strategies to counter the recession are working. We've been successful at gaining Representatives and consumers during these tough economic times. This confirms our belief in the inherent advantage of our direct-selling business model. As women around the globe are seeking income and smart value products, Avon is there to meet their needs.

In a recent interview she made a clear distinction between management and leadership, saying: "I think there is a big and significant difference between being a leader and being a manager—leaders lead from the heart. You have to be analytical and flexible. Flexibility is one of the key ingredients to being successful. If you feel like it's difficult to change, you will probably have a harder time succeeding."

With her success in leading Avon it is little wonder Ms. Jung was ranked #5 on *Fortune* magazine's "50 Most Powerful Women in Business" list; she has been on it since the list's inception. Jung is also #25 on the *Forbes* list of "The World's 100 Most Powerful Women."

with leadership things happen

Leadership

Even though Andrea Jung is one of a kind, it is assumed that anyone in management, particularly the CEO, is a leader.[1] Currently, however, controversy has arisen over this assumption. We can all think of examples where managers do not perform much, if any, leadership, as well as instances where leadership is performed by people who are not in management. Researchers have even argued that to not clearly recognize this difference is a violation of "truth in advertising" because many studies labeled "leadership" may actually be about "management."[2]

Managers versus Leaders

A key way of differentiating between the two is to argue that the role of *management* is to promote stability or to enable the organization to run smoothly, whereas the role of *leadership* is to promote adaptive or useful changes.[3] Persons in managerial positions could be involved with both management and leadership activities, or they could emphasize one activity at the expense of the other. Both management and leadership are needed, however, and if managers do not assume responsibility for both, then they should ensure that someone else handles the neglected activity. The point is that when we discuss leadership, we do not assume it is identical to management.

> **Leadership** is the process of influencing others and the process of facilitating individual and collective efforts to accomplish shared objectives.

For our purposes, we treat **leadership** as the process of influencing others to understand and agree about what needs to be done and how to do it, and the process of facilitating individual and collective efforts to accomplish shared objectives.[4] Leadership appears in two forms: (1) *formal leadership*, which is exerted by persons appointed or elected to positions of formal authority in organizations, and (2) *informal leadership*, which is exerted by persons who become influential because they have special skills that meet the needs of others. Although both types are important in organizations, this chapter will emphasize formal leadership.[5]

The leadership literature is vast—thousands of studies at last count—and consists of numerous approaches.[6] We have grouped these approaches into two chapters: Leadership Essentials, Chapter 13, and Strategic Leadership and Organizational Change, Chapter 14. This chapter focuses on trait and behavioral theory perspectives, attributional and symbolic leadership perspectives, and transformational and charismatic leadership approaches. Chapter 14 deals with such leadership challenges as how to be a moral leader, how to share leadership, how to lead across cultures, how to be a strategic leader of major units, and, of course, how to lead change. Many of the perspectives in each chapter include several models. While each of these models may be useful to you in a given work setting, we invite you to mix and match them as necessary in your setting, just as we did earlier with the motivational models discussed in Chapter 5.

Trait Leadership Perspectives

> **Trait perspectives** assume that traits play a central role in differentiating between leaders and nonleaders or in predicting leader or organizational outcomes.

For over a century scholars have attempted to identify the key characteristics that separate leaders from nonleaders. Much of this work stressed traits. **Trait perspectives** assume that traits play a central role in differentiating between leaders and nonleaders in that leaders must have the "right stuff."[7] The *great person-trait approach* reflects the attempt to use traits to separate leaders from nonleaders. This list of possible traits identified only became longer as researchers

Energy and adjustment or stress tolerance: Physical vitality and emotional resilience

Prosocial power motivation: A high need for power exercised primarily for the benefit of others

Achievement orientation: Need for achievement, desire to excel, drive to success, willingness to assume responsibility, concern for task objectives

Emotional maturity: Well-adjusted, does not suffer from severe psychological disorders

Self-confidence: General confidence in self and in the ability to perform the job of a leader

Integrity: Behavior consistent with espoused values; honest, ethical, trustworthy

Perseverance or tenacity: Ability to overcome obstacles; strength of will

Cognitive ability, intelligence, social intelligence: Ability to gather, integrate, and interpret information; intelligence, understanding of social setting

Task-relevant knowledge: Knowledge about the company, industry, and technical aspects

Flexibility: Ability to respond appropriately to changes in the setting

→ **Positive Impact on Leadership Success**

Figure 13.1 Traits with positive implications for successful leadership.

focused on the leadership traits linked to successful leadership and organizational performance. Unfortunately, few of the same traits were identified across studies. Part of the problem was inadequate theory, poor measurement of traits, and the confusion between managing and leading.

Fortunately, recent research has yielded promising results. A number of traits have been found that help identify important leadership strengths, as outlined in Figure 13.1. As it turns out, most of these traits also tend to predict leadership outcomes.[8]

Key traits of leaders include ambition, motivation, honesty, self-confidence, and a high need for achievement. They crave power not as an end in itself but as a means to achieve a vision or desired goals. At the same time, they have to be emotionally mature enough to recognize their own strengths and weaknesses, and oriented toward self-improvement. Furthermore, to be trusted, they must have authenticity; without trust, they cannot hope to maintain the loyalty of their followers. Leaders are not easily discouraged and stick to a chosen course of action as they push toward goal accomplishment. At the same time, they must be able to deal with the large amount of information they receive on a regular basis. They do not need to be brilliant, but usually exhibit above-average intelligence. In addition, leaders have a good understanding of their social setting and possess extensive knowledge concerning their industry, firm, and job.

Even with these traits, however, the individual still needs to be engaged. To lead is to influence others, and so we turn to the question of how a leader should act.

Behavioral Leadership Perspectives

How should leaders act toward subordinates? The **behavioral perspective** assumes that leadership is central to performance and other outcomes. However, instead of underlying traits, behaviors are considered. Two classic research programs—at the University of Michigan and at the Ohio State University—provide useful insights into leadership behaviors.

The **behavioral perspective** assumes that leadership is central to performance and other outcomes.

Michigan Studies   In the late 1940s, researchers at the University of Michigan sought to identify the leadership pattern that results in effective performance. From interviews of high- and low-performing groups in different organizations, the researchers derived two basic forms of leader behaviors: employee-centered and production-centered. Employee-centered supervisors are those who place strong emphasis on their subordinates' welfare. In contrast, production-centered supervisors are more concerned with getting the work done. In general, employee-centered supervisors were found to have more productive workgroups than did the production-centered supervisors.[9]

These behaviors may be viewed on a continuum, with employee-centered supervisors at one end and production-centered supervisors at the other. Sometimes, the more general terms *human-relations oriented* and *task oriented* are used to describe these alternative leader behaviors.

- A leader high in **consideration** is sensitive to people's feelings.

- A leader high in **initiating structure** is concerned with spelling out the task requirements and clarifying aspects of the work agenda.

- **Leadership grid** is an approach that uses a grid that places concern for production on the horizontal axis and concern for people on the vertical axis.

Ohio State Studies   At about the same time as the Michigan studies, an important leadership research program began at the Ohio State University. A questionnaire was administered in both industrial and military settings to measure subordinates' perceptions of their superiors' leadership behavior. The researchers identified two dimensions similar to those found in the Michigan studies: **consideration** and **initiating structure**.[10] A highly considerate leader was found to be sensitive to people's feelings and, much like the employee-centered leader, tries to make things pleasant for his or her followers. In contrast, a leader high in initiating structure was found to be more concerned with defining task requirements and other aspects of the work agenda; he or she might be seen as similar to a production-centered supervisor. These dimensions are related to what people sometimes refer to as socio-emotional and task leadership, respectively.

At first, the Ohio State researchers believed that a leader high in consideration, or socio-emotional warmth, would have more highly satisfied or better performing subordinates. Later results suggested, however, that many individuals in leadership positions should be high in both consideration and initiating structure. This dual emphasis is reflected in the leadership grid approach.[11]

Tiger Woods Masters Uncertainty

The consulting firm Accenture is running a series of ads featuring legendary golfer Tiger Woods. In one Tiger shades his eyes and looks ahead with an iron in hand, pondering a shot. The ad asks: "How can you plan ahead when you can hardly see ahead?" The leadership message is one of finding strength to master uncertainty.

The Leadership Grid   Robert Blake and Jane Mouton developed the leadership grid approach based on extensions of the Ohio State dimensions. **Leadership grid** results are plotted on a nine-position grid that places concern for production on the horizontal axis and concern for people on the vertical axis, where 1 is minimum concern and 9 is maximum concern. As an example, those with a 1/9 style—low concern for production and high concern for people—are termed "country club management." They do not emphasize task accomplishment but stress the attitudes, feelings, and social needs of people.

Similarly, leaders with a 1/1 style—low concern for both production and people—are termed "impoverished," while a 5/5 style is labeled "middle of the road." A 9/1 leader—high concern for production and low concern for people—has a "task management" style. Finally, a 9/9 leader, high on both dimensions, is considered to have a "team management" style, the ideal leader in Blake and Mouton's framework.

RESEARCH INSIGHT

Participatory Leadership and Peace

In an unusual cross-cultural organizational behavior study, Gretchen Spreitzer examined the link between business leadership practices and indicators of peace in nations. She found that earlier research suggested that peaceful societies had (1) open and egalitarian decision making, and (2) social control processes that limit the use of coercive power. These two characteristics are the hallmarks of participatory systems that empower people in the collective. She reasoned that business firms can provide open egalitarian decisions by stressing participative leadership and empowerment.

Spreitzer also recognized that broad cultural factors could also be important. The degree to which the culture is future oriented and power distance appeared relevant. And she reasoned that she needed specific measures of peace. She selected two major indicators: (a) the level of corruption, and (b) the level of unrest. The measure of unrest was a combined measure of political instability, armed conflict, social unrest, and international disputes. While she found a large leadership database that directly measured participative leadership, she developed the measures of empowerment from another apparently unrelated survey. Two items appeared relevant: the

decision freedom individuals reported (decision freedom), and the degree to which they felt they had to comply with their boss regardless of whether they agreed with an order (compliance).

You can schematically think of this research in terms of the following model.

As one might expect with exploratory research, the findings support most of her hypotheses but not all. Participative leadership was related to less corruption and less unrest as was the future-oriented aspect of culture. Regarding empowerment, there were mixed results; decision freedom was linked to less corruption and unrest but the compliance measure was only linked to more unrest.

What Do You Think?

Do you agree that when business used participatory leadership, it made the democratically based style legitimate and increased the opportunity for individuals to express their voice? What other research could be done to determine the link between leadership and peace?[13]

Source: Gretchen Spreitzer "Giving Peace a Chance: Organizational Leadership, Empowerment, and Peace," *Journal of Organizational Behavior* 28 (2007), pp. 1077–1095.

Cross-Cultural Implications   It is important to consider whether the findings of the Michigan, Ohio State, and grid studies transfer across national boundaries. Some research in the United States, Britain, Hong Kong, and Japan shows that the behaviors must be carried out in different ways in alternative cultures. For instance, British leaders are seen as considerate if they show subordinates how to use equipment, whereas in Japan the highly considerate leader helps subordinates with personal problems.[12] We will see this pattern again as we discuss other theories. The concept seems to transfer across boundaries but the actual behaviors differ. Sometimes the differences are slight but in other cases, they are not. Even subtle differences in the leader's situation can make a significant difference in precisely the type of behavior needed for success. Successful leaders adjust their influence attempts to the situation.

Situational Contingency Leadership

The trait and behavioral perspectives assume that leadership, by itself, would have a strong impact on outcomes. Another development in leadership thinking has recognized, however, that leader traits and behaviors can act in conjunction with *situational contingencies*—other important aspects of the leadership situation—to predict outcomes. Traits are enhanced by their relevance to the leader's situational contingencies.[14] For example, achievement motivation should be most effective for challenging tasks that require initiative and the assumption of personal responsibility for success. Leader flexibility should be most predictive in unstable environments or when leaders lead different people over time.

Prosocial power motivation is likely to be most important in complex organizations where decision implementation requires lots of persuasion and social influence. "Strong" or "weak" situations also make a difference. An example of a strong situation is a highly formal organization with lots of rules, procedures, and policies. Here, traits will have less impact than in a weaker, more unstructured situation. In more common terms, leaders can't show dynamism as much when the organization restricts them.

Traits sometimes have a direct relationship to outcomes or to leaders versus nonleaders. They may also make themselves felt by influencing leader behaviors (e.g., a leader high in energy engages in directive, take-charge behaviors).[15] In an attempt to isolate when particular traits and specific combinations of leader behavior and situations are important, scholars have developed a number of situational contingency theories and models. Some of these theories emphasize traits whereas others deal exclusively with leader behaviors and the setting.

Fiedler's Leadership Contingency View

Fred Fiedler's leadership contingency view argues that team effectiveness depends on an appropriate match between a leader's style, essentially a trait measure, and the demands of the situation.[16] Specifically, Fiedler considers **situational control**—the extent to which a leader can determine what his or her group is going to do as well as the outcomes of the group's actions and decisions.

To measure a person's leadership style, Fiedler uses an instrument called the **least–preferred co-worker (LPC) scale**. Respondents are asked to describe the person with whom they have been able to work least well—their

* **Situational control** is the extent to which leaders can determine what their groups are going to do and what the outcomes of their actions are going to be.

* The **least-preferred co-worker (LPC) scale** is a measure of a person's leadership style based on a description of the person with whom respondents have been able to work least well.

least preferred co-worker, or LPC—using a series of adjectives such as the following two:

Unfriendly ____ ____ ____ ____ ____ ____ ____ ____ Friendly
         1   2   3   4   5   6   7   8

Pleasant ____ ____ ____ ____ ____ ____ ____ ____ Unpleasant
       1   2   3   4   5   6   7   8

Fiedler argues that high-LPC leaders (those describing their LPC very positively) have a relationship-motivated style, whereas low-LPC leaders have a task-motivated style. Because LPC is a style and does not change across settings, the leaders' actions vary depending upon the degree of situational control. Specifically, a task-motivated leader (low LPC) tends to be nondirective in high- and low-control situations, and directive in those in between. A relationship-motivated leader tends to be the opposite. Confused? Take a look at Figure 13.2 to clarify the differences between high-LPC leaders and low-LPC leaders.

Figure 13.2 shows the task-motivated leader as having greater group effectiveness under high and low situational control and the relationship-motivated leader as having a more effective group in those in-between situations. The figure also shows that Fiedler measures the range of control with the following three variables arranged in the situational combinations indicated:

- *Leader-member relations* (good/poor)—membership support for the leader
- *Task structure* (high/low)—spelling out the leader's task goals, procedures, and guidelines in the group
- *Position power* (strong/weak)—the leader's task expertise and reward or punishment authority

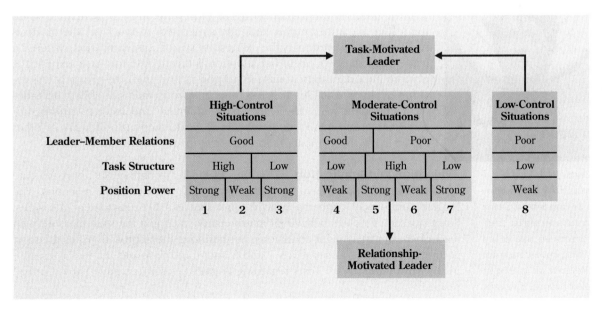

Figure 13.2 Fiedler's situational variables and their preferred leadership styles.

Consider an experienced and well-trained production supervisor of a group that is responsible for manufacturing a part for a personal computer. The leader is highly supported by his group members and can grant raises and make hiring and firing decisions. This supervisor has very high situational control and is operating in situation 1 in Figure 13.2. For such high-control situations, a task-oriented leader style is predicted as the most effective. Now consider the opposite setting. Think of the chair of a student council committee of volunteers who are unhappy about this person being the chair. They have the low-structured task of organizing a Parents' Day program to improve university-parent relations. This low-control situation also calls for a task-motivated leader who needs to behave directively to keep the group together and focus on the task; in fact, the situation demands it. Finally, consider a well-liked academic department chair who is in charge of determining the final list of students who will receive departmental honors at the end of the academic year. This is a moderate-control situation with good leader-member relations, low task structure, and weak position power, calling for a relationship-motivated leader. The leader should emphasize nondirective and considerate relationships with the faculty.

• In **leader match training**, leaders are trained to diagnose the situation to match their high and low LPC scores with situational control.

Department of Homeland Security's Janet Napolitano

Secretary of the Department of Homeland Security Janet Napolitano told the House Homeland Security Committee her priorities include better interaction with state and local governments, improving immigration enforcement, and improving the Federal Emergency Management Administration's ability to support local first-responders in a disaster.

Fiedler's Cognitive Resource Perspective   Fiedler eventually moved beyond his contingency approach by developing a cognitive resource perspective.[17] Cognitive resources are abilities or competencies. According to this approach, whether a leader should use directive or nondirective behavior depends on the following situational contingencies: (1) the leader's or subordinate group members' ability or competency, (2) stress, (3) experience, and (4) group support of the leader. Basically, cognitive resource theory is most useful because it directs us to leader or subordinate group-member ability, an aspect not typically considered in other leadership approaches.

The theory views directiveness as most helpful for performance when the leader is competent, relaxed, and supported. In this case, the group is ready, and directiveness is the clearest means of communication. When the leader feels stressed, his or her attention is diverted. In this case, experience is more important than ability. If support is low, then the group is less receptive, and the leader has less impact. Group-member ability becomes most important when the leader is nondirective and receives strong support from group members. If support is weak, then task difficulty or other factors have more impact than either the leader or the subordinates.

Evaluation and Application   The roots of Fiedler's contingency approach date back to the 1960s and have elicited both positive and negative reactions. The biggest controversy concerns exactly what Fiedler's LPC instrument measures. Some question Fiedler's behavioral interpretations that link the style measure with leader behavior in all eight conditions. Furthermore, the approach makes the most accurate predictions in situations 1 and 8 and 4 and 5; results are less consistent in the other situations.[18] Tests regarding cognitive resources have shown mixed results.[19]

In terms of application, Fiedler has developed **leader match training**, which Sears, Roebuck and Co. and other organizations have used. Leaders are trained to diagnose the situation in order to "match" their LPC score. The red arrows in Figure 13.2 suggest a "match." In cases with no "match," the training shows how each of these situational control variables can be changed to obtain a match. For instance, a leader with a low LPC and in setting 4 could change the position power to strong and gain a "match." Another way of getting a match is through leader selection or placement based on LPC scores.[20] For example, a low LPC leader would be selected for a position with high situational control, as in our earlier example of the manufacturing supervisor. A number of studies have been designed to test this leader match training. Although they are not uniformly supportive, more than a dozen such tests have found increases in group effectiveness following the training.[21]

We conclude that although there are still unanswered questions concerning Fiedler's contingency theory, especially concerning the meaning of LPC, the perspective and the leader match program have relatively strong support.[22] The approach and training program are especially useful in encouraging situational contingency thinking.

House's Path-Goal View of Leadership

Another well-known approach to situational contingencies is one developed by Robert House based on the earlier work of others.[23] House's **path-goal view of leadership** has its roots in the expectancy model of motivation discussed in Chapter 5. The term "path-goal" is used because of its emphasis on how a leader influences subordinates' perceptions of both work goals and personal goals, and the links, or paths, found between these two sets of goals.

The theory assumes that a leader's key function is to adjust his or her behaviors to complement situational contingencies, such as those found in the work setting. House argues that when the leader is able to compensate for things lacking in the setting, subordinates are likely to be satisfied with the leader. For example, the leader could help remove job ambiguity or show how good performance could lead to an increase in pay. Performance should improve as the paths by which (1) effort leads to performance—expectancy—and (2) performance leads to valued rewards—instrumentality—becomes clarified.

House's approach is summarized in Figure 13.3. The figure shows four types of leader behavior (directive, supportive, achievement oriented, and participative) and two categories of situational contingency variables (subordinate attributes and work-setting attributes). The leader behaviors are adjusted to complement the situational contingency variables in order to influence subordinate satisfaction, acceptance of the leader, and motivation for task performance.

Before delving into the dynamics of the House model, it is important to understand each component. **Directive leadership** has to do with spelling out the subordinates' tasks; it is much like the initiating structure mentioned earlier. **Supportive leadership** focuses on subordinate needs and well-being and on promoting a friendly work climate; it is similar to consideration. **Achievement-oriented leadership** emphasizes setting challenging goals, stressing excellence in performance, and showing confidence in the group members' ability to achieve high standards of performance. **Participative leadership** focuses on consulting with subordinates, and seeking and taking their suggestions into account before making decisions.

- House's **path-goal view of leadership** assumes that a leader's key function is to adjust his or her behaviors to complement situational contingencies.

- **Directive leadership** spells out the what and how of subordinates' tasks.

- **Supportive leadership** focuses on subordinate needs, well-being, and promotion of a friendly work climate.

- **Achievement-oriented leadership** emphasizes setting goals, stressing excellence, and showing confidence in people's ability to achieve high standards of performance.

- **Participative leadership** focuses on consulting with subordinates and seeking and taking their suggestions into account before making decisions.

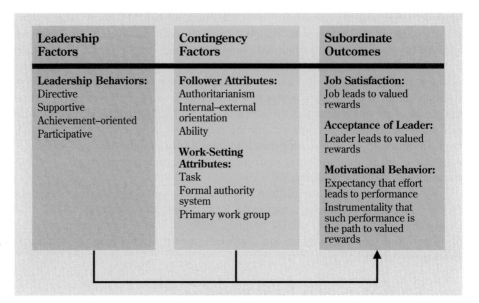

Leadership Factors	Contingency Factors	Subordinate Outcomes
Leadership Behaviors: Directive Supportive Achievement–oriented Participative	**Follower Attributes:** Authoritarianism Internal–external orientation Ability	**Job Satisfaction:** Job leads to valued rewards
	Work-Setting Attributes: Task Formal authority system Primary work group	**Acceptance of Leader:** Leader leads to valued rewards
		Motivational Behavior: Expectancy that effort leads to performance Instrumentality that such performance is the path to valued rewards

Figure 13.3 Summary of major path-goal relationships in House's leadership approach.

Important subordinate characteristics are *authoritarianism* (close-mindedness, rigidity), *internal-external orientation* (i.e., locus of control), and *ability*. The key work-setting factors are the nature of the subordinates' tasks (task structure), the *formal authority system*, and the *primary workgroup*.

Predictions from Path-Goal Theory   Directive leadership is predicted to have a positive impact on subordinates when the task is ambiguous; it is predicted to have just the opposite effect for clear tasks. In addition, the theory predicts that when ambiguous tasks are being performed by highly authoritarian and close-minded subordinates, even more directive leadership is called for.

Supportive leadership is predicted to increase the satisfaction of subordinates who work on highly repetitive tasks or on tasks considered to be unpleasant, stressful, or frustrating. In this situation the leader's supportive behavior helps compensate for adverse conditions. For example, many would consider traditional assembly-line auto worker jobs to be highly repetitive, perhaps even unpleasant or frustrating. A supportive supervisor could help make these jobs more enjoyable. Achievement-oriented leadership is predicted to encourage subordinates to strive for higher performance standards and to have more confidence in their ability to meet challenging goals. For subordinates in ambiguous, nonrepetitive jobs, achievement-oriented leadership should increase their expectations that effort leads to desired performance.

Participative leadership is predicted to promote satisfaction on nonrepetitive tasks that allow for the ego involvement of subordinates. For example, on a challenging research project, participation allows employees to feel good about dealing independently with the demands of the project. On repetitive tasks, open-minded or nonauthoritarian subordinates will also be satisfied with a participative leader. On a task where employees screw nuts on bolts hour after hour, for example, those who are nonauthoritarian will appreciate having a leader who allows them to get involved in ways that may help break up the monotony.

Evaluation and Application   House's path-goal approach has been with us for more than 30 years. Early work provided some support for the theory in general and for the particular predictions discussed earlier.[24] However, current assessments by well-known scholars have pointed out that many aspects have not been tested adequately, and there is very little current research concerning the theory.[25] House recently revised and extended path-goal theory into the theory of work-unit leadership. It's beyond our scope to discuss the details of this new theory, but as a base the new theory expands the list of leader behaviors beyond those in path-goal theory, including aspects of both leadership theory and emerging challenges of leadership.[26] It remains to be seen how much research it will generate.

In terms of application there is enough support for the original path-goal theory to suggest two possibilities. First, training could be used to change leadership behavior to fit the situational contingencies. Second, the leader could be taught to diagnose the situation and learn how to try to change the contingencies, as in leader match.

Hersey and Blanchard Situational Leadership Model

Like other situational contingency approaches, the **situational leadership model** developed by Paul Hersey and Kenneth Blanchard indicates that there is no single best way to lead.[27] Hersey and Blanchard focus on the situational contingency of maturity, or "readiness," of followers, in particular. Readiness is the extent to which people have the ability and willingness to accomplish a specific task. Hersey and Blanchard argue that "situational" leadership requires adjusting the leader's emphasis on task behaviors—for instance, giving guidance and direction—and relationship behaviors—for example, providing socioemotional support—according to the readiness of followers to perform their tasks. Figure 13.4 identifies four leadership styles: delegating, participating, selling, and telling. Each emphasizes a different combination of task and relationship behaviors by the leader. The figure also suggests the following situational matches as the best choice of leadership style for followers at each of four readiness levels.

- The Hersey and Blanchard **situational leadership model** focuses on the situational contingency of maturity or "readiness" of followers.

A "telling" style (S1) is best for low follower readiness (R1). The direction provided by this style defines roles for people who are unable and unwilling to take responsibility themselves; it eliminates any insecurity about the task that must be done.

A "selling" style (S2) is best for low-to-moderate follower readiness (R2). This style offers both task direction and support for people who are unable but willing to take task responsibility; it involves combining a directive approach with explanation and reinforcement in order to maintain enthusiasm.

A "participating" style (S3) is best for moderate-to-high follower readiness (R3). Able but unwilling followers require supportive behavior in order to increase their motivation; by allowing followers to share in decision making, this style helps enhance the desire to perform a task.

A "delegating" style (S4) is best for high readiness (R4). This style provides little in terms of direction and support for the task at hand; it allows able and willing followers to take responsibility for what needs to be done.

This situational leadership approach requires the leader to develop the capability to diagnose the demands of situations and then to choose and implement the

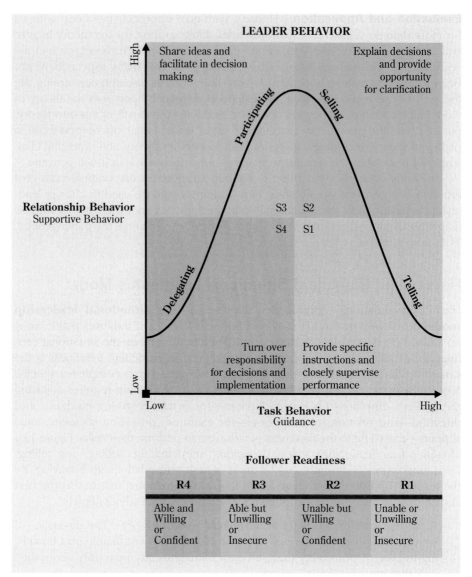

Figure 13.4 Hersey and Blanchard model of situational leadership.

appropriate leadership response. The model gives specific attention to followers and their feelings about the task at hand and suggests that an effective leader focus on emerging changes in the level of readiness of the people involved in the work.

In spite of its considerable history and incorporation into training programs by a large number of firms, this situational leadership approach has received very little systematic research attention.[28]

Graen's Leader-Member Exchange Theory

Still another situational contingency perspective is Graen's **leader-member exchange (LMX) theory**. This perspective emphasizes the quality of the working relationship between leaders and followers. An LMX scale assesses the degree to

• **Leader-member exchange theory** emphasizes the quality of the working relationship between leaders and followers.

MASTERING MANAGEMENT

BUILDING HIGH-QUALITY LEADER-MEMBER EXCHANGE RELATIONSHIPS

Building relationships with subordinates calls for a greater focus on those you lead than on the task given to you as the formal leader. With all of the positive benefits of better relations with your employees, consider doing the following:

- Meet separately with your employees during a testing phase to help each of you evaluate motives, attitudes, and potential resources to be exchanged, and establish mutual role expectations.
- For those who show the most promise during the test meeting, work toward refining the original exchange relationship and developing mutual trust, loyalty, and respect for these "in-group" members.
- Determine which of these relationships will advance to a third ("mature") stage where exchange based on self-interest is transformed into mutual commitment to the vision, mission, and objectives of the work unit.
- Reward second and third stage "in-group members" with greater status, influence, and benefits in return for extra attention from them, and remain responsive to their needs with strong reliance on persuasion and consultation.
- Follow up with day-to-day observations and discussions and work toward increasing the number of in-group members.

which leaders and followers have mutual respect for one another's capabilities, feel a deepening sense of mutual trust, and have a strong sense of obligation to one another. Taken together, these dimensions tend to establish the extent to which followers will be a part of the leader's "in-group" or "out-group."[29]

In-group followers tend to function as assistants, lieutenants, or advisers and to have higher-quality personalized exchanges with the leader than do out-group followers. The out-group followers tend to emphasize more formalized job requirements, and a relatively low level of mutual influence exists between leaders and out-group followers. The more personalized in-group exchanges typically involve a leader's emphasis on assignments to interesting tasks, delegation of important responsibilities, information sharing, and participation in the leader's decisions, as well as special benefits, such as personal support, approval, and favorable work schedules.

It is easy to say a manager should have a better leader-member exchange relationship with his or her followers. Mastering Management provides some tips on developing better relationships with an "in-group" of subordinates.[30]

Research suggests that high-quality LMX is associated with increased follower satisfaction and productivity, decreased turnover, increased salaries, and faster promotion rates. These findings are encouraging, and the approach continues to receive increasing emphasis in organizational behavior research literature worldwide. Of course, many questions remain, such as: What happens in the event of too much disparity in the treatment of in-group and out-group members? Will out-group members become resentful and sabotage team efforts? Much more needs to be learned about how the in-group/out-group exchange starts in the first place and how these relations develop and change over time.[31]

Substitutes for Leadership

A final situational contingency approach is leadership substitutes.[32] Scholars using this approach have developed a perspective indicating that sometimes hierarchical leadership makes essentially no difference. These researchers contend that certain individuals, jobs, and organization variables can serve as substitutes for leadership or neutralize a leader's impact on subordinates. Some examples of these variables are shown in Figure 13.5.

- **Substitutes for leadership** make a leader's influence either unnecessary or redundant in that they replace a leader's influence.

Substitutes for leadership make a leader's influence either unnecessary or redundant in that they replace a leader's influence. For example, in Figure 13.5 it will be unnecessary and perhaps impossible for a leader to provide the kind of task-oriented direction already available from an experienced, talented, and well-trained subordinate. In contrast, neutralizers can prevent a leader from behaving in a certain way or nullify the effects of a leader's actions. If a leader has little formal authority or is physically separated, for example, his or her leadership may be nullified even though task supportiveness may still be needed.

Research suggests some support for the general notion of substitutes for leadership.[33] First, studies involving Mexican, U.S., and Japanese workers suggests both similarities and differences between various substitutes in the countries examined. Again, there were subtle but important differences across the national samples. Second, a systematic review of 17 studies found mixed results for the substitutes theory. The review suggested a need to broaden the list of substitutes and leader behaviors. It was also apparent that the approach is especially important

Characteristics of Individuals	Impact on Leadership
Experience, ability, training	Substitutes for task-oriented leadership
Professional orientation	Substitutes for task-oriented and supportive leadership
Indifference toward organizational rewards	Neutralizes task-oriented and supportive leadership
Characteristics of Job	
Highly structured/routine	Substitutes for task-oriented leadership
Intrinsically satisfying	Substitutes for supportive leadership
Characteristics of Organization	
Cohesive work group	Substitutes for task-oriented and supportive leadership
Low leader position power	Neutralizes task-oriented and supportive leadership
Leader physically separated	Neutralizes task-oriented and supportive leadership

Figure 13.5 Some examples of leadership substitutes and neutralizers.

in examining self-directed work teams. In such teams, for example, in place of a hierarchical leader specifying standards and ways of achieving goals (task-oriented behaviors), the team might set its own standards and substitute them for those of the leader's.

Central to the substitutes for leadership perspective is the question of whether leadership makes a difference at all levels of the organization. At least one researcher has suggested that at the very top of today's complex firms, the leadership of the CEO makes little difference compared to environmental and industry forces. These leaders are typically accountable to so many groups of people for the resources they use that their leadership impact is greatly constrained, so the argument goes. Instead of a dramatic and important effect, much of the impact a top leader has is little more than symbolic. Further, much of what is described as CEO leadership is actually explanations to legitimize their actions.[34]

Such symbolic treatment of leadership occurs particularly when performance is either extremely high or extremely low or when the situation is such that many people could have been responsible for the performance. The late James Meindl and his colleagues call this phenomenon the **romance of leadership**, whereby people attribute romantic, almost magical, qualities to leadership.[35] Consider the firing of a baseball manager or football coach whose team does not perform well. Neither the owner nor anyone else is really sure why this occurred. But the owner can't fire all the players, so a new team manager is brought in to symbolize "a change in leadership" that is "sure to turn the team around."

> **Romance of leadership** is where people attribute romantic, almost magical, qualities to leadership.

Implicit Leadership

So far we have dealt with leader traits, leader behavior, and the situations facing the leader and his or her subordinates. What about the followers and their view of the setting? In the mid-1970s, researchers argued that leadership factors are in the mind of the respondent. It remains to be established whether or not they are more than that.[36] This general notion is described here in two forms. The first one is *leadership as attribution* and the second is termed *leadership prototypes*.

Leadership as Attribution

Recall from Chapter 4 that attribution theory focuses on inferences people make when trying to understand causes, assess responsibilities, and evaluate personal qualities. People often attribute a cause or causes to an outcome even though they may not really know who is responsible or why it occurred. Think about a work group or student organization that you feel performs really well. Now assume that you are asked to describe the leader on one of the leadership scales discussed earlier in the chapter. If you are like many others, the group's high performance probably encouraged you to describe the leader favorably; in other words you attributed (inferred) good things to the leader based on the group's performance. Similarly, recall that leaders themselves make attributions about subordinate performance and react differently depending on those attributions. For example, if leaders attribute an employee's poor performance to lack of effort, they may issue a reprimand, whereas if they attribute the poor performance to an external factor, such as work overload, they will probably try to fix the problem. A great deal of evidence supports attributional views of subordinates and leaders.[37]

• **Inference-based leadership attribution** emphasizes leadership effectiveness as inferred by perceived group/organizational performance.

Some researchers have concentrated on the inference processes of subordinates and leaders to develop **inference-based attribution** models. Such models emphasizes leadership effectiveness as inferred by followers based on how followers depict group or organizational performance outcomes.[38] If the group or organization is seen as performing well, they tend to attribute good leadership to the person in charge. If not, they attribute poor leadership to the head manager. While you might want to dismiss such a simplistic view, most individuals have considerable difficulty separating the performance of the unit from the performance of the unit head. Further, when good things happen, we all like to attribute success to individuals. Finally, many of the depictions of successful corporate leaders are based on an inference perspective. How could the top manager be incompetent if the organization is performing well? The CEO could be lucky or basking in the glow of a prior executive's decisions.

Leadership Prototypes

Leadership prototypes are the second form of leadership considered to be in the mind of the beholder. Here, researchers argue that people have a mental image of the characteristics that make a "good" leader or that a "real" leader would possess to be considered effective in a given situation. Leadership prototypes are an alternative way to the inference-based approach to assess leadership and are termed *recognition based*. You may not be able to define great leadership, so to speak, but you know a great leader when you see one.[39] These prototypes may be based on leadership legacies from the past as suggested in OB Savvy 13.1.[40]

• **Recognition-based leadership prototypes** base leadership effectiveness on how well a person fits characteristics the evaluator thinks describe a good or effective leader.

These **recognition-based prototypes** usually consist of a mix of specific, and more general, characteristics. For example, a prototype of a bank president would differ in many ways from that of a high-ranking military officer. However, you could expect some core characteristics reflecting leaders in our society in general—for example, integrity and self efficacy.[41] You also would expect differences in prototypes by country and by national culture. For example, a typical business leader prototype in Japan is described as responsible, educated, trustworthy, intelligent, and disciplined whereas those in the United States are portrayed as determined, goal oriented, verbally skilled, industrious, and persistent.[42] More in-depth insights on such prototypes, as related to culture, are provided by the broad-scale Project GLOBE.

A recent study suggests that national culture dimensions emphasize either an inference-based approach or a recognition-based approach in perceiving effective leaders.[43] For example, the less power-distance is valued in a culture, the more followers will emphasize an inference-based process to perceive leadership. The reasoning is that in low-power-distance societies the relative equality means that people rely upon analytical cause-effect approaches in judging both outcomes and the leader. With higher power distance there is a tendency to analyze if the leader acts consistently with a particular prototype. Are these prototypes stable? At least one study suggests that the individual aspects of a prototype were reasonably

---

OB SAVVY 13.1

Abraham Lincoln's Leadership Legacies

From an analysis of Abraham Lincoln's presidency one writer suggests leaders should:

1. Take the long view and demonstrate an unswerving commitment to purpose.
2. Practice superhuman empathy.
3. Refine your sense of timing and send clear messages.
4. Eschew power and coercion.
5. Rise above personal slights and clashing ideologies.

stable across different kinds of groups. However, across time, the dimensions changed toward more sensitivity, intelligence, dedication, and dynamism and less tyranny and masculinity.[44]

Inspirational Leadership Perspectives

One of the reasons leadership is considered so important is simply because most of us think of leaders as highly inspirational individuals—heroes and heroines. We think of prominent individuals who appear to have made a significant difference by inspiring followers to work toward great accomplishments. In the study of leadership, this inspirational aspect has been studied extensively under the notions of charismatic leadership and transformational leadership.

Charismatic Leadership

Robert House and his associates have done extensive studies of charismatic leadership.[45] This body of research has found that **charismatic leaders** are leaders who, by force of their personal abilities, are capable of having a profound and extraordinary effect on followers. These leaders are high in need for power and have high feelings of self-efficacy and conviction in the moral rightness of their beliefs. While the need for power motivates these people to want to be leaders, this need is then reinforced by their conviction of the moral rightness of their beliefs. Their feeling of self-efficacy, in turn, makes these people believe these individuals are capable of being leaders. These traits then influence such charismatic behaviors as role modeling, image building, articulating simple and dramatic goals, emphasizing high expectations, showing confidence, and arousing follower motives.

> • **Charismatic leaders** are those leaders who are capable of having a profound and extraordinary effect on followers.

Some of the more interesting and important work based on aspects of House's charismatic theory involves a study of U.S. presidents.[46] The research showed that behavioral charisma was substantially related to presidential performance and that the kind of personality traits described in House's theory, along with response to crisis among other things, predicted behavioral charisma for the sample of presidents.[47]

When it comes to charisma there is also the potential negative side of this trait as seen in infamous leaders such as Adolf Hitler and Joseph Stalin, who had been considered charismatic. Negative, or "dark-side," charismatic leaders emphasize personalized power and focus on themselves—whereas positive, or "bright-side," charismatic leaders emphasize socialized power that tends to positively empower their followers.[48] This helps explain the differences between a dark-side leader such as David Koresh, leader of the Branch Davidian sect, and a bright-side leader such as Martin Luther King, Jr.[49] Charismatic leaders often arise in difficult times. Before you start to think more about becoming a charismatic leader or following a charismatic leader, consider the eleven ethics questions in Ethics in OB.[50]

Jay Conger and Rabindra Kanungo have developed a three-stage charismatic leadership model.[51] In the initial stage the leader critically evaluates the status quo. Deficiencies in the status quo lead to formulations of future goals. Before developing these goals, the leader assesses available resources and constraints that stand in the way of the goals. The leader also assesses follower abilities, needs,

Leaders on Leadership

THE "IRON FRAU": ANGELA MERKEL

She has topped *Forbes Magazine's* list of "the most powerful women in the world" for the past four consecutive years. As Germany's Chancellor, she is the first female, the first East German, and the youngest to don the leadership mantel in the nation's history.

"Discovered" by Helmut Kohl in the early 1990s, who referred to her simply as *das Mädchen* ("the girl"), her appointment as Minister for Women and Youth made her the youngest cabinet minister in German history as well. So how did the daughter of a pastor with a talent for the natural sciences come to be leader of the world's 4th largest economy?

Her journey has been a fascinating one given that she took her first serious steps into the political realm when she was 35, just after the fall of the Berlin Wall. Before that she was an accomplished laboratory physicist working for the Academy of Sciences in Berlin-Adlershof after earning her doctorate.

Some attribute her success as a leader to her science background, a rather unique one for politicians who have typically emerged from the fields of law or political science. Having been raised outside the "clubhouse" so to speak, has provided her distinct benefits—she is free to think beyond established political paradigms and focuses instead on her own self-proclaimed style of leadership: "think, consult, and then decide."

Her early academic and professional training has given her powerful skills to observe and analyze the world around her. She is adept at simplifying complex situations, recognizing important patterns and understanding implications of possible actions. In short, she invokes the tools of science to approach problems rationally, "trusting in persuasion through argument."

She's been described as very unpretentious, authentic, modest, flexible, smart, persistent, disciplined, ambitious, strategic, robust and tough. Regardless of the characteristics one may focus on in describing her, the combination has brought her success as a leader.

"It is her open and friendly but sharp and persistent way that makes her highly influential." She has used that influence to bring "a dose of discussion, discretion and collegiality into German government and the international arena." Merkel is a successful leader who possesses an impressive combination of leadership traits and uses her experience and training to influence others in positive, constructive ways. Her logical, task-oriented side is in balance with her ability to connect with constituents. It's led to positive results thus far as many continue to watch this rising political leader.

and satisfaction levels. In the second stage, the leader formulates and articulates the goals along with an idealized future vision. Here, the leader emphasizes articulation and impression-management skills. Then, in the third stage, the leader shows how these goals and the vision can be achieved. The leader emphasizes innovative and unusual means to achieve the vision.

Martin Luther King Jr. illustrated these three stages in his nonviolent civil rights approach, thereby changing race relations in this country. Conger and

ELEVEN ETHICAL QUESTIONS FOR LEADERS AND THEIR FOLLOWERS

Being a leader is all about choices and decisions. Before you decide to influence others or follow a charismatic leader, you may want to consider the following ethical questions:

1. Have the issues been identified thoroughly or are you about to advocate a solution based on a self-serving view?
2. Who will be the winners and losers when the decision has been made; who will bear the brunt of the costs and benefits?
3. Have the appropriate stakeholders been considered; have any stakeholder's interests been purposely ignored?
4. How will your decision or followership be perceived a year from now; what are the long-term ramifications?
5. How would you feel if you were in another stakeholder's place?
6. Do you have enough information to make an informed decision to lead or follow?
7. Would you want your decision to be the standard in all situations?
8. What would the CEO say if all of the details of your decision or followership came to light?
9. If you had to stand before a court, could you defend your decision legally as the leader or a follower?
10. Would you want your family and friends to know the details of your decision as a leader or choice to follow a leader?
11. Could you explain your decision or choice of followership in court a year from now?

Check the Questions: Choose a decision situation in which you are expected to show leadership or act as devoted follower. How well do these questions hold up? How can this list be modified to become more useful?

Kanungo have argued that if leaders use behaviors such as vision articulation, environmental sensitivity, and unconventional behavior, rather than maintaining the status quo, followers will tend to attribute charismatic leadership to them. Such leaders are also seen as behaving quite differently from those labeled "non-charismatic."[52] Want to build your image as a charismatic leader? Check out OB Savvy 13.2.[53]

Finally, an especially important question about charismatic leadership is whether it is described in the same way for close-up or at-a-distance leaders. Boas Shamir examined this issue in Israel.[54] He found that descriptions of distant charismatics (e.g., former Israeli prime minister Golda Meir) and close-up charismatics (e.g., a specific teacher) were generally more different than they were similar. Figure 13.6 shows the high points of his findings. Clearly, leaders with whom followers have close contact and those with whom they seldom, if ever, have direct contact are both described as charismatic but possess quite different traits and behaviors.

OB SAVVY 13.2

Building Your Charismatic Image

- Be sensitive to the most appropriate contexts for charisma–emphasize critical evaluation and problem detection.
- Vision–use creative thinking to learn and think about profound change.
- Communication–use oral and written linguistic aspects.
- Impression management–use modeling, appearance, body language, and verbal skills.
- Empowering–communicate high-performance expectations, improve decision-making participation, loosen up bureaucratic constraints, set meaningful goals, and establish appropriate reward system.

Distant Charismatics Should Demonstrate
- Persistence
- Rhetorical skills
- Courage
- An emphasis on social courage (expressing opinions, not conforming to pressure)
- Ideological orientation

Close-up Charismatics Should Demonstrate
- Sociability
- Expertise
- Humor
- Dynamism, activity
- Physical appearance
- Intelligence
- High standards
- Originality

Both Distant and Close-up Charismatics Should Demonstrate
- Self-confidence
- Honesty
- Authoritativeness
- Sacrifice

Figure 13.6 Descriptions of characteristics of distant and close-up charismatics.

Transactional and Transformational Leadership

Building on notions originated by James MacGregor Burns, as well as on ideas from House's work, Bernard Bass has developed an approach that focuses on both transactional and transformational leadership.[55]

• **Transactional leadership** involves leader-follower exchanges necessary for achieving routine performance agreed upon between leaders and followers.

Transactional leadership involves leader-follower exchanges necessary for achieving routine performance agreed upon between leaders and followers. Transactional leadership is similar to most of the leadership approaches mentioned earlier. These exchanges involve four dimensions:

1. *Contingent rewards*—various kinds of rewards in exchange for mutually agreed-upon goal accomplishment;
2. *Active management by exception*—watching for deviations from rules and standards and taking corrective action;
3. *Passive management by exception*—intervening only if standards not met; and
4. *Laissez-faire*—abdicating responsibilities and avoiding decisions.

• **Transformational leadership** occurs when leaders broaden and elevate followers' interests and stir followers to look beyond their own interests to the good of others.

Transformational leadership goes beyond this routine accomplishment, however. For Bass, **transformational leadership** occurs when leaders broaden and elevate their followers' interests, when they generate awareness and acceptance of the group's purposes and mission, and when they stir their followers to look beyond their own self-interests to the good of others.

Transformational Leadership Dimensions

Transformational leadership has four dimensions: *charisma, inspiration, intellectual stimulation*, and *individualized consideration*. Charisma provides vision and a sense of mission, and it instills pride along with follower respect and trust. For example, Steve Jobs, who founded Apple Computer, showed charisma by emphasizing the importance of creating the Macintosh as a radical new computer and has since followed up with products such as the iPod and iPhone.

Inspiration communicates high expectations, uses symbols to focus efforts, and expresses important purposes in simple ways. As an example, in the movie

Patton, George C. Scott stood on a stage in front of his troops with a wall-sized American flag in the background and ivory-handled revolvers in holsters at his side. Soldiers were told not to die for their country but make the enemy die for his. Intellectual stimulation promotes intelligence, rationality, and careful problem solving. For instance, your boss encourages you to look at a very difficult problem in a new way. Individualized consideration provides personal attention, treats each employee individually, and coaches and advises. For example, your boss drops by and makes remarks reinforcing your worth as a person.

Bass concludes that transformational leadership is likely to be strongest at the top-management level, where there is the greatest opportunity for proposing and communicating a vision. However, for him, it is not *restricted* to the top level; it is found throughout the organization. Furthermore, transformational leadership operates *in combination with* transactional leadership. Leaders need both transformational and transactional leadership in order to be successful, just as they need to display both leadership and management abilities.[56]

Reviews have summarized a large number of studies using Bass's transformational approach. These reviews report significant favorable relationships between Bass's leadership dimensions and various aspects of performance and satisfaction, as well as extra effort, burnout and stress, and predispositions to act as innovation champions on the part of followers. The strongest relationships tend to be associated with charisma or inspirational leadership, although in most cases the other dimensions are also important. These findings are consistent with those reported elsewhere.[57] They broaden leadership outcomes beyond those cited in many leadership studies.

Issues in Charismatic and Transformational Leadership

In respect to leaders and leadership development, it is reasonable to ask: *Can people be trained in charismatic/transformational leadership?* According to research in this area, the answer is yes. Bass and his colleagues have put a lot of work into developing such training efforts. For example, they have created a workshop where leaders are given initial feedback on their scores on Bass's measures. The leaders then devise improvement programs to strengthen their weaknesses and work with the trainers to develop their leadership skills. Bass and Avolio report findings that demonstrate the beneficial effects of this training. They also report the effectiveness of team training and programs tailored to individual firms' needs.[58] Similarly, Conger and Kanungo propose training to develop the kinds of behaviors summarized in their model.

Approaches with special emphasis on vision often emphasize training. Kouzas and Posner report results of a week-long training program at AT&T. The program involved training leaders on five dimensions oriented around developing, communicating, and reinforcing a shared vision. According to Kouzas and Posner, leaders showed an average 15 percent increase in these visionary behaviors 10 months after participating in the program.[59] Similarly, Sashkin and Sashkin have developed a leadership approach that emphasizes various aspects of vision and organizational culture change. They discuss a number of ways to train leaders to be more visionary and to enhance cultural change.[60] All of these leadership training programs involve a heavy hands-on workshop emphasis so that leaders do more than just read about vision.

A second issue in leadership and leadership development involves this question: *is charismatic/transformational leadership always good?* As pointed

Lynn Willenbring's Transformational Leadership

Within a few months of being appointed CIO (Chief Information Officer) of the City of Minneapolis, Lynn Willenbring needed to hire her entire executive team, renegotiate their outsourcing contract, and deal with the I-35W bridge collapse. At the end of her first six months, she had changed the IT department's direction and built credibility for their ability to deliver.

out earlier, dark-side charismatics, such as Adolf Hitler, can have a negative effect on followers. Similarly, charismatic/transformational leadership is not always helpful. Sometimes emphasis on a vision diverts energy from more important day-to-day activities. It is also important to note that such leadership by itself is not sufficient. That leadership needs to be used in conjunction with all of the leadership theories discussed in this chapter. Finally, charismatic and transformational leadership is important not only at the top of an organization. A number of experts argue that for an organization to be successful, it must apply at all levels of organizational leadership.

Resources in The OB Skills Workbook

These learning activities from *The OB Skills Workbook* are suggested for Chapter 13.

Cases for Critical Thinking	Team and Experiential Exercises	Self-Assessment Portfolio
• The New Vice President • Southwest Airlines	• Interview a Leader • Leadership Skills Inventories • Leadership and Participation	• Student Leadership Practices Inventory • Least-Preferred Co-worker Scale • Leadership Style • "TT" Leadership

13 studyguide

Summary Questions and Answers

What is leadership?

• Leadership is the process of influencing others to understand and agree about what needs to be done and how to do it, and the process of facilitating individual and collective efforts to accomplish shared objectives.

• Leadership and management differ in that management is designed to promote stability or to make the organization run smoothly, whereas the role of leadership is to promote adaptive change.

• Trait or great-person approaches argue that leader traits have a major impact on differentiating between leaders and nonleaders or predicting leadership outcomes.

• Traits are considered relatively innate and hard to change.

• Similar to trait approaches, behavioral theories argue that leader behaviors have a major impact on outcomes.

• The Michigan and Ohio State approaches are important leader behavior theories.

• Leader behavior theories are especially suitable for leadership training.

What is situational contingency leadership?

• Leader situational contingency approaches argue that leadership, in combination with various situational contingency variables, can have a major impact on outcomes.

- The effects of traits are enhanced to the extent of their relevance to the situational contingencies faced by the leader.

- Strong or weak situational contingencies influence the impact of leadership traits.

- Fiedler's contingency theory, House's path-goal theory, Hersey and Blanchard's situational leadership theory, Graen's leader-member exchange theory, and Kerr and Jermier's substitutes for leadership theory are particularly important specific situational contingency approaches.

- Sometimes, as in the case of the substitutes for leadership approach, the role of situational contingencies replaces that of leadership, so that leadership has little or no impact in itself.

What is implicit leadership?

- Attribution theory extends traditional leadership approaches by recognizing that substantive effects cannot always be objectively identified and measured.

- Leaders form attributions about why their employees perform well or poorly and respond accordingly as do employees concerning leaders.

- Leaders and followers often infer that there is good leadership when their group performs well. This is an inferential perspective.

- Leaders and followers often have in mind a good leader prototype; compare the leader against such a prototype; and conclude that the closer the fit, the better the leadership. This is a representational perspective.

- Some contend that leadership makes no real difference and is largely symbolic; others, following the "romance of leadership" notion, embrace this symbolic emphasis and attribute almost magical qualities to leadership.

What are inspirational leadership perspectives?

- Charismatic and transformational leadership helps move followers to achieve goals that transcend their own self-interests and help transform the organization.

- Particularly important among such approaches are Bass's transformational theory and House's and Conger and Kanungo's charismatic perspectives.

- Transformational approaches are broader than charismatic ones and sometimes include charisma as one of their dimensions.

- Transformational/charismatic leadership, in general, is important because it goes beyond traditional leadership in facilitating change in the increasingly fast-moving workplace.

- In terms of charismatic/transformational leadership training, Bass and his colleagues, Conger and Kanungo, and Kouzos and Posner, among others, have developed such training programs.

- Charismatic/transformational leadership is not always good, as shown by the example of Adolf Hitler.

- Charismatic/transformational leadership is not always helpful because, even if good, it may divert energy away from other kinds of leadership.

- Charismatic/transformational leadership is important throughout the organization, as well as the top.

Key Terms

Achievement-oriented
  leadership (p. 313)
Behavioral perspective
  (p. 307)
Charismatic leaders
  (p. 321)
Consideration (p. 308)
Directive leadership
  (p. 313)
Inference-based leadership
  attribution (p. 320)
Initiating structure
  (p. 308)
Leadership (p. 306)

Leadership grid (p. 308)
Leader-member exchange
  theory (p. 316)
Leader match training
  (p. 312)
Least-preferred co-worker
  (LPC) scale (p. 310)
Participative leadership
  (p. 313)
Path-goal view of
  leadership (p. 313)
Recognition-based
  leadership prototypes
  (p. 320)

Romance of leadership
  (p. 319)
Situational control (p. 310)
Situational leadership
  model (p. 315)
Substitutes for leadership
  (p. 318)
Supportive leadership
  (p. 313)
Trait perspectives (p. 306)
Transactional leadership
  (p. 324)
Transformational leadership
  (p. 324)

Self-Test 13

Multiple Choice

1. Leadership is central, and other variables are less important, best describes _____
   theories. (a) trait and behavioral (b) attribution (c) situational contingency
   (d) substitutes for leadership

2. Leader trait and behavioral approaches assume that traits and behaviors are
   _____. (a) as equally important as other variables (b) more important than
   other variables (c) caused by other variables (d) symbolic of leadership

3. In comparing leadership and management, _____. (a) leadership promotes
   stability and management promotes change (b) leadership promotes change and
   management promotes stability (c) leaders are born but managers are developed
   (d) the two are pretty much the same

4. The earliest theory of leadership stated that individuals become leaders because of
   _____. (a) the behavior of those they lead (b) the traits they possess (c) the
   particular situation in which they find themselves (d) being very tall

5. Which leadership theory argues that a leader's key function is to act in ways that
   complement the work setting? (a) trait (b) behavioral (c) path-goal (d) multiple
   influence

6. A leadership prototype _____. (a) is useful primarily for selection and training
   (b) uses LPC as an important component (c) depicts the image of a model leader
   (d) emphasizes leadership development

7. Conger and Kanungo's model emphasizes all of the following except (a) active
   management by exception. (b) vision articulation. (c) environmental sensitivity.
   (d) unconventional behavior.

8. For situational leadership theory, _____. (a) management is substituted for
   leadership (b) position power is very important (c) there is considerable empirical
   support (d) maturity or readiness of followers is emphasized

9. Transformational leadership _____. (a) is similar to transactional leadership (b) is particularly useful in combination with transactional leadership (c) is not related to charismatic leadership (d) has been studied for more than 100 years

10. In terms of the importance of leadership, it has been argued that _____. (a) leadership makes little or no difference. (b) only charismatic leadership is important. (c) charismatic leadership is more important than transformational leadership. (d) leadership is important only in a situational contingencies context.

11. In the romance of leadership, _____. (a) supervisors are encouraged to lead each other to the altar (b) leaders are encouraged to marry each other (c) leaders are given credit for difficult-to-explain happenings (d) leadership substitutes for traditional romantic actions

12. Attributional theory _____. (a) is one important leadership direction (b) is no longer popular in studying leadership (c) helps explain Fiedler's model (d) helps explain situational leadership

13. Close-up and at-a-distance charismatic leaders _____. (a) use the same behaviors (b) exhibit a number of different behaviors (c) are hard to distinguish (d) have similar impacts on individual performance

14. In terms of charismatic or transformational leadership, _____. (a) people can be trained (b) these characteristics are inborn (c) either is as important as transactional leadership (d) both tend to become managerial in orientation

15. Leadership traits _____. (a) are largely passé (b) are excellent substitutes for behaviors (c) are now being combined with behaviors (d) are too rigid to be used in analyzing leadership

Short Response

16. Define "leadership" and contrast it with "management."

17. Discuss the role of leader trait and behavior approaches in leadership.

18. Discuss the role of situational contingency approaches in leadership.

19. Discuss implicit theories and leadership prototype.

Applications Essay

20. You have just been called in by your boss to respond to a point mentioned on television that leadership is not real and is only a figment of peoples' imaginations. Prepare a report that analyzes the pros and cons to this argument. Also describe the implications of this conclusion for your personal leadership development.

14

Leadership Challenges and Organizational Change

chapter at a glance

Some challenges of leadership and organizational change are quite new; others have been recognized for decades. In this chapter we explore moral persuasion, cultural differences, strategy, and situational change for insights on increasing your effectiveness as a leader. Don't forget to check your learning with the Summary Questions & Answers and Self-Test in the end-of-chapter Study Guide.

Organizations today cannot escape change—they must be flexible and adaptable to effectively navigate the demands that various types of change demand. Oxfam GB, a UK-based aid and development charity organization, embraces change as part of their mission: to change the world by ending global poverty.

Started in 1942 to help Greek civilian victims of war, it survived through the years by changing the way it did business, literally.

Oxfam changed the industry itself when it opened one of the world's first charity shops in 1948. Its strategy was to become a business, taking donated wares from citizens and selling them; the profits were then used to fund its growing number of programs. The wide array of items ranged "from false teeth, various stuffed animals up to a houseboat". Today the shops raise millions of dollars for the organization's causes.

Those causes include climate change, natural disasters, health and nutrition, education, debt, gender equality and trade. Oxfam addresses these issues through its campaigning, emergency response and development activities in over 70 countries.

The continuous demand for funds is an issue for any charity organization—Oxfam has continued to change the game by developing innovate solutions to funding its work and creating self-sufficiency among those in need. So, while the organization is working to change the world, it's doing so by changing the way it operates and forcing similar organizations to adapt as well.

Oxfam's latest strategic move is in response to our increasingly high tech world. The organization is successfully taking its message online to reach a broader, more global audience. This, along with its own television programming and music festivals, is helping it connect to younger generations as well.

oxfam GB: changing
the world around us

Moral Leadership

All of us are aware of recent concerns with moral leadership issues. American International Group (AIG), for example, joined the growing list of firms such as Enron and Merrill Lynch, which at one time had highly questionable leadership. It appears that leaders of various government, religious, and educational entities made decisions based on short-term individual gain rather than long-term collective benefit.

As these problems have gained attention and scrutiny, there has been a stronger emphasis in research on topics including authentic leadership, servant leadership, spiritual leadership, and ethical leadership. These are the topics we will cover in our treatment of moral leadership. Essentially the moral leader is attempting to use transcendent values to stimulate action that is considered beneficial. The challenge of moral leadership starts with who you are and what you think the job of a leader should be.

Authentic Leadership

Authentic leadership essentially argues "know thyself."[1] It involves both owning one's personal experiences (values, thoughts, emotions, and beliefs) and acting in accordance with one's true self (expressing what you really think and believe, and acting accordingly). Although no one is perfectly authentic, authenticity is something to strive for. It reflects the unobstructed operation of one's true or core self. It also underlies virtually all other aspects of leadership, regardless of the particular theory or model involved.

Those high in authenticity are thought to have optimal self-esteem, or genuine, true, stable, and congruent self-esteem, as opposed to fragile self-esteem based on outside responses. Leaders who desire authentic leadership should have genuine relationships with followers and associates and display transparency, openness, and trust.[2] All of these points draw on psychological well-being emphasized in positive psychology literature.[3] For instance, Nelson Mandela is considered authentic leaders.

Self-efficacy is a person's belief that he or she can perform adequately in a situation.

Optimism is the expectation of positive outcomes.

Hope is the tendency to look for alternative pathways to reach a desired goal.

Resilience is the ability to bounce back from failure and keep forging ahead.

In positive psychology we find a stress on **self-efficacy**, which is an individual's belief about the likelihood of successfully completing a specific task; **optimism**, the expectation of positive outcomes; **hope**, the tendency to look for alternative pathways to reach a desired goal; and **resilience**, the ability to bounce back from failure and keep forging ahead. An increase in any one of these is seen as increasing the others. These are important traits for a leader to demonstrate, and are believed to positively influence his or her followers.

Perhaps the most important aspect of authentic leadership is the notion that being a leader begins with you and your perspective on leading others. But being authentic is just one aspect of moral leadership. A second feature is your view of the leader's task.

Spiritual Leadership

In contrast to authentic leadership, spiritual leadership can be seen as a field of inquiry within the broader setting of workplace spirituality.[4] Western religious theology and practice coupled with leadership ethics and values provide much

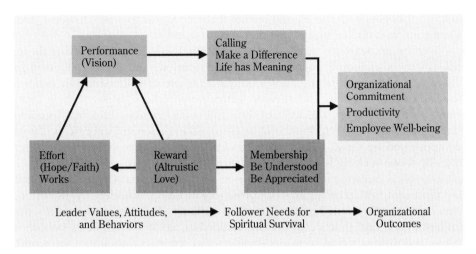

Figure 14.1 Casual model of spiritual leadership theory. [*Source:* Lewis W. Fry. Steve Vitucci, and Marie Cedillo, "Spiritual Leadership and Army Transformation: Theory, Measurement, and Establishing a Baseline," *The Leadership Quarterly* 16.5 (2005), p. 838.]

of the base for the actions of a spiritual leader. As one might expect with a view based on religion, there is considerable disagreement. One key point of contention is whether spirituality and religion are the same. To some, spirituality stems from their religion. For others, it does not. Researchers note that organized religions provide rituals, routines, and ceremonies, thereby providing a vehicle for achieving spirituality. Of course, one could be considered religious by following religious rituals but could lack spirituality, or one could reflect a strong spirituality without being religious.

Even though spiritual leadership does not yet have a strong research base in organizational behavior, there has been some research resulting in the term Spiritual Leadership Theory or SLT. It is a causal leadership approach for organizational transformation designed to create an intrinsically motivated, learning organization. Spiritual leadership includes values, attitudes, and behaviors required to intrinsically motivate the leader and others to have a sense of spiritual survival through calling and membership. In other words, the leader and followers experience meaning in their lives, believe they make a difference, and feel understood and appreciated. Such a sense of leader and follower survival tends to create value congruence across the strategic, empowered team and at the individual level; it ultimately encourages higher levels of organizational commitment, productivity, and employee well-being.

Figure 14.1 summarizes a causal model of spiritual leadership. It shows three core qualities of a spiritual leader: *Vision*—defines the destination and journey, reflects high ideals, encourages hope/faith; *Altruistic love*—trust/loyalty as well as forgiveness/acceptance/honesty, courage, and humility; *Hope/Faith*—endurance, perseverance, do what it takes, have stretch goals.

Servant Leadership

Servant leadership, developed by Robert K. Greenleaf, is based on the notion that the primary purpose of business should be to create a positive impact on the organization's employees as well as the community. In an essay he wrote about servant leadership in 1970, Greenleaf said: "The servant-leader *is* servant first . . . It begins with the natural feeling that one wants to serve, to serve *first*. Then conscious choice brings one to aspire to lead."[5]

The servant leader is attuned to basic spiritual values and, in serving these, assists others including colleagues, the organization, and society. Viewed in this way servant leadership is not a unique example of leadership but rather a special kind of service. The servant leader helps others discover their inner spirit, earns and keeps the trust of their followers, exhibits effective listening skills, and places the importance of assisting others over self-interest. It is best demonstrated by those with a vision and a desire to serve others first, rather than by those seeking leadership roles. Servant leadership is usually seen as a philosophical movement, with the support of the Greenleaf Center for Servant Development, an international nonprofit organization founded by Robert K. Greenleaf in 1964 and headquartered in Indiana. The Center promotes the understanding and practice of servant leadership, holds conferences, publishes books and materials, and sponsors speakers and seminars throughout the world.

While servant leadership is not rooted in OB research, its guiding philosophy is consistent with that of the other aspects of moral leadership discussed here. In this case, the power of modeling service is the basis for influencing others. You lead to serve and ask others to follow; their followership then becomes a special form of service.

Ethical Leadership

There is no simple definition of ethical leadership. However, many believe that ethical leadership is characterized by caring, honest, principled, fair, and balanced choices by individuals who act ethically, set clear ethical standards, communicate about ethics with followers, and reward as well as punish others based on ethical or unethical conduct.[6] Figure 14.2 summarizes the similarities and differences among ethical, authentic, spiritual, and transformational leadership. A key similarity cutting across all these dimensions is role modeling. Altruism,

	Similarities with ethical leadership	**Differences from ethical leadership**
Authentic Leadership	Key similarities: - Concern for others (altruism) - Ethical decision making - Integrity - Role modeling	Key differences: - Ethical leaders emphasize moral management (more transactional) and "other" awareness. - Authentic leaders emphasize authenticity and self-awareness.
Spiritual Leadership	Key similarities: - Concern for others (altruism) - Integrity - Role modeling	Key differences: - Ethical leaders emphasize moral management. - Spiritual leaders emphasize visioning, hope/faith; work as vocation.
Transformational Leadership	Key similarities: - Concern for others (altruism) - Ethical decision making - Integrity - Role modeling	Key differences: - Ethical leaders emphasize ethical standards and moral management (more transactional). - Transformational leaders emphasize vision, values, and intellectual stimulation.

Figure 14.2 Similarities and differences between ethical, spiritual, authentic, and transformational theories of leadership.
[*Source:* Michael E. Brown and Linda K. Trevino, "Ethical Leadership: A Review and Future Directions," *The Leadership Quarterly* 17.6 (December 2006), p. 598.]

ETHICS IN OB

COLLEGE ATHLETICS AND ETHICAL CHOICES

During a volleyball game, player A hits the ball over the net. The ball barely grazes off player B's fingers and lands out of bounds. However, the referee does not see player B touch the ball. Because the referee is responsible for calling rule violations, player B is not obligated to report the violation and lose the point. Do you "strongly agree," "agree," are "neutral" about, "disagree," or "strongly disagree" that player B should be silent. At an increasing rate, athletes are answering "strongly agree." In other words, winning is more important than fair play.

The above is one example of work conducted by Sharon Stoll, a University of Idaho faculty member and administrator, to see if athletes are as morally developed as the normal population. In a 20-year study of some 80,000 high school, college, and professional athletes, the athletes' responses on moral reasoning are worse than those of nonathletes. From the time male athletes enter big-time sports, their moral reasoning does not improve and sometimes declines. The same has also recently become true of female athletes.

As a part of a leadership role in this problem, Stoll has developed an educational program as a component of "Winning with Character." The universities of Georgia and Maryland, among other athletic programs, hold weekly group discussions with athletes about ethical problem areas.

What Would You Expect? Would you expect the ethical response differences between athletes and nonathletes? What kinds of details might you suggest be included in the weekly group discussions?

or concern for others, and integrity are also important similarities. Leaders influence others by appealing to transcendent values. In terms of differences, authentic leaders stress authenticity and self-awareness and tend to be more transactional than do the other leaders. Ethical leaders emphasize moral concerns, while spiritual leaders stress visioning, hope, and faith, as well as work as a vocation.

Transformational leaders emphasize values, vision, and intellectual stimulation. Taken as a whole, it is clear that any of these related approaches are important and ready for systematic empirical and conceptual development. Even servant leadership would lend itself to further developments.[7] Despite the lack of research, ethical leadership can and should be a driving force for improving today and tomorrow's leaders. Take a look at Ethics in OB for one example.[8]

Shared Leadership

Shared leadership is defined as a dynamic, interactive influence process among individuals in groups for which the objective is to lead one another to the achievement of group or organizational goals or both. This influence process often involves peer or lateral influence; at other times it involves upward or downward hierarchical influence. The key distinction between shared leadership

● **Shared leadership** is a dynamic, interactive influence process through which individuals in teams lead one another.

and traditional models of leadership is that the influence process involves more than just downward influence on subordinates by an appointed or elective leader. Rather, leadership is broadly distributed among a set of individuals instead of centralized in the hands of a single individual who acts in the role of a superior.[9]

Shared Leadership in Work Teams

So far our treatment of leadership has tended to treat it as vertical influence. The notion of vertical leadership is best depicted by the old Westerns of Hollywood fame. A single rider wearing a white hat and riding a white horse—the bad guys wear black hats and ride black horses—arrives in town. The townsfolk are passive and docile while they stand by and watch as the hero cleans up the town, eliminates the bad guys, and declares, "My work here is done." You should recognize that leadership is not restricted to the vertical influence of the lone figure in a white hat but extends to other people as well. Shared and vertical leadership can be more specifically illustrated in terms of self-directing work teams.

Locations of Shared Leadership   Leadership can come from outside or inside the team. Within a team, leadership can be assigned to one person, rotate across team members, or even be shared simultaneously as different needs arise across time.[10] Outside the team, leaders can be traditional, formally designated, first-level supervisors, or an outside vertical (top down) leader of a self-managing team whose duties tend to be quite different from those of a traditional supervisor. Often these nontraditional leaders are called "coordinators" or "facilitators." A key part of their job is to provide resources to their unit and serve as a liaison with other units, all without the authority trappings of traditional supervisors. Here, team members tend to carry out traditional managerial/leadership functions internal to the team along with direct performance activities.

The activities or functions vary and could involve a designated team role or even be defined more generally as a process to facilitate shared team performance. In the latter case, you are likely to see job rotation activities, along with skill-based pay, where workers are paid for the mix and depth of skills they possess as opposed to the skills of a given job assignment they might hold.

Desired Shared Conditions   The key element to successful team performance is to create and maintain conditions for that performance. While a wide variety of characteristics may be important for the success of a specific effort, five important characteristics have been identified across projects. They include (1) efficient, goal directed effort; (2) adequate resources; (3) competent, motivated performance; (4) a productive, supportive climate; and (5) a commitment to continuous improvement.

Efficient, Goal-Directed Effort   The key here is to coordinate the effort both inside and outside the team. Team leaders can play a crucial role and need to coordinate individual efforts with those of the team, as well as team efforts with those of the organization or major subunit. Among other things, such coordination calls for shared visions and goals.

Leaders Understand Diversity

Max DePree is a noted author and former CEO of the innovative furniture maker Herman Miller, Inc. He says "It is fundamental that leaders endorse the concept of persons" and that "this begins with an understanding of the diversity of people's gifts, talents, and skills."

Adequate Resources   Teams rely on their leaders to obtain enough equipment, supplies, and so on to carry out the team's goals. These are often handled by the outside facilitator and almost always involve internal and external negotiations enabling the facilitator to do his or her negotiating outside the team.

Competent, Motivated Performance   Team members need the appropriate knowledge, skills, abilities, and motivation to perform collective tasks well. Leaders may be able to influence team composition so as to enhance shared efficacy and performance. We often see this demonstrated with short-term teams such as task forces.

A Productive, Supportive Climate   Here, we are talking about high levels of cohesiveness, mutual trust, and cooperation among team members. Sometimes these aspects are part of a team's "interpersonal climate." Team leaders contribute to this climate by role-modeling and supporting relationships that build the high levels of cohesion, trust, and collaboration. Team leaders can also work to enhance shared beliefs about team efficacy and collective capability.

Commitment to Continuous Improvement and Adaptation   A successful team should be able to adapt to changing conditions. Again, both internal and external team leaders may play a role. The focus on continuous improvement may be through formal mechanisms. Often, however, teams recognize that a failure to strive for improvement actually results in a deterioration of performance.

Shared Leadership and Self-Leadership

These shared and vertical self-directing team activities tend to encourage self-leadership activities. Self-leadership can help both the individual and the team. All members, at one point or another, are expected to be leaders. Self-leadership represents a portfolio of self-influence strategies that positively influence individual behavior, thought processes, and related activities. Self-leadership activities are divided into three broad categories: behavior-focused, natural-reward, and constructive-thought-pattern strategies.[11]

Behavior-Focused Strategies   Behavior-focused strategies tend to increase self-awareness, leading to the handling of behaviors involving necessary but not always pleasant tasks. These strategies include personal observation, goal setting, reward, self-correcting feedback, and practice. Self-observation involves examining your own behavior in order to increase awareness of when and why you engage in certain behaviors. Such examination identifies behaviors that should be changed, enhanced, or eliminated. Poor performance could lead to informal self-notes documenting the occurrence of unproductive behaviors. Such heightened awareness is a first step toward behavior change.

Self-Rewards   It helps if you, as a team member, set high but reachable goals and provide yourself with rewards when they are reached. Self-rewards can be quite useful in moving behaviors toward goal attainment. Self-rewards can be real (e.g., a steak dinner) or imaginary (imagining a steak dinner). Also, such things as the rehearsal of desired behaviors you know will lead to self-established goals before the actual performance can prove quite useful. Rehearsals allow you to perfect skills that will be needed when the actual performance is required.

Innocent Identity

Coco-Cola invested $44 million in Innocent, the highly-regarded British maker of healthy smoothies. Innocent uses recycled bottles, gives 10 percent of profits to charity, and follows ethical marketing practices, all while selling a product consumers love. By not allowing Coke to have a majority stake for its millions, Innocent plans to keep its identity and integrity while gaining the advantages of Coke's global reach.

Constructive Thought Patterns   Constructive thought patterns focus on the creation or alteration of cognitive thought processes. Self-analysis and improvement of belief systems, mental imagery of successful performance outcomes, and positive self-talk can help. Developing a mental image of the necessary actions allows you to think about what needs to be accomplished and how it will be accomplished before the stress of performance takes hold.

These activities can influence and control the team members' thoughts through the use of cognitive strategies designed to facilitate ways of thinking that can positively affect performance. Where these activities occur, they tend to serve as partial substitutes for hierarchical leadership even though they may be encouraged in a shared situation in contrast to a vertical leadership setting.

A final thought is in order before we move on. Leadership should not be restricted to the traditional style of vertical leadership, nor should the focus be primarily on shared leadership. Shared leadership appears in many forms and is often used successfully in combination with vertical leadership. As with a number of the leadership approaches discussed in this book, various contingencies operate that influence the emphasis that should be devoted to each of the leadership perspectives.

Leadership across Cultures

At some point in your career you will confront the challenge of cross-cultural leadership. This may come in the form of leading team members from different cultures or it may come when you are offered your first international assignment. Or it might happen when you are asked to join in a cooperative venture with a foreign-based supplier or distributor. There are a wide variety of approaches to meeting the challenge of cross-cultural leadership. A major research project conducted by an international team of researchers provides an excellent overview of the factors you need to consider. Called project GLOBE, it outlines the common dimensions of leadership that are important, as well as the significant differences in how effective managers lead in different cultures.

The GLOBE Perspective

Project GLOBE (Global Leadership and Organizational Behavior Effectiveness Research Program) is an ambitious program involving over 17,000 managers from 951 organizations functioning in 62 nations throughout the world. The project, which is led by Robert House, has involved over 140 country co-investigators, plus a coordinating team and a number of research associates.[12]

The GLOBE approach argues that leadership variables and cultural variables can be meaningfully applied at societal and organizational levels. Congruence between cultural expectations and leadership is expected to yield superior performance. The central assumption behind the model, shown in Figure 14.3, is that the attributes and entities that differentiate a specified culture predict

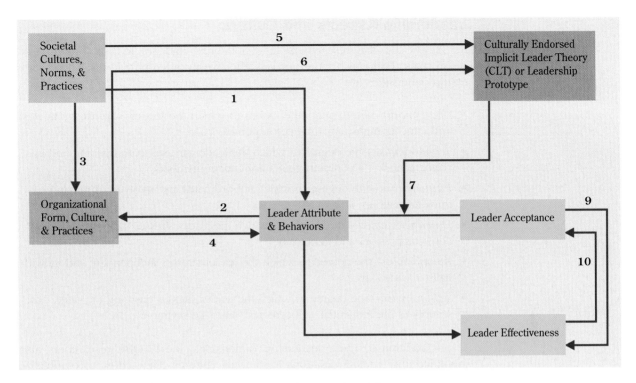

Figure 14.3 A simplified version of the original GLOBE theoretical model.
[*Source:* See Robert J. House, Paul J. Hanges, Mansour Javidan, Peter W. Dorfman, and Vipin Gupta (eds.), *Culture, Leadership, and Organizations* (Thousand Oaks, CA: Sage Publications, 2004).]

organizational practices, leader attributes, and behaviors that are most often carried out and are most effective in that culture.

A variety of leadership assumptions are evident in the Globe theoretical model as summarized in Figure 14.3. For example, societal cultural norms, values, and practices affect leaders' attributes and behaviors, as do organizational forms, cultures, and practices. Founders and organization members are immersed in their own societal cultures as well as in the prevailing practices in their industries. Societal cultural norms, values, and practices also affect organizational culture and practices. Both societal culture and organizational culture, in turn, influence the culturally endorsed leadership prototype. And, leader attributes and behaviors affect organizational forms, cultures, and practices.

As shown in the figure above as well, acceptance of leaders by followers facilitates leadership effectiveness. Leaders who are not accepted by organization members will find it more difficult and arduous to influence these members than leaders who are accepted. Leader effectiveness over time, furthermore, increases leader acceptance. Demonstrated leader effectiveness causes some members to adjust their behaviors toward the leader in positive ways. Those followers not accepting the leader are likely to leave the organization either voluntarily or involuntarily.

Leadership Aspects and Culture

So far the GLOBE researchers have identified and studied six broad-based dimensions. That can be more or less effective in different cultures. These leadership dimensions are:

- *Charismatic/value-based*—the extent to which the leader inspires, motivates, and expects high performance outcomes;
- *Team-oriented*—the degree to which the leader stresses team building and implementation of a common goal among team members;
- *Participative*—the degree to which subordinates are involved in making an implementation;
- *Humane-oriented*—the degree to which the leader stresses support, consideration, compassion, and generosity;
- *Autonomous*—the degree to which the leader stresses independent and individualistic leadership;
- *Self-protective*—the degree to which the leader stresses ensuring the safety and security of the individual, self-centered, and face saving.

In addition to these leadership dimensions, the GLOBE researchers also identified and studied variations in national cultures. They chose to emphasize cultural aspects known to have some relationship to effective leadership. The presumption was that leaders in different cultures would be required to adjust their approaches to best fit these cultural differences. In other words, effective leadership is based on a good fit of leadership approach and culture. The nine dimensions of societal cultural used in the GLOBE studies are:

1. *assertiveness:* assertive, confrontational, and aggressive in relationships versus nonconfrontational;
2. *future orientation:* future-oriented behaviors such as delaying gratification and investing in the future versus a stress on immediate gratification;
3. *gender egalitarianism:* the collective minimizes gender inequality versus asserting major differences by gender;
4. *uncertainty avoidance:* reliance on social norms, rules, etc., to alleviate future unpredictability versus adaptation to rapid change;
5. *power distance:* expectation that power is equally distributed versus large differences in the power of positions and individuals;
6. *institutional collectivism:* organization/society rewards and collective resources/action versus individual rewards;
7. *in-group collectivism:* individuals express pride, loyalty, and similar attitudes in organizations/families versus individualism;
8. *performance orientation:* the collective encourages/rewards group for performance improvement versus rewards for membership;
9. *humane orientation:* the collective encourages/rewards individuals for being fair, generous, and kind.

Sample Country	Societal Cluster	Leadership Dimensions						
		Charismatic/ Value-Based	Team-Oriented	Partici-pative	Humane-Oriented	Autono-mous	Self-Protective
Russia	Eastern Europe	M	M	L	M	H	H
Argentina	Latin America	H	H	M	M	L	H
France	Latin Europe	H	M	M	L	L	M
China	Confucian Asia	M	H	L	H	M	H
Sweden	Nordic Europe	H	M	H	L	M	L
USA	Anglo	H	M	H	H	M	L
Nigeria	Sub-Saharan Africa	M	M	M	H	L	L
India	Southern Asia	H	H	L	H	M	H
Germany	Germanic Europe	H	L	H	M	H	L
Egypt	Middle East	L	L	L	M	M	H

Figure 14.4 Summary of GLOBE comparisons for culturally endorsed leadership dimensions.
[*Source:* Mansour Javidan, Peter W. Dorfman, Mary Sully de Luque, and Robert J. House, "In the Eye of the Beholder: Cross Cultural Lessons in Leadership from Project GLOBE," *Academy of Management Perspectives* 20.7 (2006), pp. 67–90.]
Note: H = high rank; M = medium rank; L = low rank as a culturally endorsed leadership dimension.

Although each culture has its own unique pattern across these nine dimensions, nations do have enough similarities to be grouped in societal clusters. These clusters often form around geographic areas where there is a common language and an extensive pattern of interaction. For example, Argentina is a member of the Latin America societal cluster while India is a member of the Southern Asia societal cluster. Figure 14.4 shows some of the major societal clusters identified in project GLOBE and highlights a representative country for each cluster.

Culturally Endorsed Leadership Matches

So far GLOBE researchers have matched cultural and leadership dimensions for over 62 countries and collapsed them to form 10 geographic clusters. For the six broad-based leadership dimensions, Figure 14.4 shows the degree to which a particular aspect of leadership is endorsed with an H for highly endorsed, an M for moderately endorsed, and an L for not endorsed. Where an emphasis on a specific leadership dimension is matched with an H on a cultural dimension, it is labeled a **culturally endorsed leadership dimension**. This aspect of leadership is characteristic of what individuals in the culture expect from an effective leader.

Perhaps the best way to grasp this complicated perspective is to examine the patterns across the leadership dimensions by cluster in Figure 14.4. For example, in the United States the charismatic dimension is highly endorsed while the

• A **culturally endorsed leadership dimension** is one that members of a culture expect from effective leaders.

protective dimension is not. For team orientation, endorsement is medium. In Russia, the self protective dimension is culturally endorsed. Note the differences in the degree to which specific dimensions of leadership are endorsed or refuted. For instance, there is a very sharp contrast between the Anglo cluster (of which the United States is a part) and the Middle East.

Universally Endorsed Aspects of Leadership

Finally, GLOBE seeks to understand which attributes of leadership are universally endorsed. To date, across the sampled countries, some aspects of leadership are associated with effective leadership while others portray ineffective leadership. Leadership described in terms of integrity, charismatic-visionary, charismatic-inspirational, and team-oriented are almost universally endorsed as indications of outstanding leadership. Leadership described in terms of irritability, egocentricity, noncooperativeness, malevolence, being a loner, dictatorial, and ruthless are identified as indicators of ineffective leadership. Some aspects of leadership were seen as effective in only some national samples and involve leaders as being characterized as individualistic, status conscious, risk taking, or self-sacrificing.

The important point to remember is that there are dramatically different expectations for leaders in different cultures. Leading across cultures is far from simple, as this overview of the GLOBE project suggests. Throughout the book we have stressed integrity, and the discussion of shared leadership emphasizes an orientation toward a team. These aspects of leadership appear to be important in most cultures. In many respects the GLOBE perspective on leadership highlights the difficulty in prescribing exactly what a leader should do in our increasingly global economy. As your career progresses and you become more engaged in cross-cultural leadership it will be important for you to go beyond a universalist view to study cultural expectations. Each culture is unique and the pattern of cultural expectations upon leaders is also unique.

Strategic Leadership

Strategic leadership is leadership of a quasi-independent unit, department, or organization.

There are probably as many views of strategic leadership as there are scholars studying this complex subject. When the focus is on **strategic leadership** it is the study of a quasi-independent unit, department, or organization. A number of researchers focus on the top management team as a group, suggesting that if there is greater diversity in the challenges and opportunities facing the firm, the top management team should be more diverse.[13] Essentially, they indicate that a major challenge of top management is to develop an effective group process that will cope with the struggles and opportunities facing the firm. Several researchers have just focused on the chief executive officer, such as a president of the United States, but new research suggests that strategic leadership is not rooted in just the top management team or the CEO.[14] It involves a number of individuals, some of whom may be partially outside the organization such as the outside members of the board of directors. To understand the challenges of strategic management it is important to examine the roles of managers at different organizational levels.

Top Management Teams

Top management teams (TMTs) refer to the relatively small group of executives at the very top of the organization or the leaders of the firm. Often the top management team is composed of three to ten executives.[15] The composition of the top management team is important because the collective nature, temperament, outlook, and interactions among these individuals alters the choices made in the leadership of the organization.

Much of the research on top management teams uses demographic characteristics as proxies for harder-to-obtain psychological variables. Such variables as age, tenure, education, and functional background are used in this perspective. Researchers typically attempt to link such variables to various kinds of organizational outcomes, including sales growth, innovation, and executive turnover.[16]

Because of conflicting findings, researchers have been working to enrich this approach. One important review argues that a given TMT is likely to face a variety of different situations over time. Demographic composition may be relatively stable but the tasks are dynamic and variable. Sometimes team members have similar information (symmetric) and interests, and sometimes not (asymmetric). With asymmetric information and symmetric interests, there is an opportunity for the top management team to develop new innovative solutions. For example, when considering a merger, some executives may have information on the potential partner's finances, its management style and strategy, or on the partner's connections with others. The team may initially move to buy the new partner but sell off selected portions of the new business.

It is important to recognize that in today's dynamic environment it is desirable for top management teams to have a variety of skills, experiences, and emergent theories which are basically explanations of what might happen and why. Diversity of the skills and abilities of the team can promote debate and discussion, which can lead to more comprehensive, balanced, and effective initiatives for improvement.[17] Homogeneous top management groups are less likely to identify and respond to subtle but important variations. This can result in stale strategies, unresponsiveness, and dulling consistency. Of course, there are practical limits to the degree of diversity and the range of emergent theories that top management can effectively discuss. Too much variation can yield excessive discussion and paralysis by analysis.[18]

The TMT researchers argue that group process must be handled differently and effectively for dynamic versus less dynamic settings. Not only should the composition of the top management team be adjusted to the degree of change facing the firm but there should also be adjustments in group process. With change facing the firm, there needs to be more emphasis on processing information, a representation of broader interests, a strong recognition of existing power asymmetries, and additional emphasis on developing new emergent theories of action.[19]

Multiple-Level Leadership

There is a variety of leadership requirements at different levels or echelons of management. The multiple-level perspective argues that there are three organizational

Management Team Composition

The composition of a top management team can have a major influence on how an organization operates in terms of the shared culture, decision-making and management styles, and even the ethical foundation of day-to-day workplace behaviors.

Leadership at All Levels

Organizations require leadership at all levels, from top to bottom and from side to side. The types of problems leaders face vary by level, and leaders at top levels have special responsibilities since their influence cascades throughout the organization.

domains from the bottom to the top of the organization, typically consisting of no more than two managerial levels within a domain: (1) the production domain at the bottom of the organization; (2) the organization domain in the middle levels; and (3) the systems domain at the top.[20] Each domain and level gets more complex than those beneath it in terms of its leadership and managerial requirements.

One way of expressing the increasing complexity of the levels is in terms of how long it takes to see the results of the key decisions required at any given domain and level. The time frame can range from three months or so at the lowest level, which emphasizes hands-on work performance and practical judgment to solve ongoing problems, to 20 years or more at the top.

Because problems become increasingly complex from the lower levels to the upper levels of the organization, you can expect that managers at each domain and level must demonstrate increasing cognitive and behavioral complexity in order to deal with an increase in organizational complexity. One way of measuring a manager's cognitive complexity is in terms of how far into the future he or she can develop a vision. Notice that this measure is trait oriented, similar in some ways but different from intelligence. In other words, using an intelligence measure instead of a complexity measure will not do. Accompanying such vision should be an increasing range and sophistication of leadership behaviors.

This approach, or extensions of it, is notable for emphasizing the impact of top leadership as it cascades deep within the organization. One example of such cascading, indirect leadership, is the leadership-at-a-distance. Even individuals several levels above a unit can influence the style and tone of what occurs in a unit. One way of thinking about such cascading is in terms of a *leadership of* emphasis at the top and much more of a *leadership in* emphasis as the cascading moves down the organization.

The systems domain leadership at the top of an organization is normally responsible for creating complex systems, organizing acquisition of major resources, creating vision, developing strategy and policy, and identifying organizational design. These functions call for a much broader conception of leadership. In many respects *leadership of* combines leadership and management. Of course, *leadership in* is also exercised in the systems and organization domains and involves a more face-to-face approach. One example of *leadership of* is the indirect, cascading effects of an upper-domain decision concerning, say, leadership development programs to be implemented down the organization. Another example of *leadership of* is the cascading of the "intent of the commander" where middle-level leaders try to mimic what they think the top-level leader would do in their situation.[21] Examine Research Insight to see how one group of researchers linked CEO values to culture and then to organizational outcomes as the values of the CEO cascaded.[22]

This multiple-level leadership view also recognizes that regardless of the level, leaders must engage in direct supervision and must be effective followers. The saying is that, "everyone has a boss." And even most CEOs would argue that those near the top must act as a team and the notion of shared leadership at the top of the organization is clearly relevant.[23]

CEO Values Make a Difference

While there has been a lot of discussion about how the values of the CEO impact performance, there have been comparatively few comprehensive studies. Recently, Y. Berson, S. Oreg, and T. Dvir started to remedy this with a study of CEO values, organizational culture, and performance. They suggested that individuals are drawn to and stay with organizations that have value priorities similar to their own. That includes the CEO. Further, the CEO reinforces some values over others, and this has a measurable impact on the organizational culture. The organizational culture, then, emphasizes some aspects of performance over others.

They hypothesized and found the following in a study of some 22 CEOs and their firms in Israel: CEOs tend to place a high priority on self-direction or security or benevolence. This priority tends to emphasize a particular type of organizational culture. Specifically, when a CEO values self-direction, there is more cultural emphasis on innovation; when a CEO values security, there is more cultural emphasis on bureaucracy; and when a CEO values benevolence,

the culture is more supportive of its members. Then they linked aspects of organizational culture with specific elements of performance (organizational outcomes). More innovation was associated with higher sales growth. A bureaucratic culture was linked to efficiency while a supportive culture was associated with greater employee satisfaction. In sum, CEO values are linked to organizational culture which, in turn, is associated with organizational outcomes. Schematically, it looks like this:

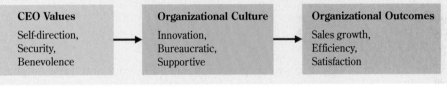

What Do You Think?

Do you think this study would transfer to firms located in North America? Is it possible that firms with an established innovative culture select a CEO that values self-direction?

Source: Yair Berson, Shaul Oreg, and Taly Dvir, "CEO values, organizational culture and firm outcomes." *Journal of Organizational Behavior* 29 (2008), pp. 615–633.

Leadership Tensions and Complexity

A strategic leadership perspective developed by Boal and Hooijberg focuses on the tensions and complexity faced by strategic leaders. This perspective is shown in Figure 14.5.[24] Notice that off to the left their approach starts the notion of tension from Emergent Theories and the Competing Values Framework (CVF).[25] It suggests a tension between flexibility versus control and internal focus versus external focus. The internal versus external focus dimension distinguishes between social actions emphasizing such internal effectiveness measures as employee satisfaction, versus a focus on external effectiveness measures such as market share and profitability. The control versus flexibility dimension contrasts actions

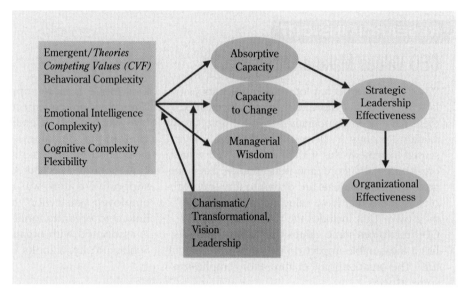

Figure 14.5 Boal and Hooijberg Perspective on Strategic Leadership. [*Source:* Kimberly B. Boal and Robert Hooijberg, "Strategic Leadership Research: Moving On." *The Leadership Quarterly* 11 (2009).]

• **Behavioral complexity** is the possession of a repertoire of leadership roles and the ability to selectively apply them.

• **Cognitive complexity** is the underlying assumption that those high in cognitive complexity process information differently and perform certain tasks better than less cognitively complex people.

focused on goal clarity and efficiency and those emphasizing adaptation to people and the external environment. As a whole, the two focus dimensions define four quadrants and eight leadership roles that address these distinct organizational demands. They emphasize the challenges leaders often face when working toward meeting the competing demands of stakeholders.

Executives who have a large repertoire of leadership roles available and know when to apply these roles are more likely to be effective than leaders who have a small role repertoire and who indiscriminately apply these roles. This repertoire and selective application is termed **behavioral complexity**. To exhibit both repetitive and selective application, executives need cognitive and behavioral complexity as well as flexibility. Of course, they may understand and see the differences between their subordinates and superiors but not be able to behaviorally differentiate so as to satisfy the demands of each group.

In terms of **cognitive complexity**, the underlying assumption is that those high in cognitive complexity process information differently and perform certain tasks better than less cognitively complex persons because they use more categories to discriminate. In other words, such complexity taps into how a person constructs meaning as opposed to what he or she thinks.

Figure 14.5 shows CVF, behavioral complexity, emotional complexity, and cognitive complexity as directly associated with absorptive capacity, capacity to change, and managerial wisdom as well as with charismatic/transformational leadership and vision. In other words, the block to the left shows the challenges and opportunities facing those at and near the top. The leadership of these individuals, alone and in combination, alter the degree to which the firm can adjust day-to-day management. As the complexity of the challenges and opportunities increase there is more stress on the organization. How it is led then becomes more important.

Organizational Competencies and Strategic Leadership   Finally, consistent with the research of Boal and Hooijberg, it is important to recognize key organizational competencies and link them with strategic leadership effectiveness and ultimately with organizational effectiveness.[26] The first key competency is absorptive capacity. **Absorptive capacity** is the ability to learn. It involves the capacity to recognize new information, assimilate it, and apply it toward new ends. It utilizes processes necessary to improve the organization-environment fit. Absorptive capacity of strategic leaders is of particular importance because those in such a position have a unique ability to change or reinforce organizational action patterns.

The second key competency is adaptive capacity. **Adaptive capacity** refers to the ability to change. Boal and Hooijberg argue that in the new, fast-changing competitive landscape, organizational success calls for strategic flexibility, that is, being able to respond quickly to competitive conditions. The third key competency is **managerial wisdom** which involves the ability to perceive variation in the environment and understand the social actors and their relationships. Thus, emotional intelligence is called for and the leader must be able to take the right action at the right moment.

An Example of the Model   Let's look at an integrative example of an engineering company that had, at one time, 100 percent of its contracts with the Department of Defense. Astute strategic leaders—those high in absorptive capacity, change, and managerial wisdom—realized that a company reorientation was necessary given the decline in the defense budget. They had to reconceptualize their organization's system. Contract bidding procedures changed; the company no longer needed to comply with numerous government regulations in terms of its contracts, and executive leaders had to acquire new customers. These leaders tended to increase the three capacities noted above, and they formulated future visions and emphasized organizational transformation. They might even have appeared charismatic, if not visionary. Strategic leaders high in behavioral complexity and emotional intelligence are likely to spot trends more quickly than others and better prepare their organizations for the future.[27]

Contexts for Leadership Action

During the recent recession, it became quite clear that leaders are facing new and unique challenges. Not only have North American-based firms fully entered the information age, they have recognized the need to innovate or die. The old titans of the industrial age, the Fords, the GMs, the U.S. Steels, today look like remnants of a bygone era. Now we send tweets, instead of sending handwritten letters, and check e-mails on our Blackberry anytime and anywhere. Our family pictures are displayed electronically instead of as paper photos in frames or albums. Increasingly, leaders in every level of the organization are confronting the necessity and challenges of continual innovation and the uncertainty of the age. Simply put, leaders need to be acutely aware of the setting in which they lead.[28] And, the leadership needed in a routine setting is not the same leadership that is needed in other contexts.[29]

• **Absorptive capacity** is the ability to learn.

• **Adaptive capacity** refers to the ability to change.

• **Managerial wisdom** is the ability to perceive variations in the environment and understand the social actors and their relationships.

Key to the Future Is Education

At the opening of the Oprah Winfrey Leadership Academy for young women in South Africa, Oprah said: "I wanted to give this opportunity to girls who had a light so bright that not even poverty could dim that light." Nelson Mandela, first president of nonapartheid South Africa, also spoke, saying: "The key to any country's future is in educating its youth."

• **Context** is the collection of opportunities and constraints that affect the occurrence and meaning of behavior and the relationships among variables.

Contextual leadership perspectives detail the conditions facing the leader and then suggest the type of leadership that is needed for success. In organizational behavior, the term **context** is used to describe the collection of opportunities and constraints that affect the occurrence and meaning of behavior as well as the relationships among variables.[30] The different contexts may be described in terms of the stability and uncertainty facing the leader and his other unit.

For most managers there are three major sources of instability. The first is market and environmental instability. During a recession, for example, the market is extremely unstable. Second is technological instability, where what is produced and how it is produced are changing. For example, competitors may be innovating rapidly but in ways your firm cannot easily predict. Finally, there is firm instability with an emphasis on process and procedure or internal administration instability. An example is an internal production and delivery system that needs changing but the instability is so great that the design changes cannot keep up with system demands. In other words, managers cannot clear the swamp because the alligators keep eating the workers.

Four Leadership Contexts   These sources of instability can be combined to depict the overall character of the opportunities and constraints facing the leader. For simplicity consider the four contexts in Figure 14.6.[31] In context 1 (Stability), stable conditions exist and the focus is on adjusting and creating

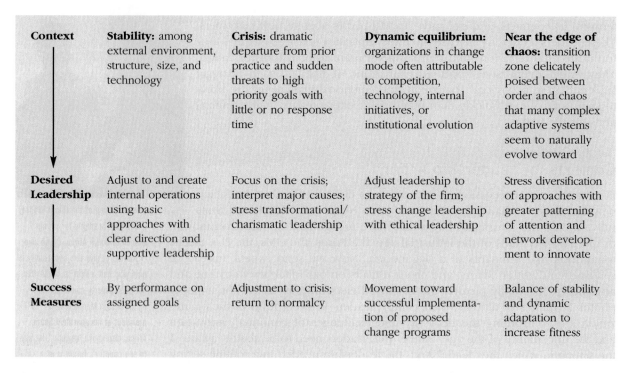

Context	**Stability:** among external environment, structure, size, and technology	**Crisis:** dramatic departure from prior practice and sudden threats to high priority goals with little or no response time	**Dynamic equilibrium:** organizations in change mode often attributable to competition, technology, internal initiatives, or institutional evolution	**Near the edge of chaos:** transition zone delicately poised between order and chaos that many complex adaptive systems seem to naturally evolve toward
Desired Leadership	Adjust to and create internal operations using basic approaches with clear direction and supportive leadership	Focus on the crisis; interpret major causes; stress transformational/ charismatic leadership	Adjust leadership to strategy of the firm; stress change leadership with ethical leadership	Stress diversification of approaches with greater patterning of attention and network development to innovate
Success Measures	By performance on assigned goals	Adjustment to crisis; return to normalcy	Movement toward successful implementation of proposed change programs	Balance of stability and dynamic adaptation to increase fitness

Figure 14.6 Four situational contexts, the desired leadership, and how to measure success.
[*Source:* Based on Osborn, Hunt, and Jauch (2002).]

internal operations to enhance system goals. This is often the context for earlier leadership perspectives. Note that to measure success, the leader should judge progress on the basis of goals assigned to his or her unit.

In context 2 (Crisis), there are identifiable and dramatic departures from prior practice and sudden threats to high priority goals, providing little or no response time. For many managers the current recession is such a crisis and calls for dramatic action and active leadership where charismatic and transformational leadership can be particularly important. While the situation appears dire, leaders are aware of factors contributing to the crisis and can develop action plans to try and weather the storm. For example, in a recession, downsizing is a way to preserve the firm until the economy improves. To judge success, the leader should monitor the degree to which the unit is coping with the crisis and make sure it is on track to return to normal operations. While those in the middle can face a crisis, in cases of a dramatic downturn the firm may even bring in a new CEO. Examine Leaders on Leadership for the case of Carol Bartz and Yahoo.

In context 3 (Dynamic Equilibrium), organizational stability occurs only within a range of shifting priorities with programmed change efforts. This is the well-known dynamic equilibrium setting found in many analyses of corporate strategy, strategic leadership, and change leadership.

Context 4 (Near the Edge of Chaos) is a transition zone poised between order and chaos. Here, the system must rapidly adjust while maintaining sufficient stability to learn.[32] While globally operating high tech firms are classic examples of those at the edge of chaos,[33] more conventional analyses of today's corporations have suggested that many firms are moving toward the edge of chaos. Why? By moving forward with a balance of exploration and exploitation they find superior performance. Poised near the edge of chaos, firms stress innovation, responsiveness, and adaptability over routine efficiency.

Near the edge of chaos, context 4 leaders operate in uncertainty where no one person can actually describe the challenges and opportunities facing the firm. The context is just too complex. With this level of complexity some of the traditional aspects of leadership are expected to yield very poor performance. For example, transformational leadership often fails simply because no single leader is capable of charting the necessary goals and paths to keep the system viable.[34] More transactional leadership appears to provide stability but often reinforces sticking to a failed approach. The challenge is to stimulate innovation while keeping the learning environment stable.

Patterning of Attention and Network Development   Recent research suggests that in order to meet context challengers, leaders need to emphasize two often neglected aspects of leadership, patterning of attention and network development.[35] **Patterning of attention** involves isolating and communicating important information from a potentially endless stream of events, actions, and outcome. The term *patterning* is used to stress the establishment of a norm where the leader is expected to ask questions, raise issues, and help gather information for unit members. The leader is not telling others what the goal is or how to reach it. Nor is the leader stressing an ideology or moral position. The leader is merely stimulating discussion among others in the setting. This discussion, in turn, produces new knowledge and information as individuals develop coping strategies.

• **Patterning of attention** involves isolating and communicating what information is important and what is given attention from a potentially endless stream of events, actions, and outcome.

Leaders on Leadership

CEO CAROL BARTZ AND THE CRISIS AT YAHOO

When Carol Bartz was asked to describe her leadership style as the new CEO of Yahoo, Inc., she said: "Fair but tough. We all work hard, and work has to be an interesting, fun place. And that has to start at the top. You have to be willing to say, I don't know, I made mistakes, and change. When somebody tells me they're going to do something, I want them to do it or tell me they're not going to do it."

Carol Bartz's management style has been described by others as mixing "bluntness" and "humor." One of her former executives at Autodesk points out

"she could get the best out of people." And that's most likely what the Yahoo Board was hoping when Bartz was appointed as the CEO. The firm had struggled under founder Jerry Yang's leadership and the intense competition from rival Google. In her new position Bartz faces a firm with low employee morale and shareholder discontent as well as pressure from financial analysts. Many believe she is well-suited to the task.

With plenty of technology experience—14 years as CEO of Autodesk and board appointments with the likes of Intel and Cisco Systems—she is known for being tough and insightful. Through it all she has fought the glass ceiling, making no bones about what she considered discrimination from a business community ruled by men. She cites an incident that occurred in a meeting with U.S. Senators. One turned to her and said: "So, how are we going to start the meeting?" Looking back on it she says: "He thought I must be the moderator. It's annoying. I don't have time for these guys, but when it's ridiculous I call them on it."

Having proven herself to be talented and skilled at leading big businesses, Bartz didn't waste any time digging in to the leadership challenges at Yahoo. Within six weeks of her appointment as CEO she was "preparing a company-wide reorganization" that reflected her "belief in a more top-down management approach." She calls Yahoo an "important property and such a great name" that needs "structure."

● **Network development** involves developing and managing the connections among individuals both inside and outside the unit or firm.

Members of a particular unit or firm may not be able to develop effective ways to compete in a very complex situation. They often need help from others and the leader may engage in network development. **Network development** involves developing and managing the connections among individuals both inside and outside the unit. With greater network development the leader expands the contacts needed to provide a greater diversity of information to the unit. This expansion of contacts may be with other units inside the firm or with a wide

MASTERING MANAGEMENT

NETWORKING LEADERSHIP FOR THE GREATER GOOD

Managers can emphasize leadership by encouraging the formation of giving circles that bring people together for a charitable purpose such as helping poor children or curing cancer. These are a number of charities that may arise informally or as a part of a formal voluntary organization such as the United Way. Here are some tips for establishing the circles.

- Find out who is interested in participating in a giving circle comprised of employees that will contribute a fixed amount of money and/or time toward a charitable cause.
- Once the circle is established, provide a schedule of meeting times and locations.
- Assign an appropriate number of people, depending on the size of the group, to bring forward a cause for support.
- Educate members in a variety of activities and organizations in order to get more people involved.
- Decide on the scope of the charitable cause, whether broad, narrow, or variable.
- Keep in touch with other volunteer organizations and giving circles.

variety of knowledgeable individuals outside the firm. For instance, key customers are often consulted in order to make changes and successfully implement product innovation.

In combination, greater patterning of attention and network development increases the size, interconnectedness, and diversity of the unit to provide a variety of world views. By increasing the depth and breadth of talent in combination with increased interaction, the chances are much greater that the unit will isolate reachable goals and evolve a sustaining way of accomplishing them. Too much patterning of attention and/or network development, however, can decrease the chances of effective adaptation. This would be the case when there is too much talk and not enough action. Managers must realize that patterning of attention and network development is a delicat balancing act. Finally, as suggested in Mastering Management, network leadership can be an important aspect of influence in many contexts. In this illustration it is used to establish a philanthropic entity.[36]

Leading Organizational Change

Leaders can also change the situation facing them and their followers. Change leadership deals with the idea that an organization needs to master the challenges of change while creating a satisfying, healthy, and effective workplace for its employees. For over a decade firms have dealt with a "new economy (that) has ushered in great business opportunities—and great turmoil."[37] The terms "turmoil" and "turbulence" are particularly salient in the current economic environment. In addition to the traditional challenges, the forces of globalization provide a number of problems and opportunities, and the new economy is constantly springing surprises on even the most experienced organizational executives. Flexibility, competence, and commitment are the rules of the day. People in the new workplace must be comfortable dealing with adaptation and continuous change, along with greater productivity, willingness to learn from the successes of others, total quality, and continuous improvement.

To deal with all of these concerns and more, we will examine leaders as change agents, phases of planned change, change strategies, and resistance to change.

Leaders as Change Agents

• **Transformational change** radically shifts the fundamental character of an organization.

While change is the watch word for most firms it is important to separate transformational from incremental change. Some of this change may be described as radical change, or frame-breaking change.[38] This is **transformational change**, which results in a major overhaul of the organization or its component systems. Organizations experiencing transformational change undergo significant shifts in basic characteristics, including the overall purpose/mission, underlying values and beliefs, and supporting strategies and structures.[39] In today's business environments, transformational changes are often initiated by a critical event, such as a new CEO, a new ownership brought about by merger or takeover, or a dramatic failure in operating results. When it occurs in the life cycle of an organization, such radical change is intense and all encompassing.[40] Examine OB Savvy 14.1 to increase the chances of successfully coping with a transformational change.

• **Incremental change** builds on the existing ways of operating to enhance or extend them in new directions.

• **Unplanned change** occurs spontaneously or randomly.

The most common form of change is **incremental change**, or frame-bending change. This type of change, being part of an organization's natural evolution, is frequent and less traumatic than other types of change. Typical incremental changes include the introduction of new products, technologies, systems, and processes. Although the nature of the organization remains relatively the same, incremental change builds on the existing ways of operating to enhance or extend them in new directions. The capability of improving continuously through incremental change is an important asset in today's demanding business environment.

The success of both radical and incremental change in organizations depends in part on change agents who lead and support the change processes. These are individuals and groups who take responsibility for changing the existing behavior patterns of another person or even the entire social system. Although change agents are sometimes consultants hired from outside the organization, most managers in today's dynamic times are expected to act in the capacity of change agents. Indeed, this responsibility is essential to the leadership role. Simply put, being an effective change agent means being effective at "change leadership."

Planned and Unplanned Change   Not all change in organizations is the result of a change agent's direction. **Unplanned changes** can occur spontaneously or randomly. They may be disruptive, such as a wildcat strike that ends in a plant closure, or beneficial, such as an interpersonal conflict that results in a new

---

OB SAVVY 14.1

Increasing Your Chances of Success with Transformational Change

- Develop a sense of urgency.
- Have a powerful guiding coalition.
- Have a compelling vision.
- Communicate the vision.
- Empower others to act.
- Celebrate short-term wins.
- Build on accomplishments.
- Institutionalize results.

procedure designed to improve the flow of work between two departments. When the forces of unplanned change appear, the goal is to act quickly in order to minimize negative consequences and maximize possible benefits. In many cases, an unplanned change can be turned into an advantage.

In contrast, **planned change** is the result of specific efforts led by a change agent. It is a direct response to someone's perception of a performance gap—a discrepancy between the desired and actual state of affairs. **Performance gaps** may represent problems to be solved or opportunities to be explored. Most planned changes are efforts intended to deal with performance gaps in ways that benefit an organization and its members. The processes of continuous improvement require constant vigilance to spot performance gaps and to take action to resolve them.

Change Is Opportunity

For Fred Smith, founder and CEO of FedEx, "change is shorthand for opportunity." He claims, "You'll get extinguished if you think you will not have to change. Organizational change calls for a high degree of trust and outstanding communication capability.

Forces and Targets for Change   The driving forces for change are ever-present in and around today's dynamic work settings. They are found in the organization-environment relationship, with mergers, strategic alliances, and divestitures among the examples of organizational attempts to redefine their relationships in challenging social and political environments. They are found in the organizational life cycle, with changes in culture and structure among the examples of how organizations must adapt as they evolve from birth through growth and toward maturity. They are found in the political nature of organizations, with changes in internal control structures, including benefits and reward systems that attempt to deal with shifting political currents.

Planned change based on any of these forces can be internally directed toward a wide variety of organizational components, most of which have already been discussed in this book. As shown in Figure 14.7, these targets include organizational purpose, strategy, structure, and people, as well as objectives, culture, tasks, and technology. When considering these targets, it must be recognized that they are highly intertwined in the workplace. Changes in any one are likely to require or involve changes in others. For example, a change in the basic tasks—what people do—is inevitably accompanied by a change in technology—the way in which tasks are accomplished. Changes in tasks and technology usually require alterations in structures, including changes in the patterns of authority and communication as well as in the roles of workers. These technological and structural changes can, in turn, necessitate changes in the knowledge, skills, and behaviors of the members of the organization.[41] In all cases, tendencies to accept easy-to-implement, but questionable, "quick fixes" to problems should be avoided.

- **Planned change** is a response to someone's perception of a performance gap—a discrepancy between the desired and actual state of affairs.
- **Performance gap** is a discrepancy between the desired and the actual conditions.

Phases of Planned Change

The failure rate of transformational organizational change is as high as 70 percent.[42] For a leader to improve his or her chances of success as a change agent, it is important to understand the normal process of change in organizations. Remember, most organizations operate on routines derived from prior success. Thus, a leader needs to think of any change effort in three phases—unfreezing, changing, and refreezing. All three phases must be handled well for a change to be successful.[43] Although the continuous nature of different changes means

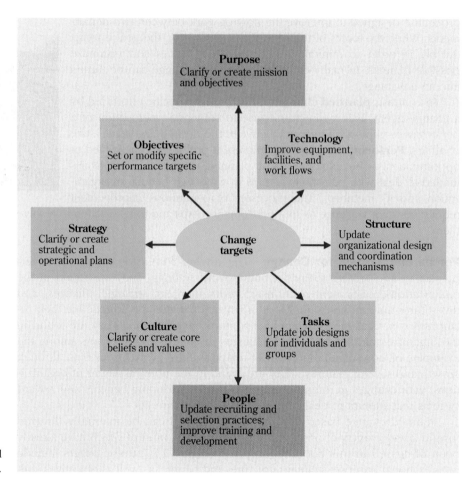

Figure 14.7 Organizational targets for planned change.

that these phases will often overlap, each phase is important and needs to be handled in a different manner. Inexperienced managers may become easily pre-occupied with the changing phase and neglect the importance of the unfreezing and refreezing stages.

Unfreezing is the stage at which a situation is prepared for change. In this stage it is the responsibility of the change agent to show the need for alterations. Have environmental changes opened new opportunities? Has someone else developed a better way to get the job done? Has performance started to slip in comparison with the competition? A manager will ask such questions when he or she is preparing for improvement. Many changes are never tried, or they fail simply because situations are not properly unfrozen to begin with.

Large units seem particularly susceptible to what is sometimes called the boiled frog phenomenon.[44] This refers to the notion that a live frog will immediately jump out when placed in a pan of hot water. When placed in cold water that is then heated very slowly, however, the frog will stay in the water until the water boils the frog to death. Organizations, too, can fall victim to similar circumstances. When change agents fail to monitor their environments, recognize

- **Unfreezing** is the stage at which a situation is prepared for change.

important trends, or sense the need to change, their organizations may slowly suffer and lose their competitive edge. Although the signals that change may be needed are available, they are not noticed or given any special attention—until it is too late. In contrast, people who are always on the alert and understand the importance of "unfreezing" in the change process are the most successful leaders.

Changing involves taking action to modify a situation by altering things, such as the people, tasks, structure, or technology of the organization. Many change agents are prone to an activity trap. They bypass the unfreezing stage and start with the changing stage prematurely or too quickly. Although their intentions may be good, the situation has not been properly prepared for change and this often leads to failure. Change is difficult in any situation, let alone having to do so without setting the proper foundations.

> • **Changing** is the stage in which specific actions are taken to create change.

Refreezing is the final stage in the planned change process. Designed to maintain the momentum of a change and eventually institutionalize it as part of the normal routine, refreezing secures the full benefits of long-lasting change. Refreezing involves positively reinforcing desired outcomes and providing extra support when difficulties are encountered. It involves evaluating progress and results, and assessing the costs and benefits of the change. And it allows for modifications to be made in the change to increase its success over time. If all of this is not done and refreezing is neglected, changes are often abandoned after a short time or incompletely implemented.

> • **Refreezing** is the stage in which changes are reinforced and stabilized.

Planned Change Strategies

There are a variety of **power change strategies** utilized to mobilize power, exert influence over others, and get people to support planned change efforts. Three pure strategies, force–coercion, rational persuasion, and shared power, are described in Figure 14.8. Each of these strategies builds from the various bases of social power. Note in particular that each power source has somewhat different implications for the planned change process.[45]

> • **Planned change strategies** consist of force–coercion, rational persuasion, and shared power.

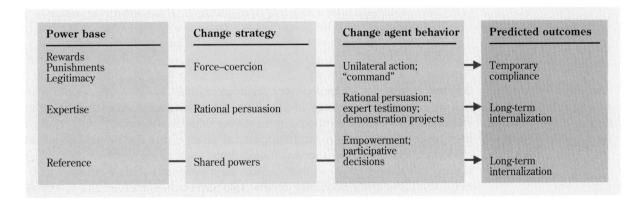

Power base	Change strategy	Change agent behavior	Predicted outcomes
Rewards Punishments Legitimacy	Force–coercion	Unilateral action; "command"	Temporary compliance
Expertise	Rational persuasion	Rational persuasion; expert testimony; demonstration projects	Long-term internalization
Reference	Shared powers	Empowerment; participative decisions	Long-term internalization

Figure 14.8 Power bases, change strategies, and predicted change outcomes.

• Force–coercion
strategy uses authority,
rewards, and punishments
to create change.

Force–Coercion

A **force–coercion strategy** uses authority, rewards, or punishments as primary inducements to change. Here, the leader acts unilaterally to "command" change through the formal authority of his or her position, to induce change via an offer of special rewards, or to bring about change via threats of punishment. People respond to this strategy mainly out of the fear of being punished if they do not comply with a change directive or out of the desire to gain a reward if they do. Coercion compliance is usually temporary and continues only as long as the leader is present. With reliance upon legitimate authority and rewards, compliance remains as long as supervision is visible and rewards keep coming. The actions as a change agent using the force–coercion strategy might match the following profile:

> You believe that people who run things are motivated by self-interest and by what the situation offers in terms of potential personal gain or loss. Since you feel that people change only in response to such motives, you try to find out where their vested interests lie and then put the pressure on. If you have formal authority, you use it. If not, you resort to whatever possible rewards and punishments you have access to and do not hesitate to threaten others with these weapons. Once you find a weakness, you exploit it and are always wise to work "politically" by building supporting alliances wherever possible.[46]

• Rational persuasion
strategy uses facts, special
knowledge, and rational
argument to create change.

Rational Persuasion

Change agents using a **rational persuasion strategy** attempt to bring about change through the use of special knowledge, empirical support, or rational arguments. This strategy assumes that rational people will be guided by reason and self-interest in deciding whether or not to support a change. Expert power is mobilized to convince others that the change will leave them better off than before. It is sometimes referred to as an empirical-rational strategy of planned change. When successful, this strategy results in a longer-lasting, more naturalized change than does force-coercion. A change agent taking the rational persuasion approach to a change situation might behave as follows:

> You believe that people are inherently rational and are guided by reason in their actions and decision making. Once a specific course of action is demonstrated to be in a person's self-interest, you assume that reason and rationality will cause the person to adopt it. Thus, you approach change with the objective of communicating—through information and facts—the essential "desirability" of change from the perspective of the person whose behavior you seek to influence. If this logic is effectively communicated, you are sure of the person who is adopting the proposed change.[47]

• Shared-power strategy
uses participatory methods
and emphasizes common
values to create change.

Shared Power

A **shared-power strategy** actively involves the people who will be affected by a change in planning and making key decisions relating to this change. Sometimes called a normative-reeducative approach, this strategy tries to develop directions and support for change through involvement and empowerment. It builds essential foundations, such as personal values, group norms, and shared goals, so that support for a proposed change emerges naturally. Managers using normative-reeducative approaches draw on the power of personal reference and share power by allowing others to participate in planning and implementing the change. Given this high level of involvement, the strategy is likely to result in a longer-lasting and internalized change. A change agent who shares power and adopts a normative-reeducative approach to change is likely to fit this profile:

> *You believe that people have complex motivations and behave as they do as a result of sociocultural norms and commitments to these norms. You also recognize that changes in these orientations involve changes in attitudes, values, skills, and significant relationships, not just changes in knowledge, information, or intellectual rationales for action and practice. Thus, when seeking to change others, you are sensitive to the supporting or inhibiting effects of group pressures and norms. In working with people, you try to find out their side of things and identify their feelings and expectations.*[48]

Resistance to Change

In organizations, **resistance to change** is any attitude or behavior that indicates unwillingness to make or support a desired alteration. Leaders often view any resistance as something that must be "overcome" in order for change to be successful. This is not always the case, however. It is helpful to view resistance to change as feedback that the leader can use to facilitate gaining change objectives.[49] The essence of this constructive approach to resistance is to recognize that when people resist change, they are defending something that is important to them that appears to be threatened.

Resistance to change is any attitude or behavior that indicates unwillingness to make or support a desired change.

Why People Resist Change   People have many reasons to resist change—fear of the unknown, insecurity, lack of a felt need to change, threat to vested interests, contrasting interpretations, and lack of resources, among other possibilities. A work team's members, for example, may resist the introduction of an advanced workstation of computers because they have never used the operating system and are apprehensive. They may wonder whether the new computers will eventually be used as justification for "getting rid" of certain members of their department, or they may believe that they have been doing their jobs just fine and do not need the new computers. These and other viewpoints often create resistance to even the best and most well-intended planned changes.

Resistance to the Change Itself   Sometimes a leader experiences resistance to the change itself. People may reject a change because they believe it is not worth their time, effort, or attention. They may believe that the proposed change asks them to do more for less. To minimize resistance in such cases, the leader should make sure that everyone who may be affected by a change knows how it satisfies the following criteria.[50]

> *Benefit*—The change should have a clear advantage for the people being asked to change; it should be perceived as "a better way."
>
> *Compatibility*—The change should be as compatible as possible with the existing values and experiences of the people being asked to change.
>
> *Complexity*—The change should be no more complex than necessary; it must be as easy as possible for people to understand and use.
>
> *Triability*—The change should be something that people can try on a step-by-step basis and make adjustments as things progress.

Resistance to the Change Strategy   Leaders must also be prepared to deal with resistance to the change strategy. Someone who attempts to bring about change via force-coercion, for example, may create resistance among individuals who resent management of leadership by "command" or the use of threatened punishment. People may resist a rational persuasion strategy in which the data are suspect or the expertise of advocates is not clear. They may resist a shared-power strategy that even appears manipulative and insincere.

Resistance to the Change Agent   Resistance to a leader implementing the change often involves personality differences and a poor history of relationships. Leaders who are isolated and aloof from other persons in the change situation, who appear self-serving, or who have a high emotional involvement in the changes are especially prone to such problems. Research indicates that leaders who differ from other persons on such dimensions as age, education, and socioeconomic status may encounter greater resistance to change.[51]

How to Deal with Resistance   An informed leader has many options available for dealing positively with resistance to change. Figure 14.9 summarizes insights into how and when each of these methods may be used to deal with resistance to change. Regardless of the chosen strategy, it is always best to remember that the presence of resistance typically suggests that something can be done to achieve a better fit among the change, the situation, and the people affected. A good leader deals with resistance to change by listening to feedback and acting accordingly.[52]

Method ⟶	Use when ⟶	Advantages ⟶	Disadvantages
Education & communication	People lack information or have inaccurate information	Creates willingness to help with the change	Can be very time consuming
Participation & involvement	Other people have important information and/or power to resist	Adds information to change planning; builds commitment to the change	Can be very time consuming
Facilitation & support	Resistance traces to resource or adjustment problems	Satisfies directly specific resource or adjustment needs	Can be time consuming; can be expensive
Negotiation & agreement	A person or group will "lose" something because of the change	Helps avoid major resistance	Can be expensive; can cause others to seek similar "deals"
Manipulation & cooptation	Other methods don't work or are too expensive	Can be quick and inexpensive	Can create future problems if people sense manipulation
Explicit & implicit coercion	Speed is important and change agent has power	Quick; overpowers resistance	Risky if people get "mad"

Figure 14.9 Methods for dealing with resistance to change.

The first approach in dealing with resistance through *educa-tion and communication*. The objective is to te... fore it is implemented and to help them under... Education and communication seem to work be... inaccurate or incomplete information. A second... and involvement. With the goal of allowing o... ment the changes, this approach asks people t... to work on task forces or committees that ma... useful when the leader does not have all the in... handle a problem situation. Here, for instance... of attention and network development by the...

Facilitation and support help to deal wit... both emotional and material—for people expe... Here a leader increases consideration by a... complaints. This is matched with greater in... provides training in the new ways, and help... pressures. Facilitation and support are high... frustrated by work constraints and difficulties...

A *negotiation and agreement approach* o... change resistors. Trade-offs are arranged to pr... assurances that the change will not be blocke... a person or group that will lose something of v...

Frustrated managers may attempt to u... covert attempts to influence others, selecti... sciously structuring events so that the desire... and co-optation are common when other ta... and experience executives find they can ga...

In a crisis, some leaders find that in orde... must resort to *explicit or implicit coercion*. ... riety of undesirable consequences if they d... the temporary compliance to the change m... storm. Unfortunately, crises are much rarer... crisis is past, even the temporary use of coe... bark on a new change program that stress...

Finally, it is important to recognize th... as it undergoes planned change. Often a... alterations in the culture of the organizatio... into the concept of organizational culture... a unique kind of planned change.

These learning activities from *The OB Skills*... ested for Chapter 14.

Case for Critical Thinking	Team and... Ex...	Self-Assessment Portfolio
• Novo Nordisk	• Interview a...	"TT" Leadership
	• Leadership Inventorie...	
	• Force-Fie...	

Resources in The OB Skills Workbook

14 study

Summary Questions and Answers

What is moral leadership

- Moral leadership includes ___ship, servant leadership, and spiritual and ethical leadership.

- Authentic leadership emp___ one's personal experiences and acting in accordance with one's tru___ ___ich underlies virtually all other aspects of leadership.

- Servant leadership is where ___ tuned to basic spiritual values and, in serving these, serves others ___gues, the organization, and society.

- Spiritual leadership is a fiel___ in the broader setting of workplace spirituality; it includes values, a___ ___aviors required to intrinsically motivate self and others to have a se___ ___rvival through calling and membership.

- Ethical leadership emphasiz___ ___s.

What is shared leadership

- Shared leadership is a dynam___ ___uence process among individuals in groups for which the objectiv___ ___nother to the achievement of group or organizational goals or bo___

- The influence process often i___ ___eral influence and at other times involves upward or downward ___ce within a team.

- Although broader than traditic___ ___ship, shared leadership may be used in combination with it.

- Self-leadership techniques can ___ve the effectiveness of shared leadership.

How do you lead across cul___

- Cross-cultural leadership empha___E (Global Leadership and Organizational Effectiveness Re___ ___hich involves 62 societies, 951 organizations, and about 140 co___ ___rs.

- It assumes that the attributes and ___ntiate a specified culture predict organizational practices and lead___ ___haviors that are most often carried out and most effective in tha___

- It identifies a number of potentia___ ___s of culture that form the basis for culturally based leader protot___

- It matches key aspects of leadersl___ aspects of culture to identify endorsed elements of leadership.

- It suggests both universally endor___ ___rship as well as those unique to a particular culture and group ___

What is strategic leadership?

- When the focus is on strategic leadership this is leadership of a quasi-independent unit, department, or organization.

- The expectations for leaders, the time frame for their actions, and the complexity of the assignments increases as one moves up the organizational hierarchy.

- Strategic leadership, as used here, includes the leadership of both the CEO and the top management team.

- Boal and Hooijberg's view of strategic leadership uses emergent theories: cognitive complexity, emotional intelligence (complexity), and behavioral complexity as well as charismatic, transformational, and visionary leadership to influence absorptive capacity, capacity to change, and managerial wisdom, which in turn influence effectiveness.

- In today's complex environment, strategic leadership needs to come from the middle of the organization and should vary by the nature of the context facing the leader.

What is organizational change leadership?

- Change leadership helps deal with the idea of an organization that masters the challenges of both radical and incremental change while still creating a satisfying, healthy, and effective employee workplace.

- Change leadership deals with leaders as change agents, phases of planned change, change strategies, and resistance to change.

- Radical or transformational change results in a major overhaul of the organization or its component systems.

- Incremental or frame-bending change as part of an organization's natural evolution is frequent and less traumatic than radical change.

- Change agents are individuals and groups who take responsibility for changing the existing behavior pattern or social system; being a change agent is an integral part of a manager's leadership role.

- Planned change strategies consist of force-coercion, rational persuasion, and shared power.

- Dealing with resistance to change involves education and communication, participation and involvement, facilitation and support, negotiation and agreement, manipulation and co-optation, and explicit or implicit agreement.

Key Terms

Rational persuasion strategy (p. 356)	Self-efficacy (p. 332)	Strategic leadership (p. 342)
Refreezing (p. 355)	Shared leadership (p. 335)	Transformational change (p. 352)
Resilience (p. 332)	Shared-power strategy (p. 356)	Unfreezing (p. 354)
Resistance to change (p. 357)		Unplanned change (p. 352)

Self-Test 14

Multiple Choice

1. Authentic Leadership is _____. (a) another name for transformational leadership (b) another name for transactional leadership (c) emphasizes acting in accordance with one's true or core self (d) is strongly supported by research findings

2. Shared leadership _____. (a) emphasizes vertical leadership (b) involves a white hat and a white horse (c) has almost totally replaced vertical leadership (d) is becoming more and more important in modern organizations

3. Project GLOBE _____. (a) considers both culture and leadership (b) is no longer a relevant program (c) was completed in 2004 (d) has nothing to do with cross-cultural leadership

4. The multiple-level strategic leadership approach _____. (a) emphasizes leadership in different organizational domains (b) is an obsolete approach to leadership (c) is a face-to-face leadership approach (d) is the latest extension to Fiedler's work

5. Boal and Hooijberg _____. (a) argue against the notion of strategic leadership theory (b) have a theory with lots of research support (c) have a theory emphasizing leadership tensions and complexity (d) have a theory that is largely obsolete

6. Authentic leadership is _____. (a) virtually the same as ethical leadership (b) not a very widely discussed approach (c) not one that emphasizes knowing thyself (d) one that might serve as a base for numerous other leadership theories

7. Servant leadership is _____. (a) virtually the same as transformational leadership (b) has much research support (c) has very little research support (d) is currently one of the more popular leadership approaches

8. Spiritual leadership is _____. (a) a kind of religion (b) beginning to develop a research stream (c) virtually the same as authentic leadership (d) ties together full-range leadership theory, shared leadership, cross-cultural leadership, and strategies leadership

9. Incremental change is _____. (a) more dramatic than radical change (b) less dramatic than radical change (c) infrequently encountered (d) usually very expensive

10. Contextual leadership _____. (a) has three levels and six domains (b) is an over-used approach (c) assumes decreasing complexity up the organization (d) stresses a leader's responsiveness to the setting

11. Change leadership _____. (a) is very widely used (b) deals with leaders as change agents, phases of planned change, change strategies, and resistance to change (c) is practically unknown (d) is of recent origin

12. Performance gaps that create potential change situations include the existence of both problems to be resolved and _____. (a) costs to be avoided (b) people to be terminated (c) problems already resolved (d) opportunities to be explored

13. The presence or absence of a felt need for change is a critical issue in which phase of change: (a) reflective. (b) evaluative. (c) unfreezing. (d) changing.

14. Which strategy relies mainly on empirical data and expert power? (a) force–coercion (b) rational persuasion (c) shared power (d) authoritative command

15. Which change strategy is limited in effectiveness because it tends to create only temporary compliance? (a) force–coercion (b) rational persuasion (c) shared power (d) normative reeducation

Short Response

16. Explain three ways in which shared leadership can be used in a self-directed work team.

17. Briefly compare and contrast the multiple-level leadership approach with the Boal and Hooijberg strategic leadership theory.

18. What should a manager do when forces for unplanned change appear?

19. What internal and external forces push for change in organizations?

Applications Essay

20. When Jorge Maldanado became general manager of the local civic recreation center, he realized that many changes would be necessary to make the facility a true community resource. Having the benefit of a new bond issue, the center had the funds for new equipment and expanded programming. All he needed to do now was get the staff committed to new initiatives. Unfortunately, his first efforts have been met with considerable resistance to change. A typical staff comment is, "Why do all these extras? Everything is fine as it is." How can Jorge use the strategies for dealing with resistance to change, as discussed in the chapter, to move the change process along?

15

Organizational Culture and Innovation

Stop by a Chick-fil-A restaurant for a tasty sandwich any day but Sunday. The co-founder of the company and the individual who started the no Sunday policy is 86-year-old Truett Cathy. He believes everyone should have a day of rest. It is part of his philosophy to put "people before profits." The family-owned firm is known in some forty U.S. states for its consistent quality and great service, and it was recently recognized as the best drive thru chain in the country.

Less well known is the fact that the company has consistently grown during the years as a chain. Chick-fil-A is headquartered in Atlanta, GA where its first restaurant was opened over sixty years ago. Today, Chick-fil-A is the second largest chicken restaurant chain in the United States, with some 1,425 restaurants in 40 states. It reached over $3 billion sales in 2008 and posted a 12 percent growth in 2009, despite the downturn in the economy.

Now, Truett's son, Dan T. Cathy, heads the firm. Dan believes the Sunday day of rest is a statement about their culture. He says: "If we take care of our team members and operators behind the counter, then they are going to do a better job on Monday. In fact I say our food tastes better on Monday because we are closed on Sunday." The president of the national Restaurant Association Educational Foundation says: "I don't think there's any chain that creates such a wonderful culture around the way they treat their people and the respect they have for their employees."

"I don't think there's any chain that creates such a wonderful culture . . ."

Like many successful firms stressing culture, key Chick-fil-A managers stress innovation and change. When commenting on the consistent years of growth, Woody Faulk, vice president of brand development, says: "It would be very easy for us to pause after such a successful year, but in doing that, we would be in jeopardy of falling into a trap of complacency." He adds: "Customer needs are constantly fluctuating, and we have to be intentional about staying ahead of and remaining relevant to those changes."

living and working together

Organizational Culture

Continuing the record of success at Chick-fil-A calls for an intricate balance among a broad range of factors. To provide stability and continuity CEO Dan T. Cathy relies upon the rich cultural traditions of Chick-fil-A. Yet, this culture tradition is matched with an emphasis on innovation to provide a balance between stability and effective change. In this chapter, we will discuss the stability and meaning provided by organizational culture and the necessity for evolutionary change provided by an emphasis on innovation.

Organizational or corporate culture is the system of shared actions, values, and beliefs that develops within an organization and guides the behavior of its members.[1] In the business setting, this system is often referred to as the corporate culture. Just as no two individual personalities are the same, no two organizational cultures are identical. Today management scholars and consultants believe that cultural differences can have a major impact on the performance of organizations and the quality of work life experienced by their members.[2] For instance, it appeared that Cantor Fitzgerald died when most of its employees died on 9/11 with the collapse of Twin Towers. Such was not the case.

- **Organizational or corporate culture** is the system of shared actions, values, and beliefs that develops within an organization and guides the behavior of its members.

Functions of Organizational Culture

Through their collective experience, members of an organization can solve two extremely important survival issues.[3] The first issue is one of external adaptation: What precisely needs to be accomplished, and how can it be done? The second is known as internal integration: How do members resolve the daily problems associated with living and working together?

External Adaptation   Issues of **external adaptation** deal with reaching goals, the tasks to be accomplished, methods used to achieve the goals, and the methods of coping with success and failure. Through their shared experiences, members may develop common views that help guide their day-to-day activities. Organizational members need to know the real mission of the organization, not just the pronouncements to key constituencies, such as stockholders. By talking to one another, members will naturally develop an understanding of how they contribute to the mission via interaction. This view may emphasize the importance of human resources. On the other hand, employees may see themselves as cogs in a machine, or a cost to be reduced.

- **External adaptation** deals with reaching goals, the tasks to be accomplished, the methods used to achieve the goals, and the methods of coping with success and failure.

Closely related to the organization's mission and view of its contribution are the questions of responsibility, goals, and methods. For instance, at 3M, employees believe that it is their responsibility to innovate and contribute creatively. They see these responsibilities reflected in achieving the goal of developing new and improved products and processes.

Each collection of individuals in an organization also tends to (1) separate more important from less important external forces, (2) develop ways to measure their accomplishments, and (3) create explanations for why goals are not always met. At Dell, the retailer of computers and consumer electronics, managers, for example, have moved away from judging their progress against specific

Leaders on Leadership

ULRICH SCHWANENGEL AND CONSOL'S EMPOWERING CULTURE

Based in Munich, Germany, ConSol Software GmbH is a high tech company involved in the "development, integration and operation of complex IT systems."

With academic training in mathematics, physics and computer science, Dr. Schwanengel started Consol in 1984.

Employee involvement, equal opportunity and work-life balance are the components of Consol's "culture of cooperation." We have guidelines like "arguments rather than directives," and we encourage employees to speak out loud and share their opinions." In 2008 the company was awarded the Bavarian Advancement of Women Prize for its policies that cater to the individual needs of female employees. Consol's health management system values work-life balance with programs that encourage physical fitness and healthy living.

The company has been voted the best place to work in Germany for the past four years and just recently was named the third best place to work in Europe.

targets to estimating the degree to which they are moving a development process forward. Instead of blaming a poor economy or upper-level managers for the firm's failure to reach a goal, Dell managers have set hard goals that are difficult to reach and have redoubled their efforts to improve participation and commitment.[4]

The final issues in external adaptation deal with two important, but often neglected, aspects of coping with external reality. First, individuals need to develop acceptable ways of telling outsiders just how good they really are. At 3M, for example, employees talk about the quality of their products and the many new, useful products they have brought to the market. Second, individuals must collectively know when to admit defeat. At 3M, the answer is easy for new projects: at the beginning of the development process, members establish "drop" points at which to quit the development effort and redirect it.[5]

In sum, external adaptation involves answering important instrumental or goal-related questions concerning coping with reality: What is the real mission? How do we contribute? What are our goals? How do we reach our goals? What external forces are important? How do we measure results? What do we do if we do not met specific targets? How do we tell others how good we are? When do we quit? Chris Connor of Sherwin-Williams expressed his firm's approach to external adaptation in terms of winning (see Leaders on Leadership).[6]

The process of **internal integration** often begins with the establishment of a unique identity; that is, each collection of individuals and each subculture within the organization develops a unique definition of itself. Through dialogue and interaction, members begin to characterize their world. They may see it as malleable or fixed, filled with opportunity or threatening. Real progress toward innovation can begin when group members collectively believe that they can

• **Internal integration** deals with the creation of a collective identity and with ways of working and living together.

The Culture at Aetna

Aetna, one of the nation's leading diversified health care benefits companies, describes its corporate culture as employees who "work together openly, share information freely and build on each other's ideas to continually create the next better way. Nothing is impossible to our Aetna team. We are eager, ambitious learners and continuous innovators. And we are succeeding. Every day."

change important parts of the world around them and that what appears to be a threat is actually an opportunity for change.

Three important aspects of working together are (1) deciding who is a member of the group and who is not, (2) developing an informal understanding of acceptable and unacceptable behavior, and (3) separating friends from enemies. These are important questions for managers as well. A key to effective total quality management, for instance, is that subgroups in the organization need to view their immediate supervisors as members of the group. The immediate supervisor is expected to represent the group to friendly higher managers. Of course, should management not be seen as friendly, the process of improving quality could quickly break down.[7]

To work together effectively, individuals need to decide collectively how to allocate power, status, and authority. They need to establish a shared understanding of who will get rewards and sanctions for specific types of actions. Too often, managers fail to recognize these important aspects of internal integration. For example, a manager may fail to explain the basis for a promotion and to show why this reward, the status associated with it, and the power given to the newly promoted individual are consistent with commonly shared beliefs. Collections of individuals also need to work out acceptable ways to communicate and to develop guidelines for friendships. Although these aspects of internal integration may appear esoteric, they are vital. For example, to function effectively as a team, team members must recognize that some members will be closer than others; friendships are inevitable.[8]

Resolving the issues of internal integration helps individuals develop a shared identity and a collective commitment. It may well lead to longer-term stability and provide a lens for members to make sense of their part of the world. In sum, internal integration involves answers to important questions associated with living together. What is our unique identity? How do we view the world? Who is a member? How do we allocate power, status, and authority? How do we communicate? What is the basis for friendship? Answering these questions is important to organizational members because the organization is more than just a place to work.[9]

Subcultures and Countercultures

While smaller firms often have a single dominant culture with a universal set of shared actions, values, and beliefs, most larger organizations contain several subcultures as well as one or more countercultures.[10]

• **Subcultures** are groups who exhibit unique patterns of values and philosophies not consistent with the dominant culture of the larger organization or social system.

Subcultures **Subcultures** are groups of individuals who exhibit a unique pattern of values and a philosophy that is not inconsistent with the organization's dominant values and philosophy.[11] While subcultures are unique, their members' values do not clash with those of the larger organization. Interestingly, strong subcultures are often found in task forces, teams, and special project groups in organizations. The subculture emerges to bind individuals working intensely together to accomplish a specific task. For example, there are strong subcultures of stress engineers and liaison engineers in the Boeing Renton plant. These highly specialized groups must solve knotty technical issues to ensure that Boeing planes are safe. Though distinct, these groups of engineers also share in the dominant values of Boeing.

Countercultures   In contrast, **countercultures** are groups where the patterns of values and philosophies outwardly reject those of the larger organization or social system.[12] When Stephen Jobs reentered Apple computer as its CEO, he quickly formed a counterculture within Apple. Over the next 18 months, numerous clashes occurred as the followers of the old CEO (Gil Amelio) fought to maintain their place and the old culture. Jobs won and Apple won. His counterculture became dominant.[13] Every large organization imports potentially important subcultural groupings when it hires employees from the larger society. In North America, for instance, subcultures and countercultures may naturally form based on ethnic, racial, gender, generational, or locational similarities. In Japanese organizations, subcultures often form based on the date of graduation from a university, gender, or geographic location. In European firms, ethnicity and language play an important part in developing subcultures, as does gender. In many less developed nations, language, education, religion, or family social status are often grounds for forming popular subcultures and countercultures.

Within an organization, mergers and acquisitions may produce adjustment problems. Employers and managers of an acquired firm may hold values and assumptions that are inconsistent with those of the acquiring firm. This is known as the "clash of corporate cultures."[14] As more firms globalize and use mergers and acquisitions to expand, often they must cope with imported subcultures and the subsequent clash of corporate cultures. For instance, when Daimler Benz purchased Chrysler Corporation, Daimler billed the purchase as a merger of equals. The corporate culture clash came quickly, however, when Chrysler managers and employees realized that Daimler executives would control the new combination and form it around the German partner. Within a few short years, Daimler executives realized they could not change the Chrysler culture and sold most of Chrysler.[15] With the recent consolidation of banks and brokerage firms, culture clashes within the huge financial services firms have become quite common. For example, Bank of America has had difficulty with the huge bonuses it gives to traders in its newly acquired Merrill Lynch unit.

• **Countercultures** are groups where the patterns of values and philosophies outwardly reject those of the larger organization or social system.

National Culture and Corporate Culture

Corporate mergers across national boundaries often serve to highlight both corporate and national cultural differences as in the case of Daimler Benz and Chrysler.[16] The difference between Sony's corporate emphasis on group achievements and Zenith's emphasis on individual engineering excellence, for example, can be traced to the Japanese emphasis on collective action versus the U.S. emphasis on individualism. National cultural values may also become embedded in the expectations of important organizational constituencies and in generally accepted solutions to problems.

When moving across national cultures, managers need to be sensitive to national cultural differences so that their actions do not violate common assumptions in the underlying national culture. To improve morale at General Electric's

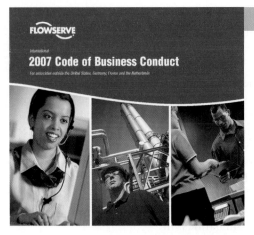

THE DILEMMA OF WHOSE ETHICS?

It often goes unsaid that the culture of the organization should be ethical. Consider Flowserve. It is a recognized world leader in supplying pumps, valves, and seals to a wide variety of industries. It has over 14,000 employees in 56 countries and offices in the Americas, Australia, Eurasia, and the Middle East. How does it develop and maintain culture across so many regions?

Its solution of maintaining an ethical culture, in part, rests on a well developed code of ethics as well as an emphasis on integrity and trust to define its character. In every location it emphasizes Commitment, Creativity, Competence, Character, Confidence, and Collaboration. Employees are to follow a well developed and very specific U.S.-based code of ethics, and are asked to report problems through the Web site or hotline. The code of ethics shows exactly how to be ethical.

"Is It Appropriate?" Is it appropriate to impose U.S.-based ethical solutions on individuals from other nations with different cultures?

French subsidiary, Chi. Generale de Radiologie, American managers invited all of the European managers to a "get-acquainted" meeting near Paris. The Americans gave out colorful t-shirts with the GE slogan, "Go for One," a typical maneuver in many American training programs. The French resented the t-shirts. One outspoken individual said, "It was like Hitler was back, forcing us to wear uniforms. It was humiliating." Firms often face problems in developing strong ethical standards, and some, like Flowserve, as featured in Ethics in OB, take extensive measures to support an ethical culture.[17]

Importing Societal Subgroups Beyond becoming culturally sensitive, difficulties often arise with importing groupings from the larger society. Some of these groupings are relevant to the organization while other may be quite destructive. At the one extreme, senior managers can merely accept societal divisions and work within the confines of the larger culture. There are three primary difficulties with this approach. First, subordinated groups, such as members of a specific religion or ethnic group, are likely to form into a counterculture and to work more diligently to change their status than to better the firm. Second, the firm may find it extremely difficult to cope with broader cultural changes. For instance, in the United States the expected treatment of women, ethnic minorities, and the disabled has changed dramatically over the last 20 years. Firms that merely accept old customs and prejudices have experienced a greater loss of key personnel and increased communication difficulties, as well as greater interpersonal conflict, than have their more progressive counterparts. Third, firms that accept and build on natural divisions from the larger culture may find it extremely difficult to develop sound international operations. For example, many Japanese firms have had substantial difficulty adjusting to the equal treatment of women in their U.S. operations.[18]

Building Upon National Cultural Diversity   At the other extreme, managers can work to eradicate all naturally occurring national subcultures and counter-cultures. Firms are groping to develop what Taylor Cox calls the multicultural organization. The **multicultural organization** is a firm that values diversity but systematically works to block the transfer of societally based subcultures into the fabric of the organization.[19] Because Cox focuses on some problems unique to the United States, his prescription for change may not apply to organizations located in other countries with much more homogeneous populations.

    Cox suggests a five-step program for developing the multicultural organization. First, the organization should develop pluralism with the objective of multi-based socialization. To accomplish this objective, members of different naturally occurring groups need to school one another to increase knowledge and information and to eliminate stereotyping. Second, the firm should fully integrate its structure so that there is no direct relationship between a naturally occurring group and any particular job—for instance, there are no distinct male or female jobs. Third, the firm must integrate the informal networks by eliminating barriers and increasing participation. That is, it must break down existing societally based informal groups. Fourth, the organization should break the linkage between naturally occurring group identity and the identity of the firm. Fifth, the organization must actively work to eliminate interpersonal conflict based on either the group identity or the natural backlash of the largest societally based grouping.

> **Multicultural organization** is a firm that values diversity but systematically works to block the transfer of societally based subcultures into the fabric of the organization.

Understanding Organizational Cultures

Some aspects of organizational culture are easy to see. Yet, not all aspects of organizational culture are readily apparent because they are buried deep in the shared experience of organizational members. It may take years to understand some deeper aspects of the culture. This complexity has led some to examine different layers of analysis ranging from easily observable to deeply hidden aspects of corporate culture.

Layers of Cultural Analysis

Figure 15.1 illustrates the observable aspects of culture, shared values, and underlying assumptions as three layers.[20] The deeper one digs, the more difficult it is to discover the culture but the more important an aspect becomes.

    The first level concerns **observable culture**, or "the way we do things around here." Important parts of an organization's culture emerge from the collective experience of its members. These emergent aspects of the culture help make it unique and may well provide a competitive advantage for the organization. Some of these aspects may be observed directly in day-to-day practices. Others may have to be discovered—for example, by asking members to tell stories of important incidents in the history of the organization. We often learn about the unique aspects of the organizational culture through descriptions of specific events.[21] By observing employee actions, listening to stories, and asking members to interpret what is going on, one can begin to understand the organization's culture. The observable culture includes the unique stories, ceremonies, and corporate rituals that make up the history of the firm or a group within the firm.

> **Observable culture** is the way things are done in an organization.

Figure 15.1 Three levels of analysis in studying organizational culture.

The Shared Passions at Microsoft

At Microsoft, they profess to "share a passion for technology and what it can do for people. It's a shared passion for innovation, exploration, and creativity, and a belief in the value of software and the difference it can make in people's lives."

The second layer recognizes that shared values can play a critical part in linking people together and can provide a powerful motivational mechanism for members of the culture. Many consultants suggest that organizations should develop a "dominant and coherent set of shared values."[22] The term shared in cultural analysis implies that the group is a whole. Not every member may agree with the shared values, but they have all been exposed to them and have often been told they are important. At General Mills, for example, innovation is part of everyone's vocabulary. Such is also the case with Microsoft.

At the deepest layer of cultural analysis are common cultural assumptions; these are the taken-for-granted truths that collections of corporate members share as a result of their joint experience. It is often extremely difficult to isolate these patterns, but doing so helps explain why culture invades every aspect of organizational life.

Stories, Rites, Rituals, and Symbols

To begin understanding a corporate culture, it is often easiest to start with stories. Organizations are rich with stories of winners and losers, successes and failures. Perhaps one of the most important stories concerns the founding of the organization. The founding story often contains the lessons learned from the heroic efforts of an embattled entrepreneur, whose vision may still guide the firm. The story of the founding may be so embellished that it becomes a **saga**—a heroic account of accomplishments.[23] Sagas are important because they are used to tell new members the real mission of the organization, how the organization operates, and how individuals can fit into the company. Rarely is the founding story totally accurate, and it often glosses over some of the more negative aspects of the founders. Such is the case with Monterey Pasta.[24]

- A **saga** is an embellished heroic account of the story of the founding of an organization.

On its Web site, the organization says of its history, "The Monterey Pasta Company was launched from a 400-square-foot storefront on Lighthouse Avenue in Monterey, California in 1989. . . . The founders started their small fresh pasta company in response to the public's growing interest in healthy gourmet foods. Customers were increasingly excited about fresh pasta given its superior quality and nutritional value, as well as ease of preparation. . . . The company soon accepted its first major grocery account. . . . In 1993, the company completed its first public offering." The Web site fails to mention another interesting aspect of the firm. An unsuccessful venture into the restaurant business in the mid-1990s provided a significant distraction, and substantial losses were incurred before the company was refocused on its successful retail business. But why ruin a good founding story?

If you have job experience, you may well have heard stories concerning the following questions: How will the boss react to a mistake? Can someone move from the bottom to the top of the company? What will get me fired? These are common story topics in many organizations.[25] Often, the stories provide valuable but hidden information about who is more equal than others, whether jobs are secure, and how things are really controlled. In essence, the stories begin to suggest how organizational members view the world and live together.

- **Rites** are standardized and recurring activities used at special times to influence the behaviors and understanding of organizational members.

Some of the most obvious aspects of organizational culture are rites and rituals.[26] **Rites** are standardized and recurring activities that are used at special times to influence the behaviors and understanding of organizational members;

rituals are systems of rites. It is common, for example, for Japanese workers and managers to start their workdays together with group exercises and singing of the "company song." Separately, the exercises and song are rites. Together, they form part of a ritual. In other settings, such as Mary Kay Cosmetics, scheduled ceremonies reminiscent of the Miss America pageant (a ritual) are used regularly to spotlight positive work achievements and reinforce high-performance expectations with awards, including gold and diamond pins and fur stoles.

Rituals and rites may be unique to particular groups within the organization. Subcultures often arise from the type of technology deployed by the unit, the specific function being performed, and the specific collection of specialists in the unit. A unique language may well maintain the boundaries of the subculture. Often, the language of a subculture, and its rituals and rites, emerge from the group as a form of jargon. In some cases, the special language starts to move outside the firm and begins to enter the larger society. For instance, look at Microsoft Word's specialized language, with such words as hyperlink, frames, and autoformat. It's a good thing they also provide a Help button defining each.

Another observable aspect of corporate culture centers on the symbols found in organizations. A **cultural symbol** is any object, act, or event that serves to transmit cultural meaning. Good examples are the corporate uniforms worn by UPS and Federal Express delivery personnel.

- **Rituals** are systems of rites.

- A **cultural symbol** is any object, act, or event that serves to transmit cultural meaning.

Cultural Rules and Roles

Organizational culture often specifies when various types of actions are appropriate and where individual members stand in the social system. These cultural rules and roles are part of the normative controls of the organization and emerge from its daily routines.[27] For instance, the timing, presentation, and methods of communicating authoritative directives are often quite specific to each organization. In one firm, meetings may follow a set rigid agenda. The manager could go into meetings to tell subordinates what to do and how to accomplish tasks. Private conversations prior to the meeting might be the place for any new ideas or critical examination. In other firms, meetings might be forums for dialogue and discussion, where managers set agendas and then let others offer new ideas, critically examine alternatives, and fully participate. Take a look at how R&R Partners uses what they call a SWARM.[28]

Shared Values, Meanings, and Organizational Myths

To describe more fully the culture of an organization, it is necessary to go deeper than the observable aspects. To many researchers and managers, shared common values lie at the very heart of organizational culture.

Shared Values Shared values help turn routine activities into valuable and important actions, tie the corporation to the important values of society, and possibly provide a very distinctive source of competitive advantage. In organizations, what works for one person is often taught to new members as the correct way to think and feel. Important values are then attributed to these solutions to everyday problems. By linking values and actions, the organization taps into some of the strongest and deepest realms of the individual. The tasks a person performs are given not only meaning but also value: what one does is not only workable

The SWARM at R&R Partners

At R&R Partners, the Las Vegas–based advertising agency and lobbying firm, there is a creative culture that permeates the entire organization, as everyone is responsible for creating new ideas. When new ideas are needed, everyone at R&R is invited into the agency's "war room" to brainstorm. These brainstorming sessions are called a SWARM.

but correct, right, and important. At Lam Research Corporation, for instance, they are very clear about their core values as they provide meaning for everyone's work.[29]

Some successful organizations share some common cultural characteristics.[30] Organizations with "strong cultures" possess a broadly and deeply shared value system. Unique, shared values can provide a strong corporate identity, enhance collective commitment, provide a stable social system, and reduce the need for formal and bureaucratic controls. For firms in a very stable domestic environment, several consultants suggest firms develop a "strong culture."[31] By this, they basically mean:

- A widely shared real understanding of what the firm stands for, often embodied in slogans;
- A concern for individuals over rules, policies, procedures, and adherence to job duties;
- A recognition of heroes whose actions illustrate the company's shared philosophy and concerns;
- A belief in ritual and ceremony as important to members and to building a common identity;
- A well-understood sense of the informal rules and expectations so that employees and managers understand what is expected of them;
- A belief that what employees and managers do is important and that it is important to share information and ideas.

A strong culture can be a double-edged sword, however. A strong culture and value system can reinforce a singular view of the organization and its environment. If dramatic changes are needed, it may be very difficult to change the organization. General Motors may have a "strong" culture, for example, but the firm faces enormous difficulty in its attempts to adapt its ways to a dynamic and highly competitive environment.

In many corporate cultures, one finds a series of common assumptions known to most everyone in the corporation: "We are different." "We are better at. . . ." "We have unrecognized talents." Cisco Systems provides an excellent example. Senior managers often share common assumptions, such as "We are good stewards" and "We are competent managers" and "We are practical innovators." Like values, such assumptions become reflected in the organizational culture.

Shared Meanings   When observing the actions within a firm, it is important to keep in mind the three levels of analysis we mentioned earlier. What you see as an outside observer may not be what organizational members experience because members may link actions to values and unstated assumptions. For instance, in the aftermath of 9/11 many saw crane operators moving wreckage from an 18-acre pile of rubble into waiting trucks. Farther up the worksite, many saw steelworkers cutting beams while police seemed to stand around talking to a few firemen. If you probe the values and assumptions about what these individuals are doing, however, you get an entirely different picture. They were not just hauling away the remnants of the twin towers at the World Trade Center complex. They were rebuilding America. These workers had infused a larger shared meaning—or sense of broader purpose—into their tasks. Through interaction

Lam Research

Lam is a major supplier of wafer fabrication equipment and related services to the semiconductor industry. They are very clear about their core values, which include achievement, honesty and integrity, innovation and continuous improvement, mutual trust and respect, open communication, ownership and accountability, teamwork, and think: customer, then company, then individual.

with one another, and as reinforced by the rest of their organizations and the larger society, their work had deeper meaning. In this deeper sense, organizational culture is a "shared" set of meanings and perceptions. In most corporations, these shared meanings and perceptions may not be as dramatic as those shared at Ground Zero, yet in most firms employees create and learn a deeper aspect of their culture.[32]

Organizational Myths   In many firms, the management philosophy is supported by a series of organizational myths. **Organizational myths** are unproven and often unstated beliefs that are accepted uncritically. Often corporate mythology focuses on cause-effect relationships and assertions by senior management that cannot be empirically supported.[33] While some may scoff at organizational myths and want to see rational, hard-nosed analysis replace mythology, each firm needs a series of managerial myths.[34] Myths allow executives to redefine impossible problems into more manageable components. Myths can facilitate experimentation and creativity, and they allow managers to govern. Of course, there is also a potential downside to the power of myths.

Three common myths may combine to present major risk problems.[35] The first common myth is the presumption that at least senior management has *no risk bias*. This myth is often expressed as, "Although others may be biased, I am able to define problems and develop solutions objectively." We are all subject to bias in varying degrees and in varying ways. As an issue becomes more complex it is much more likely there are several biased viable interpretations.

A second common myth is *the presumption of administrative competence*. Managers at all levels are subject to believing that their part of the firm is okay and just needs minor improvements in implementation. As we have documented throughout this book, such is rarely the case. In almost all firms, there is often considerable room for improvement. One particularly damaging manifestation of this myth is that new process and product innovations can be managed in the same way as older ones.

A third common myth is *the denial of trade-offs*. Most managers believe that their group, unit, or firm can avoid making undesirable trade-offs and simultaneously please nearly every constituency. Whereas the denial of trade-offs is common, it can be a dangerous myth in some firms. An emphasis on a single goal often means that other goals are neglected. For example, throughout this book we have emphasized ethics to remind the reader that ethics does not stem from the search for higher efficiency. It is a worthy goal among several.

The myths may be combined in organizational practice. Purposeful unintended consequences arise from the collective application of these three myths by a wide number of individuals.[36] Over the last decade, banks and financial institutions bought and sold mortgage-backed derivatives under the myths that they could (1) accurately judge the risk themselves and value them accurately (they were not risk biased), (2) administer these complex instruments in a manner similar to traditional mortgages (the presumption of administrative competence), and (3) gain great short-term returns without threatening long-term profitability (denial of trade-offs). These combined myths allowed the managers to dismiss collectively the potential of a systematic meltdown of the entire financial system (the unintended consequence). Yet, by the end of 2008 and the beginning of 2009 the global financial system almost collapsed from these and related problems. Was the unintended consequence

• An **organizational myth** is a commonly held cause-effect relationship or assertion that cannot be supported empirically.

How the Mighty Fall

In his new book *How the Mighty Fall*, consultant and author Jim Collins asks what can be learned from the failures of previously great companies. He likens corporate decline to a "disease"–the firm looks good on the outside but is sick on the inside. The first stage of decline is "hubris born of success," a point where arrogance in leadership leads to strategic neglect.

pursued on purpose? Yes and no. No one manager sought a meltdown. Yet, collectively, millions of mortgages were granted to individuals with questionable credit based on the assumption that housing values would increase forever. Derivatives based on these mortgages proliferated. It took unprecedented actions by many central banks and governments to avert a collapse.

And yet, mortgage-backed securities and derivatives were one of the financial system's major innovations toward the turn of the century. They were an important way to broaden the financial support for housing. Initially they appeared quite successful and provided financial institutions with a way to grow and prosper. So, we turn to the topic of innovation to delve more deeply into this important factor for growth and prosperity.

Innovation in Organizations

When analysis stresses commonly shared actions, values, and common assumptions across the entire organization it can appear that firms are static, unchanging entities. It is quite clear that much of the organization's culture and its structure emphasize stability and control. Yet, we all know the world is changing and that firms must change with it. The best organizations don't stagnate; they consistently innovate to the extent that innovation becomes a part of everyday operations.[37]

- **Innovation** is the process of creating new ideas and putting them into practice.

Innovation is the process of creating new ideas and putting them into practice.[38] It is the means by which creative ideas find their way into everyday practices, ideally practices that contribute to improved customer service or organizational productivity. There are a variety of ways to look at innovation. Here, we will examine it as a process, separate product from process innovation, and note the tensions between the early development of ideas and the task of implementation.

The Process of Innovation

The basic steps in a typical process of organizational innovation are shown in Figure 15.2. They include:

1. *Idea creation*—to create an idea through spontaneous creativity, ingenuity, and information processing
2. *Initial experimentation*—to establish the idea's potential value and application
3. *Feasibility determination*—to identify anticipated costs and benefits
4. *Final application*—to produce and market a new product or service, or to implement a new approach to operations

It takes many creative ideas to establish a base for initial experimentation. Moreover, many successful initial experiments are just not feasible. Even among the few feasible ideas, only the rare idea actually makes it into application. Finally, innovative entities benefit from and require top-management support. Senior managers can and must provide good examples for others, eliminate obstacles to innovation, and try to get things done that make innovation easier.

By emphasizing the innovation process, innovative entities often adapt a different culture from the ones typically found where more routine operations are paramount. Innovative entities look to the future, are willing to cannibalize existing products in their development of new ones, have a high tolerance for risk, have

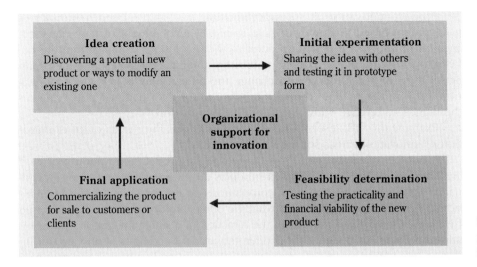

Figure 15.2 The innovation process: a case of new product development.

a high tolerance for mistakes, respect well-intentioned ideas that just do not work, prize creativity, and reward and give special attention to idea generators, information keepers, product champions, and project leaders. They also prize empowerment and emphasize communication up, down, and across all individuals in the unit.[39]

While it is convenient to depict the process as a sequential four-step affair, you should be aware that in practice the process of innovation is often quite messy. With initial experimentation, for instance, the very act of sharing ideas with others can, and often does, yield a completely new set of ideas. Even in final application, the process does not stop, as astute innovators carefully listen to customers and clients to make further improvements.

While the desire to improve financial performance is often important in stimulating innovation, it is also important to note that innovation can arise from the desire of the firm to be more legitimate in the eyes of key stakeholders, such as government regulators. For example, one recent study suggested that pressures from regulators and a prior record of poor environmental performance yielded more innovative environmental responses from firms. There was an exception, however, in that firms with greater slack resources did not respond as positively to regulatory pressures even if they had a record of poorer prior environmental performance.[40]

Product and Process Innovations

Product innovations result in the introduction of new or improved goods or services to better meet customer needs. A number of studies suggest that the key difficulty with product development is the integration across all of the units needed to move from the idea stage to final implementation.[41] Culturally, new product development often challenges existing practice, existing value structures, and common understandings. For instance, by its very definition, product innovation means that the definition of the business will change. Many firms find it difficult to cannibalize their existing product line-up in the hope new products will be even more successful. Yet, this is what often needs to be done.[42]

Product innovations introduce new goods or services to better meet customer needs.

Product innovation is so important that there have been a number of government-based initiatives to help spur the development of new products. Individuals proposing initiatives point to the revolution resulting from the development of the Internet, the hope for new green technologies, and the promise of medical breakthroughs to change the human condition. One important new study suggests that corporate culture, rather than national policy, makes the biggest difference with radical product innovation.

Examine the OB Research Insight as it highlights the results of an examination of innovation across some seventeen nations.[43]

A number of interrelated firms may share the product innovation process.[44] Generally speaking, large complex products are often combinations of individual components from a variety of corporations. At the extreme, there is open innovation where each firm knows what the others are doing. Control is exercised by a common design, often under the direction of a single integrator who maintains the dominant design. This is often the model in computer software, for instance. It is important to note that the development and control of the dominant design can be linked to extremely high profitability.[45] Further, the dominant design is often not the best technical solution—it is the solution most adopted by a large number of users.

Where the product innovation process is less open, firms often find that coordination with lead users can help provide design insights.[46] Yet, firms typically confront waning commitment to product innovation. While no solution is perfect, several studies suggest that the development of multidisciplinary teams can help maintain broader commitment. Of course, just the inclusion of individuals with diverse skills, interests, and perspectives calls for astute management. As we said—the innovation process is far from easy.

- **Process innovations** introduce into operations new and better ways of doing things.

Process innovations result in the introduction of new and better work methods and operations. Perhaps one of the most interesting and difficult types of process improvement is that of management innovation.[47] Obviously, much management innovation comes from the vast industry known as management consulting, Unfortunately, many of the new management practices coming from these outside units are more fashions and fads than workable solutions to the problems faced by individual firms. The key to successful managerial innovation often involves extensive interaction with peers, subordinates, and superiors. As astute managers try new practices they compare initial implementation with the reactions of peers and subordinates to refine and modify the practice. Often this process of trial and error takes several iterations before the practice becomes accepted well enough to provide the intended benefits.

Balancing Exploration and Exploitation

As suggested by Figure 15.2, the innovation continuum runs from exploration to exploitation.[48] In the early stages of innovation, time, energy, and effort to explore potentials are necessary. These early phases are the result of the research and development units found in so many companies. Yet, too much emphasis on exploration will yield a whole list of potential ideas for new products and processes to new clients and customers in new markets, but little pay-off. It is also important to stress *exploitation* to capture the economic value stemming from exploration.[49] **Exploitation** often focuses on refinement and reuse of existing

- **Exploitation** focuses on refinement and reuse of existing products and processes.

The Role of Firm and National Factors in Dramatic Product Innovations

Gerard Tellis, Jaideep Prabhu, and Rajesh Chandy examined the potential importance of a number of national and firm factors typically associated with dramatic product innovations for some 750 firms in 17 different nations. Specifically they examined cultural, labor, and capital based measures for each firm and each nation.

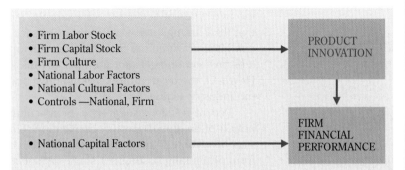

The researchers found that a firm's culture was the most important predictor of innovation and it was also related to the firm's subsequent financial performance. The important firm cultural factors included the willingness to cannibalize existing products, a strong emphasis on future markets, a high tolerance for risk, the grooming of product champions, and the implementation of incentives for innovation.

Tellis, et al. also found that the industry of the firm and its history of patents were far less important than expected. It was the firm culture that mattered for innovation. And they found that national capital factors and the population size of the nation were related to the financial performance of the firm.

The schematic depicts their initial model of national and firm factors predicting innovation.

What Do You Think?

Does this model and research do a good job of exploring how firm and national factors can influence product innovation? What further questions on this topic might you suggest for attention by researchers? Is there a difference between what is needed for an innovation and what is needed for making the innovation pay off financially?

Source: Gerard J. Tellis, Jaideep C. Prabhu, & Rajesh K. Chandy, "Radical Innovation Across Nations: The Preeminence of Corporate Culture," *Journal of Marketing*, (2009) Vol. 73 #1, pp. 3–23.

products and processes. Refining an existing product to make it more saleable in a new market is an example of exploitation. Of course, too much emphasis on exploitation and the firm loses its competitive edge because its products become obsolete and its processes less effective and efficient than those of competitors.

The admonition to balance exploration and exploitation sounds very simple but it comes with a major problem. **Exploration** calls for the organization and its managers to stress freedom and radical thinking and therefore opens the firm to big changes—or what some call radical innovations.[50] While some radical departures are built upon existing competencies, often the adoption of a radically new product or process means that the existing knowledge within a firm is invalidated.[51] Conversely, an emphasis on exploitation stresses control and evolutionary development. Such exploitation can be planned with tight budgets, careful

Exploration calls for the organization and its managers to stress freedom and radical thinking and therefore opens the firm to big changes—or what some call radical innovations.

forecasts, and steady implementation. It is often much easier to stress exploitation because most organizations have a structure and culture that emphasize stability and control.[52]

Managers may attempt to solve this tension between exploration and exploitation in a variety of ways. One partial solution is to have separate units for the two types of activities. For example, some firms rely heavily upon cooperative R&D arrangements with other firms for exploration and keep a tight rein on exploitation within the firm.[53] Others rely upon middle managers to reconcile the tensions stemming from attempts to link explorative and exploitative groups. However, the desired mix of explorative and exploitative may well depend upon the industry setting.

Recent research suggests a more culturally oriented solution based on the notion of an ambidextrous organization. First, managers must recognize the tension between exploration and exploitation. Second, they should realize that one form of thinking based on a single perspective is inappropriate. Third, managers need to discuss with their subordinates the paradoxes arising from simultaneously thinking about big ideas and sound incremental improvements. Fourth, managers must encourage subordinates to embrace these paradoxes and use them as motivations to provide creative solutions.[54]

Managing Organizational Culture and Innovation

Good managers are able to reinforce and support an existing strong culture. They are also able to help build resilient cultures in situations where they are absent. The best managers also recognize that effectively managing organization culture involves incorporation of the innovation process as well.

MASTERING MANAGEMENT

BECOMING A BETTER CULTURE MANAGER

To develop a strong management culture, consider the following:

- Emphasize a shared understanding of what the unit stands for.
- Stress a concern for members over rules and procedures.
- Talk about heroes of the past and their contributions.
- Develop rituals and ceremonies for the members.
- Reinforce informal rules and expectations consistent with shared values.
- Promote the sharing of ideas and information.
- Provide employees with emotional support.
- Make a commitment to understand all members.
- Support progressive thinking by all members.

Management Philosophy and Strategy

The process of managing organizational culture calls for a clear understanding of the organizational subculture at the top and a firm recognition of what can and cannot be changed. The first step in managing an organizational culture is for management to recognize its own subculture. Key aspects of the top-management subculture are often referred to in the OB literature by the term management philosophy. A **management philosophy** links key goal-related strategic issues with key collaboration issues and comes up with a series of general ways by which the firm will manage its affairs.[55] A well-developed management philosophy is important because it links strategy to a more basic understanding of how the firm is to operate. Specifically, it (1) establishes generally understood boundaries for all members of the firm, (2) provides a consistent way of approaching new and novel situations, and (3) helps hold individuals together by assuring them of a known path toward success. In other words, it is the way in which top management addresses the questions of external adaptation.

> A **management philosophy** links key goal-related issues with key collaboration issues to come up with general ways by which the firm will manage its affairs.

When the management philosophy stresses security and stability, management reinforces such values as benevolence. Such firms tend to be less innovative than when the management philosophy is more self-directive and reinforces risk taking. When the management philosophy stresses reaching out to others, embracing novel situations, and collectively developing a new path toward new visions of success, there is greater innovation.[56]

For instance, Cisco Systems has a clearly identified management philosophy linking the strategic concerns of growth, profitability, and customer service with observable aspects of culture and selected desired underlying values. In the case of Cisco Systems' growth and profitability, customer service is linked to (1) empowering employees to generate the best ideas quickly and to implement them successfully, (2) hiring the best people because the ideas and intellectual assets of these colleagues drive success, and (3) developing and disseminating information to compete in the world of ideas. While elements of a management philosophy may be formally documented in a corporate plan or statement of business philosophy, it is the well-understood fundamentals these written documents signify that form the heart of a well-developed management philosophy.[57]

Building, Reinforcing, and Changing Culture

Managers can modify the visible aspects of culture, such as the language, stories, rites, rituals, and sagas. They can change the lessons drawn from common stories and even encourage individuals to see the reality they see. Because of their positions, senior managers can interpret situations in new ways and can adjust the meanings attached to important corporate events. They can create new rites and rituals. Executives can back these initiatives with both their words and their actions. This takes time and enormous energy, but the long-run benefits can also be great.

One of the key ways management influences the organizational culture is via the reward systems it establishes. In many larger U.S.-based firms the reward system matches the overall strategy of the firm and reinforces the culture emerging from day-to-day activities. Two patterns of reward systems, strategies, and

Culture at
Cousin's Subs

Christine Specht, the Chief Operating Officer of Cousin's Subs, notes the importance of culture and her intention to keep stressing the key attributes her father instilled. She notes, "Our food is better; our sandwiches are bigger. More importantly, they are made by people who really care about serving the guests. . . . we have a great organizational culture of people who really care about the company and the guest."

corporate cultures are common. The first is a steady-state strategy matched with hierarchal rewards and consistent with what can be labeled a clan culture.

Specifically, rewards emphasize and reinforce a culture characterized by long-term commitment, fraternal relationships, mutual interests, and collegiality with heavy pressures to conform from peers and with superiors acting as mentors. Firms with this pattern were in such industries as power generation, chemicals, mining, and pharmaceuticals. In contrast was a second pattern where the strategy stressed evolution and change. Here the rewards emphasized and reinforced a more market culture. That is, rewards emphasized a contractual link between employee and employer, focused on short-term performance, and stressed individual initiative with very little pressures from peers to conform and with supervisors acting as resource allocators. Firms with this pattern were often in such industries as restaurants, consumer products, and industrial services.[58]

Beyond reward systems, top managers can set the tone for a culture and for cultural change. Managers at Aetna Life and Casualty Insurance built on its humanistic traditions to provide basic skills to highly motivated but under-qualified individuals. Even in the highly cost-competitive steel industry, Nucor executives built on basic entrepreneurial values in U.S. society to reduce the number of management levels by half.

Each of these examples illustrates how managers can help foster a culture that provides answers to important questions concerning external adaptation and internal integration. Recent work on the linkages between corporate culture and financial performance reaffirms the importance of an emphasis on helping employees adjust to the environment. It also suggests that this emphasis alone is not sufficient. Neither is an emphasis solely on stockholders or customers associated with long-term economic performance. Instead, managers must work to emphasize all three issues simultaneously.

The need to provide a balanced emphasis can be seen when executives violate ethical and legal standards as in the case of misleading earning statements. One key study found that while the fines levied for "cooking the books" may appear small, other costs were far more substantial. The real costs to these firms came from a loss of the reputation in the business community. Customers lost confidence, suppliers demanded greater assurances, and, of course, the entire financial community undervalued the firm so that loan costs were higher, stock prices were lower, and scrutiny was more extensive. How big is big? The fines averaged about $23 million a firm. The estimated financial cost from the loss of reputation was estimated at 7.5 times the average fine. That yielded a loss of some $196 million.[59]

Early research on culture and cultural change often emphasized direct attempts by senior management to alter the values and assumptions of individuals by re-socializing them—that is, trying to change their hearts so that their minds and actions would follow.[60] The goal was to establish a clear, consistent organization-wide consensus. More recent work suggests that this unified approach of working through values may not be either possible or desirable.[61]

Trying to change people's values from the top down without also changing how the organization operates and recognizes the importance of individuals does not work very well. Look again at the example of Cisco Systems. Here managers realized that maintaining a dynamic, change-oriented culture is a mix of managerial actions, decisions about technology, and initiatives from all employees. The values are not set and imposed from someone on high. The shared values emerge, and they are not identical across all of Cisco's operating sites. For instance, subtle but important differences emerge across their operations in Silicon Valley, the North Carolina operation, and the Australian setting.

It is also a mistake for managers to attempt to revitalize an organization by dictating major changes and ignoring shared values. Although things may change a bit on the surface, a deeper look often shows whole departments resisting change and many key people unwilling to learn new ways. Such responses may indicate that the managers responsible are insensitive to the effects of their proposed changes on shared values. They fail to ask whether the changes are contrary to the important values of participants within the firm, a challenge to historically important corporatewide assumptions, and inconsistent with important common assumptions derived from the national culture, outside the firm.

Tensions Between Cultural Stability and Innovation

While organizational cultures help individuals cope with external adaptation and internal integration, the enduring pattern of observable actions, shared values, and common assumptions often does not evolve as quickly as required by innovations. **Organizational cultural lag** is a condition where dominant cultural patterns are inconsistent with new emerging innovations.[62] As we suggested earlier, observable aspects of organizational culture such as rites, rituals, and cultural symbols often have powerful underlying meaning to organizational members. In a way they are symbols of prior successful ways to cope with external adaptation and internal integration. Individuals are often wary of abandoning the successful for an unproven new approach. One scholar notes that there can be a major "cultural drag on innovation from cultural legacies."[63] These legacy effects come from an overreliance on rule following and reinforcement of old existing patterns of action.

Thus, one of the key challenges to management in promoting innovation where there are widely held and strong attached-to shared values and common assumptions is to show how they apply to the new innovations. When managers see an opportunity to develop new visions, create new strategies, and move the organization in new directions, they need to balance rule changing and rule following.[64] If left uncontrolled, rule changing can yield run-away industry change that can quickly lead to chaos. While rule following can lead to a more stable industry structure and/or controlled industry change, there is also a danger of reinforcing cultural lag.

> **Organizational cultural lag** is a condition where dominant cultural patterns are inconsistent with new emerging innovations.

Resources in
The OB Skills
Workbook

These learning activities from *The OB Skills Workbook* are suggested for Chapter 15.

Case for Critical Thinking	Team and Experiential Exercises	Self-Assessment Portfolio
• Never on Sunday	• How We View Differences	• Are You Cosmopolitan?
	• Workgroup Culture	• Team Effectiveness
	• Fast-Food Technology	• Which Culture Fits You?
	• Alien Invasion	

15 study guide

Summary Questions and Answers

What is organizational culture?

- Organizational or corporate culture is the system of shared actions, values, and beliefs that develops within an organization and guides the behavior of its members.

- The functions of the corporate culture include responding to both external adaptation and internal integration issues.

- Most organizations contain a variety of subcultures, and a few have countercultures that can sometimes become the source of potentially harmful conflicts.

- The corporate culture also reflects the values and implicit assumptions of the larger national culture.

How do you understand an organizational culture?

- Organizational cultures may be analyzed in terms of observable actions, shared values, and common assumptions (the taken-for-granted truths).

- Observable aspects of culture include the stories, rites, rituals, and symbols that are shared by organization members.

- Cultural rules and roles specify when various types of actions are appropriate and where individual members stand in the social system.

- Shared meanings and understandings help everyone know how to act and expect others to act in various circumstances.

- Common assumptions are the taken-for-granted truths that are shared by collections of corporate members.

What is innovation, and why is it important?

- Innovation is the process of creating new ideas and then implementing them in practical applications.

- Steps in the innovation process normally include idea generation, initial experimentation, feasibility determination, and final application.

- Common features of highly innovative organizations include supportive strategies, cultures, structures, staffing, and senior leadership.

- Product innovations result in improved goods or services; process innovations result in improved work methods and operations.

- Process innovations introduce into operations new and better ways of doing things.

- While it is necessary to balance exploration and exploitation, it is difficult to accomplish.

How to manage organizational culture and innovation

- Executives may manage many aspects of the observable culture directly.

- Nurturing shared values among the membership is a major challenge for executives.

- Adjusting actions to common understandings limits the decision scope of even the CEO.

- There are tensions between the tendency for cultural stability in most firms and the need to innovate.

Key Terms

Countercultures (p. 369)
Cultural symbol (p. 373)
Exploitation (p. 378)
Exploration (p. 379)
External adaptation
    (p. 366)
Innovation (p. 376)
Internal integration
    (p. 367)

Management philosophy
    (p. 381)
Multicultural organization
    (p. 371)
Observable culture (p. 371)
Organizational cultural lag
    (p. 383)
Organizational or corporate
    culture (p. 366)

Organizational myth (p. 375)
Process innovations (p. 378)
Product innovations (p. 377)
Rites (p. 372)
Rituals (p. 373)
Sagas (p. 372)
Subcultures (p. 368)

Self-Test 15

Multiple Choice

1. Culture concerns all of the following except _____. (a) the collective concepts shared by members of a firm (b) acquired capabilities (c) the personality of the leader (d) the beliefs of members

2. The three levels of cultural analysis highlighted in the text concern _____. (a) observable culture, shared values, and common assumptions (b) stories, rites, and rituals (c) symbols, myths, and stories (d) manifest culture, latent culture, and observable artifacts

3. External adaptation concerns _____. (a) the unproven beliefs of senior executives (b) the process of coping with outside forces (c) the vision of the founder (d) the processes working together

4. Internal integration concerns _____. (a) the process of deciding the collective identity and how members will live together (b) the totality of the daily life of members as they see and describe it (c) expressed unproven beliefs that are accepted uncritically and used to justify current actions (d) groups of individuals with a pattern of values that rejects those of the larger society

5. When Japanese workers start each day with the company song, this is an example of a(n) _____. (a) symbol (b) myth (c) underlying assumption (d) ritual

6. _____ is a sense of broader purpose that workers infuse into their tasks as a result of interaction with one another. (a) A rite (b) A cultural symbol (c) A foundation myth (d) A shared meaning

7. The story of a corporate turnaround attributed to the efforts of a visionary manager is an example of _____. (a) a saga (b) a foundation myth (c) internal integration (d) a latent cultural artifact

8. The process of creating new ideas and putting them into practice is _____. (a) innovation (b) creative destruction (c) product innovation (d) process innovation

9. Any object, act, or event that serves to transmit cultural meaning is called _____. (a) a saga (b) a cultural symbol (c) a cultural lag (d) a cultural myth

10. Groups where the patterns of values outwardly reject those of the larger organization are _____. (a) external adaptation rejectionist (b) cultural lag (c) countercultures (d) organizational myths

11. Groups with unique patterns of values and philosophies that are consistent with the dominant organizational culture are called _____. (a) countercultures (b) subcultures (c) sagas (d) rituals

12. A _____ links key goal-related issues with key collaboration issues to come up with general ways by which the firm will manage its affairs. (a) managerial philosophy (b) cultural symbol (c) ritual (d) saga

13. Commonly held cause-effect relationships that cannot be empirically supported are referred to as _____. (a) cultural lags (b) rituals (c) management philosophy (d) organizational myths

14. The patterns of values and philosophies that outwardly reject those of the larger organization or social system are called _____. (a) sagas (b) organizational development (c) rituals (d) countercultures

15. _____ is a condition where dominant cultural patterns are inconsistent with new emerging innovations. (a) Organizational cultural lag (b) Management philosophy (c) Internal integration (d) External adaptation

Short Response

16. Describe the five steps Taylor Cox suggests need to be developed to help generate a multicultural organization or pluralistic company culture.

17. List the three aspects that help individuals and groups work together effectively and illustrate them through practical examples.

18. Give an example of how cultural rules and roles affect the atmosphere in a college classroom. Provide specific examples from your own perspective.

19. What are the major elements of a strong corporate culture?

Applications Essay

20. Discuss why managers should balance exploration and exploitation when seeking greater innovation.

16

Organizational Goals and Structures

n the US, Southwest Airlines' low-cost, no-frills approach to domestic air travel and the unconventional personality of its founder, Herb Kelleher, took the country's airline industry by storm. Even through tough economic times it achieved an unprecedented thirty five consecutive years of profit from 1973 to 2008.

Ryanair, Europe's low-cost, no frills, short-haul airline based in Dublin, Ireland also has a CEO with a colorful personality and, while it has broken into the European market successfully, the similarities end there.

In 2006 Ryanair was voted the world's most disliked airline, a title that causes more amusement than worry to CEO Michael O'Leary, described alternately as charming and offensive. One of the most successful businessmen in Ireland, O'Leary

is "known for thick-skinned aggression, outrageous public statements and an implacable belief that short-haul airline passengers will endure nearly every imaginable indignity as long as the tickets are cheap and the planes are on time."[1]

To O'Leary, "no frills" means bare-bones travel—no seat-back recliners or seat-back products. Almost every service comes at a charge such as online check-in, luggage check-in, a wheelchair charge, and charges for in-flight drinks and food. Always looking to push the low-cost strategy further, he's planning on decreasing the number of toilets on board and charging for their use, levying a "fat tax" for passengers that exceed the airline's standard body weight, and eventually having passengers carry their own luggage to the aircraft.

He takes "low-cost" to the extreme in both the airline's pricing model as well as its approach to management. Staff pay for their own training, uniforms, meals and unionization is not allowed. This management style has lead to low employee morale, high turnover and poor customer service.

Yet stellar customer service isn't what Ryanair promises. They promise low fares, on-time departure and arrival, few cancellations and few lost bags.

And right now anyhow, many air travelers seem to be okay with that because Ryanair, despite disgruntled employees and offended customers, continues to succeed as the low-cost leader in Europe's airline industry. This is in stark contrast to the airline mentioned at the beginning of this case—Southwest Airlines.

Both airlines share a common goal—be the most successful low-cost leader in their respective markets and both have achieved that goal. However, the manner in which they've each pursued that goal demonstrates the multiple means by which our goals can be reached. Southwest is admired for its employee-centered culture and for its zany, but friendly customer service while Ryanair is criticized for its stingy employee policies and for its poor treatment of customers.

ryanair's thrifty take on air travel stirs controversy

Organizational Goals

The notion that organizations have goals is very familiar to us simply because our world is one of organizations.[2] Most of us are born, go to school, work, and retire in organizations. Without organizations and their limited, goal-directed behavior, modern societies would simply cease to function. We would need to revert to older forms of social organization based on royalty, clans, and tribes. Organizational goals are so pervasive we rarely give them more than passing notice. Michael O'Leary, CEO of Ryanair, is very clear about his organization's goals and how to achieve them. Simply put, Ryanair is the first and most successful low-cost, no-frills European airline.

While the company wins no awards as a friendly, customer-centered airline, it has attracted the attention of the industry and, from its various questionable marketing campaigns, the media. But again, O'Leary is clear about his company's goal—no frills means no frills and low cost is a culture that is well engrained in each area of the organization's operations. No one—customers, competitors, shareholders, or employees are surprised by O'Leary's decisions or policies because they match the company goals quite well.

No firm can be all things to all people. By selecting goals, firms also define who they are and what they will try to become. The choice of goals involves the type of contribution the firm makes to the larger society and the types of outputs it seeks. Managers decide how to link conditions considered desirable for enhanced survival prospects with its societal and output desires.[3] From these basic choices, executives can work with subordinates to develop ways of accomplishing the chosen targets. As we saw with Force 10 Hoops, LLC, the goals of the firm should be consistent and compatible with the way in which it is organized.

- **Societal goals** reflect the intended contributions of an organization to the broader society.
- **Mission statements** are written statements of organizational purpose.

Societal Goals

Hope Labs

Pam Omidyar, an immunology researcher and gaming enthusiast, founded the nonprofit Hope Labs, to "improve the health and quality of life of young people with chronic illness." It produced the video game Re-Mission where players move the nanorobot Roxxi through the body of a cancer patient to destroy cancer cells. The game helps young patient stick to their medication schedules.

Organizations do not operate in a social vacuum but rather they reflect the needs and desires of the societies in which they operate. **Societal goals** reflect an organization's intended contributions to the broader society.[4] Organizations normally serve a specific societal function or an enduring need of the society. Astute top-level managers build on the professed societal contribution of the organization by relating specific organizational tasks and activities to higher purposes. By contributing to the larger society, organizations gain legitimacy, a social right to operate, and more discretion for their nonsocietal goals and operating practices. By claiming to provide specific types of societal contributions, an organization can also make legitimate claims over resources, individuals, markets, and products. For instance, would you not want a higher salary to work for a tobacco firm than a health food store? Tobacco firms are heavily taxed and under increasing pressure for regulation because their societal contribution is highly questionable.

Often, the social contribution of the firm is a part of its mission statement. **Mission statements** are written statements of organizational purpose. Weaving a mission statement together with an emphasis on implementation to provide direction and motivation is an executive order of the first magnitude. A good mission statement says whom the firm will serve and how it will go about accomplishing its societal purpose.[5]

We would expect to see the mission statement of a political party linked to generating and allocating power for the betterment of citizens. Mission statements for universities often profess to both develop and disseminate knowledge. Courts are expected to integrate the interests and activities of citizens. Finally, business firms are expected to provide economic sustenance and material well-being.[6]

Organizations that can more effectively translate the positive character of their societal contribution into a favorable image have an advantage over firms that neglect this sense of purpose. Executives who link their firm to a desirable mission can lay claim to important motivational tools that are based on a shared sense of noble purpose. Some executives and consultants talk of a "strategic vision" which links highly desirable and socially appealing goals to the contributions a firm intends to make.[7] The first step, as shown in Mastering Management 16.1, is a clear compelling mission statement.

ATA Engineering Inc.

ATA is a small engineering consulting firm in San Diego. Its 84 employees are all owners and the organization is designed for collaboration and teamwork. When a job candidate is interviewed, at least 8–10 staffers participate; an objection by any one will veto the candidate.

Output Goals

Organizations need to refine their societal contributions in order to target their efforts toward a particular group.[8] In the United States, for example, it is generally expected that the primary beneficiary of business firms is the stockholder. Interestingly, in Japan employees are much more important, and stockholders are considered as important as banks and other financial institutions. Although each organization may have a primary beneficiary, its mission statement may also recognize the interests of many other parties. Thus, business mission statements often include service to customers, the organization's obligations to employees, and its intention to support the community.

As managers consider how they will accomplish their firm's mission, many begin with a very clear statement of which business they are in.[9] This statement can form the basis for long-term planning and may help prevent huge organizations from diverting too many resources to peripheral areas. For some corporations, answering the question of which business they are in may yield a more

---

MASTERING MANAGEMENT 16.1

SETTING THE MISSION

One key managerial skill is setting desirable, realistic, and achievable goals. This starts with a mission statement that should be short, link highly desirable and socially appealing goals to the focus of the unit, and state the contributions intended.

Lobar Inc. is one of the few private Pennsylvania-based family-owned general contractors. Lobar, a forty-year-old, third-generation firm has become a multi-million dollar enterprise concentrating on construction services for Pennsylvania, Maryland, New Jersey, New York, and West Virginia. Their mission statement is quite clear: ". . . to provide superior construction services." Historically, Lobar managers have added to this simple statement by striving for excellence in customer relations and construction quality. They want prospective customers to want Lobar, Inc. to do their construction project no matter how large or small.

• **Output goals** are the goals that define the type of business an organization is in.

detailed statement concerning their products and services. These product and service goals provide an important basis for judging the firm. **Output goals** define the type of business an organization is in and provide some substance to the more general aspects of mission statements.

Systems Goals

Historically, fewer than 10 percent of the privately owned businesses founded in a typical year can be expected to survive to their twentieth birthday.[10] The survival rate for public organizations is not much better. Even in organizations for which survival is not an immediate problem, managers seek specific types of conditions within their firms that minimize the risk of demise and promote survival. These conditions are positively stated as systems goals.

• **Systems goals** are concerned with conditions within the organization that are expected to increase its survival potential.

Systems goals are concerned with the conditions within the organization that are expected to increase the organization's survival potential. The list of systems goals is almost endless, since each manager and researcher links today's conditions to tomorrow's existence in a different way. For many organizations, however, the list includes growth, productivity, stability, harmony, flexibility, prestige, and human-resource maintenance. In some businesses, analysts consider market share and current profitability important systems goals. Other recent studies suggest that innovation and quality are also considered important.[11]

In a very practical sense, systems goals represent short-term organizational characteristics that higher-level managers wish to promote. Systems goals often must be balanced against one another. For instance, a productivity and efficiency drive, if taken too far, may reduce the flexibility of an organization even in a downturn. For example, PepsiCo's CEO Indra Nooyi, eliminated plants and over 3,000 jobs, yet she also knows she must expand PepsiCo's operations in China.[12]

Often different parts of the organization are asked to pursue different types of systems goals. For example, higher-level managers may expect to see their production operations strive for efficiency while pressing for innovation from their R&D lab and promoting stability in their financial affairs. The relative importance of different systems goals can vary substantially across various types of organizations. Although we may expect the University of British Columbia or the University of New South Wales to emphasize prestige and innovation, few expect such businesses as Pepsi or Coke to subordinate growth and profitability to prestige. We expect to see some societal expectations and output desires used to justify the incorporation of some systems goals.

Systems goals are important to firms because they provide a road map that helps them link together various units of their organization to assure survival. Well-defined systems goals are practical and easy to understand; they focus the manager's attention on what needs to be done. Accurately stated systems goals also offer managers flexibility in devising ways to meet important targets. They can be used to balance the demands, constraints, and opportunities facing the firm. Recent research suggests incorporating integrity and ethics into the desired system goals characteristics.

The choices managers make regarding systems goals should naturally form a basis for dividing the work of the firm—a basis for developing a formal structure. In other words, to insure success, management needs to match decisions regarding what to accomplish with choices concerning an appropriate way to reach these goals.

THE BUSINESS CASE FOR INTEGRITY AND ETHICS AS SYSTEM GOALS

One of the important keystones for promoting ethical behavior is integrity. Very simply, integrity is a match between the statements of an individual and his or her actions. Recently a group of OB researchers asked whether there was any link between managerial integrity and the satisfaction and commitment of their subordinates and whether there might be differences across nations.

Across a dozen studies in different types of firms and different nations, the answer was the same. The greater the degree of managerial integrity, as judged by subordinates, the higher the satisfaction and commitment. So what has this to do with ethics? Many studies are documenting the important business case for firms to be ethical. If executives want key employees to stay, then it is smart, as well as right, to promote integrity.

> *Is It All about Integrity? If it is both smart and right to promote integrity, why do managers say it is so difficult to maintain their integrity? How would changing circumstances make managerial integrity a challenge?*

Hierarchy and Control

The formal structure shows the planned configuration of positions, job duties, and the lines of authority among different parts of the enterprise.[13] The configuration selected provides the organization with specific strengths to reach toward some goals more than others. Traditionally, the formal structure of the firm has also been called the division of labor. Some still use this terminology to isolate decisions concerning formal structure from choices regarding the division of markets and/or technology. We will deal with environmental and technology issues after we discuss the structure as a foundation for managerial action. Here, we emphasize that the formal structure outlines the jobs to be done, the person(s) (in terms of position) who is (are) to perform specific activities, and the ways the total tasks of the organization are to be accomplished. In other words, the formal structure is the skeleton of the firm. See Leaders on Leadership on the structural change instituted by Irene Rosenfeld, CEO of Kraft Foods.

Organizations as Hierarchies

In larger organizations, there is a clear separation of authority and duties by hierarchical rank. That is, firms are vertically specialized. This separation represents **vertical specialization**, a hierarchical division of labor that distributes formal authority and establishes where and how critical decisions are to be made. This division creates a hierarchy of authority—an arrangement of work positions in order of increasing authority.[14]

The Organization Chart   **Organization charts** are diagrams that depict the formal structures of organizations. A typical chart shows the various positions, the position holders, and the lines of authority that link them to one another.

* **Vertical specialization** is a hierarchical division of labor that distributes formal authority.

* **Organization charts** are diagrams that depict the formal structures of organizations.

Leaders on Leadership

IRENE ROSENFELD CHAIRMAN AND CEO KRAFT FOODS

Kraft is the newest old firm you know well. On April 2, 2007 Kraft Foods became an independent firm (a spin-off from a large conglomerate) with Irene Rosenfeld as its CEO. She promised a new Kraft Foods with a company built upon great people and iconic brands that would consistently deliver top-tier performance. Kraft Foods has some of the best known brands in the United States including Kraft cheeses, Maxwell House coffees, Oscar Mayer meats, Jell-O, Kool-Aid, and, of course Oreo cookies (one of Irene's favorites). Kraft Foods is the world's second largest food company with annual revenues of $42 billion

and some 100,000 employees operating across 150 countries.

As the new/old firm became independent, CEO Rosenfeld took a hard look at the strategy and structure of the emerging food giant. Some brands did not seem to fit well into the overall business and were eliminated. This included Post Cereals. Others needed a fresh approach. To create a reliable, consistent platform for growth she led the effort to fundamentally change the structure. She stressed a mindset of candor, courage, and action to open honest discussion. The goal: to learn from what is working well and fix what is not working. The challenge: to strike a balance between global and local decision making. The result: putting more decision making in the hands of local market leaders.

Along with decentralization, each product and brand leader was asked to refocus on emerging trends to "reframe" each category of products to

make each more relevant to consumers. To balance the emphasis on individual products, CEO Rosenfeld also stresses the potential power of Kraft as an organization. She initiated a new sales initiative to give store managers a single point of contact for all Kraft products. This initiative helps Kraft leverage overall growth across all brands. Further, she recognized the necessity to constantly drive down costs without compromising quality. The overall slogan to capture her multi-pronged approach: Make Today Delicious.

So how has the new Kraft done? In 2007 Irene was named Chairman in addition to CEO. The latest financial results for the first-quarter of 2009 showed that profits rose 10 percent, beating analyst predictions. As Edward Jones analyst Matt Arnold noted, "Rosenfeld's restructuring has made Kraft more entrepreneurial and less centralized."

Figure 16.1 presents a partial organization chart for a large university. The total chart allows university employees to locate their positions in the structure and to identify the lines of authority linking them with others in the organization. For instance, in this figure, the treasurer reports to the vice president of administration, who, in turn, reports to the president of the university.

While an organization chart may clearly indicate who reports to whom, it is also important to recognize that it does not show how work is completed, who exercises the most power over specific issues, or how the firm will respond to its environment. An organization chart is just the beginning to an understanding

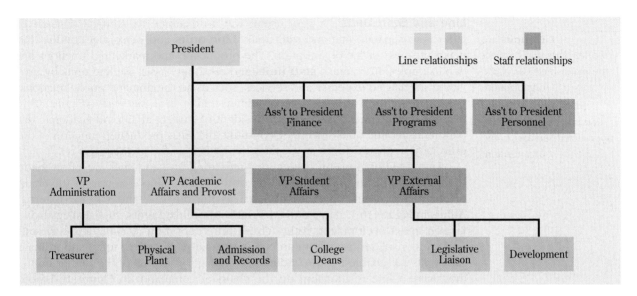

Figure 16.1 A partial organization chart for a state university.

of how a firm organizes its work. In firms facing constant change, the formal chart may be quickly out of date. However, organization charts can be important to the extent that they accurately represent the "chain of command."

The chain of command is a listing of who reports to whom up and down the firm and shows how executives, managers, and supervisors are hierarchically connected. Traditional management theory suggests that each individual should have one boss and each unit one leader. Under these circumstances, there is a "unity of command." Unity of command is considered necessary to avoid confusion, to assign accountability to specific individuals, and to provide clear channels of communication up and down the organization.

Span of Control   The number of individuals reporting to a supervisor is called the **span of control**. Narrower spans of control are expected when tasks are complex, when subordinates are inexperienced or poorly trained, or when tasks call for team effort. Unfortunately, narrow spans of control yield many organizational levels. The excessive number of levels is not only expensive, but it also makes the organization unresponsive to necessary change. Communications in such firms often become less effective because they are successively screened and modified so that subtle but important changes are ignored. Furthermore, with many levels, managers are removed from the action and become isolated.

New information technologies now allow organizations to broaden the span of control, flatten their formal structures, and still maintain control of complex operations. At Nucor, for instance, senior managers pioneered the development of "minimills" for making steel and developed what they call "lean" management. At the same time, management has expanded the span of control with extensive employee education and training backed by sophisticated information systems. The result: Nucor has four levels of management from the bottom to the top.[15]

* **Span of control** refers to the number of individuals reporting to a supervisor.

> • **Line units** are workgroups that conduct the major business of the organization.
>
> • **Staff units** assist the line units by performing specialized services to the organization.

Line and Staff Units   A very useful way to examine the vertical division of labor is to separate line and staff units. **Line units** and personnel conduct the major business of the organization. The production and marketing functions are two examples. In contrast, **staff units** and personnel assist the line units by providing specialized expertise and services, such as accounting and public relations. For example, the vice president of administration in a university (Figure 16.1) heads a staff unit, as does the vice president of student affairs. All academic departments are line units since they constitute the basic production function of the university.

Two additional useful distinctions regarding line and staff are often made in firms. One distinction is the nature of the relationship of a unit in the chain of command. A staff department, such as the office of the V.P. for External Affairs in Figure 16.1, may be divided into subordinate units, such as Legislative Liaison and Development. Although all units reporting to a higher-level staff unit are considered staff from an organizational perspective, some subordinate staff units are charged with conducting the major business of the higher unit—they have a line relationship up the chain of command. In Figure 16.1 both Legislative Liaison and Development are staff units with a line relationship to the unit immediately above them in the chain of command—the V.P. for External Affairs. Why the apparent confusion? It is a matter of history, with the notion of line and staff originally coming from the military with its emphasis on command. In a military sense, the V.P. for External Affairs is the commander of this staff effort—the individual responsible for this activity and the one held accountable.

A second useful distinction for both line and staff units concerns the amount and types of contacts each maintains with outsiders to the organization. Some units are mainly internal in orientation; others are more external in focus. In general, internal line units (e.g., production) focus on transforming raw materials and information into products and services, whereas external line units (e.g., marketing) focus on maintaining linkages to suppliers, distributors, and customers. Internal staff units (e.g., accounting) assist the line units in performing their function. Normally, they specialize in specific technical or financial areas. External staff units (e.g., public relations) also assist the line units, but the focus of their actions is on linking the firm to its environment and buffering internal operations. To recap: the Legislative Liaison unit is external staff with a line relationship to the office of the V.P. for External Affairs.

Staff units can be assigned predominantly to senior-, middle-, or lower-level managers. When staff is assigned predominantly to senior management, the capability of senior management to develop alternatives and make decisions is expanded. When staff is at the top, senior executives can directly develop information and alternatives and check on the implementation of their decisions. Here, the degree of vertical specialization in the firm is comparatively lower because senior managers plan, decide, and control via their centralized staff. With new information technologies, fewer firms are placing most staff at the top. They are replacing internal staff with information systems and placing talented individuals farther down the hierarchy. For instance, executives at giant international glass bottle maker OI have shifted staff from top management to middle management. When staff are moved to the middle of the organization, middle managers now have the specialized help necessary to expand their role.

Cooperative Land O' Lakes

Land O' Lakes, the butter company you know from the grocery store, is a cooperative that sells dairy products and helps farmer members buy supplies. The cooperative is organized into divisions for (a) dairy operations, (b) feed, (c) seed, and (d) crop nutrients and crop protection products.

Many firms are also beginning to ask whether certain staff should be a permanent part of the organization at all. Some are outsourcing many of their staff functions. Manufacturing firms are spinning off much of their accounting, personnel, and public relations activities to small, specialized firms.[16] Outsourcing by large firms has been a boon for smaller corporations.

For some time, firms have used information technology to streamline operations and reduce staff to lower costs and raise productivity.[17] One way to facilitate these actions is to provide line managers and employees with information and managerial techniques designed to expand on their analytical and decision-making capabilities—that is, to replace internal staff.[18]

Controls Are a Basic Feature

When considering the firm's hierarchy, vertical specialization with its division of labor that distributes formal authority is only half of the picture. Distributing formal authority calls for control. **Control** is the set of mechanisms used to keep action or outputs within predetermined limits. Control deals with setting standards, measuring results versus standards, and instituting corrective action. We should stress that effective control occurs before action actually begins. For instance, in setting standards, managers must decide what will be measured and how accomplishment will be determined. While there are a wide variety of organizational controls, they are roughly divided into output, process, and social controls.

- **Control** is the set of mechanisms used to keep actions and outputs within predetermined limits.

Output Controls   Earlier in this chapter, we suggested that systems goals are a road map that ties together the various units of the organization to achieve a practical objective. Developing targets or standards, measuring results against these targets, and taking corrective action are all steps involved in developing output controls.[19] **Output controls** focus on desired targets and allow managers to use their own methods to reach defined targets. Most modern organizations use output controls as part of an overall method of managing by exception.

- **Output controls** are controls that focus on desired targets and allow managers to use their own methods for reaching defined targets.

Output controls are popular because they promote flexibility and creativity and they facilitate dialogue concerning corrective actions. Reliance on outcome controls separates what is to be accomplished from how it is to be accomplished. Thus, the discussion of goals is separated from the dialogue concerning methods. This separation can facilitate the movement of power down the organization, as senior managers are reassured that individuals at all levels will be working toward the goals senior management believes are important, even as lower-level managers innovate and introduce new ways to accomplish these goals.

Process Controls   Few organizations run on outcome controls alone. Once a solution to a problem is found and successfully implemented, managers do not want the problem to recur, so they institute process controls. **Process controls** attempt to specify the manner in which tasks are accomplished. There are many types of process controls, but three groups have received considerable attention: (1) policies, procedures, and rules; (2) formalization and standardization; and (3) total quality management controls. Before we discuss each of these, check OB Savvy 16.1 for a note of caution.

- **Process controls** are controls that attempt to specify the manner in which tasks are to be accomplished.

Policies, Procedures, and Rules   Most organizations implement a variety of policies, procedures, and rules to help specify how goals are to be accomplished. Usually, we think of a *policy* as a guideline for action that outlines important objectives and broadly indicates how an activity is to be performed. A policy allows for individual discretion and minor adjustments without direct clearance by a higher-level manager. *Procedures* indicate the best method for performing a task, show which aspects of a task are the most important, or outline how an individual is to be rewarded.

Many firms link *rules* and *procedures*. Rules are more specific, rigid, and impersonal than policies. They typically describe in detail how a task or a series of tasks is to be performed, or they indicate what cannot be done. They are designed to apply to all individuals, under specified conditions. For example, most car dealers have detailed instruction manuals for repairing a new car under warranty, and they must follow very strict procedures to obtain reimbursement from the manufacturer for warranty work.

Rules, procedures, and policies are often employed as substitutes for direct managerial supervision. Under the guidance of written rules and procedures, the organization can specifically direct the activities of many individuals. It can ensure virtually identical treatment across even distant work locations. For example, a McDonald's hamburger and fries taste much the same whether they are purchased in Hong Kong, Indianapolis, London, or Toronto simply because the ingredients and the cooking methods follow written rules and procedures.

• **Formalization** is the written documentation of work rules, policies, and procedures.

Formalization and Standardization   **Formalization** refers to the written documentation of rules, procedures, and policies to guide behavior and decision making. Beyond substituting for direct management supervision, formalization is often used to simplify jobs. Written instructions allow individuals with less training to perform comparatively sophisticated tasks. Written procedures may also be available to ensure that a proper sequence of tasks is executed, even if this sequence is performed only occasionally.

• **Standardization** is the degree to which the range of actions in a job or series of jobs is limited.

Most organizations have developed additional methods for dealing with recurring problems or situations. **Standardization** is the degree to which the range of allowable actions in a job or series of jobs is limited so that actions are performed in a uniform manner. It involves the creation of guidelines so that similar work activities are repeatedly performed in a similar fashion. Such standardized methods may come from years of experience in dealing with typical situations, or they may come from outside training. For instance, if you are late in paying your credit card, the bank will automatically send you a notification and start an internal process of monitoring your account.

Total Quality Management   The process controls discussed so far—policies, procedures, rules, formalization, and standardization—represent the lessons of experience within an organization. That is, managers institute these process controls based on experience typically one at a time. Often there is no overall philosophy for using control to improve the overall operations of the company. Another way to institute process controls is to establish a total quality management process within the firm.

The late W. Edwards Deming is the modern-day founder of the total quality management movement.[20] When Deming's ideas were not generally accepted in the United States, he found an audience in Japan. Thus, to some managers, Deming's ideas appear in the form of the best Japanese business practices.

The heart of Deming's approach is to institute a process approach to continual improvement based on statistical analyses of the firm's operations. Around this core idea, Deming built a series of 14 points for managers to implement. As they are shown in Mastering Management 16.2, note the emphasis on everyone working together using statistical controls to improve continually. All levels of management are to be involved in the quality program. Managers are to improve supervision, train employees, retrain employees in new skills, and create a structure that pushes the quality program. Where the properties of the firm's outcomes are well defined, as in most manufacturing operations, Deming's system and emphasis on quality work well, especially when implemented in conjunction with empowerment and participative management.

Centralization and Decentralization

Different firms use very different mixes of vertical specialization, output controls, process controls, and managerial techniques to allocate the authority or discretion to act.[21] The farther up the hierarchy of authority the discretion to spend money, to hire people, and to make similar decisions is moved, the greater the degree of **centralization**. The more such decisions are delegated, or moved down the hierarchy of authority, the greater the degree of **decentralization**.

• **Centralization** is the degree to which the authority to make decisions is restricted to higher levels of management.

• **Decentralization** is the degree to which the authority to make decisions is given to lower levels in an organization's hierarchy.

MASTERING MANAGEMENT 16.2

DEMING'S 14 POINTS OF QUALITY MANAGEMENT

1. Create a consistency of purpose in the company to (a) innovate, (b) put resources into research and education, and (c) put resources into maintaining equipment and new production aids.
2. Learn a new philosophy of quality to improve every system.
3. Require statistical evidence of process control and eliminate financial controls on production.
4. Require statistical evidence of control in purchasing parts; this will mean dealing with fewer suppliers.
5. Use statistical methods to isolate the sources of trouble.
6. Institute modern on-the-job training.
7. Improve supervision to develop inspired leaders.
8. Drive out fear and instill learning.
9. Break down barriers between departments.
10. Eliminate numerical goals and slogans.
11. Constantly revamp work methods.
12. Institute massive training programs for employees in statistical methods.
13. Retrain people in new skills.
14. Create a structure that will push, every day, on the above 13 points.

Greater centralization is often adopted when the firm faces a single major threat to its survival. Thus, it is little wonder that armies tend to be centralized and that firms facing bankruptcy increase centralization. Recent research even suggests that governmental agencies may improve their performance via centralization when in a defensive mode.[22]

Greater decentralization generally provides higher subordinate satisfaction and a quicker response to a diverse series of unrelated problems. Decentralization also assists in the on-the-job training of subordinates for higher-level positions. Decentralization is now a popular approach in many industries. For instance, Union Carbide is pushing responsibility down the chain of command, as are SYSCO and Hewlett-Packard. In each case, the senior managers hope to improve both performance quality and organizational responsiveness. Closely related to decentralization is the notion of participation. Many people want to be involved in making decisions that affect their work. Participation results when a manager delegates some authority for such decision making to subordinates in order to include them in the choice process. Employees may want a say both in what the unit objectives should be and in how they may be achieved.[23]

Firms such as Intel Corporation, Eli Lilly, Texas Instruments, and Hoffmann-LaRoche have also experimented by moving decisions down the chain of command and increasing participation. Governmental agencies find that increasing decentralization helps them effectively explore innovations.[24] Firms have generally found that just cutting the number of organizational levels was insufficient. They also needed to alter their controls toward quality, to stress constant improvement, and to change other basic features of the organization. As these firms changed their degree of vertical specialization, they also changed the division of work among units or the firm's horizontal specialization.

Organizing and Coordinating Work

● **Horizontal specialization** is a division of labor through the formation of work units or groups within an organization.

Managers must divide the total task into separate duties and group similar people and resources together.[25] Organizing work is formally known as horizontal specialization. **Horizontal specialization** is a division of labor that establishes specific work units or groups within an organization. This aspect of the organization is also called departmentation. There are several pure forms of departmentation. Whenever managers divide tasks and group similar types of skills and resources together, they must also be concerned with how each group's individual efforts will integrate with others. Integration across the firm is the subject of coordination. As noted below, managers use a mix of personal and impersonal methods of coordination to tie the efforts of departments together.

Traditional Types of Departments

● **Functional departmentation** is grouping individuals by skill, knowledge, and action yields.

Since the pattern of departmentation is so visible and important in a firm, managers often refer to their pattern of departmentation as the departmental structure. While most firms use a mix of various types of departments, it is important to look at the traditional types and what they do and do not provide the firm.

Functional Departments Grouping individuals by skill, knowledge, and action yields a pattern of **functional departmentation**. Recall that Figure 16.1 shows

Major Advantages and Disadvantages of Functional Specialization	
Advantages	**Disadvantages**
1. Yields very clear task assignments, consistent with an individual's training.	1. May reinforce the narrow training of individuals.
2. Individuals within a department can easily build on one another's knowledge, training, and experience.	2. May yield narrow, boring, and routine jobs.
3. Provides an excellent training ground for new managers.	3. Communication across technical area is complex and difficult.
4. It is easy to explain.	4. "Top-management overload" with too much attention to cross-functional problems.
5. Takes advantage of employee technical quality.	5. Individuals may look up the organizational hierarchy for direction and reinforcement rather than focus attention on products, services, or clients.

Figure 16.2 Major advantages and disadvantages of functional specialization.

the partial organization chart for a large university in which each department has a technical specialty. Marketing, finance, production, and personnel are important functions in business. In many small firms, this functional pattern dominates. Even large firms use this pattern in technically demanding areas. Figure 16.2 summarizes the advantages and disadvantages of the functional pattern. With all of these advantages, it is not surprising that the functional form is extremely popular. It is used in most organizations, particularly toward the bottom of the hierarchy. The extensive use of functional departments also has some disadvantages. Organizations that rely heavily on functional specialization may expect the following tendencies to emerge over time: an emphasis on quality from a technical standpoint, rigidity to change, and difficulty in coordinating the actions of different functional areas.

Divisional Departments   In **divisional departments** individuals and resources are grouped by products, territories, services, clients, or legal entities.[26] Figure 16.3 shows a divisional pattern of organization grouped around products, regions, and customers for three divisions of a conglomerate. This pattern is often used to meet diverse external threats and opportunities. As shown in Figure 16.3, the major advantages of the divisional pattern are its flexibility in meeting external demands, spotting external changes, integrating specialized individuals deep within the organization, and focusing on the delivery of specific products to specific customers. Among its disadvantages are duplication of effort by function, the tendency for divisional goals to be placed above corporate interests, and conflict among divisions. It is also not the structure most desired for training individuals in technical areas; firms relying on this pattern may fall behind technically to competitors with a functional pattern.

Many larger, geographically dispersed organizations that sell to national and international markets may rely on departmentation by geography. The savings in time, effort, and travel can be substantial, and each territory can adjust to regional differences. Organizations that rely on a few major customers may organize their people and resources by client. Here, the idea is to focus attention on the needs of the individual customer. To the extent that customer needs are unique, departmentation by customer can also reduce confusion and increase synergy. Organizations expanding internationally may also form divisions to meet the demands of complex host-country ownership requirements. For example, NEC, Sony, Nissan, and many

Divisional departmentation groups individuals and resources by products, territories, services, clients, or legal entities.

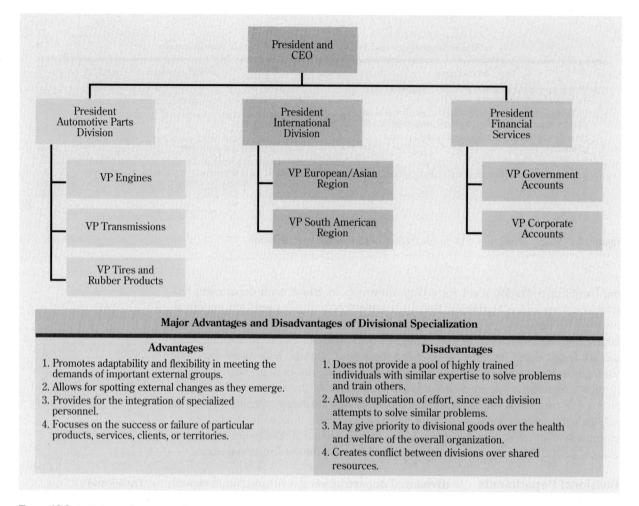

Figure 16.3 A divisional pattern of departmentation.

other Japanese corporations have developed U.S. divisional subsidiaries to service their customers in the U.S. market. Some huge European-based corporations such as Philips and Nestlé have also adopted a divisional structure in their expansion to the United States. Similarly, most of the internationalized U.S.-based firms, such as IBM, GE, and DuPont, have incorporated the divisional structure as part of their internalization programs.

Matrix Structures   Originally from the aerospace industry, a third unique form of departmentation called the matrix structure was developed and is now becoming more popular.[27] In aerospace efforts, projects are technically very complex, involving hundreds of subcontractors located throughout the world. Precise integration and control are needed across many sophisticated functional specialties and corporations. This is often more than a functional or divisional structure can provide, for many firms do not want to trade the responsiveness of the divisional form for the technical emphasis provided by the functional form. Thus, **matrix departmentation** uses both the functional and divisional forms simultaneously.

• **Matrix departmentation** is a combination of functional and divisional patterns wherein an individual is assigned to more than one type of unit.

Figure 16.4 shows the basic matrix arrangement for an aerospace program. Note the functional departments on one side and the project efforts on the other. Workers and supervisors in the middle of the matrix have two bosses—one functional and one project.

The major advantages and disadvantages of the matrix form of departmentation are summarized in Figure 16.4. The key disadvantage of the matrix method is the loss of unity of command. Individuals can be unsure as to what their jobs are, whom they report to for specific activities, and how various managers are to administer the effort. It can also be a very expensive method because it relies on individual managers to coordinate efforts deep within the firm. Despite these limitations, the matrix structure provides a balance between functional and divisional concerns. Many problems can be resolved at the working level, where the balance among technical, cost, customer, and organizational concerns can be dealt with.

NBBJ, the world's third largest architectural practice, manages a very broad range of projects. To meet these diverse challenges, NBBJ uses a matrix structure to draw specialists from its global offices to complete major design projects. NBBJ executives use senior contact staff in a local design studio to identify and focus on the specific needs of a client. They matrix across the global locations to supplement a local studio's staff.[28] Many organizations also use elements of the matrix structure without officially using the term matrix. For example, special project teams, coordinating committees, and task forces can be the beginnings

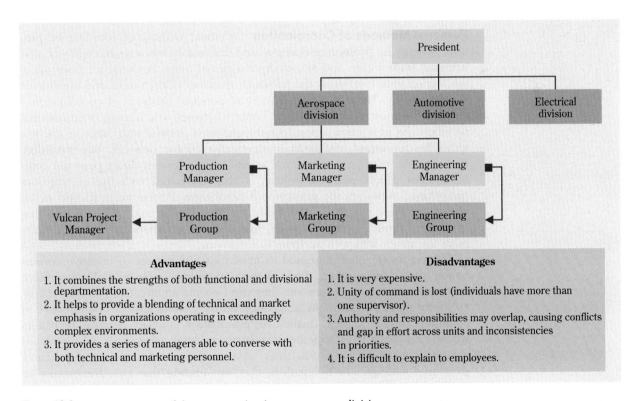

Advantages

1. It combines the strengths of both functional and divisional departmentation.
2. It helps to provide a blending of technical and market emphasis in organizations operating in exceedingly complex environments.
3. It provides a series of managers able to converse with both technical and marketing personnel.

Disadvantages

1. It is very expensive.
2. Unity of command is lost (individuals have more than one supervisor).
3. Authority and responsibilities may overlap, causing conflicts and gap in effort across units and inconsistencies in priorities.
4. It is difficult to explain to employees.

Figure 16.4 A matrix pattern of departmentation in an aerospace division.

of a matrix. These temporary structures can be used within a predominantly functional or divisional form and without upsetting the unity of command or hiring additional managers.

Which form of departmentation should be used? As the matrix concept suggests, it is possible to departmentalize by two different methods at the same time. Actually, organizations often use a mixture of departmentation forms. It is often desirable to divide the effort (group people and resources) by two methods at the same time in order to balance the advantages and disadvantages of each. These mixed forms help firms use their division of labor to capitalize on environmental opportunities, capture the benefits of larger size, and realize the potential of new technologies in pursuit of its strategy.

Coordination

- **Coordination** is the set of mechanisms used in an organization to link the actions of its subunits into a consistent pattern.

Whatever is divided up horizontally in two departments must also be integrated.[29] **Coordination** is the set of mechanisms that an organization uses to link the actions of their units into a consistent pattern. This linkage includes mechanisms to link managers and staff units, operating units with each other, and divisions with each other. Coordination is needed at all levels of management, not just across a few scattered units. Much of the coordination within a unit is handled by its manager. Smaller organizations may rely on their management hierarchy to provide the necessary consistency and integration. As the organization grows, however, managers become overloaded. The organization then needs to develop more efficient and effective ways of linking work units to one another.

Personal Methods of Coordination   Personal methods of coordination produce synergy by promoting dialogue and discussion, innovation, creativity, and learning, both within and across organizational units. Personal methods allow the organization to address the particular needs of distinct units and individuals simultaneously. There is a wide variety of personal methods of coordination.[30] Perhaps the most popular is direct contact between and among organizational members. As new information technologies have moved into practice, the potential for developing and maintaining effective contact networks has expanded. For example, many executives use e-mail to supplement direct personal communication. Direct personal contact is also associated with the ever-present "grapevine." Although the grapevine is notoriously inaccurate in its role as the corporate rumor mill, it is often both accurate enough and quick enough that managers cannot ignore it. Instead, managers need to work with and supplement the rumor mill with accurate information.

Managers are often assigned to numerous committees to improve coordination across departments. Even though committees are generally expensive and have a very poor reputation, they can become an effective personal mechanism for mutual adjustment across unit heads. Committees can be effective in communicating complex qualitative information and in helping managers whose units must work together to adjust schedules, workloads, and work assignments to increase productivity. As more organizations develop flatter structures with greater delegation, they are finding that task forces can be quite useful. Whereas committees tend to be long lasting, task forces are typically formed with a more limited agenda. Individuals from different parts of the

Coordination in Temporary Organizations

In today's world, many individuals have jobs that take them to a number of different temporary settings such as a corporate task force, an alliance, or a special project. Coordinating the actions of the members in these temporary arrangements is often a problem. However, new research by Beth Bechky offers some insight. She studied the workers on a movie set—not the actors or producer—but the crew who set up and run the equipment, shoot the movie, and make sure the sound is perfect. These individuals are generally "independent" contractors whose work must mesh quickly even though they have only been together a few hours.

How do they do it in the short-lived organization of a movie set? According to Bechky, they negotiate their roles with each other. Each has his or her own specialization and assignment but these must be coordinated with all others. While each recognizes his or her and the others' career progression (some have more experience and they are looked to for help), all recognize that the current assignment is one among the many they want in the future. All are on their best behavior so they will be hired for the next movie.

To successfully coordinate, Bechky found that the more experienced crew may provide enthusiastic thanks and very polite admonishing to the other less-experienced crew members. To enforce an emerging order and maintain coordination, all will use humor, polite ribbing, sarcastic comments, and teasing. Public display of anger is rare and frowned upon. With these mechanisms, it only takes a few hours for the crew to emerge as an integrated unit.

To transfer the findings to a student group, try and build a simplified model of the factors mentioned in the description. It might look somewhat like this:

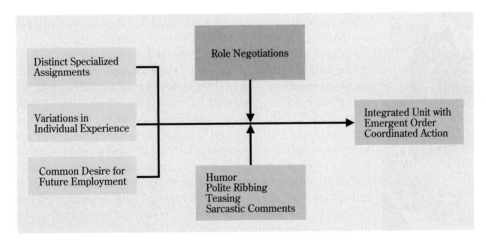

Pick a temporary student group to perform a team case study with majors in different areas (such as accounting, finance, management). See if the members self-assign to specialized areas based on their major. Look for variations in experience and check if there is a common desire for high performance. As the group starts work on the project, observe if they negotiate distinct roles. Do they use humor, polite ribbing, teasing, or sarcastic comments to coalesce? Do they form an integrated group with an identified order and coordinated action or do just a few actually run the show?

Questions

Would you expect a student group to form-up much the way the professionals do? If the student group does not use humor or teasing, what do they use to gain coordinated action?

Source: Beth A. Bechky, "Gaffers, gofers, and grips: Role-based coordination in temporary organizations" *Organization Science* 17.1 (2006), pp. 3–23.

organization are assembled into a task force to identify and solve problems that cut across different departments.

No magic is involved in selecting the appropriate mix of personal coordination methods and tailoring them to the individual skills, abilities, and experience of subordinates. Managers need to know the individuals involved, their preferences, and the accepted approaches in different organizational units. As the Research Insights feature suggests, different personal methods can be tailored to match different individuals and the settings in which they operate. Personal methods are only one important part of coordination. The manager may also establish a series of impersonal mechanisms.

Impersonal Methods of Coordination   Impersonal methods of coordination produce synergy by stressing consistency and standardization so that individual pieces fit together. Impersonal coordination methods are often refinements and extensions of process controls with an emphasis on formalization and standardization. Larger organizations often have written policies and procedures, such as schedules, budgets, and plans that are designed to mesh the operations of several units into a whole by providing predictability and consistency.

Shiseido Increases Profits by Consolidating

At Shiseido, Japan's largest cosmetic company with a global reach into Europe, North America, and China, President and CEO Shinzo Maeda recently announced the results of a three-year effort to reorganize North American operations by consolidating three large separate divisions into one integrated unit. The goal was to increase coordination. The results were a dramatic increase in sales and profits as the once separate divisions were able to focus as one unit.

Historically, firms used specialized departments to coordinate across units. However, this method is very expensive and often results in considerable rigidity. The most highly developed form of impersonal coordination comes with the adoption of a matrix structure. As noted earlier, this form of departmentation is designed to coordinate the efforts of diverse functional units. Many firms are using cross-functional task forces instead of maintaining specialized departments or implementing a matrix.

The final example of impersonal coordination mechanisms is undergoing radical change in many modern organizations. Originally, management information systems were developed and designed so that senior managers could coordinate and control the operations of diverse subordinate units. These systems were intended to be computerized substitutes for schedules, budgets, and the like. In some firms, the management information system still operates as a combined process control and impersonal coordination mechanism. In the hands of astute managers, however, the management information system becomes an electronic network, linking individuals throughout the organization. Using decentralized communication systems that connect all members allows once centralized systems to evolve into a supplement to personal coordination.

In the United States there is an aversion to controls, as the culture prizes individuality, democracy, and individual free will. Managers often institute controls under the title of coordination. Since some of the techniques are used for both, many managers suggest that all efforts at control are for coordination. It is extremely important to separate these two functions simply because the reactions to controls and coordination are quite different. The underlying logic of control involves setting targets, measuring performance, and taking corrective action to meet goals normally assigned by higher management. Thus, many employees see an increase in controls as a threat based on a presumption that they have been doing something wrong. The logic of coordination is to get unit actions and interactions meshed together into a unified whole. While control involves the vertical exercise of formal authority involving targets, measures, and corrective action, coordination stresses cooperative problem solving.

Experienced employees recognize the difference between controls and coordination regardless of what the boss calls it.[31] Increasing controls rarely solves problems of coordination, and emphasizing coordination to solve control issues rarely works.

Bureaucracy and Beyond

In the developed world, most firms are bureaucracies. In OB this term has a very special meaning, beyond its negative connotation. The famous German sociologist Max Weber suggested that organizations would thrive if they became bureaucracies by emphasizing legal authority, logic, and order.[32] Ideally, **bureaucracies** rely on a division of labor, hierarchical control, promotion by merit with career opportunities for employees, and administration by rule.

Weber argued that the rational and logical idea of bureaucracy was superior to building the firm based on charisma or cultural tradition. The "charismatic" ideal-type organization was overly reliant on the talents of one individual and could fail when the leader leaves. Too much reliance on cultural traditions blocked innovation, stifled efficiency, and was often unfair. Since the bureaucracy prizes efficiency, order, and logic, Weber hoped that it could also be fair to employees and provide more freedom for individual expression than is allowed when tradition dominates or dictators rule. Many interpreted Weber as suggesting that bureaucracy or some variation of this ideal form, although far from perfect, would dominate modern society.[33] For large organizations the bureaucratic form is predominant. Yet, as noted in OB Savvy 16.2, this comes at some costs as well. While charismatic leadership and cultural traditions are still important today, it is the rational, legal, and efficiency aspects of the firm that characterize modern corporations.

Just as interpretations of Weber have evolved over time, so has the notion of a bureaucracy.[34] We will discuss two popular basic types of bureaucracies: the mechanistic structure and machine bureaucracy and the organic structure and professional bureaucracy as well as some hybrid approaches. Each type is a different mix of the basic elements discussed in this chapter, and each mix yields firms with a slightly different blend of capabilities and natural tendencies. That is, each type of bureaucracy allows the firm to pursue some goals more easily than others.

- **Bureaucracy** is an ideal form of organization, the characteristics of which were defined by the German sociologist Max Weber.

- **Mechanistic type of machine bureaucracy** emphasizes vertical specialization and control with impersonal coordination and a heavy reliance on standardization, formalization, rules, policies, and procedures.

Mechanistic Structures and the Machine Bureaucracy

The **mechanistic type of bureaucracy** emphasizes vertical specialization and control.[35] Organizations of this type stress rules, policies, and procedures; specify techniques for decision making; and emphasize developing well-documented control systems backed by a strong middle management and supported by a centralized staff. There is often extensive use of the

---

OB SAVVY 16.2

Negative Aspects of Large Bureaucracies

Most large firms are bureaucracies; expect to see the following to some degree or another:

1. Overspecialization with conflicts between highly specialized units
2. Overreliance on the chain of command rather than bottom-up problem solving
3. Objectification of senior executives as rulers rather than problem solvers for others
4. Overemphasis on conformity
5. Rules become ends in and of themselves

functional pattern of departmentation throughout the firm. Henry Mintzberg uses the term *machine bureaucracy* to describe an organization structured in this manner.[36]

The mechanistic design results in a management emphasis on routine for efficiency. Firms often used this design in pursuing a strategy of becoming a low-cost leader. Until the implementation of new information systems, most large-scale firms in basic industries were machine bureaucracies. Included in this long list were all of the auto firms, banks, insurance companies, steel mills, large retail establishments, and government offices. Efficiency was achieved through extensive vertical and horizontal specialization tied together with elaborate controls and impersonal coordination mechanisms.

There are, however, limits to the benefits of specialization backed by rigid controls. Employees do not like rigid designs, so motivation becomes a problem. Unions further solidify narrow job descriptions by demanding fixed work rules and regulations to protect employees from the extensive vertical controls. Key employees may leave. In short, using a machine bureaucracy can hinder an organization's capacity to adjust to subtle external changes or new technologies.

Organic Structures and the Professional Bureaucracy

* **Organic type or professional bureaucracy** emphasizes horizontal specialization, extensive use of personal coordination, and loose rules, policies, and procedures.

The **organic type** is much less vertically oriented than its mechanistic counterpart is; it emphasizes horizontal specialization. Procedures are minimal, and those that do exist are not as formalized. The organization relies on the judgments of experts and personal means of coordination. When controls are used, they tend to back up professional socialization, training, and individual reinforcement. Staff units are placed toward the middle of the organization. Because this is a popular design in professional firms, Mintzberg calls it a professional bureaucracy.[37]

Your university is probably a professional bureaucracy that looks like a broad, flat pyramid with a large bulge in the center for the professional staff. Power in this ideal type rests with knowledge. Furthermore, there was often an elaborate staff to "help" the line managers. Often the staff had very little formal power, other than to block action. Control is enhanced by the standardization of professional skills and the adoption of professional routines, standards, and procedures. Other examples of organic types include most hospitals and social service agencies.

Although not as efficient as the machine bureaucracy, the professional bureaucracy is better for problem solving and for serving individual customer needs. Since lateral relations and coordination are emphasized, centralized direction by senior management is less intense. Thus, this type is good at detecting external changes and adjusting to new technologies, but at the sacrifice of responding to central management direction.[38] Firms using this pattern found it easier to pursue product quality, quick response to customers, and innovation as strategies.

Hybrid Structures

Many very large firms found that neither the mechanistic nor the organic approach was suitable for all of their operations. Adopting a machine bureaucracy would overload senior management and yield too many levels of management. Yet, adopting an organic type would mean losing control and becoming too inefficient. Senior managers may opt for one of a number of hybrid types.

We have already briefly introduced two of the more common hybrid types. One is an extension of the divisional pattern of departmentation, and sometimes called a divisional firm. Here, the firm is composed of quasi-independent divisions so that different divisions can be more or less organic or mechanistic. While the divisions may be treated as separate businesses, they often share a similar mission and systems goals.[39] When adopting this hybrid type, each division can pursue a different strategy. Land O' Lakes, for instance, is a divisional cooperative.

A second hybrid is the true conglomerate. A **conglomerate** is a single corporation that contains a number of unrelated businesses. On the surface, these firms look like divisionalized firms, but when the various businesses of the divisions are unrelated, the term conglomerate is applied.[40] For instance, General Electric is a conglomerate that has divisions in unrelated businesses and industries, ranging from producing light bulbs, to designing and servicing nuclear reactors, to building jet engines, to operating the National Broadcasting Company. Many state and federal entities are also, by necessity, conglomerates. For instance, a state governor is the chief executive officer of those units concerned with higher education, welfare, prisons, highway construction and maintenance, police, and the like.

The conglomerate type also simultaneously illustrates three important points. (1) All structures are combinations of the basic elements. (2) There is no one best structure—it all depends on a number of factors such as the size of the firm, its environment, its technology, and, of course, its strategy. (3) The firm does not stand alone but is part of a larger network of firms that competes against other networks.

● **Conglomerates** are firms that own several different unrelated businesses.

Resources in The OB Skills Workbook

These learning activities from *The OB Skills Workbook* are suggested for Chapter 16.

Cases for Critical Thinking	Team and Experiential Exercises	Self-Assessment Portfolio
• First Community Financial	• Tinker Toys	• Twenty-First-Century Manager
	• Organizations Alive	• Organizational Design Preference
	• Fast-Food Technology	
	• Alien Invasion	

16 studyguide

Summary Questions and Answers

What are the different types of organizational goals?

• Societal goals: organizations make specific contributions to society and gain legitimacy from these contributions.

• A societal contribution focused on a primary beneficiary may be represented in the firm's mission statement.

- Output goals: as managers consider how they will accomplish their firm's mission, many begin with a very clear statement of which business they are in.

- Firms often specify output goals by detailing the types of specific products and services they offer.

- Systems goals: corporations have systems goals to show the conditions managers believe will yield survival and success.

- Growth, productivity, stability, harmony, flexibility, prestige, and human-resource maintenance are examples of systems goals.

What are the hierarchical aspects of organizations?

- The formal structure is also known as the firm's division of labor.

- The formal structure defines the intended configuration of positions, job duties, and lines of authority among different parts of the enterprise.

- Vertical specialization is used to allocate formal authority within the organization and may be seen on an organization chart.

- Vertical specialization is the hierarchical division of labor that specifies where formal authority is located.

- Typically, a chain of command exists to link lower-level workers with senior managers.

- The distinction between line and staff units also indicates how authority is distributed, with line units conducting the major business of the firm and staff providing support.

- Managerial techniques, such as decision support and expert computer systems, are used to expand the analytical reach and decision-making capacity of managers to minimize staff.

- Control is the set of mechanisms the organization uses to keep action or outputs within predetermined levels.

- Output controls focus on desired targets and allow managers to use their own methods for reaching these targets.

- Process controls specify the manner in which tasks are to be accomplished through (1) policies, rules, and procedures; (2) formalization and standardization; and (3) total quality management processes.

- Firms are learning that decentralization often provides substantial benefits.

How is work organized and coordinated?

- Horizontal specialization is the division of labor that results in various work units and departments in the organization.

- Three main types or patterns of departmentation are observed: functional, divisional, and matrix. Each pattern has a mix of advantages and disadvantages.

- Organizations may successfully use any type, or a mixture, as long as the strengths of the structure match the needs of the organization.

- Coordination is the set of mechanisms an organization uses to link the actions of separate units into a consistent pattern.

- Personal methods of coordination produce synergy by promoting dialogue, discussion, innovation, creativity, and learning.

- Impersonal methods of control produce synergy by stressing consistency and standardization so that individual pieces fit together.

What are bureaucracies and what are the common forms?

- The bureaucracy is an ideal form based on legal authority, logic, and order that provides superior efficiency and effectiveness.

- Mechanistic, organic, and hybrid are common types of bureaucracies.

- Hybrid types include the divisionalized firm and the conglomerate. No one type is always superior to the others.

Key Terms

Bureaucracy (p. 407)
Centralization (p. 399)
Conglomerates (p. 409)
Control (p. 397)
Coordination (p. 404)
Decentralization (p. 399)
Divisional departmentation (p. 401)
Formalization (p. 398)
Functional departmentation (p. 400)

Horizontal specialization (p. 400)
Line units (p. 396)
Matrix departmentation (p. 402)
Mechanistic type or machine bureaucracy (p. 407)
Mission statements (p. 390)
Organic type or professional bureaucracy (p. 408)

Organization charts (p. 393)
Output controls (p. 397)
Output goals (p. 392)
Process controls (p. 397)
Societal goals (p. 390)
Span of control (p. 395)
Staff units (p. 396)
Standardization (p. 398)
Systems goals (p. 392)
Vertical specialization (p. 393)

Self-Test 16

Multiple Choice

1. The major types of goals for most organizations are _____. (a) societal, personal, and output (b) societal, output and systems (c) personal and impersonal (d) profits, corporate responsibility, and personal (e) none of the above

2. The formal structures of organizations may be shown in a(n) _____. (a) environmental diagram (b) organization chart (c) horizontal diagram (d) matrix depiction (e) labor assignment chart

3. A major distinction between line and staff units concerns _____. (a) the amount of resources each is allowed to utilize (b) linkage of their jobs to the goals of the firm (c) the amount of education or training they possess (d) their use of computer information systems (e) their linkage to the outside world

4. The division of labor by grouping people and material resources deals with _____. (a) specialization (b) coordination (c) divisionalization (d) vertical specialization (e) goal setting

5. Control involves all but _____. (a) measuring results (b) establishing goals (c) taking corrective action (d) comparing results with goals (e) selecting manpower

6. Grouping individuals and resources in the organization around products, services, clients, territories, or legal entities is an example of _____ specialization. (a) divisional (b) functional (c) matrix (d) mixed form (e) outsourced specialization

7. Grouping resources into departments by skill, knowledge, and action is the _____ pattern. (a) functional (b) divisional (c) vertical (d) means-end chains (e) matrix

8. A matrix structure _____. (a) reinforces unity of command (b) is inexpensive (c) is easy to explain to employees (d) gives some employees two bosses (e) yields a minimum of organizational politics

9. _____ is the concern for proper communication enabling the units to understand one another's activities. (a) Control (b) Coordination (c) Specialization (d) Departmentation (e) Division of Labor

10. Compared to the machine bureaucracy (mechanistic type), the professional bureaucracy (organic type) _____. (a) is more efficient for routine operations (b) has more vertical specialization and control (c) is larger (d) has more horizontal specialization and coordination mechanism (e) is smaller

11. Written statements of organizational purpose are called _____. (a) mission statements (b) formalization (c) mean-ends chains (d) formalization

12. _____ is grouping individuals by skill, knowledge, and action yields. (a) Divisional departmentation (b) Functional departmentation (c) Hybrid structuration (d) Matrix departmentation

13. The division of labor through the formation of work units or groups within an organization is called _____. (a) control (b) vertical specialization (c) horizontal specialization (d) coordination

14. _____ is the set of mechanisms used in an organization to link the actions of its subunits into a consistent pattern. (a) Departmentation (b) Coordination (c) Control (d) Formal authority

15. The set of mechanisms used to keep actions and outputs within predetermined limits is called _____. (a) coordination (b) vertical specialization (c) control (d) formalization

16. _____ describes how formal authority is distributed and establishes where and how critical decisions are to be made. (a) Vertical/horizontal specialization (b) Centralization/decentralization (c) Control/coordination (d) Bureaucratic/charismatic

17. Grouping people together by skill, knowledge, and action yields a _____ pattern of departmentation. (a) functional (b) divisional (c) matrix (d) dispersed

18. _____ in an organization provide specialized expertise and services. (a) Staff units and personnel (b) Line units and personnel (c) Cross-functional teams (d) Auditing units

19. One of the advantages of a _____ is that it helps provide a blending of technical and market emphases in organizations operating in exceedingly complex environments. (a) functional structure (b) matrix structure (c) divisional structure (d) conglomerate structure

20. _____ goals are the goals that define the type of business an organization is in. (a) Divisional (b) Systems (c) Societal (d) Output

Short Response

21. Compare and contrast output goals with systems goals.

22. Describe the types of controls that are used in organizations.

23. What are the major advantages and disadvantages of functional departmentation?

24. What are the major advantages and disadvantages of matrix departmentation?

Applications Essay

25. Describe some of the side effects of organizational controls in a large mechanistically structured organization, such as the United States Postal Service.

17

Strategy, Technology, and Organizational Design

chapter at a glance

Organizations use strategy, technology, and design options to respond to opportunities and challenges in their competitive landscapes. Here's what to look for in Chapter 17. Don't forget to check your learning with the Summary Questions & Answers and Self-Test in the end-of-chapter Study Guide.

WHY ARE STRATEGY AND ORGANIZATIONAL LEARNING IMPORTANT?

Strategy

Organizational Learning

Linking Strategy and Organizational Learning

HOW DOES STRATEGY INFLUENCE ORGANIZATIONAL DESIGN?

Organizational Design and Strategic Decisions

Organizational Design and Co-Evolution

Organizational Design and Growth

HOW DOES TECHNOLOGY INFLUENCE ORGANIZATIONAL DESIGN?

Operations Technology and Organizational Design

Adhocracy as a Design Option for Innovation and Learning

Information Technology

HOW DOES THE ENVIRONMENT INFLUENCE ORGANIZATIONAL DESIGN?

Environmental Complexity

Organizational Networks and Alliances

Fusajiro Yamauchi created Nintendo back in 1889 as a producer and marketer of playing cards (for the Japanese game Hanafuda). Earlier ventures to expand the business were unsuccessful (e.g., a taxi company, a hotel chain, TV network, and a food company), but its entry into the home video game console market back in the mid-1970s brought the company much success and has revolutionized the video gaming industry.[1]

Saturo Iwata became Nintendo's CEO in 2002. His passion for innovation and collaboration has lead Nintendo down a revolutionary path with the remarkable success of Wii. Introduced in 2006, it is the best selling console system in the world and Nintendo has used it to appeal to a broader target market including females and older users by developing games that are more practical, attractive and interactive.

"Almost every review of the Wii has been accompanied by real excitement of the kind that has been unknown to the video game industry for so long few recognized it."[1] Wii has transformed the industry by making video games a social activity which will impact game development for years to come.

Nintendo has some of the brightest minds in the industry; Shigeru Miyamoto, once a student product developer, joined the company back in the 1970s. If the name doesn't sound familiar, then perhaps some of his creations will: Donkey Kong, Mario Brothers, Zelda. It's Nintendo's innovative culture that appeals to specialists like Miyamoto. "Part of Nintendo's culture is to praise people for doing something different."[1]

Collaboration is key and the organization is designed to allow its development teams great leeway in producing some of the industry's most popular products. According to Miyamoto, "Nintendo is the company which makes the most innovative products. I am not sure that I would be able to make games like that elsewhere. At Nintendo I can make the games which I want."

The success of its products is uniquely shared by the CEO with his teams. Demonstrating considerable humility, Iwata deflects praise for his company's achievements by shining the spotlight directly on them. Nintendo's website features interviews with the developers of many of the company's success stories and the interviewer is none other than Iwata himself. This is his creative way of showcasing the talent this company relies on for its innovative successes and sharing a bit of the spotlight in the process.

nintendo: from playing cards to wii and beyond

Strategy and Organizational Learning

The world in which organizations now operate provides countless demands and constraints, as well as alternatives and choices for survival and growth. This world is also constantly changing, and doing so in fundamental ways. To be successful, organizations need, at a minimum, a sound strategy and the ability to learn.

Strategy

• **Strategy** positions the organization in the competitive environment and implements actions to compete successfully.

When Nintendo introduced Wii, it reflected a significant strategic change for the company and forced change within the industry itself. **Strategy** is the process of positioning the organization in the competitive environment and implementing actions to compete successfully. It is a pattern in a stream of decisions.[2] Choosing the types of contributions the firm intends to make to the larger society, precisely whom it will serve, and exactly what it will provide to others are conventional ways in which the firm begins the pattern of decisions and corresponding implementations that define its strategy.

The strategy process is ongoing. It should involve individuals at all levels of the firm to ensure that there is a recognizable, consistent pattern—yielding a superior capability over rivals—up and down the firm and across all of its activities. This recognizable pattern involves many facets to develop a sustainable and unique set of dynamic capabilities. Nintendo has established itself as the industry leader in innovation through its introduction of Wii. The technology has altered the gaming landscape by, as noted in the case, making the gaming experience a social activity and developing the types of games that appeal to entirely different markets. With its army of top-notch engineers in an environment that celebrates creativity and innovation, Nintendo has positioned itself ahead of its major competitors by developing and successfully implementing a winning strategy.

Obviously, a successful strategy does not evolve in a vacuum but is driven by the goals emphasized, the size of the enterprise, the nature of the technology used by the firm, and its setting as well as the structure used to implement the strategy. In this chapter, we will emphasize the development of dynamic capabilities via organizational learning as an enduring feature of a successful strategy. We emphasize organizational learning because learning will be critical for firms competing in the 21st century.

Organizational Learning

• **Organizational learning** is the process of knowledge acquisition, information distribution, information interpretation, and organizational retention.

Organizational learning is the process of acquiring knowledge and using information to adapt successfully to changing circumstances. For organizations to learn, they must engage in knowledge acquisition, information distribution, information interpretation, and organizational retention in adapting successfully to changing circumstances.[3] In simpler terms, organizational learning involves the adjustment of the actions based on the organization's experience and that of others. The challenge is doing to learn and learning to do.

How Organizations Acquire Knowledge   Firms obtain information in a variety of ways and at different rates during their histories. Perhaps the most important information is obtained from sources outside the firm at the time of its founding. During the firm's initial years, its managers copy, or mimic, what they believe are the successful practices of others.[4] As they mature, however, firms can also acquire knowledge through experience and systematic search.

Mimicry   **Mimicry** is important to the new firm because (1) it provides workable, if not ideal, solutions to many problems; (2) it reduces the number of decisions that need to be analyzed separately, allowing managers to concentrate on more critical issues; and (3) it establishes legitimacy or acceptance by employees, suppliers, and customers and narrows the choices calling for detailed explanation. One of the key factors involved in examining mimicry is the extent to which managers attempt to isolate cause-effect relationships. Simply copying others without attempting to understand the issues involved often leads to failure. When mimicking others, managers need to adjust for the unique circumstances of their corporation. See OB Savvy 17.1 for tips about Process Benchmarking.

> **OB SAVVY 17.1**
>
> ## Tips for Better Process Benchmarking
>
> When learning how to improve an administrative process from others, consider the following:
>
> 1. Carefully define the process by comparing current operations with best practices either inside or outside the firm.
> 2. Organize a systematic effort by developing a plan, identifying who will be studied, and determining who will conduct the study, where it will be done, and how it will be conducted.
> 3. After conducting the comparison between your current practices and best practices, prioritize the findings by ease of implementation and projected benefit, recognizing the differences between the unit to be copied and your current unit.
> 4. Consider applicability of the proposed changes—do they make sense and can they be applied?
> 5. Discuss implementation with all affected parties and monitor implementation for lessons learned.

Experience   A primary way to acquire knowledge is through experience. All organizations and managers can learn in this manner. Besides learning-by-doing, managers can also systematically embark on structured programs to capture the lessons to be learned from failure and success. For instance, a well-designed research and development program allows managers to learn as much through failure as through success.[5]

Learning-by-doing in an intelligent way is at the heart of many Japanese corporations, with their emphasis on statistical quality control, quality circles, and other such practices. Many firms have discovered that numerous small improvements can cumulatively add up to a major improvement in both quality and efficiency. The major problem with emphasizing learning-by-doing is the inability to forecast precisely what will change and how it will change. Managers need to believe that improvements can be made, listen to suggestions, and actually implement the changes. It is much more difficult to do than to say, however.[6]

Vicarious Learning   Vicarious learning involves capturing the lessons of others' experiences. Typically, successful vicarious learning involves both scanning and grafting.[7]

Scanning involves looking outside the firm and bringing back useful solutions. At times, these solutions are applied to recognized problems. More often, these solutions float around management until they are needed to solve a problem.[8] Astute managers can contribute to organizational learning by scanning external sources, such as competitors, suppliers, industry consultants, customers, and leading firms. For instance, by reverse engineering the competitor's products (developing the engineering drawings and specifications from the existing product), an organization can quickly match all standard product features. By systematically exploring the proposed developments from suppliers, a firm may become a lead user and be among the first to capitalize on the developments of suppliers.

Grafting is the process of acquiring individuals, units, or firms to bring in useful knowledge. Almost all firms seek to hire experienced individuals from other firms simply because experienced individuals may bring with them a completely new series of solutions. Contracting out or outsourcing is the reverse of

- **Mimicry** is the copying of the successful practices of others.

- **Scanning** is looking outside the firm and bringing back useful solutions to problems.

- **Grafting** is the process of acquiring individuals, units, and/or firms to bring in useful knowledge to the organization.

grafting and involves asking outsiders to perform a particular function. Whereas virtually all organizations contract out and outsource, the key question for managers is often what to keep.

Information Distribution and Interpretation   Once information is obtained, managers must establish mechanisms to distribute relevant information to the individuals who may need it. A primary challenge in larger firms is to locate quickly who has the appropriate information and who needs specific types of information.

Although data collection is helpful, it is not enough. Data are not information; the information must be interpreted. Information within organizations is a collective understanding of the firm's goals and of how the data relate to one of the firm's stated or unstated objectives within the current setting. Unfortunately, a number of common problems often thwarts the process of developing multiple interpretations.[9]

Chief among the problems of interpretation are self-serving interpretations. Among managers, the ability to interpret events, conditions, and history to their own advantage is almost universal. Managers and employees alike often see what they have seen in the past or see what they want to see. Rarely do they see what is or can be.

Retention   Organizations contain a variety of mechanisms that can be used to retain useful information.[10] Six important retention mechanisms are individuals, transformation procedures, formal structures, ecology, external archives, and internal information technologies (IT).

1. *Individuals* are the most important storehouses of information for organizations. Organizations that retain a large and comparatively stable group of experienced individuals are expected to have a higher capacity to acquire, retain, and retrieve information. Collectively, these individuals hold memory via rich, vivid, and meaningful stories that outlive those who experienced the event.

2. Transformation mechanisms such as documents, rule books, written procedures, and even standard but unwritten methods of operation are all *transformation mechanisms* used to store accumulated information. In cases where operations are extremely complex but rarely needed, written sources of information are often invaluable.

3. The organization's *formal structure* and the positions in an organization are less obvious but equally important mechanisms for storing information. When an aircraft lands on the deck of a U.S. Navy aircraft carrier, there are typically dozens of individuals on the deck, apparently watching the aircraft land. Each person on the deck is there for a specific purpose. Each can often trace his or her position to a specific accident that would not have occurred had some individual originally been assigned that position.

4. *Physical structures* (or *ecology*, in the language of learning theorists) are potentially important mechanisms used to store information. For example, a traditional way of ordering parts and subcomponents in a factory is known as the "two-bin" system. One bin is always kept in reserve. Once an individual opens the reserve bin, he or she automatically orders replacements. In this way, the plant never runs out of components.

5. *External archives* can be tapped to provide valuable information in larger organizations. Former employees, stock market analysts, suppliers, distributors, and the media can be important sources of valuable information. These

external archives are important because they may provide a view of events quite different from that held in the organization.

6. Finally, internal information technology of a firm, or its *IT System*, can provide a powerful and individually tailored mechanism for storing information. All too often, however, managers are not using their IT systems strategically and are not tapping into them as mechanisms for retention.

Linking Strategy and Organizational Learning

As this quick overview of strategy and learning suggests, there are many strategies and many ways to learn. Historically, these two concepts have been discussed separately. Often strategy is linked to economic perspectives of the firm whereas learning is discussed with organizational change. Today, however, many OB scholars recognize that to compete successfully in the 21st century global economy, individuals, units, and firms will need to learn continually. A firm based in a developed nation cannot successfully compete with firms based in developing counties just by being more efficient any more than an individual in Western Europe or North America can afford to work for the same wages as laborers from developing countries. There is just too much difference in the labor rates.

Production technology now spreads globally; transportation of goods is cheap and the delivery of many services cuts across national boundaries. However, this does not mean firms in developed nations are doomed. Firms can know more about their local markets; they can carefully select what they produce, what services they provide, what they buy, and how to build capability. They must learn and use their strategy to provide the necessary balance between exploration and exploitation of new ideas.[11] They must be capable of sustained learning at the organizational level to capture the lessons from exploring new technologies and exploiting existing markets.[12]

It is important to emphasize that sustaining a competitive strategy with consistent learning involves more than just a commitment by individuals; it calls for a systematic adjustment of the organization's structure and processes to alterations in the size and scope of operations, the technology selected, and the environmental setting. The process involved in making these dynamic adjustments is known as organizational design.

Strategy and Organizational Design

Organizational design is the process of choosing and implementing a structural configuration.[13] It goes beyond just indicating who reports to whom and what types of jobs are contained in each department. The design process takes the basic structural elements and molds them to the firm's desires, demands, constraints, and choices. The choice of an appropriate organizational design is contingent upon several factors, including the size of the firm, its operations and information technology, its environment, and, of course, the strategy it selects for growth and survival.

For example, IBM's senior management has selected a form of organization for each component of IBM that matches that component's contribution to the whole. The overall organizational design matches the technical challenges facing IBM, allows it to adjust to new developments, and helps it shape its competitive

- **Organizational design** is the process of choosing and implementing a structural configuration for an organization.

Naoki Abe is a research staff
member at IBM where he has been
engaged in the development of novel
machine learning methods and their
application to problems in business
analytics and optimization. His
research activities range from cost-
sensitive learning, sampling
schemes, reinforcement learning,
and their applications to business
intelligence. He currently is engaged
in research in machine learning,
data mining, and their applications
to problems in business analytics.

landscape. Above all, the design promotes the development of individual skills and abilities, but different designs stress different skills and abilities. See, for instance, the activities IBM supports for Naoki Abe in its Yorktown Research Center. As we discuss each major contingency factor, we will highlight the design option the firm's managers need to consider and link these options to aspects of innovation and learning.[14]

Organizational Design and Strategic Decisions

To show the intricate intertwining of strategy and organizational design, it is important to reiterate and extend the dualistic notion of strategy.[15] Recall that strategy is a positioning of the firm in its environment to provide it with the capability to succeed. Strategy is also a pattern in the stream of decisions. Here we will emphasize that what the firm intends to do must be backed up by capabilities for implementation in a setting that facilitates success.

Historically, executives were told that firms had available a limited number of economically determined generic strategies that were built upon the foundations of such factors as efficiency and innovation.[16] If the firm wanted efficiency it should adopt the machine bureaucracy (many levels of management backed with extensive controls replete with written procedures). If it wanted innovation, it should adopt a more organic form (fewer levels of management with an emphasis on coordination). Today the world of corporations is much more complex and executives have found much more sophisticated ways of competing.

Now many senior executives emphasize the skills and abilities that their firms need to compete and to remain agile and dynamic in a rapidly changing world.[17] The structural configuration or organizational design of the firm should not only facilitate the types of accomplishment desired by senior management, but also allow individuals to experiment, grow, and develop competencies so that the strategy of the firm can evolve.[18] Over time, the firm may develop specific administrative and technical skills as middle and lower-level managers institute minor adjustments to solve specific problems. As they learn, so can their firms if the individual learning of employees can be transferred across and up the organization's hierarchy. As the skills of employees and managers develop, they may be recognized by senior management and become a foundation for revisions in the overall strategy of the firm.

Organizational Design and Co-Evolution

With astute senior management, the firm can co-evolve. That is, the firm can adjust to both internal and external changes even as it shapes some of the challenges facing it. Co-evolution is a process.[19] One aspect of this process is repositioning the firm in its setting as the setting changes. A shift in the environment may call for adjusting the firm's scale of operations. Senior management can also guide the process of positioning and repositioning in the environment. Co-evolution may call for changes in technology. For instance, a firm can introduce new products into new markets. It can change parts of its environment by joining with others to compete. However, senior management must also have the necessary internal capabilities if it is to shape its environment. It cannot introduce new products without extensive product development capabilities or rush into a new market it does not understand. Shaping capabilities via the organization's design is a dynamic aspect of co-evolution.

The second aspect of strategy is a pattern in the stream of decisions. In a recent poll of some 750 CEOs, Samuel Palmisano, CEO of IBM, reported that two-thirds of the respondents reported being inundated with change and new competitors. Most saw that their primary focus would be to adjust their firm's processes, management, and culture to the new learning challenges. Most called for collaboration with other firms and suggested that they would emphasize learning to innovate.[20]

The organizational design can reinforce a focus and provide a setting for the continual development of employee skills. As the environment, strategy, and technology shift, we will see shifts in design and the resulting capabilities. IBM was once known as *big blue*, a button-down, white-shirt, blue-tie-and-black-shoe, second-to-market imitator with the bulk of its business centered on mainframe computers. The company is now a major hub in e-commerce and is on the cutting edge as an integrator across systems, equipment, and service. To remain successful, IBM will continue to rely upon the willingness of employees to take chances, refine their skills, and work together creatively.

The interplay of forces helps mold and shape the behavior in organizations and the development of competencies through a firm's organizational design. Even with co-evolution, managers must maintain a recognizable pattern of choices in the design that leads to accomplishing a broadly shared view of where the firm is going.

Fab India

A premium retail brand in India, Fab India sells hand-woven products produced by 20,000+ artisan workers. It is also unique in its strategy of inviting them to become shareholders and setting up centers to specialize in each region's special crafts. CEO William Bissell says: "We're somewhere between the 17th century, with our artisan suppliers, and the 21st century with our consumers."

Organizational Design and Growth

Most organizations want to grow, and as they grow, the organizational design of the firm needs to be attuned to its size. For many reasons, large organizations cannot be bigger versions of their smaller counterparts. When the number of individuals in a firm is increased arithmetically, the number of possible interconnections between these individuals increases geometrically. In other words, the direct interpersonal contact among all members in an organization must be managed. The design of small firms is directly influenced by its core operations technology, whereas larger firms have many core operations technologies in a wide variety of much more specialized units. In short, larger organizations are often more complex than smaller firms. While all larger firms are bureaucracies, smaller firms need not be. In larger firms, additional complexity calls for a more sophisticated organizational design. Such is not the case for the small firm.

Smaller Size and the Simple Design   The **simple design** is a configuration involving one or two ways of specializing individuals and units. Vertical specialization and control typically emphasize levels of supervision without elaborate formal mechanisms (for example, rulebooks and policy manuals), and the majority of the control resides in the manager. Thus, the simple design tends to minimize bureaucracy and rest more heavily on the leadership of the manager.

The simple design pattern is appropriate for many small firms, such as family businesses, retail stores, and small manufacturing firms.[21] The strengths of the simple design are simplicity, flexibility, and responsiveness to the desires of a central manager—in many cases, the owner. Because a simple design relies heavily on the manager's personal leadership, however, this configuration is only as effective as is the senior manager.

Simple design is a configuration involving one or two ways of specializing individuals and units.

For example, B&A Travel is a comparatively small travel agency owned by Helen Druse. Reporting to Helen is a part-time staff member, Jane Bloom, for accounting and finance. Joan Wiland heads the operations arm. Joan supervises eight travel agents and keeps the dedicated computer system operating. Each of the lead travel agents specializes in a geographical area, and all but Sue Connely and Bart Merve take client requests for all types of trips. Sue is in charge of three major business accounts, and Bart heads a tour operation. Both of these agents report directly to Helen. Coordination is achieved through their dedicated intranet and Internet connections. Joan uses weekly meetings and a lot of personal contact by Helen and Joan to coordinate everyone. Control is enhanced by the computerized reservation system they all use. Helen makes sure each agent has a monthly sales target, and she routinely chats with important clients about their level of service. Helen realizes that developing participation from even the newest associate is an important tool in maintaining a "fun" atmosphere.

Read the Leaders on Leadership feature for this chapter and the story about G24i's leadership team. This small high-tech producer in the solar-power business has a simple structure to implement its strategy. The backgrounds of the leadership team clearly reflect the competencies they bring to help this new and innovative start-up to succeed.[22]

The Perils of Growth and Age　As organizations age and begin to grow beyond their simple structure they become more rigid, inflexible, and resistant to change.[23] Managerial scripts become routines, and both managers and employees begin to believe their prior success will continue into the future without an emphasis on innovation or learning. The organization or department becomes subject to routine scripts.

• A **managerial script** is a series of well-known routines for problem identification and alternative generation and analysis common to managers within a firm.

A **managerial script** is a series of well-known routines for problem identification and alternative generation and analysis common to managers within a firm.[24] Different organizations have different scripts, often based on what has worked in the past. In a way, the script is a ritual that reflects the "memory banks" held by the corporation. Managers become bound by what they have seen. The danger is that they may not be open to what actually is occurring. They may be unable to unlearn.

The script may be elaborate enough to provide an apparently well-tested series of solutions based on the firm's experience. Typically, older firms are structured for efficiency. Their organizational design emphasizes repetition, volume processing, and routine. In order to learn, the organization needs to be able to unlearn, switch routines to obtain information quickly, and provide various interpretations of events rather than just tap into external archives.

Few managers question a successful script. Consequently, they start solving today's problems with yesterday's solutions. Managers are trained, both in the classroom and on the job, to initiate corrective action within the historically shared view of the world. That is, managers often initiate small, incremental improvements based on existing solutions instead of creating new approaches to identify underlying problems.

For larger organizations a key challenge is eliminating the vertical, horizontal, external, and geographic barriers that block desired action, innovation, and learning.[25] These barriers include an overemphasis on vertical relations that can block communication up and down the firm; an overemphasis on functions, product lines, or organizational units that blocks effective coordination;

Leader on Leadership

THE LEADERSHIP TEAM AT G24i

What would bring a California politician, an Irish high-tech salesman and a chemist to Cardiff Wales? G24i. G24 Innovations is a new solar cell manufacturer. G24i utilizes the latest breakthrough in material science and nanotechnology to create a new class of advanced solar cells that are the closest that humankind has come to replicating nature's photosynthesis. It produces a thin, extremely flexible film that converts light energy into electrical energy even in low light and indoors.

The California politician is Robert M. Hertzberg, Chairman and Founder, G24 Innovations.

Hertzberg was twice Speaker of the California State Assembly, 2000–2002 and in this capacity, was instrumental in drafting legislative solutions to the California Energy Crisis. As Chairman of G24i, Mr. Hertzberg directs renewable energy policy issues and works on many aspects of company activities. He is the "green entrepreneur."

John Hartnett, the Irish high-tech salesman, is Chief Executive Officer. Prior to joining G24i, Mr. Hartnett was senior vice-president of global markets at Palm, Inc., where he was responsible for worldwide sales, service, and support. He has over 20 years of senior management experience across sales, marketing, and operations in the U.S. and Ireland. As for the chemist, Dr. Kevin Tabor, Director of Science and Research for G24i, holds a PhD in chemistry and has been a member of the scientific community for over 26 years. Dr. Tabor previously served as Director of Manufacturing and Technology at Solar Integrated Technologies where he managed the installation and commissioning of a

new generation, large (3-meter-wide), high throughput (180-MW-design capacity) manufacturing plant for production of flexible photovoltaic panels.

Their strategy is to use new technology to develop products for markets in developing countries. One product uses the thin film is a "power station" for cell phones. In a developing country, it can be miles to the nearest power source. By embedding the solar energy strip into clothing or other items exposed to light, users will be able to recharge their cell phones without utilizing their car batteries, the comparatively expensive option available now.

In the future, expect to see the solar energy film used in awnings, shades, and windows to cut conventional energy use or to power remote security surveillance systems and billboards. Now with some seventy employees, G24i appears poised for rapid growth. In the next phase, it will be a more sophisticated structure. For now what matters is the team and the skills they bring to manage this start-up.

maintaining rigid lines of demarcation between the firm and its partners that isolate it from others; and reinforcing natural cultural, national, and geographical borders that can limit globally coordinated action. In breaking down such barriers, the goal is not necessarily to eliminate them altogether, but to make them more permeable.[26]

There are several major factors associated with the inability to dynamically co-evolve and develop a cycle with positive benefits, but three are obvious from current research.[27] One is organizational inertia. It is very difficult to change an organization, and the larger the organization, the more inertia it often has. A second is hubris. Too few senior executives are willing to challenge their own actions or those of their firms because they see a history of success. A third is the issue of detachment. Executives often believe they can manage far-flung, diverse operations through analysis of reports and financial records. They lose touch and fail to make the needed unique and special adaptations required of all firms.

Inertia, hubris, and detachment are common maladies, but they are not the automatic fate of all corporations. Firms can successfully co-evolve. As we have repeatedly demonstrated, managers are constantly trying to reinvent their firms. They hope to initiate a benefit cycle—a pattern of successful adjustment followed by further improvements.[28] General Mills, IBM, Cisco, and Microsoft are examples of firms experiencing a benefit cycle. In this cycle, the same problems do not keep recurring as the firm develops adequate mechanisms for learning. The firm has few major difficulties with the learning process, and managers continually attempt to improve knowledge acquisition, information distribution, information interpretation, and organizational memory.

Technology and Organizational Design

Although the design for an organization should reflect its size, it must also be adjusted to fit technological opportunities and requirements.[29] Successful organizations are said to arrange their internal structures to meet the dictates of their dominant "operations technologies" or workflows and, more recently, information technology opportunities.[30] **Operations technology** is the combination of resources, knowledge, and techniques that creates a product or service output for an organization.[31] **Information technology** is the combination of machines, artifacts, procedures, and systems used to gather, store, analyze, and disseminate information for translating it into knowledge.[32]

- **Operations technology** is the combination of resources, knowledge, and techniques that creates a product or service output for an organization.

- **Information technology** is the combination of machines, artifacts, procedures, and systems used to gather, store, analyze, and disseminate information for translating it into knowledge.

Operations Technology and Organizational Design

As researchers in OB have charted the links between operations technology and organizational design, two common classifications for operations technology have received considerable attention: Thompson's and Woodward's classifications.

Thompson's View of Technology   James D. Thompson classified technologies based on the degree to which the technology could be specified and the degree of interdependence among the work activities with categories called intensive, mediating, and long-linked.[33] Under *intensive technology*, there is uncertainty as to how to produce desired outcomes. A group of specialists must be brought together interactively to use a variety of techniques to solve problems. Examples are found in a hospital emergency room or a research and development laboratory. Coordination and knowledge exchange are of critical importance with this kind of technology.

Mediating technology links parties that want to become interdependent. For example, banks link creditors and depositors and store money and information to facilitate such exchanges. Whereas all depositors and creditors are indirectly interdependent, the reliance is pooled through the bank. The degree of coordination among the individual tasks with pooled technology is substantially reduced, and information management becomes more important than coordinated knowledge application.

Under *long-linked technology*, also called mass production or industrial technology, the way to produce the desired outcomes is known. The task is broken down into a number of sequential steps. A classic example is the automobile assembly line. Control is critical, and coordination is restricted to making the sequential linkages work in harmony.

Joan Woodward also divides technology into three categories: small-batch, mass production, and continuous-process manufacturing.[34] In units of *small-batch production*, a variety of custom products are tailor-made to fit customer specifications, such as tailor-made suits. The machinery and equipment used are generally not very elaborate, but considerable craftsmanship is often needed. In *mass production*, the organization produces one or a few products through an assembly-line system. The work of one group is highly dependent on that of another, the equipment is typically sophisticated, and the workers are given very detailed instructions. Automobiles and refrigerators are produced in this way.

Organizations using *continuous-process technology* produce a few products using considerable automation. Classic examples are automated chemical plants and oil refineries. Millennium Chemicals' operations are a good example of what Woodward called continuous-process manufacturing. As the Ethics in OB suggests, innovative firms such as Millennium Chemicals are infusing ethics into day-to-day operations and making ethics a part of a recognizable pattern we have called strategy.

From her studies, Woodward concluded that the combination of structure and technology was critical to the success of the organizations. When technology and organizational design were matched properly, a firm was more successful. Specifically, successful small-batch and continuous-process plants had flexible structures with small workgroups at the bottom; more rigidly structured plants were less successful. In contrast, successful mass-production operations were rigidly structured and had large workgroups at the bottom. Since Woodward's studies, various other investigations supported this technological imperative. Today we recognize that operations technology is just one factor involved in the success of an organization.[35]

ETHICS IN OB

AT MILLENNIUM INORGANIC CHEMICALS ETHICS IS A PART OF ITS DESIGN AND STRATEGY

National Titanium Dioxide Company Ltd. ("Cristal") and Millennium Inorganic Chemicals (MIC) combined to form the world's second-largest producer of titanium dioxide and a leading producer of titanium chemicals. Cristal and MIC operate nine manufacturing plants in six countries and employ more than 3,700 people worldwide. Millennium Inorganic Chemicals is committed to protecting its employees, its neighbors, and the environment. As a critical component of who it is and what it wishes to be, its commitment to safety, health, and environmental stewardship is a prominent part of its company culture. MIC has a moral obligation to protect its employees, its neighbors, and the environment. As a critical component of who it is and what it wishes to be, its stated commitment is prominently included on its Web site.

Ethics for Stockholder Returns: Do you believe that a company integrating ethics into its strategy and design can provide great returns to stockholders as well?

Adhocracy as a Design Option for Innovation and Learning

The influence of operations technology is clearly seen in small organizations and in specific departments within large firms. In some instances, managers and employees simply do not know the appropriate way to service a client or to produce a particular product. This is an extreme example of Thompson's intensive type of technology, and it may be found in some small-batch processes where a team of individuals must develop a unique product for a particular client.

Mintzberg suggests that at these technological extremes, the "adhocracy" may be an appropriate design.[36] An **adhocracy** is characterized by

- few rules, policies, and procedures;
- substantial decentralization;
- shared decision making among members;
- extreme horizontal specialization (as each member of the unit may be a distinct specialist);
- few levels of management; and
- virtually no formal controls.

> **Adhocracy** emphasizes shared, decentralized decision making; extreme horizontal specialization; few levels of management; the virtual absence of formal controls; and few rules, policies, and procedures.

This design emphasizes innovation and learning. The adhocracy is particularly useful when an aspect of the firm's operations technology presents two sticky problems:

1. the tasks facing the firm vary considerably and provide many exceptions, as in a management consulting firm, or
2. problems are difficult to define and resolve.[37]

The adhocracy places a premium on professionalism and coordination in problem solving.[38] Large firms may use temporary task forces, form special committees, and even contract with consulting firms to provide the creative problem identification and problem solving that the adhocracy promotes. For instance, Microsoft creates autonomous departments to encourage talented employees to develop new software programs. Allied Chemical and 3M set up quasi-autonomous groups to work through new ideas.

We should note, however, that the adhocracy is notoriously inefficient. Further, many managers are reluctant to adopt this form because they appear to lose control of day-to-day operations. The implicit strategy consistent with the adhocracy is a stress on quality and individual service as opposed to efficiency. With more advanced information technology, firms are beginning to combine an adhocracy with bureaucratic elements based on advanced information systems.

Information Technology

Recall that we defined information technology as the combination of machines, artifacts, procedures, and systems used to gather, store, analyze, and disseminate information.[39] Information technology (IT), the Web, and the computer are virtually inseparable and they have fundamentally changed the organization design of firms to capture new competencies.[40] While some suggest that IT refers only to computer-based systems used in the management of the enterprise, we take a broader view.[41] With substantial collateral advances in telecommunication options, advances in the computer as a machine are much less profound than how information technology is transforming how firms manage all of their parts.

From an organizational standpoint, IT can be used, among other things, as a partial substitute for some operations as well as some process controls and impersonal methods of coordination. IT has a strategic capability as well as a capability for transforming information to knowledge. For instance, most financial firms could not exist without IT, because it is now the base for the industry. Early adopters created new segments of the industry with both major contributions to our economy and major new threats. With IT, exotic international financial products are available today, which did not exist 20 years ago. And financial institutions created completely new aspects of their industry based on IT, such as exotic derivatives; it is now painfully obvious that these new aspects of the industry outpaced the ability of management to control them. Information technology, just as operations technology, can yield great good or great harm.

IT as a Substitute   Old bureaucracies prospered and dominated other firms, in part, because they provided efficient production through specialization and through how they managed their information. Where the organization used mediating technology or long-linked technology, the machine bureaucracy ran rampant. In these firms, rules, policies, and procedures, as well as other process controls, could be rigidly enforced based on very scant information.[42] Such was the case for the U.S. post office: postal clerks had rules telling them how to hold their hands when sorting mail.

In many organizations, the initial implementation of IT displaced the most routine, highly specified, and repetitive jobs.[43] A second wave of substitution replaced process controls and informal coordination mechanisms. Management discovered that written rules, policies, and procedures could be replaced with a decision support system (DSS) that programmed repetitive routine choices into a computer-based system. For instance, if you apply for a credit card, a computer program will check your credit history and other financial information. If your application passes several preset tests, you are issued a credit card.

IT to Add Capability   IT has also long been recognized for its potential to add capability.[44] For many years, scholars have talked of using IT to improve the efficiency, speed of responsiveness, and effectiveness of operations. Married to machines, IT became advanced manufacturing technology when computer-aided design (CAD) was combined with computer-aided manufacturing (CAM) to yield the automated manufacturing cell. More complex decision-support systems have provided middle and lower-level managers with programs to aid in analyzing complex problems rather than merely ratifying routine choices. Computer-generated reports now give senior executives the opportunity to track the individual sales performance of every salesperson from top to bottom.

Now instead of substituting for existing operations, or process controls, IT provides individuals deep within the organization with the information they need to plan, coordinate with others, and control their own operations. Connectivity is the watchword of today and with parallel developments in telecommunications, a whole world of electronic commerce, teleconferencing—with combinations of data, pictures, and sound—and cell phones has opened new opportunities for companies. For example, textbooks now provide you with Web exercises and other opportunities for online learning in each chapter.

IT systems can also empower individuals, expanding their jobs and making them both interesting and challenging. The emphasis on narrowly defined jobs replete with process controls imposed by middle management can be transformed to broadly envisioned, interesting jobs based on IT-embedded processes with output controls. The IT system can handle the routine operations while individuals deep within the organization deal with the exceptions. For example, you can order plumbing supplies to update a bath or kitchen from Moen directly. Their Web site provides pictures of the products, specifications, and a phone number if you need help. The Moen representatives are there to provide the needed technical assistance and design help while their Web site provides the product information.[45]

For the production segments of firms using long-linked technology such as in auto assembly plants and canneries, IT is now linked to total quality management (TQM) programs and embedded in the machinery. Data on operations now transform into knowledge of operations and are used to improve quality and efficiency. This means that firms have had to rethink their view of employees as brainless robots. To make TQM work with IT, all employees must plan, do, and control. Combining IT and TQM with empowerment and participation is fundamental for success.[46]

The Virtual Organization and IT Opportunities   Shortly before the turn of the last century, e-business exploded upon the scene.[47] Today e-business is integrated into the virtual organization just as on-site project teams morphed into virtual project teams.

E- Business and IT   Whether it is business to business (B2B) or business to consumers (B2C), there is a whole new set of firms with information technology at the core of their operations. One of the more flamboyant early entrants to the B2C world is the now-familiar Amazon.com. Opened in 1995 to sell books directly to customers via the Internet, it rapidly expanded to toys and games, health and beauty products, groceries, computers and video games, as well as cameras and photography. It is now a virtual general store with one of the best-recognized Web site addresses available.

It is interesting to examine the transformation in the design of this firm to illustrate the notion of co-evolution and the ability to learn with advanced IT. Initially, Amazon.com was organized as a simple structure. As it grew, it became more complex by adding divisions devoted to each of its separate product areas. To remain flexible and promote growth in both the volume of operations and the capabilities of employees, it did not develop an extensive bureaucracy. There are still very few levels of management. It built separate organizational components based on product categories (divisional structure) with minimal rules, policies, and procedures. In other words, the organizational design it adopted appeared relatively conventional.[48]

What was not conventional was the use of IT for learning about customers and for coordinating and tracking operations. Although their Web site is not particularly advanced technically, you can easily order a book, track the delivery, and feel confident it will arrive as promised. In recent years, Amazon.com has used its IT prowess to develop strategic alliances with brick and mortar firms and it effectively changed the competitive landscape.

In comparison to Amazon.com, many other new dot-com firms adopted a variation of the adhocracy as their design pattern. The thinking was that e-business was fundamentally different from the old bricks-and-mortar operations. Thus, an entirely new structural configuration was needed to accommodate the development of new e-products and services. The managers of these firms forgot two important liabilities of the adhocracy as they grew. First, there are limits on the size of an effective adhocracy. Second, the actual delivery of their products and services did not require continual product innovation but rested more on responsiveness to clients and maintaining efficiency. The design did not deliver what they needed. In common terms they had great Web sites, but they were grossly inefficient. Many of these businesses died almost as quickly as they were formed.

The Emergence of the Virtual Organization

As IT has become widespread, firms are finding it can be the basis for a new way to compete. Some executives have started to develop "virtual organizations."[49] A **virtual organization** is an ever-shifting constellation of firms, with a lead corporation, that pools skills, resources, and experiences to thrive jointly. This ever-changing collection most likely has a relatively stable group of actors (usually independent firms) that normally includes customers, research centers, suppliers, and distributors all connected to each other. The lead firm possesses a critical competence that all need and therefore directs the constellation. While this critical competence may be a key operations technology or access to customers, it always includes IT as a base for connecting the firms. Across time, members of the constellation come and go during shifts in technology or alterations in environmental conditions. It is also important to stress that key customers are an integral part of a virtual organization. Not only do customers purchase from the company, they also participate in the development of new products and services. Thus, the virtual organization co-evolves by incorporating many types of firms.

The virtual organization works if it operates by some unique rules and is led in a most untypical way. First, the production system that yields the products and services that customers desire needs to be a partner network among independent firms where they are bound together by mutual trust and collective survival. As customers desire change, the proportion of work done by any member firm might also change and the membership itself may change. In a similar fashion, the introduction of a new operations technology could shift the proportion of work among members or call for the introduction of new members.

Second, this partner network needs to develop and maintain (a) an advanced information technology (rather than just face-to-face interaction), (b) trust and cross-owning of problems and solutions, and (c) a common shared culture. Developing these characteristics is a very tall order, but the virtual organization can be highly resilient, extremely competent, innovative, and reasonably efficient— characteristics that are usually trade-offs. The virtual organization can effectively compete on a global scale in very complex settings using advanced operations and information technologies.

The role of the lead firm is also quite unusual and actually makes a network of firms a virtual organization. The lead firm must take responsibility for the whole constellation and coordinate the actions and evolution of autonomous member firms. Executives in the lead firm need to have the vision to see how the network of participants will both effectively compete with consistent

A **virtual organization** is an ever-shifting constellation of firms, with a lead corporation, that pool skills, resources, and experiences to thrive jointly.

> **MASTERING MANAGEMENT**
>
> **BECOMING A BETTER VIRTUAL PROJECT MANAGER**
>
> When you manage a "virtual" project,
>
> - Establish a set of mutually reinforcing motives for participation including a share in success.
> - Stress self-governance and make sure there are a manageable number of high-quality contributors.
> - Outline a set of rules that members can adapt to their individual needs.
> - Encourage joint monitoring and sanctions of member behavior.
> - Stress shared values, norms, and behavior.
> - Develop effective work structures and processes via project management software.
> - Emphasize the use of technology for communication and norms about how to use it.

enough patterns to be recognizable and still rapidly adjust to technological and environmental changes. Executives should not only communicate this vision and inspire individuals in the independent member firms, but also treat members as if they are volunteers. To accomplish this across independent firms, the lead corporation and its members need to rethink how they are internally organized and managed.[49]

Even before the complete development of a virtual organization, more than likely you will be involved with a "virtual" network of task forces and temporary teams to both define and solve problems. Here the members will only connect electronically. Recent work on participants of the virtual teams suggests you will need to rethink what it means to "manage." Instead of telling others what to do, you will need to treat your colleagues as unpaid volunteers who expect to participate in governing the meetings and who are tied to the effort only by a commitment to identify and solve problems.[50] Mastering Management provides guidelines to think about when managing a project in a virtual environment.[51]

Environment and Organizational Design

An effective organizational design also reflects powerful external forces as well as size and technological factors. Organizations, as open systems, need to receive input from the environment and in turn to sell output to their environment. Therefore, understanding the environment is important.[52]

• The **general environment** is the set of cultural, economic, legal-political, and educational conditions found in the areas in which the organization operates.

The **general environment** is the set of cultural, economic, legal-political, and educational conditions found in the areas in which the organization operates. Firms expanding globally encounter multiple general environments. Once, firms could separate foreign and domestic operations into almost separate operating entities, but this is rarely the case now. Today consumers and employees are responding to a series of global issues such as global warming, fair trade, and sustainability. Firms sourcing from developing countries are changing their sourcing practices to conform to expectations in developed nations, as illustrated by the Fairtrade movement. Here, farmers are encouraged to develop sustainable farming and are paid more for their products.[53]

The owners, suppliers, distributors, government agencies, and competitors with which an organization must interact to grow and survive constitute its **specific environment**. A firm typically has much more choice in the composition of its specific environment than its general environment. Although it is often convenient to separate the general and specific environmental influences on the firm, managers need to recognize the combined impact of both. Choosing some businesses, for instance, means entering global competition with advanced technologies.

Environmental Complexity

A basic concern to address when analyzing the environment of the organization is its complexity. A more complex environment provides an organization with more opportunities and more problems. **Environmental complexity** refers to the magnitude of the problems and opportunities in the organization's environment, as evidenced by three main factors: the degree of richness, the degree of interdependence, and the degree of uncertainty stemming from both the general and the specific environment.

Environmental Richness
Overall, the environment is richer when the economy is growing, when individuals are improving their education, and when everyone that the organization relies upon is prospering. For businesses, a richer environment means that economic conditions are improving, customers are spending more money, and suppliers (especially banks) are willing to invest in the organization's future. In a rich environment, more organizations survive, even if they have poorly functioning organizational designs. A richer environment is also filled with more opportunities and dynamism—the potential for change. The organizational design must allow the company to recognize these opportunities and capitalize on them.

The opposite of richness is decline. For business firms, the current general recession is a good example of a leaner environment. While corporate reactions do vary, it is instructive to examine typical responses to decline. In the United States, firms have traditionally reacted to decline first by issuing layoffs to non-supervisory workers and by moving the layoffs up the organizational ladder as the environment becomes leaner. Many European firms find it difficult to cut full-time employees quickly because of European employment laws. In sustained periods of decline, many European firms therefore turn to national governments for help. Much like U.S.-based firms, European-based firms view changes in organizational design as a last but increasingly necessary resort as they compete globally.

Environmental Interdependence
The link between external interdependence and organizational design is often subtle and indirect. The organization may co-opt powerful outsiders by including them. For instance, many large corporations have financial representatives from banks and insurance companies on their boards of directors. The organization may also adjust its overall design strategy to absorb or buffer the demands of a more powerful external element. Perhaps the most common adjustment is the development of a centralized staff department to

Ensuring Sustainability and a Fair Price

Cadbury's Dairy Milk bar will be "Fairtrade" certified in the UK and Ireland by the end of 2009, and *Mars* is working with Rainforest Alliance to source sustainably all of their cocoa by 2020, starting with Rainforest Alliance certification for its Galaxy bar in 2010. Fairtrade is an organization that works to ensure a minimum price for farmers.

• The **specific environment** is the set of owners, suppliers, distributors, government agencies, and competitors with which an organization must interact to grow and survive.

• **Environmental complexity** is the magnitude of the problems and opportunities in the organization's environment as evidenced by the degree of richness, interdependence, and uncertainty.

Corning's Global Reach

While Corning is an innovation-driven firm engaged in a variety of advanced materials and technologies, it does not commercialize its new products alone. Instead it relies upon alliances with over 50 affiliated companies in 16 countries to distribute its products.

handle an important external group. For instance, few large U.S. corporations lack some type of centralized governmental relations group. Where service to a few large customers is critical, the organization's departmentation is likely to switch from a functional to a divisionalized form.[54]

Uncertainty and Volatility   Environmental uncertainty and volatility can be particularly damaging to large bureaucracies. In times of change, investments quickly become outmoded, and internal operations no longer work as expected. The obvious organizational design response to uncertainty and volatility is to opt for a more flexible organic form. At the extremes, movement toward an adhocracy may be important. However, these pressures may run counter to those that come from large size and operations technology. In these cases, it may be too hard or too time consuming for some organizations to make the design adjustments. Thus, the organization may continue to struggle while adjusting its design just a little bit at a time. Some firms can deal with the conflicting demands from environmental change and need for internal stability by developing alliances.

Using Networks and Alliances

In today's complex global economy, organizational design must go beyond the traditional boundaries of the firm.[55] Firms must learn to co-evolve by altering their environment. Two ways are becoming more popular: (1) the management of networks, and (2) the development of alliances. Many North American firms are learning from their European and Japanese counterparts to develop networks of linkages to the key firms they rely upon. In Europe, for example, one finds *informal combines* or *cartels*. Here, competitors work cooperatively to share the market in order to decrease uncertainty and improve favorability for all. Except in rare cases, these arrangements are often illegal in the United States.

In Japan, the network of relationships among well-established firms in many industries is called a *keiretsu*. There are two common forms. The first is a bank-centered *keiretsu*, in which firms link to one another directly through cross-ownership and historical ties to one bank. The Mitsubishi group is a good example of a company that grew through cross-ownership. In the second type, a *vertical keiretsu*, a key manufacturer is at the hub of a network of supplier firms or distributor firms. The manufacturer typically has both long-term supply contracts with members and cross-ownership ties. These arrangements help isolate Japanese firms from stockholders and provide a mechanism for sharing and developing technology. Toyota is an example of a firm at the center of a *vertical keiretsu*.

A specialized form of network organization is evolving in U.S.-based firms as well. Here, the central firm specializes in core activities, such as design, assembly, and marketing, and works with a small number of participating suppliers on a long-term basis for both component development and manufacturing efficiency. The central firm is the hub of a network where others need it more than it needs any other member. Although Nike was a leader in the development of these relationships, now it is difficult to find a large U.S. firm that does not outsource extensively. Executives seeking to find cheap sources of foreign labor often justify outsourcing from the U.S. firms. However, as a design option,

RESEARCH INSIGHT

Changing the Environment to Learn More

Researchers Thomas Keil, Markku Maula, Henri Schildt, and Shaker Zahra examined the learning development actions of 110 of the largest U.S.-based firms in the computer, electronics, and communication equipment industries. Did firms that developed joint ventures with others, established alliances, funded initiatives by other firms (corporate venture capital investments), or acquired others learn enough to develop more patents?

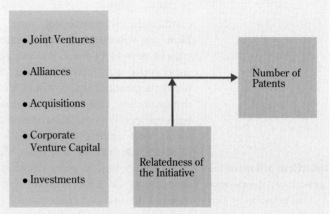

Further, they examined whether the degree of relatedness to existing business on each of these different types of initiatives increased the number of patents. Specifically, they rated each of the initiatives as within the existing industry, related to the industry of the firm, or unrelated. They expected that related initiatives would yield the greatest learning because they balanced novelty and experience. There was too little to learn from related initiatives and too much of a gap in knowledge to learn from unrelated initiatives.

They found that more joint ventures, more alliances, more acquisitions, and more corporate venture capital investments were related to more patents. This outcome was expected and seems to confirm common sense. What was unusual was the pattern for each of these initiatives when considering the degree of relatedness. There was an inverted U-shaped pattern for joint ventures, alliances, and acquisitions when linking relatedness and the number of patents.

Specifically, there were modest increases for initiatives within the industry of the firm, much more dramatic increases for initiatives related to current businesses, and modest increases for initiatives unrelated to current businesses. The biggest surprise was for acquisitions. Firms learned the most from acquisitions within their main business. They learned less from acquisitions unrelated or related to existing businesses.

What Do You Think?

Was the challenge of integrating a new firm so great that it negated the opportunity to learn from the new firm? Do you think these results apply to firms in other industries?

Source: Thomas Keil, Markku Maula, Henri Schildt, and Shaker Zahra, "The Effect of Governance Modes and Relatedness of External Business Development Activities on Innovative Performance," *Strategic Management Journal* 29 (2008), pp. 895–907.

managers should examine how this alternative fits with the firm's strategy and technology as well. For instance, if the firm markets high quality products matched with service, outsourcing may be inconsistent with the service requirements needed for success. Customers could move to firms that do not outsource service.

Being at the hub of a network can provide a greater opportunity to innovate and gain greater financial returns. Hiring capable individuals with experience in developing new products helps. Combine these two traits, and firms generate substantially more innovation and gain substantially more financial returns.[56]

More extreme variations of network design are emerging to meet apparently conflicting environmental, size, and technological demands simultaneously. Firms are spinning off staff functions to reduce their overall size and take advantage of new IT options. For example, many call centers for computer technology support are outsourced to India. With too much outsourcing, firms become too highly dependent upon others, lose the ability to be flexible and respond to new opportunities, and may lose valuable information. For example, the use of foreign call centers cuts information flowing from customers to the core firm. With these new environmental challenges and technological opportunities, firms must choose and not just react blindly.

> **Interfirm alliances** are announced cooperative agreements or joint ventures between two independent firms.

Another option is to develop **interfirm alliances**, which are cooperative agreements or joint ventures between two independent firms.[57] Often, these agreements involve corporations that are headquartered in different nations. In high-tech areas, such as robotics, semiconductors, advanced materials (ceramics and carbon fibers), and advanced information systems, a single company often does not have all of the knowledge necessary to bring new products to the market. Alliances are quite common in such high-technology industries. Via their international alliances, high-tech firms seek to develop technology and to ensure that their solutions standardize across regions of the world.

Developing and effectively managing an alliance is a managerial challenge of the first order. Firms are asked to cooperate rather than compete. The alliance's sponsors normally have different and unique strategies, cultures, and desires for the alliance itself. Both the alliance managers and sponsoring executives must be patient, flexible, and creative in pursuing the goals of the alliance and each sponsor. It is little wonder that some alliances are terminated prematurely.[58]

Of course, alliances are but one way of altering the environment. The firm can also invest in the projects of other firms via corporate venture capital. It may acquire other companies to bring their expertise directly into the firm. All of these can be beneficial.[59] However, these initiatives need to be related to the strategy of the firm and its technology. Examine the Research Insight to see how much firms learned from the use of joint ventures, established alliances and acquisitions (both partial and complete).[60]

Resources in *The OB Skills Workbook*

These learning activities from *The OB Skills Workbook* are suggested for Chapter 17.

Case for Critical Thinking	Team and Experiential Exercises	Self-Assessment Portfolio
• Mission Management and Trust	• Tinker Toys • Organizations Alive • Alien Invasion	• A 21st-Century Manager • Group Effectiveness • Organizational Design Preferences

17 studyguide

Why are strategy and organizational learning important?

- Strategy is the process of positioning the organization in the competitive environment and implementing actions to compete successfully. It is a pattern in a stream of decisions.

- Organizational learning is the process of acquiring knowledge and using information to adapt successfully to changing circumstances.

- For organizations to learn, they must engage in knowledge acquisition, information distribution, information interpretation, and organizational retention in adapting successfully to changing circumstances.

- Firms use mimicry, experience, vicarious learning, scanning, and grafting to acquire information.

- Firms established mechanisms to convert information into knowledge. Chief among the problems of interpretation are self-serving interpretations.

- Firms retain information via individuals, transformation mechanisms, formal structure, physical structure, external archives, and their IT system.

- To compete successfully, individuals, units, and firms will need to constantly learn because of changes in the scope of operations, technology, and the environment.

What is organizational design, and how is it linked to strategy?

- Organizational design is the process of choosing and implementing a structural configuration for an organization.

- Organizational design is a way to implement the positioning of the firm in its environment.

- Organizational design provides a basis for a consistent stream of decisions.

- Strategy and organizational design are interrelated, and must evolve with changes in size, technology, and the environment.

- The design of a large organization is far more complex than that of a small firm. Smaller firms often adopt a simple structure because it works, is cheap, and stresses the influence of the leader.

- With growth and aging, firms become subject to routine managerial scripts. Large organizations will need to systematically break down boundaries limiting learning.

How does technology influence organizational design?

- Operations technology and organizational design should be interrelated to insure the firm produces the desired goods and/or services.

- Adhocracy is an organizational design used in technology intense settings.

- Information technology is the combination of machines, artifacts, procedures, and systems used to gather, store, analyze, and disseminate information for translating it into knowledge.

- IT provides an opportunity to change the design by substitution, for learning, and to capture strategic advantages.

- IT forms the basis for the virtual organization.

How does the environment influence organizational design?

- Organizations, as open systems, need to receive inputs from the environment and, in turn, to sell outputs to their environment.

- The environment is more complex when it is richer and more interdependent with higher volatility and greater uncertainty.

- The more complex the environment, the greater the demands on the organization, and firms should respond with more complex designs.

- Firms need not stand alone but can develop network relationships and alliances to cope with greater environmental complexity.

- By honing the knowledge gained in this text you can develop the skills to compete successfully in the 21st century and become a leader.

Key Terms

Adhocracy (p. 426)
Environmental complexity
  (p. 431)
General environment
  (p. 430)
Grafting (p. 417)
Information technology
  (p. 424)

Interfirm alliances (p. 434)
Organizational design
  (p. 419)
Organizational learning
  (p. 416)
Operations technology
  (p. 424)
Managerial script (p. 422)

Mimicry (p. 417)
Scanning (p. 417)
Simple design (p. 421)
Specific environment
  (p. 431)
Strategy (p. 416)
Virtual organization
  (p. 429)

Self-Test 17

Multiple Choice

1. The design of the organization needs to be adjusted to all but _____.
   (a) the environment of the firm (b) the strategy of the firm (c) the size of the firm (d) the operations and information technology of the firm (e) the personnel to be hired by the firm

2. _____ is the combination of resources, knowledge, and techniques that creates a product or service output for an organization. (a) Information technology (b) Strategy (c) Organizational learning (c) Operations technology (d) The general environment (e) The benefit cycle

3. _____ is the combination of machines, artifacts, procedures, and systems used to gather, store, analyze, and disseminate information for translating it into knowledge (a) The specific environment (b) Strategy (c) Operations technology (d) Information technology (e) Organizational decline

4. Which of the following is an accurate statement about an adhocracy? (a) The design facilitates information exchange and learning. (b) There are many rules and policies. (c) Use of IT is always minimal. (d) It handles routine problems efficiently. (e) It is quite common in older industries.

5. The set of cultural, economic, legal-political, and educational conditions in the areas in which a firm operates is called the _____. (a) task environment (b) specific environment (c) industry of the firm (d) environmental complexity (e) general environment

6. The segment of the environment that refers to the other organizations with which an organization must interact in order to obtain inputs and dispose of outputs is called _____. (a) the general environment (b) the strategic environment (c) the learning environment (d) the technological setting (e) the specific environment

7. _____ are announced cooperative agreements or joint ventures between two independent firms. (a) Mergers (b) Acquisitions (c) Interfirm alliances (d) Adhocracies (e) Strategic configurations

8. The process of knowledge acquisition, organizational retention, and information distribution and interpretation is called _____. (a) vicarious learning (b) experience (c) organizational learning (d) an organizational myth (e) a self-serving interpretation

9. Three methods of vicarious learning are _____. (a) scanning, grafting, and contracting out (b) grafting, contracting out, and mimicry (c) maladaptive specialization, scanning, and grafting (d) scanning, grafting, and mimicry (e) experience, mimicry, and scanning

10. Three important factors that block information interpretation are _____. (a) detachment, scanning, and common myths (b) self-serving interpretations, detachment, and common myths (c) managerial scripts, maladaptive specialization, and common myths (d) contracting out, common myths, and detachment (e) common myths, managerial scripts, and self-serving interpretations

11. Regarding the organizational design for a small firm compared to a large firm, _____. (a) they are almost the same (b) they are fundamentally different (c) a large firm is just a larger version of a small one (d) the small firm has more opportunity to use information technology

12. Organizations with well-defined and stable operations technologies _____. (a) have more opportunity to substitute decision support systems (DSS) for managerial judgment than do firms relying on more variable operations technologies (b) have less opportunity to substitute decision support systems for managerial judgment than do firms relying on more variable operations technologies (c) are less able to develop international alliances (d) are more able to develop international alliances

13. Adhocracies tend to favor _____. (a) vertical specialization and control (b) horizontal specialization and coordination (c) extensive centralization (d) a rigid strategy

14. With extensive use of IT, _____. (a) more staff are typically added (b) firms can use IT (c) firms can move internationally (d) firms can reduce redundancy

15. Environmental complexity _____. (a) refers to the set of alliances formed by senior management (b) refers to the overall level of problems and opportunities stemming from munificence, interdependence, and volatility (c) is restricted to the general environment of organizations (d) is restricted to other organizations with which an organization must interact in order to obtain inputs and dispose of outputs

16. The strategy of a firm _____. (a) is the process of positioning the organization in the competitive environment and implementing actions to compete successfully. It is a pattern in a stream of decisions (b) is only a process of positioning the organization to compete (c) is only a pattern in a stream of decisions (d) is a process of acquiring knowledge, organizational retention, and distributing and interpreting information

17. An organizational alliance is _____. (a) an extreme example of an adhocracy (b) an announced cooperative agreements or joint venture between two independent firms (c) always short-lived (d) a sign of organizational weakness

18. Copying of the successful practices of others is called _____. (a) mimicry (b) scanning (c) grafting (d) strategy

19. _____ is the process of choosing and implementing a structural configuration for an organization. (a) Strategy (b) Organizational design (c) Grafting (d) Scanning

20. The process of acquiring individuals, units, and/or firms to bring in useful knowledge to the organization is called _____. (a) grafting (b) strategy (c) scanning (d) mimicry

Short Response

21. Explain why a large firm could not use a simple structure.

22. Explain the deployment of IT and its uses in organizations.

23. Describe the effect operations technology has on an organization from both Thompson's and Woodward's points of view.

24. What are the three primary determinants of environmental complexity?

Applications Essay

25. Why would Ford Motors want to shift to a matrix design organization for the design and development of cars and trucks but not do so in its manufacturing and assembly operations?

THE OB SKILLS WORKBOOK

Featuring
The Jossey-Bass/Pfeiffer
Classroom Collection

Pfeiffer
An Imprint of WILEY

JOSSEY-BASS
An Imprint of WILEY
Now you know.

SUGGESTED USES AND APPLICATIONS OF WORKBOOK MATERIALS

1. Learning Styles

Activity	Suggested Part	Overview
1. Learning Styles Inventory— Online at: www.wiley.com/ go/global/schermerhorn	1	This online inventory provides insight into a person's relative strengths on seven alternative approaches to learning, described as: visual learner, print learner, auditory learner, interactive learner, haptic learner, kinesthetic learner, and olfactory learner.
2. Study Tips for Different Learning Styles	1	This reading included in the workbook provides study tips for learners with different tendencies and strengths.

2. Student Leadership Practices Inventory by Kouzes and Posner

Activity	Suggested Part	Overview
1. Student Leadership Practices Inventory— Student Workbook	All	This workbook includes a worksheet to help interpret feedback and plan improvement in each leadership practice assessed, sections on how to compare scores with the normative sample and how to share feedback with constituents, and more than 140 actual steps students can take to get results.
2. Student Leadership Practices Inventory— Self	All	This 30-item inventory will help students evaluate their performance and effectiveness as a leader. Results from the simple scoring process help students prepare plans for personal leadership development.
3. Student Leadership Practices Inventory— Observer	All	This version of the LPI is used by others to assess the individual's leadership tendencies, thus allowing for comparison with self-perceptions.

3. Self-Assessment Portfolio

See companion Web site for online versions of many assessments: www.wiley.com/go/global/schermerhorn

Assessment	Suggested Chapter	Cross-References and Integration
1. Managerial Assumptions	1 Organizational Behavior Today	leadership
2. A Twenty-First-Century Manager	1 Organizational Behavior Today 14 Leadership Challenges and Organizational Change 16 Organizational Goals and Structures 17 Strategy, Technology, and Organizational Design	leadership; decision making; globalization

Assessment	Suggested Chapter	Cross-References and Integration
3. *Turbulence Tolerance Test*	1 Organizational Behavior Today 2 Individual Differences, Values, and Diversity	perception; individual differences; organizational change and stress
4. *Global Readiness Index*	3 Emotions, Attitudes, and Job Satisfaction 14 Leadership Challenges and Organizational Change	diversity; culture; leading; perception; management skills; career readiness
5. *Personal Values*	3 Emotions, Attitudes, and Job Satisfaction 6 Motivation and Performance	perception; diversity and individual differences; leadership
6. *Intolerance for Ambiguity*	4 Perception, Attribution, and Learning	perception; leadership
7. *Two-Factor Profile*	5 Motivation Theories 6 Motivation and Performance	job design; perception; culture; human resource management
8. *Are You Cosmopolitan?*	6 Motivation and Performance 15 Organizational Culture and Innovation	diversity and individual differences; organizational culture
9. *Group Effectiveness*	7 Teams in Organizations 8 Teamwork and Team Performance 15 Organizational Culture and Innovation 17 Strategy, Technology, and Organizational Design	organizational designs and cultures; leadership
10. *Least Preferred Co-worker Scale*	13 Foundations for Leadership	diversity and individual differences; perception; group dynamics and teamwork
11. *Leadership Style*	13 Foundations for Leadership	diversity and individual differences; perception; group dynamics and teamwork
12. *"TT" Leadership Style*	11 Communication and Collaboration 13 Foundations for Leadership	diversity and individual differences; perception; group dynamics and teamwork
13. *Empowering Others*	8 Teamwork and Team Performance 11 Communication and Collaboration 12 Power and Politics	leadership; perception and attribution
14. *Machiavellianism*	12 Power and Politics	leadership; diversity and individual differences
15. *Personal Power Profile*	12 Power and Politics	leadership; diversity and individual differences
16. *Your Intuitive Ability*	9 Creativity and Decision Making	diversity and individual differences

Assessment	Suggested Chapter	Cross-References and Integration
17. Decision-Making Biases	7 Teams in Organizations 9 Creativity and Decision Making	teams and teamwork; communication; perception
18. Conflict Management Strategies	10 Conflict and Negotiation	diversity and individual differences; communication
19. Your Personality Type	2 Individual Differences, Values, and Diversity	diversity and individual differences; job design
20. Time Management Profile	2 Individual Differences, Values, and Diversity	diversity and individual differences
21. Organizational Design Preference	16 Organizational Goals and Structures 17 Strategy, Technology, and Organizational Design	job design; diversity and individual differences
22. Which Culture Fits You?	15 Organizational Culture and Innovation	perception; diversity and individual differences

 ## 4. Team and Experiential Exercises

Selections from The Pfeiffer Annual Training

Activity	Suggested Part	Overview
A. Sweet Tooth: Bonding Strangers into a Team	Parts 1, 3, 4	Perception, teamwork, decision making, communication
B. Interrogatories: Identifying Issues and Needs	Parts 1, 3, 4	Current issues, group dynamics, communication
C. Decode: Working with Different Instructions	Parts 3, 4	Decision making, leadership, conflict, teamwork
D. Choices: Learning Effective Conflict Management Strategies	Parts 1, 2, 3, 4, 5	Conflict, negotiation, communication, decision making
E. Internal/External Motivators: Encouraging Creativity	Parts 2, 4, 5	Creativity, motivation, job design, decision making
F. Quick Hitter: Fostering the Creative Spirit	Parts 4, 5	Creativity, decision making, communication

Additional Team and Experiential Exercises

Exercise	Suggested Chapter	Cross-References and Integration
1. My Best Manager	1 Introducing Organizational Behavior 3 Emotions, Attitudes, and Job Satisfaction	leadership

Exercise	Suggested Chapter	Cross-References and Integration
2. *Graffiti Needs Assessment*	1 Introducing Organizational Behavior	human resource management; communication
3. *My Best Job*	1 Introducing Organizational Behavior 6 Motivation and Performance	motivation; job design; organizational cultures
4. *What Do You Value in Work?*	5 Motivation Theories	diversity and individual differences; performance management and rewards; motivation; job design; decision making
5. *My Asset Base*	3 Emotions, Attitudes, and Job Satisfaction 4 Perception, Attribution, and Learning	perception and attribution; diversity and individual differences; groups and teamwork; decision making
6. *Expatriate Assignments*	4 Perception, Attribution, and Learning 15 Organizational Culture and Innovation	perception and attribution; diversity and individual differences; decision making
7. *Cultural Cues*	14 Leadership Challenges and Organizational Change	perception and attribution; diversity and individual differences; decision making; communication; conflict; groups and teamwork
8. *Prejudice in Our Lives*	3 Emotions, Attitudes, and Job Satisfaction	perception and attribution; decision making; conflict; groups and teamwork
9. *How We View Differences*	3 Emotions, Attitudes, and Job Satisfaction 4 Perception, Attribution, and Learning 15 Organizational Culture and Innovation	culture; international; diversity and individual differences; decision making; communication; conflict; groups and teamwork
10. *Alligator River Story*	4 Perception, Attribution, and Learning	diversity and individual differences; decision making; communication; conflict; groups and teamwork
11. *Teamwork and Motivation*	5 Motivation Theories	performance management and rewards; groups and teamwork
12. *The Downside of Punishment*	5 Motivation Theories	motivation; perception and attribution; performance management and rewards
13. *Tinkertoys*	6 Motivation and Performance 16 Organizational Goals and Structures 17 Strategy, Technology, and Organizational Design	organizational structure; design and culture; groups and teamwork
14. *Job Design Preferences*	6 Motivation and Performance	motivation; job design; organizational design; change
15. *My Fantasy Job*	6 Motivation and Performance	motivation; individual differences; organizational design; change
16. *Motivation by Job Enrichment*	6 Motivation and Performance	motivation; job design; perception; diversity and individual differences; change

Exercise	Suggested Chapter	Cross-References and Integration
17. *Annual Pay Raises*	5 Motivation Theories 6 Motivation and Performance	motivation; learning and reinforcement; perception and attribution; decision making; groups and teamwork
18. *Serving on the Boundary*	7 Teams in Organizations	intergroup dynamics; group dynamics; roles; communication; conflict; stress
19. *Eggsperiential Exercise*	7 Teams in Organizations	group dynamics and teamwork; diversity and individual differences; communication
20. *Scavenger Hunt—Team Building*	8 Teamwork and Team Performance	groups; leadership; diversity and individual differences; communication; leadership
21. *Work Team Dynamics*	8 Teamwork and Team Performance	groups; motivation; decision making; conflict; communication
22. *Identifying Team Norms*	8 Teamwork and Team Performance	groups; communication; perception and attribution
23. *Workgroup Culture*	8 Teamwork and Team Performance 15 Organizational Culture and Innovation	groups; communication; perception and attribution; job design; organizational culture
24. *The Hot Seat*	8 Teamwork and Team Performance	groups; communication; conflict and negotiation; power and politics
25. *Interview a Leader*	12 Power and Politics 13 Foundations for Leadership	performance management and rewards; groups and teamwork; new workplace; organizational change and stress
26. *Leadership Skills Inventories*	13 Foundations for Leadership	individual differences; perception and attribution; decision making
27. *Leadership and Participation in Decision Making*	13 Foundations for Leadership	decision making; communication; motivation; groups; teamwork
28. *My Best Manager: Revisited*	12 Power and Politics	diversity and individual differences; perception and attribution
29. *Active Listening*	11 Communication and Collaboration	group dynamics and teamwork; perception and attribution
30. *Upward Appraisal*	6 Motivation and Performance 11 Communication and Collaboration	perception and attribution; performance management and rewards
31. *360° Feedback*	6 Motivation and Performance 11 Communication and Collaboration	communication; perception and attribution; performance management and rewards
32. *Role Analysis Negotiation*	9 Creativity and Decision Making	communication; group dynamics and teamwork; perception and attribution; communication; decision making
33. *Lost at Sea*	9 Creativity and Decision Making	communication; group dynamics and teamwork; conflict and negotiation
34. *Entering the Unknown*	9 Creativity and Decision Making 10 Conflict and Negotiation	communication; group dynamics and teamwork; perception and attribution

Exercise	Suggested Chapter	Cross-References and Integration
35. *Vacation Puzzle*	10 Conflict and Negotiation	conflict and negotiation; communication; power; leadership
36. *The Ugli Orange*	9 Creativity and Decision Making 10 Conflict and Negotiation	communication; decision making
37. *Conflict Dialogues*	10 Conflict and Negotiation	conflict; communication; feedback; perception; stress
38. *Force-Field Analysis*	9 Creativity and Decision Making	decision making; organization structures, designs, cultures
39. *Organizations Alive!*	16 Organizational Goals and Structures 17 Strategy, Technology, and Organizational Design	organizational design and culture; performance management and rewards
40. *Fast-Food Technology*	15 Organizational Culture and Innovation 16 Organizational Goals and Structures	organizational design; organizational culture; job design
41. *Alien Invasion*	15 Organizational Culture and Innovation 16 Organizational Goals and Structures 17 Strategy, Technology, and Organizational Design	organizational structure and design; international; diversity and individual differences; perception and attribution
42. *Power Circles Exercise*	12 Power and Politics	influence; power; leadership; change management

5. Cases for Critical Thinking

Case	Suggested Chapter	Cross-References and Integration
1a. *Trader Joe's*	1 Introducing Organizational Behavior	human resource management; organizational cultures; innovation; information technology; leadership
1b. *Management Training Dilemma*	1 Introducing Organizational Behavior	ethics and decision making; communication; conflict and negotiation
2. *Ursula Burns, Xerox*	2 Individual Differences, Values, and Diversity	diversity and individual differences; perception and attribution; performance management; job design; communication; conflict; decision making
3. *Louise Quam, Tysvar, LLC*	3 Emotions, Attitudes, and Job Satisfaction	organizational cultures; globalization; innovation; motivation
4. *MagRec, Inc.*	4 Perception, Attribution, and Learning	ethics and diversity; organizational structure, design, and culture; decision making; organizational change

Case	Suggested Chapter	Cross-References and Integration
5. *It Isn't Fair*	5 Motivation Theories	perception and attribution; performance management and rewards; communication; ethics and decision making
6a. *Perfect Pizzeria*	6 Motivation and Performance	organizational design; motivation; performance management and rewards
6b. *Hovey and Beard*	6 Motivation and Performance	organizational cultures; globalization; communication; decision making
7. *The Forgotten Group Member*	7 Teams in Organizations	teamwork; motivation; diversity and individual differences; perception and attribution; performance management and rewards; communication; conflict; leadership
8. *NASCAR's Racing Teams*	7 Teams in Organizations	organizational cultures; leadership; motivation and reinforcement; communication
9. *Decisions, Decisions*	9 Creativity and Decision Making	organizational structure; organizational cultures; change and innovation; group dynamics and teamwork; diversity and individual differences
10. *The Missing Raise*	10 Conflict and Negotiation	change; innovation and stress; job designs; communication; power and politics
11. *The Poorly Informed Walrus*	11 Communication and Collaboration	diversity and individual differences; perception and attribution
12. *Faculty Empowerment*	12 Power and Politics	change; innovation and stress; job designs; communication; power and politics
13a. *The New Vice President*	13 Foundations for Leadership	leadership; performance management and rewards; diversity and individual differences; communication; conflict and negotiation; power and influence
13b. *Southwest Airlines*	14 Leadership Challenges and Organizational Change	leadership; performance management and rewards; diversity and individual differences; communication; conflict and negotiation; power and influence
14. *Novo Nordisk*	14 Leadership Challenges and Organizational Change	leadership; performance management and rewards; diversity and individual differences; communication; conflict and negotiation; power and influence
15. *Never on a Sunday*	15 Organizational Culture and Innovation	ethics and diversity; organizational structure, design, and culture; decision making; organizational change
16. *First Community Financial*	16 Organizational Goals and Structures	organizational structure, designs, and culture; performance management and rewards
17. *Mission Management and Trust*	17 Strategy, Technology, and Organizational Design	organizational structure, designs, and culture; performance management and rewards

LEARNING STYLE INVENTORY

This is a Wiley resource—www.wiley.com/go/global/schermerhorn

Step 1.

Take the Learning Style Instrument at www.wiley.com/go/global/schermerhorn

Step 2.

The instrument will give you scores on seven learning styles:

1. Visual learner—focus on visual depictions such as pictures and graphs
2. Print learner—focus on seeing written words
3. Auditory learner—focus on listening and hearing
4. Interactive learner—focus on conversation and verbalization
5. Haptic learner—focus on sense of touch or grasp
6. Kinesthetic learner—focus on physical involvement
7. Olfactory learner—focus on smell and taste

Step 3.

Consider your top four rankings among the learning styles. They suggest your most preferred methods of learning.

Step 4.

Read the following study tips for the learning styles. Think about how you can take best advantage of your preferred learning styles.

WHAT ARE LEARNING STYLES?

Have you ever repeated something to yourself over and over to help remember it? Or does your best friend ask you to draw a map to someplace where the two of you are planning to meet, rather than just tell her the directions? If so, then you already have an intuitive sense that people learn in different ways. Researchers in learning theory have developed various categories of learning styles. Some people, for example, learn best by reading or writing. Others learn best by using various senses—seeing, hearing, feeling, tasting, or even smelling. When you understand how you learn best, you can make use of learning strategies that will optimize the time you spend studying. To find out what your particular learning style is, go to www.wiley.com/college/boone and take the learning styles quiz you find there. The quiz will help you determine your primary learning style:

| Visual Learner | Auditory Learner | Haptic Learner | Olfactory Learner |
| Print Learner | Interactive Learner | Kinesthetic Learner | |

Then, consult the information below and on the following pages for study tips for each learning style. This information will help you better understand your learning style and how to apply it to the study of business.

Study Tips for Visual Learners

If you are a Visual Learner, you prefer to work with images and diagrams. It is important that you see information.

Visual Learning
- Draw charts/diagrams during lecture.
- Examine textbook figures and graphs.
- Look at images and videos on WileyPLUS and other Web sites.

- Pay close attention to charts, drawings, and handouts your instructor uses.
- Underline; use different colors.
- Use symbols, flowcharts, graphs, different arrangements on the page, white spaces.

Visual Reinforcement
- Make flashcards by drawing tables/charts on one side and definition or description on the other side.
- Use art-based worksheets; cover labels on images in text and then rewrite the labels.

Study Tips for Visual Learners (Continued)

- Use colored pencils/markers and colored paper to organize information into types.
- Convert your lecture notes into "page pictures." To do this:
  - Use the visual learning strategies outlined above.
  - Reconstruct images in different ways.
  - Redraw pages from memory.
  - Replace words with symbols and initials.
  - Draw diagrams where appropriate.
  - Practice turning your visuals back into words.

If visual learning is your weakness: If you are not a Visual Learner but want to improve your visual learning, try re-keying tables/charts from the textbook.

Study Tips for Print Learners

If you are a Print Learner, reading will be important but writing will be much more important.

Print Learning

- Write text lecture notes during lecture.
- Read relevant topics in textbook, especially textbook tables.
- Look at text descriptions in animations and Web sites.
- Use lists and headings.
- Use dictionaries, glossaries, and definitions.
- Read handouts, textbooks, and supplementary library readings.
- Use lecture notes.

Print Reinforcement

- Rewrite your notes from class, and copy classroom handouts in your own handwriting.

- Make your own flashcards.
- Write out essays summarizing lecture notes or text book topics.
- Develop mnemonics.
- Identify word relationships.
- Create tables with information extracted from textbook or lecture notes.
- Use text-based worksheets or crossword puzzles.
- Write out words again and again.
- Reread notes silently.
- Rewrite ideas and principles into other words.
- Turn charts, diagrams, and other illustrations into statements.

- Practice writing exam answers.
- Practice with multiple choice questions.
- Write paragraphs, especially beginnings and endings.
- Write your lists in outline form.
- Arrange your words into hierarchies and points.

If print learning is your weakness: If you are not a Print Learner but want to improve your print learning, try covering labels of figures from the textbook and writing in the labels.

Study Tips for Auditory Learners

If you are an Auditory Learner, then you prefer listening as a way to learn information. Hearing will be very important, and sound helps you focus.

Auditory Learning

- Make audio recordings during lecture. Do not skip class; hearing the lecture is essential to understanding.
- Play audio files provided by instructor and textbook.
- Listen to narration of animations.
- Attend lecture and tutorials.
- Discuss topics with students and instructors.
- Explain new ideas to other people.
- Leave spaces in your lecture notes for later recall.
- Describe overheads, pictures, and visuals to somebody who was not in class.

Auditory Reinforcement

- Record yourself reading the notes and listen to the recording.
- Write out transcripts of the audio files.
- Summarize information that you have read, speaking out loud.
- Use a recorder to create self-tests.
- Compose "songs" about information.
- Play music during studying to help focus.
- Expand your notes by talking with others and with information from your textbook.

- Read summarized notes out loud.
- Explain your notes to another auditory learner.
- Talk with the instructor.
- Spend time in quiet places recalling the ideas.
- Say your answers out loud.

If auditory learning is your weakness: If you are not an Auditory Learner but want to improve your auditory learning, try writing out the scripts from pre-recorded lectures.

Study Tips for Interactive Learners

If you are an Interactive Learner, you will want to share your information. A study group will be important.

Interactive Learning
- Ask a lot of questions during lecture or TA review sessions.
- Contact other students, via e-mail or discussion forums, and ask them to explain what they learned.

Interactive Reinforcement
- "Teach" the content to a group of other students.

- Talking to an empty room may seem odd, but it will be effective for you.
- Discuss information with others, making sure that you both ask and answer questions.
- Work in small group discussions, making a verbal and written discussion of what others say.

If interactive learning is your weakness: If you are not an Interactive Learner but want to improve your interactive learning, try asking your study partner questions and then repeating them to the instructor.

Study Tips for Haptic Learners

If you are a Haptic Learner, you prefer to work with your hands. It is important to physically manipulate material.

Haptic Learning
- Take blank paper to lecture to draw charts/tables/diagrams.
- Using the textbook, run your fingers along the figures and graphs to get a "feel" for shapes and relationships.

Haptic Reinforcement
- Trace words and pictures on flashcards.

- Perform electronic exercises that involve drag-and-drop activities.
- Alternate between speaking and writing information.
- Observe someone performing a task that you would like to learn.
- Make sure you have freedom of movement while studying.

If haptic learning is your weakness: If you are not a Haptic Learner but want to improve your haptic learning, try spending more time in class working with graphs and tables while speaking or writing down information.

Study Tips for Kinesthetic Learners

If you are a Kinesthetic Learner, it will be important that you involve your body during studying.

Kinesthetic Learning
- Ask permission to get up and move during lecture.
- Participate in role-playing activities in the classroom.
- Use all your senses.
- Go to labs; take field trips.
- Listen to real-life examples.
- Pay attention to applications.
- Use trial-and-error methods.
- Use hands-on approaches.

Kinesthetic Reinforcement
- Make flashcards; place them on the floor, and move your body around them.
- Move while you are teaching the material to others.
- Put examples in your summaries.
- Use case studies and applications to help with principles and abstract concepts.
- Talk about your notes with another Kinesthetic person.

- Use pictures and photographs that illustrate an idea.
- Write practice answers.
- Role-play the exam situation.

If kinesthetic learning is your weakness: If you are not a Kinesthetic Learner but want to improve your kinesthetic learning, try moving flashcards to reconstruct graphs and tables, etc.

Study Tips for Olfactory Learners

If you are an Olfactory Learner, you will prefer to use the senses of smell and taste to reinforce learning. This is a rare learning modality.

Olfactory Learning
- During lecture, use different scented markers to identify different types of information.

Olfactory Reinforcement
- Rewrite notes with scented markers.
- If possible, go back to the computer lab to do your studying.

- Burn aromatic candles while studying.
- Try to associate the material that you're studying with a pleasant taste or smell.

If olfactory learning is your weakness: If you are not an Olfactory Learner but want to improve your olfactory learning, try burning an aromatic candle or incense while you study, or eating cookies during study sessions.

STUDENT LEADERSHIP PRACTICES INVENTORY

STUDENT WORKBOOK

James M. Kouzes
Barry Z. Posner, Ph.D.
Jossey-Bass Publishers • San Francisco

Jossey-Bass/Pfeiffer Classroom Collection

ISBN: 0-7879-4425-4

Jossey-Bass is a registered trademark of Jossey-Bass Inc., a Wiley Company.

Printed in the United States of America.

Jossey-Bass books and products are available through most bookstores. To contact Jossey-Bass directly, call (888) 378-2537, fax to (800) 605-2665, or visit our Web site at www.josseybass.com.

Substantial discounts on bulk quantities of Jossey-Bass books are available to corporations, professional associations, and other organizations. For details and discount information, contact the special sales department at Jossey-Bass.

Printing 10 9 8 7 6 5 4 3 2

This book is printed on acid-free, recycled stock that meets or exceeds the minimum GPO and EPA requirements for recycled paper.

CONTENTS

> **People** WHO BECOME
> leaders
> DON'T *always* **seek**
> THE **challenges**
> THEY **face.**
> CHALLENGES
> *also* SEEK **leaders.**

1
Leadership: What People Do When They're Leading

" *L*eadership is everyone's business."* That's the conclusion we have come to after nearly two decades of research into the behaviors and actions of people who are making a difference in their organizations, clubs, teams, classes, schools, campuses, communities, and even their families. We found that leadership is an observable, learnable set of practices. Contrary to some myths, it is not a mystical and ethereal process that cannot be understood by ordinary people. Given the opportunity for feedback and practice, those with the desire and persistence to lead—to make a difference—can substantially improve their ability to do so.

The *Leadership Practices Inventory* (LPI) is part of an extensive research project into the everyday actions and behaviors of people, at all levels and across a variety of settings, as they are leading. Through our research we identified five practices that are common to all leadership experiences. In collaboration with others, we extended our findings to student leaders and to school and college environments and created the student version of the LPI.[1] The LPI is a tool, not a test, designed to assess your current leadership skills. It will identify your areas of strength as well as areas of leadership that need to be further developed.

The *Student LPI* helps you discover the extent to which you (in your role as a leader of a student group or organization) engage in the following five leadership practices:

Challenging the Process. Leaders are pioneers—people who seek out new opportunities and are willing to change the status quo. They innovate, experiment, and explore ways to improve the organization. They treat mistakes as learning experiences. Leaders also stay prepared to meet whatever challenges may confront them. *Challenging the Process* involves

- Searching for opportunities
- Experimenting and taking risks

As an example of Challenging the Process, one student related how innovative thinking helped him win a student class election: "I challenged the process in more than one way. First, I wanted people to understand that elections are not necessarily popularity contests, so I campaigned on the issues and did not promise things that could not possibly be done. Second, I challenged the incumbent positions. They thought they would win easily because they were incumbents, but I showed them that no one has an inherent right to a position."

---

[1]For more information on our original work, see *The Leadership Challenge: How to Keep Getting Extraordinary Things Done in Organizations* (Jossey-Bass Publishers).

Challenging the Process for a student serving as treasurer of her sorority meant examining and abandoning some of her leadership beliefs: "I used to believe, 'If you want to do something right, do it yourself.' I found out the hard way that this is impossible to do. . . . One day I was ready to just give up the position because I could no longer handle all of the work. My adviser noticed that I was overwhelmed, and she turned to me and said three magic words: 'Use your committee.' The best piece of advice I would pass along about being an effective leader is that it is okay to experiment with letting others do the work."

Inspiring a Shared Vision.

Leaders look toward and beyond the horizon. They envision the future with a positive and hopeful outlook. Leaders are expressive and attract other people to their organization and teams through their genuineness. They communicate and show others how their interests can be met through commitment to a common purpose. *Inspiring a Shared Vision* involves

- Envisioning an uplifting future
- Enlisting others in a common vision

Describing his experience as president of his high school class, one student wrote: "It was our vision to get the class united and to be able to win the spirit trophy. . . . I told my officers that we could do anything we set our minds on. Believe in yourself and believe in your ability to accomplish things."

Enabling Others to Act. Leaders
infuse people with energy and confidence, developing relationships based on mutual trust. They stress collaborative goals. They actively involve others in planning, giving them discretion to make their own decisions. Leaders ensure that

people feel strong and capable. *Enabling Others to Act* involves

- Fostering collaboration
- Strengthening people

It is not necessary to be in a traditional leadership position to put these principles into practice. Here is an example from a student who led his team as a team member, not from a traditional position of power: "I helped my team members feel strong and capable by encouraging everyone to practice with the same amount of intensity that they played games with. Our practices improved throughout the year, and by the end of the year had reached the point I was striving for: complete involvement among all players, helping each other to perform at our very best during practice times."

Modeling the Way. Leaders are clear about their personal values and beliefs. They keep people and projects on course by behaving consistently with these values and modeling how they expect others to act. Leaders also plan projects and break them down into achievable steps, creating opportunities for small wins. By focusing on key priorities, they make it easier for others to achieve goals. *Modeling the Way* involves

- Setting the example
- Achieving small wins

Working in a business environment taught one student the importance of Modeling the Way. She

writes: "I proved I was serious because I was the first one on the job and the last one to leave. I came prepared to work and make the tools available to my crew. I worked alongside them and in no way portrayed an attitude of superiority. Instead, we were in this together."

Encouraging the Heart. Leaders encourage people to persist in their efforts by linking recognition with accomplishments and visibly recognizing contributions to the common vision. They express pride in the achievements of the group or organization, letting others know that their efforts are appreciated. Leaders also find ways to celebrate milestones. They nurture a team spirit, which enables people to sustain continued efforts. *Encouraging the Heart* involves

- Recognizing individual contributions
- Celebrating team accomplishments

While organizing and running a day camp, one student recognized volunteers and celebrated accomplishments through her actions. She explains: "We had a pizza party with the children on the last day of the day camp. Later, the volunteers were sent thank you notes and 'valuable volunteer awards' personally signed by the day campers. The pizza party, thank you notes, and awards served to encourage the hearts of the volunteers in the hopes that they might return for next year's day camp."

Somewhere,
sometime,
THE *leader within*
EACH OF **US**
MAY **get**
THE CALL
to STEP **forward.**

2
Questions Frequently Asked About the *Student LPI*

Question 1: What are the right answers?

Answer: There are no universal right answers when it comes to leadership. Research indicates that the more frequently you are perceived as engaging in the behavior and actions identified in the *Student LPI,* the more likely it is that you will be perceived as an effective leader. The higher your scores on the Student LPI-Observer, the more others perceive you as (1) having personal credibility, (2) being effective in running meetings, (3) successfully representing your organization or group to nonmembers, (4) generating a sense of enthusiasm and cooperation, and (5) having a high-performing team. In addition, findings show a strong and positive relationship between the extent to which people report their leaders engaging in this set of five leadership practices and how motivated, committed, and productive they feel.

Question 2: How reliable and valid is the Student LPI?

Answer: The question of reliability can be answered in two ways. First, the *Student LPI* has shown sound psychometric properties. The scale for each leadership practice is internally reliable, meaning that the statements within each practice are highly correlated with one another. Second, results of multivariate analyses indicate that the statements within each leadership practice are more highly correlated (or associated) with one another than they are between the five leadership practices.

In terms of validity (or "So what difference do the scores make?"), the *Student LPI* has good face validity and predictive validity. This means, first, that the results make sense to people. Second, scores on the *Student LPI* significantly differentiate high-performing leaders from their less successful counterparts. Whether measured by the leader, his or her peers, or student personnel administrators, those student leaders who engage more frequently, rather than less frequently, in the five leadership practices are more effective.

Question 3: Should my perceptions of my leadership practices be consistent with the ratings other people give me?

Answer: Research indicates that trust in the leader is essential if other people (for example, fellow members of a group, team, or organization) are going to follow that person over time. People must experience the leader as believable, credible, and trustworthy. Trust—whether in a leader or any other person—is developed through consistency in behavior. Trust is further established when words and deeds are congruent.

This does not mean, however, that you will always be perceived in exactly the same way by every person in every situation. Some people may not see you as often as others do, and therefore they may rate you differently on the same behavior. Some people simply may not know you as well as others do. Also you may appropriately behave differently in different situations, such as in a crisis versus during more stable times. Others may have different expectations of you, and still others may perceive the rating descriptions (such as "once in a while" or "fairly often") differently.

Therefore, the key issue is not whether your self-ratings and the ratings from others are exactly the same, but whether people perceive consistency between what you say you do and what you actually do. The only way you can know the answer to this question is to solicit feedback. The Student LPI-Observer has been designed for this purpose.

Research indicates that people tend to see themselves more positively than others do. The Student LPI-Self norms are consistent with this general trend; scores on the Student LPI-Self tend to be somewhat higher than scores on the Student LPI-Observer. *Student LPI* scores also tend to be higher than LPI scores of experienced managers and executives in the private and public sector.

Question 4: Can I change my leadership practices?

Answer: It is certainly possible—even for experienced people—to learn new skills. You will increase your chances of changing your behavior if you receive feedback on what level you have achieved with a particular skill, observe a positive model of that skill, set some improvement goals for yourself, practice the skill, ask for updated feedback on your performance, and then set new goals. The practices that are assessed with the *Student LPI* fall into the category of learnable skills.

But some things can be changed only if there is a strong and genuine inner desire to make a difference. For example, enthusiasm for a cause is unlikely to be developed through education or job assignments; it must come from within.

Use the information from the *Student LPI* to better understand how you currently behave as a leader, both from your own perspective and from the perspective of others. Note where there are consistencies and inconsistencies. Understand which leadership behaviors and practices you feel comfortable engaging in and which you feel uncomfortable with. Determine which leadership behaviors and practices you can improve on, and take steps to improve your leadership skills and gain confidence in leading other people and groups. The following sections will help you to become more effective in leadership.

> **Perhaps** NONE OF
> us knows
> OUR *true strength*
> UNTIL **challenged**
> TO **bring**
> *it* forth.

3
Recording Your Scores

On pages W-18 through W-21 are grids for recording your *Student LPI* scores. The first grid (Challenging the Process) is for recording scores for items 1, 6, 11, 16, 21, and 26 from the Student LPI-Self and Student LPI-Observer. These are the items that relate to behaviors involved in Challenging the Process, such as searching for opportunities, experimenting, and taking risks. An abbreviated form of each item is printed beside the grid as a handy reference.

In the first column, which is headed "Self-Rating," write the scores that you gave yourself. If others were asked to complete the Student LPI-Observer and if the forms were returned to you, enter their scores in the columns (A, B, C, D, E, and so on) under the heading "Observers' Ratings." Simply transfer the numbers from page W-18 of each Student LPI-Observer to your scoring grids, using one column for each observer. For example, enter the first observer's scores in column A, the second observer's scores in column B, and so on. The grids provide space for the scores of as many as ten observers.

After all scores have been entered for Challenging the Process, total each column in the row marked "Totals." Then add all of the totals for observers; do not include the "self" total. Write this grand total in the space marked "Total of All Observers' Scores." To obtain the average, divide the grand total by the number of people who completed the Student LPI-Observer. Write this average in the blank provided. The sample grid shows how the grid would look with scores for self and five observers entered.

Sample Grid with Scores from Self and Five Observers

	SELF-RATING	OBSERVERS' RATINGS										TOTAL OF ALL OBSERVERS' SCORES
		A	B	C	D	E	F	G	H	I	J	
1. Seeks challenge	5	4	2	4	4	2						
6. Keeps current	4	4	3	4	4	3						
11. Initiates experiment	3	3	2	2	2	1						
16. Looks for ways to improve	4	3	2	3	5	3						
21. Asks "What can we learn?"	2	3	2	3	3	2						
26. Lets others take risks	5	3	3	2	3	2						
TOTALS	23	20	14	18	21	13						86

TOTAL SELF-RATING: _____23_____   AVERAGE OF ALL OBSERVERS: _____17.2_____

The other four grids should be completed in the same manner.

The second grid (Inspiring a Shared Vision) is for recording scores to the items that pertain to envisioning the future and enlisting the support of others. These include items 2, 7, 12, 17, 22, and 27.

The third grid (Enabling Others to Act) pertains to items 3, 8, 13, 18, 23, and 28, which involve fostering collaboration and strengthening others.

The fourth grid (Modeling the Way) pertains to items about setting an example and planning small wins. These include items 4, 9, 14, 19, 24, and 29.

The fifth grid (Encouraging the Heart) pertains to items about recognizing contributions and celebrating accomplishments. These are items 5, 10, 15, 20, 25, and 30.

Grids for Recording Student LPI Scores

Scores should be recorded on the following grids in accordance with the instructions on page W-17. As you look at individual scores, remember the rating system that was used:

- "1" means that you *rarely or seldom* engage in the behavior.
- "2" means that you engage in the behavior *once in a while*.
- "3" means that you *sometimes* engage in the behavior.
- "4" means that you engage in the behavior *fairly often*.
- "5" means that you engage in the behavior *very frequently*.

After you have recorded all of your scores and calculated the totals and averages, turn to page W-21 and read the section on interpreting scores.

Challenging the Process

	SELF-RATING	OBSERVERS' RATINGS									
		A	B	C	D	E	F	G	H	I	J
1. Seeks challenge											
6. Keeps current											
11. Initiates experiment											
16. Looks for ways to improve											
21. Asks "What can we learn?"											
26. Lets others take risks											
TOTALS											

TOTAL OF ALL OBSERVERS' SCORES

TOTAL SELF-RATING: _____

AVERAGE OF ALL OBSERVERS: _____

Inspiring a Shared Vision

	SELF-RATING	OBSERVERS' RATINGS									
		A	B	C	D	E	F	G	H	I	J
2. Describes ideal capabilities											
7. Looks ahead and communicates future											
12. Upbeat and positive communicator											
17. Finds common ground											
22. Communicates purpose and meaning											
27. Enthusiastic about possibilities											
TOTALS											

TOTAL OF ALL OBSERVERS' SCORES

TOTAL SELF-RATING: _____

AVERAGE OF ALL OBSERVERS: _____

Enabling Others to Act

	SELF-RATING	OBSERVERS' RATINGS									
		A	B	C	D	E	F	G	H	I	J
3. Includes others in planning											
8. Treats others with respect											
13. Supports decisions of others											
18. Fosters cooperative relationships											
23. Provides freedom and choice											
28. Lets others lead											
TOTALS											

TOTAL OF ALL OBSERVERS' SCORES

TOTAL SELF-RATING: _____   AVERAGE OF ALL OBSERVERS: _____

Modeling the Way

	SELF-RATING	OBSERVERS' RATINGS									
		A	B	C	D	E	F	G	H	I	J
4. Shares beliefs about leading											
9. Breaks projects into steps											
14. Sets personal example											
19. Talks about guiding values											
24. Follows through on promises											
29. Sets clear goals and plans											
TOTALS											

TOTAL OF ALL OBSERVERS' SCORES

TOTAL SELF-RATING: _____   AVERAGE OF ALL OBSERVERS: _____

Encouraging the Heart

	SELF-RATING	OBSERVERS' RATINGS									
		A	B	C	D	E	F	G	H	I	J
5. Encourages other people											
10. Recognizes people's contributions											
15. Praises people for job well done											
20. Gives support and appreciation											
25. Finds ways to publicly celebrate											
30. Tells others about group's good work											
TOTALS											

TOTAL OF ALL OBSERVERS' SCORES

TOTAL SELF-RATING: _____   AVERAGE OF ALL OBSERVERS: _____

> THE unique ROLE
> OF leaders
> IS TO *take us*
> TO places
> WE'VE never
> *been* before.

4

Interpreting Your Scores

This section will help you to interpret your scores by looking at them in several ways and by making notes to yourself about what you can do to become a more effective leader.

Ranking Your Ratings

Refer to the previous chapter, "Recording Your Scores." On each grid, look at your scores in the blanks marked "Total Self-Rating." Each of these totals represents your responses to six statements about one of the five leadership practices. Each of your totals can range from a low of 6 to a high of 30.

In the blanks that follow, write "1" to the left of the leadership prac-

tice with the highest total self-rating, "2" by the next-highest total self-rating, and so on. This ranking represents the leadership practices with which you feel most comfortable, second-most comfortable, and so on. The practice you identify with a "5" is the practice with which you feel least comfortable.

Again refer to the previous chapter, but this time look at your scores in the blanks marked "Average of All Observers." The number in each blank is the average score given to you by the people you asked to complete the Student LPI-Observer. Like each of your total self-ratings, this number can range from 6 to 30.

In the blanks that follow, write "1" to the right of the leadership practice with the highest score, "2" by the next-highest score, and so on. This ranking represents the leadership practices that others feel you use most often, second-most often, and so on.

Self		Observers
_____	Challenging the Process	_____
_____	Inspiring a Shared Vision	_____
_____	Enabling Others to Act	_____
_____	Modeling the Way	_____
_____	Encouraging the Heart	_____

Comparing Your Self-Ratings to Observers' Ratings

To compare your Student LPI-Self and Student LPI-Observer assessments, refer to the "Chart for Graphing Your Scores" on the next page. On the chart, designate your scores on the five leadership practices (Challenging, Inspiring, Enabling, Modeling, and Encouraging) by marking each of these points with a capital "S" (for "Self"). Connect the five resulting "S" scores" with a *solid line* and label the end of this line "Self" (see sample chart below).

If other people provided input through the Student LPI-Observer, designate the average observer scores (see the blanks labeled "Average of All Observers" on the scoring grids) by marking each of the points with a capital "O" (for "Observer"). Then connect the five resulting "O scores" with a *dashed line* and label the end of this line "Observer" (see sample chart). Completing this process will provide you with a graphic representation (one solid and one dashed line) illustrating the relationship between your self-perception and the observations of other people.

Chart for Graphing Your Scores

Percentile	Challenging the Process	Inspiring a Shared Vision	Enabling Others to Act	Modeling the Way	Encouraging the Heart
100%	30 / 29 / 28	30 / 29	30	30 / 29 / 28	30
	27	28	29		29
90%	26	27		27	
	25	26	28	26	28
80%		25 (O)			27
	24		25 (S)	25	
70%					26
	23	24 (S)	26	24	
60%		23			Self
	22		(O)	(O) 23	
50%			25		Observer 24
		22			
40%	(S)	21	24	(S)	23
		20			
30%	20		23	21	22
		19		20	21
20%	19 (O)	18	22	19	20
	18	17	21		19
10%	17	16 / 15	20	18	18
	16 / 15	14	19 / 18	17 / 16	17 / 16

Chart for Graphing Your Scores

Percentile	Challenging the Process	Inspiring a Shared Vision	Enabling Others to Act	Modeling the Way	Encouraging the Heart
100%	30	30	30	30	30
	29	29		29	
	28			28	
		28	29		29
	27			27	
		27			
90%	26				28
			28	26	
	25	26			
					27
80%					
	24	25	27	25	
					26
70%					
		24		24	
	23		26		
60%					25
		23			
	22			23	
50%					24
		22	25		
				22	
40%	21				23
		21	24		
		20			
30%	20			21	22
		19	23		21
				20	
20%	19	18	22	19	20
	18	17	21		19
10%	17	16	20	18	18
		15	19	17	17
	16	14	18	16	16
	15				

Percentile Scores

Look again at the "Chart for Graphing Your Scores." The column to the far left represents the Student LPI-Self percentile rankings for more than 1,200 student leaders. A percentile ranking is determined by the percentage of people who score at or below a given number. For example, if your total self-rating for "Challenging" is at the 60th percentile line on the "Chart for Graphing Your Scores," this means that you assessed yourself higher than 60 percent of all people who have completed the *Student LPI;* you would be in the top 40 percent in this leadership practice. Studies indicate that a "high" score is one at or above the 70th percentile, a "low" score is one at or below the 30th percentile, and a score that falls between those ranges is considered "moderate."

Using these criteria, circle the "H" (for "High"), the "M" (for "Moderate"), or the "L" (for "Low") for each leadership practice on the "Range of Scores" table below. Compared to other student leaders around the country, where do your leadership practices tend to fall? (Given a "normal distribution," it is expected that most people's scores will fall within the moderate range.)

Range of Scores

In my perception				In others' perception			
Practice	**Rating**			**Practice**	**Rating**		
Challenging the Process	H	M	L	Challenging the Process	H	M	L
Inspiring a Shared Vision	H	M	L	Inspiring a Shared Vision	H	M	L
Enabling Others to Act	H	M	L	Enabling Others to Act	H	M	L
Modeling the Way	H	M	L	Modeling the Way	H	M	L
Encouraging the Heart	H	M	L	Encouraging the Heart	H	M	L

Exploring Specific Leadership Behaviors

Looking at your scoring grids, review each of the thirty items on the *Student LPI* by practice. One or two of the six behaviors within each leadership practice may be higher or lower than the rest. If so, on which specific items is there variation? What do these differences suggest? On which specific items is there agreement? Please write your thoughts in the following space.

Challenging the Process

_____

_____

_____

_____

Inspiring a Shared Vision

_____

_____

_____

_____

_____

Enabling Others to Act

_____

_____

_____

_____

_____

_____

Modeling the Way

_____

_____

_____

_____

_____

_____

_____

_____

_____

_____

**Comparing Observers'
Responses to One Another**

Study the Student LPI-Observer scores for each of the five leadership practices. Do some respondents' scores differ significantly from others? If so, are the differences localized in the scores of one or two people? On which leadership practices do the respondents agree? On which practices do they disagree? If you try to behave basically the same with all the people who assessed you, how do you explain the difference in ratings? Please write your thoughts in the following space.

_____

_____

_____

_____

_____

_____

_____

_____

_____

_____

_____

_____

_____

_____

> **Wanting** TO LEAD AND
> **believing** THAT
> YOU *can lead* ARE THE
> **departure** POINTS
> ON THE PATH TO **leadership.**
> LEADERSHIP IS AN ART—
> A *performing* **art**—
> AND THE **instrument**
> IS THE **self.**

5
Summary and Action-Planning Worksheets
· ·

Take a few moments to summarize your *Student LPI* feedback by completing the following Strengths and Opportunities Summary Worksheet. Refer to the "Chart for Graphing Your Scores," the "Range of Scores" table, and any notes you have made.

After the summary worksheet you will find some suggestions for getting started on meeting the leadership challenge. With these suggestions in mind, review your *Student LPI* feedback and decide on the actions you will take to become an even more effective leader. Then complete the Action-Planning Worksheet to spell out the steps you will take. (One Action-Planning Worksheet is included in this workbook, but you may want to develop action plans for several practices or behaviors. You can make copies of the blank form before you fill it in or just use a separate sheet of paper for each leadership practice you plan to improve.)

**Strengths and Opportunities
Summary Worksheet**

Strengths

Which of the leadership practices and behaviors are you most comfortable with? Why? Can you do more?

_____

_____

_____

_____

_____

_____

Areas for Improvement

What can you do to use a practice more frequently? What will it take to feel more comfortable?

_____
_____
_____
_____
_____
_____
_____

The following are ten suggestions for getting started on meeting the leadership challenge.

Prescriptions for Meeting the Leadership Challenge

Challenge the Process
- Fix something
- Adopt the "great ideas" of others

Inspire a Shared Vision
- Let others know how you feel
- Recount your "personal best"

Enable Others to Act
- Always say "we"
- Make heroes of other people

Model the Way
- Lead by example
- Create opportunities for small wins

Encourage the Heart
- Write "thank you" notes
- Celebrate, and link your celebrations to your organization's values

Action-Planning Worksheet

1. What would you like to be better able to do?

_____
_____
_____
_____

_____
_____
_____
_____
_____
_____

2. What specific actions will you take?

_____
_____
_____
_____
_____
_____
_____
_____

3. What is the first action you will take? Who will be involved? When will you begin?

Action _____

_____

People Involved _____

_____
_____
_____

Target Date _____

4. Complete this sentence: "I will know I have improved in this leadership skill when . . ."

_____
_____
_____
_____

5. When will you review your progress? _____

About the Authors

*J*ames M. Kouzes is chairman of TPG/Learning Systems, which makes leadership work through practical, performance-oriented learning programs. In 1993 *The Wall Street Journal* cited Jim as one of the twelve most requested "nonuniversity executive-education providers" to U.S. companies. His list of past and present clients includes AT&T, Boeing, Boy Scouts of America, Charles Schwab, Ciba-Geigy, Dell Computer, First Bank System, Honeywell, Johnson & Johnson, Levi Strauss & Co., Motorola, Pacific Bell, Stanford University, Xerox Corporation, and the YMCA.

Barry Z. Posner, PhD, is dean of the Leavey School of Business, Santa Clara University, and professor of organizational behavior. He has received several outstanding teaching and leadership awards, has published more than eighty research and practitioner-oriented articles, and currently is on the editorial review boards for *The Journal of Management Education, The Journal of Management Inquiry,* and *The Journal of Business Ethics.* Barry also serves on the board of directors for Public Allies and for The Center for Excellence in Non-Profits. His clients have ranged from retailers to firms in health care, high technology, financial services, manufacturing, and community service agencies.

Kouzes and Posner are coauthors of several best-selling and award-winning leadership books. *The Leadership Challenge: How to Keep Getting Extraordinary Things Done in Organizations* (2nd ed., 1995), with over 800,000 copies in print, has been reprinted in fifteen languages, has been featured in three video programs, and received a Critic's Choice award from the nation's newspaper book review editors. *Credibility: How Leaders Gain and Lose It, Why People Demand It* (1993) was chosen by *Industry Week* as one of the five best management books of the year. Their latest book is *Encouraging the Heart: A Leader's Guide to Rewarding and Recognizing Others* (1998).

STUDENT LEADERSHIP PRACTICES INVENTORY—SELF

Your Name: _____

Instructions

On the next two pages are thirty statements describing various leadership behaviors. Please read each statement carefully. Then rate *yourself* in terms of *how frequently* you engage in the behavior described. *This is not a test* (there are no right or wrong answers).

Consider each statement in the context of the student organization (for example, club, team, chapter, group, unit, hall, program, project) with which you are most involved. The rating scale provides five choices:

(1) If you RARELY or SELDOM do what is described in the statement, circle the number one (1).
(2) If you do what is described ONCE IN A WHILE, circle the number two (2).
(3) If you SOMETIMES do what is described, circle the number three (3).
(4) If you do what is described FAIRLY OFTEN, circle the number four (4).
(5) If you do what is described VERY FREQUENTLY or ALMOST ALWAYS, circle the number five (5).

Please respond to every statement.

In selecting the response, be realistic about the extent to which you *actually* engage in the behavior. Do *not* answer in terms of how you would like to see yourself or in terms of what you should be doing. Answer in terms of how you *typically behave*. The usefulness of the feedback from this inventory will depend on how honest you are with yourself about how frequently you actually engage in each of these behaviors.

For example, the first statement is "I look for opportunities that challenge my skills and abilities." If you believe you do this "once in a while," circle the number 2. If you believe you look for challenging opportunities "fairly often," circle the number 4.

When you have responded to all thirty statements, please turn to the response sheet on the back page and transfer your responses as instructed. Thank you.

STUDENT LEADERSHIP PRACTICES INVENTORY-SELF

How frequently do you typically engage in the following behaviors and actions? *Circle* the number that applies to each statement.

1 SELDOM OR RARELY	2 ONCE IN A WHILE	3 SOMETIMES	4 FAIRLY OFTEN	5 VERY FREQUENTLY

1. I look for opportunities that challenge my skills and abilities.	1	2	3	4	5
2. I describe to others in our organization what we should be capable of accomplishing.	1	2	3	4	5
3. I include others in planning the activities and programs of our organization.	1	2	3	4	5
4. I share my beliefs about how things can be run most effectively within our organization.	1	2	3	4	5
5. I encourage others as they work on activities and programs in our organization.	1	2	3	4	5
6. I keep current on events and activities that might affect our organization.	1	2	3	4	5
7. I look ahead and communicate about what I believe will affect us in the future.	1	2	3	4	5
8. I treat others with dignity and respect.	1	2	3	4	5
9. I break our organization's projects down into manageable steps.	1	2	3	4	5
10. I make sure that people in our organization are recognized for their contributions.	1	2	3	4	5
11. I take initiative in experimenting with the way we do things in our organization.	1	2	3	4	5
12. I am upbeat and positive when talking about what our organization is doing.	1	2	3	4	5
13. I support the decisions that other people in our organization make on their own.	1	2	3	4	5
14. I set a personal example of what I expect from other people.	1	2	3	4	5
15. I praise people for a job well done.	1	2	3	4	5
16. I look for ways to improve whatever project or task I am involved in.	1	2	3	4	5
17. I talk with others about how their own interests can be met by working toward a common goal.	1	2	3	4	5
18. I foster cooperative rather than competitive relationships among people I work with.	1	2	3	4	5
19. I talk about the values and principles that guide my actions.	1	2	3	4	5
20. I give people in our organization support and express appreciation for their contributions.	1	2	3	4	5
21. I ask, "What can we learn from this experience?" when things do not go as we expected.	1	2	3	4	5
22. I speak with conviction about the higher purpose and meaning of what we are doing.	1	2	3	4	5
23. I give others a great deal of freedom and choice in deciding how to do their work.	1	2	3	4	5
24. I follow through on the promises and commitments I make in this organization.	1	2	3	4	5
25. I find ways for us to celebrate our accomplishments publicly.	1	2	3	4	5
26. I let others experiment and take risks even when outcomes are uncertain.	1	2	3	4	5
27. I show my enthusiasm and excitement about what our organization is doing.	1	2	3	4	5
28. I provide opportunities for others to take on leadership responsibilities.	1	2	3	4	5
29. I make sure that we set goals and make specific plans for the projects we undertake.	1	2	3	4	5
30. I make it a point to tell others about the good work done by our organization.	1	2	3	4	5

Transferring the Scores

After you have responded to the thirty statements on the previous two pages, please transfer your responses to the blanks below. This will make it easier to record and score your responses. Notice that the numbers of the statements are listed *horizontally*. Make sure that the number you assigned to each statement is transferred to the appropriate blank. Fill in a response for every item.

1. _____   2. _____   3. _____   4. _____   5. _____

6. _____   7. _____   8. _____   9. _____   10. _____

11. _____   12. _____   13. _____   14. _____   15. _____

16. _____   17. _____   18. _____   19. _____   20. _____

21. _____   22. _____   23. _____   24. _____   25. _____

26. _____   27. _____   28. _____   29. _____   30. _____

Further Instructions

Please write your name here: _____

Please bring this form with you to the workshop (seminar or class) or return this form to:

_____

_____

_____

_____

If you are interested in feedback from other people, ask them to complete the Student LPI-Observer, which provides you with perspectives on your leadership behaviors as perceived by others.

Jossey-Bass is a registered trademark of Jossey-Bass Inc., a Wiley Company.

Printed in the United States of America.

Jossey-Bass Publishers
350 Sansome Street
San Francisco, California 94104
(888) 378-2537
Fax (800) 605-2665

www.josseybass.com

Printing 10 9 8 7 6 5 4 3

This instrument is printed on acid-free, recycled stock that meets or exceeds the minimum GPO and EPA requirements for recycled paper.

ISBN: 0-7879-4426-2

STUDENT LEADERSHIP PRACTICES INVENTORY — OBSERVER

Name of Leader: _____

Instructions

On the next two pages are thirty descriptive statements about various leadership behaviors. Please read each statement carefully. Then rate *the person who asked you to complete this form* in terms of *how frequently* he or she typically engages in the described behavior. *This is not a test* (there are no right or wrong answers).

Consider each statement in the context of the student organization (for example, club, team, chapter, group, unit, hall, program, project) with which that person is most involved or with which you have had the greatest opportunity to observe him or her. The rating scale provides five choices:

(1) If this person RARELY or SELDOM does what is described in the statement, circle the number one (1).
(2) If this person does what is described ONCE IN A WHILE, circle the number two (2).
(3) If this person SOMETIMES does what is described, circle the number three (3).
(4) If this person does what is described FAIRLY OFTEN, circle the number four (4).
(5) If this person does what is described VERY FREQUENTLY or ALMOST ALWAYS, circle the number five (5).

Please respond to every statement.

In selecting the response, be realistic about the extent to which this person *actually* engages in the behavior. Do *not* answer in terms of how you would like to see this person behaving or in terms of what this person should be doing. Answer in terms of how he or she *typically behaves*. The usefulness of the feedback from this inventory will depend on how honest you are about how frequently you observe this person actually engaging in each of these behaviors.

For example, the first statement is, "He or she looks for opportunities that challenge his or her skills and abilities." If you believe this person does this "once in a while," circle the number 2. If you believe he or she looks for challenging opportunities "fairly often," circle the number 4.

When you have responded to all thirty statements, please turn to the response sheet on the back page and transfer your responses as instructed. Thank you.

STUDENT LEADERSHIP PRACTICES INVENTORY—OBSERVER

How frequently does this person typically engage in the following behaviors and actions? *Circle* the number that applies to each statement:

1	2	3	4	5
SELDOM OR RARELY	ONCE IN A WHILE	SOMETIMES	FAIRLY OFTEN	VERY FREQUENTLY

He or she:

1. looks for opportunities that challenge his or her skills and abilities.	1	2	3	4	5
2. describes to others in our organization what we should be capable of accomplishing.	1	2	3	4	5
3. includes others in planning the activities and programs of our organization.	1	2	3	4	5
4. shares his or her beliefs about how things can be run most effectively within our organization.	1	2	3	4	5
5. encourages others as they work on activities and programs in our organization.	1	2	3	4	5
6. keeps current on events and activities that might affect our organization.	1	2	3	4	5
7. looks ahead and communicates about what he or she believes will affect us in the future.	1	2	3	4	5
8. treats others with dignity and respect.	1	2	3	4	5
9. breaks our organization's projects down into manageable steps.	1	2	3	4	5
10. makes sure that people in our organization are recognized for their contributions.	1	2	3	4	5
11. takes initiative in experimenting with the way we do things in our organization.	1	2	3	4	5
12. is upbeat and positive when talking about what our organization is doing.	1	2	3	4	5
13. supports the decisions that other people in our organization make on their own.	1	2	3	4	5
14. sets a personal example of what he or she expects from other people.	1	2	3	4	5
15. praises people for a job well done.	1	2	3	4	5
16. looks for ways to improve whatever project or task he or she is involved in.	1	2	3	4	5
17. talks with others about how their own interests can be met by working toward a common goal.	1	2	3	4	5
18. fosters cooperative rather than competitive relationships among people he or she works with.	1	2	3	4	5
19. talks about the values and principles that guide his or her actions.	1	2	3	4	5
20. gives people in our organization support and expresses appreciation for their contributions.	1	2	3	4	5
21. asks "What can we learn from this experience?" when things do not go as we expected.	1	2	3	4	5
22. speaks with conviction about the higher purpose and meaning of what we are doing.	1	2	3	4	5
23. gives others a great deal of freedom and choice in deciding how to do their work.	1	2	3	4	5
24. follows through on the promises and commitments he or she makes in this organization.	1	2	3	4	5
25. finds ways for us to celebrate our accomplishments publicly.	1	2	3	4	5
26. lets others experiment and take risks even when outcomes are uncertain.	1	2	3	4	5
27. shows his or her enthusiasm and excitement about what our organization is doing.	1	2	3	4	5
28. provides opportunities for others to take on leadership responsibilities.	1	2	3	4	5
29. makes sure that we set goals and make specific plans for the projects we undertake.	1	2	3	4	5
30. makes it a point to tell others about the good work done by our organization.	1	2	3	4	5

Transferring the Scores

After you have responded to the thirty statements on the previous two pages, please transfer your responses to the blanks below. This will make it easier to record and score your responses. Notice that the numbers of the statements are listed *horizontally*. Make sure that the number you assigned to each statement is transferred to the appropriate blank. Fill in a response for every item.

1. _____   2. _____   3. _____   4. _____   5. _____

6. _____   7. _____   8. _____   9. _____   10. _____

11. _____   12. _____   13. _____   14. _____   15. _____

16. _____   17. _____   18. _____   19. _____   20. _____

21. _____   22. _____   23. _____   24. _____   25. _____

26. _____   27. _____   28. _____   29. _____   30. _____

Further Instructions

The above scores are for (name of person): _____

Please bring this form with you to the workshop (seminar or class) or return this form to:

_____

_____

_____

_____

ISBN: 0-7879-4427-0

Printed in the United States of America.

Jossey-Bass Publishers
350 Sansome Street
San Francisco, California 94104
(888) 378-2537
Fax (800) 605-2665

www.josseybass.com

Printing 10 9 8 7 6 5 4 3 2 1

 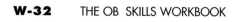

SELF-ASSESSMENT PORTFOLIO

Find online versions of many assessments at www.wiley.com/go/global/schermerhorn

Managerial Assumptions

Instructions

Read the following statements. Write "Yes" if you agree with the statement, or "No" if you disagree with it. Force yourself to take a "yes" or "no" position for every statement.

1. Are good pay and a secure job enough to satisfy most workers?

2. Should a manager help and coach subordinates in their work?

3. Do most people like real responsibility in their jobs?

4. Are most people afraid to learn new things in their jobs?

5. Should managers let subordinates control the quality of their work?

6. Do most people dislike work?

7. Are most people creative?

8. Should a manager closely supervise and direct work of subordinates?

Source: Schermerhorn, John R., Jr., *Management*, 5th ed. (New York, John Wiley & Sons, Inc., 1996), p. 51. By permission.

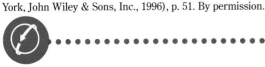

9. Do most people tend to resist change?
10. Do most people work only as hard as they have to?
11. Should workers be allowed to set their own job goals?
12. Are most people happiest off the job?
13. Do most workers really care about the organization they work for?
14. Should a manager help subordinates advance and grow in their jobs?

Scoring

Count the number of "yes" responses to items 1, 4, 6, 8, 9, 10, 12; write that number here as [X = ____]. Count the number of "yes" responses to items 2, 3, 5, 7, 11, 13, 14; write that score here [Y = ____].

Interpretation

This assessment gives insight into your orientation toward Douglas McGregor's Theory X (your "X" score) and Theory Y (your "Y" score) assumptions. You should review the discussion of McGregor's thinking in Chapter 1.1 and consider further the ways in which you are likely to behave toward other people at work. Think, in particular, about the types of "self-fulfilling prophecies" you are likely to create.

A Twenty-First-Century Manager

Instructions

Rate yourself on the following personal characteristics. Use this scale.

> S = Strong, I am very confident with this one.
> G = Good, but I still have room to grow.
> W = Weak, I really need work on this one.
> ? = Unsure, I just don't know.

1. *Resistance to stress:* The ability to get work done even under stressful conditions.
2. *Tolerance for uncertainty:* The ability to get work done even under ambiguous and uncertain conditions.
3. *Social objectivity:* The ability to act free of racial, ethnic, gender, and other prejudices or biases.
4. *Inner work standards:* The ability to personally set and work to high-performance standards.
5. *Stamina:* The ability to sustain long work hours.
6. *Adaptability:* The ability to be flexible and adapt to changes.
7. *Self-confidence:* The ability to be consistently decisive and display one's personal presence.
8. *Self-objectivity:* The ability to evaluate personal strengths and weaknesses and to understand one's motives and skills relative to a job.
9. *Introspection:* The ability to learn from experience, awareness, and self-study.

10. *Entrepreneurism:* The ability to address problems and take advantage of opportunities for constructive change.

Scoring

Give yourself 1 point for each S, and 1/2 point for each G. Do not give yourself points for W and ? responses. Total your points and enter the result here [PMF = ____].

Interpretation

This assessment offers a self-described *profile of your management foundations* (*PMF*). Are you a perfect 10, or is your PMF score something less than that? There shouldn't be too many 10s around. Ask someone who knows you to assess you on this instrument. You may be surprised at the differences between your PMF score as self-described and your PMF score as described by someone else. Most of us, realistically speaking, must work hard to grow and develop continually in these and related management foundations. This list is a good starting point as you consider where and how to further pursue the development of your managerial skills and competencies. The items on the list are recommended by the American Assembly of Collegiate Schools of Business (AACSB) as skills and personal characteristics that should be nurtured in college and university students of business administration. Their success—and yours—as twenty-first-century managers may well rest on (1) an initial awareness of the importance of these basic management foundations and (2) a willingness to strive continually to strengthen them throughout your work career.

Source: See *Outcome Management Project,* Phase I and Phase II Reports (St. Louis: American Assembly of Collegiate Schools of Business, 1986 & 1987).

Turbulence Tolerance Test

Instructions

The following statements were made by a 37-year-old manager in a large, successful corporation. How would you like to have a job with these characteristics? Using the following scale, write your response to the left of each statement.

> 4 = I would enjoy this very much; it's completely acceptable.
>
> 3 = This would be enjoyable and acceptable most of the time.
>
> 2 = I'd have no reaction to this feature one way or another, or it would be about equally enjoyable and unpleasant.
>
> 1 = This feature would be somewhat unpleasant for me.
>
> 0 = This feature would be very unpleasant for me.

_____ 1. I regularly spend 30 to 40 percent of my time in meetings.

_____ 2. Eighteen months ago my job did not exist, and I have been essentially inventing it as I go along.

_____ 3. The responsibilities I either assume or am assigned consistently exceed the authority I have for discharging them.

_____ 4. At any given moment in my job, I have on average about a dozen phone calls to be returned.

_____ 5. There seems to be very little relation between the quality of my job performance and my actual pay and fringe benefits.

_____ 6. About 2 weeks a year of formal management training is needed in my job just to stay current.

_____ 7. Because we have very effective equal employment opportunity (EEO) in my company and because it is thoroughly multinational, my job consistently brings me into close working contact at a professional level with people of many races, ethnic groups and nationalities, and of both sexes.

_____ 8. There is no objective way to measure my effectiveness.

_____ 9. I report to three different bosses for different aspects of my job, and each has an equal say in my performance appraisal.

_____ 10. On average, about a third of my time is spent dealing with unexpected emergencies that force all scheduled work to be postponed.

_____ 11. When I have to have a meeting of the people who report to me, it takes my secretary most of a day to find a time when we are all available, and even then I have yet to have a meeting where everyone is present for the entire meeting.

_____ 12. The college degree I earned in preparation for this type of work is now obsolete, and I probably should go back for another degree.

_____ 13. My job requires that I absorb 100–200 pages of technical materials per week.

_____ 14. I am out of town overnight at least one night per week.

_____ 15. My department is so interdependent with several other departments in the company that all distinctions about which departments are responsible for which tasks are quite arbitrary.

Source: Peter B. Vail, _Managing as a Performance Art: New Ideas for a World of Chaotic Change_ (San Francisco: Jossey-Bass, 1989), pp. 8–9. Used by permission.

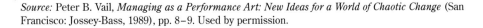

____ 16. In about a year I will probably get a promotion to a job in another division that has most of these same characteristics.

____ 17. During the period of my employment here, either the entire company or the division I worked in has been reorganized every year or so.

____ 18. While there are several possible promotions I can see ahead of me, I have no real career path in an objective sense.

—— 19. While there are several possible promotions I can see ahead of me, I think I have no realistic chance of getting to the top levels of the company.

____ 20. While I have many ideas about how to make things work better, I have no direct influence on either the business policies or the personnel policies that govern my division.

____ 21. My company has recently put in an "assessment center" where I and all other managers will be required to go through an extensive battery of psychological tests to assess our potential.

____ 22. My company is a defendant in an antitrust suit, and if the case comes to trial, I will probably have to testify about some decisions that were made a few years ago.

____ 23. Advanced computer and other electronic office technology is continually being introduced into my division, necessitating constant learning on my part.

____ 24. The computer terminal and screen I have in my office can be monitored in my bosses' offices without my knowledge.

Scoring

Total your responses and divide the sum by 24; enter the score here [TTT = ____].

Interpretation

This instrument gives an impression of your tolerance for managing in turbulent times—something likely to characterize the world of work well into the future. In general, the higher your TTT score, the more comfortable you seem to be with turbulence and change—a positive sign. For comparison purposes, the average scores for some 500 MBA students and young managers was 1.5–1.6. The test's author suggests the TTT scores may be interpreted much like a grade point average in which 4.0 is a perfect A. On this basis, a 1.5 is below a C! How did you do?

ASSESSMENT 4

Global Readiness Index

Instructions

Use the scale to rate yourself on each of the following items to establish a baseline measurement of your readiness to participate in the global work environment.

Rating Scale

```
1 = Very Poor
2 = Poor
3 = Acceptable
4 = Good
5 = Very Good
```

Source: Developed from "Is Your Company Really Global," *Business Week* (December 1, 1997).

____ 1. I understand my own culture in terms of its expectations, values, and influence on communication and relationships.

____ 2. When someone presents me with a different point of view, I try to understand it rather than attack it.

____ 3. I am comfortable dealing with situations where the available information is incomplete and the outcomes unpredictable.

____ 4. I am open to new situations and am always looking for new information and learning opportunities.

____ 5. I have a good understanding of the attitudes and perceptions toward my culture as they are held by people from other cultures.

6. I am always gathering information about other countries and cultures and trying to learn from them.

7. I am well informed regarding the major differences in government, political systems, and economic policies around the world.

8. I work hard to increase my understanding of people from other cultures.

9. I am able to adjust my communication style to work effectively with people from different cultures.

10. I can recognize when cultural differences are influencing working relationships and adjust my attitudes and behavior accordingly.

Interpretation

To be successful in the twenty-first-century work environment, you must be comfortable with the global economy and the cultural diversity that it holds. This requires a *global mind-set* that is receptive to and respectful of cultural differences, *global knowledge* that includes the continuing quest to know and learn more about other nations and cultures, and *global work skills* that allow you to work effectively across cultures.

Scoring

The goal is to score as close to a perfect "5" as possible on each of the three dimensions of global readiness. Develop your scores as follows.

Items $(1 + 2 + 3 + 4)/4$
= ____ Global Mind-Set Score

Items $(5 + 6 + 7)/3$
= ____ Global Knowledge Score

Items $(8 + 9 + 10)/3$
= ____ Global Work Skills Score

ASSESSMENT 5

Personal Values

Instructions

Below are 16 items. Rate how important each one is to you on a scale of 0 (not important) to 100 (very important). Write the numbers 0–100 on the line to the left of each item.

Not important				Somewhat important				Very important		
0	10	20	30	40	50	60	70	80	90	100

____ 1. An enjoyable, satisfying job.

____ 2. A high-paying job.

____ 3. A good marriage.

____ 4. Meeting new people; social events.

____ 5. Involvement in community activities.

____ 6. My religion.

____ 7. Exercising, playing sports.

____ 8. Intellectual development.

____ 9. A career with challenging opportunities.

____ 10. Nice cars, clothes, home, etc.

____ 11. Spending time with family.

____ 12. Having several close friends.

____ 13. Volunteer work for not-for-profit organizations, such as the cancer society.

Source: Robert N. Lussier, *Human Relations in Organizations,* 2nd ed. (Homewood, IL: Richard D. Irwin, 1993). By permission.

____ 14. Meditation, quiet time to think, pray, etc.
____ 15. A healthy, balanced diet.
____ 16. Educational reading, TV, self-improvement programs, etc.

Scoring

Transfer the numbers for each of the 16 items to the appropriate column below, then add the two numbers in each column.

	Professional	Financial	Family	Social
	1. ____	2. ____	3. ____	4. ____
	9. ____	10. ____	11. ____	12. ____
Totals	____	____	____	____

	Community	Spiritual	Physical	Intellectual
	5. ____	6. ____	7. ____	8. ____
	13. ____	14. ____	15. ____	16. ____
Totals	____	____	____	____

Interpretation

The higher the total in any area, the higher the value you place on that particular area. The closer the numbers are in all eight areas, the more well-rounded you are. Think about the time and effort you put forth in your top three values. Is it sufficient to allow you to achieve the level of success you want in each area? If not, what can you do to change? Is there any area in which you feel you should have a higher value total? If yes, which, and what can you do to change?

ASSESSMENT 6

Intolerance for Ambiguity

Instructions

To determine your level of tolerance (intolerance) for ambiguity, respond to the following items. PLEASE RATE EVERY ITEM; DO NOT LEAVE ANY ITEM BLANK. Rate each item on the following seven-point scale:

1	2	3	4	5	6	7
strongly disagree	moderately disagree	slightly disagree		slightly agree	moderately agree	strongly agree

Rating

____ 1. An expert who doesn't come up with a definite answer probably doesn't know too much.

____ 2. There is really no such thing as a problem that can't be solved.

____ 3. I would like to live in a foreign country for a while.

____ 4. People who fit their lives to a schedule probably miss the joy of living.

____ 5. A good job is one where what is to be done and how it is to be done are always clear.

Source: Based on Budner, S. Intolerance of Ambiguity as a Personality Variable, *Journal of Personality,* Vol. 30, No. 1, (1962), pp. 29–50.

_____ 6. In the long run it is possible to get more done by tackling small, simple problems rather than large, complicated ones.

_____ 7. It is more fun to tackle a complicated problem than it is to solve a simple one.

_____ 8. Often the most interesting and stimulating people are those who don't mind being different and original.

_____ 9. What we are used to is always preferable to what is unfamiliar.

_____ 10. A person who leads an even, regular life in which few surprises or unexpected happenings arise really has a lot to be grateful for.

_____ 11. People who insist upon a yes or no answer just don't know how complicated things really are.

_____ 12. Many of our most important decisions are based on insufficient information.

_____ 13. I like parties where I know most of the people more than ones where most of the people are complete strangers.

_____ 14. The sooner we all acquire ideals, the better.

_____ 15. Teachers or supervisors who hand out vague assignments give a chance for one to show initiative and originality.

_____ 16. A good teacher is one who makes you wonder about your way of looking at things.

_____ Total

Scoring

The scale was developed by S. Budner. Budner reports test–retest correlations of .85 with a variety of samples (mostly students and health care workers). Data, however, are more than 30 years old, so mean shifts may have occurred. Maximum ranges are 16–112, and score ranges were from 25 to 79, with a grand mean of approximately 49.

The test was designed to measure several different components of possible reactions to perceived threat in situations which are new, complex, or insoluble. Half of the items have been reversed.

To obtain a score, first _reverse_ the scale score for the eight "reverse" items, 3, 4, 7, 8, 11, 12, 15, and 16 (i.e., a rating of 1 = 7, 2 = 6, 3 = 5, etc.), then add up the rating scores for all 16 items.

Interpretation

Empirically, low tolerance for ambiguity (high intolerance) has been positively correlated with:

• Conventionality of religious beliefs
• High attendance at religious services
• More intense religious beliefs
• More positive views of censorship
• Higher authoritarianism
• Lower Machiavellianism

The application of this concept to management in the 1990s is clear and relatively self-evident. The world of work and many organizations are full of ambiguity and change. Individuals with a _higher_ tolerance for ambiguity are far more likely to be able to function effectively in organizations and contexts in which there is a high turbulence, a high rate of change, and less certainty about expectations, performance standards, what needs to be done, and so on. In contrast, individuals with a lower tolerance for ambiguity are far more likely to be unable to adapt or adjust quickly in turbulence, uncertainty, and change. These individuals are likely to become rigid, angry, stressed, and frustrated when there is a high level of uncertainty and ambiguity in the environment. High levels of tolerance for ambiguity, therefore, are associated with an ability to "roll with the punches" as organizations, environmental conditions, and demands change rapidly.

Two-Factor Profile

Instructions

On each of the following dimensions, distribute a total of 10 points between the two options. For example:

Summer weather   (7) ....(3) Winter weather

1. Very responsible job   (___) ....(___) Job security

2. Recognition for   (___) ....(___) Good relations
   work accomplishments   with co-workers

3. Advancement   (___) ....(___) A boss who knows
   opportunities at work   his/her job well

4. Opportunities to grow   (___) ....(___) Good working
   and learn on the job   conditions

5. A job that I can   (___) ....(___) Supportive rules,
   do well   policies of employer

6. A prestigious or   (___) ....(___) A high base wage
   high-status job   or salary

Scoring

Summarize your total scores for all items in the *left-hand column* and write it here:
MF = ___.
Summarize your total scores for all items in the *right-hand column* and write it here:
HF = ___.

Interpretation

The "MF" score indicates the relative importance that you place on motivating or satisfier factors in Herzberg's two-factor theory. This shows how important job content is to you. The "HF" score indicates the relative importance that you place on hygiene or dissatisfier factors in Herzberg's two-factor theory. This shows how important job context is to you.

Are You Cosmopolitan?

Instructions

Answer the questions using a scale of 1 to 5: 1 representing "strongly disagree"; 2, "somewhat disagree"; 3, "neutral"; 4, "somewhat agree"; and 5, "strongly agree."

____ 1. You believe it is the right of the professional to make his or her own decisions about what is to be done on the job.

Source: Developed from Joseph A. Raelin, *The Clash of Cultures, Managers and Professionals* (Harvard Business School Press, 1986).

2. You believe a professional should stay in an individual staff role regardless of the income sacrifice.

____ 3. You have no interest in moving up to a top administrative post.

____ 4. You believe that professionals are better evaluated by professional colleagues than by management.

____ 5. Your friends tend to be members of your profession.

____ 6. You would rather be known or get credit for your work outside rather than inside the company.

____ 7. You would feel better making a contribution to society than to your organization.

____ 8. Managers have no right to place time and cost schedules on professional contributors.

Scoring and Interpretation

A "cosmopolitan" identifies with the career profession, and a "local" identifies with the employing organization. Total your scores. A score of 30–40 suggests a cosmopolitan work orientation, 10–20 a "local" orientation, and 20–30 a mixed orientation.

● ● ● ● ● ● ASSESSMENT 9 ●

Group Effectiveness

Instructions

For this assessment, select a specific group you work with or have worked with; it can be a college or work group. For each of the eight statements below, select how often each statement describes the group's behavior. Place the number 1, 2, 3, or 4 on the line next to each of the 8 numbers.

Usually	Frequently	Occasionally	Seldom
1	2	3	4

____ 1. The members are loyal to one another and to the group leader.

____ 2. The members and leader have a high degree of confidence and trust in each other.

____ 3. Group values and goals express relevant values and needs of members.

____ 4. Activities of the group occur in a supportive atmosphere.

____ 5. The group is eager to help members develop to their full potential.

____ 6. The group knows the value of constructive conformity and knows when to use it and for what purpose.

____ 7. The members communicate all information relevant to the group's activity fully and frankly.

____ 8. The members feel secure in making decisions that seem appropriate to them.

Scoring

____ Total. Add up the eight numbers and place an X on the continuum below that represents the score.

Effective group   8 . . . 16 . . . 24 . . . 32   Ineffective group

Interpretation

The lower the score, the more effective the group. What can you do to help the group become more effective? What can the group do to become more effective?

Least Preferred Co-worker Scale

Instructions

Think of all the different people with whom you have ever worked—in jobs, in social clubs, in student projects, or whatever. Next, think of the *one person* with whom you could work *least* well—that is, the person with whom you had the most difficulty getting a job done. This is the one person—a peer, boss, or subordinate—with whom you would least want to work. Describe this person by circling numbers at the appropriate points on each of the following pairs of bipolar adjectives. Work rapidly. There are no right or wrong answers.

Pleasant	8 7 6 5 4 3 2 1	Unpleasant
Friendly	8 7 6 5 4 3 2 1	Unfriendly
Rejecting	1 2 3 4 5 6 7 8	Accepting
Tense	1 2 3 4 5 6 7 8	Relaxed
Distant	1 2 3 4 5 6 7 8	Close
Cold	1 2 3 4 5 6 7 8	Warm
Supportive	8 7 6 5 4 3 2 1	Hostile
Boring	1 2 3 4 5 6 7 8	Interesting
Quarrelsome	1 2 3 4 5 6 7 8	Harmonious
Gloomy	1 2 3 4 5 6 7 8	Cheerful
Open	8 7 6 5 4 3 2 1	Guarded
Backbiting	1 2 3 4 5 6 7 8	Loyal
Untrustworthy	1 2 3 4 5 6 7 8	Trustworthy
Considerate	8 7 6 5 4 3 2 1	Inconsiderate
Nasty	1 2 3 4 5 6 7 8	Nice
Agreeable	8 7 6 5 4 3 2 1	Disagreeable
Insincere	1 2 3 4 5 6 7 8	Sincere
Kind	8 7 6 5 4 3 2 1	Unkind

Scoring

This is called the "least preferred co-worker scale" (LPC). Compute your LPC score by totaling all the numbers you circled; enter that score here [LPC = ____].

Interpretation

The LPC scale is used by Fred Fiedler to identify a person's dominant leadership style. Fiedler believes that this style is a relatively fixed part of one's personality and is therefore difficult to change. This leads Fiedler to his contingency views, which suggest that the key to leadership success is finding (or creating) good "matches" between style and situation. If your score is 73 or above, Fiedler considers you a "relationship-motivated" leader; if your score is 64 and below, he considers you a "task-motivated" leader. If your score is between 65 and 72, Fiedler leaves it up to you to determine which leadership style is most like yours.

Source: Fred E. Fiedler and Martin M. Chemers. *Improving Leadership Effectiveness: The Leader Match Concept,* 2nd ed. (New York: John Wiley & Sons, Inc., 1984). Used by permission.

Leadership Style

Instructions

The following statements describe leadership acts. Indicate the way you would most likely act if you were leader of a workgroup, by circling whether you would most likely behave in this way:

> always (A); frequently (F); occasionally (O); seldom (S); or never (N)

A F O S N 1. Act as group spokesperson.
A F O S N 2. Encourage overtime work.
A F O S N 3. Allow members complete freedom in their work.
A F O S N 4. Encourage the use of uniform procedures.
A F O S N 5. Permit members to solve their own problems.
A F O S N 6. Stress being ahead of competing groups.
A F O S N 7. Speak as a representative of the group.
A F O S N 8. Push members for greater effort.
A F O S N 9. Try out ideas in the group.
A F O S N 10. Let the members work the way they think best.
A F O S N 11. Work hard for a personal promotion.
A F O S N 12. Tolerate postponement and uncertainty.
A F O S N 13. Speak for the group when visitors are present.
A F O S N 14. Keep the work moving at a rapid pace.
A F O S N 15. Turn members loose on a job.
A F O S N 16. Settle conflicts in the group.
A F O S N 17. Focus on work details.
A F O S N 18. Represent the group at outside meetings.
A F O S N 19. Avoid giving the members too much freedom.
A F O S N 20. Decide what should be done and how it should be done.
A F O S N 21. Push for increased production.
A F O S N 22. Give some members authority to act.
A F O S N 23. Expect things to turn out as predicted.
A F O S N 24. Allow the group to take initiative.
A F O S N 25. Assign group members to particular tasks.
A F O S N 26. Be willing to make changes.
A F O S N 27. Ask members to work harder.
A F O S N 28. Trust members to exercise good judgment.
A F O S N 29. Schedule the work to be done.
A F O S N 30. Refuse to explain my actions.
A F O S N 31. Persuade others that my ideas are best.
A F O S N 32. Permit the group to set its own pace.
A F O S N 33. Urge the group to beat its previous record.
A F O S N 34. Act without consulting the group.
A F O S N 35. Ask members to follow standard rules.

T _____   P _____

Scoring

1. Circle items 8, 12, 17, 18, 19, 30, 34, and 35.
2. Write the number 1 in front of a *circled item number* if you responded S (seldom) or N (never) to that item.

3. Write a number 1 in front of *item numbers not circled* if you responded A (always) or F (frequently).
4. Circle the number 1's which you have written in front of items 3, 5, 8, 10, 15, 18, 19, 22, 24, 26, 28, 30, 32, 34, and 35.
5. *Count the circled number 1's.* This is your score for leadership *concern for people.* Record the score in the blank following the letter P at the end of the questionnaire.
6. *Count the uncircled number 1's.* This is your score for leadership *concern for task.* Record this number in the blank following the letter T.

ASSESSMENT 12

"TT" Leadership Style

Instructions

For each of the following 10 pairs of statements, divide 5 points between the two according to your beliefs, perceptions of yourself, or according to which of the two statements characterizes you better. The 5 points may be divided between the a and b statements in any one of the following ways: 5 for a, 0 for b; 4 for a, 1 for b; 3 for a, 2 for b; 1 for a, 4 for b; 0 for a, 5 for b, but not equally (2 1/2) between the two. Weigh your choices between the two according to the one that characterizes you or your beliefs better.

1. (a) As leader I have a primary mission of maintaining stability.
   (b) As leader I have a primary mission of change.
2. (a) As leader I must cause events.
   (b) As leader I must facilitate events.
3. (a) I am concerned that my followers are rewarded equitably for their work.
   (b) I am concerned about what my followers want in life.
4. (a) My preference is to think long range: what might be.
   (b) My preference is to think short range: what is realistic.
5. (a) As a leader I spend considerable energy in managing separate but related goals.
   (b) As a leader I spend considerable energy in arousing hopes, expectations, and aspirations among my followers.

6. (a) Although not in a formal classroom sense, I believe that a significant part of my leadership is that of teacher.
   (b) I believe that a significant part of my leadership is that of facilitator.
7. (a) As leader I must engage with followers at an equal level of morality.
   (b) As leader I must represent a higher morality.
8. (a) I enjoy stimulating followers to want to do more.
   (b) I enjoy rewarding followers for a job well done.
9. (a) Leadership should be practical.
   (b) Leadership should be inspirational.
10. (a) What power I have to influence others comes primarily from my ability to get people to identify with me and my ideas.
    (b) What power I have to influence others comes primarily from my status and position.

Scoring

Circle your points for items 1b, 2a, 3b, 4a, 5b, 6a, 7b, 8a, 9b, 10a and add up the total points you allocated to these items; enter the score here [**T** = ____]. Next, add up the total points given to the uncircled items 1a, 2b, 3a, 4b, 5a, 6b, 7a, 8b, 9a, 10b; enter the score here [T = ____].

Interpretation

This instrument gives an impression of your tendencies toward "transformational" leadership (your **T** score) and "transactional" leadership (your T score). You may want to refer to the discussion of these concepts in Chapter 4. Today, a lot of attention is being given to the transformational aspects of leadership—those personal qualities that inspire a sense of vision and desire for extraordinary accomplishment in followers. The most successful leaders of the future will most likely be strong in both "T"s.

Source: Questionnaire by W. Warner Burke, Ph.D. Used by permission.

Empowering Others

Instructions

Think of times when you have been in charge of a group—this could be a full-time or part-time work situation, a student workgroup, or whatever. Complete the following questionnaire by recording how you feel about each statement according to this scale.

> 1 = Strongly disagree
> 2 = Disagree
> 3 = Neutral
> 4 = Agree
> 5 = Strongly agree

When in charge of a group I find:

____ 1. Most of the time other people are too inexperienced to do things, so I prefer to do them myself.

____ 2. It often takes more time to explain things to others than just to do them myself.

____ 3. Mistakes made by others are costly, so I don't assign much work to them.

____ 4. Some things simply should not be delegated to others.

____ 5. I often get quicker action by doing a job myself.

____ 6. Many people are good only at very specific tasks, and thus can't be assigned additional responsibilities.

____ 7. Many people are too busy to take on additional work.

____ 8. Most people just aren't ready to handle additional responsibilities.

____ 9. In my position, I should be entitled to make my own decisions.

Scoring

Total your responses; enter the score here [____].

Interpretation

This instrument gives an impression of your *willingness to delegate.* Possible scores range from 9 to 45. The higher your score, the more willing you appear to be to delegate to others. Willingness to delegate is an important managerial characteristic. It is essential if you—as a manager—are to "empower" others and give them opportunities to assume responsibility and exercise self-control in their work. With the growing importance of empowerment in the new workplace, your willingness to delegate is well worth thinking about seriously.

Source: Questionnaire adapted from L. Steinmetz and R. Todd, *First Line Management,* 4th ed. (Homewood, IL: BPI/Irwin, 1986), pp. 64–67. Used by permission.

Machiavellianism

Instructions

For each of the following statements, circle the number that most closely resembles your attitude.

Statement	Disagree A Lot	A Little	Neutral	Agree A Little	A Lot
1. The best way to handle people is to tell them what they want to hear.	1	2	3	4	5
2. When you ask someone to do something for you, it is best to give the real reason for wanting it rather than reasons that might carry more weight.	1	2	3	4	5
3. Anyone who completely trusts someone else is asking for trouble.	1	2	3	4	5
4. It is hard to get ahead without cutting corners here and there.	1	2	3	4	5
5. It is safest to assume that all people have a vicious streak, and it will come out when they are given a chance.	1	2	3	4	5
6. One should take action only when it is morally right.	1	2	3	4	5
7. Most people are basically good and kind.	1	2	3	4	5
8. There is no excuse for lying to someone else.	1	2	3	4	5
9. Most people forget more easily the death of their father than the loss of their property.	1	2	3	4	5
10. Generally speaking, people won't work hard unless forced to do so.	1	2	3	4	5

Scoring and Interpretation

This assessment is designed to compute your Machiavellianism (Mach) score. Mach is a personality characteristic that taps people's power orientation. The high-Mach personality is pragmatic, maintains emotional distance from others, and believes that ends can justify means. To obtain your Mach score, add up the numbers you checked for questions 1, 3, 4, 5, 9, and 10. For the other four questions, reverse the numbers you have checked, so that 5 becomes 1; 4 is 2; and 1 is 5. Then total both sets of numbers to find your score. A random sample of adults found the national average to be 25. Students in business and management typically score higher.

The results of research using the Mach test have found: (1) men are generally more Machiavellian than women; (2) older adults tend to have lower Mach scores than younger adults; (3) there is no significant difference between high Machs and low Machs on measures of intelligence or ability; (4) Machiavellianism is not significantly related to demographic characteristics such as educational level or marital status; and (5) high Machs tend to be in professions that emphasize the control and manipulation of people—for example, managers, lawyers, psychiatrists, and behavioral scientists.

Source: From R. Christie and F. L. Geis, *Studies in Machiavellianism* (New York: Academic Press, 1970). By permission.

Personal Power Profile

Contributed by Marcus Maier, Chapman University

Instructions
Below is a list of statements that may be used in describing behaviors that supervisors (leaders) in work organizations can direct toward their subordinates (followers). First, carefully read each descriptive statement, thinking in terms of *how you prefer to influence others*. Mark the number that most closely represents how you feel. Use the following numbers for your answers.

> 5 = Strongly agree
> 4 = Agree
> 3 = Neither agree nor disagree
> 2 = Disagree
> 1 = Strongly disagree

To influence others, I would prefer to:	Strongly Disagree	Disagree	Neither Agree nor Disagree	Agree	Strongly Agree
1. Increase their pay level	1	2	3	4	5
2. Make them feel valued	1	2	3	4	5
3. Give undesirable job assignments	1	2	3	4	5
4. Make them feel like I approve of them	1	2	3	4	5
5. Make them feel that they have commitments to meet	1	2	3	4	5
6. Make them feel personally accepted	1	2	3	4	5
7. Make them feel important	1	2	3	4	5
8. Give them good technical suggestions	1	2	3	4	5
9. Make the work difficult for them	1	2	3	4	5
10. Share my experience and/or training	1	2	3	4	5
11. Make things unpleasant here	1	2	3	4	5
12. Make being at work distasteful	1	2	3	4	5
13. Influence their getting a pay increase	1	2	3	4	5
14. Make them feel like they should satisfy their job requirements	1	2	3	4	5
15. Provide them with sound job-related advice	1	2	3	4	5
16. Provide them with special benefits	1	2	3	4	5
17. Influence their getting a promotion	1	2	3	4	5
18. Give them the feeling that they have responsibilities to fulfill	1	2	3	4	5
19. Provide them with needed technical knowledge	1	2	3	4	5
20. Make them recognize that they have tasks to accomplish	1	2	3	4	5

Source: Modified version of T. R. Hinken and C. A. Schriesheim, "Development and Application of New Scales to Measure the French and Raven (1959) Bases of Social Power," *Journal of Applied Psychology,* Vol. 74 (1989), pp. 561–567.

Scoring

Using the grid below, insert your scores from the 20 questions and proceed as follows: *Reward power*—sum your response to items 1, 13, 16, and 17 and divide by 4. *Coercive power*—sum your response to items 3, 9, 11, and 12 and divide by 4. *Legitimate power*—sum your response to questions 5, 14, 18, and 20 and divide by 4. *Referent power*—sum your response to questions 2, 4, 6, and 7 and divide by 4. *Expert power*—sum your response to questions 8, 10, 15, and 19 and divide by 4.

Reward	Coercive	Legitimate	Referent	Expert
1 ___	3 ___	5 ___	2 ___	8 ___
13 ___	9 ___	14 ___	4 ___	10 ___
16 ___	11 ___	18 ___	6 ___	15 ___
17 ___	12 ___	20 ___	7 ___	19 ___
Total ___	___	___	___	___
Divide by 4 ___	___	___	___	___

Interpretation

A high score (4 and greater) on any of the five dimensions of power implies that you prefer to influence others by employing that particular form of power. A low score (2 or less) implies that you prefer not to employ this particular form of power to influence others. This represents your power profile. Your overall power position is not reflected by the simple sum of the power derived from each of the five sources. Instead, some combinations of power are synergistic in nature—they are greater than the simple sum of their parts. For example, referent power tends to magnify the impact of other power sources because these other influence attempts are coming from a "respected" person. Reward power often increases the impact of referent power, because people generally tend to like those who give them things that they desire. Some power combinations tend to produce the opposite of synergistic effects, such that the total is less than the sum of the parts. Power dilution frequently accompanies the use of (or threatened use of) coercive power.

ASSESSMENT 16

Intuitive Ability

Instructions

Complete this survey as quickly as you can. Be honest with yourself. For each question, select the response that most appeals to you.

1. When working on a project, do you prefer to:
   (a) Be told what the problem is but be left free to decide how to solve it?
   (b) Get very clear instructions about how to go about solving the problem before you start?
2. When working on a project, do you prefer to work with colleagues who are:
   (a) Realistic?
   (b) Imaginative?

3. Do you most admire people who are:
   (a) Creative?
   (b) Careful?
4. Do the friends you choose tend to be:
   (a) Serious and hard working?
   (b) Exciting and often emotional?
5. When you ask a colleague for advice on a problem you have, do you:
   (a) Seldom or never get upset if he or she questions your basic assumptions?
   (b) Often get upset if he or she questions your basic assumptions?
6. When you start your day, do you:
   (a) Seldom make or follow a specific plan?
   (b) Usually first make a plan to follow?

Source: AIM Survey (El Paso, TX: ENFP Enterprises, 1989). Copyright © 1989 by Weston H. Agor. Used by permission.

7. When working with numbers do you find that you:
    (a) Seldom or never make factual errors?
    (b) Often make factual errors?
8. Do you find that you:
    (a) Seldom daydream during the day and really don't enjoy doing so when you do it?
    (b) Frequently daydream during the day and enjoy doing so?
9. When working on a problem, do you:
    (a) Prefer to follow the instructions or rules when they are given to you?
    (b) Often enjoy circumventing the instructions or rules when they are given to you?
10. When you are trying to put something together, do you prefer to have:
    (a) Step-by-step written instructions on how to assemble the item?
    (b) A picture of how the item is supposed to look once assembled?
11. Do you find that the person who irritates you *the most* is the one who appears to be:
    (a) Disorganized?
    (b) Organized?
12. When an expected crisis comes up that you have to deal with, do you:
    (a) Feel anxious about the situation?
    (b) Feel excited by the challenge of the situation?

Scoring

Total the number of "a" responses circled for questions 1, 3, 5, 6, 11; enter the score here [A = ____]. Total the number of "b" responses for questions 2, 4, 7, 8, 9, 10, 12; enter the score here [B = ____]. Add your "a" and "b" scores and enter the sum here [A + B = ____]. This is your *intuitive score.* The highest possible intuitive score is 12; the lowest is 0.

Interpretation

In his book *Intuition in Organizations* (Newbury Park, CA: Sage, 1989), pp. 10–11, Weston H. Agor states: "Traditional analytical techniques . . . are not as useful as they once were for guiding major decisions. . . . If you hope to be better prepared for tomorrow, then it only seems logical to pay some attention to the use and development of intuitive skills for decision making." Agor developed the prior survey to help people assess their tendencies to use intuition in decision making. Your score offers a general impression of your strength in this area. It may also suggest a need to further develop your skill and comfort with more intuitive decision approaches.

<hr>

● ● ● ● ● ASSESSMENT 17 ●

Decision-Making Biases

Instructions

How good are you at avoiding potential decision-making biases? Test yourself by answering the following questions:

1. Which is riskier:
    (a) driving a car on a 400-mile trip?
    (b) flying on a 400-mile commercial airline flight?
2. Are there more words in the English language:
    (a) that begin with "r"?
    (b) that have "r" as the third letter?
3. Mark is finishing his MBA at a prestigious university. He is very interested in the arts and at one time considered a career as a musician. Is Mark more likely to take a job:
    (a) in the management of the arts?
    (b) with a management consulting firm?

4. You are about to hire a new central-region sales director for the fifth time this year. You predict that the next director should work out reasonably well since the last four were "lemons" and the odds favor hiring at least one good sales director in five tries. Is this thinking
    (a) correct?
    (b) incorrect?
5. A newly hired engineer for a computer firm in the Boston metropolitan area has 4 years' experience and good all-around qualifications. When asked to estimate the starting salary for this employee, a chemist with very little knowledge about the profession or industry guessed an annual salary of $35,000. What is your estimate?
    $____ per year

Scoring

Your instructor will provide answers and explanations for the assessment questions.

<hr>

Source: Incidents from Max H. Bazerman, *Judgment in Managerial Decision Making,* 3rd ed. (New York: John Wiley & Sons, Inc., 1994), pp. 13–14. Used by permission.

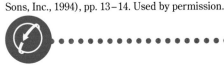

Interpretation

Each of the preceding questions examines your tendency to use a different judgmental heuristic. In his book *Judgment in Managerial Decision Making,* 3rd ed. (New York: John Wiley & Sons, 1994), pp. 6–7, Max Bazerman calls these heuristics "simplifying strategies, or rules of thumb" used in making decisions. He states, "In general, heuristics are helpful, but their use can sometimes lead to severe errors. . . . If we can make managers aware of the potential adverse impacts of using heuristics, they can then decide when and where to use them." This assessment offers an initial insight into your use of such heuristics. An informed decision maker understands the heuristics, is able to recognize when they appear, and eliminates any that may inappropriately bias decision making.

Test yourself further. Before hearing from your instructor, go back and write next to each item the name of the judgmental heuristic (see Chapter 2 text discussion) that you think applies.

Then write down a situation that you have experienced and in which some decision-making bias may have occurred. Be prepared to share and discuss this incident with the class.

ASSESSMENT 18

Conflict Management Strategies

Instructions

Think of how you behave in conflict situations in which your wishes differ from those of others. In the space to the left, rate each of the following statements on a scale of "1" "not at all" to "5" "very much."

When I have a conflict at work, school, or in my personal life, I do the following:

____ **1.** I give in to the wishes of the other party.
____ **2.** I try to realize a middle-of-the-road solution.
____ **3.** I push my own point of view.
____ **4.** I examine issues until I find a solution that really satisfies me and the other party.
____ **5.** I avoid a confrontation about our differences.
____ **6.** I concur with the other party.
____ **7.** I emphasize that we have to find a compromise solution.
____ **8.** I search for gains.
____ **9.** I stand for my own and the other's goals.
____ **10.** I avoid differences of opinion as much as possible.
____ **11.** I try to accommodate the other party.
____ **12.** I insist we both give in a little.
____ **13.** I fight for a good outcome for myself.
____ **14.** I examine ideas from both sides to find a mutually optimal solution.
____ **15.** I try to make differences seem less severe.
____ **16.** I adapt to the other party's goals and interests.
____ **17.** I strive whenever possible towards a fifty-fifty compromise.
____ **18.** I do everything to win.
____ **19.** I work out a solution that serves my own as well as other's interests as much as possible.
____ **20.** I try to avoid a confrontation with the other person.

Scoring

Total your scores for items as follows.
Yielding tendency: 1+6+11+16 = ____.

Source: This instrument is described in Carsten K. W. De Drew, Arne Evers, Bianca Beersma, Esther S. Kluwer, and Aukje Nauta, "A Theory-Based Measure of Conflict Management Strategies in the Workplace," *Journal of Organizational Behavior,* vol. 22 (2001), pp. 645–668. Used by permission.

Compromising tendency: $2+7+12+17 =$ ____.
Forcing tendency: $3+8+13+18 =$ ____.
Problem-solving tendency: $4+9+14+19 =$ ____.
Avoiding tendency: $5+10+15+20 =$ ____.

Interpretation

Each of the scores above approximates one of the conflict management styles discussed in the chapter. Look back to Figure 15.4 and make the match ups. Although each style is part of management, only collaboration or problem solving leads to true conflict resolution. You should consider any patterns that may be evident in your scores and think about how to best handle the conflict situations in which you become involved.

ASSESSMENT 19

Your Personality Type

Instructions

How true is each statement for you?

	Not True at All		Not True or Untrue		Very True
1. I hate giving up before I'm absolutely sure that I'm licked.	1	2	3	4	5
2. Sometimes I feel that I should not be working so hard, but something drives me on.	1	2	3	4	5
3. I thrive on challenging situations. The more challenges I have, the better.	1	2	3	4	5
4. In comparison to most people I know, I'm very involved in my work.	1	2	3	4	5
5. It seems as if I need 30 hours a day to finish all the things I'm faced with.	1	2	3	4	5
6. In general, I approach my work more seriously than most people I know.	1	2	3	4	5
7. I guess there are some people who can be nonchalant about their work, but I'm not one of them.	1	2	3	4	5
8. My achievements are considered to be significantly higher than those of most people I know.	1	2	3	4	5
9. I've often been asked to be an officer of some group or groups.	1	2	3	4	5

Scoring

Add all your scores to create a total score = ____.

Interpretation

Type A personalities (hurried and competitive) tend to score 36 and above. Type B personalities (relaxed) tend to score 22 and below. Scores of 23–35 indicate a balance or mix of Type A and Type B.

Source: From *Job Demands and Worker Health* (HEW Publication No. [NIOSH] 75–160) (Washington, DC: US Department of Health, Education and Welfare, 1975), pp. 253–254.

Time Management Profile

Instructions

Complete the following questionnaire by indicating "Y" (yes) or "N" (no) for each item. Be frank and allow your responses to create an accurate picture of how you tend to respond to these kinds of situations.

____ 1. When confronted with several items of similar urgency and importance, I tend to do the easiest one first.

____ 2. I do the most important things during that part of the day when I know I perform best.

____ 3. Most of the time I don't do things someone else can do; I delegate this type of work to others.

____ 4. Even though meetings without a clear and useful purpose upset me, I put up with them.

____ 5. I skim documents before reading them and don't complete any that offer a low return on my time investment.

____ 6. I don't worry much if I don't accomplish at least one significant task each day.

____ 7. I save the most trivial tasks for that time of day when my creative energy is lowest.

____ 8. My workspace is neat and organized.

____ 9. My office door is always "open"; I never work in complete privacy.

____ 10. I schedule my time completely from start to finish every workday.

____ 11. I don't like "to do" lists, preferring to respond to daily events as they occur.

____ 12. I "block" a certain amount of time each day or week that is dedicated to high-priority activities.

Scoring

Count the number of "Y" responses to items 2, 3, 5, 7, 8, 12. [Enter that score here ____.] Count the number of "N" responses to items 1, 4, 6, 9, 10, 11. [Enter that score here ____.] Add together the two scores.

Interpretation

The higher the total score, the closer your behavior matches recommended time management guidelines. Reread those items where your response did not match the desired one. Why don't they match? Do you have reasons why your behavior in this instance should be different from the recommended time management guideline? Think about what you can do (and how easily it can be done) to adjust your behavior to be more consistent with these guidelines. For further reading, see Alan Lakein, *How to Control Your Time and Your Life* (New York: David McKay), and William Oncken, *Managing Management Time* (Englewood Cliffs, NJ: Prentice Hall, 1984).

Source: Suggested by a discussion in Robert E. Quinn, Sue R. Faerman, Michael P. Thompson, and Michael R. McGrath, *Becoming a Master Manager: A Contemporary Framework* (New York: John Wiley & Sons, Inc., 1990), pp. 75–76.

Organizational Design Preference

Instructions

To the left of each item, write the number from the following scale that shows the extent to which the statement accurately describes your views.

5 = strongly agree

4 = agree somewhat

3 = undecided

2 = disagree somewhat

1 = strongly disagree

I prefer to work in an organization where:

1. Goals are defined by those in higher levels.
2. Work methods and procedures are specified.
3. Top management makes important decisions.
4. My loyalty counts as much as my ability to do the job.

Source: John F. Veiga and John N. Yanouzas, *The Dynamics of Organization Theory: Gaining a Macro Perspective* (St. Paul, MN: West, 1979), pp. 158–160. Used by permission.

5. Clear lines of authority and responsibility are established.
6. Top management is decisive and firm.
7. My career is pretty well planned out for me.
8. I can specialize.
9. My length of service is almost as important as my level of performance.
10. Management is able to provide the information I need to do my job well.
11. A chain of command is well established.
12. Rules and procedures are adhered to equally by everyone.
13. People accept authority of a leader's position.
14. People are loyal to their boss.
15. People do as they have been instructed.
16. People clear things with their boss before going over his or her head.

Scoring
Total your scores for all questions. Enter the score here [____].

Interpretation
This assessment measures your preference for working in an organization designed along "organic" or "mechanistic" lines. The higher your score (above 64), the more comfortable you are with a mechanistic design; the lower your score (below 48), the more comfortable you are with an organic design. Scores between 48 and 64 can go either way. This organizational design preference represents an important issue in the new workplace. Indications are that today's organizations are taking on more and more organic characteristics. Presumably, those of us who work in them will need to be comfortable with such designs.

···· **ASSESSMENT 22** ·

Which Culture Fits You?

Instructions
Check one of the following organization "cultures" in which you feel most comfortable working.

1. A culture that values talent, entrepreneurial activity, and performance over commitment; one that offers large financial rewards and individual recognition.
2. A culture that stresses loyalty, working for the good of the group, and getting to know the right people; one that believes in "generalists" and step-by-step career progress.
3. A culture that offers little job security; one that operates with a survival mentality, stresses that every individual can make a difference, and focuses attention on "turnaround" opportunities.
4. A culture that values long-term relationships; one that emphasizes systematic career development, regular

Source: Developed from Carol Hymowitz, "Which Corporate Culture Fits You?" *Wall Street Journal* (July 17, 1989), p. B1.

training, and advancement based on gaining of functional expertise.

Scoring
These labels identify the four different cultures: 1 = "the baseball team," 2 = "the club," 3 = "the fortress," and 4 = "the academy."

Interpretation
To some extent, your future career success may depend on working for an organization in which there is a good fit between you and the prevailing corporate culture. This assessment can help you learn how to recognize various cultures, evaluate how well they can serve your needs, and recognize how they may change with time. A risk taker, for example, may be out of place in a "club" but fit right in with a "baseball team." Someone who wants to seek opportunities wherever they may occur may be out of place in an "academy" but fit right in with a "fortress."

†EAM AND eXPERIENTIAL eXERCISES

Selections from The Pfeiffer Training Annuals

A. SWEET TOOTH: BONDING STRANGERS INTO A TEAM

Procedure:

The general idea is just to relax, have fun, and get to know one another while completing a task. Form groups of five. All groups in the room will be competing to see which one can first complete the following items with the name of a candy bar or sweet treat. The team that completes the most items correctly first will win a prize.

Source: Robert Allan Black, *The 2002 Annual Volume 1, Training/© 2002 John Wiley & Sons, Inc.*

1. Pee Wee . . ., baseball player.
2. Dried up cows.
3. Kids' game minus toes.
4. Not bad and more than some.
5. Explosion in the sky.
6. Polka. . . .
7. Rhymes with Bert's, dirts, hurts.
8. Happy place to drink.
9. Drowning prevention device.
10. Belongs to a mechanic from Mayberry's cousin.

11. They're not "lesses"; they're. . . .
12. Two names for a purring pet.
13. Takes 114 licks to get to the center of these.
14. Sounds like asteroids.
15. A military weapon.
16. A young flavoring.
17. Top of mountains in winter.
18. To catch fish you need to. . . .
19. Sounds like riddles and fiddles.

Questions for discussion:
- What lessons about effective teamwork can be learned from this activity?
- What caused each subgroup to be successful?
- What might be learned about effective teamwork from what happened during this activity?
- What might be done next time to increase the chances of success?

Variation
- Have the individual subgroups create their own lists of clues for the names of candies/candy bars/sweets. Collect the lists and make a grand list using one or two from each group's contribution. Then hold a competition among the total group.

B. INTERROGATORIES: IDENTIFYING ISSUES AND NEEDS

Procedure:

This activity is an opportunity to discover what issues and questions people have brought to the class. The instructor will select from the topic list below. Once a topic is raised, participants should ask any questions they have related to that topic. No one is to *answer* a question at this time. The goal is to come up with as many questions as possible in the time allowed. Feel free to build on a question already asked, or to share a completely different question.

Interrogatories Starter Topic List

- Class requirements
- Coaching
- Communication
- Customers
- Instant messaging
- Job demands
- Leadership
- Management
- Meetings

- Mission
- Performance appraisal
- Personality
- Priorities
- Project priorities
- Quality
- Rules
- Service

- Social activities
- Success
- Task uncertainty
- Teamwork
- Time
- Training
- Values
- Work styles

Questions for discussion:
- How did you feel about this process?
- What common themes did you hear?
- What questions would you most like to have answered?

Source: Cher Holton, *The 2002 Annual: Volume 1, Training/© 2002 John Wiley & Sons, Inc.*

C. DECODE: WORKING WITH DIFFERENT INSTRUCTIONS

Procedure:

1. You are probably familiar with codes and cryptograms from your childhood days. In a cryptogram, each letter in the message is replaced by another letter of the alphabet. For example, LET THE GAMES BEGIN! May become this cryptogram:

YZF FOZ JUKZH CZJVQ!

In the cryptogram Y replaces L, Z replaces E, F replaces T, and so on. Notice that the same letter substitutions are used throughout this cryptogram: Every E in the sentence is replaced by a Z, and every T is replaced by an F.

Here's some information to help you solve cryptograms:

Letter Frequency

The most commonly used letters of the English language are *e, t, a, i, o, n, s, h,* and *r.*

The letters that are most commonly found at the beginning of words are *t, a, o, d,* and *w.*

The letters that are most commonly found at the end of words are *e, s, d,* and *t.*

Word Frequency

One-letter words are either *a* or *I.*

The most common two-letter words are *to, of, in, it, is, as, at, be, we, he, so, on, an, or, do, if, up, by,* and *my.*

The most common three-letter words are *the, and, are, for, not, but, had, has, was, all, any, one, man, out, you, his, her,* and *can.*

The most common four-letter words are *that, with, have, this, will, your, from, they, want, been, good, much, some,* and *very.*

2. The goal of the activity is to learn to work together more effectively in teams. Form into groups of four to seven members each. Have members briefly share their knowledge of solving cryptogram puzzles.

3. In this exercise all groups will be asked to solve the same cryptogram. If a team correctly and completely solves the cryptogram within two minutes, it will earn two hundred points. If it takes more than two minutes but fewer than three minutes, the team will earn fifty points.

4. Before working on the cryptogram, each participant will receive an Instruction Sheet with hints on how to solve cryptograms. Participants can study this sheet for two minutes only. They may not mark up the Instruction Sheet but they may take notes on an index card or a blank piece of paper. The Instruction Sheets will be taken back after two minutes.

5. At any time a group can send one of its members to ask for help from the instructor. The instructor will decode any *one* of the words in the cryptogram selected by the group member.

6. After the points are tallied, the instructor will lead class discussion.

DECODE CRYPTOGRAM

ISV'B   JZZXYH BPJB BPH SVQE

_____

UJE BS UCV CZ BS FSYTHBH.

_____

ZSYHBCYHZ BPH AHZB UJE BS

_____

UCV CZ BS FSSTHWJBH UCBP

_____

SBPHWZ—Z. BPCJMJWJOJV

_____

Source: Sivasailam "Thiagi" Thiagarajan, *The 2003 Annual: Volume 1, Training/© 2003 John Wiley & Sons, Inc.*

D. CHOICES: LEARNING EFFECTIVE CONFLICT MANAGEMENT STRATEGIES

Procedure: Form teams of three.

Assume you are a group of top managers who are responsible for an organization of seven departments. Working as a team, choose an appropriate strategy to intervene in the situations below when the conflict must be managed in some way. Your choices are *withdrawal, suppression, integration, compromise,* and *authority.* Refer to the list below for some characteristics of each strategy. Write your team's choice following each situation number. Engage in discussion led by the instructor.

CHOICES: STRATEGIES AND CONTINGENCIES

Withdrawal Strategy

Use When (Advantages)
- Choosing sides is to be avoided
- Critical information is missing
- The issue is outside the group
- Others are competent and delegation is appropriate
- You are powerless

Be Aware (Disadvantages)
- Legitimate action ceases
- Direct information stops
- Failure can be perceived
- Cannot be used in a crisis

Suppression (and Diffusion) Strategy

Use When (Advantages)
- A cooling down period is needed
- The issue is unimportant
- A relationship is important

Be Aware (Disadvantages)
- The issue may intensify
- You may appear weak and ineffective

Integration Strategy

Use When (Advantages)
- Group problem solving is needed
- New alternatives are helpful
- Group commitment is required
- Promoting openness and trust

Be Aware (Disadvantages)
- Group goals must be put first
- More time is required for dialogue
- It doesn't work with rigid, dull people

Compromise Strategy

Use When (Advantages)
- Power is equal
- Resources are limited
- A win-win settlement is desired

Be Aware (Disadvantages)
- Action (a third choice) can be weakened
- Inflation is encouraged
- A third party may be needed for negotiation

Authority Strategy

Use When (Advantages)
- A deadlock persists
- Others are incompetent
- Time is limited (crisis)
- An unpopular decision must be made
- Survival of the organization is critical

Be Aware (Disadvantages)
- Emotions intensify quickly
- Dependency is promoted
- Winners and losers are created

Source: Chuck Kormanski, Sr., and Chuck Kormanski, Jr., *The 2003 Annual: Volume 1, Training/*© 2003 John Wiley & Sons, Inc.

Situation #1

Two employees of the support staff have requested the same two-week vacation period. They are the only two trained to carry out an essential task using a complex computer software program that cannot be mastered quickly. You have encouraged others to learn this process so there is more backup for the position, but heavy workloads have prevented this from occurring.

Situation #2

A sales manager has requested a raise because there are now two salespeople on commission earning higher salaries. The work performance of this individual currently does not merit a raise of the amount requested, mostly due to the person turning in critical reports late and missing a number of days of work. The person's sales group is one of the highest rated in the organization, but this may be the result of having superior individuals assigned to the team, rather than to the effectiveness of the manager.

Situation #3

It has become obvious that the copy machine located in a customer service area is being used for a variety of personal purposes, including reproducing obscene jokes. A few copies have sometimes been found lying on or near the machine at the close of the business day. You have mentioned the matter briefly in the organization's employee newsletter, but recently you have noticed an increase in the activity. Most of the office staff seems to be involved.

Situation #4

Three complaints have filtered upward to you from long-term employees concerning a newly hired individual. This person has a pierced nose and a visible tattoo. The work performance of the individual is adequate and the person does not have to see customers; however, the employees who have complained allege that the professional appearance of the office area has been compromised.

Situation #5

The organization has a flex-time schedule format that requires all employees to work the core hours of 10 A.M. to 3 P.M., Monday through Friday. Two department managers have complained that another department does not always maintain that policy. The manager of the department in question has responded by citing recent layoffs and additional work responsibilities as reasons for making exceptions to policy.

Situation #6

As a result of a recent downsizing, an office in a coveted location is now available. Three individuals have made a request to the department manager for the office. The manager has recommended that the office be given to one of the three. This individual has the highest performance rating, but was aided in obtaining employment with the company by the department manager, who is a good friend of the person's family. Colleagues prefer not to work with this individual, as there is seldom any evidence of teamwork.

Situation #7

Two department managers have requested a budget increase in the areas of travel and computer equipment. Each asks that your group support this request. The CEO, not your group, will make the final decision. You are aware that increasing funds for one department will result in a decrease for others, as the total budget figures for all of these categories are set.

Situation #8

Few of the management staff attended the Fourth of July picnic held at a department manager's country home last year. This particular manager, who has been a loyal team player for the past twenty-one years, has indicated that he/she plans to host the event again this year. Many of you have personally found the event to be boring, with little to do but talk and eat. Already a few of the other managers have suggested that the event be held at a different location with a new format or else be cancelled.

Situation #9

It has come to your attention that a manager and a subordinate in the same department are having a romantic affair openly in the building. Both are married to other people. They have been taking extended lunch periods, yet both remain beyond quitting time to complete their work. Colleagues have begun to complain that neither is readily available mid-day and that they do not return messages in a timely manner.

Situation #10

Two loyal department managers are concerned that a newly hired manager who is wheelchair-bound has been given too much in the way of accommodations beyond what is required by the Americans with Disabilities Act. They have requested similar changes to make their own work lives easier. Specifically, they cite office size and location on the building's main floor as points of contention.

E. INTERNAL/EXTERNAL MOTIVATORS: ENCOURAGING CREATIVITY

Procedure:

1. This interactive, experience-based activity is designed to increase participants' awareness of creativity and creative processes. Begin by thinking of a job that you now hold or have held. Then complete Questions 1 and 2 from the Internal/External Motivators Questionnaire (see below).
2. Form into groups. Share your questionnaire results and make a list of responses to Question 1.
3. Discuss and compare rankings of major work activities listed for Question 2. Make a list with at least two responses from each participant.
4. Individually record your answers to Questions 3 and 4 below. Then share your answers and again list member responses within your group.
5. Individually, compare your responses to Questions 1 and 2 with your responses to Questions 3 and 4. Then answer Question 5. Again, share with the group and make a group list of answers to Question 5 for the recorder, who is to record these answers on the flip chart. (Ten minutes.)

Questions for Discussion:

- What was the most important part of this activity for you?
- What have you learned about motivation?
- What impact will having done this activity have for you back in the workplace?
- How will what you have learned change your leadership style or future participation in a group?
- What will you do differently based on what you have learned?

INTRINSIC/EXTRINSIC MOTIVATORS QUESTIONNAIRE

1. How could you do your job in a more creative manner? List some ways in the space below:

2. List four or five major work activities or jobs you perform on a regular basis in the left-hand boxes on the following chart. Use a seven-point scale that ranges from 1 (low) to 7 (high) to rate each work activity on three separate dimensions: (a) level of difficulty, (b) potential to motivate you, and (c) opportunity to add value to the organization.

Source: Elizabeth A. Smith, *The 2003 Annual: Volume 1, Training/© 2003 John Wiley & Sons, Inc.*

Major Work Activity	Level of Difficulty	Potential to Motivate	Opportunity to Add Value
1.			
2.			
3.			
4.			
5.			

3. List five motivators or types of rewards that would encourage you to do your job in a more creative manner.

4. List three motivators or types of rewards from Question 3 above that you believe would *definitely increase your creativity.* Indicate whether these motivators are realistic or unrealistic in terms of your job or work setting. Indicate whether each is intrinsic or extrinsic.

Motivators	Realistic/ Unrealistic	Intrinsic	Extrinsic
1.			
2.			
3.			

5. List three types of work activities you like to perform and the motivators or rewards that would stimulate and reinforce your creativity.

Work Activity	Rewards That Reinforce Creativity
1.	
2.	
3.	

F. QUICK HITTER: FOSTERING THE CREATIVE SPIRIT

Part A Procedure:

1. Write the Roman numeral nine (IX) on a sheet of paper.
2. Add one line to make six. After you have one response, try for others.

Questions for discussion:

• What does solving this puzzle show us about seeing things differently?
• Why don't some people consider alternatives easily?
• What skills or behaviors would be useful for us to develop our ability to see different points of view?

Part B Procedure:

1. Rent the video or DVD of "Patch Adams." In this video Patch (Robin Williams) is studying to become a doctor, but he does not look, act, or think like a traditional doctor. For Patch, humor is the best medicine. He is always willing to do unusual things to make his patients laugh. Scenes from this video can be revealing to an OB class.

2. Show the first Patch Adams scene (five minutes)—this is in the psychiatric hospital where Patch has admitted himself after a failed suicide attempt. He meets Arthur in the hospital. Arthur is obsessed with showing people four fingers of his hand and asking them: "How many fingers can you see?" Everybody says four. The scene shows Patch visiting Arthur to find out the solution. Arthur's answer is: "If you only focus on the problem, you will never see the solution. Look further. You have to see what other people do not see."

3. Engage the class in discussion of these questions and more:
   • How does this film clip relate to Part A of this exercise?
   • What restricts our abilities to look beyond what we see?
   • How can we achieve the goal of seeing what others do not see?

4. Show the second Patch Adams scene (five minutes)—this is when Patch has left the hospital and is studying medicine. Patch and his new friend Truman are having breakfast. Truman is reflecting on the human mind and on the changing of behavioral patterns (the adoption of programmed answers) as a person grows older. Patch proposes to carry out the Hello Experiment. The objective of the experiment is "to change the programmed answer by changing the usual parameters."

5. Engage the class in discussion of these questions and more:
   • What is a programmed answer?
   • What is the link between our programmed answers and our abilities to exhibit creativity?
   • How can we "deprogram" ourselves?

6. Summarize the session with a wrap-up discussion of creativity, including barriers and ways to encourage it.

Source: Mila Gascó Hernández and Teresa Torres Coronas, *The 2003 Annual: Volume 1, Training/© 2003 John Wiley & Sons, Inc.*

Additional Team and Experiential Exercises

EXERCISE 1

My Best Manager

Procedure

1. Make a list of the attributes that describe the best manager you ever worked for. If you have trouble identifying an actual manager, make a list of attributes you would like the manager in your next job to have.
2. Form a group of four or five persons and share your lists.
3. Create one list that combines all the unique attributes of the "best" managers represented in your group. Make sure that you have all attributes listed, but list each only once. Place a check mark next to those that were reported by two or more members. Have one of your members prepared to present the list in general class discussion.
4. After all groups have finished Step 3, spokespersons should report to the whole class. The instructor will make a running list of the "best" manager attributes as viewed by the class.
5. Feel free to ask questions and discuss the results.

EXERCISE 2

Graffiti Needs Assessment: Involving Students in the First Class Session

Contributed by Barbara K. Goza, Visiting Associate Professor, University of California at Santa Cruz, and Associate Professor, California State Polytechnic University, Pomona. From *Journal of Management Education*, 1993.

Procedure

1. Complete the following sentences with as many endings as possible.
   1. When I first came to this class, I thought . . .
   2. My greatest concern this term is . . .
   3. In 3 years I will be . . .
   4. The greatest challenge facing the world today is . . .
   5. Organizational behavior specialists do . . .
   6. Human resources are . . .
   7. Organizational research is . . .
   8. The most useful question I've been asked is . . .
   9. The most important phenomenon in organizations is . . .
   10. I learn the most when . . .
2. Your instructor will guide you in a class discussion about your responses. Pay careful attention to similarities and differences among various students' answers.

EXERCISE 3

My Best Job

Procedure

1. Make a list of the top five things you expect from your first (or next) full-time job.
2. Exchange lists with a nearby partner. Assign probabilities (or odds) to each goal on your partner's list to indicate how likely you feel it is that the goal can be

accomplished. (*Note:* Your instructor may ask that everyone use the same probabilities format.)

3. Discuss your evaluations with your partner. Try to delete superficial goals or modify them to become more substantial. Try to restate any unrealistic goals to make them more realistic. Help your partner do the same.

4. Form a group of four to six persons. Within the group, have everyone share what they now consider to be the most "realistic" goals on their lists. Elect a spokesperson to share a sample of these items with the entire class.

5. Discuss what group members have individually learned from the exercise. Await further class discussion led by your instructor.

EXERCISE 4

What Do You Value in Work?

Procedure

1. The following nine items are from a survey conducted by Nicholas J. Beutell and O. C. Brenner ("Sex Differences in Work Values," *Journal of Vocational Behavior,* Vol. 28, pp. 29–41, 1986). Rank the nine items in terms of how important (9 = most important) they would be to you in a job.

How important is it to you to have a job that:
____ Is respected by other people?
____ Encourages continued development of knowledge and skills?
____ Provides job security?
____ Provides a feeling of accomplishment?
____ Provides the opportunity to earn a high income?
____ Is intellectually stimulating?
____ Rewards good performance with recognition?
____ Provides comfortable working conditions?
____ Permits advancement to high administrative responsibility?

2. Form into groups as designated by your instructor. Within each group, the *men in the group* will meet to develop a consensus ranking of the items as they think the *women* in the Beutell and Brenner survey ranked them. The reasons for the rankings should be shared and discussed so they are clear to everyone. The *women in the group* should not participate in this ranking task. They should listen to the discussion and be prepared to comment later in class discussion. A spokesperson for the men in the group should share the group's rankings with the class.

3. (*Optional*) Form into groups as designated by your instructor, but with each group consisting entirely of men or women. Each group should meet and decide which of the work values members of the *opposite* sex ranked first in the Beutell and Brenner survey. Do this again for the work value ranked last. The reasons should be discussed, along with reasons that each of the other values probably was not ranked first . . . or last. A spokesperson for each group should share group results with the rest of the class.

Source: Adapted from Roy J. Lewicki, Donald D. Bowen, Douglas T. Hall, and Francine S. Hall, *Experiences in Management and Organizational Behavior,* 3rd ed. (New York: John Wiley & Sons, Inc., 1988), pp. 23–26. Used by permission.

My Asset Base

A business has an asset base or set of resources that it uses to produce a good or service of value to others. For a business, these are the assets or resources it uses to achieve results, including capital, land, patented products or processes, buildings and equipment, raw materials, and the human resources or employees, among others.

Each of us has an asset base that supports our ability to accomplish the things we set out to do. We refer to our personal assets as *talents, strengths,* or *abilities.* We probably inherit our talents from our parents, but we acquire many of our abilities and strengths through learning. One thing is certain: we feel very proud of the talents and abilities we have.

Procedure

1. Printed here is a T chart that you are to fill out. On the right-hand side of the T, list four or five of your accomplishments—*things you have done of which you are most proud.* Your accomplishments should only include those things for which you can take credit, those *things for which you are primarily responsible.* If you are proud of the sorority to which you belong, you may be justifiably proud, but don't list it unless you can argue that the sorority's excellence is due primarily to your efforts. However, if you feel that having been invited to join the sorority is a major accomplishment for you, then you may include it.

   When you have completed the right-hand side of the chart, fill in the left-hand side by listing *talents, strengths,* and *abilities* that you have that have enabled you to accomplish the outcomes listed on the right-hand side.

My Asset Base

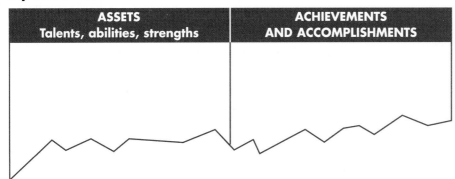

ASSETS Talents, abilities, strengths	ACHIEVEMENTS AND ACCOMPLISHMENTS

2. Share your lists with other team members. As each member shares his or her list, pay close attention to your own perceptions and feelings. Notice the effect this has on your attitudes toward the other team members.
3. Discuss these questions in your group:
   1. How did your attitudes and feelings toward other members of the team change as you pursued the activity? What does this tell you about the process whereby we come to get to know and care about people?
   2. How did you feel about the instructions the instructor provided? What did you expect to happen? Were your expectations accurate?

Source: Adapted from Donald D. Bowen et al., *Experiences in Management and Organizational Behavior,* 4th ed. (New York: John Wiley & Sons, Inc., 1997).

Expatriate Assignments

Contributed by Robert E. Ledman, Morehouse College

This exercise focuses on issues related to workers facing international assignments. It illustrates that those workers face a multitude of issues. It further demonstrates that managers who want employees to realize the maximum benefits of international assignments should be aware of, and prepared to deal with, those issues. Some of the topics that are easily addressed with this exercise include the need for culture and language training for the employees and their families and the impact that international assignments may have on an employee's family and how that may affect an employee's willingness to seek such assignments.

Procedure

1. Form into "families" of four or five. Since many students today have only one parent at home, it is helpful if some groups do not have students to fill both parental roles in the exercise. Each student is assigned to play a family member and given a description of that person.

2. Enter into a 20-minute discussion to explore how a proposed overseas assignment will affect the family members. Your goal is to try to reach a decision about whether the assignment should be taken. You must also decide whether the entire family or only the family member being offered the assignment will relocate. The assignment is for a minimum of two years, with possible annual extensions resulting in a total of four years, and your family, or the member offered the assignment, will be provided, at company expense, one trip back to the states each year for a maximum period of 15 days. The member offered the assignment will not receive any additional housing or cost-of-living supplements described in the role assignment if he or she chooses to go overseas alone and can expect his or her living expenses to exceed substantially the living allowance being provided by the company. In your discussion, address the following questions:

   1. What are the most important concerns your family has about relocating to a foreign country?
   2. What information should you seek about the proposed host country to be able to make a more informed decision?

3. What can the member offered the assignment do to make the transition easier if he or she goes overseas alone? If the whole family relocates?
4. What should the member offered the assignment do to ensure that this proposed assignment will not create unnecessary stress for him or her and the rest of the family?
5. What lessons for managers of expatriate assignees are presented by the situation in this exercise?

Try to reach some "family" consensus. If a consensus is not possible, however, resolve any differences in the manner you think the family in the role descriptions would ultimately resolve any differences.

3. Share your answers with the rest of the class. Explain the rationale for your answers and answer questions from the remainder of the class.
4. (*Optional*) After each group has reported on a given question, the instructor may query the class about how their answers are consistent, or inconsistent, with common practices of managers as described in the available literature.

Descriptions of Family Members
Person Being Offered Overseas Assignment

This person is a middle- to upper-level executive who is on a fast track to senior management. He or she has been offered the opportunity to manage an overseas operation, with the assurance of a promotion to a vice presidency upon return to the states. The company will pay all relocation expenses, including selling costs for the family home and the costs associated with finding a new home upon return. The employer will also provide language training for the employee and cultural awareness training for the entire family. The employee will receive a living allowance equal to 20 percent of his or her salary. This should be adequate to provide the family a comparable standard of living to that which is possible on the employee's current salary.

Spouse of the Person Offered an Overseas Assignment (Optional)

This person is also a professional with highly transferable skills and experience for the domestic market. It is unknown how easily he or she may be able to find

Source: Robert E. Ledman, Gannon University. Presented in the Experiential Exercise Track of the 1996 ABSEL Conference and published in the *Proceedings* of that conference.

employment in the foreign country. This person's income, though less than his or her spouse's, is necessary if the couple is to continue paying for their child's college tuition and to prepare for the next child to enter college in two years. This person has spent 15 years developing a career, including completing a degree at night.

Oldest Child

This child is a second-semester junior in college and is on track to graduate in 16 months. Transferring at this time would probably mean adding at least one semester to complete the degree. He or she has been dating the same person for over a year; they have talked about getting married immediately after graduation, although they are not yet formally engaged.

Middle Child

This child is a junior in high school. He or she has already begun visiting college campuses in preparation for applying in the fall. This child is involved in a number of school activities; he or she is a photographer for the yearbook and plays a varsity sport. This child has a learning disability for which services are being provided by the school system.

Youngest Child

This child is a middle school student, age 13. He or she is actively involved in Scouting and takes piano lessons. This child has a history of medical conditions that have required regular visits to the family physician and specialists. This child has several very close friends who have attended the same school for several years.

EXERCISE 7

Cultural Cues

Contributed by Susan Rawson Zacur and W. Alan Randolph, University of Baltimore

Introduction

In the business context, culture involves shared beliefs and expectations that govern the behavior of people. In this exercise, *foreign culture* refers to a set of beliefs and expectations different from those of the participant's home culture (which has been invented by the participants).

Procedure

1. (10–15 minutes) Divide into two groups, each with color-coded badges. For example, the blue group could receive blue Post-it notes and the yellow group could receive yellow Post-it notes. Print your first name in bold letters on the badge and wear it throughout the exercise.

   Work with your group members to invent your own cultural cues. Think about the kinds of behaviors and words that will signify to all members that they belong together in one culture. For each category provided below, identify and record at least one important attribute for your culture.

Cultural Cues:	Your Culture:
Facial expression:	_____
Eye contact (note: you must have some eye contact in order to observe others):	_____
Handshake:	_____
Body language (note: must be evident while standing):	_____
Key words or phrases:	_____

Source: Adapted by Susan Rawson Zacur and W. Alan Randolph from *Journal of Management Education,* Vol. 17, No. 4 (November 1993), pp. 510–516.

Once you have identified desirable cultural aspects for your group, practice them. It is best to stand with your group and to engage one another in conversations involving two or three people at a time. Your aim in talking with one another is to learn as much as possible about each other—hobbies, interests, where you live, what your family is like, what courses you are taking, and so on, all the while practicing the behaviors and words on the previous page. It is not necessary for participants to answer questions of a personal nature truthfully. Invention is permissible because the conversation is only a means to the end of cultural observation. Your aim at this point is to become comfortable with the indicators of your particular culture. Practice until the indicators are second nature to you.

2. Now assume that you work for a business that has decided to explore the potential for doing business with companies in a different culture. You are to learn as much as possible about another culture. To do so, you will send from one to three representatives from your group on a "business trip" to the other culture. These representatives must, insofar as possible, behave in a manner that is consistent with your culture. At the same time, each representative must endeavor to learn as much as possible about the people in the other culture, while keeping eyes and ears open to cultural attributes that will be useful in future negotiations with foreign businesses. (*Note:* At no time will it be considered ethical behavior for the representative to ask direct questions about the foreign culture's attributes. These must be gleaned from firsthand experience.)

   While your representatives are away, you will receive one or more exchange visitors from the other culture, who will engage in conversation as they attempt to learn more about your organizational culture. You must strictly adhere to the cultural aspects of your own culture while you converse with the visitors.

3. (5–10 minutes) All travelers return to your home cultures. As a group, discuss and record what you have learned about the foreign culture based on the exchange of visitors. This information will serve as the basis for orienting the next representatives who will make a business trip.

4. (5–10 minutes) Select one to three different group members to make another trip to the other culture to check out the assumptions your group has made about the other culture. This "checking out" process will consist of actually practicing the other culture's cues to see whether they work.

5. (5–10 minutes) Once the traveler(s) have returned and reported on findings, as a group prepare to report to the class what you have learned about the other culture.

EXERCISE 8

Prejudice in Our Lives

Contributed by Susan Schor of Pace University and Annie McKee of The Wharton School, University of Pennsylvania, with the assistance of Ariel Fishman of The Wharton School

Procedure

1. As a large class group, generate a list of groups that tend to be targets of prejudice and stereotypes in our culture—such groups can be based on gender, race, ethnicity, sexual orientation, region, religion, and so on. After generating a list, either as a class or in small groups, identify a few common positive and negative stereotypes associated with each group. Also consider relationships or patterns that exist between some of the lists. Discuss the implications for groups that have stereotypes that are valued in organizations versus groups whose stereotypes are viewed negatively in organizations.

2. As an individual, think about the lists you have now generated, and list those groups with which you identify. Write about an experience in which you

were stereotyped as a member of a group. Ask yourself the following questions and write down your thoughts:

1. What group do I identify with?
2. What was the stereotype?
3. What happened? When and where did the incident occur? Who said what to whom?
4. What were my reactions? How did I feel? What did I think? What did I do?
5. What were the consequences? How did the incident affect myself and others?

3. Now, in small groups, discuss your experiences. Briefly describe the incident and focus on how the incident made you feel. Select one incident from the ones shared in your group to role-play for the class. Then, as a class, discuss your reactions to each role play. Identify the prejudice or stereotype portrayed, the feelings the situation evoked, and the consequences that might result from such a situation.

4. Think about the prejudices and stereotypes you hold about other people. Ask yourself, "What groups do I feel prejudice toward? What stereotypes do I hold about members of each of these groups?" How may such a prejudice have developed—did a family member or close friend or television influence you to stereotype a particular group in a certain way?

5. Now try to identify implications of prejudice in the workplace. How do prejudice and stereotypes affect workers, managers, relationships between people, and the organization as a whole? Consider how you might want to change erroneous beliefs as well as how you would encourage other people to change their own erroneous beliefs.

EXERCISE 9

How We View Differences

Contributed by Barbara Walker

Introduction

Clearly, the workplace of the future will be much more diverse than it is today: more women, more people of color, more international representation, more diverse lifestyles and ability profiles, and the like. Managing a diverse workforce and working across a range of differences is quickly becoming a "core competency" for effective managers.

Furthermore, it is also becoming clear that diversity in a work team can significantly enhance the creativity and quality of the team's output. In today's turbulent business environment, utilizing employee diversity will give the manager and the organization a competitive edge in tapping all of the available human resources more effectively. This exercise is an initial step in the examination of how we work with people whom we see as different from us. It is fairly simple, straightforward, and safe, but its implications are profound.

Source: Exercise developed by Barbara Walker, a pioneer on work on valuing differences. Adapted for this volume by Douglas T. Hall. Used by permission of Barbara Walker.

Procedure

1. Read the following:

Imagine that you are traveling in a rental car in a city you have never visited before. You have a one-hour drive on an uncrowded highway before you reach your destination. You decide that you would like to spend the time listening to some of your favorite kind of music on the car radio.

The rental car has four selection buttons available, each with a preset station that plays a different type of music. One plays *country music,* one plays *rock,* one plays *classical,* and one plays *jazz.* Which type of music would you choose to listen to for the next hour as you drive along? (Assume you want to relax and just stick with one station; you don't want to bother switching around between stations.)

2. Form into groups based on the type of music that you have chosen. All who have chosen country will meet in an area designated by the instructor. Those who chose rock will meet in another area, and so on. In your groups, answer the following question. Appoint one member to be the spokesperson to report your answers back to the total group.

Question

For each of the other groups, what words would you use to describe people who like to listen to that type of music?

3. Have each spokesperson report the responses of her or his group to the question in Step 2. Follow with class discussion of these additional questions:
    1. What do you think is the purpose or value of this exercise?
    2. What did you notice about the words used to describe the other groups? Were there any *surprises* in this exercise for you?
    3. Upon what sorts of data do you think these images were based?
    4. What term do we normally use to describe these generalized perceptions of another group?
    5. What could some of the consequences be?
    6. How do the perceptual processes here relate to other kinds of intergroup differences, such as race, gender, culture, ability, ethnicity, health, age, nationality, and so on?
    7. What does this exercise suggest about the ease with which intergroup stereotypes form?
    8. What might be ways an organization might facilitate the valuing and utilizing of differences between people?

EXERCISE 10

Alligator River Story

The Alligator River Story

There lived a woman named Abigail who was in love with a man named Gregory. Gregory lived on the shore of a river. Abigail lived on the opposite shore of the same river. The river that separated the two lovers was teeming with dangerous alligators. Abigail wanted to cross the river to be with Gregory. Unfortunately, the bridge had been washed out by a heavy flood the previous week. So she went to ask Sinbad, a riverboat captain, to take her across. He said he would be glad to if she would consent to go to bed with him prior to the voyage. She promptly refused and went to a friend named Ivan to explain her plight. Ivan did not want to get involved at all in the situation. Abigail felt her only alternative was to accept Sinbad's terms. Sinbad fulfilled his promise to Abigail and delivered her into the arms of Gregory. When Abigail told Gregory about her amorous escapade in order to cross the river, Gregory cast her aside with disdain. Heartsick and rejected, Abigail turned to Slug with her tail of woe. Slug, feeling compassion for Abigail, sought out Gregory and beat him brutally. Abigail was overjoyed at the sight of Gregory getting his due. As the sun set on the horizon, people heard Abigail laughing at Gregory.

Procedure

1. Read "The Alligator River Story."
2. After reading the story, rank the five characters in the story beginning with the one whom you consider the most offensive and end with the one whom you consider the least objectionable. That is, the character who seems to be the most reprehensible to you should be entered first in the list following the story, then the second most reprehensible, and so on, with the least reprehensible or objectionable being entered fifth. Of course, you will have your own reasons as to why you rank them in the order that you do. Very briefly note these too.
3. Form groups as assigned by your instructor (at least four persons per group with gender mixed).
4. Each group should:
    1. Elect a spokesperson for the group
    2. Compare how the group members have ranked the characters
    3. Examine the reasons used by each of the members for their rankings
    4. Seek consensus on a final group ranking
5. Following your group discussions, you will be asked to share your outcomes and reasons for agreement or nonagreement. A general class discussion will then be held.

Source: From Sidney B. Simon, Howard Kirschenbaum, and Leland Howe, *Values Clarification, The Handbook,* rev. ed., copyright © 1991, Values Press, P.O. Box 450, Sunderland, MA. 01375.

Teamwork and Motivation

Contributed by Dr. Barbara McCain, Oklahoma City University

Procedure

1. Read this situation.

You are the *owner* of a small manufacturing corporation. Your company manufactures widgets—a commodity. Your widget is a clone of nationally known widgets. Your widget, "WooWoo," is less expensive and more readily available than the nationally known brand. Presently, the sales are high. However, there are many rejects, which increases your cost and delays the delivery. You have 50 employees in the following departments: sales, assembly, technology, and administration.

2. In groups, discuss methods to motivate all of the employees in the organization—rank them in terms of preference.

3. Design an organization motivation plan that encourages high job satisfaction, low turnover, high productivity, and high-quality work.

4. Is there anything special you can do about the minimum-wage service worker? How do you motivate this individual? On what motivation theory do you base your decision?

5. Report to the class your motivation plan. Record your ideas on the board and allow all groups to build on the first plan. Discuss additions and corrections as the discussion proceeds.

Worksheet

Individual Worker	Team Member
Talks	
Me oriented	
Department focused	
Competitive	
Logical	
Written messages	
Image	
Secrecy	
Short-term sighted	
Immediate results	
Critical	
Tenure	

Directions: Fill in the right-hand column with descriptive terms. These terms should suggest a change in behavior from individual work to teamwork.

The Downside of Punishment

Contributed by Dr. Barbara McCain, Oklahoma City University

Procedure

There are numerous problems associated with using punishment or discipline to change behavior. Punishment creates negative effects in the workplace. To better understand this, work in your group to give an example of each of the following situations:

1. Punishment may not be applied to the person whose behavior you want to change.

2. Punishment applied over time may suppress the occurrence of socially desirable behaviors.

3. Punishment creates a dislike of the person who is implementing the punishment.

4. Punishment results in undesirable emotions such as anxiety and aggressiveness.

5. Punishment increases the desire to avoid punishment.

6. Punishing one behavior does not guarantee that the desired behavior will occur.

7. Punishment follow-up requires allocation of additional resources.

8. Punishment may create a communication barrier and inhibit the flow of information.

Source: Adapted from class notes: Dr. Larry Michaelson, Oklahoma University.

EXERCISE 13

Tinker Toys

Contributed by Bonnie McNeely, Murray State University

Materials Needed
Tinker Toy sets.

Source: Adapted from Bonnie McNeely, "Using the Tinker Toy Exercise to Teach the Four Functions of Management," *Journal of Management Education,* Vol. 18, No. 4 (November 1994), pp. 468–472.

Procedure
1. Form groups as assigned by the instructor. The mission of each group or temporary organization is to build the tallest possible Tinker Toy tower. Each group should determine worker roles: at least four students will be builders, some will be consultants who offer suggestions, and the remaining students

will be observers who remain silent and complete the observation sheet provided below.

2. Rules for the exercise:

1. Fifteen minutes allowed to plan the tower, but *only 60 seconds* to build.

2. No more than two Tinker Toy pieces can be put together during the planning.

3. All pieces must be put back in the box before the competition begins.

4. Completed tower must stand alone.

Observation Sheet

1. What planning activities were observed?

   Did the group members adhere to the rules?

2. What organizing activities were observed?

   Was the task divided into subtasks? Division of labor?

3. Was the group motivated to succeed? Why or why not?

4. Were any control techniques observed?

   Was a timekeeper assigned?

   Were backup plans discussed?

5. Did a clear leader emerge from the group?

   What behaviors indicated that this person was the leader?

   How did the leader establish credibility with the group?

6. Did any conflicts within the group appear?

   Was there a power struggle for the leadership position?

EXERCISE 14

Job Design Preferences

Procedure

1. Use the left column to rank the following job characteristics in the order most important *to you* (1—highest to 10—lowest). Then use the right column to rank them in the order you think they are most important *to others*.

   ____ Variety of tasks   ____
   ____ Performance feedback   ____
   ____ Autonomy/freedom in work ____
   ____ Working on a team   ____
   ____ Having responsibility   ____
   ____ Making friends on the job ____

_____ Doing all of a job, not part _____
_____ Importance of job to others _____
_____ Having resources to do well _____
_____ Flexible work schedule _____

2. Form workgroups as assigned by your instructor. Share your rankings with other group members. Discuss where you have different individual preferences and where your impressions differ from the preferences of others. Are there any major patterns in your group—for either the "personal" or the "other" rankings? Develop group consensus rankings for each column. Designate a spokesperson to share the group rankings and results of any discussion with the rest of the class.

EXERCISE 15

My Fantasy Job

Contributed by Lady Hanson, California State Polytechnic University, Pomona

Procedure

1. Think about a possible job that represents what you consider to be your ideal or "fantasy" job. For discussion purposes, try to envision it as a job you would hold within a year of finishing your current studies. Write down a brief description of that job in the space below. Start the description with the following words—*My fantasy job would be* . . .

2. Review the description of the Hackman/Oldham model of Job Characteristics Theory offered in the textbook. Note in particular the descriptions of the core characteristics. Consider how each of them could be maximized in your fantasy job. Indicate in the spaces that follow how specific parts of your fantasy job will fit into or relate to each of the core characteristics.

   1. Skill variety: _____

   2. Task identity: _____

   3. Task significance: _____

   4. Autonomy: _____

   5. Job feedback: _____

3. Form into groups as assigned by your instructor. In the group have each person share his or her fantasy job and the descriptions of its core characteristics. Select one person from your group to tell the class as a whole about her or his fantasy job. Be prepared to participate in a general discussion regarding the core characteristics and how they may or may not relate to job performance and job satisfaction. Consider also the likelihood that the fantasy jobs of class members are really attainable—in other words: Can "fantasy" become fact?

Motivation by Job Enrichment

Contributed by Diana Page, University of West Florida

Procedure

1. Form groups of five to seven members. Each group is assigned one of the following categories:
    1. Bank teller
    2. Retail sales clerk
    3. Manager, fast-food service (e.g., McDonald's)
    4. Wait person
    5. Receptionist
    6. Restaurant manager
    7. Clerical worker (or bookkeeper)
    8. Janitor
2. As a group, develop a short description of job duties for the job your group has been assigned. The list should contain approximately four to six items.
3. Next, using job characteristics theory, enrich the job using the specific elements described in the theory. Develop a new list of job duties that incorporate any or all of the core job characteristics suggested by Richard Hackman and Greg Oldham, such as skill variety, task identity, and so on. Indicate for each of the new job duties which job characteristic(s) was/were used.
4. One member of each group should act as the spokesperson and will present the group's ideas to the class. Specifically describe one or two of the old job tasks. Describe the modified job tasks. Finally, relate the new job tasks the group has developed to specific job core characteristics such as skill variety, skill identity, and so on.
5. The group should also be prepared to discuss these and other follow-up questions:
    1. How would a manager go about enlarging but not enriching this job?
    2. Why was this job easy or hard?
    3. What are the possible constraints on actually accomplishing this enrichment in the workplace?
    4. What possible reasons are there that a worker would *not* like to have this newly enriched job?

Annual Pay Raises

Procedure

1. Read the following job descriptions and decide on a percentage pay increase for each of the eight employees.
2. Make salary increase recommendations for each of the eight managers that you supervise. There are no formal company restrictions on the size of raises you give, but the total for everyone should not exceed the $10,900 (a 4 percent increase in the salary pool) that has been budgeted for this purpose. You have a variety of information on which to base the decisions, including a "productivity index" (PI), which

Industrial Engineering computes as a quantitative measure of operating efficiency for each manager's work unit. This index ranges from a high of 10 to a low of 1. Indicate the percentage increase *you* would give each manager in the blank space next to each manager's name. Be prepared to explain why.

_____ *A. Alvarez*   Alvarez is new this year and has a tough workgroup whose task is dirty and difficult. This is a hard position to fill, but you don't feel Alvarez is particularly good. The word around is that the other managers agree with you. PI = 3. Salary = $33,000.

_____ *B. J. Cook*   Cook is single and a "swinger" who enjoys leisure time. Everyone laughs at the problems B.J. has getting the work out, and you feel it certainly is lacking. Cook has been in the job two years. PI = 3. Salary = $34,500.

_____ *Z. Davis*   In the position three years, Davis is one of your best people, even though some of the other managers don't agree. With a spouse who is independently wealthy, Davis doesn't need money but likes to work. PI = 7. Salary = $36,600.

_____ *M. Frame*   Frame has personal problems and is hurting financially. Others gossip about Frame's performance, but you are quite satisfied with this second-year employee. PI = 7. Salary = $34,700.

_____ *C. M. Liu*   Liu is just finishing a fine first year in a tough job. Highly respected by the others, Liu has a job offer in another company at a 15 percent increase in salary. You are impressed, and the word is that the money is important. PI = 9. Salary = $34,000.

_____ *B. Ratin*   Ratin is a first-year manager whom you and the others think is doing a good job. This is a bit surprising since Ratin turned out to be a "free spirit" who doesn't seem to care much about money or status. PI = 9. Salary = $33,800.

_____ *H. Smith*   Smith is a first-year manager recently divorced and with two children to support as a single parent. The others like Smith a lot, but your evaluation is not very high. Smith could certainly use extra money. PI = 5. Salary = $33,000.

_____ *G. White*   White is a big spender who always has the latest clothes and a new car. In the first year on what you would call an easy job, White doesn't seem to be doing very well. For some reason, though, the others talk about White as the "cream of the new crop." PI = 5. Salary = $33,000.

3. Convene in a group of four to seven persons and share your raise decision.
4. As a group, decide on a new set of raises and be prepared to report them to the rest of the class. Make sure that the group spokesperson can provide the rationale for each person's raise.
5. The instructor will call on each group to report its raise decisions. After discussion, an "expert's" decision will be given.

EXERCISE 18

Serving on the Boundary

Contributed by Joseph A. Raelin, Boston College

Procedure

The objective of this exercise is to experience what it is like being on the boundary of your team or organization and to experience the boundary person's divided loyalties.

1. As a full class, decide on a stake you are willing to wager on this exercise. Perhaps it will be 5¢ or 10¢ per person or even more.

2. Form into teams. Select or elect one member from your team to be an expert. The expert will be the person most competent in the field of international geography.
3. The experts will then form into a team of their own.
4. The teams, including the expert team, are going to be given a straightforward question to work on. Whichever team comes closest to deriving the correct answer will win the pool from the stakes already collected. The question is any one of the following as assigned by the instructor: (a) What is the airline distance between Beijing and Moscow (in miles)? (b) What is the highest point in Texas (in feet)? (c) What was the number of American battle deaths in the Revolutionary War?
5. Each team should now work on the question, including the expert team. However, after all the teams come up with a verdict, the experts will be allowed to return to their "home" team to inform the team of the expert team's deliberations.
6. The expert team members are now asked to reconvene as an expert team. They should determine their final answer to the question. Then, they are to face a decision. The instructor will announce that for a period of up to two minutes, any expert may either return to their home team (to sink or swim with the answer of the home team) or remain with the expert team. As long as two members remain in the expert team, it will be considered a group and may vie for the pool. Home teams, during the two-minute decision period, can do whatever they would like to do—within bounds of normal decorum—to try to persuade their expert member to return.
7. After the two minutes are up, teams will hand in their verdicts to the question, and the team with the closest answer (up or down) will be awarded the pool.
8. Class members should be prepared to discuss the following questions:
   1. What did it feel like to be a boundary person (the expert)?
   2. What could the teams have done to corral any of the boundary persons who chose not to return home?

EXERCISE 19

Eggsperiential Exercise

Contributed by Dr. Barbara McCain, Oklahoma City University

Materials Needed
1 raw egg per group
6 plastic straws per group

1 yard of plastic tape
1 large plastic jar

Procedure
1. Form into equal groups of five to seven people.
2. The task is to drop an egg from the chair onto the plastic without breaking the egg. Groups can evaluate the materials and plan their task for 10 minutes. During this period the materials may not be handled.
3. Groups have 10 minutes for construction.
4. One group member will drop the egg while standing on top of a chair in front of the class. One by one a representative from each group will drop their eggs.
5. Optional: Each group will name the egg.
6. Each group discusses their individual/group behaviors

during this activity. Optional: This analysis may be summarized in written form. The following questions may be utilized in the analysis:
1. What kind of group is it? Explain.
2. Was the group cohesive? Explain.
3. How did the cohesiveness relate to performance? Explain.
4. Was there evidence of groupthink? Explain.
5. Were group norms established? Explain.
6. Was there evidence of conflict? Explain.
7. Was there any evidence of social loafing? Explain.

Scavenger Hunt—Team Building

Contributed by Michael R. Manning and Paula J. Schmidt, New Mexico State University

Introduction

Think about what it means to be a part of a team—a successful team. What makes one team more successful than another? What does each team member need to do in order for their team to be successful? What are the characteristics of an effective team?

Procedure

1. Form teams as assigned by your instructor. Locate the items on the list below while following these important rules:
   1. Your team *must stay together at all times*—that is, you cannot go in separate directions.
   2. Your team must return to the classroom in the time allotted by the instructor.
   The team with the most items on the list will be declared the most successful team.
2. Next, reflect on your team's experience. What did each team member do? What was your team's strategy? What made your team effective? Make a list of the most important things your team did to be successful. Nominate a spokesperson to summarize your team's discussion for the class. What items were similar between teams? That is, what helped each team to be effective?

Source: Adapted from Michael R. Manning and Paula J. Schmidt, *Journal of Management Education,* Building Effective Work Teams: A Quick Exercise Based on a Scavenger Hunt (Thousand Oaks, CA: Sage Publications, 1995), pp. 392–398. Used by permission. Reference for list of items for scavenger hunt from C. E. Larson and F. M. Lafas, *Team Work: What Must Go Right/What Can Go Wrong* (Newbury Park, CA: Sage Publications, 1989).

Items for Scavenger Hunt

Each item is to be identified and brought back to the classroom.

1. A book with the word "team" in the title.
2. A joke about teams that you share with the class.
3. A blade of grass from the university football field.
4. A souvenir from the state.
5. A picture of a team or group.
6. A newspaper article about a team.
7. A team song to be composed and performed for the class.
8. A leaf from an oak tree.
9. Stationery from the dean's office.
10. A cup of sand.
11. A pine cone.
12. A live reptile. (*Note:* Sometimes a team member has one for a pet or the students are ingenious enough to visit a local pet store.)
13. A definition of group "cohesion" that you share with the class.
14. A set of chopsticks.
15. Three cans of vegetables.
16. A branch of an elm tree.
17. Three unusual items.
18. A ball of cotton.
19. The ear from a prickly pear cactus.
20. A group name.

(*Note:* Items may be substituted as appropriate for your locale.)

Work Team Dynamics

Introduction

Think about your course work team, a work team you are involved in for another course, or any other team suggested by the instructor. Indicate how often each of the following statements accurately reflects your experience in the team. Use this scale:

Source: Adapted from William Dyer, *Team Building,* 2nd ed. (Reading, MA: Addison-Wesley, 1987), pp. 123–125.

1 = Always   2 = Frequently   3 = Sometimes   4 = Never

_____ 1. My ideas get a fair hearing.

_____ 2. I am encouraged for innovative ideas and risk taking.

_____ 3. Diverse opinions within the team are encouraged.

_____ 4. I have all the responsibility I want.

_____ 5. There is a lot of favoritism shown in the team.

_____ 6. Members trust one another to do their assigned work.

_____ 7. The team sets high standards of performance excellence.

_____ 8. People share and change jobs a lot in the team.

_____ 9. You can make mistakes and learn from them on this team.

_____ 10. This team has good operating rules.

Procedure

Form groups as assigned by your instructor. Ideally, this will be the team you have just rated. Have all team members share their ratings, and make one master rating for the team as a whole. Circle the items on which there are the biggest differences of opinion. Discuss those items and try to find out why they exist. In general, the better a team scores on this instrument, the higher its creative potential. If everyone has rated the same team, make a list of the five most important things members can do to improve its operations in the future. Nominate a spokesperson to summarize the team discussion for the class as a whole.

EXERCISE 22

Identifying Team Norms

Procedure

1. Choose an organization you know quite a bit about.
2. Complete the questionnaire below, indicating your responses using one of the following:

> 1. Strongly agree or encourage it.
> 2. Agree with it or encourage it.
> 3. Consider it unimportant.
> 4. Disagree with or discourage it.
> 5. Strongly disagree with or discourage it.

_If_ an employee in this organization were to . . . _Most other employees would:_

1. Show genuine concern for the problems that face the organization and make suggestions about solving them . . .   _____

2. Set very high personal standards of performance . . .   _____

3. Try to make the workgroup operate more like a team when dealing with issues or problems . . .   _____

4. Think of going to a supervisor with a problem . . .   _____

5. Evaluate expenditures in terms of the benefits they will provide for the organization . . .   _____

6. Express concern for the well-being of other members of the organization . . . ____
7. Keep a customer or client waiting while looking after matters of personal convenience . . . ____
8. Criticize a fellow employee who is trying to improve things in the work situation . . . ____
9. Actively look for ways to expand his or her knowledge to be able to do a better job . . . ____
10. Be perfectly honest in answering this questionnaire . . . ____

Scoring

A = +2, B = +1, C = 0, D = −1, E = −2

1. Organizational/Personal Pride
   Score ____
2. Performance/Excellence
   Score ____
3. Teamwork/Communication
   Score ____
4. Leadership/Supervision
   Score ____
5. Profitability/Cost-Effectiveness
   Score ____

6. Colleague/Associate Relations
   Score ____
7. Customer/Client Relations
   Score ____
8. Innovativeness/Creativity
   Score ____
9. Training/Development
   Score ____
10. Candor/Openness
    Score ____

EXERCISE 23

Workgroup Culture

Contributed by Conrad N. Jackson, MPC Inc.

Procedure

The bipolar scales on this instrument can be used to evaluate a group's process in a number of useful ways. Use it to measure where you see the group to be at present. To do this, *circle* the number that best represents *how you see the culture of the group.* You can also indicate how you think the group *should* function by using a different symbol, such as a square (**) or a caret (^), to indicate how you saw the group at some time in the past.

1. If you are assessing your own group, have everyone fill in the instrument, summarize the scores, then discuss their bases (what members say and do that has led to these interpretations) and implications. This is often an extremely productive intervention to improve group or team functioning.

2. If you are assessing another group, use the scores as the basis for your feedback. Be sure to provide specific feedback on behavior *you have observed* in addition to the subjective interpretations of your ratings on the scales in this instrument.

3. The instrument can also be used to compare a group's self-assessment with the assessment provided by another group.

1. Trusting	1 : 2 : 3 : 4 : 5	Suspicious
2. Helping	1 : 2 : 3 : 4 : 5	Ignoring, blocking
3. Expressing feelings	1 : 2 : 3 : 4 : 5	Suppressing feelings
4. Risk taking	1 : 2 : 3 : 4 : 5	Cautious
5. Authenticity	1 : 2 : 3 : 4 : 5	Game playing
6. Confronting	1 : 2 : 3 : 4 : 5	Avoiding
7. Open	1 : 2 : 3 : 4 : 5	Hidden, diplomatic

Source: Adapted from Donald D. Bowen, et al., *Experiences in Management and Organizational Behavior,* 4th ed. (New York: John Wiley & Sons, Inc., 1997.)

The Hot Seat

Contributed by Barry R. Armandi, SUNY–Old Westbury

Procedure
1. Form into groups as assigned by your instructor.
2. Read the following situation.

A number of years ago, Professor Stevens was asked to attend a departmental meeting at a university. He had been on leave from the department, but a junior faculty member discreetly requested that he attend to protect the rights of the junior faculty. The Chair, or head of the department, was a typical Machiavellian, whose only concerns were self-serving. Professor Stevens had had a number of previous disagreements with the Chair. The heart of the disagreements centered around the Chair's abrupt and domineering style and his poor relations with the junior faculty, many of whom felt mistreated and scared.

The department was a conglomeration of different professorial types. Included in the mix were behavioralists, generalists, computer scientists, and quantitative analysts. The department was embedded in the school of business, which had three other departments. There was much confusion and concern among the faculty, since this was a new organizational design. Many of the faculty were at odds with each other over the direction the school was now taking.

At the meeting, a number of proposals were to be presented that would seriously affect the performance and future of certain junior faculty, particularly those who were behavioral scientists. The Chair, a computer scientist, disliked the behaviorists, who he felt were "always analyzing the motives of people." Professor Stevens, who was a tenured full professor and a behaviorist, had an objective to protect the interests of the junior faculty and to counter the efforts of the Chair.

Including Professor Stevens, there were nine faculty present. The accompanying diagram below shows the seating

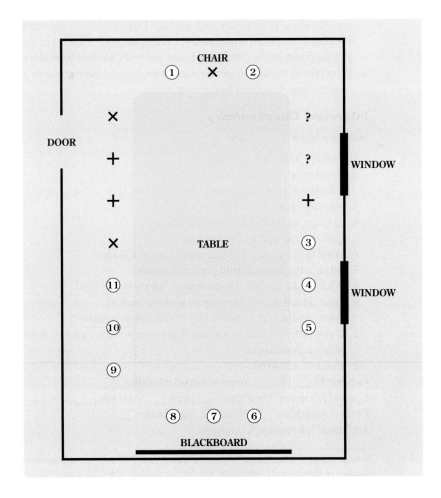

arrangement and the layout of the room. The **×**s signify those faculty who were allies of the Chair. The **+**s are those opposed to the Chair and supportive of Professor Stevens, and the **?**s were undecided and could be swayed either way. The circled numbers represent empty seats. Both **?**s were behavioralists, and the **+** next to them was a quantitative analyst. Near the door, the first **×** was a generalist, the two **+**s were behavioralists, and the second **×** was a quantitative analyst. The diagram shows the seating of everyone but Professor Stevens, who was the last one to enter the room. Standing at the door, Professor Stevens

surveyed the room and within 10 seconds knew which seat was the most effective to achieve his objective.

3. Answer the following questions in your group.
    1. Which seat did Professor Stevens select and why?
    2. What is the likely pattern of communication and interaction in this group?
    3. What can be done to get this group to work harmoniously?

EXERCISE 25

Interview a Leader

Contributed by Bonnie McNeely, Murray State University

Procedure

1. Make an appointment to interview a leader. It can be a leader working in a business or nonprofit organization, such as a government agency, school, and so on. Base the interview on the form provided here, but feel free to add your own questions.
2. Bring the results of your interview to class. Form into groups as assigned by your instructor. Share the responses from your interview with your group and compare answers. What issues were similar? Different? Were the stress levels of leaders working in nonprofit organizations as high as those working in for-profit firms? Were you surprised at the number of hours per week worked by leaders?
3. Be prepared to summarize the interviews done by your group as a formal written report if asked to do so by the instructor.

Interview Questionnaire

Student's Name _____ Date _____

1. Position in the organization (title):
2. Number of years in current position:
   Number of years of managerial experience:
3. Number of people directly supervised:
4. Average number of hours worked a week:
5. How did you get into leadership?
6. What is the most rewarding part of being a leader?
7. What is the most difficult part of your job?
8. What would you say are the *keys to success* for leaders?
9. What advice do you have for an aspiring leader?
10. What type of ethical issues have you faced as a leader?
11. If you were to enroll in a leadership seminar, what topics or issues would you want to learn more about?
12. (Student question)

Gender: M _____ F _____ Years of formal education _____
Level of job stress: Very high _____ High _____ Average _____ Low _____
Profit organization _____ Nonprofit organization _____
Additional information/Comments:

_____

Source: Adapted from Bonnie McNeely, "Make Your Principles of Management Class Come Alive," *Journal of Management Education,* Vol. 18, No. 2 (May 1994), pp. 246–249.

Leadership Skills Inventories

Procedure
1. Look over the skills listed below and ask your instructor to clarify those you do not understand.
2. Complete each category by checking either the "Strong" or "Needs Development" category in relation to your own level with each skill.
3. After completing each category, briefly describe a situation in which each of the listed skills has been utilized.
4. Meet in your groups to share and discuss inventories. Prepare a report summarizing major development needs in your group.

Instrument

	Strong	Needs Development	Situation
Communication	_____	_____	_____
Conflict management	_____	_____	_____
Delegation	_____	_____	_____
Ethical behavior	_____	_____	_____
Listening	_____	_____	_____
Motivation	_____	_____	_____
Negotiation	_____	_____	_____
Performance appraisal and feedback	_____	_____	_____
Planning and goal setting	_____	_____	_____
Power and influence	_____	_____	_____
Presentation and persuasion	_____	_____	_____
Problem solving and decision making	_____	_____	_____
Stress management	_____	_____	_____
Team building	_____	_____	_____
Time management	_____	_____	_____

Leadership and Participation in Decision Making

Procedure
1. For the 10 situations described here, decide which of the three styles you would use for that unique situation. Place the letter A, P, or L on the line before each situation's number.

      A—authority; make the decision alone without additional inputs.
      P—consultative; make the decision based on group inputs.
      L—group; allow the group to which you belong to make the decision.

Decision Situations

_____ 1. You have developed a new work procedure that will increase productivity. Your boss likes the idea and wants you to try it within a few weeks. You view your employees as fairly capable and believe that they will be receptive to the change.

_____ 2. The industry of your product has new competition. Your organization's revenues have been dropping. You have been told to lay off three of your ten employees in two weeks. You have been the supervisor for over one year. Normally, your employees are very capable.

_____ 3. Your department has been facing a problem for several months. Many solutions have been tried and have failed. You finally thought of a solution, but you are not sure of the possible consequences of the change required or its acceptance by the highly capable employees.

_____ 4. Flextime has become popular in your organization. Some departments let each employee start and end work whenever they choose. However, because of the cooperative effort of your employees, they must all work the same eight hours. You are not sure of the level of interest in changing the hours. Your employees are a very capable group and like to make decisions.

_____ 5. The technology in your industry is changing faster than the members of your organization can keep up. Top management hired a consultant who has given the recommended decision. You have two weeks to make your decision. Your employees are capable, and they enjoy participating in the decision-making process.

_____ 6. Your boss called you on the telephone to tell you that someone has requested an order for your department's product with a very short delivery date. She asked that you call her back with the decision about taking the order in 15 minutes. Looking over the work schedule, you realize that it will be very difficult to deliver the order on time. Your employees will have to push hard to make it. They are cooperative, capable, and enjoy being involved in decision making.

_____ 7. A change has been handed down from top management. How you implement it is your decision. The change takes effect in one month. It will personally affect everyone in your department. The acceptance of the department members is critical to the success of the change. Your employees are usually not too interested in being involved in making decisions.

_____ 8. You believe that productivity in your department could be increased. You have thought of some ways that may work, but you're not sure of them. Your employees are very experienced; almost all of them have been in the department longer than you have.

_____ 9. Top management has decided to make a change that will affect all of your employees. You know that they will be upset because it will cause them hardship. One or two may even quit. The change goes into effect in 30 days. Your employees are very capable.

_____ 10. A customer has offered you a contract for your product with a quick delivery date. The offer is open for two days. Meeting the contract deadline would require employees to work nights and weekends for six weeks. You cannot require them to work overtime. Filling this profitable contract could help get you the raise you want and feel you deserve. However, if you take the contract and don't deliver on time, it will hurt your chances of getting a big raise. Your employees are very capable.

2. Form groups as assigned by your instructor. Share and compare your choices for each decision situation. Reconcile any differences and be prepared to defend your decision preferences in general class discussion.

My Best Manager: Revisited

Contributed by J. Marcus Maier, Chapman University

Procedure

1. Refer to the list of qualities—or profiles—the class generated earlier in the course for the "Best Manager."
2. Looking first at your Typical Managers profile, suppose you took this list to 100 average people on the street (or at the local mall) and asked them whether ____ (Trait X, quality Y) was "more typical of men or of women in our culture." What do you think *most* of them would say? That ____ (X, Y etc.) is more typical of *women*? or of *men*? or of neither/both?[1] Do this for every trait on your list(s). (5 minutes)
3. Now do the same for the qualities we generated in our Best Manager profile. (5 min.)
4. A straw vote is taken, one quality at a time, to determine the class's overall gender identification of each trait, focusing on the Typical Managers profile (10–15 min.). Then this is repeated for the Best Manager profile (10–15 min.).[2]
5. Discussion. What do you see in the data this group has generated? How might you interpret these results? (15–20 min.)

Source: Based on Maier's 1993 article, "The Gender Prism," *Journal of Management Education,* 17(3), 285–314. 1994 Fritz Roethlisberger Award Recipient for Best Paper (Updated, 1996).

[1] This gets the participants to move outside of their *own* conceptions to their awareness of *societal* definitions of masculinity and femininity.

[2] This is done by a rapid show of hands, looking for a clear majority vote. An "f" (for "feminine") is placed next to those qualities that a clear majority indicate are more typical of women, an "m" (for "masculine") next to those qualities a clear majority indicate would be more typical of men. (This procedure parallels the median-split method used in determining Bem Sex Role Inventory classifications.) If no clear majority emerges (i.e., if the vote is close), the trait or quality is classified as "both" (f/m). The designations "masculine" or "feminine" are used (rather than "men" or "women") to underscore the *socially constructed* nature of each dimension.

Active Listening

Contributed by Robert Ledman, Morehouse College

Procedure

1. Review active listening skills and behaviors as described in the textbook and in class.
2. Form into groups of three. Each group will have a listener, a talker, and an observer (if the number of students is not evenly divisible by three, two observers are used for one or two groups).
3. The "talkers" should talk about any subject they wish, but only *if* they are being actively listened to. Talkers should stop speaking as soon as they sense active listening has stopped.
4. The "listeners" should use a list of active listening skills and behaviors as their guide, and practice as many of them as possible to be sure the talker is kept

---

Source: Adapted from the presentation entitled "An Experiential Exercise to Teach Active Listening," presented at the Organizational Behavior Teaching Conference, Macomb, IL, 1995.

talking. Listeners should contribute nothing more than "active listening" to the communication.

5. The "observer" should note the behaviors and skills used by the listener and the effects they seemed to have on the communication process.

6. These roles are rotated until each student has played every role.

7. The instructor will lead a discussion of what the observers saw and what happened with the talkers and listeners. The discussion focuses on what behaviors from the posted list have been present, which have been absent, and how the communication has been affected by the listener's actions.

EXERCISE 30

Upward Appraisal

Procedure

1. Form workgroups as assigned by your instructor.
2. The instructor will leave the room.
3. Convene in your assigned workgroups for a period of 10 minutes. Create a list of comments, problems, issues, and concerns you would like to have communicated to the instructor in regard to the course experience to date. *Remember,* your interest in the exercise is twofold: (a) to communicate your feelings to the instructor and (b) to learn more about the process of giving and receiving feedback.
4. Select one person from the group to act as spokesperson in communicating the group's feelings to the instructor.
5. The spokespersons should briefly convene to decide on what physical arrangement of chairs, tables, and so forth is most appropriate to conduct the feedback session. The classroom should then be rearranged to fit the desired specifications.
6. While the spokespersons convene, persons in the remaining groups should discuss how they expect the forthcoming communications event to develop. Will it be a good experience for all parties concerned? Be prepared to critically observe the actual communication process.
7. The instructor should be invited to return, and the feedback session will begin. Observers should make notes so that they may make constructive comments at the conclusion of the exercise.
8. Once the feedback session is complete, the instructor will call on the observers for comments, ask the spokespersons for reactions, and open the session to discussion.

EXERCISE 31

360° Feedback

Contributed by Timothy J. Serey, Northern Kentucky University

Introduction

The time of performance reviews is often a time of genuine anxiety for many organizational members. On the one hand, it is an important organizational ritual and a key part of the Human Resource function. Organizations usually codify the process and provide a mechanism to appraise performance. On the other hand, it is rare for managers to feel comfortable with this process. Often, they feel discomfort over "playing God." One possible reason for this is that managers rarely receive formal training about how to provide feedback. From the manager's point of view, if done properly, giving feedback is at the very heart of his or her job as "coach" and "teacher." It is an investment in the professional development of another person, rather than the punitive element we so often associate with hearing from "the boss." From the subordinate's perspective, most people want to know where they stand, but this is usually tempered by a fear of "getting it in the neck." In many organizations, it is rare to receive straight, non-sugar-coated feedback about where you stand.

Procedure

1. Review the section of the book dealing with feedback before you come to class. It is also helpful if individuals make notes about their perceptions and feelings about the course *before* they come to class.
2. Groups of students should discuss their experiences, both positive and negative, in this class. Each group should determine the dimensions of evaluating the class itself *and* the instructor. For example, students might select criteria that include the practicality of the course, the way the material is structured and presented (e.g., lecture or exercises), and the instructor's style (e.g., enthusiasm, fairness).
3. Groups select a member to represent them in a subgroup that next provides feedback to the instructor before the entire class.
4. The student audience then provides the subgroup with feedback about their effectiveness in this exercise. That is, the larger class provides feedback to the subgroup about the extent to which students actually put the principles of effective feedback into practice (e.g., descriptive, not evaluative; specific, not general).

Source: Adapted from Timothy J. Serey, *Journal of Management Education,* Vol. 17, No. 2 (May 1993). © 1993 by Sage Publications, Inc. Reprinted by permission of Sage Publications.

EXERCISE 32

Role Analysis Negotiation

Contributed by Paul Lyons, Frostburg State University

Introduction

A role is the set of various behaviors people expect from a person (or group) in a particular position. These role expectations occur in all types of organizations, such as one's place of work, school, family, clubs, and the like. Role ambiguity takes place when a person is confused about the expectations of the role. And sometimes, a role will have expectations that are contradictory—for example, being loyal to the company when the company is breaking the law.

The Role Analysis Technique, or RAT, is a method for improving the effectiveness of a team or group. RAT helps to clarify role expectations, and all organization members have responsibilities that translate to expectations. Determination of role requirements, by consensus—involving all concerned—will ultimately result in more effective and mutually satisfactory behavior. Participation and collaboration in the definition and

Source: Adapted from Paul Lyons, "Developing Expectations with the Role Analysis Technique," *Journal of Management Education.* Vol. 17, No. 3 (August 1993), pp. 386–389. © Sage Publications.

analysis of roles by group members should result in clarification regarding who is to do what as well as increase the level of commitment to the decisions made.

Procedure

Working alone, carefully read the course syllabus that your instructor has given you. Make a note of any questions you have about anything for which you need clarification or understanding. Pay particular attention to the performance requirements of the course. Make a list of any questions you have regarding what, specifically, is expected of you in order for you to be successful in the course. You will be sharing this information with others in small groups.

EXERCISE 33

Lost at Sea

Introduction

Consider this situation. You are adrift on a private yacht in the South Pacific when a fire of unknown origin destroys the yacht and most of its contents. You and a small group of survivors are now in a large raft with oars. Your location is unclear, but you estimate being about 1,000 miles south–southwest of the nearest land. One person has just found in her pockets five $1 bills and a packet of matches. Everyone else's pockets are empty. The following items are available to you on the raft.

	A	B	C
Sextant	____	____	
Shaving mirror	____	____	
5 gallons of water	____	____	
Mosquito netting	____	____	
1 survival meal	____	____	
Maps of Pacific Ocean	____	____	
Floatable seat cushion	____	____	
2 gallons oil-gas mix	____	____	
Small transistor radio	____	____	
Shark repellent	____	____	
20 square feet black plastic	____	____	
1 quart of 20-proof rum	____	____	
15 feet of nylon rope	____	____	
24 chocolate bars	____	____	
Fishing kit	____	____	

Source: Adapted from "Lost at Sea: A Consensus-Seeking Task," in *The 1975 Handbook for Group Facilitators*. Used with permission of University Associates, Inc.

Procedure

1. *Working alone,* rank in Column A the 15 items in order of their importance to your survival ("1" is most important and "15" is least important).
2. *Working in an assigned group,* arrive at a "team" ranking of the 15 items and record this ranking in Column B. Appoint one person as group spokesperson to report your group rankings to the class.
3. *Do not write in Column C* until further instructions are provided by your instructor.

EXERCISE 34

Entering the Unknown

Contributed by Michael R. Manning, New Mexico State University; Conrad N. Jackson, MPC Inc., Huntsville, Alabama; and Paula S. Weber, New Mexico Highlands University

Procedure

1. Form into groups of four or five members. In each group spend a few minutes reflecting on members' typical entry behaviors in new situations and their behaviors when they are in comfortable settings.
2. According to the instructor's directions, students count off to form new groups of four or five members each.
3. The new groups spend the next 15–20 minutes getting to know each other. There is no right or wrong way to proceed, but all members should become more aware of their entry behaviors. They should act in ways that can help them realize a goal of achieving comfortable behaviors with their group.
4. Students review what has occurred in the new groups, giving specific attention to the following questions:
    1. What topics did your group discuss (content)? Did these topics involve the "here and now" or were they focused on "there and then"?
    2. What approach did you and your group members take to the task (process)? Did you try to initiate or follow? How? Did you ask questions? Listen? Respond to others? Did you bring up topics?
    3. Were you more concerned with how you came across or with how others came across to you? Did you play it safe? Were you open? Did you share things even though it seemed uncomfortable or risky? How was humor used in your group? Did it add or detract?
    4. How do you feel about the approach you took or the behaviors you exhibited? Was this hard or easy? Did others respond the way you had anticipated? Is there some behavior you would like to do more of, do better, or do less of?
    5. Were your behaviors the ones you had intended (goals)?
5. Responses to these questions are next discussed by the class as a whole. (*Note:* Responses will tend to be mixed within a group, but between groups there should be more similarity.) This discussion helps individuals become aware of and understand their entry behaviors.
6. Optional individuals have identified their entry behaviors; each group can then spend 5–10 minutes discussing members' perceptions of each other:
    1. What behaviors did they like or find particularly useful? What did they dislike?

2. What were your reactions to others? What ways did they intend to come across? Did you see others in the way they had intended to come across?
(Alternatively, if there is concern about the personal nature of this discussion, ask the groups to discuss what they liked/didn't like without referring to specific individuals.)

Vacation Puzzle

Contributed by Barbara G. McCain and Mary Khalili, Oklahoma City University

Procedure

Can you solve this puzzle? Give it a try and then compare your answers with those of classmates. Remember your communicative skills!

Puzzle

Khalili, McCain, Middleton, Porter, and Quintaro teach at Oklahoma City University. Each gets two weeks of vacation a year. Last year, each took his or her first week in the first five months of the year and his or her second week in the last five months. If each professor took each of his or her weeks in a different month from the other professors, in which months did each professor take his or her first and second week?

Here are the facts:

1. McCain took her first week before Khalili, who took *hers* before Porter; for their second week, the order was reversed.
2. The professor who vacationed in March also vacationed in September.
3. Quintaro did not take her first week in March or April.
4. Neither Quintaro nor the professor who took his or her first week in January took his or her second week in August or December.
5. Middleton took her second week before McCain but after Quintaro.

Month	Professor
January	
February	
March	
April	
May	
June	
July	
August	
September	
October	
November	
December	

Source: Adapted to classroom activity by Dr. Mary Khalili.

The Ugli Orange

Introduction

In most work settings, people need other people to do their job, benefit the organization, and forward their career. Getting things done in organizations requires us to work together in cooperation, even though the ultimate objectives of those other people may be different from our own. Your task in the present exercise is learning how to achieve this cooperation more effectively.

Procedure

1. The class will be divided into pairs. One student in each pair will read and prepare the role of Dr. Roland, and one will play the role of Dr. Jones (role descriptions to be distributed by instructor). Students should read their respective role descriptions and prepare to meet with their counterpart (see Steps 2 and 3).
2. At this point the group leader will read a statement. The instructor will indicate that he or she is playing

the role of Mr. Cardoza, who owns the commodity in question. The instructor will tell you
  1. How long you have to meet with the other
  2. What information the instructor will require at the end of your meeting
After the instructor has given you this information, you may meet with the other firm's representative and determine whether you have issues you can agree to.
3. Following the meetings (negotiations), the spokesperson for each pair will report any agreements reached to the entire class. The observer for any pair will report on negotiation dynamics and the process by which agreement was reached.
4. Questions to consider:
  1. Did you reach a solution? If so, what was critical to reaching that agreement?
  2. Did you and the other negotiator trust one another? Why or why not?
  3. Was there full disclosure by both sides in each group? How much information was shared?
  4. How creative and/or complex were the solutions? If solutions were very complex, why do you think this occurred?
  5. What was the impact of having an "audience" on your behavior? Did it make the problem harder or easier to solve?

Source: Adapted from Hall et al., *Experiences in Management and Organizational Behavior,* 3rd ed. (New York: John Wiley and Sons, Inc.), 1988. Originally developed by Robert J. House. Adapted by D. T. Hall and R. J. Lewicki, with suggested modifications by H. Kolodny and T. Ruble.

Conflict Dialogues

Contributed by Edward G. Wertheim, Northeastern University

Procedure

1. Think of a conflict situation at work or at school and try to re-create a segment of the dialogue that gets to the heart of the conflict.
2. Write notes on the conflict dialogue using the following format

Introduction

- Background
- My goals and objectives

- My strategy
- Assumptions I am making

Dialogue (re-create part of the dialogue below and try to put what you were really thinking in parentheses).

- *Me:*
- *Other:*
- *Me:*
- *Other, etc.*

3. Share your situation with members of your group. Read the dialogue to them, perhaps asking someone to play the role of "other."
4. Discuss with the group:
    1. The style of conflict resolution you used (confrontation, collaboration, avoidance, etc.)
    2. The triggers to the conflict, that is, what really set you off and why
    3. Whether or not you were effective
    4. Possible ways of handling this differently
5. Choose one dialogue from within the group to share with the class. Be prepared to discuss your analysis and also possible alternative approaches and resolutions for the situation described.

EXERCISE 38

Force-Field Analysis

Procedure

1. Choose a situation in which you have high personal stakes (for example, how to get a better grade in course X; how to get a promotion; how to obtain a position).
2. Using a version of the Sample Force-Field Analysis Form on the next page, apply the technique to your situation.
    1. Describe the situation as it now exists.
    2. Describe the situation as you would like it to be.
    3. Identify those "driving forces"—the factors that are presently helping to move things in the desired direction.
    4. Identify those "restraining forces"—the factors that are presently holding things back from moving in the desired direction.
3. Try to be as specific as possible in terms of the above in relation to your situation. You should attempt to be exhaustive in your listing of these forces. List them all!
4. Now go back and classify the strength of each force as weak, medium, or strong. Do this for both the driving and the restraining forces.
5. At this point you should rank the forces regarding their ability to influence or control the situation.
6. In small groups share your analyses. Discuss the usefulness and drawbacks to using this method for personal situations and its application to organizations.
7. Be prepared to share the results of your group's discussion with the rest of the class.

Sample Force-Field Analysis Form

Current Situation:	Situation as You Would Like It to Be:
Driving Forces:	**Restraining Forces:**

• • • • • • **EXERCISE 39** •

Organizations Alive!

Contributed by Bonnie L. McNeely, Murray State University

Procedure

1. Find a copy of the following items from actual organizations. These items can be obtained from the company where you now work, a parent's workplace, or the university. Universities have mission statements, codes of conduct for students and faculty, organizational charts, job descriptions, performance appraisal forms, and control devices. Some student organizations also have these documents. All the items do not have to come from the same organization. *Bring these items to class.*

1. Mission statement
2. Code of ethics
3. Organizational chart
4. Job description
5. Performance appraisal form
6. Control device

2. Form groups in class as assigned by your instructor. Share your items with the group, as well as what you learned while collecting these items. For example, did you find that some firms have a mission, but it is not written down? Did you find that job descriptions existed, but they were not really used or had not been updated in years?

Source: Adapted from Bonnie L. McNeely, "Make Your Principles of Management Class Come Alive," *Journal of Management Education,* Vol. 18, No. 2 (May 1994), pp. 246–249.

• • • • • • **EXERCISE 40** •

Fast-Food Technology

Contributed by D. T. Hall, Boston University, and F. S. Hall, University of New Hampshire

Introduction

A critical first step in improving or changing any organization is *diagnosing* or analyzing its present functioning.

Many change and organization development efforts fall short of their objectives because this important step was not taken or was conducted superficially. To illustrate this, imagine how you would feel if you went to your doctor complaining of stomach pains and he recommended surgery without conducting any tests, without obtaining any further information, and without a careful physical examination. You would probably switch doctors! Yet managers often attempt major changes with correspondingly little diagnostic work in advance. (It could be said that they undertake vast projects with half-vast ideas.)

In this exercise, you will be asked to conduct a group diagnosis of two different organizations in the fast-food business. The exercise will provide an opportunity to integrate much of the knowledge you have gained in other exercises and in studying other topics. Your task will be to describe the organizations as carefully as you can in terms of several key organizational concepts. Although the organizations are probably very familiar to you, try to step back and look at them as though you were seeing them for the first time.

Procedure

1. In groups of four or six people, your assignment is described below.

One experience most people in this country have shared is that of dining in the hamburger establishment known as McDonald's. In fact, someone has claimed that twenty-fifth-century archeologists may dig into the ruins of our present civilization and conclude that twentieth-century religion was devoted to the worship of golden arches.

Your group, Fastalk Consultants, is known as the shrewdest, most insightful, and most overpaid management consulting firm in the country. You have been hired by the president of McDonald's to make recommendations for improving the motivation and performance of personnel in their franchise operations. Let us assume that the key job activities in franchise operations are food preparation, order-taking and dealing with customers, and routine cleanup operations.

Recently the president of McDonald's has come to suspect that his company's competitors—such as Burger King, Wendy's, Jack-in-the-Box, Dunkin' Donuts, various pizza establishments, and others—are making heavy inroads into McDonald's market. He has also hired a market research firm to investigate and compare the relative merits of the sandwiches, french fries, and drinks served in McDonald's and the competitor, and has asked the market research firm to assess the advertising campaigns of the two organizations. Hence, you will not need to be concerned with marketing issues, except as they may have an impact on employee behavior. The president wants *you* to look into the *organization* of the franchises to determine the strengths and weaknesses of each. Select a competitor that gives McDonald's a good "run for its money" in your area.

The president has established an unusual contract with you. *He wants you to make your recommendations based upon your observations as a customer.* He does not want you to do a complete diagnosis with interviews, surveys, or behind-the-scenes observations. He wants your report in two parts. Remember, the president wants concrete, specific, and practical recommendations. Avoid vague generalizations such as "improve communications" or "increase trust." Say very clearly *how* management can improve organizational performance. Substantiate your recommendations by reference to one or more theories of motivation, leadership, small groups, or job design.

Part I

Given his organization's goals of profitability, sales volume, fast and courteous service, and cleanliness, the president of McDonald's wants an analysis that will *compare and contrast McDonald's and the competitor* in terms of the following concepts:
- Organizational goals
- Organizational structure
- Technology
- Environment
- Employee motivation
- Communication
- Leadership style
- Policies/procedures/rules/standards
- Job design
- Organizational climate

Part II

Given the corporate goals listed under Part I, what specific actions might McDonald's management and franchise owners take in the following areas to achieve these goals (profitability, sales volume, fast and courteous service, and cleanliness)?
- Job design and workflow
- Organizational structure (at the individual restaurant level)
- Employee incentives
- Leadership
- Employee selection

How do McDonald's and the competition differ in these aspects? Which company has the best approach?

2. Complete the assignment by going as a group to one McDonald's and one competitor's restaurant. If possible, have a meal in each place. To get a more valid comparison, visit a McDonald's and a competitor located in the same area. After observing each restaurant, meet with your group and prepare your 10-minute report to the executive committee.
3. In class, each group will present its report to the rest of the class, who will act as the executive committee. The group leader will appoint a timekeeper to be sure

• •

that each group sticks to its 10-minute time limit. Possible discussion questions include:

1. What similarities are there between the two organizations?
2. What differences are there between the organizations?
3. Do you have any "hunches" about the reasons for the particular organizational characteristics you found? For example, can you try to explain why one organization might have a particular type of structure? Incentive system? Climate?
4. Can you try to explain one set of characteristics in terms of some other characteristics you found? For example, do the goals account for structure? Does the environment explain the structure?

Alien Invasion

Procedure

This is an exercise in organizational culture. You will be assigned to a team (if you are not already in one) and instructed to visit an organization by your instructor.

1. Visit the assigned site as a team working under conditions set forth in the "situation" below.
2. Take detailed notes on the cultural forms that you observe.
3. Prepare a presentation for the class that describes these forms and draw any inferences you can about the nature of the culture of the organization—its ideologies, values, and norms of behavior.
4. Be sure to explain the basis of your inferences in terms of the cultural forms observed.

You will have 20 minutes to report your findings, so plan your presentation carefully. Use visual aids to help your audience understand what you have found.

Situation

You are Martians who have just arrived on Earth in the first spaceship from your planet. Your superiors have ordered you to learn as much about Earthlings and the way they behave as you can without doing anything to make them aware that you are Martians. It is vital for the future plans of your superiors that you do nothing to disturb the Earthlings. Unfortunately, Martians communicate by emitting electromagnetic waves and are incapable of speech, so you cannot talk to the natives. Even if you did, it is reported by the usually reliable Bureau of Interplanetary Intelligence that Earthlings may become cannibalistic if annoyed. However, the crash course in Earth languages taught by the bureau has enabled you to read the language.

Remember, these instructions limit your data collection to observation and request that you *not* talk to the "natives." There are two reasons for this instruction. First, your objective is to learn what the organization does when it is simply going about its normal business and not responding to a group of students asking questions. Second, you are likely to be surprised at how much you can learn by simply observing if you put your mind to it. Many skilled managers employ this ability in sensing what is going on as they walk through their plant or office area.

Since you cannot talk to people, some of the cultural forms (legends, sagas, etc.) will be difficult to spot unless you are able to pick up copies of the organization's promotional literature (brochures, company reports, advertisements) during your visit. Do not be discouraged, because the visible forms such as artifacts, setting, symbols, and (sometimes) rituals can convey a great deal about the culture. Just keep your eyes, ears, and antennae open!

Source: Adapted from Donald D. Bowen et al., *Experiences in Management and Organizational Behavior,* 4th ed. (New York: John Wiley & Sons, Inc., 1997).

Power Circles

Contributed by Marian C. Schultz, University of West Florida

This exercise is designed to examine power and influence in the classroom setting. Specifically, it allows you to identify the combination of power bases used by your instructor in accomplishing his or her objectives for the course.

Procedure

1. Recall that the instructor's power includes the following major bases: (a) the authority that comes from the instructor's position (position power), (b) the knowledge, skill, and expertise of the instructor in the subject area (expert power), and (c) the regard in which you personally hold the instructor (referent power).

2. Indicate the configuration of power that is most evident in the way the instructor behaves in the course overall and according to the following "power circle." This circle can be filled in to represent the relative emphasis on the three power bases (e.g., 60 percent position, 30 percent expert, and 10 percent referent). Use the grid at the right to draw/fill in the circle to show the profile of instructor's power. The instructor will also complete a self-perceived power circle profile.

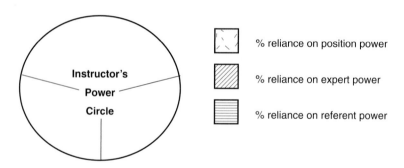

3. Consider also some possible special situations in which the instructor would have to use his or her power in the classroom context. Draw one power circle for each of the following situations, showing for each the power profile most likely to be used by the instructor to accomplish his or her goal.
   o Instructor wants to change the format of the final examination.
   o Instructor wants to add an additional group assignment to course requirements.
   o Instructor wants to have students attend a special two-hour guest lecture on a Saturday morning.
   o Instructor wants students to come to class better prepared for discussions of assigned material.
   o The instructor will also complete a self-perceived power circle profile for each situation.

4. Share your power circles with those developed by members of your assigned group. Discuss the profiles and the reasons behind them in the group. Appoint one group member as spokesperson to share results in general class discussion. Discuss with the group the best way to communicate this feedback effectively to the instructor in the presence of all class members, and help prepare the spokesperson for the feedback session.

5. Have the instructor share his or her power profiles with the class. Ask the instructor to comment on any differences between the self-perceptions and the views of the class. Comment as a class on the potential significance to leaders and managers of differences in the way they perceive themselves and the ways they are perceived by others.
6. Discuss with the instructor and class how people may tend to favor one or more of the power bases (i.e., to develop a somewhat predictable power circle profile). Discuss as well how effective leaders and managers need to use power contingently, and modify their use of different power bases and power circle profiles to best fit the needs of specific influence situations.

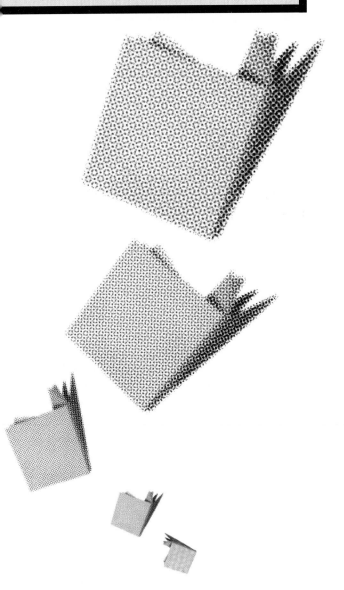

CASES FOR CRITICAL THINKING

Trader Joe's

While vacationing in the Caribbean, founder "Trader" Joe Coulombe, discovered a way to differentiate his 7-Eleven–style corner stores from those of his competitors. Joe observed that consumers are more likely to try new things while on vacation. With a nautical theme and cheerful guides sporting Hawaiian shirts, Joe transformed his stores into oases of value by replacing humdrum sundries with exotic, one-of-a-kind foods priced persuasively below any reasonable competitor.[1]

For over fifty years, Trader Joe's has competed with such giants as Whole Foods and Dean & DeLuca. So what is its recipe for success? The company applies its pursuit of value to every facet of its operations. Buyers travel all over the world in search of great tasting foods and beverages. By focusing on natural ingredients, inspiring flavors, and buying direct from the producer whenever possible, Trader Joes' is able to keep costs down. The chain prides itself on its thriftiness and cost-saving measures, proclaiming, "We run a pretty lean ship," "Every penny we save is a penny you save," and "Our CEO doesn't even have a secretary."[2]

"When you look at food retailers," says Richard George, professor of food marketing at St. Joseph's University, "there is the low end, the big middle, and then there is the cool edge—that's Trader Joe's."[3] But how does Trader Joe's compare with other stores with an edge, such as Whole Foods? Both obtain products locally and from all over the world. Each values employees and strives to offer the highest quality. However, there's no mistaking that Trader Joe's is cozy and intimate, whereas Whole Foods' spacious stores offer an abundance of choices. By limiting its stock and selling quality products at low prices, Trader Joe's sells twice as much per square foot than other supermarkets.[4] Most retail mega-markets, such as Whole Foods, carry between 25,000 and 45,000 products; Trader Joe's stores carry only 1,500 to 2,000.[5] But this scarcity benefits both Trader Joe's and its customers. According to Swarthmore professor Barry Schwartz, author of *The Paradox of Choice: Why Less Is More*, "Giving people too much choice can result in paralysis. . . . [R]esearch shows that the more options you offer, the less likely people are to choose any."[6]

Despite the lighthearted tone suggested by marketing materials and in-store ads, Trader Joe's aggressively courts friendly, customer-oriented employees by writing job descriptions highlighting desired soft skills ("ambitious and adventurous, enjoy smiling and have a strong sense of values") as much as actual retail experience.[7]

Trader Joe's connects with its customers because of the culture of product knowledge and customer involvement that its management cultivates among store employees. Trader Joe's considers its responsible, knowledgeable, and friendly "crew" to be critical to its success. Therefore they nurture their employees with a promote-from-within philosophy.

Each employee is encouraged to taste and learn about the products and to engage customers to share what they've experienced. Most shoppers recall instances when helpful crew members took the time to locate or recommend particular items. Says one employee,

"Our customers don't just come here to buy a loaf of bread. They can do that anywhere. They come to try new things. They come to see a friendly face. They come because they know our names and we know theirs. But most of all, they come because we can tell them why not all Alaskan salmon has to come from Alaska or the difference between a Shiraz and a Syrah. The flow of ideas and information at the store level is always invigorating."[8]

When it comes to showing its appreciation for its employees, Trader Joe's puts its money where its mouth is. Those who work for Trader Joe's earn considerably more than their counterparts at other chain grocers. Starting benefits include medical, dental, and vision insurance, company-paid retirement, paid vacation, and a 10% employee discount.[9] Being a privately owned company and a little media shy, Trader Joe's has been keeping some of its financial information confidential these days, but would say that managers make in the neighborhood of $100K per year.

Outlet managers are highly compensated, substantially more so than at other retailers, partly because they know the Trader Joe's system inside and out (managers are hired only from within the company). Future leaders enroll in training programs such as Trader Joe's University that foster in them the loyalty necessary to run stores according to both company and customer expectations, teaching managers to imbue their part-timers with the customer-focused attitude shoppers have come to expect.[10]

So it came as a horrifying surprise to many of those shoppers that Trader Joe's had a new nickname: "Traitor Joe's." The usually environmentally friendly company fared the worst of the national chains on Greenpeace's recently released seafood sustainability scorecard. Greenpeace's study, *Carting Away the Oceans: How Grocery Stores are Emptying the Seas*, ranked 20 supermarket companies by assessing their seafood policies and checked to see whether they sold fish off the red list—fish that are over fished and need to be conserved in order to survive.[11] Greenpeace surveys found Trader Joe's sells 15 of the 22 red list seafoods: Alaskan pollock, Atlantic cod, Atlantic salmon, Atlantic sea scallops, Chilean sea bass, Greenland halibut, monkfish, ocean quahog, orange roughy, red snapper, redfish, South Atlantic albacore tuna, swordfish, tropical shrimp, and yellowfin tuna.[12] Customers who trust Trader Joe's to offer the most nutritious, sustainable, organic foods felt deceived. Trader Joe's was quick to respond and post this to the action alerts on their Web site: "We listen to our customers. Hearing recent feedback, our goal is to offer seafood options that fit customer needs ranging from food safety and taste, to concern over the environment."[13]

Now let's see if the company puts those words into action. As consumers are increasingly mindful of how and where each dollar is spent, Trader Joe's simply can't afford not to.

Discussion Questions

1. How does Trader Joe's design jobs for increased job satisfaction and higher performance?
2. In what ways does Trader Joe's demonstrate the importance of each responsibility in the management process—planning, organizing, leading, and controlling?
3. Describe the methods that show Trader Joe's knows the importance of human capital.
4. Explain the value chain as it pertains to Trader Joe's.
5. Research Question: What do the blogs and current news reports say? Is Trader Joe's a management benchmark for others to follow? In what areas relevant to Organizational Behavior does the firm have an edge on the competition? ∎

Management Training Dilemma

Developed by John R. Schermerhorn, Jr., Ohio University

Shane Alexander is the personnel director of the Central State Medical Center. One of her responsibilities is to oversee the hospital's supervisory training programs. Recently Shane attended a professional conference where a special "packaged" training program was advertised for sale. The package includes a set of videotaped lectures by a distinguished management consultant plus a workbook containing readings, exercises, cases, tests, and other instructional aids. The subjects covered in the program include motivation, group dynamics, communication skills, leadership effectiveness, performance appraisal, and the management of planned change.

In the past Shane felt that the hospital had not lived up to its supervisory training goals. One of the reasons for this was the high cost of hiring external consultants to do the actual instruction. This packaged program was designed, presumably, so that persons from within the hospital could act as session coordinators. The structure of the program provided through the videotapes and workbook agenda was supposed to substitute for a consultant's expertise. Because of this, Shane felt that use of the packaged program could substantially improve supervisory training in the hospital.

The cost of the program was $3,500 for an initial purchase of the videotapes plus 50 workbooks. Additional workbooks were then available at $8 per copy. Before purchasing the program, Shane needed the approval of the senior administrative staff.

At the next staff meeting Shane proposed purchasing the training program. She was surprised at the response. The hospital president was noncommittal; the vice-president was openly hostile; and the three associate administrators were varied in their enthusiasm. It was the vice-president's opinion that dominated the discussion. He argued that to invest in such a program on the assumption that it would lead to improved supervisory practices was unwise. "This is especially true in respect to the proposed program," he said. "How could such a package possibly substitute for the training skills of an expert consultant?"

Shane argued her case and was left with the following challenge. The administrators would allow $1,000 to be spent to rent the program with 30 workbooks. It would be up to Shane to demonstrate through a trial program that an eventual purchase would be worth-while.

There were 160 supervisors in the hospital. The program was designed to be delivered in eight $2\frac{1}{2}$ hour sessions. It was preferred to schedule one session per week, with no more than 15 participants per session.

Shane knew that she would have to present very strong evidence to gain administrative support for the continued use of the program. Given the opportunity, she decided to implement a trial program in such a way that conclusive evidence on the value of the packaged training would be forthcoming.

Review Questions

1. If you were Shane, what type of research design would you use to test this program? Why?
2. How would the design actually be implemented in this hospital setting?
3. What would be your research hypothesis? What variables would you need to measure to provide data that could test this hypothesis? How would you gather these data?
4. Do you think the administrator's request for "proof before purchase" was reasonable? Why or why not? ∎

Xerox

At Xerox, Diversity equals Success. The equation certainly has worked for them! According to Fortune magazine's annual reputation survey, Xerox is the world's most admired company in the computer industry. According to Anne Mulcahy, Xerox Chairman and former CEO, "Diversity is about more than race and gender. It's about more than numbers. It's about inclusion. Diversity means creating an environment where all employees can grow to their fullest potential." Xerox knows that employees with different ways of thinking, and different ways of perceiving the world, are employees who create innovative solutions. In a business like Xerox, whose lifeblood is fresh ideas, this variety of perspectives is a priceless resource—and a key to achieving critical business results.[1]

Innovation keeps Xerox at the forefront of their industry. In fact, nearly 5% of revenue is dedicated to Research & Development and Engineering. Says Mulcahy, "Investing in innovation was indeed the best decision I've ever made. Despite the economic slowdown in technology spending, Xerox is still the prominent player in our industry, with a No. 1 revenue share. And at a time when we had a bunker-like mentality to save our company, we also empowered a small but entrepreneurial team to create our services business. Good thing we did. The offerings from Xerox Global Services have never been more relevant for our customers, who are knocking on our door looking for any way to save money . . . We're able to move quickly on these opportunities right now because we decided to fund innovation back then." With sales of $17.6 billion, Xerox is the world's largest technology-and-services company specializing in document management.[2, 3]

Xerox provides the document industry's broadest portfolio of offerings. Digital systems include color and black-and-white printing and publishing systems, digital presses and "book factories," advanced and basic multifunction systems, laser and solid ink network printers, copiers, and fax machines. No competitor can match Xerox's services expertise, which includes: helping businesses develop online document archives, analyzing how employees can most efficiently share documents and knowledge in the office, operating in-house print shops or mailrooms, and building Web-based processes for personalizing direct mail, invoices, brochures and more. Xerox also offers associated software, support and even supplies such as toner, paper and ink.[3]

By recognizing and respecting diversity and empowering individuality, Xerox creates productive people and an innovative company. Theirs is a corporate culture of inclusion whose commitment to diversity can be traced back to its very first chairman, Joseph C. Wilson. Chairman Wilson took proactive steps to create a more diverse workforce in response to race riots in the 1960s. With then Xerox President C. Peter McCullough, Wilson called for increased hiring of African Americans in an effort to achieve equality among its workforce. Throughout the 1970s Xerox established an internal affirmative action office and began to hire a significant number of minority employees.[4]

Xerox placed emphasis on the advancement of minorities and females in the 1980s. It was during this time that Barry Rand, an African American, was named the first minority president of a division. Xerox's Balanced Workforce Strategy (BWF) aimed to achieve unbiased representation for women and minorities throughout the organization at all times, including throughout times of restructuring. During the influx of women in its workforce Xerox recognized their struggle balancing work and family commitments. In response, Xerox Human Resources (HR) initiated "flex time" and other HR policies to maintain a high level of productivity and satisfaction among its workforce.[5]

In the 1990s sexual orientation was included in the company's Equal Opportunity/Affirmative Action and On-discrimination policy, Galaxe Pride at Work (a caucus group for gay, lesbian, bisexual and transgender employees) was established, and Xerox began to provide domestic partner benefits for gay, lesbian, bisexual and transgender employees. Annual diversity

employee roundtables with senior managers were initiated, providing employees the opportunity to engage in unfiltered communication with management about best practices, strengths and weaknesses of Xerox's diversity initiatives.[6]

Xerox's view on a diverse work force is most eloquently expressed by Xerox Chairman Anne M. Mulcahy:

I'm convinced diversity is a key to success. Experience tells us that the most diverse companies—companies ruled by a hierarchy of imagination and filled with people of all ages, races, and backgrounds—are the most successful over time. Somehow, diversity breeds creativity. Maybe it's because people with different backgrounds challenge each other's underlying assumptions, freeing everybody from convention and orthodoxy. We provide a shining proof point that diversity in all its wonderful manifestations is good for business . . . good for our country . . . and good for people.[7]

Xerox is proud to say that women and minorities make up 52% of their workforce. About 42.5 percent of Xerox senior executives are women or people of color or both. The employee roster is made up of over 30% African-Americans, Latinos, Asians and Native Americans. In fact, Xerox has been rated as one of the Top 10 companies in hiring minorities, women, disabled and gay and lesbian employees by *Fortune, Forbes, Working Mother, Latino Style,* and *Enable* magazines. They are among *Working Mother*'s top 100 family friendly companies for women—and have been for the past 15 years.[8]

In 2007 Ursula Burns was named the first African American, female president of Xerox Corporation. In July 2009 she succeeded Anne M. Mulcahy as CEO. It was the first female to female hand-off in Fortune 500 history. Burns' philosophy echoes Mulcahy's:

"The power of our people development model is that it recognizes the value of diversity from entry-level positions to the top seats. When you've been at it as long as we have, the bench gets pretty strong of next generation leaders who represent the real world: black, white, male, female, Hispanic, Asian from different religions and with different beliefs. What they all have in common is strong skills, a solid work ethic, commitment and a will to win."[9]

With Ursula Burns at the helm, and a 100 percent rating on the Corporate Equality Index by the Human Rights Campaign

Foundation, there's no doubt about it—Xerox's commitment to diversity is still going strong.[10]

Review Questions

1. How would Xerox define diversity? How has its definition changed over the years?
2. What are the seven reasons why Xerox should be motivated to diversify their workforce? Illustrate how Xerox shows it values workplace diversity.
3. Research question: Compare Xerox to other Fortune 500 companies. How are women and minorities represented at the highest levels of each organization? How can these statistics be improved upon? ■

CASE 3
Lois Quam
....
Founder and Chief Executive Officer, Tysvar, LLC

After accompanying Will Steger on a trip to Norway and the Arctic Circle, Lois Quam's interest in global climate change was sparked. There she witnessed firsthand the astonishing changes in the polar ice masses and the resulting impact on wildlife. Inspired by Steger's call for action to reduce global climate change, in 2009 Lois Quam left Piper Jaffray, a leading international investment bank, to become the founder and CEO of Tysvar, LLC, a privately held, Minnesota-based New Green Economy and health care reform incubator.[1]

"I'm focused on ways to finding solutions to really significant problems and taking those ideas to full potential," Quam said. "Piper [Jaffray] does a wonderful job financing companies. I want to bring the green economy to reality in a way that is much broader than financing. I want to focus on areas where I can make the most difference bringing the green economy to scale."[2]

Tysvar works with investors who can create the change they wish to see in the world rather than simply reacting to events as they unfold. The company is a strategic advisor and incubator of ideas, organizations, and people working to facilitate and build the New Green Economy (NGE) to scale. Tysvar's goal is to contribute to a viable, profitable, and socially responsible industry of sustainability, clean tech-

nology, and renewable energy sources.[3]

Lois Quam believes the New Green Economy will produce high quality jobs, improve our national security via less dependence on foreign fuels, and prevent the most damaging consequence of all: irreversible and diminishing climate change. She and Tysvar are committed to establishing universal health care reform in America. They believe universal health care is the answer for dependable, affordable health care for all Americans and that it is necessary to help rebuild the American economy and restore American competitiveness worldwide.[4]

Conscientiously working to play their part to create a more sustainable world for the next generation, Tysvar's efforts include new creation of NGE industries, jobs, and investment opportunities, contributing to building NGE public policy frameworks, trade for import/export of clean technologies, and renewable energy sources around the world.[5]

"We stand on the brink of a very exciting time in the world," according to Quam. The interest in developing renewable energy sources to replace dwindling fossil fuel supplies and reduce carbon dioxide emissions is worldwide. "It is a very difficult time in the financial markets right now to do this, but that will change. Good companies will find ways to get things done."[6]

"I am an optimist about our future," said Quam, "Which is why I started Tysvar. The challenges we face from climate change are immense, but so are our capabilities, and the rewards and benefits to humanity are even greater in the New Green Economy."[7]

Lois Quam named her company after Tysvar, the hometown of her grandfather, Nels Quam.

Tysvar is a majestically beautiful area in western Norway which is becoming a clean technology hub as part of Norway's growing NGE leadership and will soon be the site of the world's largest off-shore wind farm.[8]

In founding Tysvar, I am following in the footsteps of my grandparents who journeyed from their homeland of Norway to Minnesota. They came bringing with them a set of enduring values and a search for a place where they could make a great difference. They embodied—and gave to me—the unquestionable knowledge that life was about serving others starting with your own loved ones. They also were about creating institutions that grew to serve others in impressive ways.

For my generation, we leave the past to build here in America the new institutions required for a better future. [9]

Lois Quam has continually worked for a better tomorrow. In 2005, Quam was named Norwegian American of the Year. She believes there is much to learn from Norway: From balancing work and life, allowing parents to fully participate in the economy while still being active parents, to how successfully Norway is immersing itself in new energy technologies such as wind and biomass. As an arctic oil producing nation with a carbon tax since 1993, Norway has reinvested its oil wealth to become a world leader in renewable energy.[10, 11]

Internationally recognized as a visionary and leader on universal health-care reform and the emerging NGE, Lois Quam embodies the skill sets needed to succeed in this new economy. Named in 2006 by Fortune magazine as one of America's "50 Most Powerful Women," Quam has worked as head of Strategic Investments, Green Economy &

Health at Piper Jaffray, a leading international investment bank; served as president and CEO of the Public and Senior Markets segment at UnitedHealth Group, a $30 billion division she helped create and run; chaired the Minnesota Health Care Access Commission, which led to legislation that brought health insurance to tens of thousands of Minnesotans; and served as a senior advisor to Hillary Clinton's task force on health care reform. She graduated magna cum laude from Macalester College in St. Paul and went on to attend the University of Oxford as a Rhodes Scholar, earning a master's degree in philosophy, politics, and economics.[12]

On Earth Day Lois Quam gave a speech at the University of St. Thomas on the emerging opportunities in the New Green Economy (NGE) after which she said, "I enjoyed sharing . . . how we can all use these key capabilities as a platform for doing something you love. Imagine: helping to build the NGE with a purposeful passion. It doesn't get much better than that!"[13]

In another speech she illustrated her philosophy:

The change required to combat climate change and conserve biodiversity will create a change in business and society similar to the Industrial Revolution. The new energy realities require nothing short of an energy revolution, a thorough retooling of our energy economy in ways that match up with the realities of the 21st century. It will affect every aspect of daily life and business, creating an immense set of opportunities for investors, businesses and individuals.

For investors, there are highly diverse and immense opportunities to create and scale new sources of energy, adapt our current methods of production and improve daily life in ways that drive down global warming emissions.

It will also create unprecedented depth and breadth of opportunities for businesses and investors . . . . clean energy will always be in strong demand . . . the world will always have massive energy needs, and they will always have to be balanced against the needs of the environment . . . the clean energy industry is fueled by the laws of nature—and there is no force as powerful or promising.

Think about what we can achieve working together at this conference and as a region . . . and think about the time sometime in the future when our work is reaching critical mass, when our environment is safer and our energy is cleaner, when we too will have our eureka moments, our moments of life-changing and world-changing discovery.[14]

As individuals, organizations, and countries answer the call for action, we look forward to achieving Lois Quam's vision of the future.

Review Questions

1. How does Lois Quam use emotions and moods in her speeches to convey her viewpoint? Cite examples to support your statements.
2. Based on what you have learned about Lois Quam, create hypotheses about the attitudes of her colleagues at Tysvar while using the three basic components of attitudes in your theories.
3. Research question: Search news reports, Web sites, and blogs to find out more information on Lois Quam and Tysvar. How is the company faring in its quest to make the world cleaner and safer for future generations? What implications might that have on Tysvar's employees, their attitudes, and job satisfaction? ■

CASE 4
MAGREC, Inc.
....
Developed by Mary McGarry, Empire State College and Barry R. Armandi, SUNY-Old Westbury

Background

MagRec, Incorporated was started by Mr. Leed, a brilliant engineer (he has several engineering patents) who was a group manager at Fairchild Republic. The company's product was magnetic recording heads, a crucial device used for reading, writing, and erasing data on tapes and disks.

Like any other startup, MagRec had a humble beginning. It struggled during the early years, facing cash-flow and technical problems. After a slow start, it grew rapidly and gained 35 percent of the tape head market, making it the second-largest supplier in North America. Financially, the company suffered heavily because of price erosions caused by Far East competition. Unlike all its competitors, the company resisted moving its manufacturing operations offshore. But the company accumulated losses to a point of bankruptcy. Finally MagRec entered a major international joint venture and received many new sales orders. Things looked good again. But . . .

Pat's Dilemma

When Fred Marsh promoted me to Sales Manager, I was in seventh heaven. Now, six months later, I feel I am in hell. This is the first time in my life that I am really on my own. I have been working with other people all my life. I tried my best and what I could not solve, I took upstairs. Now it's different because I am the boss (or am I?). Fred has taught me a lot. He was my mentor and gave me this job when he became vice president. I have always respected him and listened to his judgment. Now thinking back I wonder whether I should have listened to him at all on this problem.

It started one late Friday evening. I had planned to call my West Coast customer, Partco, to discuss certain contract clauses. I wanted to nail this one fast (Partco had just been acquired by Volks, Inc.). Partco was an old customer in fact, through good and bad it had always stayed with us. It was also a *major* customer. I was about to call Partco when Dinah Coates walked in clutching a file. I had worked with Dinah for three years. She was good. I knew that my call to Partco would have to wait. Dinah had been cleaning out old files and came across a report about design and manufacturing defects in Partco heads. The report had been written nine years ago. The cover memo read as follows:

To: Ken Smith, Director of Marketing
From: Rich Grillo, V.P. Operations
Sub: Partco Head Schedule

This is to inform you that due to pole-depth problems in design, the Partco heads (all 514 in test) have failed. They can't reliably meet the reading requirements. The problem is basically a design error in calculations. It can be corrected. However, the fix will take at least six months.

Meanwhile Ron Scott in production informs me that the entire 5,000 heads (the year's production) have already been pole-slotted, thus they face the same problem.

Ken, I don't have to tell you how serious this is, but how can we OK and ship them to Partco knowing that they'll cause read error problems in the field? My engineering and manufacturing people realize this is the number one priority. By pushing the Systems Tech job back we will be back on track in less than six months. In the interim I can modify Global Widgets heads. This will enable us to at least continue shipping some product to Partco. As a possible alternate I would like to get six Partco drives. Michaels and his team feel that with quick and easy changes in the drives tape path they can get the head to work. If this is true we should be back on track within six to eight weeks.

A separate section of the report reads as follows:

Confidential
(Notes from meeting with Don Updyke and Rich Grillo)

Solution to Partco heads problem
All Partco heads can be reworked (.8 hrs. ea.—cost insignificant) to solve Partco's read problems by grinding an extra three-thousandths of an inch off the top of the head. This will reduce the overall pole depth to a point where no read errors occur. The heads will fully meet specifications in all respects except one, namely life. Don estimates that due to the reduced chrome layer (used for wear) the heads' useful life will be 2500 hours instead of 6000 hours of actual usage.

Our experience is that no customer keeps accurate records to tell actual usage and life. Moreover, the cost is removed since Partco sells drives to MegaComputer, who sells systems to end-users. The user at the site hardly knows or rarely complains about extra costs such as the replacement of a head 12 to 18 months down the line instead of the normal 2 years. Besides, the service technicians always innovatively believe in and offer plausible explanations—such as the temperature must be higher than average—or they really must be using the computer a lot.

I have directed that the heads be reworked and shipped to Partco. I also instructed John to tell Partco that due to inclement weather this week's shipment will be combined with next week's shipment.

Dinah was flabbergasted. The company planned to sell products deliberately that it knew would not meet life requirements, she said, "risking our reputation as a quality supplier. Partco and others buy our heads thinking they are the best. Didn't we commit fraud through outright misrepresentation?"

Dinah insisted I had to do something. I told her I would look into the matter and get back to her by the end of next week.

Over the weekend I kept thinking about the Partco issue. We had no customer complaints. Partco had always been extremely pleased with our products and technical support. In fact, we were their sole suppliers. MegaComputer had us placed on the preferred, approved ship to stock, vendors list. It was a fact that other vendors were judged against our standards. MegaComputer's Quality Control never saw our product or checked it.

Monday morning I showed the report to Fred. He immediately recollected it and began to explain the situation to me.

MagRec had been under tremendous pressure and was growing rapidly at the time. "That year we had moved into a new 50,000 sq. ft. building and went from 50 or 60 employees to over 300. Our sales were increasing

dramatically." Fred was heading Purchasing at the time and every week the requirements for raw materials would change. "We'd started using B.O.A.s (Broad Order Agreements, used as annual purchasing contracts) guaranteeing us the right to increase our numbers by 100 percent each quarter. The goal was to maintain the numbers. If we had lost Partco then, it could have had a domino effect and we could have ended up having no customers left to worry about."

Fred went on to explain that it had only been a short-term problem that was corrected within the year and no one ever knew it existed. He told me to forget it and to move the file into the back storage room. I conceded. I thought of all the possible hassles. The thing was ancient history anyway. Why should I be concerned about it? I wasn't even here when it happened.

The next Friday Dinah asked me what I had found out. I told her Fred's feelings on the matter and that I felt he had some pretty good arguments regarding the matter. Dinah became angry. She said I had changed since my promotion and that I was just as guilty as the crooks who'd cheated the customers by selling low-life heads as long-life heads. I told her to calm down. The decision was made years ago. No one got hurt and the heads weren't defective. They weren't causing any errors.

I felt bad but figured there wasn't much to do. The matter was closed as far as I was concerned, so I returned to my afternoon chores. Little was I to know the matter was not really closed.

That night Fred called me at 10:00. He wanted me to come over to the office right away. I quickly changed, wondering what the emergency was. I walked into Fred's office. The coffee was going. Charlie (Personnel Manager) was there.

Rich Grillo (V.P. Operations) was sitting on the far side of Fred's conference table. I instinctively headed there for that was the designated smoking corner.

Ken (Director of Marketing) arrived 15 minutes later. We settled in. Fred began the meeting by thanking everyone for coming. He then told them about the discovery of the Partco file and filled them in on the background. The problem now was that Dinah had called Partco and gotten through to their new vice president, Tim Rand. Rand had called Fred at 8 P.M. at home and said he was personally taking the Red Eye to find out what this was all about. He would be here in the morning.

We spent a grueling night followed by an extremely tense few weeks. Partco had a team of people going through our tests, quality control, and manufacturing records. Our production slipped, and overall morale was affected.

Mr. Leed personally spent a week in California assuring Partco that this would never happen again. Though we weathered the storm, we had certain losses. We were never to be Partco's sole source again. We still retained 60 percent of their business but had to agree to lower prices. The price reduction had a severe impact. Although Partco never disclosed to anyone what the issues were (since both companies had blanket nondisclosure agreements), word got around that Partco was paying a lower price. We were unable to explain to our other customers why Partco was paying this amount. Actually I felt the price word got out through Joe Byrne (an engineer who came to Partco from Systems Tech and told his colleagues back at Systems Tech that Partco really knew how to negotiate prices down). He was unaware, however, of the real issues. Faced with customers who perceived they were being treated inequitably, we experienced problems. Lowering prices meant incurring losses; not lowering them meant losing customers. The next two financial quarters saw sales dollars decline by 40 percent. As the sales manager, I felt pretty rotten presenting my figures to Fred.

With regard to Dinah, I now faced a monumental problem. The internal feeling was she should be avoided at all costs. Because of price erosions, we faced cutbacks. Employees blamed her for production layoffs. The internal friction kept mounting. Dinah's ability to interface effectively with her colleagues and other departments plummeted to a point where normal functioning was impossible.

Fred called me into his office two months after the Partco episode and suggested that I fire Dinah. He told me that he was worried about results. Although he had nothing personally against her, he felt that she must go because she was seriously affecting my department's overall performance. I defended Dinah by stating that the Partco matter would blow over and given time I could smooth things out. I pointed out Dinah's accomplishments and stated I really wanted her to stay. Fred dropped the issue, but my problem persisted.

Things went from bad to worse. Finally, I decided to try to solve the problem myself. I had known Dinah well for many years and had a good relationship with her before the incident. I took her to lunch to address the issue. Over lunch, I acknowledged the stress the Partco situation had put on her and suggested that she move away for a while to the West Coast, where she could handle that area independently.

Dinah was hurt and asked why I didn't just fire her already. I responded by accusing her of causing the problem in the first place by going to Partco.

Dinah came back at me, calling me a lackey for having taken her story to Fred and having brought his management message back. She said I hadn't even attempted a solution and that I didn't have the guts to stand up for what was right. I was only interested in protecting my backside and keeping Fred happy. As her manager, I should have protected her and taken some of the heat off her back. Dinah refused to transfer or to quit. She told me to go ahead and fire her, and she walked out.

I sat in a daze as I watched Dinah leave the restaurant. What the heck went wrong? Had Dinah done the morally right thing? Was I right in defending MagRec's position? Should I have taken a stand with Fred? Should I have gone over Fred's head to Mr. Leed? Am I doing the right thing? Should I listen to Fred and fire Dinah? If not, how do I get my department back on track? What am I saying? If Dinah is right, shouldn't I be defending her rather than MagRec?

Review Questions

1. Place yourself in the role of the manager. What should you do now? After considering what happened, would you change any of your behaviors?
2. Do you think Dinah was right? Why or why not? If you were she and you had it to do all over again, would you do anything differently? If so, what and why?
3. Using cognitive dissonance theory, explain the actions of Pat, Dinah, and Fred. ■

CASE 5
It Isn't Fair
• •

Developed by Barry R. Armandi, SUNY–Old Westbury

Mary Jones was in her senior year at Central University and interviewing for jobs. Mary was in the top 1 percent of her class, active in numerous extracurricular activities, and highly respected by her professors. After the interviews, Mary was offered positions with every company with which she interviewed. After much thought, she decided to take the offer from Universal Products, a multinational company. She felt that the salary was superb ($40,000), there were excellent benefits, and there was good potential for promotion.

Mary started work a few weeks after graduation and learned her job assignments and responsibilities thoroughly and quickly. Mary was asked on many occasions to work late because report deadlines were often moved forward. Without hesitation she said "Of course!" even though as an exempt employee she would receive no overtime.

Frequently she would take work home with her and use her personal computer to do further analyses. At other times she would come into the office on weekends to monitor the progress of her projects or just to catch up on the ever-growing mountain of correspondence.

On one occasion her manager asked her to take on a difficult assignment. It seemed that the company's Costa Rican manufacturing facility was having production problems. The quality of one of the products was highly questionable, and the reports on the matter were confusing. Mary was asked to be part of a team to investigate the quality and reporting problems. The team stayed in poor accommodations for the entire three weeks they were there. This was because of the plant's location near its resources, which happened to be in the heart of the jungle. Within the three-week period the team had located the source of the quality problem, corrected it, and altered the reporting documents and processes. The head of the team, a quality engineer, wrote a note to Mary's manager stating the following: "Just wanted to inform you of the superb job Mary Jones did down in Costa Rica. Her suggestions and insights into the reporting system were invaluable. Without her help we would have been down there for another three weeks, and I was getting tired of the mosquitoes. Thanks for sending her."

Universal Products, like most companies, has a yearly performance review system. Since Mary had been with the company for a little over one year, it was time for her review. Mary entered her manager's office nervous, since this was her first review ever and she didn't know what to expect. After closing the door and exchanging the usual pleasantries, her manager, Tom, got right to the point.

Tom: Well, Mary, as I told you last week this meeting would be for your annual review. As you are aware, your performance and compensation are tied together. Since the philosophy of the company is to reward those who perform, we take these reviews very sincerely. I have spent a great deal of time thinking about your performance over the

past year, but before I begin I would like to know your impressions of the company, your assignments, and me as a manager.

Mary: Honestly, Tom, I have no complaints. The company and my job are everything I was led to believe. I enjoy working here. The staff are all very helpful. I like the team atmosphere, and my job is very challenging. I really feel appreciated and that I'm making a contribution. You have been very helpful and patient with me. You got me involved right from the start and listened to my opinions. You taught me a lot and I'm very grateful. All in all I'm happy being here.

Tom: Great, Mary, I was hoping that's the way you felt because from my vantage point, most of the people you worked with feel the same. But before I give you the qualitative side of the review, allow me to go through the quantitative appraisal first. As you know, the rankings go from 1 (lowest) to 5 (highest). Let's go down each category and I'll explain my reasoning for each.

Tom starts with category one (Quantity of Work) and ends with category ten (Teamwork). In each of the categories, Tom has either given Mary a 5 or a 4. Indeed, only two categories have a 4 and Tom explains these are normal areas for improvement for most employees.

Tom: As you can see, Mary, I was very happy with your performance. You have received the highest rating I have ever given any of my subordinates. Your attitude, desire, and help are truly appreciated. The other people on the Costa Rican team gave you glowing reports, and speaking with the plant manager, she felt that you helped her understand the reporting system better than anyone else. Since your performance has

been stellar, I'm delighted to give you a 10 percent increase effective immediately!

Mary: (mouth agape, and eyes wide) Tom, frankly I'm flabbergasted! I don't know what to say, but thank you very much. I hope I can continue to do as fine a job as I have this last year. Thanks once again.

After exchanging some parting remarks and some more thank-you's, Mary left Tom's office with a smile from ear to ear. She was floating on air! Not only did she feel the performance review process was uplifting, but her review was outstanding and so was her raise. She knew from other employees that the company was only giving out a 5 percent average increase. She figured that if she got that, or perhaps 6 or 7, she would be happy. But to get 10 percent . . . wow!! Imagine . . .

Sue: Hi, Mary! Lost in thought? My, you look great. Looks like you got some great news. What's up?

Susan Stevens was a recent hire, working for Tom. She had graduated from Central University also, but a year after Mary. Sue had excelled while at Central, graduating in the top 1 percent of her class. She had laudatory letters of recommendation from her professors and was into many after-school clubs and activities.

Mary: Oh, hi, Sue! Sorry, but I was just thinking about Universal and the opportunities here.

Sue: Yes, it truly is . . .

Mary: Sue, I just came from my performance review and let me tell you, the process isn't that bad. As a matter of fact I found it quite rewarding, if you get my drift. I got a wonderful review, and can't wait till next year's. What a great company!

Sue: You can say that again! I couldn't believe them hiring me right out of college at such a good salary. Between you and me, Mary, they started me at $45,000. Imagine that? Wow, was I impressed. I just couldn't believe that they would . . . Where are you going, Mary? Mary? What's that you say, "It isn't fair"? What do you mean? Mary? Mary . . .

Review Questions

1. Indicate Mary's attitudes before and after meeting Sue. If there was a change, why?
2. What do you think Mary will do now? Later?
3. What motivation theory applies best to this scenario? Explain. ■

CASE 6A
Perfect Pizzeria
....

Perfect Pizzeria in Southville, in deep southern Illinois, is the second-largest franchise of the chain in the United States. The headquarters is located in Phoenix, Arizona. Although the business is prospering, employee and managerial problems exist.

Each operation has one manager, an assistant manager, and from two to five night managers. The managers of each pizzeria work under an area supervisor. There are no systematic criteria for being a manager or becoming a manager trainee. The franchise has no formalized training period for the manager. No college education is required. The managers for whom the case observer worked during a four-year period were relatively young (ages 24 to 27) and only one had completed college. They came from the ranks of night managers or assistant managers, or both. The night managers were chosen for their ability to perform the duties of the regular employees. The assistant managers worked a two-hour shift during the luncheon period five days a week to gain knowledge about bookkeeping and management. Those becoming managers remained at that level unless they expressed interest in investing in the business.

The employees were mostly college students, with a few high school students performing the less challenging jobs. Since Perfect Pizzeria was located in an area with few job opportunities, it had a relatively easy task of filling its employee quotas. All the employees, with the exception of the manager, were employed part time and were paid the minimum wage.

The Perfect Pizzeria system is devised so that food and beverage costs and profits are computed according to a percentage. If the percentage of food unsold or damaged in any way is very low, the manager gets a bonus. If the percentage is high, the manager does not receive a bonus; rather, he or she receives only his or her normal salary.

There are many ways in which the percentage can fluctuate. Since the manager cannot be in the store 24 hours a day, some employees make up for their paychecks by helping themselves to the food. When a friend comes in to order a pizza, extra ingredients are put on the friend's pizza. Occasional nibbles by 18 to 20 employees throughout the day at the meal table also raise the percentage figure. An occasional bucket of sauce may be spilled or a pizza accidentally burned.

In the event of an employee mistake, the expense is supposed to come from the individual. Because of peer pressure, the night manager seldom writes up a bill for the erring employee. Instead, the establishment takes the loss and the error goes unnoticed until the end of the month when the inventory is taken. That's when the manager finds out that the percentage is high and that there will be no bonus.

In the present instance, the manager took retaliatory measures. Previously, each employee was entitled to a free pizza, salad, and all the soft drinks he or she could drink for every 6 hours of work. The manager raised this figure from 6 to 12 hours of work. However, the employees had received these 6-hour benefits for a long time. Therefore, they simply took advantage of the situation whenever the manager or the assistant was not in the building. Although the night manager theoretically had complete control of the operation in the evenings, he did not command the respect that the manager or assistant manager did. This was because he received the same pay as the regular employees, he could not reprimand other employees, and he was basically the same age or sometimes even younger than the other employees.

Thus, apathy grew within the pizzeria. There seemed to be a further separation between the manager and his workers, who started out as a closely knit group. The manager made no attempt to alleviate the problem, because he felt it would iron itself out. Either the employees that were dissatisfied would quit or they would be content to put up with the new regulations. As it turned out, there was a rash of employee dismissals. The manager had no problem filling the vacancies with new workers, but the loss of key personnel was costly to the business.

With the large turnover, the manager found that he had to spend more time in the building, supervising and sometimes taking the place of inexperienced workers. This was in direct violation of the franchise regulation, which stated that a manager would act as a supervisor and at no time take part in the actual food preparation. Employees were not placed under strict supervision with the manager working alongside them. The operation no longer worked smoothly because of differences between the remaining experienced workers and the manager concerning the way in which a particular function should be performed.

After a two-month period, the manager was again free to go back to his office and leave his subordinates in charge of the entire operation. During this two-month period, the percentage had returned to the previous low level, and the manager received a bonus each month. The manager felt that his problems had been resolved and that conditions would remain the same, since the new personnel had been properly trained.

It didn't take long for the new employees to become influenced by the other employees. Immediately after the manager had returned to his supervisory role, the percentage began to rise. This time the manager took a bolder step. He cut out any benefits that the employees had—no free pizzas, salads, or drinks. With the job market at an even lower ebb than usual, most employees were forced to stay. The appointment of a new area supervisor made it impossible for the manager to "work behind the counter," since the super-

visor was centrally located in Southville.

The manager tried still another approach to alleviate the rising percentage problem and maintain his bonus. He placed a notice on the bulletin board stating that if the percentage remained at a high level, a lie detector test would be given to all employees. All those found guilty of taking or purposefully wasting food or drinks would be immediately terminated. This did not have the desired effect on the employees, because they knew if they were all subjected to the test, all would be found guilty and the manager would have to dismiss all of them. This would leave him in a worse situation than ever.

Even before the following month's percentage was calculated, the manager knew it would be high. He had evidently received information from one of the night managers about the employees' feelings toward the notice. What he did not expect was that the percent-

age would reach an all-time high. That is the state of affairs at the present time.

Review Questions

1. Consider the situation where the manager changed the time period required to receive free food and drink from 6 to 12 hours of work. Try to apply each of the motivational approaches to explain what happened. Which of the approaches offers the most appropriate explanation? Why?
2. Repeat Question 1 for the situation where the manager worked beside the employees for a time and then later returned to his office.
3. Repeat Question 1 for the situation as it exists at the end of the case.
4. Establish and justify a motivational program based on one or a combination of motivation theories to deal with the situation as it exists at the end of the case. ■

CASE 6B
Hovey and Beard Company
....

Source: Abridged and adapted from George Strauss and Alex Bavelas, "Group Dynamics and Intergroup Relations" (under the title "The Hovey and Beard Case"), in *Money and Motivation*, ed. William F. Whyte (New York: Harper & Row, 1955).

The Hovey and Beard Company manufactures a variety of wooden toys, including animals, pull toys, and the like.[1] The toys were manufactured by a transformation process that began in the wood room. There, toys were cut, sanded, and partially assembled. Then the toys were dipped into shellac and sent to the painting room.

In years past, the painting had been done by hand, with each employee working with a given toy until its painting was completed. The toys were predominantly two-colored, although a few required more colors. Now in response to increased demand for the toys, the painting operation was changed so that the painters sat in a line by an endless chain of hooks. These hooks moved continuously in front of the painters and passed into a long horizontal oven. Each painter sat in a booth designed to carry away fumes and to backstop excess paint. The painters would take a toy from a nearby tray, position it in a jig inside the painting cubicle, spray on the color according to a pattern, and then hang the toy on a passing hook. The rate at which the hooks moved was calculated by the engineers so that each painter, when fully trained, could hang a painted toy on each hook before it passed beyond reach.

The painters were paid on a group bonus plan. Since the operation was new to them, they received a learning bonus that decreased by regular amounts each month. The learning bonus was scheduled to vanish in six months, by which time it was expected that they would be on their own—that is, able to meet the production standard and earn a group bonus when they exceeded it.

By the second month of the training period, trouble developed. The painters learned more slowly than had been anticipated and it began to look as though their production would stabilize far below what was planned. Many of the hooks were going by empty. The painters complained that the hooks moved too fast and that the engineer had set the rates wrong. A few painters quit and had to be replaced with new ones. This further aggravated the learning problem. The team spirit that the management had expected to develop through the group bonus was not in evidence except as an expression of what the engineers called "resistance." One painter, whom the group regarded as its leader (and the management regarded as the ring-leader), was outspoken in taking the complaints of the group to the supervisor. These complaints were that the job

was messy, the hooks moved too fast, the incentive pay was not correctly calculated, and it was too hot working so close to the drying oven.

A consultant was hired to work with the supervisor. She recommended that the painters be brought together for a general discussion of the working conditions. Although hesitant, the supervisor agreed to this plan.

The first meeting was held immediately after the shift was over at 4 P.M. It was attended by all eight painters. They voiced the same complaints again: the hooks went by too fast, the job was too dirty, and the room was hot and poorly ventilated. For some reason, it was this last item that seemed to bother them most. The supervisor promised to discuss the problems of ventilation and temperature with the engineers, and a second meeting was scheduled. In the next few days the supervisor had several talks with the engineers. They, along with the plant superintendent, felt that this was really a trumped-up complaint and that the expense of corrective measures would be prohibitively high.

The supervisor came to the second meeting with some apprehensions. The painters, however, did not seem to be much put out. Rather, they had a proposal of their own to make. They felt that if several large fans were set up to circulate the air around their feet, they would be much more comfortable. After some discussion, the supervisor agreed to pursue the idea. The supervisor and the consultant discussed the idea of fans with the superintendent. Three large propeller-type fans were purchased and installed.

The painters were jubilant. For several days the fans were moved about in various positions until they were placed to the satisfaction of the group. The painters seemed com-

pletely satisfied with the results, and the relations between them and the supervisor improved visibly.

The supervisor, after this encouraging episode, decided that further meetings might also prove profitable. The painters were asked if they would like to meet and discuss other aspects of the work situation. They were eager to do this. Another meeting was held and the discussion quickly centered on the speed of the hooks. The painters maintained that the engineer had set them at an unreasonably fast speed and that they would never be able to fill enough of them to make a bonus.

The discussion reached a turning point when the group's leader explained that it wasn't that the painters couldn't work fast enough to keep up with the hooks but that they couldn't work at that pace all day long. The supervisor explored the point. The painters were unanimous in their opinion that they could keep up with the belt for short periods if they wanted to. But they didn't want to because if they showed they could do this for short periods then they would be expected to do it all day long. The meeting ended with an unprecedented request by the painters: "Let us adjust the speed of the belt faster or slower depending on how we feel." The supervisor agreed to discuss this with the superintendent and the engineers.

The engineers reacted negatively to the suggestion. However, after several meetings it was granted that there was some latitude within which variations in the speed of the hooks would not affect the finished product. After considerable argument with the engineers, it was agreed to try out the painters' idea.

With misgivings, the supervisor had a control with a dial marked "low, medium, fast" installed at the booth of the group leader. The speed of the belt could now be adjusted anywhere between the lower and upper limits that the engineers had set.

The painters were delighted and spent many lunch hours deciding how the speed of the belt should be varied from hour to hour throughout the day. Within a week the pattern had settled down to one in which the first half hour of the shift was run on a medium speed (a dial setting slightly above the point marked "medium"). The next two and a half hours were run at high speed, and the half hour before lunch and the half hour after lunch were run at low speed. The rest of the afternoon was run at high speed with the exception of the last 45 minutes of the shift, which was run at medium.

The constant speed at which the engineers had originally set the belt was actually slightly below the "medium" mark on the control dial; the average speed at which the painters were running the belt was on the high side of the dial. Few, if any, empty hooks entered the oven, and inspection showed no increase of rejects from the paint room.

Production increased, and within three weeks (some two months before the scheduled ending of the learning bonus) the painters were operating at 30 to 50 percent above the level that had been expected under the original arrangement. Naturally, their earnings were correspondingly higher than anticipated. They were collecting their base pay, earning a considerable piece-rate bonus, and still benefiting from the learning bonus. They were earning more now than many skilled workers in other parts of the plant.

Management was besieged by demands that the inequity between the earnings of the painters and those of other workers in the plant be taken care of. With growing irritation between the superintendent and the supervisor, the engineers and supervisor, and the superintendent and engineers, the situation came to a head when the superintendent revoked the learning bonus and returned the painting operation to its original status: the hooks moved again at their constant, time-studied, designated speed. Production dropped again and within a month all but two of the eight painters had quit. The supervisor stayed on for several months, but, feeling aggrieved, left for another job.

1. How does the painters' job score on the core job characteristics before and after the changes were made? How can the positive impact of the job redesign be explained?
2. Was the learning bonus handled properly in this case? How can its motivational impact be explained? What alternative approaches could have been taken with similar motivational results?
3. How do you explain the situation described in the last paragraph of the case? How could this outcome have been avoided by appropriate managerial actions? ■

CASE 7
The Forgotten Group Member

Developed by Franklin Ramsoomair, Wilfred Laurier University

The Organizational Behavior course for the semester appeared to promise the opportunity to learn, enjoy, and practice some of the theories and principles in the textbook and class discussions. Christine Spencer was a devoted, hard-working student who had been maintaining an A–average to date. Although the skills and knowledge she had acquired through her courses were important, she was also very concerned about her grades. She felt that grades were paramount in giving her a competitive edge when looking for a job and, as a third-year student, she realized that she'd soon be doing just that.

Sunday afternoon. Two o'clock. Christine was working on an accounting assignment but didn't seem to be able to concentrate. Her courses were working out very well this semester, all but the OB. Much of the mark in that course was to be based on the quality of groupwork, and so she felt somewhat out of control. She recollected the events of the past five weeks. Professor Sandra Thiel had divided the class into groups of five people and had given them a major group assignment worth 30 percent of the final grade. The task was to analyze a seven-page case and to come up with a written analysis. In addition, Sandra had asked the groups to present the case in class, with the idea that the rest of the class members would be "members of the board of directors of the company" who would be listening to how the manager and her team dealt with the problem at hand.

Christine was elected "Team Coordinator" at the first group meeting. The other members of the group were Diane, Janet, Steve, and Mike. Diane was quiet and never volunteered suggestions, but when directly asked, she would come up with high-quality ideas. Mike was the clown. Christine remembered that she had suggested that the group should get together before every class to discuss the day's case. Mike had balked, saying "No way!! This is an 8:30 class, and I barely make it on time anyway! Besides, I'll miss my *Happy Harry* show on television!" The group couldn't help but laugh at his indignation. Steve was the businesslike individual, always wanting to ensure that group meetings were guided by an agenda and noting the tangible results achieved or not achieved at the end of every meeting. Janet was the reliable one who would always have more for the group than was expected of her. Christine saw herself as meticulous and organized and as a person who tried to give her best in whatever she did.

It was now week 5 into the semester, and Christine was deep in thought about the OB assignment. She had called everyone to arrange a meeting for a time that would suit them all, but she seemed to be running into a roadblock. Mike couldn't make it, saying that he was working that night as a member of the campus security force. In fact, he seemed to miss most meetings and would send in brief notes to Christine, which she was supposed to discuss for him at the group meetings. She wondered how to deal with this. She also remembered the incident last week. Just before class started, Diane, Janet, Steve, and she were joking with one another before class. They were laughing and enjoying themselves before Sandra came in. No one noticed that Mike had

slipped in very quietly and had unobtrusively taken his seat.

She recalled the cafeteria incident. Two weeks ago, she had gone to the cafeteria to grab something to eat. She had rushed to her accounting class and had skipped breakfast. When she got her club sandwich and headed to the tables, she saw her OB group and joined them. The discussion was light and enjoyable as it always was when they met informally. Mike had come in. He'd approached their table. "You guys didn't say you were having a group meeting," he blurted. Christine was taken aback.

We just happened to run into each other. Why not join us?"

"Mike looked at them, with a noncommittal glance. "Yeah . . . right," he muttered, and walked away.

Sandra Thiel had frequently told them that if there were problems in the group, the members should make an effort to deal with them first. If the problems could not be resolved, she had said that they should come to her. Mike seemed so distant, despite the apparent camaraderie of the first meeting.

An hour had passed, bringing the time to 3 P.M., and Christine found herself biting the tip of her pencil. The written case analysis was due next week. All the others had

done their designated sections, but Mike had just handed in some rough handwritten notes. He had called Christine the week before, telling her that in addition to his course and his job, he was having problems with his girlfriend. Christine empathized with him. Yet, this was a group project! Besides, the final mark would be peer evaluated. This meant that whatever mark Sandra gave them could be lowered or raised, depending on the group's opinion about the value of the contribution of each member. She was definitely worried. She knew that Mike had creative ideas that could help to raise the overall mark. She was also concerned for him. As she listened to the music in the background, she wondered what she should do.

Review Questions

1. How could an understanding of the stages of group development assist Christine in leadership situations such as this one?
2. What should Christine understand about individual membership in groups in order to build group processes that are supportive of her work group's performance?
3. Is Christine an effective group leader in this case? Why or why not? ∎

CASE 8
NASCAR'S Racing Teams UPDATE
• •

Developed by David S. Chappell, Ohio University, modified by Hal Babson, Columbus State Community College and John R. Schermerhorn, Jr., Ohio University

The most popular team sport, based on total spectator audience, is not basketball, baseball, football, or even soccer: it is stock car racing. The largest stock car racing group in the world is the National Association for Stock Car Auto Racing (NASCAR), which recently celebrated its 60th year. The NASCAR Nextel Cup Series kicks off in February and runs through November. Along the way it serves as a marketing powerhouse.

Not only are over 12 million fans attracted to NASCAR's races, but another 250 million watch races on television. Drivers are involved in cable network shows as well as syndicated radio shows each week. NASCAR's official Web site, at www.nascar.com, consistently ranks among the top league sites on the Internet and generates well over 1 billion page views year-after-year.[1] Companies such as the Coca-Cola Co. take advantage of NASCAR's popularity with merchandise, collectibles, apparel, accessories, toys, and other marketing tie-ins. The race cars themselves have been described by some as "200 mile-per-hour billboards."

Jeff Gordon is one of NASCAR's most successful and well-known drivers; he's been a sensation ever since he started racing go-carts and quarter-midget cars at the age of 5. But as the driver of a successful race car he represents just the most visible part of an incredibly complex racing organization—a high-performance system whose ultimate contribution takes place on race day. For several years a team known as the Rainbow Warriors handled Gordon's car. Their leader was crew chief Ray Evernham, recognized by many as one of the very best in the business. Posted on the wall of his workshop was this sign:

Success is a ruthless competitor, for it flatters and nourishes our weaknesses and lulls us into complacency.

While Gordon represented the star attraction, many believed that it was Evernham who pulled the whole act together. He was responsible for a group of over 120 technicians and mechanics with an annual budget estimated between $10 and $12 million! And he had strong opinions as to what it takes to consistently finish

first: painstaking preparation, egoless teamwork, and thoroughly original strategizing—principles that apply to any high-performance organization.

Evernham believed that teams needed to experiment with new methods and processes. When he assembled his Rainbow Warriors pit crew, none of them had Nextel/Winston Cup experience and none worked on the car in any other capacity. With the use of a pit crew coach, the Rainbow Warriors provide Gordon with an approximately one-second advantage with each pit stop, which, at a speed of 200 miles per hour, equates to 300 feet of race track. "When you coach and support a superstar like Jeff Gordon, you give him the best equipment possible, you give him the information he needs, and then you get out of the way. But racing is a team sport. Everyone who races pretty much has the same car and the same equipment. What sets us apart is our people. I like to talk about our "team IQ"—because none of us is as smart as all of us.

Said Evernham, "I think a lot about people, management, and psychology: Specifically, how can I motivate my guys and make them gel as a team? I surround them with ideas about teamwork. I read every leadership book I can get my hands on. One thing that I took from my reading is the idea of a 'circle of strength.' When the Rainbow Warriors meet, we always put our chairs in a circle. That's a way of saying that we're stronger as a team than we are on our own."

Evernham backed up this belief in team by emphasizing team performance over individual performance. When the car won a race, everyone shared in the prize money. In addition, when Evernham earned money through personal-service activities such as speaking tours and

autograph signings, he shared what he earned with the team. "I wouldn't be in a position to earn that income if it weren't for the team. Everyone should feel as if his signature is on the finished product."

Steve Letarte had some pretty big shoes to fill when he became Jeff Gordon's crew chief. After a series of ups and downs including a brutal 2008 season, Gordon, Letarte, and their #24 crew appear reinvigorated and have positioned themselves as one of NASCAR's leaders.

It's not only the fans who have noticed what goes on in the NASCAR pit crews and racing teams. The next time you fly on United Airlines check out the ground crews. You might notice some similarities with the teams handling pit stops for NASCAR racers. In fact, there's a good chance the members of the ramp crews have been through what has been called "Pit Crew U."[2] United is among many organizations that are sending employees to Pit Instruction and Training in Mooresville, North Carolina. At the same facility where real racing crews train, United's ramp workers learn to work under pressure while meeting the goals of teamwork, safety, and job preparedness. The objective is to replace work practices that may sometimes result in aircraft delays and service inadequacies—things that a NASCAR team must avoid in order to stay competitive in races. "It's stuff you can carry back like cleaning up your work area, being set up for that airplane to arrive like the pit crews are ready for that car to get here," said Marc Abbatacola of Chicago's O'Hare International Airport.[3]

Joe Konkel agreed: "The PIT training supports all the major principles of Georgia-Pacific . . . the need for everyone to have the necessary skill, commitment, ownership, and teamwork to advance the vision. Safety, compliance, and efficiency work together and become a result of this focus. This fosters pride, ownership, and a clear understanding of each person's individual advantage as part of the team."[4]

High-performance teams may be inherited, but must be maintained. They do not happen by chance; rather, they are the result of good recruiting and meticulous attention to learning every detail of the job.

Review Questions

1. In what ways do Evernham's leadership tactics prove consistent with the characteristics and ideas on high performance teams and teamwork advanced in the text?

2. How might the 2008 season have shaped Steve Letarte and his crew, their cohesiveness, and team norms?

3. What can someone who takes over a highly successful team from a leader like Evernham do to maintain and even improve team success in the future?

4. Research question: Pit crews are often in the news. See what you can find out about pit crew performance. Ask: What distinguishes the "high performance" pit crews from the "also rans?" ■

CASE 9
Decisions, Decisions

Developed by John R. Schermerhorn, Jr.

The Case of the Wedding Ring

Setting—A woman is preparing for a job interview.

Dilemma—She wants the job desperately and is worried that her marital status might adversely affect the interview.

Decision—Should she or should she not wear her diamond engagement ring?

Considerations—When queried for a column in *The Wall Street Journal*, some women claimed that they would try to hide their marital status during a job interview.[1] One says: "Although I will never remove my wedding band, I don't want anyone to look at my engagement ring and think, she doesn't need this job, what is she doing working?" Even the writer remembers that she considered removing her engagement ring some years back when applying for a job. "I had no idea about the office culture," she said. "I didn't want anyone making assumptions, however unreasonable, about my commitment to work."

Wellness or Invasive Coercion?

Setting—Scotts Miracle-Gro Company, Marysville, Ohio.

Dilemma—Corporate executives are concerned about rising health-care costs. CEO Jim Hagedorn backs an aggressive wellness program and anti-smoking campaign to improve health of employees and reduce health-care costs for the firm. Scott employees are asked to take extensive health-risk assessments; failure to do so increases their health insurance premiums by $40 a month. Employees found to have "moderate to high" health risks are assigned health coaches and given action plans; failure to comply adds another $67 per month. In states where the practice is legal, the firm will not hire a smoker and tests new employees for nicotine use. In response to complaints that the policy is intrusive, Hagedorn says: "If people understand the facts and still choose to smoke, it's suicidal. And we can't encourage suicidal behavior."

Decision—Is Hagedorn doing the right thing by leading Scott's human resource policies in this direction?

Considerations—Joe Pellegrini's life was probably saved by his employer. After urging from a Scott's health coach he saw his doctor about weight and cholesterol concerns. This led to a visit with a heart specialist who inserted two stents, correcting a 95% blockage. Scott Rodrigues' life was changed by his employer; he is suing Scott's for wrongful dismissal. A smoker, he claims that he was fired after failing a drug test for nicotine even though he wasn't informed about the test and had been told the company would help him stop smoking. CEO Hagedorn says: "This is an area where CEOs are afraid to go. A lot of people are watching to see how badly we get sued."[2]

Super Sales Woman Won't Ask for Raise

Setting—A woman is described as a "productive star" and "super-successful" member of an 18 person sales force.[3]

Dilemma—She finds out that both she and the other woman

salesperson are being paid 20% less than the men. Her sister wants her to talk with her boss and ask for more pay. She says: "No, I'm satisfied with my present pay and I don't want to 'rock the boat'." The sister can't understand how and why she puts up with this situation, allowing herself to be paid less than a man for at least equal and quite possibly better performance.

Considerations—In the past ten years women have lost ground relative to men when it comes to pay; whereas they previously earned 75.7 cents for each dollar earned by a man, a decade later they are earning 74.7 cents. Some claim that one explanation for the wage gap and its growing size is that women tolerate the situation and allow it to continue, rather than confronting the gap in their personal circumstances and trying to change it.

Wal-Mart Goes Public with Annual Bonuses

Setting—Wal-Mart executives released to the public information on the annual bonuses paid to store employees.[4]

Dilemma—Wal-Mart's founder, Sam Walton, started the bonus program in 1986 as a way of linking employees with the firm's financial success. Historically Wal-Mart did not divulge the annual bonuses. Recently the firm has received considerable negative publicity regarding the wages paid to employees and the benefits they are eligible to receive. But a spokesperson indicated that going public with the bonuses was not a response to such criticism. A former human resource executive at the firm says: "This is just an example of how they really treat their people well and they're putting it out there to let the facts speak for themselves."

Considerations—Some 813,759 employees shared a bonus pool of $529.8 million. A current employee said she received "substantially over $1,000," and that this was higher than the prior year's bonus. Wal-Mart is planning to give the bonuses on a quarterly basis to link them more frequently with performance. One of the firm's critics, WakeUpWalMart.com, was critical, charging: "Wal-Mart values are so misplaced that it gives executives hundreds of millions in bonuses and the mere crumbs to associates."

Review Questions

1. Use the decision-making model presented in the chapter to map the decisions being made in these situations. Identify how, where, and why different decisions might be made.
2. What are the issues involved in these situations? How are they best addressed by the decision makers?
3. Find other decision-making examples that raise similar issues and quandaries. Share them with classmates and analyze the possible decisions. ∎

CASE 10
The Case of the Missing Raise

Prepared by John R. Schermerhorn, Jr., Ohio University

It was late February, and Marsha Lloyd had just completed an important long-distance telephone call with Professor Fred Massie, head of the Department of Management at Central University. During the conversation Marsha accepted an offer to move from her present position at Private University, located in the East, to Central in the Midwest as an Assistant Professor. Marsha and her husband John then shared the following thoughts.

Marsha: "Well, it's final."
John: "It's been a difficult decision, but I know it will work out for the best."
Marsha: "Yes, however, we are leaving many things we like here."
John: "I know, but remember, Professor Massie is someone you respect a great deal and he is offering you a challenge to come and introduce new courses at Central. Besides, he will surely be a pleasure to work for."
Marsha: "John we're young, eager and a little adventurous. There's no reason we shouldn't go."
John: "We're going dear."

Marsha Lloyd began the fall semester eagerly. The points discussed in her earlier conversations with Fred were now real challenges, and she was teaching new undergraduate and graduate courses in Central's curriculum. Overall, the transition to Central had been pleasant. The nine faculty members were warm in welcoming her, and Marsha felt it would be good working with them. She also felt comfortable with the performance standards that appeared to exist in the department. Although it was certainly not a "publish or perish" situation, Fred had indicated during the recruiting process that research and publications would be given increasing weight along with teaching and service in future departmental decisions. This was consistent with Marsha's personal belief that a professor should live up to each of these responsibilities. Although there was some conflict in evidence among the faculty over what weighting and standards should apply to these performance areas, she sensed some consensus that the multiple responsibilities should be respected.

It was April, and spring vacation time. Marsha was sitting at home reflecting upon her experiences to date at Central. She was pleased. Both she and John had adjusted very well to Midwestern life. Although there were things they both missed from their prior location, she was in an interesting new job and they found the rural environment of Central very satisfying. Marsha had also received positive student feedback on her fall semester courses, had presented two papers at a recent professional meeting, and had just been informed that two of her papers would be published by a journal. This was a good record and she felt satisfied. She had been working hard and it was paying off.

The spring semester had ended and Marsha was preoccupied. It was time, she thought, for an end-of-the-year performance review by Fred Massie. This anticipation had been stimulated, in part, by a recent meeting of the College faculty in which the Dean indicated that a 7% pay raise pool was now available for the coming year. He was encouraging department chairpersons to distribute this money differentially based on performance merit. Marsha had listened closely to the Dean and liked what she heard. She felt this meant that Central was really trying

to establish a performance-oriented reward system. Such a system was consistent with her personal philosophy and, indeed, she taught such reasoning in her courses.

Throughout May, Marsha kept expecting to have a conversation with Fred Massie on these topics. One day, the following memo appeared in her faculty mailbox.

MEMORANDUM
TO: Fellow Faculty
FROM: Fred
RE: Raises for Next Year

The Dean has been most open about the finances of the College as evidenced by his detail and candor regarding the budget at the last faculty meeting. Consistent with that philosophy I want to provide a perspective on raises and clarify a point or two.

The actual dollars available to our department exclusive of the chairman total 7.03%. In allocating those funds I have attempted to reward people on the basis of their contribution to the life of the Department and the University, as well as professional growth and development. In addition, it was essential this year to adjust a couple of inequities which had developed over a period of time. The distribution of increments was the following:

| 5% or less | 3 | 7 + %–9% | 3 |
| 5 + %–7% | 2 | More than 9% | 2 |

Marsha read the memo with mixed emotions. Initially, she was upset that Fred had obviously made the pay raise decisions without having spoken first with her about her performance. Still, she felt good because she was sure to be one of those receiving a 9 + % increase. "Now," she mused to herself, "it will be good to sit down with Fred and discuss not only this past year's efforts, but my plans for next year's as well."

Marsha was disappointed when Fred did not contact her for such a

discussion. Furthermore, she found herself frequently involved in informal conversations with other faculty members who were speculating over who received the various pay increments.

One day Carla Block, a faculty colleague, came into Marsha's office and said she had asked Fred about her raise. She received a 7 + % increase, and also learned that the two 9 + % increases had been given to senior faculty members. Marsha was incredulous. "It can't be," she thought, "I was a top performer this past year. My teaching and publications records are strong, and I feel I've been a positive force in the department." She felt Carla could be mistaken and waited to talk the matter out with Fred.

A few days later another colleague reported to Marsha the results of a similar conversation with Fred. This time Marsha exploded internally. She felt she deserved just reward.

The next day Marsha received a computerized notice on her pay increment from the Accounting Office. Her raise was 7.2%. That night, after airing her feelings with John, Marsha telephoned Fred at home and arranged to meet with him the next day.

Fred Massie knocked on the door to Marsha's office and entered. The greetings were cordial. Marsha began the conversation. "Fred, we've always been frank with one another and now I'm concerned about my raise," she said. "I thought I had a good year, but I understand that I've received just an average raise." Fred Massie was a person who talked openly, and Marsha could trust him. He responded to Marsha in this way.

Yes, Marsha, you are a top performer. I feel you have made great contributions to the Department. The two 9 + % raises went to correct "inequities" that had built up over a period of time for two senior people. I felt that since the money was available this year that I had a responsibility to make the adjustments. If we don't consider them, you received one of the three top raises, and I consider any percentage differences between these three very superficial. I suppose I could have been more discriminating at the lower end of the distribution, but I can't give zero increments. I know you had a good year. It's what I expected when I hired you. You haven't let me down. From your perspective I know you feel you earned an "A," and I agree. I gave you a "B +". I hope you understand why.

Marsha sympathized with Fred's logic and felt good having spoken with him. Although she wasn't happy, she understood Fred's position. Her final comment to Fred was this. "You know, it's not the absolute dollar value of the raise that hurts. It's the sense of letdown. Recently, for example, I turned down an extensive consulting job that would have paid far more than the missing raise. I did so because I felt it would require too many days away from the office. I'm not sure my colleagues would make that choice."

In the course of a casual summer conversation, Carla mentioned to Marsha that she heard two of the faculty who had received 4 + % raises had complained to Fred and the Dean. After lodging the complaints they had received additional salary increments. "Oh great," Marsha responded to herself, "I thought I had put this thing to rest."

About three weeks later, Marsha, Fred, Carla, and another colleague were in a meeting with the Dean. Although the meeting was on a separate matter, something was said which implied that Carla had also received an additional pay increment. Marsha confronted the Dean and learned that this was the case. Carla had protested to Fred and the

Dean, and they raised her pay on the justification that an historical salary inequity had been overlooked. Fred was visibly uncomfortable as a discussion ensued on how salary increments should be awarded and what had transpired in the department in this respect.

Fred eventually excused himself to attend another meeting. Marsha and the others continued to discuss the matter with the Dean and the conversation became increasingly heated. Finally, they each rose to terminate the meeting and Marsha felt compelled to say one more thing. "It's not that I'm not making enough money," she said to the Dean, "but I just don't feel I received my fair share, especially in terms of your own stated policy of rewarding faculty on the basis of performance merit."

With that remark, Marsha left the meeting. As she walked down the hall to her office, she said to herself, "Next year there will be no turning down consulting jobs because of a misguided sense of departmental responsibility."

Review Questions

1. What is Marsha's conflict management style and how has it influenced events in this case? What were Marsha's goals and what conflict management style would have worked best in helping her achieve them?
2. What is Fred's conflict management style and how has it influenced events in this case?
3. Once Marsha found out what her raise was to be, how could she have used the notion and elements of distributive negotiation to create a situation where Fred would make a raise adjustment that was favorable and motivating for her? ■

CASE 11
The Poorly Informed Walrus
....

Developed by Barbara McCain, Oklahoma City University

"How's it going down there?" barked the big walrus from his perch on the highest rock near the shore. He waited for the good word.

Down below the smaller walruses conferred hastily among themselves. Things weren't going well at all, but none of them wanted to break the news to the Old Man. He was the biggest and wisest walrus in the herd, and he knew his business, but he had such a terrible temper that every walrus in the herd was terrified of his ferocious bark.

"What will we tell him?" whispered Basil, the second-ranking walrus. He well remembers how the

Old Man had raved and ranted at him the last time the herd had caught less than its quota of herring, and he had no desire to go through that experience again. Nevertheless, the walrus noticed for several weeks that the water level in the nearby Arctic bay had been falling constantly, and it had become necessary to travel much farther to catch the dwindling supply of herring. Someone should tell the Old Man; he would probably know what to do. But who? and how?

Finally Basil spoke up: "Things are going pretty well, Chief," he said. The thought of the receding water line made his heart grow heavy, but he went on: "As a matter of fact, the beach seems to be getting larger."

The Old Man grunted. "Fine, fine," he said. "That will give us a bit more elbow room." He closed his eyes and continued basking in the sun.

The next day brought more trouble. A new herd of walruses moved in down the beach and, with the supply of herring dwindling, this invasion could be dangerous. No one wanted to tell the Old Man, though only he could take the steps necessary to meet this new competition.

Reluctantly, Basil approached the big walrus, who was still sunning himself on the large rock. After some smalltalk, he said, "Oh, by the way, Chief, a new herd of walruses seems to have moved into our territory." The Old Man's eyes snapped open, and he filled his great lungs in preparation for a mighty bellow. But Basil added quickly, "Of course, we don't anticipate any trouble. They don't look like herring eaters to me. More likely interested in minnows. And as you know, we don't bother with minnows ourselves."

The Old Man let out the air with a long sigh. "Good, good," he said. "No point in our getting excited over nothing then, is there?"

Things didn't get any better in the weeks that followed. One day, peering down from the large rock, the Old Man noticed that part of the herd seemed to be missing. Summoning Basil, he grunted peevishly. "What's going on, Basil? Where is everyone?" Poor Basil didn't have the courage to tell the Old Man that many of the younger walruses were leaving every day to join the new herd. Clearing his throat nervously, he said, "Well

Chief, we've been tightening up things a bit. You know, getting rid of some of the dead wood. After all, a herd is only as good as the walruses in it."

"Run a tight ship, I always say," the Old Man grunted. "Glad to hear that all is going so well."

Before long, everyone but Basil had left to join the new herd, and Basil realized that the time had come to tell the Old Man the facts. Terrified but determined, he flopped up to the large rock. "Chief," he said, "I have bad news. The rest of the herd has left you." The old walrus was so astonished that he couldn't even work up a good bellow. "Left

me?" he cried. "All of them? But why? How could this happen?"

Basil didn't have the heart to tell him, so he merely shrugged helplessly.

"I can't understand it," the old walrus said. "And just when everything was going so well."

Review Questions

1. What barriers to communication are evident in this fable?
2. What communication "lessons" does this fable offer to those who are serious about careers in the new workplace? ■

CASE 12
Faculty Empowerment and the Changing University Environment

Source: Developed by John Bowen, Columbus State Community College

In a typical university, the instructor enjoys a very high level of empowerment and opportunity for creativity in achieving course objectives. Within general limitations of the course description, instructors tend to have a good deal of flexibility in selecting course content, designing instructional activities, and selecting assignments. This allows them to tailor courses in varying ways to do what may seem to work best in a given situation. For example, an instructor teaching a course four times a year may design one section to cover course content in a somewhat different manner or with a slightly different focus due to the unique background and interests of the students. Since not all students learn or can be effectively evaluated in exactly the same way, an instructor normally is able to respond to varying situations by the way in which the text is used, the specific activities assigned, and choice of tests and other means of measuring student performance.

One of the settings in which instructor empowerment has been especially functional is the presence of adult learners (those working full-time and attending school part-time, or returning to school after substantial work experience).

Often adult learners have quite different needs than the more traditional student. Course variations that include unique learning opportunities that tap their work experiences and that accommodate the nature of their work schedules are often necessary. Flexibility and responsiveness by the instructor is also important. A major news event may create intense student interest in a course-related topic, but it might not occur at the specific point in the course in which the topic was scheduled to be covered, and the level of interest might require more time being allocated to the discussion than was originally planned. Assignment schedules and requirements are also a challenge when dealing with adult learners. Not all have work schedules such that they have the same amount of work week after week, but instead they may have variations in workloads that may include substantial travel commitments.

Where instructors have a good deal of empowerment, quality of education is maintained through instructor selection and development and through oversight by department heads. The supervision often includes reviews of any changes in course plans, learning activities, exams, assignments, and syllabus. This is facilitated by reviews of student feedback and through personal observation of the instructor conducting a class.

Regardless of the extent to which such quality control measures may or may not work, competition among colleges and universities is beginning to have an impact on faculty empowerment. In the past, schools tended to focus on a given geographic area, certain fields of study, or a particular class of students. Thus, competitive pressures were often relatively minimal. Today competition in the education market is not just local or even national, but is becoming increasingly global. Accelerating the trend is the use of online classes that can enable students in distant locations to take classes over the Internet.

The need to compete for revenues and to contain costs has also produced pressure for universities to operate more like businesses. This has, in some cases, resulted in more standardization of courses and instructional methods, consequently reducing the traditional empowerment of instructors. As an example of what is being done, consider two universities: Upstate University and Downstate University. Upstate and Downstate share two commonalities: (1) each sees their primary target student market as the working adult and (2) each is increasing the use of standardization in instructional methods.

Upstate University focuses on the working adult: 82 percent of its 8,200 students are employed and the average age is 32. It still holds traditional face-to-face classes on its main campus and in nearby communities, but its programs now include standardized online courses (including a program for military personnel) in both masters and undergraduate degree programs. It has developed a "Balanced Learning Format" approach involving standardized quality, content, and delivery for its courses—both online and traditional courses.

Downstate University was started to provide a means through which poor but qualified students could work and pay for their education. The school offers both undergraduate and masters degree programs. Enrollment at the main campus is now approximately 2,000 students but it has over 19,000 other students attending around the nation and around the world. Those students attend classes online and at 37 other campuses in 20 states—most of those students are working adults.

Upstate has standardized its courses so that certain specific activities and points are to be covered in each class session. The instructor does not set the assignments (problems, text questions, etc.). Rather, the

student taking the course can go online and see what is required for both the instructor and student. The amount of time to be devoted to particular discussion or activities must follow a given script for each class session or at least be within guidelines in which some flexibility may exist. As a result, all instructors covering a given class session will be following the same script—often saying and doing much the same thing. This approach largely limits creativity to the person or persons involved in developing and modifying the course. Any ideas to change the course would normally have to be approved by that developer. Changes are infrequent, however, perhaps because some instructors might be unwilling to contact the course developer and take the time to argue the need for a change.

Downstate is modifying its courses in ways that are similar to the approach taken at Upstate, although not identical. Standardized test banks are being used. Objective test questions are to be randomly selected from within the test banks and scored by computer, thus reducing subjective evaluation (and any possible favoritism) by individual instructors.

At both Upstate and Downstate, online instruction is playing an increasingly important role. The goal is to assure that all online interaction between students and instructors is proper and consistent with school policies. Online classes are conducted so that any communication must be either at the class Web site or through use of the school's own e-mail system. Thus the institution can monitor not only what goes on in the "electronic classroom" (the Web site for the course) but also in what might be comparable to the private chats which traditional students in the past had in the instructor's office. Furthermore, to the extent that a course is online and that all activity is completed using either the course Web site or the school's e-mail system, protection is provided to both students and instructors. There is always proof available that an assignment was or was not received on time; student complaints or grade challenges are much more verifiable.

From the perspective of administration at both universities, the approach to more standardization ensures uniformity of quality in instructional delivery across settings, students, and instructors. It also provides a benefit in regards to the recruitment of adjunct (part-time) instructors that are increasingly used. Since not all such instructors have the same level of creativity and experience, having a standardized course and common script for all to follow is presumed to help maintain quality of instruction across instructors and course sections. Many instructors—especially those who have taught in the past under empowered conditions, find the new developments at both Upstate and Downstate frustrating. They believe that their prerogatives and talents as professionals are not being fully respected.

Review Questions

1. Would you rather be a student in a class that has been standardized or one in which the instructor has a high degree of empowerment? Why?
2. What issues involving power and politics are involved in moving from a setting that encouraged faculty empowerment to one that required much more standardization of instruction? How would you deal with those issues if you were involved in university administration?
3. In the specific case of adult learners and use of multiple instructors, is it possible to reach a compromise between standardization and empowerment so that the benefits of standardization can be obtained while still allowing for the flexibility that comes with empowerment? How can this apply to courses taught online versus face-to-face? ◼

CASE 13
The New Vice President
....

[*Note:* Please read only those parts identified by your instructor. Do not read ahead.]

Part A

When the new president at Mid-West U took over, it was only a short time before the incumbent vice president announced his resignation. Unfortunately, there was no one waiting in the wings, and a hiring freeze prevented a national search from commencing.

Many faculty leaders and former administrators suggested that the president appoint Jennifer Treeholm, the Associate Vice President for Academic Affairs, as interim. She was an extremely popular person on campus and had 10 years of experience in the role of associate vice president. She knew everyone and everything about the campus. Jennifer, they assured him, was the natural choice. Besides, Jennifer *deserved* the job. Her devotion to the school was unparalleled, and her energy knew no bounds. The new president, acting on advice from many campus leaders, appointed Jennifer interim vice president for a term of up to three years. He also agreed that she could be a candidate for the permanent position when the hiring freeze was lifted.

Jennifer and her friends were ecstatic. It was high time more women moved into important positions on campus. They went out for dinner to their every-Friday-night watering hole to celebrate and reflect on Jennifer's career.

Except for a brief stint outside of academe, Jennifer's entire career had been at Mid-West U. She started out teaching Introductory History, then, realizing she wanted to get on the tenure track, went back to school and earned her Ph.D. at Metropolitan U while continuing to teach at Mid-West. Upon completion of her degree, she was appointed as an assistant professor and eventually earned the rank of associate based on her popularity and excellent teaching.

Not only was Jennifer well liked, but she devoted her entire life, it seemed, to Mid-West, helping to form the first union, getting grants, writing skits for the faculty club's annual follies, and going out of her way to befriend everyone who needed support.

Eventually, Jennifer was elected president of the Faculty Senate. After serving for two years, she was offered the position of associate vice president. During her 10 years as associate vice president, she handled most of the academic complaints, oversaw several committees, wrote almost all of the letters and reports

Source: Adapted from Donald D. Bowen et al., *Experiences in Management and Organizational Behavior.* 4th ed. (New York: Wiley, 1997).

for the vice president, and was even known to run personal errands for the president. People just knew they could count on Jennifer.

Review Questions

1. At this point, what are your predictions about Jennifer as the interim vice president?
2. What do you predict will be her management/leadership style?
3. What are her strengths? Her weaknesses? What is the basis for your assessment?

After you have discussed Part A, please read Part B.

Part B

Jennifer's appointment as interim vice president was met with great enthusiasm. Finally the school was getting someone who was "one of their own," a person who understood the culture, knew the faculty, and could get things done.

It was not long before the campus realized that things were not moving and that Jennifer, despite her long-standing popularity, had difficulty making tough decisions. Her desire to please people and to try to take care of everyone made it difficult for her to choose opposing alternatives. (To make matters worse, she had trouble planning, organizing, and managing her time.)

What was really a problem was that she did not understand her role as the number-two person at the top of the organization. The president expected her to support him and his decisions without question. Over time the president also expected her to implement some of his decisions—to do his dirty work. This became particularly problematic when it involved firing people or saying "no" to old faculty cronies. Jennifer also found herself uncomfortable with the other members of the president's senior staff.

Although she was not the only woman (the general counsel, a very bright, analytical woman was part of the group), Jennifer found the behavior and decision-making style to be different from what she was used to.

Most of the men took their lead from the president and discussed very little in the meetings. Instead, they would try to influence decisions privately. Often a decision arrived in a meeting as a "fait accompli." Jennifer felt excluded and wondered why, as vice president, she felt so powerless.

In time, she and the president spent less and less time together talking and discussing how to move the campus along. Although her relations with the men on the senior staff were cordial, she talked mostly to her female friends.

Jennifer's friends, especially her close-knit group of longtime female colleagues, all assured her that it was because she was "interim." "Just stay out of trouble," they told her. Of course this just added to her hesitancy when it came to making tough choices.

As the president's own image on campus shifted after his "honeymoon year," Jennifer decided to listen to her friends rather than follow the president's lead. After all, her reputation on campus was at stake.

Review Questions

1. What is the major problem facing Jennifer?
2. What would you do if you were in her position?
3. Would a man have the same experience as Jennifer?
4. Are any of your predictions about her management style holding up?

Part C

When the hiring freeze was lifted and Jennifer's position was able to be filled, the president insisted on a national search. Jennifer and her friends felt this was silly, given that she was going into her third year in the job. Nonetheless, she entered the search process.

After a year-long search, the Search Committee met with the president. The external candidates were not acceptable to the campus. Jennifer, they recommended, should only be appointed on a permanent basis if she agreed to change her management style.

The president mulled over his dilemma, then decided to give Jennifer the benefit of the doubt and the opportunity. He appointed her permanent provost, while making the following private agreement with her.

1. She would organize her office and staff and begin delegating more work to others.
2. She would "play" her number-two position, backing the president and echoing his position on the university's vision statement.
3. She would provide greater direction for the Deans who report to her.

Jennifer agreed to take the position. She was now the university's first female vice president and presided over a council of 11 deans, three of whom were her best female friends. Once again, they sought out their every-Friday-night watering hole for an evening of dinner and celebration.

Review Questions

1. If you were Jennifer, would you have accepted the job?
2. What would you do as the new, permanent, vice president?
3. Will Jennifer change her management style? If so, in what ways?
4. What are your predictions for the future?

Part D

Although people had predicted that things would be better once Jennifer

• •

was permanently in the job, things in fact became more problematic. People now expected Jennifer to be able to take decisive action. She did not feel she could.

Every time an issue came up, she would spend weeks, sometimes months, trying to get a sense of the campus. Nothing moved once it hit her office. After a while, people began referring to the vice president's office as "the black hole" where things just went in and disappeared.

Her immediate staff were concerned and frustrated. Not only did she not delegate effectively, but her desire to make things better led her to try to do more and more herself.

The vice president's job also carried social obligations and requests. Here again, she tried to please everyone and often ran from one evening obligation to another, trying to show her support and concern for every constituency on campus. She was exhausted, overwhelmed, and knowing the mandate under which she was appointed, anxious about the president's evaluation of her behavior.

The greatest deterioration occurred within her Dean's Council. Several of the male Deans, weary of waiting for direction from Jennifer regarding where she was taking some of the academic proposals of the president, had started making decisions without Jennifer's approval.

"Loose cannons," was how she described a couple of them. "They don't listen. They just march out there on their own."

One of the big problems with two of the deans was that they just didn't take "no" for an answer when it came from Jennifer. Privately, each conceded that her "no" sounded like a "maybe." She always left room open to renegotiate.

Whatever the problem, and there were several by now, Jennifer's ability to lead was being questioned. Although her popularity was as high as ever, more and more people on campus were expressing their frustrations with what sometimes appeared as mixed signals from her and the president and sometimes was seen as virtually no direction. People wanted priorities. Instead, crisis management reigned.

Review Questions

1. If you were president, what would you do?
2. If you were Jennifer, what would you do?

Conclusion

Jennifer had a few "retreats" with her senior staff. Each time, she committed herself to delegate more, prioritize, and work on time management issues, but within 10 days or so, everything was back to business as usual.

The president decided to hire a person with extensive corporate experience to fill the vacant position of Vice President of Finance and Administration. The new man was an experienced team player who had survived mergers, been fired and bounced back, and had spent years in the number-two position in several companies. Within a few months he had earned the respect of the campus as well as the president and was in fact emerging as the person who really ran the place. Meanwhile, the president concentrated on external affairs and fundraising.

Jennifer felt relieved. Her role felt clearer. She could devote herself to academic and faculty issues and she was out from under the pressure to play "hatchet man."

As she neared the magic age for early retirement, she began to talk more and more about what she wanted to do next. ∎

CASE 14
Novo Nordisk & Southwest Airlines
••

During the last decade, it seemed no matter where we looked we found evidence of the erosion of business ethics and the basic concepts of right and wrong. Respected corporations and individuals who spent years building their reputations of integrity seemingly lost theirs overnight—perhaps forever. But some companies hold themselves to a higher set of standards and recognize that their business practices have lasting and worldwide effects. Let's look at one example from the United States—Southwest Airlines, and another—Novo Nordisk from "across the pond."

Southwest Airlines has grown from a regional Texan carrier into one of the most profitable and beloved airlines in American history. Its success springs from its core values, developed by Herb Kelleher, cofounder and former CEO, and embraced daily by the company's 35,000 employees: humor, altruism, and "LUV" (the company's NYSE stock ticker symbol).[1]

At Southwest Airlines they believe that low costs are crucial; change is inevitable; innovation is necessary; and leadership is essential—particularly during troubling economic times. "Our competitors take drastic/short sighted measures to compete with us on the price level . . . They make draconian reductions in their employees' salaries, wages, benefits, and pensions. In doing so, they ultimately sacrifice their most important assets—their employees and their employees' goodwill."[2]

Southwest applies this philosophy in an organizational culture that respects employees and their ideas. As executive vice president, Colleen Barrett started a "culture committee" made up of employees from different functional areas and levels. The committee meets quarterly to brainstorm ideas for maintaining Southwest's corporate spirit and image. All managers, officers, and directors are expected to "get out in the field," meeting and talking with employees to understand their jobs. Employees are encouraged to use their creativity and sense of humor to make their jobs—and the customers' experiences—more enjoyable. Gate agents are given books of games to play with passengers waiting for delayed flights. Flight agents might imitate Elvis or Mr. Rogers when making announcements.[3]

To encourage employees to treat one another as well as they treat their customers, departments examine linkages within Southwest to see what their "internal customers" need. The provisioning department, for example, whose responsibility is to provide the snacks and drinks for each flight, selects a flight attendant as "customer of the month." The provisioning department's own board of directors makes the selection decision. Other departments have sent pizza and ice cream to their internal cus-

tomers. Employees write letters commending the work of other employees or departments that are valued as much as letters from external customers. When problems occur between departments, employees work out solutions in supervised meetings.

Employees exhibit the same attitude of altruism and "luv" (also Southwest's term for its relationship with its customers) toward other groups as well. A significant portion of Southwest employees volunteer at Ronald McDonald Houses throughout Southwest's service territory.[4] When the company purchased a small regional airline, employees sent cards and company T-shirts to their new colleagues to welcome them into the Southwest family.

Southwest Airlines is a low-cost operator. But, according to Harvard University professor John Kotter, setting the standard for low costs in the airline industry does not mean Southwest is *cheap*. "Cheap is trying to get your prices down by nibbling costs off everything . . . [Firms such as Southwest Airlines] are thinking 'efficient,' which is very different . . . They recognize that you don't necessarily have to take a few pennies off of everything. Sometimes you might even spend more."[5] By using only one type of plane in its fleet, Southwest saves on pilot training and aircraft maintenance costs.[6] The *cheap* paradigm would favor used planes, but Southwest's choice for high productivity over lower capital expenditures has given it the youngest fleet of aircraft in the industry.

By using each plane an average of 13 hours daily, Southwest is also able to make more trips with fewer planes than any other airline. It has won the monthly "Triple Crown" distinction—Best On-Time Record, Best Baggage Handling, and Fewest Customer Complaints—more than

30 times. The company has created employee satisfaction by focusing on its internal "Customers," who are then positively motivated to show the same degree of concern for external customers.

When Herb Kelleher relinquished his role as Southwest's CEO, investors worried because so much of Southwest's success came from Kelleher's unique management and leadership. But events showed that Kelleher's successor, Colleen Barrett, was well prepared to handle the challenges of maintaining Southwest's culture and success.

Now, Barrett has retired and 22-year employee of the firm Gary Kelly has taken the helm. Kelly is navigating Southwest Airlines through one of the industry's most turbulent periods by expanding into new markets, adding flights to heavily trafficked domestic airports, and seeking cross-border alliances with foreign carriers. The airline remains steadfast against charging customers for checking suitcases and using pillows, as rivals have done. Some analysts question if management has made the right call by not charging for these services, which are generating hundreds of millions of dollars for rivals.[7] Even without the extra revenue Southwest Airlines continues to post profits; perhaps flyers continue to choose Southwest over the competition because they're not being "nickled and dimed" for everything from pillows to packs of peanuts. In fact, Southwest recently earned the top spot in *Fortune* magazine's Most Admired Airline list and is the only airline to make the magazine's top 20 list in its annual survey assessing corporate reputations.[8]

Headquartered in Denmark, Novo Nordisk is another company whose concerns run beyond the financial bottom line. Novo Nordisk not only manufactures and markets pharmaceutical products and services, it also realizes that *responsible business is good business.*

One of the world's leading producers of insulin, Novo Nordisk also makes insulin analogues, injection devices, and diabetes education materials. Its products include analogues Levemir and NovoRapid and the revolutionary FlexPen, a pre-filled insulin injection tool. In addition to its diabetes portfolio, the firm has products in the areas of hemostasis management (blood clotting), human growth hormone, and hormone replacement therapy.[9]

Today, diabetes is recognized as a pandemic. Novo Nordisk rallies the attention of policy makers and influencers to improve the quality of life for those with diabetes, to find a cure for Type 1 diabetes, and to prevent the onset of Type 2 diabetes. The company has framed a strategy for inclusive access to diabetes care. The ambition to ultimately defeat diabetes is at the core of Novo Nordisk's vision. Much like one finds at Southwest, this vision puts the company's objectives in perspective and inspires employees in their work. It is a beacon that keeps everyone's focus on creating long-term shareholder value and leveraging the company's unique qualities to gain competitive advantage.

In making decisions and managing their business, Novo Nordisk uses their Triple Bottom Line business principle to balance three considerations: Is it economically viable? Is it socially responsible? And is it environmentally sound? This ensures that decision-making balances financial growth with corporate responsibility, short-term gains with long-term profitability, and shareholder return with other stakeholder interests. The Triple Bottom Line is built into their corporate governance structures, manage-ment tools, individual performance assessments and rewards.

Novo Nordisk strives to manage their business in a way that ensures corporate profitability and growth, while it seeks to leave a positive economic footprint in the community. Their environmentally sound decisions address the company's impact on the world as well as the bioethical implications of its activities. As part of Novo Nordisk's ambitious non-financial targets they aim to achieve a 10% reduction in their company's CO_2 emissions by 2014, compared with 2004 emission levels. In 2009 it was announced that the company had already reduced CO_2 emissions by 9% and water consumption by 17% even as production and sales increased![10] Novo Nordisk considers the people who rely on the company's products and its employees, as well as the impact of their business on society.

Novo Nordisk adopted the Balanced Scorecard as the company-wide management tool for its measuring progress. As part of their payment package, individuals are rewarded for performance that meets or exceeds the financial and non-financial targets in the Balanced Scorecard. Financial performance is guided by a set of four long-term targets focusing on growth, profitability, financial return and cash generation. Non-financial performance targets include job creation, the ability to manage environmental impacts and optimize resource efficiency, and social impacts related to employees, patients and communities.[11]

Corporate sustainability—the ability to sustain and develop their business in the long-term perspective, in harmony with society—has made a meaningful difference to Novo Nordisk's business, and they believe it is a driver of their business success. Surveys indicate that ethical behavior in business today is the number one driver of reputation for pharmaceutical companies. Any company that is not perceived by the public as behaving in an ethical manner is likely to lose business, and it takes a long time to regain trust.

Southwest Airline's perpetual profitability stems not from miserliness but from attention to customers, value, and sensible cost savings. For Novo Nordisk, a business with integrity and innovation, their commitment to corporate sustainability has always been based on values. For both companies doing the right thing is making a direct return on their bottom line.

Review Questions

1. What leadership style dominates at Southwest and Novo Nordisk? What could each company learn from the other? Cite examples to support your opinion.

2. How does each company's leadership influence its organizational design and shape its competitive strategy?

3. Describe each company's philosophy in relation to transformational change, planned and unplanned change, and the strategies they've used to create change.

4. Research Question: Has Gary Kelly brought his own personal leadership style to Southwest? How well is he doing? Can he keep Southwest moving forward in the turbulent environment of the airlines industry?

5. Research Question: Check up on the strides Novo Nordisk has made for diabetes recently. Have they made any progress and garnered the attention of influential people or organizations? How might cultural expectations and leadership enhance or limit their success? ■

CASE 15
Never on a Sunday

Developed by Anne C. Cowden, California State University, Sacramento and John R. Schermerhorn, Jr., Ohio University

McCoy's Building Supply Centers of San Marcos, Texas, have been in continuous successful operation for over 70 years in an increasingly competitive retail business. McCoy's is one of the nation's largest family-owned and -managed building-supply companies, serving 10 million customers a year in a regional area currently covering New Mexico, Texas, Oklahoma, Arkansas, Mississippi, and Louisiana. McCoy's strategy has been to occupy a niche in the market of small and medium-sized cities.

McCoy's grounding principle is acquiring and selling the finest-quality products that can be found and providing quality service to customers. As an operations-oriented company. McCoy's has always managed without many layers of management. Managers are asked to concentrate on service-related issues in their stores: get the merchandise on the floor, price it, sell it, and help the customer carry it out. The majority of the administrative workload is handled through headquarters so that store employees can concentrate on customer service. The top management team (Emmett McCoy and his two sons, Brian and Mike, who serve as co-presidents) has established 11 teams of managers drawn from the different regions McCoy's stores cover. The teams meet regularly to discuss new products, better ways for product delivery, and a host of items integral to maintaining customer satisfaction. Team leadership is rotated among the managers.

McCoy's has a workforce of 70 percent full-time and 30 percent part-time employees. McCoy's philosophy values loyal, adaptable, skilled employees as the most essential element of its overall success. To operationalize this philosophy, the company offers extensive on-the-job training. The path to management involves starting at the store level and learning all facets of operations before advancing into a management program. All management trainees are required to relocate to a number of stores. Most promotions come from within. Managers are rarely recruited from the outside. This may begin to change as the business implements more technology requiring greater reliance on college-educated personnel.

Permeating all that McCoy's does is a strong religious belief, including a strong commitment to community. The firm has a long-standing reputation of fair dealing that is a source of pride for all employees.

Many McCoy family members are Evangelical Christians who believe in their faith through letting their "feet do it"—that is, showing their commitment to God through action, not just talk. Although their beliefs and values permeate the company's culture in countless ways, one very concrete way is reflected in the title of this case: Never on a Sunday. Even though it's a busy business day for retailers, all 103 McCoy's stores are closed on Sunday.

Atlanta, Georgia

Courteous service fuels growth at Chick-fil-A. But don't plan on stopping in for a chicken sandwich on a Sunday; all of the chain's 1,250 stores are closed. It is a tradition started by 85-year-old founder Truett Cathy, who believes that employees deserve a day of rest. Known as someone who believes in placing "people before profits," Truett has built a successful and fast growing fast-food franchise.

Headquartered in Atlanta, where its first restaurant was opened, Chick-fil-A is wholly owned by Truett's family and is now headed by his son. It has a reputation as a great employer, processing about 10,000 inquiries each year for 100 open restaurant operator jobs. Chick-fil-A's turnover among restaurant operators is only 3%, compared to an industry average as high as 50%. It is also a relatively inexpensive franchise, costing $5,000, compared to the $50,000 that is typical of its competitors.

The president of the National Restaurant Association Educational Foundation says: "I don't think there's any chain that creates such a wonderful culture around the way they treat their people and the respect they have for their employees."

Truett asks his employees to always say "my pleasure" when thanked by a customer. He says: "It's important to keep people happy." The results seem to speak for themselves. Chick-fil-A is the twenty-fifth largest restaurant chain in the United States, and reached over $2 billion in sales in 2006.[1]

Review Questions

1. How have the personal beliefs of the McCoy and Cathy families influenced the organizational cultures of their firms?
2. What lessons for developing high-performance organizational cultures can these two cases provide for other firms that aren't family run?
3. What would be the challenges for a new leader who is interested in moving her organization in the direction of the McCoy or Chick-fil-A cultures? ■

CASE 16
First Community Financial

Developed by Marcus Osborn, RSR Partners

First Community Financial is a small business lender that specializes in asset-based lending and factoring for a primarily small-business clientele. First Community's business is generated by high-growth companies in diverse industries, whose capital needs will not be met by traditional banking institutions. First Community Financial will lend in amounts up to $1 million, so its focus is on small business. Since many of the loans that it administers are viewed by many banks as high-risk loans, it is important that the sales staff and loan processors have a solid working relationship. Since the loans and factoring deals that First Community finances are risky, the interest that it charges is at prime plus 6 percent or sometimes higher.

First Community is a credible player in the market because of its history and the human resource policies of the company. The company invests in its employees and works to assure that turnover is low. The goal of this strategy is to develop a consistent, professional team that has more expertise than its competitors.

Whereas Jim Adamany, president and CEO, has a strong history in the industry and is a recognized expert in asset-based lending and factoring, First Community has one of the youngest staff and management teams in the finance industry. In the banking industry, promotions are slow in coming, because many banks employ conservative personnel programs. First Community, however, has recruited young, ambitious people who are specifically looking to grow with the company. As the company grows, so will the responsibility and rewards for these young executives. In his early thirties, for example, Matt Vincent is a vice president; at only 28, Brian Zcray is director of marketing.

Since First Community has a diverse product line, it must compete in distinct markets. Its factoring products compete with small specialized factoring companies. Factoring is a way for businesses to improve their cash flow by selling their invoices at a discount. Factoring clients are traditionally the smallest clients finance companies must serve. Education about the nature of the product is crucial if the company is to be successful, since this is often a new approach to financing for many companies. First Community's sales staff is well trained in understanding its product lines and acts as the client's representative as they work through the approval process.

To assure the loans or factoring deals fit within the risk profile of the company, First Community must ask many complex financial questions. Many small businesses are intimidated by credit officers, so First Community handles all of these inquiries through the business development officers. The business development officers, in turn, must understand the needs of their credit officers, who are attempting to minimize risk to the company while maintaining a friendly rapport with the client. By centralizing the client contract through educated sales representatives, First Community is able to ask the hard financial questions and still keep the clients interested in the process. A potential customer can be easily discouraged by a credit administrator's strong questioning about financial background. Utilizing the business development officers as an intermediary reduces the fear of many applicants about the credit approval process. Thus, a sales focus is maintained throughout the recruitment and loan application process.

Internally at First Community Financial there is a continual pressure between the business development staff and the credit committee. The business development staff is focused on bringing in new clients. Their compensation is in large part dependent on how many deals they can execute for the company. Like sales staff in any industry, they are aggressive and always look for new markets for business. The sales staff sells products from both the finance department and the factoring department, so they must interact with credit officers from each division. In each of these groups are credit administrators specifically responsible for ensuring that potential deals meet the lending criteria of the organization. While the business development officer's orientation is to bring in more and more deals, the credit administrator's primary goal is to limit bad loans.

The pressure develops when business development officers bring in potential loans that are rejected by the credit administrators. Since the business development officers have some experience understanding the credit risks of their clients, they often understand the policy reasoning for denying or approving a loan. The business development officers have additional concerns that their loans that have potential to be financed are approved because many of the referral sources of the sales staff will only refer deals to companies that are lending. If First Community fails to help many of a bank's referral clients, that source of business may dry up, as bankers refer deals to other lending institutions.

These structural differences are handled by focused attempts at improving communication. As noted before, the First Community staff experiences an extremely low turnover rate. This allows for the development of a cohesive team. With a cohesive staff, the opportunity to maintain frank and open communication helps bridge the different orientations of the sales staff and the administration divisions. A simple philosophy that the opinions of all staff are to be respected is continually implemented.

Since approving a loan is often a policy decision, the sales staff and the loan administrators can have an open forum to discuss whether a loan will be approved. CEO Jim Adamany approves all loans, but since he values the opinions of all of his staff, he provides them all an opportunity to communicate. Issues such as the loan history for an applicant's industry, current bank loan policies, and other factors can be openly discussed from multiple perspectives.

Review Questions

1. What coordinative mechanisms does First Community use to manage the potential conflict between its sales and finance/auditing functions?
2. What qualities should First Community emphasize in hiring new staff to ensure that its functional organizational structure will not yield too many problems?
3. What are the key types of information transfer that First Community needs to emphasize, and how is this transmitted throughout the firm?
4. Why might a small finance company have such a simple structure while a larger firm might find this structure inappropriate? ■

CASE 17
Mission Management and Trust
....
Developed by Marcus Osborn, RSR Partners

With more than 500 business and political leaders in attendance from across the state of Arizona, CEO Carmen Barmudez of Mission Management and Trust accepted the prestigious ATHENA Award. The ATHENA, which is presented by the Arizona Chamber of Commerce, is annually awarded to companies that have a demonstrated track record in promoting women's issues within their company and the community. The 50-pound bronze statue that was presented to Mission Management and Trust was particularly special for the company's leadership because it was a tangible demonstration of their commitment to the community and to women's issues.

Mission Management and Trust is a small, newly formed company of just eight employees that has already made great headway in an industry that is dominated by giant corporations. When it began, Mission was the first minority- and women-owned trust company in the nation.

The trust management industry provides services to individuals, organizations, and companies who want their assets managed and protected by specialized outside firms. Mission Management provides personal service to its customers at a level of sophistication that is unusual for a firm of its small size.

Understanding that the trust management business is highly competitive, Mission developed a unique strategy that highlighted socially conscious policies combined with good business relations.

When the company was formed, it was created with more than the goal of just making a profit. Founder Carmen Bermúdez started Mission with three principal goals in mind. "1. To run a top-quality trust company; 2. To promote within the company and, by example, increase opportunities for women and minorities; and 3. To donate a portion of all revenue to charitable projects supported by clients and staff." As these statements demonstrate, Mission Management and Trust was created with a specific purpose that was focused not just on the business of trust management but on the responsibility of being a good corporate citizen.

Even with these lofty goals, Mission faced the problem of finding clients who not only wanted quality services but were not hindered by some of the potential sacrifices a socially conscious investment company might make. Many investors want a high rate of return for their trusts, and social policy is of a much lesser concern. This was not the market Mission wanted to address, so it had to be selective in developing a client base.

Mission needed to find clients that fit its social philosophy about investing and corporate responsibility. The ideal customers would be individuals and organizations that were committed to socially conscious policies and wanted an investment strategy that reflected this commitment. Mission found a perfect niche in the market with religious institutions. Churches and other civic organizations across the nation have trusts that they use to fund special projects and maintain operating expenses. They need effective service, but in many cases these organizations must be mindful of investing in companies and other projects that do not reflect their ideals. For example, a trust company that invests in companies in the highly profitable liquor and cigarette industries would not be consistent with the philosophy of many religious organizations. Mission services this niche by developing an organization that is structurally designed to make socially conscious decisions.

Mission has already begun to meet one of its principal goals, which is to donate a portion of its profits to charities. It donated $4,500

to causes ranging from Catholic Community Services to the Jewish Community Center scholarship program. These donations not only fulfill a goal of the organization but assist in the socially conscious client recruitment. Mission's target client base will find Mission a much more attractive trust company because of its charity programs. A religious organization can be comforted with the reality that some of the dollars it spends on trust management will be recycled into causes it promotes itself. The Mission policy makes good social policy, but it also makes good marketing sense. Understanding your clients is crucial to developing a small business, and Mission has mastered this principle.

Mission makes the most of its commitment to charitable causes by keeping its clients informed about the trust's activities and, more importantly, its community activities. *The Mission Bell,* a regular publication of Mission Management and Trust, details news and issues about the trust industry, company activities, and, most importantly, how Mission's social responsibility philosophy is being implemented. The name *Mission Bell* is more consistent with a religious publication than a corporate investing sheet, but it is consistent with its clients' needs. The name of the publication and its content clarifies Mission's role and purpose. For example, the *Mission Bell* summer issue presented articles on new hires, breaking investment news, and an article about how Mission is working with other groups to support socially responsible corporate investing. Thus, the Mission philosophy is clearly defined in its marketing and communication strategies.

To be consistent with the goals of the organizations, Carmen Bermúdez collected a small staff of highly experienced individuals whose backgrounds and principles

fit Mission's ideals. She frequently comments that the best business decision she ever made was "giving preference to intelligent, talented, compatible people whose main attribute was extensive experience." Mission employees are not just experts in the field of finance but leaders in their communities. These dual qualifications fulfill three important requirements that are crucial for the company's success. First, community involvement creates an appreciation of the investment sensitivities that are required by the organizations that Mission services. Second, individuals who are involved in the community have well-developed contacts that can be useful in business recruitment. Finally, socially active employees are committed to the purpose of the organization and help unify the corporate culture within Mission.

The Mission case is a clear example of how matching a philosophy with a market can bear solid results. Mission's commitment to its ideals is evident and reflected in all of its business practices. When human resources, investing, marketing, and strategic planning decisions are made with unified goals in mind, the chances are good that a strong, successful corporate culture will develop.

Review Questions

1. How do the mission elements of Mission Management differ from most firms?
2. Does donating to charity before the firm is fully established mean that Mission is not demonstrating financial prudence?
3. Could Mission's unique mission contribute to effective coordination as well as adjustment to the market?
4. Would Mission's unique mission still yield success with more traditional investors? ■

Notes

Case 1 References

[1] Deborah Orr, "The Cheap Gourmet," *Forbes* (April 10, 2006).

[2] www.traderjoes.com/how_we_do_biz.html accessed July 10, 2009.

[3] Deborah Orr, "The Cheap Gourmet," *Forbes* (April 10, 2006).

[4] Business Week Online. February 21, 2008.

[5] Kerry Hannon. "Let Them Eat Ahi Jerky," *U.S. News & World Report* (July 7, 1997).

[6] Marianne Wilson, "When Less is More," *Chain Store Age* (November 2006).

[7] Irwin Speizer, "The Grocery Chain That Shouldn't Be," *Fast Company* (February 2004).

[8] http://www.traderjoes.com/meet_our_crew.html accessed July 10, 2009.

[9] www.traderjoes.com/benefits.html accessed July 10, 2009.

[10] Irwin Speizer, "Shopper's Special," *Workforce Management* (September 2004).

[11] http://www.huffingtonpost.com/2009/07/13/the-greenpeace-vs-trader_n_230891.html (accessed July 22, 2009).

[12] http://go.greenpeaceusa.org/seafood/scorecards/trader-joes.pdf (accessed July 22, 2009.)

[13] http://www.traderjoes.com/action_issues.asp (accessed July 22, 2009)

Case 2 References

[1] How Xerox Diversity Breeds Business Success. (Accessed August 3, 2009 at http://a1851.g.akamaitech.net/f/1851/2996/24h/cacheB.xerox.com/downloads/usa/en/d/Diversity_Brochure_2006.pdf)

[2] http://a1851.g.akamaitech.net/f/1851/2996/24h/cacheB.xerox.com/downloads/usa/en/x/Xerox_Fact_Sheet_Who_We_Are_Today.pdf (accessed July 7, 2009)

[3] http://www.xerox.com/go/xrx/template/019d.jsp?view=Factbook&id=Overview&Xcntry=USA&Xlang=en_US&Xseg=xnet (accessed July 7, 2009)

[4] http://www.xerox.com/downloads/usa/en/n/nr_Xerox_Diversity_Timeline_2008.pdf (accessed July 7, 2009)

[5] Ibid.

[6] Ibid.

[7] http://www.xeroxcareers.com/working-xerox/diversity.aspx (accessed July 7, 2009)

[8] http://www.xeroxcareers.com/docs/Diversity_Brochure.pdf (accessed July 7, 2009)

[9] How Xerox Diversity Breeds Business Success.

[10] http://www.hrc.org/documents/HRC_Corporate_Equality_Index_2009.pdf (accessed July 8, 2009)

Case 3 References

[1] http://www.linkedin.com/in/loisquam (accessed July 18, 2009)

[2] http://www.startribune.com/business/42640682.html (accessed July 5, 2009)

[3] http://tysvar.com

[4] http://tysvar.com/our-vision/ (accessed July 5, 2009)

[5] Ibid

[6] www.morrissuntribune.com/articles/index.cfm?id=16258&se (accessed July 18, 2009)

[7] http://tysvar.com/our-work/ (accessed July 5, 2009)

[8] http///tysvar.com; http://tysvar.com/green-blog/ (accessed July 5, 2009)

[9] http://tysvar.com/green-blog/ (accessed July 5, 2009)

[10] http://tcbmag.blogs.com/debatable/2008/02/qa-with-lois-qu.htmlQ (accessed July 5, 2009)

[11] http://www.linkedin.com/in/loisquam (accessed July 18, 2009)

[12] http://tysvar.com/lois-quam.com (accessed July 5, 2009)

[13] http://tysvar.com/our-work (accessed July 5, 2009)

[14] http://www.piperjaffray.com/pdf/lois_quam_speech.pdf (accessed July 18, 2009)

Case 8 References

[1] http://www.nascar.com/guides/about/nascar/ accessed July 13, 2009.

[2] Information from Susan Carey, "Racing to Improve," *The Wall Street Journal* (March 24, 2006).

[3] http://www.visitpit.com/about-us/testimonials/ accessed July 13, 2009.

[4] Ibid.

Case 9 References

[1] Information from Sara Schaefer Munoz, "Is Hiding Your Wedding Band Necessary at a Job Interview?" *The Wall Street Journal* (March 15, 2007), p. D3.

[2] Information and quotes from "Get Healthy—Or Else," *Business Week* (February 26, 2007), cover story; and, "Wellness—or Orwellness?" *Business Week* (March 19, 2007), cover story.

[3] Information from "Anne Fisher, "Why Women Get Paid Less," *Fortune* (March 20, 2007), retrieved from www.fortune.com.

[4] Information from Marcus Kabel, "Wal-Mart Goes Public with Annual Bonuses," *The Columbus Dispatch* (March 23, 2007), pp. H1, H2.

Case 14 References

[1] Southwest Airlines Corporate Fact Sheet, at www.swamedia.com/swamedia/fact_sheet.pdf (accessed May 25, 2009. see also James Campbell Quick, "Crafting and Organizational Culture: Herb's Hand at Southwest Airlines," *Organizational Dynamics*, vol. 21 (August 1992), p. 47.

[2] http://www.swamedia.com/swamedia/speeches/fred_taylor_speech.pdf (accessed July 22, 2009).

[3] Colleen Barrett, "Pampering Customers on a Budget," *Working Woman* (April 1993), pp. 19–22.

[4] Southwest Airlines Corporate Fact Sheet.

[5] Did We Say Cheap?" *Inc.* (October 1997), p. 60.

[6] Southwest Airlines Corporate Fact Sheet.

[7] Adapted from Mike Esterl. "Southwest Airlines CEO Flies Unchartered Skies." *The Wall Street Journal*. (March 25, 2009), p. B1.

[8] *The World's Most Admired Companies. FORTUNE*, (March 16, 2009).

Adapted from http://www.novonordisk.com/sustainability/default.asp.

[9] www.hoovers.com (accessed July 22, 2009).

[10] http://www.environmentalleader.com/2009/02/05/novo-nordisk-cuts-co2-emissions-9/ accessed July 12, 2009.

[11] Ibid.

Case 15 Reference

[1] Information from "Daniel Yee, "Chick-Fil-A Recipe Winning Customers," *The Columbus Dispatch* (September 9, 2006), p. D1.

Glossary

360° evaluation gathers evaluations from a job-holder's bosses, peers, and subordinates, as well as internal and external customers and self-ratings.

Absorptive capacity is the ability to learn.

Accommodation, or **smoothing** involves playing down differences and finding areas of agreement.

Achievement-oriented leadership emphasizes setting goals, stressing excellence, and showing confidence in people's ability to achieve high standards of performance.

Active listening encourages people to say what they really mean.

Activity measures of performance assess inputs in terms of work efforts.

Adaptive capacity refers to the ability to change.

Adhocracy emphasizes shared, decentralized decision making; extreme horizontal specialization; few levels of management; the virtual absence of formal controls; and few rules, policies, and procedures.

Affect is the range of feelings in the forms of emotions and moods that people experience in their life context.

Agency theory suggests that public corporations can function effectively even though their managers are self-interested and do not automatically bear the full consequences of their managerial actions.

Americans with Disabilities Act is a federal civil-rights statute that protects the rights of people with disabilities.

Amoral manager fails to consider the ethics of a decision or behavior.

Anchoring and adjustment heuristic bases a decision on incremental adjustments to an initial value determined by historical precedent or some reference point.

Arbitration a neutral third party acts as judge with the power to issue a decision binding for all parties.

Attitude is a predisposition to respond positively or negatively to someone or something.

Attribution is the process of creating explanations for events.

Authoritarianism is a tendency to adhere rigidly to conventional values and to obey recognized authority.

Authoritative command uses formal authority to end conflict.

Availability heuristic bases a decision on recent events relating to the situation at hand.

Avoidance involves pretending a conflict does not really exist.

Awareness of others is being aware of behaviors, preferences, styles, biases, personalities, etc. of others.

Bargaining zone is the range between one party's minimum reservation point and the other party's maximum.

Behavioral complexity is the possession of a repertoire of leadership roles and the ability to selectively apply them.

Behavioral decision model views decision makers as acting only in terms of what they perceive about a given situation.

Behavioral perspective assumes that leadership is central to performance and other outcomes.

Behaviorally anchored rating scale links performance ratings to specific and observable job-relevant behaviors.

Brainstorming involves generating ideas through "freewheeling" and without criticism.

Bureaucracy is an ideal form of organization, the characteristics of which were defined by the German sociologist Max Weber.

Centralization is the degree to which the authority to make decisions is restricted to higher levels of management.

Centralized communication networks link group members through a central control point.

Certain environments provide full information on the expected results for decision-making alternatives.

Changing is the stage in which specific actions are taken to create change.

Channel richness indicates the capacity of a channel to convey information.

Charismatic leaders are those leaders who are capable of having a profound and extraordinary effect on followers.

Classical decision model views decision makers as acting in a world of complete certainty.

Coalition power is the ability to control another's behavior indirectly because the individual owes an obligation to you or another as part of a larger collective interest.

Coercive power is the extent to which a manager can deny desired rewards or administer punishment to control other people.

Cognitive complexity is the underlying assumption that those high in cognitive complexity process information differently and perform certain tasks better than less cognitively complex people.

Cognitive dissonance is experienced inconsistency between one's attitudes and or between attitudes and behavior.

Cohesiveness is the degree to which members are attracted to a group and motivated to remain a part of it.

Collaboration involves recognition that something is wrong and needs attention through problem solving.

Communication is the process of sending and receiving symbols with attached meanings.

Communication channels are the pathways through which messages are communicated.

Competition seeks victory by force, superior skill, or domination.

Compressed work week allows a full-time job to be completed in fewer than the standard five days.

Compromise occurs when each party gives up something of value to the other.

Conceptual skill is the ability to analyze and solve complex problems.

Confirmation trap is the tendency to seek confirmation for what is already thought to be true and not search for disconfirming information.

Conflict occurs when parties disagree over substantive issues or when emotional antagonisms create friction between them.

Conflict resolution occurs when the reasons for a conflict are eliminated.

Conglomerates are firms that own several different unrelated businesses.

Consideration is sensitive to people's feelings.

Consultative decisions are made by one individual after seeking input from or consulting with members of a group.

Context is the collection of opportunities and constraints that affect the occurrence and meaning of behavior and the relationships among variables.

Contingency thinking seeks ways to meet the needs of different management situations.

Continuous reinforcement administers a reward each time a desired behavior occurs.

Contrast effect occurs when the meaning of something that takes place is based on a contrast with another recent event or situation.

Control is the set of mechanisms used to keep actions and outputs within predetermined limits.

Controlling monitors performance and takes any needed corrective action.

Coordination is the set of mechanisms used in an organization to link the actions of its subunits into a consistent pattern.

Coping is a response or reaction to distress that has occurred or is threatened.

Countercultures are groups where the patterns of values and philosophies outwardly reject those of the larger organization or social system.

Counterproductive work behaviors intentionally disrupt relationships or performance at work.

Creativity generates unique and novel responses to problems.

Crisis decision occurs when an unexpected problem can lead to disaster if not resolved quickly and appropriately.

Criteria questions assess a decision in terms of utility, rights, justice, and caring.

Critical incident diaries record actual examples of positive and negative work behaviors and results.

Cross-functional team has members from different functions or work units.

Cultural symbol is any object, act, or event that serves to transmit cultural meaning.

Culturally endorsed leadership dimension is one that members of a culture expect from effective leaders.

Culture is the learned and shared way of thinking and acting among a group of people or society.

Decentralization is the degree to which the authority to make decisions is given to lower levels in an organization's hierarchy.

Decentralized communication networks members communicate directly with one another.

Decision making is the process of choosing a course of action to deal with a problem or opportunity.

Decision making is the process of choosing among alternative courses of action.

Defensiveness occurs when individuals feel they are being attacked and they need to protect themselves.

Delphi technique involves generating decision-making alternatives through a series of survey questionnaires.

Dependent variables are outcomes of practical value and interest that are influenced by independent variables.

Directive leadership spells out the what and how of subordinates' tasks.

Disability is any form of impairment or handicap.

Disconfirmation occurs when an individual feels his or her self-worth is being questioned.

Display rules govern the degree to which it is appropriate to display emotions.

Disruptive behaviors in teams harm the group process and limit team effectiveness.

Distress is a negative impact on both attitudes and performance.

Distributed leadership is the sharing of responsibility for meeting group task and maintenance needs.

Distributive justice is the degree to which all people are treated the same under a policy.

Distributive negotiation focuses on positions staked out or declared by the parties involved, each of whom is trying to claim certain portions of the available pie.

Diversity–consensus dilemma is the tendency for diversity in groups to create process difficulties even as it offers improved potential for problem solving.

Divisional departmentation groups individuals and resources by products, territories, services, clients, or legal entities.

Dogmatism leads a person to see the world as a threatening place and to regard authority as absolute.

Downward communication follows the chain of command from top to bottom.

Dysfunctional conflict works to the group's or organization's disadvantage.

Effective manager helps others achieve high levels of both performance and satisfaction.

Effective negotiation occurs when substance issues are resolved and working relationships are maintained or improved.

Emotion and mood contagion is the spillover of one's emotions and mood onto others.

Emotional adjustment traits are traits related to how much an individual experiences emotional distress or displays unacceptable acts.

Emotional conflict involves interpersonal difficulties that arise over feelings of anger, mistrust, dislike, fear, resentment, and the like.

Emotional dissonance is inconsistency between emotions we feel and those we try to project.

Emotional intelligence is an ability to understand emotions and manage relationships effectively.

Emotional intelligence is the ability to manage oneself and one's relationships effectively.

Emotional labor is a situation where a person displays organizationally desired emotions in a job.

Emotion-focused coping mechanisms regulate emotions or distress.

Emotions are strong positive or negative feelings directed toward someone or something.

Employee engagement is a positive feeling or strong sense of connection with the organization.

Employee involvement team   meets regularly to address workplace issues.

Employee stock ownership plans   give stock to employees or allow them to purchase stock at special prices.

Empowerment   is the process by which managers help others to acquire and use the power needed to make decisions affecting themselves and their work.

Encoding   is the process of translating an idea or thought into a message consisting of verbal, written, or nonverbal symbols (such as gestures), or some combination of them.

Environmental complexity   is the magnitude of the problems and opportunities in the organization's environment as evidenced by the degree of richness, interdependence, and uncertainty.

Equity theory   posits that people will act to eliminate any felt inequity in the rewards received for their work in comparison with others.

ERG theory   identifies existence, relatedness, and growth needs.

Escalating commitment   is the tendency to continue a previously chosen course of action even when feedback suggests that it is failing.

Ethics   is the philosophical study of morality.

Ethics mindfulness   is an enriched awareness that causes one to consistently behave with ethical consciousness.

Ethnocentrism   is the tendency to believe one's culture and its values are superior to those of others.

Eustress   is a stress that has a positive impact on both attitudes and performance.

Existence needs   are desires for physiological and material well-being.

Expectancy   is the probability that work effort will be followed by performance accomplishment.

Expectancy theory   argues that work motivation is determined by individual beliefs regarding effort/performance relationships and work outcomes.

Expert power   is the ability to control another's behavior because of the possession of knowledge, experience, or judgment that the other person does not have but needs.

Exploitation   focuses on refinement and reuse of existing products and processes.

Exploration   calls for the organization and its managers to stress freedom and radical thinking and therefore opens the firm to big changes— or what some call radical innovations.

External adaptation   deals with reaching goals, the tasks to be accomplished, the methods used to achieve the goals, and the methods of coping with success and failure.

Extinction   discourages a behavior by making the removal of a desirable consequence contingent on its occurrence.

Extrinsic rewards   are valued outcomes given by some other person.

Feedback   communicates how one feels about something another person has done or said.

Filtering   senders convey only certain parts of relevant information.

FIRO-B theory   examines differences in how people relate to one another based on their needs to express and receive feelings of inclusion, control, and affection.

Flaming   is expressing rudeness when using e-mail or other forms of electronic communication.

Flexible working hours   gives individuals some amount of choice in scheduling their daily work hours.

Force–coercion strategy   uses authority, rewards, and punishments to create change.

Forced distribution   in performance appraisal forces a set percentage of persons into predetermined rating categories.

Formal channels   follow the official chain of command.

Formal teams   are official and designated to serve a specific purpose.

Formalization   is the written documentation of work rules, policies, and procedures.

Framing error   is solving a problem in the context perceived.

Functional conflict   results in positive benefits to the group.

Functional departmentation   is grouping individuals by skill, knowledge, and action yields.

Functional silos problem   occurs when members of one functional team fail to interact with others from other functional teams.

Fundamental attribution error   overestimates internal factors and underestimates external factors as influences on someone's behavior.

Gain sharing   rewards employees in some proportion to productivity gains.

Garbage can model   views problems, solutions, participants, and choice situations as all mixed together in a dynamic field of organizational forces.

General environment   is the set of cultural, economic, legal-political, and educational conditions found in the areas in which the organization operates.

Grafting   is the process of acquiring individuals, units, and/or firms to bring in useful knowledge to the organization.

Grapevine   transfers information through networks of friendships and acquaintances.

Graphic rating scales   in performance appraisal assigns scores to specific performance dimensions.

Group dynamics   are the forces operating in teams that affect the ways members work together.

Groupthink   is the tendency of cohesive group members to lose their critical evaluative capabilities.

Growth needs   are desires for continued personal growth and development.

Halo effect   uses one attribute to develop an overall impression of a person or situation.

Heterogeneous teams   members differ on many characteristics.

Heuristics   are simplifying strategies or "rules of thumb" used to make decisions.

Hierarchy of needs theory   offers a pyramid of physiological, safety, social, esteem, and self-actualization needs.

High-context cultures   words convey only part of a message, while the rest of the message must be inferred from body language and additional contextual cues.

Higher-order needs   in Maslow's hierarchy are esteem and self-actualization.

Hindsight trap   is a tendency to overestimate the degree to which an event that has already taken place could have been predicted.

Homogeneous teams   members share many similar characteristics.

Hope   is the tendency to look for alternative pathways to reach a desired goal.

Horizontal specialization   is a division of labor through the formation of work units or groups within an organization.

Human skill   is the ability to work well with other people.

Hygiene factors   in the job context are sources of job dissatisfaction.

Immoral manager   chooses to behave unethically.

Impression management   is the systematic attempt to influence how others perceive us.

Inclusion   is the degree to which an organization's culture respects and values diversity.

Inclusion   is the focus of an organization's culture on welcoming and supporting all types and groups of people.

Incremental change   builds on the existing ways of operating to enhance or extend them in new directions.

Independent variables   are presumed causes that influence dependent variables.

Individual decisions   or authority decisions, are made by one person on behalf of the team.

Individual differences   are the ways in which people are similar and how they vary in their thinking, feeling, and behavior.

Individualism–collectivism   is the tendency of members of a culture to emphasize individual self-interests or group relationships.

Inference-based leadership attribution   emphasizes leadership effectiveness as inferred by perceived group/organizational performance.

Influence   is a behavioral response to the exercise of power.

Informal channels   do not follow the chain of command.

Informal groups   are unofficial and emerge to serve special interests.

Information power   is the access to and/or the control of information.

Information technology   is the combination of machines, artifacts, procedures, and systems used to gather, store, analyze, and disseminate information for translating it into knowledge.

In-group   occurs when individuals feel part of a group and experience favorable status and a sense of belonging.

Initiating structure   is concerned with spelling out the task requirements and clarifying aspects of the work agenda.

Innovation   is the process of creating new ideas and putting them into practice.

Instrumental values   reflect a person's beliefs about the means to achieve desired ends.

Instrumentality   is the probability that performance will lead to various work outcomes.

Integrative negotiation   focuses on the merits of the issues, and the parties involved try to enlarge the available pie rather than stake claims to certain portions of it.

Interactional justice   is the degree to which the people are treated with dignity and respect in decisions affecting them.

Interactional transparency   is the open and honest sharing of information.

Interfirm alliances   are announced cooperative agreements or joint ventures between two independent firms.

Intergroup conflict   occurs among groups in an organization.

Intermittent reinforcement   rewards behavior only periodically.

Internal integration   deals with the creation of a collective identity and with ways of working and living together.

Interorganizational conflict   occurs between organizations.

Interpersonal barriers   occur when individuals are not able to objectively listen to the sender due to things such as lack of trust, personality clashes, a bad reputation, stereotypes/prejudices, etc.

Interpersonal conflict   occurs between two or more individuals in opposition to each other.

Inter-team dynamics   are relationships between groups cooperating and competing with one another.

Intrapersonal conflict   occurs within the individual because of actual or perceived pressures from incompatible goals or expectations.

Intrinsic rewards   are valued outcomes received directly through task performance.

Intuitive thinking   approaches problems in a flexible and spontaneous fashion.

Job burnout   is a loss of interest in or satisfaction with a job due to stressful working conditions.

Job design   is the process of specifying job tasks and work arrangements.

Job enlargement   increases task variety by combining into one job two or more tasks that were previously assigned to separate workers.

Job enrichment   builds high-content jobs that involve planning and evaluating duties normally done by supervisors.

Job involvement   is the extent to which an individual is dedicated to a job.

Job rotation   increases task variety by periodically shifting workers among jobs involving different tasks.

Job satisfaction   is a positive feeling about one's work and work setting.

Job satisfaction   is the degree to which an individual feels positive or negative about a job.

Job sharing   one full-time job is split between two or more persons who divide the work according to agreed-upon hours.

Job simplification   standardizes work to create clearly defined and highly specialized tasks.

Lack-of-participation error   occurs when important people are excluded from the decision-making process.

Lateral communication   is the flow of messages at the same levels across organizations.

Law of effect   is that behavior followed by pleasant consequences is likely to be repeated; behavior followed by unpleasant consequences is not.

Leader match training   leaders are trained to diagnose the situation to match their high and low LPC scores with situational control.

Leader-member exchange theory   emphasizes the quality of the working relationship between leaders and followers.

Leadership grid   is an approach that uses a grid that places concern for production on the horizontal axis and concern for people on the vertical axis.

Leadership   is the process of influencing others and the process of facilitating individual and collective efforts to accomplish shared objectives.

Leading   creates enthusiasm to work hard to accomplish tasks successfully.

Leaking pipeline   is a phrase coined to describe how women have not reached the highest levels of organizations.

Learning   is an enduring change in behavior that results from experience.

Least-preferred co-worker (LPC) scale   is a measure of a person's leadership style based on a description of the person with whom respondents have been able to work least well.

Legitimate power   or formal authority is the extent to which a manager can use the "right of command" to control other people.

Lifelong learning   is continuous learning from everyday experiences.

Line units   are workgroups that conduct the major business of the organization.

Locus of control   is the extent a person feels able to control his or her own life and is concerned with a person's internal–external orientation.

Long-term/short-term orientation   is the degree to which a culture emphasizes long-term or short-term thinking.

Low-context cultures   messages are expressed mainly by the spoken and written word.

Lower-order needs   in Maslow's hierarchy are physiological, safety, and social.

Machiavellianism   causes someone to view and manipulate others purely for personal gain.

Maintenance activities   support the emotional life of the team as an ongoing social system.

Management by objectives, or **MBO**   is a process of joint goal setting between a supervisor and a subordinate.

Management philosophy   links key goal-related issues with key collaboration issues to come up with general ways by which the firm will manage its affairs.

Managerial script   is a series of well-known routines for problem identification and alternative generation and analysis common to managers within a firm.

Managerial wisdom   is the ability to perceive variations in the environment and understand the social actors and their relationships.

Managers   are persons who support the work efforts of other people.

Masculinity–femininity   is the degree to which a society values assertiveness or relationships.

Matrix departmentation   is a combination of functional and divisional patterns wherein an individual is assigned to more than one type of unit.

Mechanistic type of machine bureaucracy   emphasizes vertical specialization and control with impersonal coordination and a heavy reliance on standardization, formalization, rules, policies, and procedures.

Mediation   a neutral third party tries to engage the parties in a negotiated solution through persuasion and rational argument.

Merit pay   links an individual's salary or wage increase directly to measures of performance accomplishment.

Mimicry   is the copying of the successful practices of others.

Mission statement   describes the organization's purpose for stakeholders and the public.

Mission statements   are written statements of organizational purpose.

Models   are simplified views of reality that attempt to explain real-world phenomena.

Moods   are generalized positive and negative feelings or states of mind.

Moral dilemma   involves a choice between two or more ethically uncomfortable alternatives.

Moral manager   makes ethical behavior a personal goal.

Moral problem   poses major ethical consequences for the decision maker or others.

Motivation   accounts for the level and persistence of a person's effort expended at work.

Motivation   refers to forces within an individual that account for the level, direction, and persistence of effort expended at work. Content theories profile different needs that may motivate individual behavior.

Motivator factors   in the job content are sources of job satisfaction.

Multicultural organization   is a firm that values diversity but systematically works to block the transfer of societally based subcultures into the fabric of the organization.

Multiculturalism   refers to pluralism and respect for diversity in the workplace.

Multiskilling   is where team members are each capable of performing many different jobs.

Mum effect   occurs when people are reluctant to communicate bad news.

Need for achievement (nAch)   is the desire to do better, solve problems, or master complex tasks.

Need for affiliation (nAff)   is the desire for friendly and warm relations with others.

Need for power (nPower)   is the desire to control others and influence their behavior.

Negative reinforcement   strengthens a behavior by making the avoidance of an undesirable consequence contingent on its occurrence.

Negotiation   is the process of making joint decisions when the parties involved have different preferences.

Network development   involves developing and managing the connections among individuals both inside and outside the unit or firm.

Noise   is anything that interferes with the effectiveness of communication.

Nominal group technique involves structured rules for generating and prioritizing ideas.

Nonprogrammed decisions are created to deal specifically with a problem at hand.

Nonverbal communication occurs through facial expressions, body motions, eye contact, and other physical gestures.

Norms are rules or standards for the behavior of group members.

Observable culture is the way things are done in an organization.

Open systems transform human and material resource inputs into finished goods and services.

Operant conditioning is the control of behavior by manipulating its consequences.

Operations technology is the combination of resources, knowledge, and techniques that creates a product or service output for an organization.

Optimism is the expectation of positive outcomes.

Optimizing decisions give the absolute best solution to a problem.

Organic type or professional bureaucracy emphasizes horizontal specialization, extensive use of personal coordination, and loose rules, policies, and procedures.

Organization charts are diagrams that depict the formal structures of organizations.

Organizational behavior is the study of individuals and groups in organizations.

Organizational behavior modification is the use of extrinsic rewards to systematically reinforce desirable work behavior and discourage undesirable behavior.

Organizational citizenship behaviors are the extras people do to go the extra mile in their work.

Organizational commitment is the loyalty of an individual to the organization.

Organizational cultural lag is a condition where dominant cultural patterns are inconsistent with new emerging innovations.

Organizational culture is a shared set of beliefs and values within an organization.

Organizational design is the process of choosing and implementing a structural configuration for an organization.

Organizational governance is the pattern of authority, influence, and acceptable managerial behavior established at the top of the organization.

Organizational justice is an issue of how fair and equitable people view workplace practices.

Organizational learning is the process of acquiring knowledge and using information to adapt to changing circumstances.

Organizational learning is the process of knowledge acquisition, information distribution, information interpretation, and organizational retention.

Organizational myth is a commonly held cause-effect relationship or assertion that cannot be supported empirically.

Organizational or corporate culture is the system of shared actions, values, and beliefs that develops within an organization and guides the behavior of its members.

Organizational politics is the management of influence to obtain ends not sanctioned by the organization or to obtain sanctioned ends through nonsanctioned means and the art of creative compromise among competing interests.

Organizations are collections of people working together to achieve a common purpose.

Organizing divides up tasks and arranges resources to accomplish them.

Out-group occurs when one does not feel part of a group and experiences discomfort and low belongingness

Output controls are controls that focus on desired targets and allow managers to use their own methods for reaching defined targets.

Output goals are the goals that define the type of business an organization is in.

Output measures of performance assess achievements in terms of actual work results.

Paired comparison in performance appraisal compares each person with every other.

Parochialism assumes the ways of your culture are the only ways of doing things.

Participative leadership focuses on consulting with subordinates and seeking and taking their suggestions into account before making decisions.

Path-goal view of leadership assumes that a leader's key function is to adjust his or her behaviors to complement situational contingencies.

Patterning of attention involves isolating and communicating what information is important and what is given attention from a potentially endless stream of events, actions, and outcome.

Perception is the process through which people receive and interpret information from the environment.

Performance gap is a discrepancy between the desired and the actual conditions.

Performance-contingent pay is that you earn more when you produce more and earn less when you produce less.

Personal conception traits represent individuals' major beliefs and personal orientation concerning a range of issues concerning social and physical setting.

Personal wellness involves the pursuit of one's job and career goals with the support of a personal health promotion program.

Personality is the overall combination of characteristics that capture the unique nature of a person as that person reacts to and interacts with others.

Personality traits enduring characteristics describing an individual's behavior.

Physical distractions include interruptions from noises, visitors, etc., that interfere with communication.

Planned change is a response to someone's perception of a performance gap—a discrepancy between the desired and actual state of affairs.

Planned change strategies consist of force–coercion, rational persuasion, and shared power.

Planning sets objectives and identifies the actions needed to achieve them.

Political savvy is knowing how to negotiate, persuade, and deal with people regarding goals they will accept.

Positive reinforcement strengthens a behavior by making a desirable consequence contingent on its occurrence.

Power distance is a culture's acceptance of the status and power differences among its members.

Power is the ability to get someone else to do something you want done or the ability to make things happen or get things done the way you want.

Power-oriented behavior is action directed primarily at developing or using relationships in which other people are willing to defer to one's wishes.

Presence-aware tools are software that allow a user to view others' real-time availability status and readiness to communicate.

Proactive personality is the disposition that identifies whether or not individuals act to influence their environments.

Problem-focused coping mechanisms manage the problem that is causing the distress.

Problem-solving style reflects the way a person gathers and evaluates information when solving problems and making decisions.

Problem-solving team is set up to deal with a specific problem or opportunity.

Procedural justice is the degree to which rules are always properly followed to implement policies.

Process controls are controls that attempt to specify the manner in which tasks are to be accomplished.

Process innovations introduce into operations new and better ways of doing things.

Process power is the control over methods of production and analysis.

Process theories examine the thought processes that motivate individual behavior.

Product innovations introduce new goods or services to better meet customer needs.

Profit sharing rewards employees in some proportion to changes in organizational profits.

Programmed decisions simply implement solutions that have already been determined by past experience as appropriate for the problem at hand.

Projection assigns personal attributes to other individuals.

Proxemics involves the use of space as people interact.

Psychological contract is an unwritten set of expectations about a person's exchange of inducements and contributions with an organization.

Punishment discourages a behavior by making an unpleasant consequence contingent on its occurrence.

Quality circle team meets regularly to address quality issues.

Ranking in performance appraisal orders each person from best to worst.

Rational persuasion is the ability to control another's behavior because, through the individual's efforts, the person accepts the desirability of an offered goal and a reasonable way of achieving it.

Rational persuasion strategy uses facts, special knowledge, and rational argument to create change.

Receiver is the individual or group of individuals to whom a message is directed.

Recognition-based leadership prototypes base leadership effectiveness on how well a person fits characteristics the evaluator thinks describe a good or effective leader.

Referent power is the ability to control another's behavior because of the individual's desire to identify with the power source.

Refreezing is the stage in which changes are reinforced and stabilized.

Reinforcement is the delivery of a consequence as a result of behavior.

Relatedness needs are desires for satisfying interpersonal relationships.

Relationship management is the ability to establish rapport with others to build good relationships.

Reliability means a performance measure gives consistent results.

Representative power is the formal right conferred by the firm to speak for and to a potentially important group.

Representativeness heuristic bases a decision on similarities between the situation at hand and stereotypes of similar occurrences.

Resilience is the ability to bounce back from failure and keep forging ahead.

Resistance to change is any attitude or behavior that indicates unwillingness to make or support a desired change.

Restricted communication networks link subgroups that disagree with one another's positions.

Reward power is the extent to which a manager can use extrinsic and intrinsic rewards to control other people.

Risk environments provide probabilities regarding expected results for decision-making alternatives.

Risk management involves anticipating risks and factoring them into decision making.

Rites are standardized and recurring activities used at special times to influence the behaviors and understanding of organizational members.

Rituals are systems of rites.

Role ambiguity occurs when someone is uncertain about what is expected of him or her.

Role conflict occurs when someone is unable to respond to role expectations that conflict with one another.

Role is a set of expectations for a team member or person in a job.

Role negotiation is a process for discussing and agreeing upon what team members expect of one another.

Role overload occurs when too much work is expected of the individual.

Role underload occurs when too little work is expected of the individual.

Romance of leadership is where people attribute romantic, almost magical, qualities to leadership.

Rule of conformity is the greater the cohesiveness the greater the conformity of members to team norms.

Saga is an embellished heroic account of the story of the founding of an organization.

Satisficing decisions choose the first alternative that appears to give an acceptable or satisfactory resolution of the problem.

Scanning is looking outside the firm and bringing back useful solutions to problems.

Schemas are cognitive frameworks that represent organized knowledge developed through experience about people, objects, or events.

Scientific management used systematic study of job components to develop practices to increase people's efficiency at work.

Selective listening individuals block out information or only hear things that match preconceived notions.

Selective perception is the tendency to define problems from one's own point of view.

Self-awareness is the ability to understand our emotions and their impact on us and others.

Self-awareness means being aware of one's own behaviors, preferences, styles, biases, personalities, etc.

Self-concept is the view individuals have of themselves as physical, social, spiritual, or moral beings.

Self-conscious emotions arise from internal sources, and **social emotions** derive from external sources.

Self-efficacy is a person's belief that he or she can perform adequately in a situation.

Self-efficacy is a person's belief that she or he is capable of performing a task.

Self-efficacy is an individual's belief about the likelihood of successfully completing a specific task.

Self-esteem is a belief about one's own worth based on an overall self-evaluation.

Self-fulfilling prophecy is creating or finding in a situation that which you expected to find in the first place.

Self-management is the ability to think before acting and control disruptive impulses.

Self-managing teams are empowered to make decisions to manage themselves in day-to-day work.

Self-monitoring is a person's ability to adjust his or her behavior to external situational (environmental) factors.

Self-serving bias underestimates internal factors and overestimates external factors as influences on someone's behavior.

Semantic barriers involve a poor choice or use of words and mixed messages.

Sender is a person or group trying to communicate with someone else.

Shaping is positive reinforcement of successive approximations to the desired behavior.

Shared leadership is a dynamic, interactive influence process through which individuals in teams lead one another.

Shared-power strategy uses participatory methods and emphasizes common values to create change.

Simple design is a configuration involving one or two ways of specializing individuals and units.

Situational control is the extent to which leaders can determine what their groups are going to do and what the outcomes of their actions are going to be.

Situational leadership model focuses on the situational contingency of maturity or "readiness" of followers.

Skill is an ability to turn knowledge into effective action.

Skill-based pay rewards people for acquiring and developing job-relevant skills.

Social awareness is the ability to empathize and understand the emotions of others.

Social capital is a capacity to get things done due to relationships with other people.

Social facilitation is the tendency for one's behavior to be influenced by the presence of others in a group.

Social identity theory is a theory developed to understand the psychological basis of discrimination.

Social learning theory describes how learning occurs through interactions among people, behavior, and environment.

Social loafing occurs when people work less hard in groups than they would individually.

Social network analysis identifies the informal structures and their embedded social relationships that are active in an organization.

Social traits are surface-level traits that reflect the way a person appears to others when interacting in social settings.

Societal goals reflect the intended contributions of an organization to the broader society.

Span of control refers to the number of individuals reporting to a supervisor.

Specific environment is the set of owners, suppliers, distributors, government agencies, and competitors with which an organization must interact to grow and survive.

Spotlight questions expose a decision to public scrutiny and full transparency.

Staff units assist the line units by performing specialized services to the organization.

Stakeholders are people and groups with an interest or "stake" in the performance of the organization.

Standardization is the degree to which the range of actions in a job or series of jobs is limited.

Status congruence involves consistency between a person's status within and outside a group.

Status differences are differences between persons of higher and lower ranks.

Stereotype assigns attributes commonly associated with a group to an individual.

stereotyping occurs when people make a generalization, usually exaggerated or oversimplified (and potentially offensive) that is used to describe or distinguish a group.

Stigma is a phenomenon whereby an individual is rejected as a result of an attribute that is deeply discredited by his/her society, is rejected as a result of the attribute.

Stock options give the right to purchase shares at a fixed price in the future.

Strategic leadership is leadership of a quasi-independent unit, department, or organization.

Strategy guides organizations to operate in ways that outperform competitors.

Strategy positions the organization in the competitive environment and implements actions to compete successfully.

Stress is tension from extraordinary demands, constraints, or opportunities.

Subcultures are groups who exhibit unique patterns of values and philosophies not consistent with the dominant culture of the larger organization or social system.

Substantive conflict involves fundamental disagreement over ends or goals to be pursued and the means for their accomplishment.

Substitutes for leadership make a leader's influence either unnecessary or redundant in that they replace a leader's influence.

Supportive communication principles are a set of tools focused on joint problem solving.

Supportive leadership focuses on subordinate needs, well-being, and promotion of a friendly work climate.

Synergy is the creation of a whole greater than the sum of its parts.

Systematic thinking approaches problems in a rational and analytical fashion.

Systems goals are concerned with conditions within the organization that are expected to increase its survival potential.

Task activities directly contribute to the performance of important tasks.

Task performance is the quantity and quality of work produced.

Team is a group of people holding themselves collectively accountable for using complimentary skills to achieve a common purpose.

Team-building is a collaborative way to gather and analyze data to improve teamwork.

Team decisions are made by all members of the team.

Teamwork occurs when team members live up to their collective accountability for goal accomplishment.

Technical skill is an ability to perform specialized tasks.

Telecommuting is work done at home or from a remote location using computers and advanced telecommunications.

Terminal values reflect a person's preferences concerning the "ends" to be achieved.

Title VII of the Civil Rights Act of 1964 protects individuals against employment discrimination on the basis of race and color, national origin, sex, and religion.

Trait perspectives assume that traits play a central role in differentiating between leaders and nonleaders or in predicting leader or organizational outcomes.

Transactional leadership involves leader-follower exchanges necessary for achieving routine performance agreed upon between leaders and followers.

Transformational change radically shifts the fundamental character of an organization.

Transformational leadership occurs when leaders broaden and elevate followers' interests and stir followers to look beyond their own interests to the good of others.

Two-factor theory identifies job context as the source of job dissatisfaction and job content as the source of job satisfaction.

Type A orientations are characterized by impatience, desire for achievement, and a more competitive nature than Type B.

Type B orientations are characterized by an easygoing and less competitive nature than Type A.

Uncertain environments provide no information to predict expected results for decision-making alternatives.

Uncertainty avoidance is the cultural tendency to be uncomfortable with uncertainty and risk in everyday life.

Unfreezing is the stage at which a situation is prepared for change.

Universal design is the practice of designing products, buildings, public spaces, and programs to be usable by the greatest number of people.

Unplanned change occurs spontaneously or randomly.

Upward communication is the flow of messages from lower to higher organizational levels.

Valence is the value to the individual of various work outcomes.

Validity means a performance measure addresses job-relevant dimensions.

Value chain is a sequence of activities that creates valued goods and services for customers.

Value congruence occurs when individuals express positive feelings upon encountering others who exhibit values similar to their own.

Values   are broad preferences concerning appropriate courses of action or outcomes.

Vertical specialization   is a hierarchical division of labor that distributes formal authority.

Virtual communication networks   link team members through electronic communication.

Virtual organization   is an ever-shifting constellation of firms, with a lead corporation, that pool skills, resources, and experiences to thrive jointly.

Virtual teams   work together through computer mediation.

Work sharing   is when employees agree to work fewer hours to avoid layoffs.

Workforce diversity   describes how people differ on attributes such as age, race, ethnicity, gender, physical ability, and sexual orientation.

Workforce diversity   is a mix of people within a workforce who are considered to be, in some way, different from those in the prevailing constituency.

Zone of indifference   is the range of authoritative requests to which a subordinate is willing to respond without subjecting the directives to critical evaluation or judgment.

Self-Test Answers

Self-Test 1

MULTIPLE CHOICE

1. b **2.** d **3.** c **4.** c **5.** c **6.** c **7.** a **8.** a **9.** d **10.** d **11.** a **12.** c **13.** c **14.** c **15.** b

SHORT RESPONSE

16. OB as a scientific discipline has the following characteristics: a) It is an interdisciplinary body of knowledge, drawing upon insights from such allied social sciences as sociology and psychology. b) OB researchers use scientific methods to develop and test models and theories about human behavior in organizations. c) OB focuses on application, trying to develop from science practical insights that can improve organizations. d) OB uses contingency thinking, trying to fit explanations to situations rather than trying to find "one best" answer that fits all situations.

17. The term "valuing diversity" is used to describe behavior that respects individual differences. In the workplace this means respecting the talents and potential contributions of people from different races and of different genders, ethnicities, and ages, for example.

18. An effective manager is one who is able to work with and support other people so that long-term high performance is achieved. This manager is able to maintain an environment for sustainable high performance by creating conditions for job satisfaction as well as high task performance.

19. Mintzberg would say that the executive would be very busy throughout the day and would work long hours. He would note that the day would be fragmented as the executive worked on many different tasks while subject to interruptions. He would point out that the day would be very communication intensive, with the executive interacting with other people in a variety of scheduled and unscheduled meetings and communicating by telephone and other electronic media.

APPLICATIONS ESSAY

20. Carla is about to lead an important discussion since the world of work will certainly be different by the time these sixth graders are ready to enter the workforce. As they look ahead, she should encourage them to consider the following points:

- Commitment to ethical behavior
- Importance of knowledge and experience in the form of "human capital"
- Less emphasis on boss-centered "command and control"
- Emphasis on teamwork
- Emphasis on use of computers and information technology
- Respect for people and their work expectations
- More people working for themselves and more job/employer shifting by people; fewer people working a lifetime for one organization

Of course, one of Carla's greatest challenges will be to express these concepts in words and examples that sixth graders will understand. Your answer should reflect that use of language and examples.

Self-Test 2

MULTIPLE CHOICE

1. c **2.** b **3.** d **4.** a **5.** a **6.** d **7.** a **8.** a **9.** d **10.** c **11.** c **12.** b **13.** c **14.** c

SHORT RESPONSE

15. The dimension of individualism-collectivism reflects different cultural emphases, and it appears in both the Hofstede and Trompenaars frameworks. As pointed out by Hofstede, for example, individualistic cultures tend to emphasize individual reward systems, whereas collectivist cultures emphasize teamwork. OB should help us become more aware of how cultural differences may affect the management of individuals and groups in various settings.

16. In high-power distance cultures managers are likely to be respected by subordinates and expected to exercise authority in their assigned roles. In low-power distance cultures the distinction between manager and subordinate may be more casual, and subordinates will expect to be more involved in decisions affecting them and their work.

17. Demographic characteristics are important for a number of reasons: (1) they serve as the basis for managing diversity; (2) there are various nondiscrimination laws affecting them; (3) they are often erroneously used stereotypically to categorize individuals; and (4) they can form the basis of a bio-data approach to help select employees.

18. Stress can be both constructive and destructive. Up to a certain point, stress is beneficial to performance because it helps to stimulate effort and even creativity. Beyond that point, stress becomes harmful because anxiety and other problems detract from performance. Thus the relationship between stress and performance is curvilinear; too little or too much stress has a negative effect on performance, whereas moderate stress has a positive effect on performance. The problem is finding the "friction" point where stress can be maintained for any given individual at the moderate level.

APPLICATIONS ESSAY

19. Your boss needs to use selected demographic, aptitude and ability, personality, and value and attitude characteristics of individuals to help match specific job and organizational requirements. Along with this, your boss can use the kinds of accountability, development, and recruitment practices designed to manage a diverse, nontraditional workforce effectively.

Self-Test 3

MULTIPLE CHOICE

1. d **2.** a **3.** a **4.** a **5.** a **6.** b **7.** a **8.** a **9.** a **10.** d
11. d **12.** b **13.** a **14.** d **15.** c

SHORT RESPONSE

16. Emotions and moods are both part of what is called affect, or the range of feelings that people experience in their life context. An emotion is a strong positive or negative feeling directed toward someone or something. It is usually intense, not long-lasting, and always associated with a source—someone or something that makes you feel the way you do. An example is the positive emotion of elation a student feels when congratulated by an instructor. A mood is a more generalized positive and negative feeling or state of mind that may persist for some time. An example is someone who wakes up and just fells "grouchy" that day. See Figure 3.2 for additional material to fit this answer.

17. Anger: often bad, stops someone from being taken advantage of; empathy: often good, encourages being taken advantage of.

18. (1) Work itself: responsibility, interest, and growth; (2) Quality of supervision: technical and social support; (3) Relationships with co-workers: social harmony and respect; (4) Promotion opportunities: chances for further advancement; (5) Pay: adequacy and perceived equity vis-à-vis others. Although it depends on the individual and the context, in general each of these can be considered equally important.

19. Cognitive dissonance describes a state of inconsistency between an individual's attitudes and his or her behavior. Such inconsistency can result in changing attitudes, changing future behavior, or developing new ways to explain the inconsistency. The amount of control an individual has over the situation and the magnitude of the reward tend to influence which of these actions will be chosen.

APPLICATIONS ESSAY

20. The heart of the issue rests with the satisfaction—performance relationship as discussed in this chapter. Does satisfaction cause performance? It appears that satisfaction alone is no guarantee of high-level job performance. Although a satisfied worker is likely not to quit and to have good attendance, his or her performance still remains uncertain. In the integrated model of motivation, performance is a function not only of motivation and effort, but also of individual attributes and organizational support. Thus I would be cautious in focusing only on creating satisfied workers and high-performing ones. I would try to make sure that the rewards for performance create satisfaction. I would also try to make sure that the satisfied worker has the right abilities, training, and other support needed to perform a job really well. Assuming that satisfaction alone will always lead to high performance seems risky at best; it leaves too many other important considerations left untouched, an example of which is described in the study of satisfaction in groups across time.

Self-Test 4

MULTIPLE CHOICE

1. b **2.** c **3.** b **4.** b **5.** d **6.** c **7.** b **8.** a **9.** a **10.** d
11. c **12.** c **13.** c **14.** a **15.** b

SHORT RESPONSE

16. A model similar to that in Figure 4.2 should be drawn to include a brief discussion of the perception process as discussed in the chapter.

17. There are six perceptual distortions listed and discussed in the chapter—stereotype, halo effect, selective perception, projection, contrast, and self-fulfilling prophecies. You may select any two and briefly note how they distort the perceptual process.

18. Figure 4.7 summarizes the underlying similarities and differences between classical and operant conditioning. Elaborate on the summary shown in the figure and use and explain different examples than those in the figures or the Pavlov's dog example.

19. Reinforcement learning is a function of its consequences, social learning theory. Emphasizes observational learning and the importance of perception and attribution. Thus, people respond to how their perceptions and attributions help define consequences, and not to the objective consequences as emphasized in reinforcement learning. Social learning theory may be elaborated through an explanation of Figure 4.6 and contrasted with reinforcement as shown through the different reinforcement strategies in Figure 4.9.

APPLICATIONS ESSAY

20. A good example to illustrate attribution is the fundamental attribution error as opposed to the self-serving bias. You should explain the fundamental attribution error as the tendency to underestimate the influence of situational factors and to overestimate the influence of personal factors in evaluating someone else's behaviors. In contrast, the self-serving bias is the tendency to deny personal responsibility for performance problems but accept personal responsibility for performance success. Then follow up with an example of each and implications for managing the department.

Self-Test 5

MULTIPLE CHOICE

1. a **2.** d **3.** b **4.** d **5.** d **6.** d **7.** c **8.** a **9.** c **10.** c
11. b **12.** d **13.** a **14.** a **15.** b

SHORT RESPONSE

16. Basically, this principle states that when one level of need is unsatisfied (or frustrated) the individual can revert back (or regress) to seek further satisfaction of a lower level need. For example, if a need for psychological growth in one's job is frustrated the person may regress back to place more emphasis on satisfying relatedness needs.

17. According to Herzberg the job content or satisfier factors are what really motivate people to work hard. They include such things as feelings of responsibility, opportunities for advancement and growth, and job challenges. In order to build these things into jobs and make them more motivational Herzberg recommends job enrichment—that is adding job content factors by moving into a job things traditionally done by higher levels such as planning and controlling responsibilities.

18. Distributive justice is when everyone is treated by the same rules with no one getting special favors or exceptions; procedural justice is when all rules and procedures are properly followed.

19. Expectancy theory states that Motivation = Expectancy $\times$ Instrumentality $\times$ Valence. The presence of multiplication signs creates the "multiplier effect." This means that a "0" in expectancy or instrumentality or valence creates a "0" for motivation. In other words, the multiplier effect is that all three factors—expectancy, instrumentality, valence— must be positive in order for motivation to be positive.

APPLICATIONS ESSAY

20. The issue in this case boils down to motivation to work hard. A job might provide lots of satisfactions for someone—relationships, good pay, etc., and they may not work hard because there is no link between receiving the need satisfactions and doing a really good job every day. To apply the needs theories of motivation managers need to link opportunities for need satisfaction with tasks and activities that are important to getting the job done well. In this case, as perhaps Person B would be suggesting, individuals will work hard because they are satisfying important needs by doing important job-relevant things.

Self-Test 6

MULTIPLE CHOICE

1. d **2.** c **3.** b **4.** b **5.** a **6.** c **7.** b **8.** d **9.** c **10.** d
11. c **12.** d **13.** d **14.** a **15.** a

SHORT RESPONSE

16. In a traditional evaluation the employee's performance is evaluated by the supervisor. In the 360° evaluation the employee's performance is evaluated by those with whom he or she works, including supervisor, peers, subordinates, and perhaps even customers. The 360° evaluation also typically includes a self-evaluation. When the results of all evaluations are analyzed and compared, the employee has a good sense of his or her accomplishments and areas for improvement. This evaluation can then be discussed with the supervisor.

17. A halo error in performance appraisal occurs when one attribute or behavior inappropriately influences the overall appraisal. For example, an individual may have a unique style of dress but be a very high performer. If the evaluator lets his or her distaste for the dress style negatively bias the overall performance evaluation, a halo error has occurred. A recency error occurs when a performance appraisal is biased due to the influence of recent events. In other words, the performance appraisal is based on most recent performance and may not be an accurate reflection of performance for a full evaluation period. For example, I might have a very bad week just prior to an evaluation due to family problems. If my supervisor uses that week's performance to negatively bias the evaluation even though for the prior six months I had been a very strong performer, recency error would have occurred.

18. It is a moderator variable. In other words, it sets the condition under which an individual will or will not respond positively to the job characteristics. When an individual is high in growth-need strength, the prediction is that he or she will respond positively to a job high in the core characteristics and therefore largely enriched. However, when the individual has low-growth-need strength, the prediction is that he or she will not respond positively to high core characteristics and may be dissatisfied and less productive in such enriched job conditions.

19. The compressed workweek, or 4–40 schedule, offers employees the advantage of a three-day weekend. However, it can cause problems for the employer in terms of ensuring that operations are covered adequately during the normal five-day workweek. Also, the compressed workweek will entail more complicated work scheduling. In addition, some employees find that the schedule is tiring and can cause family adjustment problems.

APPLICATIONS ESSAY

20. There are many things that can be done to use rewards and performance management well in the context of student organizations. On the reward side the most appropriate thing is to make sure that those who get the benefits from the organization are the ones who do the work. For example, if there is a fund-raiser to support a student trip, only those who actively raise the money should get financial support for the trip. And possibly, the financial support should be proportionate to the amount of time and effort each person contributed to raising the funds. Also it is probably quite common that little or no evaluation is done of how people perform in offices and special assignments in the student organizations. Many possible ways of creating and using more formal evaluation systems could be established. For example, officers could be rated on a BARS scale developed by the membership to reflect the desirable officer behaviors. These ratings could take place every month or two, and individuals who perform poorly can be counseled or removed, while those who perform well can be praised and continued.

Self-Test 7

MULTIPLE CHOICE

1. a **2.** b **3.** d **4.** c **5.** b **6.** d **7.** b **8.** d **9.** d **10.** c **11.** b **12.** c **13.** d **14.** c **15.** c

SHORT RESPONSE

16. Teams are potentially good for organizations for several reasons. They are good for people, they can improve creativity, they sometimes make the best decisions, they gain commitment to decisions, they help control the behavior of their members, and they can help to counterbalance the effects of large organization size.

17. Permanent formal groups appear on organization charts and serve an ongoing purpose. These groups may include departments, divisions, teams, and the like. Temporary groups are created to solve a specific problem or perform a defined task and are then disbanded. Examples are committees, cross-functional task forces, and project teams.

18. Required behaviors are formally expected of team members. They are part of the group's formal structure and represent conditions of membership that are "required" to be exhibited. Emergent behaviors are not formally required of members. They "emerge" spontaneously as members work and relate together. They are part of the informal structure of the group.

19. Self-managing teams take different forms. A common pattern, however, involves empowering team members to make decisions about the division of labor and scheduling, to develop and maintain the skills needed to perform several different jobs for the team, to help train one another to learn those jobs, and to help select new team members.

APPLICATIONS ESSAY

20. Saw your message and wanted to respond. Don't worry. There is no reason at all that a great design engineer can't run a high-performance project team. Go into the job with confidence, but try to follow some basic guidelines as you build and work with the team. First off, remember that a "team" isn't just a "group." You have to make sure that the members identify highly with the goals and will hold themselves collectively accountable for results—and that includes you. I suggest that you communicate high-performance standards right from the beginning. Set the tone in the first team meeting and even create a sense of urgency to get things going. Be sure that the members have the right skills, and find ways to create some early "successes" for them. Don't let them drift apart; make sure they spend a lot of time together. Give lots of positive feedback as the project develops and, perhaps most importantly, model the expected behaviors yourself. Go for it!

Self-Test 8

MULTIPLE CHOICE

1. d   **2.** a   **3.** a   **4.** b   **5.** b   **6.** c   **7.** c   **8.** a   **9.** b
10. b   **11.** a   **12.** c   **13.** a   **14.** a   **15.** c

SHORT RESPONSE

16. Team building usually begins when someone notices that a problem exists or may develop in the group. Members then work collaboratively to gather data, analyze the situation, plan for improvements, and implement the plan. Everyone is expected to participate in each step, and the group as a whole is expected to benefit from continuous improvement.

17. To help build positive norms, a team leader must first act as a positive role model. She or he should carefully select members for the team and be sure to reinforce and reward members for performing as desired. She or he should also hold meetings to review performance, provide feedback, and discuss and agree on goals.

18. A basic rule of group dynamics is that members of highly cohesive groups tend to conform to group norms. Thus, when group norms are positive for performance, the conformity is likely to create high-performance outcomes. When the norms are negative, however, the conformity is likely to create low-performance outcomes.

19. Intergroup competition can create problems in the way groups work with one another. Ideally, an organization is a cooperative system in which groups are well integrated and help one another out as needed. When groups get competitive, however, there is a potential dysfunctional side. Instead of communicating with one another, they decrease communication. Instead of viewing one another positively, they develop negative stereotypes of one another. Instead of viewing each other as mutual partners in the organization, they become hostile and view one another more as enemies. Although intergroup competition can be good by adding creative tension and encouraging more focused efforts, this potential negative side should not be forgotten.

APPLICATIONS ESSAY

20. I would tell Alejandro that consensus and unanimity are two different, but related, things. Consensus occurs through extensive discussion and much "give and take," in which group members share ideas and listen carefully to one another. Eventually, one alternative emerges that is preferred by most. Those who disagree, however, know that they have been listened to and have had a fair chance to influence the decision outcome. Consensus, therefore, does not require unanimity. What it does require is the opportunity for any dissenting members to feel they have been able to speak and be sincerely listened to. A decision by unanimity that generates 100 percent agreement on an issue may be the ideal state of affairs, but it is not always possible to achieve. Thus, Alejandro should always try to help members work intensively together, communicate well with one another, and sincerely share ideas and listen. However, he should not be concerned for complete unanimity on every issue. Rather, consensus should be the agreed-upon goal in most cases.

Self-Test 9

MULTIPLE CHOICE

1. c   **2.** b   **3.** a   **4.** c   **5.** b   **6.** d   **7.** a   **8.** c   **9.** a
10. c   **11.** b   **12.** a   **13.** b   **14.** c   **15.** d

SHORT RESPONSE

16. Heuristics are simplifying strategies, or "rules of thumb," that people use to make decisions. They make it easier for individuals to deal with uncertainty and limited information, but they can also lead to biased results. Common heuristics include availability-making decisions based on recent events; representativeness-making decisions based on similar events; and anchoring and adjustment making decisions based on historical precedents.

17. Individual, or authority, decisions are made by the manager or team leader acting alone based on information that he or she possesses. Consultative decisions are made by the manager or team leader after soliciting input from other persons. Group decisions are made when the manager or team leader asks others to participate in problem solving. The ideal form of the group decision is true consensus.

18. Escalating commitment is the tendency to continue with a previously chosen course of action even though feedback indicates that it is not working. This can lead to waste of time, money, and other resources, in addition to the sacrificing of the opportunity to pursue a course of action offering more valuable results. Escalating commitment is encouraged by the popular adage, "If at first you don't succeed try, try, again." Another way to look at it is "throwing good money after bad."

19. Most people are too busy to respond personally to every problem that comes their way. The effective manager and team leader knows when to delegate decisions to others, how to set priorities, and when to abstain from acting altogether. Questions to ask include: Is the problem easy to deal with? Might the problem resolve itself? Is this my decision to make? Is this a solvable problem within the context of the organization?

APPLICATIONS ESSAY

20. This is what I would say in the mentoring situation. First, teams can be great for creativity but they have to be set up and then led so that their creative potential is fully realized. To start with the team needs to have at least some highly creative members. They bring to the team context valuable insights, new ideas, and enthusiasm for finding new ways of doing things. These are people who already have strong creativity skills such as high energy, resourcefulness, intuition, lateral thinking. With people like this as part of the team it will have a strong baseline of team creativity skills in place. Then it is important to give this team management and organizational support to harness this creativity potential. The team leader has to believe in and want team creativity, he or she has to be patient and allow time for creative processes to work, and he or she also needs to make sure the team has all the resources it needs to do creative work. An organizational culture in which creativity is valued is also an asset since it provides a broader context of support for what the team is trying to accomplish. When people throughout the organization value creativity it tends to pull others along and also support their creative efforts. When creativity is expected and even evaluated as part of performance appraisals it is also further encouraged by the surrounding organizational context.

Self-Test 10

MULTIPLE CHOICE

1. c **2.** a **3.** b **4.** b **5.** d **6.** b **7.** a **8.** c **9.** d **10.** c **11.** a **12.** c **13.** c **14.** a **15.** b

SHORT RESPONSE

16. Managers can be faced with the following conflict situations: vertical conflict—conflict that occurs between hierarchical levels; horizontal conflict—conflict that occurs between those at the same hierarchical level; line-staff conflict—conflict that occurs between line and staff representatives; role conflict—conflict that occurs when the communication of task expectations is inadequate or upsetting.

17. The major indirect conflict management approaches include the following: appeals to common goals—involves focusing the attention of potentially conflicting parties on one mutually desirable conclusion; hierarchical referral—using the chain of command for conflict resolution; organizational redesign—including decoupling, buffering, linking pins, and liaison groups; use of myths and scripts—managing superficially through behavioral routines (scripts) or to hide conflict by denying the necessity to make a tradeoff in conflict resolution.

18. You should acknowledge that different styles may be appropriate under different conditions. Avoidance is the extreme form of nonattention and is most commonly used when the issue is trivial, when more important issues are pressing, or when individuals need to cool off. An accommodation strategy is used when an issue is more important to the other party than it is to you, or to build social credits.

19. Distributive negotiation focuses on staking out positions and claiming portions of the available "pie." It usually takes the form of hard negotiation—the parties maximize their self-interests and hold out to get their own way—or soft negotiation—one party is willing to make concessions in order to reach an agreement. Distributive negotiation can lead to competition, compromise, or accommodation, but it tends to be win-lose oriented in all cases. Integrative negotiation focuses on the merits of an issue and attempts to enlarge the available "pie." It may lead to avoidance, compromise, or collaboration. It tends to be more win-win oriented and seeks to satisfy the needs and interests of all parties.

APPLICATIONS ESSAY

20. When negotiating the salary for your first job, you should attempt to avoid the common pitfalls of negotiation. These include falling prey to the myth of the "fixed pie"; nonrational escalation of conflict, such as trying to compare the proposed salary to the highest offer you have heard; overconfidence; and ignoring other's needs (the personnel officer probably has a fixed limit). While the initial salary may be very important to you, you should also recognize that it may not be as significant as what type of job you will have and whether you will have an opportunity to move up in the firm.

Self-Test 11

MULTIPLE CHOICE

1. d **2.** c **3.** a **4.** b **5.** a **6.** d **7.** a **8.** d **9.** a **10.** a **11.** b **12.** a **13.** a **14.** d **15.** a

SHORT RESPONSE

16. Channel richness is a useful concept for managers because it describes the capacity of a communication channel to convey and move information. For example, if a manager wants to convey basic and routine information to a lot of people, a lean channel such as the electronic bulletin or written memorandum may be sufficient. However, if the manager needs to convey a complicated message and one that may involve some uncertainty, a richer channel such as the face-to-face meeting may be necessary. Simply put, the choice of channel may have a lot of impact on the effectiveness of a communication attempt.

17. Informal communication channels are very important in today's organizations. The modern workplace places great emphasis on cross-functional relationships and communication. Employee involvement and participation in decision-making are very important. This requires that people know and talk with one another, often across departmental lines. Progressive organizations make it easy for people to interact and meet outside of formal work assignments and relationships. When people know one another, they can more easily and frequently communicate with one another.

18. Status effects can interfere with the effectiveness of communication between lower and higher levels in an organization. Lower-level members are concerned about how the higher-level members will respond, especially if the information being communicated is negative or unfavorable. In such cases, a tendency exists to filter or modify the information to make it as attractive as possible to the recipient. The result is that high-level decision makers in organizations sometimes act on inaccurate or incomplete information. Although their intentions are good, they just aren't getting good information from their subordinates.

APPLICATIONS ESSAY

19. Organizations depend on communication flowing upward, downward, and laterally. Rapid developments in technology have led to a heavy reliance on computers to assist in the movement of this information. E-mail is one part of an electronic organizational communication system. Research suggests that people may fall prey to the "impersonality" of computer-based operations and that the personal or face-to-face side of communication may suffer. Rather than eliminate e-mail and other forms of computer-mediated communication, however, the managing director should work hard to establish proper e-mail protocols and provide many other avenues for communication. The managing director can serve as a role model in his or her use of e-mail, in being regularly available for face-to-face interactions, by holding regular meetings, and by "wandering around" frequently to meet and talk with people from all levels. In addition, the director can make sure that facility designs and office arrangements support interaction and make it less easy for people to disappear behind computer screens. Finally, the director must actively encourage communication of all types and not allow himself or herself to get trapped into serving as a classic example of the "e-mail boss."

Self-Test 12

MULTIPLE CHOICE

1. d **2.** a **3.** d **4.** d **5.** c **6.** b **7.** a **8.** c **9.** d
10. a **11.** b **12.** a **13.** d **14.** a **15.** d

SHORT RESPONSE

16. For the first part of the question, you should consider the notions of reward, coercive, legitimate, expert, and referent power. The response should recognize the difference between position sources and personal sources. The second part of the question concerns the power of lower level participants in organizational settings. Link the sources of power with Bernard's acceptance theory of authority.

17. The text introduces five basic guidelines for increasing position power. They are (1) increase your centrality and criticality in the organization; (2) increase the personal discretion and flexibility of your job; (3) build into your job

tasks that are difficult to evaluate; (4) increase the visibility of your job performance; (5) increase the relevance of your tasks to the organization. The text also identifies three basic guidelines for acquiring personal power. They are: (1) increase your knowledge and information as it relates to the job; (2) increase your personal attractiveness; (3) increase your effort in relation to key organizational tasks.

18. The text identifies seven basic strategies of managerial influence: reason, friendliness, coalition, bargaining, assertiveness, higher authority, and sanctions. You should be able to express them in everyday language along with an example. Each of these strategies is available to the manager in the downward influence attempt; however, the choices in upward attempts may be more limited. In the exercise of upward influence, influence attempts can be expected frequently to include assertiveness, friendliness, and reason.

19. Organizational politics is formally defined as "the management of influence to obtain ends not sanctioned by the organization or to obtain sanctioned ends through nonsanctioned means." Yet it can also be viewed as the art of creative compromise among competing interests. You should be able to express these apparently conflicting views in everyday language that communicates a sense of understanding. It is important that politics not be viewed as an entirely dysfunctional phenomenon that can result in people becoming dissatisfied and feeling emotionally distraught or estranged from the organizational situation. In particular, the functional aspects of organizational politics include helping managers to overcome personal inadequacies, cope with change, channel personal contacts, and substitute for formal authority.

APPLICATIONS ESSAY

20. While the financial implications to stockholders from merger and acquisition seems to vary considerably, one lesson is quite clear—the senior executive of the acquiring firm gains power and influence. Further, a chief reason for senior executives involuntarily leaving firms is being taken over by another corporation. Thus, some executives believe that it is merge or be merged so they would rather be on the acquiring end.

Self-Test 13

MULTIPLE CHOICE

1. a **2.** b **3.** b **4.** b **5.** c **6.** c **7.** a **8.** d **9.** b
10. a **11.** c **12.** a **13.** b **14.** a **15.** c

SHORT RESPONSE

16. Leadership is the process of influencing others and facilitating effort in order to accomplish shared objectives. Leadership tends to emphasize adaptive or useful change, whereas management is designed to promote stability or to enable the organization to run smoothly.

17. Leader trait and behavior approaches assume that, in a given setting, leadership (as opposed to other variables) is central to task performance and satisfaction-related outcomes.

18. Situational contingency approaches to leadership assume that leader traits or behaviors act in conjunction with situational contingencies (other important aspects of the leadership situation) to determine outcomes.

19. Implicit leadership is in the mind of the respondent and is discussed in the text in two forms: Leadership as attribution (inference-based) and leadership prototypes. Leadership as attribution argues that followers tend to describe a leader of a high performing group or organization favorably; in other words, they infer good leadership or real leadership to such an individual and if the group is not performing well, poor leadership is inferred. In the leadership prototype approach, people are seen as having a mental image of the characteristics that make a good or real leader in a given situation. This is sometimes termed recognition-based (you know a good leader when you see one). The characteristics range from specific to general for different kinds of leaders and across different cultures.

APPLICATIONS ESSAY

20. You are asked to respond on the point that leadership is not real and is only a figment of people's imaginations. You might start by arguing there is some truth to the argument, but it neglects the fact that leadership can also be real, where if it had not been exhibited certain outcomes would not have occurred. So the argument here, as in many cases, would be one of moderation—leadership can be real but it also can be inference- or recognition-based. That is, leadership can be seen as a mixture of both. The report can also use some examples of inference- and recognition-based leadership and how these relate to the more traditional treatment of leadership as a real phenomenon. One also could extend the discussion to leadership and management differences and similarities and how they relate to this point.

Self-Test 14

MULTIPLE CHOICE

1. c **2.** d **3.** a **4.** a **5.** c **6.** d **7.** c **8.** b **9.** b **10.** d
11. b **12.** d **13.** c **14.** b **15.** a

SHORT RESPONSE

16. Three ways in which shared leadership can be used in self-directed work teams are (1) behavior-focused strategies that tend to increase self-awareness, leading to the behaviors involving necessary but not always pleasant tasks; (2) self rewards in conjunction with behavior-focused strategies; and (3) constructive thought patterns that focus on the creation or alteration of cognitive thought processes. The student should then elaborate on each of these along the lines of the discussion in the chapter.

17. The multiple-level approach argues that organizations comprise three domains from bottom to top, with two managerial levels within each domain. The domains from bottom to top are production, organization, and systems. Each domain and level gets more complex in terms of managerial and leadership requirements. Managerial leader cognitive and behavioral complexity should match the additional complexity requirements at each domain and level. The Boal and Hooijberg approach essentially builds absorptive capacity, capacity to change, and managerial wisdom around charismatic, transformational, and vision leadership and their interaction with behavioral, social, and cognitive complexity. These characteristics are argued to be related to strategic leadership effectiveness and organizational effectiveness. Essentially, the student should elaborate and provide examples for the above frameworks and then do a compare and contrast treatment.

18. Not all change in organizations is planned. Unplanned change—that which occurs spontaneously or by surprise—can be useful. The appropriate goal in managing unplanned change is to act immediately once the change is recognized to minimize any negative consequences and maximize any possible benefits. The goal is to take best advantage of the change situation by learning from the experience.

19. External forces for change are found in the relationship between an organization and its environment. Examples are the pressures of mergers, strategic alliances, and divestitures. Internal forces for change include those found in different lifecycle demands as the organization passes from birth through growth and toward maturity. Internal forces also include the political nature of organizations as reflected in authority and reward systems.

APPLICATIONS ESSAY

20. Jorge may begin his attempts to deal with resistance to change by using education and communication. Through one-on-one discussions, group presentations, and even visits to other centers he can better inform his staff about the nature and logic of the changes. He should also utilize participation and involvement by allowing others (for examples, in a series of task forces) to help choose the new equipment and design the new programs. In all this he should offer enough facilitation and support to help everyone deal with any hardships the changes may cause. He should be especially alert to listen to any problems and complaints that may arise. On certain matters, Jorge might use negotiation and agreement to exchange benefits for staff support. In the extreme case, manipulation and cooperation through covert attempts to influence others might be used to achieve needed support, although this is not advisable. Similarly, explicit or implicit coercion would use force to get people to accept change at any cost. My advice would be to stick with the first four strategies as much as possible and avoid the latter two.

Self-Test 15

MULTIPLE CHOICE

1. c **2.** a **3.** b **4.** a **5.** d **6.** d **7.** a **8.** a **9.** b
10. c **11.** b **12.** a **13.** d **14.** d **15.** a

SHORT RESPONSE

16. Cox's theory is designed for organizations that are located in the United States. His ideas may not be easily expanded to multinational corporations headquartered in other cultures. Cox believes that it is important for culturally divergent groups within an organization to communicate and educate one another. This helps subgroups become more tolerant and interactive with other portions of the organization. Second, the organization needs to make sure that one type of cultural group is not segregated into one type of position. When cultural subgroups are spread throughout the organization, the levels of interaction increase as the stereotyping decreases. The company also needs to help restructure many of its informal lines of communication. By encouraging the integration of the informal communication, subgroups become more involved with one another. The organization must also ensure that no one group is associated with the company's outside image. A company that is perceived to be uniform in its culture attracts individuals who are from a similar culture. Finally, Cox states that interpersonal conflict that is based on group identity needs to be controlled.

17. Groups first need to define who is in the group and who is not. Criteria for both formal and informal groups need to be established to provide a framework for membership. Second, the group needs to set standards of behavior. These standards should consist of a series of informal rules that describe proper behavior and activities for the members. Finally, group members need to identify the friends and adversaries of the group. The identification process helps the group build alliances throughout the organization when they attempt to get projects and ideas completed.

18. If you have not had full-time employment, think seriously about this question because it is designed to help you appreciate the importance of organizational rules and roles. Formal rules should be covered to show that they help dictate procedures individuals use. Informal interaction should be discussed as well. Such questions as, "How are subgroups treated?" "Do different instructors have different rules?" and "Are Seniors treated differently from Sophomores in this system?" could all be potential subtopics.

19. The first element is the need for a widely shared philosophy. Although this first element seems vague, an effec-

tive company philosophy is anything but abstract. An organization member needs to be exposed to what the firm stands for. The firm's mission needs to be articulated often and throughout the organization. Organizations should put people ahead of rules and general policy mandates. When staffers feel included and important in a system they feel more loyal and accepting of the culture. Every company has heroes or individuals who have succeeded beyond expectations. Companies with strong company cultures allow the stories of these individuals to become well known throughout the organization. Through these stories, workers need to make sure that they understand the rituals and ceremonies that are important to the company's identity. Maintaining and enhancing these rituals helps many organizations keep a strong corporate culture. Informal rules and expectations must be evident so that workers understand what is expected of them and the organization. Finally, employees need to realize that their work is important; their work and knowledge should be networked throughout the company. The better the communication system in the company, the better the company's culture.

APPLICATIONS ESSAY

20. An overemphasis on exploration is likely to yield a great number of new ideas, programs, and initiatives, but comparatively little effective commercialization. In contrast, an over emphasis on exploitation often results in small incremental changes to existing products in existing markets and does not yield the changes often dictated by environmental and technological change. Thus, most OB researchers stress the need for some type of balance. There are a variety of ways to do this. The most ambitious is to develop an ambidextrous organization that stresses both. Often, however, senior managers ask some parts to stress exploration and other exploitation. Here they recognize the tension and are prepared to reconcile opposing views.

Self-Test 16

MULTIPLE CHOICE

1. b **2.** b **3.** b **4.** c **5.** d **6.** a **7.** a **8.** d **9.** b **10.** d
11. a **12.** b **13.** c **14.** b **15.** c **16.** b **17.** a **18.** a
19. b **20.** d

SHORT RESPONSE

21. Output goals are designed to help an organization define its overall mission and to help define the kind of business it is in. Output goals can often help define the types of products and the relationships that the company has with its consumers. Output goals often help demonstrate how a company fits into society. The second kind of organizational goal is the systems goal. A systems goal helps the company realize what behaviors it needs to maintain for its survival. The systems goal provides the means for the ends. It is important to recognize the importance of systems goals for day-to-day operations.

22. Control is the set of mechanisms used to keep action and/or outputs within predetermined limits. Two types of controls are often found in organizations. Output controls focus on desired targets to allow managers discretion in using different methods for reaching these targets. Process controls attempt to specify the manner in which tasks are accomplished. Policies, procedures, and rules as well as formalization and standardization can be seen as types of process controls. Total Quality Management can be seen as a systemic way of managing processes within the firm and thus be viewed as a control mechanism.

23. The first advantage is that functional specialization can yield clear task assignments that replicate an individual's training and experience. Functional specialization also provides the ability for departmental colleagues to build upon one another's knowledge and experience. The functional approach also provides an excellent training ground for new managers. Finally, this system is easy to explain because members can understand the role of each group even though they do not understand a particular individual's functions. There are some major disadvantages to the system as well. The system may reinforce overspecialization. Many jobs within the system may become boring and too routine. The lines of communication within the organization may become overly complex. Top management is often overloaded with too many problems that should be addresses at a lower level. Many top managers spend too much time dealing with cross-functional issues. Finally, many individuals look up in the hierarchy for reinforcement instead of focusing their attention on products, services, and clients.

24. A matrix combines the strengths of both the functional a division departmentation. For instance, divisional specialization provides the organization with adaptability and flexibility to meet important demands of key external groups. With the matrix this emphasis is blended with a stress on technical affairs found under functional departmentation. Unfortunately, there is a cost for this blending. Unity of command is lost. The authority and responsibilities of managers may overlap causing conflict. And this form may be expensive.

APPLICATIONS ESSAY

25. The notion that the Postal Service is a mechanistic bureaucracy is important because it suggests that there are already many controls built into the system by the division of labor. You should recognize several primary side effects that are exhibited when control mechanisms are placed on an individual in an organization such as the Postal Service. There is often a difficulty in balancing organizational controls. As one control is emphasized, others may be neg-

lected. Controls often force managers to emphasize the "quick fix" instead of long-term planning. Often, controls lead to solutions that are not customized to specific problems (i.e., "across the board cuts"). Planning and documentation can become burdensome and limit the amount of action that actually occurs. Managers often become more concerned with internal paperwork than with problem solving or customers. And there are far too many supervisors and managers. Controls that are vaguely designed are often ineffective and unrealistic. As a result, the manager may interpret the control, as he or she wants. The "do the best you can" goal that is commonly given to managers in the Postal Service is an example of this concept. Controls that are inserted drastically and harshly often cause panic among managers and administrators. A swift change in the territories of postal delivery clerks is an example. Finally, many goals and controls are inserted without the appropriate resources. This practice can make the attainment of goals difficult, if not impossible.

Self-Test 17

MULTIPLE CHOICE

1. d   **2.** d   **3.** d   **4.** a   **5.** d   **6.** d   **7.** c   **8.** c   **9.** c   **10.** d   **11.** b   **12.** a   **13.** b   **14.** b   **15.** b   **16.** a   **17.** b   **18.** a   **19.** b   **20.** a

SHORT RESPONSE

21. There are a number of ways to answer this question. Actually, a very large firm could use a simple structure but its chances of reaching its goals and surviving would be small. As the firm grows so does the complexity inside and individuals become overwhelmed if the firm does not evolve into a bureaucracy. Recall that a bureaucracy involved labor that is divided so that each worker was specialized. Every worker would have well-defined responsibilities and authorities. To complement this specialization, the organization should be arranged hierarchically. Authority should be arranged from the bottom up. A worker should be promoted only on the basis of merit and technical competence. Most importantly, employees are to work under rules and guidelines that were impersonal and applied to all staffers equally.

22. Information technology is the combination of machines, artifacts, procedures, and systems used to gather, store, analyze, and disseminate information for translating it into knowledge. It can be used as (a) a partial substitute for some operations as well as some process controls and impersonal methods of coordination, (b) a capability for transforming information to knowledge for learning and (c) a strategic capability.

23. James Thompson believed that technology could be divided into three categorie—intensive, mediating, or long linked. An intensive technology occurs when uncertainty exists as to how to produce the desired outcomes. Teams of specialists are brought together to pool knowledge and resources to solve the problem. An interdependence among specialists develops because all parties need one another to fulfill the project successfully. This technology often occurs in the research and development portion of organizations. A mediating technology allows various parties to become interdependent. For example, the ATM network that most banks utilize allows customers to bank at other institutions and still be tied to their home bank, automatically. Without this technology, the banking industry would not be so well linked. The technology helps determine the nature of the banks' relationships with one another. Finally, Thompson believed that long-linked technologies had a unique effect on organizations as well. Long-linked technology is more commonly known as industrial technology. This type of knowledge allows organizations to produce goods in mass quantities. The assembly line designed by Henry Ford is one of the early examples of long-linked technology. Thompson uses these distinctions to highlight the various impacts that technology has on organizations. His approach differs greatly from Joan Woodward's approach, which focuses more on the mode of production. Woodward divides technology into three areas: small-batch manufacturing, mass production, and continuous process custom goods. Crafts persons are often characterized as small producers who must alter production to fit the needs of each client. Mass production technology deals with production of uniform goods for a mass market. The production design is altered to maximize speed while limiting product styles. The last type of technology deals with continuous-process technology. Oil refineries and chemical plants are classic examples of this type of technology. These industries are intensely automated and produce the same products without variation.

24. We define environmental complexity as an estimate of the magnitude of the problems and opportunities in an organization's environment as influenced by three main factors: degree of richness, degree of interdependence, and degree of uncertainty. Environmental richness, is shown by an environment that is improving around the company. The economy is growing, and people are investing and spending money. Internally, the company may be growing, and its employees may be prospering as well. In a rich environment, organizations can succeed despite their poor organizational structure. An environment that is not rich allows only well-organized companies to survive in the long run. The second major factor in environmental complexity is the level of interdependence. This factor focuses on the relationships an organization needs to develop to compete in a certain setting. How free is that organization to conduct business? Uncertainty and volatility are the final factors that make up complexity. Organizations must decide how to deal with markets and environments that are continually changing and where the rate of change is changing.

APPLICATIONS ESSAY

25. In the design and development of cars and trucks, Ford must recognize both the voice of the customer and a whole series of extremely complex technical requirements. If the company violates either the customer requirements or the technical requirements, it will not be able to develop a profitable vehicle. In the product and assembly plants these conflict forces are not as prominent, and the firm may opt for a simpler structure.

Notes

Chapter 1

ENDNOTES

[1] Great Place to Work Institute Europe. (2009). 100 Best Workplaces in Europe. *European Great Place to Work Magazine, 2009;* www.microsoft.com/emea/presscentre/pressreleases/LargeWorkplacePR_210509.mspx.

[2] For a general overview. See Jay W. Lorsch (ed.), *Handbook of Organizational Behavior* (Englewood Cliffs. NJ: Prentice Hall, 1987); and, Julian Barling, Cary Li Cooper, Stewart Clegg (Eds.), the Sage Handbook of Organizational Behavior: Volumes l and 2 (San Francisco, CA: sage, 2009).

[3] Jeffrey Pfeffer and Robert I. Sutton, *Hard Facts, Dangerous Half-Truths, and Total Nonsense: Profiting from Evidence-Based Management* (Boston: Harvard Business School Press, 2006). See also Jeffrey Pfeffer and Robert I. Sutton, "Management Half-Truths and Nonsense," *California Management Review* 48.3, (2006), pp. 77–100; and Jeffrey Pfeffer and Robert I. Sutton, Evidence-Based Management, *Harvard Business Review* (January, 2006), R0601E.

[4] Geert Hofslede. "Cultural Constraints in Management Theories," *Academy of Management Executive* 7 (1993), pp. 81–94.

[5] John Huey, "Managing in the Midst of Chaos," *Fortune* (April 5, 1993), pp. 38–18. See also Tom Peters, *Thriving on Chaos* (New York: Knopf, 1991); Jay R. Galbraith, Edward E. Lawler III, and Associates, *Organizing for the Future: The New Logic for Managing Organizations* (San Francisco: Jossey-Bass, 1993); William H. Davidow and Michael S. Malone, *The Virtual Corporation: Structuring and Revitalizing the Corporation of the 21st Century* (New York HarperBusiness, 1993); Charles Handy, *The Age of Unreason* (Boston: Harvard Business School Press, 1994); Peter Drucker, *Managing in a Time of Great Change* (New York: Truman Talley, 1995); Peter Drucker, *Management Challenges for the 21st Century* (New York: Harper, 1999).

[6] For historical foundations see Jay A. Conger, *Winning 'Em Over: A New Model for Managing in the Age of Persuasion* (New York: Simon & Schuster, 1998), pp. 180–181; Stewart D. Friedman, Perry Christensen, and Jessica DeGroot, "Work and Life: The End of the Zero-Sum Game," *Harvard Business Review* (November/December 1998), pp. 119–129; C. Argyris, "Empowerment: The Emperor's New Clothes," *Harvard Business Review* (May/June 1998), pp. 98–105.

[7] Robert B. Reich, "The Company of the Future," *Fast Company* (November 1998), p. 124ff.

[8] For more on mission statements see Patricia Jones and Larry Kahaner, "Say It and Live It: The 50 Corporate Mission Statements That Hit the Mark" (New York: Currency/Doubleday, 1995); John Graham and Wendy Havlick, *Mission Statements: A Guide to the Corporate and Nonprofit Sectors* (New York: Garland, 1995).

[9] James C. Collins and Jerry L. Porras, "Building Your Company's Vision," *Harvard Business Review* (September/October 1996), pp. 65–77.

[10] These mission statements and others are found on corporate Web sites.

[11] See Michel E. Porter, *Competitive Strategy Techniques for Analyzing Industries and Competitors* (New York: Free Press, 1980); *Competitive Advantage: Creating and Sustaining Superior Performance* (New York: Free Press, 1986); Gary Hamel and C. K. Prahalad, "Strategic Intent," *Harvard Business Review* (May/June 1989), pp. 63–76; Richard A. D'Aveni, *Hyper Competition: Managing the Dynamics of Strategic Managing* (New York: Free Press, 1994).

[12] Edgar Schein, *Organizational Culture and Leadership*, 2nd ed. (San Francisco: Jossey-Bass, 1997); Edgar Schein, *The Corporate Culture Survival Guide* (San Francisco: Jossey-Bass, 1999). See also Terrence E. Daeal and Alan A. Kennedy, *Corporate Cultures: The Rites and Rituals of Corporate Life* (Reading, MA: Addison Wesley, 1982).

[13] Rajiv Dutta, "eBay's Meg Whitman on Building a Company's Culture." *BusinessWeek* (March 27, 2009): www.businessweek.com.

[14] Roger O. Crockett, "How P&G Finds—And Keeps—A Prized Workforce," *BusinessWeek* (April 20, 2009), p. 55.

[15] Ibid.

[16] See the OCI and other resources at www.humansynergistics.com.

[17] Robert A. Cooke and J. L Szurnal, "Measuring Normative Beliefs and Shared Behavioral Expectations in Organizations: The Reliability and Validity of the Organizational Culture Inventory," *Psychological Reports* 72 (1993), pp. 1299–1330.

[18] Ibid; Robert A. Cooke and J. L. Szurnal, "Using the Organizational Culture Inventory to Understand the Operating Cultures of Organizations," in N. M. Ashkanasy, C. P. M. Wilerom, and M. F. Peterson (eds.), *Handbook of Organizational Culture and Climate* (Thousand Oaks, CA: Sage, 2000), pp. 147–162.

[19] A baseline report on diversity in the American workplace is *Workforce 2000: Work and Workers in the 21st Century* (Indianapolis: Hudson Institute, 1987). For comprehensive discussions see Martin M. Chemers, Stuart Oskamp, and Mark A. Costanzo, *Diversity in Organization: New Perspectives for a Changing Workplace* (Beverly Hills: Sage, 1995); Robert T. Golembiewski, *Managing Diversity in Organizations* (Tuscaloosa: University of Alabama Press, 1995).

[20] See Taylor Cox Jr., "The Multicultural Organization," *Academy of Management Executive* 5 (1991), pp. 34–47; *Cultural Diversity in Organizations: Theory, Research and Practice* (San Francisco: Bernett-Koehler, 1993).

[21] R. Roosevelt Thomas Jr., *Beyond Race and Gender* (New York: AMACOM, 1992), p. 10; see also R. Roosevelt Thomas Jr., "From 'Affirmative Action' to 'Affirming Diversity,'" *Harvard Business Review* (November/December 1990), pp. 107–117; R. Roosevelt Thomas Jr., with Marjorie I. Woodruff, *Building a House for Diversity* (New York: AMACOM, 1999).

[22] "In CEO pay, Another Gender Gap," *BusinessWeek* (November 24, 2008), p. 22; "The View from the Kitchen Table," *Newsweek* (January 26, 2009), p. 29; and, Del Jones, "Women Slowly Gain on Men," *USA Today* (January 2, 2009), p. 6B; Catalyst research reports at *www.catalyst.org*; "Nicking the Glass Ceiling," *BusinessWeek* (June 9, 2009), p. 18.

[23] We're Getting Old," *The Wall Street Journal* (March 26, 2009), p. D2; and Les Christie, "Hispanic Population Boom Fuels Rising U.S. Diversity," *CnnMoney*: www.cnn.com; and Betsy Towner, "The New Face of 50+ America," *AARP Bulletin* (June, 2009), p. 31. See also U.S. Census Bureau reports at www.factfinder.census.gov.

[24] Cox, op. cit.; Thomas, 1990, 1992, op. cit.

[25] Thomas and Woodruff (1991).

[26] See Thomas and Woodruff, op. cit; Thomas, 1990, 1992, op. cit.

[27] "In CEO Pay, another Gender gap, "op. cit.; Jones, op. cit.; Catalyst, op. cit.

[28] William M. Bulkeley, "Xerox Names Burns Chief as Mulcahy Retires Early," *The Wall Street Journal* (May 22, 2009), pp. B1, B2.

[29] For more on the management process, see John R. Schermerhorn Jr., *Management*, 10th ed. (Hoboken, NJ: Wiley, 2010).

[30] The review is from Henry Mintzberg, *The Nature of Managerial Work* (New York: Harper & Row, 1973). For related and further developments, see Morgan W. McCall Jr., Ann M. Morrison, and Robert L. Hannan, *Studies of Managerial Work: Results and Methods*, Technical Report No. 9 (Greensboro, NC: Center for Creative Leadership, 1978); John P. Kotter, *The General Managers* (New York: Free Press, 1982); Fred Luthans, Stuart Rosenkrantz, and Harry Hennessey, "What Do Successful Managers Really Do?" *Journal of Applied Behavioral Science* 21.2 (1985), pp. 255–270; Robert E. Kaplan, *The Warp and Woof of the General Manager's Job*, Technical Report No. 27 (Greensboro, NC: Center for Creative Leadership, 1986); Fred Luthans, Richard M. Hodgetts, and Stuart A. Rosenkrantz, *Real Managers* (New York: HarperCollins, 1988).

[31] Mintzberg (1973). See also Henry Mintzberg, *Mintzberg on Management* (New York: Free Press, 1989); "Rounding Out the Manager's Job," *Sloan Management Review* (Fall 1994), pp. 11–26.

[32] Kotter (1982), "What Effective General Managers Really Do," *Harvard Business Review* 60 (November/December 1982), p. 161. See Kaplan (1986).

[33] Herminia Ibarra, "Managerial Networks," Teaching Note: 9-495-039, Harvard Business School Publishing, Boston, MA.

[34] Robert L. Katz, "Skills of an Effective Administrator, *Harvard Business Review* 52 (September/October 1974), p. 94. See also Richard E. Royatzis, *The Competent Manager: A Model for Effective Performance* (New York: Wiley, 1982).

[35] Daniel Goleman, *Emotional Intelligence* (New York: Bantam, 1995); Daniel Goleman, *Working with Emotional Intelligence* (New York: Bantam, 1998). See also Daniel Goleman "What Makes a Leader," *Harvard Business Review* (November/December 1998), pp. 93–102; and "Leadership That Makes a Difference," *Harvard Business Review* (March/April 2000), pp. 79–90, quote from p. 80.

[36] Archie B. Carroll, "In Search of the Moral Manager," *Business Horizons* (March/April 2001), pp. 7–15.

[37] Mahzarin R. Banagji, Max H. Bazerman, and Dolly Chugh, "How (Un)ethical are You?" *Harvard Business Review* (December 2003).

[38] Terry Thomas, John R. Schermerhorn Jr., and John W. Dinehart, "Strategic Leadership of Ethical Behavior in Business," *Academy of Management Executive* (2004).

[39] See Peter Senge, The Fifth Discipline (New York: Harper, 1990); D. A. Garvin, "Building a Learning Organization," *Harvard Business Review* (November/December 1991), pp. 78–91; Chris Argyris, *On Organizational Learning*, 2nd ed. (Malden, MA: Blackwell, 1999).

[40] For a discussion of experiential learning, see D. Christopher Kayes, "Experiential Learning and Its Critics: Preserving the Role of Experience in Management Learning and Education," *Academy of Management Learning and Education* 1.2, (2002), pp. 137–149.

[41] Institute for Learning Styles, *Perceptual Modality Preferences Survey*: www.learningstyles.org.

[42] Ibid.

FEATURE NOTES

Opener/Microsoft Europe: Great Place to Work Institute Europe. (2009). 100 Best Workplaces in Europe. *European Great Place to Work Magazine, 2009;* www.microsoft.com/emea/presscentre/pressreleases/ LargeWorkplacePR_210509.mspx

Ethics in OB: Rakesh Khuran and Nitin Horia, "It's Time to Make Management a True Profession," *Harvard Business Review* (October, 2008), pp. 70–77; Daniel Trotta, "Frustrated Americans Cheer Obama's Tough Auto Moves," Reuters (March 30, 2009): www.reuters.com.

Leaders on Leadership/Rod Jones: Information from http://www.ey.com/AU/en/Newsroom/News-releases/Australian-education-leader-vies-for-world-entrepreneur-title; http://www.navitasworld.com/index.htm

Mastering Management: Reported in Eric Schmidt and Hal Varian, "Google: Ten Golden Rules," *Newsweek* (December 2, 2005); reported on msnbc.com (retrieved September 17, 2006).

MARGIN PHOTOS

Global Forum for Responsible Management Education—Information from "Academic Leaders from 43 Countries Renew Commitment to Responsible Management Education," The Levin Institute (December 5, 2008): www.levin.suny.edu/globalforum. Overflowing Brain—Torkel Klingberg, *The Overflowing Brain: Information Overload and the Limits of Working Memory* (New York: Oxford University Press, 2009); *Umsobomvu Youth Fund/Malose Kekana*—Information from Sharon Shinn, "The Business of Dreams," *Bi₂Ed* (November/December, 2008), pp. 18–24.

Chapter 2

ENDNOTES

[1] Great Place to Work Institute Europe. (2009). 100 Best Workplaces in Europe. *European Great Place to Work Magazine, 2009;* www.atp.dk

[2] See Dorothy Leonard and Susan Strauss, "Putting Your Company's Whole Brain to Work," *Harvard Business Review* 75.4 Jul–Aug 1997, pp. 110–121. Also, Daniel Pink's *A Whole New Mind: Why Right-Brainers Will Rule the Future* (New York: Riverhead Books, 2005).

[3] Viktor Gecas, "The Self-Concept," in *Annual Review of Sociology* 8, ed. Ralph H. Turner and James F. Short Jr. (Palo Alto, CA: Annual Review, 1982), p.3. Also see Arthur P. Brief and Ramon J. Aldag, "The Self in Work Organizations: A Conceptual Review," *Academy of Management Review* (January 1981), pp. 75–88; Jerry J. Sullivan, "Self Theories and Employee Motivation," *Journal of Management* (June 1989), pp. 345–363.

[4] Compare Philip Cushman, "Why the Self Is Empty," *American Psychologist* (May 1990), pp. 599–611.

[5] Based in part on a definition in Gecas, 1982, p. 3.

[6] Suggested by J. Brockner, *Self-Esteem at Work* (Lexington, MA: Lexington Books, 1988), p. 144; John A. Wagner III and John R. Hollenbeck, *Management of Organizational Behavior* (Englewood Cliffs, NJ: Prentice-Hall, 1992), pp. 100–101.

[7] See N. Brody, *Personality: In Search of Individuality* (San Diego, CA: Academic Press, 1988), pp. 68–101; C. Holden, "The Genetics of Personality," *Science* (August 7, 1987), pp. 598–601.

[8] See Geert Hofstede, 1984.

[9] Chris Argyris, *Personality and Organization* (New York: Harper & Row, 1957); Daniel J. Levinson, *The Seasons of a Man's Life* (New York: Knopf, 1978); Gail Sheehy, *New Passages* (New York: Ballantine Books, 1995).

[10] R. Jacob, "The Resurrection of Michael Dell," *Fortune* (August 1995), pp. 117–128.

[11] M. R. Barrick and M. K. Mount, "The Big Five Personality Dimensions and Job Performance: A Meta Analysis," *Personnel Psychology* 44 (1991), pp. 1–26; M. R. Barrick and M. K. Mount, "Autonomy as a Moderator of the Relationships between the Big Five Personality Dimensions and Job Performance," *Journal of Applied Psychology* (February 1993), pp. 111–118.

[12] See Jim C. Nunnally, *Psychometric Theory*, 2nd ed. (New York: McGraw-Hill, 1978), chapter 14.

[13] See "Computerized Personality Tests Spawn a Culture of Cheating," from *The Wall Street Journal*, posted on Ethics Newsline on Jan. 12, 2009. http://www.globalethics.org/newsline/2009/01/12/personality-tests-2/print/. "Nearly One-Fourth of Workers Admit to Lying About Lateness," posted on Ethics Newsline, May 19, 2008. http://www.globalethics.org/newsline/2008/05/19/lying-about-lateness/. "One-Third of Workers 'Called in Sick With Fake Excuses in the Last Year': Survey," posted on Ethics Newsline, December 4, 2006. http://www.globalethics.org/newsline/2006/12/04/one-third-of-workers-called-in-sick-with-fake-excuses-in-the-last-year-survey/. Mary Uhl-Bien, "The Demands on Ethics and Leadership," Report of the Gallup Leadership Institute at the College of Business Administration, University of Nebraska, 2007.

[14] See David A. Whetten and Kim S. Cameron, *Developing Management Skills*, 3rd ed. (New York: HarperCollins, 1995), p. 72.

[15] Raymond G. Hunt, Frank J. Kryzstofiak, James R. Meindl, and Abdalla M. Yousry, "Cognitive Style and Decision Making," *Organizational Behavior and Human Decision Processes* 44.3 (1989), pp. 436–453. For additional work on problem-solving styles, see Ferdinand A. Gul, "The Joint and Moderating Role of Personality and Cognitive Style on Decision Making," *Accounting Review* (April 1984), pp. 264–277; Brian H. Kleiner, "The Interrelationship of Jungian Modes of Mental Functioning with Organizational Factors: Implications for Management Development," *Human Relations* (November 1983), pp. 997–1012; James L. McKenney and Peter G. W. Keen, "How Managers' Minds Work," *Harvard Business Review* (May–June 1974), pp. 79–90.

[16] Some examples of firms using the Myers-Briggs Type Indicators are given in J. M. Kunimerow and L. W. McAllister, "Team Building with the Myers-Briggs Type Indicator: Case Studies," *Journal of Psychological Type* 15 (1988), pp. 26–32; G. H. Rice Jr. and D. P. Lindecamps, "Personality Types and Business Success of Small Retailers," *Journal of Occupational Psychology* 62 (1989), pp. 177–182; B. Roach, *Strategy Styles and Management Types: A Resource Book for Organizational Management Consultants* (Stanford, CA: Balestrand, 1989).

[17] J. B. Rotter, "Generalized Expectancies for Internal versus External Control of Reinforcement," *Psychological Monographs* 80 (1966), pp. 1–28.

[18] See J. Michael Crant, "Proactive Behavior in Organizations," *Journal of Management* 26 (2000), pp. 435–462. See also T. S. Bateman, and J. M. Crant, "The proactive component of organizational behavior," *Journal of Organizational Behavior* 14 (1993), pp. 103–118.

[19] Don Hellriegel, John W. Slocum Jr., and Richard W. Woodman, *Organizational Behavior*, 5th ed. (St. Paul, MN: West, 1989), p. 46; Wagner and Hollenbeck (1992), chapter 4.

[20] Niccolo Machiavelli, *The Prince*, trans. George Bull (Middlesex, UK: Penguin, 1961).

[21] Richard Christie and Florence L. Geis, *Studies in Machiavellianism* (New York: Academic Press, 1970).

[22] See M. Snyder, *Public Appearances/Private Realities: The Psychology of Self-Monitoring* (New York: Freeman, 1987).

[23] Snyder, 1987.

[24] Adapted from R. W. Bonner, "A Short Scale: A Potential Measure of Pattern A Behavior," *Journal of Chronic Diseases* 22 (1969). Used by permission.

[25] See Meyer Friedman and Ray Roseman, *Type A Behavior and Your Heart* (New York: Knopf, 1974). For another view, see Walter Kiechel III, "Attack of the Obsessive Managers," *Fortune* (February 16, 1987), pp. 127–128.

[26] Arthur P. Brief, Randall S. Schuler, and Mary Van Sell, *Managing Job Stress* (Boston: Little, Brown, 1981).

[27] See Orlando Behling and Arthur L. Darrow, *Managing Work-Related Stress* (Chicago: Science Research Associates, 1984).

[28] Behling and Darrow, 1984.

[29] M. J. Burke, A. P. Brief, and J. M. George, "The Role of Negative Affectivity in Understanding Relations between Self-Reports of Stressors and Strains: A Comment on the Applied Psychology Literature," *Journal of Applied Psychology* 78 (1993), pp. 402–412; D. Watson and L. A. Clark, "Negative Affectivity: The Disposition to Experience Aversive Emotional States" *Psychological Bulletin* 96 (1984), pp. 465–490.

[30] A review of research is available in Steve M. Jex, *Stress and Job Performance* (Thousand Oaks, CA: Sage, 1998).

[31] "Couples Dismayed at Long Workdays, New Study Finds," *Columbus Dispatch* (January 23, 1999), p. 5A.

[32] See H. Selye, *The Stress of Life*, rev. ed. (New York: McGraw-Hill, 1976).

[33] Jeffrey Pfeffer, *The Human Equation: Building Profits by Putting People First* (Boston: Harvard Business School Press, 1998). Quotations are from Alan M. Webber, "Danger: Toxic Company," *Fast Company* (November 1998), p. 152.

[34] See John D. Adams, "Health, Stress and the Manager's Life Style," *Group and Organization Studies* 6 (1981), pp. 291–301.

[35] See Susan Folkman "Personal Control and Stress and Coping Processes: A Theoretical Analysis," *Journal of Personality and Social Psychology*, 1984, Vol. 46, No. 4, p. 844.

[36] "Attitude is Everything," adapted by Rachel Fleming '00 from the pamphlet "Your Attitude and You" by Channing L. Bete Co., Inc. copyright Academic Skills Center, Dartmouth College 2001. http://www.dartmouth.edu/~acskills/success/stress.html, accessed May 5, 2009.

[37] Information from Mike Pramik, "Wellness Programs Give Businesses Healthy Bottom Line," *Columbus Dispatch* (January 18, 1999), pp. 10–11.

[38] Pramik, 1999.

[39] Pfeffer, 1998.

[40] See P. E. Jacob, J. J. Flink, and H. L. Schuchman, "Values and Their Function in Decision Making," *American Behavioral Scientist* 5, suppl. 9 (1962), pp. 6–38.

[41] See M. Rokeach and S. J. Ball Rokeach, "Stability and Change in American Value Priorities, 1968–1981," *American Psychologist* (May 1989), pp. 775–784.

[42] Milton Rokeach, *The Nature of Human Values* (New York: Free Press, 1973).

[43] See W. C. Frederick and J. Weber, "The Values of Corporate Managers and Their Critics: An Empirical Description and Normative Implications," *Business Ethics Research Issues and Empirical Studies*, ed. W. C. Frederick and L. E. Preston (Greenwich, CT: JAI Press, 1990), pp. 123–144.

[44] Gordon Allport, Philip E. Vernon, and Gardner Lindzey, *Study of Values* (Boston: Houghton Mifflin, 1931).

[45] Adapted from R. Tagiuri, "Purchasing Executive: General Manager or Specialist?" *Journal of Purchasing* (August 1967), pp. 16–21.

46 Bruce M. Meglino and Elizabeth C. Ravlin, "Individual Values in Organizations: Concepts, Controversies and Research," *Journal of Management* 24 (1998), pp. 351–389.

47 Meglino and Ravlin, 1998.

48 Daniel Yankelovich, *New Rules! Searching for Self-Fulfillment in a World Turned Upside Down* (New York: Random House, 1981); Daniel Yankelovich, Hans Zetterberg, Burkhard Strumpel, and Michael Shanks, *Work and Human Values: An International Report on Jobs in the 1980s and 1990s* (Aspen, CO: Aspen Institute for Humanistic Studies, 1983); William Fox, *American Values in Decline: What We Can Do* (Gainesville, FL: 1st Books Library, 2001).

49 See D. Jamieson and Julia O'Mara, *Managing Workplace 2000* (San Francisco: Jossey-Bass, 1991), pp. 28–29.

50 Geert Hofstede, *Culture's Consequences: International Differences in Work-Related Values*, 2nd ed. (Beverly Hills, CA: Sage, 2001); Fons Trompenaars and Charles Hampden-Turner, *Riding the Waves of Culture: Understanding Cultural Diversity in Global Business*, 2nd ed. (New York: McGraw-Hill, 1998). For an excellent discussion of culture, see also "Culture: The Neglected Concept," in *Social Psychology Across Cultures*, 2nd ed., Peter B. Smith and Michael Harris Bond (Boston: Allyn & Bacon, 1998). See also Michael H. Hoppe, "An Interview with Geert Hofstede," *Academy of Management Executive* 18 (2004), pp. 75–79; Harry C. Triandis, "The Many Dimensions of Culture," *Academy of Management Executive* 18 (2004), pp. 88–93.

51 Geert Hofstede, *Culture and Organizations: Software of the Mind* (London: McGraw-Hill, 1991).

52 Hofstede, 2001; Geert Hofstede and Michael H. Bond, "The Confucius Connection: From Culture Roots to Economic Growth," *Organizational Dynamics* 16 (1988), pp. 4–21.

53 Hofstede, 2001.

54 Chinese Culture Connection, "Chinese Values and the Search for Culture-Free Dimensions of Culture," *Journal of Cross-Cultural Psychology* 18 (1987), pp. 143–164.

55 Hofstede and Bond, 1988; Geert Hofstede, "Cultural Constraints in Management Theories," *Academy of Management Executive* 7 (1993), pp. 81–94. For a further discussion of Asian and Confucian values, see also Jim Rohwer, Asia Rising: *Why America Will Prosper as Asia's Economies Boom* (New York: Simon & Schuster, 1995).

56 For an example, see John R. Schermerhorn Jr. and Michael H. Bond, "Cross-Cultural Leadership Dynamics in Collectivism + High Power Distance Settings," *Leadership and Organization Development Journal* 18 (1997), pp. 187–193.

57 Accessed May 5, 2009 from htttp://www.diversityhotwire.com/business/diversity_statistics.html#fem_workforce.

58 Rob McInnes, "Workforce Diversity: Changing the Way You Do Business," accessed May 3, 2009 from http://www.diversityworld.com/Diversity/workforce_diversity.htm.

59 Adapted from Rob McInnes, Diversity World www.diversityworld.com.

60 Accessed May 4, 2009 from http://www.catalyst.org/publication/207/women-in-management-1950-present. Note: this category excludes farm.

61 See Lois Joy, "Advancing Women Leaders: The Connection between Women Corporate Board Directors and Women Corporate Officers." Catalyst, 2008. email: info@catalyst.org; www.catalyst.org.

62 Joy, 2008.

63 See Catalyst report "The Double-Bind Dilemma for Women in Leadership: *Damned if You Do, Doomed if You Don't,*" 2007. email: info@catalyst.org; www.catalyst.org.

64 http://www.catalyst.org/publication/132/us-women-in-business, published in March 2009.

65 Joy, 2008.

66 See Lynda Gratton "Inspiring Women: Corporate Best Practice in Europe," The Lehman Brothers Centre for Women in Business, 2007.

67 See Catalyst report "The Double-Bind Dilemma for Women in Leadership: *Damned if You Do, Doomed if You Don't,*" 2007. email: info@catalyst.org; www.catalyst.org.

68 See Catalyst report "The Double-Bind Dilemma for Women in Leadership: *Damned if You Do, Doomed if You Don't,*" 2007. email: info@catalyst.org; www.catalyst.org.

69 See Catalyst report "The Double-Bind Dilemma for Women in Leadership: *Damned if You Do, Doomed if You Don't,*" 2007. email: info@catalyst.org; www.catalyst.org.

70 See Catalyst report "The Double-Bind Dilemma for Women in Leadership: *Damned if You Do, Doomed if You Don't,*" 2007. email: info@catalyst.org; www.catalyst.org; "The Leaking Pipeline: Where are our Female Leaders?" Pricewaterhouse Coopers report, March 2008. PwC Gender Advisory Council, www.pwc.com/women.

71 Accessed May 5, 2009 from http://www.eeoc.gov/types/race.html.

72 See Katharine Esty, "From Diversity to Inclusion," April 30, 2007, http://www.boston.com/jobs/nehra/043007.shtml, downloaded May 3, 2009.

73 Esty, 2007.

74 See Henri Tajfel and John Turner, (1979), "An Integrative Theory of Intergroup Conflict," in Austin, G. William; Worchel, Stephen. *The Social Psychology of Intergroup Relations*. Monterey, CA: Brooks-Cole. pp. 94–109.

75 See Carol Mithers, "Workplace Wars," in *Ladies' Home Journal,* May 2009, pp. 104–109.

76 Mithers, 2009.

77 http://www.accessiblesociety.org/topics/ada/index.htm

78 http://www.accessiblesociety.org/topics/ada/index.htm

79 Fernandez (1991); Patrick Digh, "Finding New Talent in a Tight Market," *Mosaics* 4.3 (March–April, 1998), pp. 1, 4–6.

80 See Fernandez, 1991, p. 236; "Diversity News: Age Discrimination Unrest in Britain," *Mosaics* 4.2 (March–April 1998), p. 4.

81 http://www.hawking.org.uk/index.php/about-stephen/questionsandanswers.

[82] http://www.pollingreport.com/civil.htm.//

[83] See Lauren Prince, "Marketers: Buying Power of Gays to Exceed $835 Billion." Dec. 8, 2007. Accessed May 4, 2009 from http://www.gfn.com/recordDetails.php?page_id=19&section_id=18&pcontent_id=2,//

[84] http://www.eeoc.gov/facts/fs-orientation_parent_marital_political.html.

[85] See "The Workplace Improves for Gay Americans," Dec. 17, 2007 GFN News. Accessed May 5, 2009 from http://www.gfn.com/recordDetails.php?page_id=19&section_id=22&pcontent_id=18.

[86] See "Where Are The Gay-Friendly Companies?" accessed Jan. 11, 2008 from http://www.gfn.com/recordDetails.php?page_id=19&section_id=22&pcontent_id=152.

[87] See "The Workplace Improves for Gay Americans," Dec 17, 2007 GFN News. Accessed May 5, 2009 from http://www.gfn.com/recordDetails.php?page_id=19&section_id=22&pcontent_id=18.

[88] See "The Workplace Improves for Gay Americans," Dec 17, 2007 GFN News. Accessed May 5 2009 from http://www.gfn.com/recordDetails.php?page_id=19&section_id=22&pcontent_id=18.

[89] See "Where Are The Gay-Friendly Companies?" Jan 11, 2008. Accessed from http://www.gfn.com/recordDetails.php?page_id=19&section_id=22&pcontent_id=152.

[90] http://www.catalystwomen.org/press_room/factsheets/factwoc3.htm. Accessed May 4, 2009.

FEATURE NOTES

Opener/ATP Denmark: Great Place to Work Institute Europe. (2009). 100 Best Workplaces in Europe. *European Great Place to Work Magazine, 2009;* www.atp.dk.

Research Insight: Arvey, R., Zhang, Z., Avolio, B., and Krueger, R. (2007). Developmental and Genetic Determinants of Leadership Role Occupancy among Women. *Journal of Applied Psychology,* 92(3), 693–706.

Ethics in OB: See "Computerized Personality Tests Spawn a Culture of Cheating," from *The Wall Street Journal,* posted on Ethics Newsline on Jan. 12, 2009. http://www.globalethics.org/newsline/2009/01/12/personality-tests-2/print/. "Nearly One-Fourth of Workers Admit to Lying About Lateness," posted on Ethics Newsline, May 19, 2008.

Mastering Management: "Attitude is Everything," adapted by Rachel Fleming '00 from the pamphlet "Your Attitude and You" by Channing L. Bete Co., Inc. copyright Academic Skills Center, Dartmouth College 2001.http://www.dartmouth.edu/~acskills/success/stress.html, accessed May 5, 2009.

Leaders on Leadership: http://www.hawking.org.uk/index.php/about-stephen/questionsandanswers.

MARGIN PHOTOS

Whole Brain—See Dorothy Leonard and Susan Strauss, "Putting Your Company's Whole Brain to Work," *Harvard Business Review* 75.4 Jul–Aug 1997, pp. 110–121. Also, Daniel Pink's *A Whole New Mind: Why Right-Brainers Will Rule the Future* (New York: Riverhead Books, 2005).

Chapter 3

ENDNOTES

[1] These concept definitions and discussions are based on J. M. George, "Trait and State Affect," p. 45 in *Individual Differences in Behavior in Organizations,* ed. K. R. Murphy (San Francisco: Jossey-Bass, 1996); N. H. Frijda, "Moods, Emotion Episodes and Emotions," pp. 381–403 in *Handbook of Emotions,* M. Lewis and J. M. Haviland (ed.) (New York: Guilford Press, 1993); H. M. Weiss and R. Cropanzano, "Affective Events Theory: A Theoretical Discussion of the Structure, Causes, and Consequences of Affective Experiences at Work," pp. 17–19 in *Research in Organizational Behavior,* 18, eds. B. M. Staw and L. L. Cummings (Greenwich, CT: JAI Press, 1996); P. Ekman and R. J. Davidson, eds., *The Nature of Emotions: Fundamental Questions* (Oxford, UK: Oxford University Press, 1994); Frijda, 1993, p. 381.

[2] For an example see Mary Ann Hazen, "Grief and the Workplace," *Academy of Management Perspective,* Vol. 22 (August 2008), pp. 78–86.

[3] J. A. Fuller, J. M. Stanton, G. G. Fisher, C. Spitzmuller, S. S. Russell, and P. C. Smith, "A Lengthy Look at the Daily Grind: Time Series Analysis of Events, Mood, Stress, and Satisfaction," *Journal of Applied Psychology* 88 (2003), pp. 1019–1033; C. J. Thoreson, S. A. Kaplan, A. P. Barsky, C. R. Warren, and K. de Chermont, "The Affective Underpinnings of Job Perceptions and Attitudes; A Meta-Analytic Review and Integration," *Psychological Bulletin* 129 (2003), pp. 914–925.

[4] Daniel Goleman, "Leadership That Gets Results," *Harvard Business Review* (March–April 2000), pp. 78–90. See also his books *Emotional Intelligence* (New York: Bantam Books, 1995) and *Working with Emotional Intelligence* (New York: Bantam Books, 1998).

[5] See Davies, L. Stankow and R. D. Roberts "Emotion and Intelligence: In Search of an Elusive Construct," *Journal of Personality and Social Psychology* 75 (1998), pp. 989–1015; I. Greenstein, *The Presidential Difference: Leadership Style from FDR to Clinton* (Princeton, NJ: Princeton University Press, 2001); Goleman, op. cit. (2000).

[6] Goleman, op. cit. (1998).

[7] J. P. Tangney and K. W. Fischer, eds., *"Self-conscious Emotions: The Psychology of Shame, Guilt, Embarrassment and Price* (New York: Guilford Press 1995); J. L. Tracy and R. W. Robbins, "Putting the Self into Self-Conscious Emotions: A Theoretical Model," *Psychological Inquiry* 15 (2004), pp. 103–125; D. Keltner and C. Anderson, "Saving Face for Darwin: The Functions and Uses of Embarrassment," *Current Directions in Psychological Science* 9 (2000), pp. 187–192; J. S. Beer, E. A. Heery, D. Keltner, D. Scabini,

and R. T. Knight, "The Regulatory Function of Self-Conscious Emotion: Insights from Patients with Orbitofrontal Damage," *Journal of Personality and Social Psychology* 85 (2003), pp. 594–604; R. P. Vecchio, "Explorations of Employee Envy: Feeling Envious and Feeling Envied," *Cognition and Emotion* 19 (2005), pp. 69–81; C. F. Poulson II, "Shame and Work," pp. 490–541 in *Emotions in the Workplace: Research, Theory, and Practice*, eds. N. M. Ashkanasy, W. Zerby, and C. E. J. Hartel (Westport, CT: Quorum Books).

[8] Diane Brady, "Charm Offensive," *BusinessWeek* (June 26, 2006), pp. 76–80.

[9] Lewis and Haviland, op. cit.

[10] Damon Darlin and Matt Richtel, "Chairwoman Leaves Hewlett in Spying Furor," *The Wall Street Journal* (September 23, 2006), pp. A1, A9.

[11] R. E. Lucas, A. E. Clark, Y. Georgellis, and E. Deiner, "Unemployment Alters the Set Points for Life Satisfaction," *Psychological Science* 15 (2004), pp. 8–13; C. Graham, A. Eggers, and S. Sukhtaner, "Does Happiness Pay?: An Exploration Based on Panel Data from Russia," *Journal of Economic Behaviour and Organization* Vol. 55 (November 2004), pp. 319–342; C. J. Howell, R. T. Howell, and K. A. Schwabe, "Does Wealth Enhance Life Satisfaction for People Who Are Materially Deprived?: Exploring the Association among the Orang Asli of Peninsular Malaysia," *Social Indicators Research* (in press, 2006); G. L. Clore, N. Schwartz, and M. Conway, "Affective Causes and Consequences of Social Information Processing," pp. 323–417 in *Handbook of Social Cognition*, Vol. 1, eds. R. S. Wyer Jr. and T. K. Srull (Hillsdale, NJ: Erlbaum, 1994); K. D. Vohs, R. F. Baumeister, and G. Lowenstein, *Do Emotions Help or Hurt Decision Making?* (New York: Russell Sage Foundation Press, in press 2006); H. M. Weiss, J. P. Nicholas, and C. S. Daus, "An Examination of the Joint Effects of Affective Experiences and Job Beliefs on Job Satisfaction and Variations in Affective Experiences over Time," *Organizational Behavior and Human Decision Processes* 78 (1999), pp. 1–24; N. M. Ashkanasy "Emotion and Performance," *Human Performance* 17 (2004), pp. 137–144.

[12] See Robert G. Lord, Richard J. Klimoski, and Ruth Knafer (Eds.), *Emotions in the Workplace: Understanding the Structure and Role of Emotions in Organizational Behavior* (San Francisco: Jossey-Bass, 2002); Roy L. Payne and Cary L. Cooper (Eds.), *Emotions at Work: Theory Research and Applications for Management* (Chichester, UK: John Wiley & Sons, 2004); Daniel Goleman and Richard Boyatzis, "Social Intelligence and the Biology of Leadership," *Harvard Business Review* (September, 2008), Reprint R0809E.

[13] Caroline Bartel and Richard Saavedra, "The Collective Construction of Work Group Moods," *Administrative Science Quarterly*, Vol. 45 (June 2000), pp. 197–231.

[14] Joyce E. Bono and Remus Ilies, "Charisma, Positive Emotions and Mood Contagion," *Leadership Quarterly* 17 (2006), pp. 317–334; Goleman and Boyatzis, op. cit.

[15] Daniel Goleman, Richard Boyatzis, and Annie McKie, *Primal Leadership: Realizing the Power of Emotional Intelligence* (Boston, MA: Harvard Business School Publishing, 2002); Quote from "Managing the Mood Is Crucial When Times Are Tough," *Financial Times* (March 24, 2009).

[16] Quote from ibid.

[17] S. M. Kruml and D. Geddes, "Catching Fire without Burning Out: Is There an Ideal Way to Perform Emotional Labor?" pp. 177–188 in N. M. Ashkanasy, C. E. J. Hartel, and W. J. Zerby (eds.), *Emotions in the Workplace* (New York: Quorum, 2000).

[18] A. Grandey, "Emotional Regulation in the Workplace: A New Way to Conceptualize Emotional Labor," *Journal of Occupational Health Psychology* 5.1 (2000), pp. 95–110; R. Cropanzano, D. E. Rupp, and Z. S. Byrne, "The Relationship of Emotional Exhaustion to Work Attitudes, Job Performance and Organizational Citizenship Behavior," *Journal of Applied Psychology* (2003), pp. 160–169.

[19] W. Tasi and Y. Huang, "Mechanisms Linking Employee Affective Delivery and Customer Behavioral Intentions," *Journal of Applied Psychology* 87 (2002), pp. 1001–1008.

[20] M. Eid and E. Diener, "Norms for Experiencing Emotions in Different Cultures: Inter- and Intranational Differences," *Journal of Personality & Social Psychology* 81.5 (2001), pp. 869–885.

[21] Ibid. (2001).

[22] B. Mesquita, "Emotions in Collectivist and Individualist Contexts," *Journal of Personality and Social Psychology* 80.1 (2001), pp. 68–74.

[23] D. Rubin, "Grumpy German Shoppers Distrust the Wal-Mart Style," *Seattle Times* (December 30, 2001), p. a15; A. Rafaeli, "When Cashiers Meet Customers: An Analysis of Supermarket Cashiers," *Academy of Management Journal* (1989), pp. 245–273.

[24] H. M. Weiss and R. Cropanzano, "An Affective Events Approach to Job Satisfaction," pp. 1–74 in *Research in Organizational Behavior*, Vol. 18, ed. B. M. Staw and L. L. Cummings (Greenwich, CT: JAI Press, 1996); N. M. Ashkanasy and C. S. Daus, "Emotion in the Workplace: New Challenges for Managers," *Academy of Management Executive* 16 (2002), pp. 76–86.

[25] A. G. Miner and C. L. Hulin, *Affective Experience at Work: A Test of Affective Events Theory.* Poster presented at the 15th annual conference of the Society for Industrial and Organizational Psychology (2000).

[26] See L. Cosmides and J. Tooby (eds.), "Evolutionary Psychology and the Emotions," pp. 91–115; in *Handbook of Emotions*, 2nd ed., M. Lewis and J. M. Haviland-Jones (eds.), (New York: Guilford Press, 2000).

[27] Information and quote from Joann S. Lublin, "How One Black Woman Lands Her Top Jobs: Risks and Networking," *The Wall Street Journal* (March 4, 2003), p. B1.

[28] Compare Martin Fishbein and Icek Ajzen, *Belief, Attitude, Intention and Behavior: An Introduction to Theory and Research* (Reading, MA: Addison-Wesley, 1973).

[29] See A. W. Wicker, "Attitude Versus Action: The Relationship of Verbal and Overt Behavioral Responses to Attitude Objects," *Journal of Social Issues* (Autumn 1969), pp. 41–78.

[30] L. Festinger, *A Theory of Cognitive Dissonance* (Palo Alto, CA: Stanford University Press, 1957).

[31] See "The Things They Do for Love," *Harvard Business Review* (December, 2004), pp. 19–20.

[32] Tony DIRomualdo, "The High Cost of Employee Disengagement" (July 7, 2004), www.wistechnology.com.

[33] Information from Sue Shellenbarger, "Employers Are Finding It Doesn't Cost Much to Make a Staff Happy," *The Wall Street Journal* (November 19, 1997), p. B1; see also "Job Satisfaction on the Decline," *The Conference Board* (July 2002).

[34] See for example Remus Ilies, Kelly Schwind Wilson, and David T. Wagner, "The Spillover of Daily Job Satisfaction onto Employees' Family Lives: The Facilitating Role of Work-Family Integration," *Academy of Management Journal* 52 (February 2009), pp. 87–102.

[35] See W. E. Wymer and J. M. Carsten, "Alternative Ways to Gather Opinions," *HR Magazine* 37.4 (April 1992), pp. 71–78.

[36] The Job Descriptive Index (JDI) is available from Dr. Patricia C. Smith, Department of Psychology, Bowling Green State University; the Minnesota Satisfaction Questionnaire (MSQ) is available from the Industrial Relations Center and Vocational Psychology Research Center, University of Minnesota.

[37] Salary.com, "Survey Shows Impact of Downturn on Job Satisfaction," *OH&S: Occupational Health and Safety* (February 7, 2009), www.ohsonline.com.

[38] See ibid.; Timothy A. Judge, "Promote Job Satisfaction Through Mental Challenge," Chapter 6 in Edwin A. Locke (ed.), *The Blackwell Handbook of Principles of Organizational Behavior* (Malden, MA: Blackwell, 2004); "U.S. Employees More Dissatisfied with Their Jobs," *Associated Press* (February 28, 2005), www.msnbc.com; "U.S. Job Satisfaction Keeps Falling, The Conference Board Reports Today," The Conference Board (February 28, 2005), www.conference-board.org; Salary.com, op. cit. (2009).

[39] Information from *What Workers Want: A Worldwide Study of Attitudes to Work and Work-Life Balance* (London: FDS International Limited, 2007).

[40] B. M. Staw, "The Consequences of Turnover," *Journal of Occupational Behavior* 1 (1980), pp. 253–273; J. P. Wanous, *Organizational Entry* (Reading, MA: Addison-Wesley, 1980).

[41] C. N. Greene, "The Satisfaction-Performance Controversy," *Business Horizons* 15 (1972), pp. 31–41; M. T. Iaffaldano and P. M. Muchinsky, "Job Satisfaction and Job Performance: A Meta-Analysis," *Psychological Bulletin* 97 (1985), pp. 251–273; D. Organ, "A Reappraisal and Reinterpretation of the Satisfaction-Causes-Performance Hypothesis," *Academy of Management Review* 2 (1977), pp. 46–53; P. Lorenzi, "A Comment on Organ's Reappraisal of the Satisfaction-Causes-Performance Hypothesis," *Academy of Management Review* 3 (1978), pp. 380–382.

[42] Salary.com, op. cit. (2009).

[43] Tony DIRomualdo, "The High Cost of Employee Disengagement" (July 7, 2004), www.wistechnology.com.

[44] Dennis W. Organ, *Organizational Citizenship Behavior: The Good Soldier Syndrome* (Lexington, MA: Lexington Books, 1988); Dennis W. Organ, "Organizational Citizenship Behavior: It's Constructive Cleanup Time," *Human Performance*, 10 (1997), pp. 85–97.

[45] See Mark C. Bolino and William H. Turnley, "Going the Extra Mile: Cultivating and Managing Employee Citizenship Behavior," *Academy of Management Executive*, vol. 17 (August 2003), pp. 60–67.

[46] See Venetta I. Coleman and Walter C. Borman, "Investigating the Underlying Structure of the Citizenship Performance Domain," *Human Resource Management Review* 10 (2000), pp. 115–126.

[47] Sandra L. Robinson and Rebecca J. Bennett, "A Typology of Deviant Workplace Behaviors: A Multidimensional Scaling Study," *Academy of Management Journal* 38 (1995), pp. 555–572.

[48] Reeshad S. Dalal, "A Meta-Analysis of the Relationship Among Organizational Citizenship Behavior and Counterproductive Work Behavior," *Journal of Applied Psychology* 90 (2005), pp. 1241–1255.

[49] Timothy A. Judge and Remus Ilies, "Affect and Job Satisfaction: A Study of Their Relationship at Work and at Home," *Journal of Applied Psychology* 89 (2004), pp. 661–673.

[50] Ilies et al., op. cit. (2009).

[51] See Benjamin Schneider, Paul J. Hanges, D. Brent Smith, and Amy Salvaggio, "Which Comes First: Employee Attitudes or Organizational, Financial, and Market Performance?" *Journal of Applied Psychology* 88.5 (2003), pp. 836–851.

[52] See Satoris S. Culbertson, "Do Satisfied Employees Mean Satisfied Customers?" *The Academy of Management Perspectives* 23 (February 2009), pp. 76–77.

[53] L. W. Porter and E. E. Lawler III, *Managerial Attitudes and Work Performance* (Homewood, IL: Irwin, 1968).

[54] Schneider, Hanges, Smith, and Salvaggio, op. cit.

[55] Ibid.

FEATURE NOTES

Opener/Ibukun Awosika: www.theconvention.org/board.html; www.allafrica.com/stories; www.spicenigeria.com/blessing-ibukun-awosika

Ethics in OB: Information and quotes from "Daniel Yee, "Chick-fil-A Recipe Winning Customers," *The Columbus Dispatch* (September 9, 2006), p. D1; Tom Murphy, "Chick-fil-A Plans Aggressive Product Rollout Initiatives," *Rocky Mount Telegram* (May 28, 2008), www.rockymount-telegram.com/ "Chick-fil-A Reaches 20,000th Scholarship Milestone," (July 28, 2005), Chick-fil-A press release, www.csrwire.com/.

Leaders on Leadership/Margarita Barney Almeida: Information from www.ashoka.org.

MARGIN PHOTOS

Life Is Good—Information from Leigh Buchanan, "Life Lessons, *Inc.* (June 6, 2006), www.inc.com/magazine/; "A Fortune Coined from Cheerfulness Entrepreneurship," *Financial Times* (May 20, 2009); www.lifeisgood.com/about/.

Employee morale—Information from *What Workers Want: A Worldwide Study of Attitudes to Work and Work-Life Balance* (London: FDS International Limited, 2007); *Millennials*—Information and quotes from "The 'Millennials' Are Coming," *CBS 60 Minutes* (November 11.2007); Brittany Hite, "Employers Rethink How they Give Feedback," *The Wall Street Journal* (October 13, 2008), p. B5; Shelly Banjo, "A Perfect Match?" *The Wall Street Journal* (October 13, 2009), p. R9; Olga Kharif, "Raised on the Web and Ready for Business," *Business-Week* (December 8, 2008), pp. 77–78; Emma Jacobs, "Reality Check for Gen Y and Its Managers," *Financial Times* (May 14, 2009). See also Ron Alsop, *The Trophy Kids Grow Up* (New York: Dow Jones, 2008).

Chapter 4

ENDNOTES

[1] H. R. Schiffmann, *Sensation and Perception: An Integrated Approach*, 3rd ed. (New York: Wiley, 1990).

[2] Example from John A. Wagner III and John R. Hollenbeck, *Organizational Behavior*, 3rd ed. (Upper Saddle River, NJ: Prentice-Hall, 1998), p. 59.

[3] See Georgia T. Chao and Steve W. J. Kozlowski, "Employee Perceptions on the Implementation of Robotic Manufacturing Technology," *Journal of Applied Psychology* 71 (1986), pp. 70–76; Steven F. Cronshaw and Robert G. Lord, "Effects of Categorization, Attribution, and Encoding Processes in Leadership Perceptions," *Journal of Applied Psychology* 72 (1987), pp. 97–106.

[4] See Robert G. Lord, "An Information Processing Approach to Social Perceptions, Leadership, and Behavioral Measurement in Organizations," pp. 87–128 in B. M. Staw and L. L. Cummings (eds.), *Research in Organizational Behavior* 7 (Greenwich, CT: JAI Press, 1985); T. K. Srull and R. S. Wyer, *Advances in Social Cognition* (Hillsdale, NJ: Erlbaum, 1988); U. Neisser, *Cognitive and Reality* (San Francisco: Freeman, 1976), p. 112.

[5] See J. G. Hunt, *Leadership: A New Synthesis* (Newbury Park, CA: Sage, 1991), ch. 7; R. G. Lord and R. J. Foti, "Schema Theories, Information Processing, and Organizational Behavior," pp. 20–48 in H. P. Simms Jr. and D. A. Gioia (eds.), *Thinking Organization* (San Francisco: Jossey-Bass, 1986); S. T. Fiske and S. E. Taylor, *Social Cognition* (Reading, MA: Addison-Wesley, 1984).

[6] Quotation from Sheila O'Flanagan, "Underestimate Casual Dressers at Your Peril," *Irish Times* (July 22, 2005).

[7] See William L. Gardner and Mark J. Martinko, "Impression Management in Organizations," *Journal of Management* (June 1988), p. 332.

[8] See B. R. Schlenker, *Impression Management: The Self-Concept, Social Identity, and Interpersonal Relations* (Monterey, CA: Brooks/Cole, 1980); W. L. Gardner and M. J. Martinko, "Impression Management in Organizations," *Journal of Management* (June 1988), p. 332; R. B. Cialdini, "Indirect Tactics of Image Management: Beyond Banking" in *Impression Management in the Organization*, R. A. Giacolini and P. Rosenfeld (eds.) (Hillsdale, NJ: Erlbaum, 1989), pp. 45–71; and Sandy Wayne and Robert Liden, "Effects of Impression Management on Performance Ratings," *Academy of Management Journal* (February 2005), pp. 232–252.

[9] See, for example, Stephan Thernstrom and Abigail Thernstrom, *America in Black and White* (New York: Simon & Schuster, 1997); David A. Thomas and Suzy Wetlaufer, "A Question of Color: A Debate on Race in the U. S. Workspace, "*Harvard Business Review* Vol. 2 (September–October 1997), pp. 118–132.

[10] Information from "Misconceptions about Women in the Global Arena Keep Their Number Low," www.catalyst-women.org/home.html.

[11] These examples are from Natasha Josefowitz, *Paths to Power* (Reading, MA: Addison-Wesley, 1980), p. 60. For more on gender issues, see Gray N. Powell (ed.), *Handbook of Gender and Work* (Thousand Oaks, CA: Sage, 1999).

[12] For a recent report on age discrimination, see Joseph C. Santora and William J. Seaton, "Age Discrimination: Alive and Well in the Workplace?" *The Academy of Management Perspectives* 22 (May 2008), pp. 103–104.

[13] Survey reported in Kelly Greene, "Age Is Still More Than a Number," *The Wall Street Journal* (April 10, 2003), p. D2.

[14] "Facebook Gets Down to Business, "*BusinessWeek* (April 20, 2009), p. 30.

[15] Dewitt C. Dearborn and Herbert A. Simon, "Selective Perception: A Note on the Departmental Identification of Executives," *Sociometry* 21 (1958), pp. 140–144.

[16] J. Sterling Livingston, "Pygmalion in Management," *Harvard Business Review* (July–August 1969), pp. 81–89.

[17] D. Eden and A. B. Shani, "Pygmalion Goes to Boot Camp," *Journal of Applied Psychology* 67 (1982), pp. 194–199.

[18] See H. H. Kelley, "Attribution in Social Interaction," in E. Jones et al. (eds.), *Attribution: Perceiving the Causes of Behavior* (Morristown, NJ: General Learning Press, 1972).

[19] See Terence R. Mitchell, S. G. Green, and R. E. Wood, "An Attribution Model of Leadership and the Poor Performing Subordinate," Barry Staw and Larry L. Cummings (eds.), pp. 197–234, in *Research in Organizational Behavior* (New York: JAI Press, 1981); John H. Harvey and Gifford Weary, "Current Issues in Attribution Theory and Research," *Annual Review of Psychology* 35 (1984), pp. 427–459.

[20] See F. Fosterling, "Attributional Retraining: A Review," *Psychological Bulletin* (November 1985), pp. 496–512.

[21] See J. M. Crant and T. S. Bateman, "Assignment of Credit and Blame for Performance Outcomes," *Academy of Management Journal* (February 1993), pp. 7–27; E. C. Pence, W. E. Pendelton, G. H. Dobbins, and J. A. Sgro, "Effects of Causal Explanations and Sex Variables on Recommendations for Corrective Actions Following Employee Failure," *Organizational Behavior and Human Performance* (April 1982), pp. 227–240.

[22] R. M. Steers, S. J. Bischoff, and L. H. Higgins, "Cross Cultural Management Research," *Journal of Management Inquiry*, Vol. 1 (December 1992), pp. 325–326; J. G. Miller, "Culture and the Development of Everyday Causal Explanation," *Journal of Personality and Social Psychology* 46 (1984), pp. 961–978.

[23] Albert Bandura, *Social Learning Theory* (Englewood Cliffs, NJ: Prentice-Hall, 1977); and Albert Bandura, *Self-Efficacy: The Exercise of Control* (New York: W. H. Freeman, 1997).

[24] See, for example, A. M. Morrison, R. P. White, and E. Van Velsor, *Breaking the Glass Ceiling* (Reading, MA: Addison-Wesley, 1987); J. D. Zalesny and J. K. Ford, "Extending the Social Information Processing Perspective: New Links to Attitudes, Behaviors and Perceptions," *Organizational Behavior and Human Decision Processes* 47 (1990), pp. 205–246; M. E. Gist, C. Schwoerer, and B. Rosen, "Effects of Alternative Training Methods of Self-Efficacy and Performance in Computer Software Training," *Journal of Applied Psychology* 74 (1989), pp. 884–891; D. D. Sutton and R. W. Woodman, "Pygmalion Goes to Work: The Effects of Supervisor Expectations in a Retail Setting," *Journal of Applied Psychology* 74 (1989), pp. 943–950; M. E. Gist, "The Influence of Training Method on Self-Efficacy and Idea Generation among Managers," *Personnel Psychology* 42 (1989), pp. 787–805.

[25] Bandura, op. cit., 1977 and 1997.

[26] See M. E. Gist, "Self Efficacy: Implications in Organizational Behavior and Human Resource Management," *Academy of Management Review* 12 (1987), pp. 472–485; A. Bandura, "Self-Efficacy Mechanisms in Human Agency," *American Psychologist* 37 (1987), pp. 122–147.

[27] For good overviews of reinforcement-based views, see W. E. Scott Jr. and P. M. Podsakoff, *Behavioral Principles in the Practice of Management* (New York: Wiley, 1985); Fred Luthans and Robert Kreitner, *Organizational Behavior Modification and Beyond* (Glenview, IL: Scott Foresman, 1985).

[28] For some of B. F. Skinner's work, see *Walden Two* (New York: Macmillan, 1948); *Science and Human Behavior* (New York: Macmillan, 1953); *Contingencies of Reinforcement* (New York: Appleton-Century-Crofts, 1969).

[29] Fred Luthans and Robert Kreitner, *Organizational Behavior Modification* (Glenview, IL: Scott Foresman, 1975); Fred Luthans and Robert Kreitner, *Organizational Behavior Modification and Beyond* (Glenview, IL: Scott Foresman, 1985); and Fred Luthans and Alexander D. Stajkovic, "Reinforce for Performance: The Need to Go Beyond Pay and Even Rewards," *Academy of Management Executive* 13 (1999), pp. 49–57.

[30] E. L. Thorndike, *Animal Intelligence* (New York: Macmillan, 1911), p. 244.

[31] Example adapted from Luthans and Kreitner (1985), op. cit., 1985.

[32] Luthans and Kreitner, op. cit., 1985.

[33] Both laws are stated in Keith L. Miller, *Principles of Everyday Behavior Analysis* (Monterey, CA: Brooks/Cole, 1975), p. 122.

[34] This example is based on a study by Barbara Price and Richard Osborn, "Shaping the Training of Skilled Workers," working paper (Detroit: Department of Management, Wayne State University, 1999).

[35] A. R. Korukonda and James G. Hunt, "Pat on the Back Versus Kick in the Pants: An Application of Cognitive Inference to the Study of Leader Reward and Punishment Behavior," *Group and Organization Studies* 14 (1989), pp. 299–234.

[36] Edwin A. Locke, "The Myths of Behavior Mod in Organizations," *Academy of Management Review* 2 (October 1977), pp. 543–553. For a counterpoint, see Jerry L. Gray, "The Myths of the Myths about Behavior Mod in Organizations: A Reply to Locke's Criticisms of Behavior Modification," *Academy of Management Review* 4 (January 1979), pp. 121–129.

[37] Robert Kreitner, "Controversy in OBM: History, Misconceptions, and Ethics," in Lee Frederiksen (ed.), *Handbook of Organizational Behavior Management* (New York: Wiley, 1982), pp. 71–91.

[38] W. E. Scott Jr. and P. M. Podsakoff, *Behavioral Principles in the Practice of Management* (New York: Wiley, 1985); also see W. Clay Hamner, "Reinforcement Theory and Contingency Management in Organizational Settings," in Richard M. Steers and Lyman W. Porters (eds.), *Motivation and Work Behavior* (4th ed.) (New York: McGraw-Hill, 1987), pp. 139–165; Luthans and Kreitner, op. cit. (1985); Charles C. Manz and Henry P. Sims Jr., *Superleadership* (New York: Berkeley, 1990).

FEATURE NOTES

Opener/Zainab Salbi: Information and quotes from Aina Hunter, "Making the Men of Iraq Listen," *The Village Voice* (March 9, 2005), www.villagevoice.com; *Women for Women International Annual Report* (Washington: Women for Women International, 2007); "Zainab Salbi, Founder and CEO, Women for Women International," www.womenforwomen.org (retrieved March 25, 2009). See also Zainab Salbi and Laurie Becklund, *Between Two*

Worlds: Escape from Tyranny: Growing Up in the Shadow of Saddam (New York: Gotham, 2006).

Ethics in OB: Information from Deloitte LLP, "Leadership Counts: 2007 Deloitte & Touce USA Ethics & Workplace Survey Results," *Kiplinger Business Resource Center* (June 2007), www.kiplinger.com.

Leaders on Leadership: Information and quotes from the corporate Web sites and from The Entrepreneur's Hall of Fame, www.1tbn.com/halloffame.html; *Knowledge@Wharton,* "The Importance of Being Richard Branson," Wharton School Publishing (June 3, 2005), www.whartonsp.com.

Mastering Management: Developed from William C. Byham, "Start Networking Right Away (Even If You Hate It)," *Harvard Business Review* (January 2009), p. 22.

MARGIN PHOTOS

Donna Byrd—Information from Temple Hemphill, "Bull Market: Now is the Time to Take Advantage of Web 2.0," *BlackMBA* (Winter 2008/2009), pp. 63–66; *Elsewhere class*—Information from Dalton Conley, "Welcome to Elsewhere," *Newsweek* (January 26, 2009), pp. 25–26; *Google/Procter & Gamble*—Information from Ellen Byron, "A New Odd Couple: Google, P&G Swap Workers to Spur Innovation," *The Wall Street Journal* (November 19, 2008), pp. A1, A18.

Chapter 5

ENDNOTES

[1] See John P. Campbell, Marvin D. Dunnette, Edward E. Lawler III, and Karl E. Weick Jr., *Managerial Behavior Performance and Effectiveness* (New York: McGraw-Hill, 1970), ch. 15.

[2] Geert Hofstede, "Cultural Constraints in Management Theories," *Academy of Management Executive* 7 (February 1993), pp. 81–94.

[3] Geert Hofstede, *Culture's Consequences: International Differences in Work-Related Values*, abridged ed. (Beverly Hills: Sage, 1984); Geert Hofstede, *Cultures Consequences: Comparing Values, Behaviors, Institutions across Nations* (Thousand Oaks, CA: Sage, 2001).

[4] Abraham Maslow, *Eupsychian Management* (Homewood, IL: Irwin, 1965); Abraham Maslow, *Motivation and Personality*, 2nd ed. (New York: Harper & Row, 1970).

[5] Lyman W. Porter, "Job Attitudes in Management: Perceived Importance of Needs as a Function of Job Level," *Journal of Applied Psychology* 47 (April 1963), pp. 141–148.

[6] Douglas T. Hall and Khalil E. Nougaim, "An Examination of Maslow's Need Hierarchy in an Organizational Setting," *Organizational Behavior and Human Performance* 3 (1968), pp. 12–35; John M. Ivancevich, "Perceived Need Satisfactions of Domestic versus Overseas Managers," *Journal of Applied Psychology* 54 (August 1969), pp. 274–278.

[7] Mahmoud A. Wahba and Lawrence G. Bridwell, "Maslow Reconsidered: A Review of Research on the Need Hierarchy Theory," *Academy of Management Proceedings* (1974), pp. 514–520; Edward E. Lawler III and J. Lloyd Shuttle, "A Causal Correlation Test of the Need Hierarchy Concept," *Organizational Behavior and Human Performance* 7 (1973), pp. 265–287.

[8] Nancy J. Adler (2nd ed.), *International Dimensions of Organizational Behavior* (Boston: PWS-Kent, 1991), p. 153; Richard M. Hodgetts and Fred Luthans, *International Management* (New York: McGraw-Hill, 1991), ch. 11.

[9] Clayton P. Alderfer, "An Empirical Test of a New Theory of Human Needs," *Organizational Behavior and Human Performance* 4 (1969), pp. 142–175; Clayton P. Alderfer, *Existence, Relatedness, and Growth* (New York: Free Press, 1972); Benjamin Schneider and Clayton P. Alderfer, "Three Studies of Need Satisfaction in Organization," *Administrative Science Quarterly* 18 (1973), pp. 489–505.

[10] Lane Tracy, "A Dynamic Living Systems Model of Work Motivation," *Systems Research* 1 (1984), pp. 191–203; John Rauschenberger, Neal Schmidt, and John E. Hunter, "A Test of the Need Hierarchy Concept by a Markov Model of Change in Need Strength," *Administrative Science Quarterly* 25 (1980), pp. 654–670.

[11] Sources pertinent to this discussion are David C. McClelland, *The Achieving Society* (New York: Van Nostrand, 1961); David C. McClelland, "Business, Drive and National Achievement," *Harvard Business Review* 40 (July/August 1962), pp. 99–112; David C. McClelland, "That Urge to Achieve," *Think* (November/December 1966), pp. 19–32; G. H. Litwin and R. A. Stringer, *Motivation and Organizational Climate* (Boston: Division of Research, Harvard Business School, 1966), pp. 18–25.

[12] George Harris, "To Know Why Men Do What They Do: A Conversation with David C. McClelland," *Psychology Today* 4 (January 1971), pp. 35–39.

[13] David C. McClelland and David H. Burnham, "Power Is the Great Motivator," *Harvard Business Review* 54 (March/April 1976), pp. 100–110; David C. McClelland and Richard E. Boyatzis, "Leadership Motive Pattern and Long-Term Success in Management," *Journal of Applied Psychology* 67 (1982), pp. 737–743.

[14] P. Miron and D. C. McClelland, "The Impact of Achievement Motivation Training in Small Businesses," *California Management Review* (Summer 1979), pp. 13–28.

[15] The complete two-factor theory is well explained by Herzberg and his associates in Frederick Herzberg, Bernard Mausner, and Barbara Bloch Synderman, *The Motivation to Work*, 2nd ed. (New York: Wiley, 1967); Frederick Herzberg, "One More Time: How Do You Motivate Employees?" *Harvard Business Review* 46 (January/February 1968), pp. 53–62.

[16] From Herzberg, (1968), op. cit.

[17] See Robert J. House and Lawrence A. Wigdor, "Herzberg's Dual-Factor Theory of Job Satisfaction and Motivation: A Review of the Evidence and a Criticism," *Personnel Psychology* 20 (Winter 1967), pp. 369–389.

[18] Adler, op. cit.; Nancy J. Adler and J. T. Graham, "Cross Cultural Interaction: The International Comparison Fallacy," *Journal of International Business Studies* (Fall 1989), pp. 515–537; Frederick Herzberg, "Workers' Needs: The Same Around the World," *Industry Week* (September 27, 1987), pp. 29–32.

[19] See, for example, J. Stacy Adams, "Toward an Understanding of Inequality," *Journal of Abnormal and Social Psychology* 67 (1963), pp. 422–436; J. Stacy Adams, "Inequity in Social Exchange," in L. Berkowitz (ed.), *Advances in Experimental Social Psychology* 2 (New York: Academic Press, 1965), pp. 267–300.

[20] Adams, op. cit. (1965).

[21] These issues are discussed in C. Kagitcibasi and J. W. Berry, "Cross-Cultural Psychology: Current Research and Trends," *Annual Review of Psychology* 40 (1989), pp. 493–531.

[22] See Blair Sheppard, Roy J. Lewicki, and John Minton, *Organizational Justice: The Search for Fairness in the Workplace* (New York: Lexington Books, 1992); Jerald Greenberg, *The Quest for Justice on the Job: Essays and Experiments* (Thousand Oaks, CA: Sage, 1995); Robert Folger and Russell Cropanzano, *Organizational Justice and Human Resource Management* (Thousand Oaks, CA: Sage, 1998); and Mary A. Konovsky, "Understanding Procedural Justice and Its Impact on Business Organizations," *Journal of Management* 26 (2000), pp. 489–511.

[23] Interactional justice is described by Robert J. Bies, "The Predicament of Injustice: The Management of Moral Outrage," in L. L. Cummings and B. M. Staw (eds.), *Research in Organizational Behavior* 9 (Greenwich, CT: JAI Press, 1987), pp. 289–319. The example is from Carol T. Kulik and Robert L. Holbrook, "Demographics in Service Encounters: Effects of Racial and Gender Congruence on Perceived Fairness," *Social Justice Research* 13 (2000), pp. 375–402.

[24] Victor H. Vroom, *Work and Motivation* (New York: Wiley, 1964).

[25] Ibid.

[26] See Terence R. Mitchell, "Expectancy Models of Job Satisfaction, Occupational Preference and Effort: A Theoretical, Methodological, and Empirical Appraisal," *Psychological Bulletin* 81 (1974), pp. 1053–1077; Mahmoud A. Wahba and Robert J. House, "Expectancy Theory in Work and Motivation: Some Logical and Methodological Issues," *Human Relations* 27 (January 1974), pp. 121–147; Terry Connolly, "Some Conceptual and Methodological Issues in Expectancy Models of Work Performance Motivation," *Academy of Management Review* 1 (October 1976), pp. 37–47; and Terrence Mitchell, "Expectancy-Value Models in Organizational Psychology," in N. Feather (ed.), *Expectancy, Incentive and Action* (New York: Erlbaum & Associates, 1980).

[27] See Adler, op. cit.

[28] Edwin A. Locke, Karyll N. Shaw, Lise M. Saari, and Gary P. Latham, "Goal Setting and Task Performance: 1969–1980," *Psychological Bulletin* 90 (July/November 1981), pp. 125–152; Edwin A. Locke and Gary P. Latham, "Work Motivation and Satisfaction: Light at the End of the Tunnel," *Psychological Science* 1.4 (July 1990), pp. 240–246; Edwin A. Locke and Gary Latham, *A Theory of Goal Setting and Task Performance* (Englewood Cliffs, NJ: Prentice Hall, 1990).

[29] Edwin A. Locke and Gary P. Latham, "Has Goal Setting Gone Wild, or Have Its Attackers Abandoned Good Scholarship?" *The Academy of Management Perspective* 23 (February 2009), pp. 17–23.

[30] Gary P. Latham and Edwin A. Locke, "Goal Setting—A Motivational Technique That Works," *Organizational Dynamics* 8 (Autumn 1979), pp. 68–80; Gary P. Latham and Timothy P. Steele, "The Motivational Effects of Participation versus Goal-Setting on Performance," *Academy of Management Journal* 26 (1983), pp. 406–417; Miriam Erez and Frederick H. Kanfer, "The Role of Goal Acceptance in Goal Setting and Task Performance," *Academy of Management Review* 8 (1983), pp. 454–463; R. E. Wood and E. A. Locke, "Goal Setting and Strategy Effects on Complex Tasks," in B. Staw and L. L. Cummings (eds.), *Research in Organizational Behavior* (Greenwich, CT: JAI Press, 1990).

[31] See E. A. Locke and G. P. Latham, "Work Motivation and Satisfaction," *Psychological Science* 1.4 (July 1990), p. 241.

[32] For recent debate on goal setting, see Lisa D. Ordóñez, Maurice E. Schwitzer, Adam D. Galinsky, and Max H. Bazerman, "Goals Gone Wild: The Systematic Side Effects of Overprescribing Goal Setting," *The Academy of Management Perspective* 23 (February 2009), pp. 6–16; Locke and Latham, op. cit. (2009).

[33] Ibid.

[34] For a good review of MBO, see Anthony P. Raia, *Managing by Objectives* (Glenview, IL: Scott Foresman, 1974).

[35] Ibid. Steven Kerr summarizes the criticisms well in "Overcoming the Dysfunctions of MBO," *Management by Objectives* 5.1, 1976.

FEATURE NOTES

Opener/Executive Women: Information from Carol Hymowitz, "Women Tell Women: Life in the Top Jobs Is Worth the Effort," *The Wall Street Journal* (November 20, 2006), p. B1; Miguel Helft, "Yahoo's New Chief Makes Decisive Appearance," *The New York Times* (January 16, 2009), www.nytimes.com/; Jessica E. Vascellaro, "Yahoo CEO Set to Install Top-Down Management," *The Wall Street Journal* (February 23, 2009), p. B1.

Ethics in OB: John Woods, *Leaving Microsoft to Change the World* (New York: HarperCollins, 2006).

Leaders on Leadership/Piscines Ideales: Information from www.csrhellas.org; www.ideales.gr; Great Place to Work Institute Europe. (2009). 100 Best Workplaces in Europe. *European Great Place to Work Magazine, 2009.*

Mastering Management: Developed from Boris Groysberg, Andrew N. McLean, and Nitin Nohria, "Are Leaders Portable?" *Harvard Business Review* (May, 2006); and, "Psychological Capital (PsyCap) Measurement, Development, and Performance Impact," *Briefings Report 2006-01* (Gallup Leadership Institute); Fred Luthans, James B. Avey, Bruce J. Avoilio, Steven M. Norman, and Gwendolyn M. Combs, "Psychological Capital Development: Toward a Micro-Intervention," *Journal of Organizational Behavior* 27 (2006), pp. 387–393.

MARGIN PHOTOS

Working Mother Media—Quote from Information from workingmother.com (retrieved September 29, 2006); *AJ's Music Café*—Information from Micheline Maynard, "Nation's Scorn Wounds Detroit's Pride," *The Columbus Dispatch* (March 30, 2009), p. C8; *American Red Cross/Theresa Bischoff*—Information from Rika Nazem, "First Responder," STERNbusiness (Fall/Winter, 2008), p. 7.

Chapter 6

ENDNOTES

[1] For complete reviews of theory, research, and practice see Edward E. Lawler III, *Pay and Organizational Effectiveness* (New York: McGraw-Hill, 1971); Edward E. Lawler III, *Pay and Organizational Development* (Reading, MA: Addison-Wesley, 1981); Edward E. Lawler III, "The Design of Effective Reward Systems," in Jay W. Lorsch (ed.), *Handbook of Organizational Behavior* (Englewood Cliffs, NJ: Prentice-Hall, 1987), pp. 255–271.

[2] Reasons for Pay Raises," *BusinessWeek* (May 29, 2006), p. 11.

[3] As an example, see D. B. Balkin and L. R. Gómez-Mejia (eds.), *New Perspectives on Compensation* (Englewood Cliffs, NJ: Prentice-Hall, 1987).

[4] Jone L. Pearce, "Why Merit Pay Doesn't Work: Implications from Organization Theory," in Balkin and Gómez-Mejia op. cit. (1987), pp. 169–178; Jerry M. Newman, "Selecting Incentive Plans to Complement Organizational Strategy," in Balkin and Gómez-Mejia op. cit. (1987), pp. 214–224; Edward E. Lawler III, "Pay for Performance: Making It Work," *Compensation and Benefits Review* 21 (1989), pp. 55–60.

[5] See Daniel C. Boyle, "Employee Motivation That Works," *HR Magazine* (October 1992), pp. 83–89; Kathleen A. McNally, "Compensation as a Strategic Tool," *HR Magazine* (July 1992), pp. 59–66.

[6] Erin White, "How to Reduce Turnover," *The Wall Street Journal* (November 21, 2005), p. B5.

[7] See Brian Graham-Moore, "Review of the Literature," in Brian Graham-Moore and Timothy L. Ross (eds.), *Gainsharing* (Washington, DC: Bureau of National Affairs, 1990), p. 20.

[8] S. E. Markham, K. D. Scott, and B. L. Little, "National Gainsharing Study: The Importance of Industry Differences," *Compensation and Benefits Review* (January/February 1992), pp. 34–45.

[9] Jeffrey Pfeffer and John F. Veiga, "Putting People First for Organizational Success," *Academy of Management Executive* 13 (May 1999), pp. 37–48.

[10] L. R. Gómez-Mejia, D. B. Balkin, and R. L. Cardy, *Managing Human Resources* (Englewood Cliffs, NJ: Prentice-Hall, 1995), pp. 410–411.

[11] N. Gupta, G. E. Ledford, G. D. Jenkins, and D. H. Doty, "Survey Based Prescriptions for Skill-Based Pay," *American Compensation Association Journal* 1.1 (1992), pp. 48–59; L. W. Ledford, "The Effectiveness of Skill-Based Pay," *Perspectives in Total Compensation* 1.1 (1991), pp. 1–4.

[12] Mina Kines, "P&G's Leadership Machine," *Fortune* (April 14, 2009).

[13] For more details, see G. P. Latham and K. N. Wexley, *Increasing Productivity through Performance Appraisal* (2nd ed.); Stephen J. Carroll and Craig E. Schneier, *Performance Appraisal and Review Systems* (Glenview, IL: Scott Foresman, 1982).

[14] See George T. Milkovich and John W. Boudreau, *Personnel/Human Resource Management: A Diagnostic Approach*, 5th ed. (Plano, TX: Business Publications, 1988).

[15] Mark R. Edwards and Ann J. Ewen, *360-Degree Feedback: The Powerful New Tool for Employee Feedback and Performance Improvement* (New York: Amacom, 1996).

[16] For discussion of many of these errors, see David L. Devries, Ann M. Morrison, Sandra L. Shullman, and Michael P. Gerlach, *Performance Appraisal on the Line* (Greensboro, NC: Center for Creative Leadership, 1986), ch. 3.

[17] Frederick W. Taylor, *The Principles of Scientific Management* (New York: Norton, 1967).

[18] Frederick Herzberg, "One More Time: How Do You Motivate Employees?" *Harvard Business Review* 46 (January/February 1968), pp. 53–62.

[19] For a complete description, see J. Richard Hackman and Greg R. Oldham, *Work Redesign* (Reading, MA: Addison-Wesley, 1980).

[20] See J. Richard Hackman and Greg Oldham, "Development of the Job Diagnostic Survey," *Journal of Applied Psychology* 60 (1975), pp. 159–170.

[21] For forerunner research, see Charles L. Hulin and Milton R. Blood, "Job Enlargement, Individual Differences, and Worker Responses," *Psychological Bulletin* 69 (1968), pp. 41–55: Milton R. Blood and Charles L. Hulin. "Alienation, Environmental Characteristics and Worker Responses," *Journal of Applied Psychology* 51 (1967), pp. 284–290.

22 Gerald Salancik and Jeffrey Pfeffer, "An Examination of Need-Satisfaction Models of Job Attitudes," *Administrative Science Quarterly* 22 (1977), pp. 427–456; Gerald Salancik and Jeffrey Pfeffer, "A Social Information Processing Approach to Job Attitude and Task Design." *Administrative Science Quarterly* 23 (1978), pp. 224–253.

23 For overviews, see Allan R. Cohen and Herman Gadon, *Alternative Work Schedules: Integrating Individual and Organizational Needs* (Reading, MA: Addison-Wesley, 1978); and Jon L. Pearce, John W. Newstrom, Randall B. Dunham, and Alison E. Barber, *Alternative Work Schedules* (Boston: Allyn & Bacon, 1989). See also Sharon Parker and Toby Wall, *Job and Work Design* (Thousand Oaks, CA: Sage, 1998).

26 C. Latack and L. W. Foster, "Implementation of Compressed Work Schedules: Participation and Job Redesign as Critical Factors for Employee Acceptance," *Personnel Psychology* 38 (1985), pp. 75–92.

28 Olga Kharif, "Chopping Hours, Not Heads," *BusinessWeek* (January 5, 2009), p. 85.

29 Sue Shellenbarger, "Does Avoiding a 9-to-5 Grind Make You a Target for Layoffs?" *The Wall Street Journal* (April 22, 2009), p. D1.

32 Mararet Harding, "Uncommon Co-Workers," *The Columbus Dispatch* (March 22, 2009), p. D1.

33 "Hurting, But Often Uncounted," *BusinessWeek* (April 20, 2009), p. 20.

FEATURE NOTES

Opener/Unimerco: Great Place to Work Institute Europe. (2009). 100 Best Workplaces in Europe. *European Great Place to Work Magazine, 2009;* www.unimerco.com

Leaders on Leadership/Haruka Nishimatsu: Information from www.cnn.com, original interview by Kyung Lah, CNN, Tokyo

Mastering Management: Information from Sue Shellenbarger, "The Mommy Drain: Employers Beef Up Perks to Lure New Mothers Back to Work," *The Wall Street Journal* (September 28, 2006), p. D1.

Ethics in OB: Information from Reuters, "Coming to Work Sick Afflicts Biz," *Economic Times Bangalore* (January 28, 2007), p. 14; www.webmd.com/.

MARGIN PHOTOS

Amazon.com–Information from Erin White, "How to Reduce Turnover," *The Wall Street Journal* (November 21, 2005), p. B5.

Phoenix Bats—Information from Scott Priestle, "Hitting It Off," *The Columbus Dispatch* (March 31, 2009).

In-N-Out Burger—Stacy Perman, "In-N-Out Burger: Professionalizing Fast Food," *BusinessWeek* (April 9, 2009); Stacy Perman, "Fast Food, Family Feuds," *The Wall Street Journal* (April 15, 2009), p. A. 13.

Jelly Columbus—Information from Mararet Harding, "Uncommon Co-Workers," *The Columbus Dispatch* (March 22, 2009), p. D1.

Chapter 7

ENDNOTES

1 See, for example, Jon R, Katzenbach and Douglas K. Smith, "The Discipline of Teams," *Harvard Business Review* (March/April 1993a), pp. 111–120; Jon R. Katzenbach and Douglas K. Smith, *The Wisdom of Teams: Creating the High-Performance Organization* (Boston: Harvard Business School Press, 1993b).

2 Katzenbach and Smith (1993a), op. cit., p. 112.

3 Information from Scott Thurm, "Teamwork Raises Everyone's Game," *The Wall Street Journal* (November 7, 2005), p. B7.

4 Ibid.

5 Katzenbach and Smith (1993a, 1993b), op. cit.

6 For a good overview, see Greg L. Stewart, Charles C. Manz, and Henry P. Sims, *Team Work and Group Dynamics* (New York: Wiley, 1999).

7 Katzenbach and Smith (1993a, 1993b), op. cit.

8 See Jon R. Katzenbach, "The Myth of the Top Management Team," *Harvard Business Review* 75 (November/December 1997), pp. 83–91.

9 Information from Stratford Shermin, "Secrets of HP's 'Muddled' Team," *Fortune* (March 18, 1996), pp. 116–120.

10 See Stewart, Manz, and Sims (1999), pp. 43–44.

11 Rensis Likert, *New Patterns of Management* (New York: McGraw-Hill, 1961).

12 Jay A. Conger, *Winning 'Em Over: A New Model for Managing in the Age of Persuasion* (New York: Simon & Schuster, 1998).

13 Ibid., p. 191.

14 See Jay R. Galbraith, *Designing Organizations* (San Francisco: Jossey-Bass, 1998).

15 Robert P. Steel, Anthony J. Mento, Benjamin L. Dilla, Nestor Ovalle, and Russell F. Lloyd, "Factors Influencing the Success and Failure of Two Quality Circles Programs," *Journal of Management* 11.1 (1985), pp. 99–119; Edward E. Lawler III and Susan A. Mohrman, "Quality Circles: After the Honeymoon," *Organizational Dynamics* 15.4 (1987), pp. 42–54.

16 See D. Duarte and N. Snyder, *Mastering Virtual Teams: Strategies, Tools, and Techniques That Succeed* (San Francisco: Jossey-Bass, 1999); Jessica Lipnack and Jeffrey Stamps, *Virtual Teams: Reaching across Space, Time, and Organizations with Technology* (New York: Wiley, 1997).

17 For reviews see Wayne F. Cascio, "Managing a Virtual Workplace," *Academy of Management Executive*, vol. 14 (2000), pp. 81–90; Sheila Simsarian Webber, "Virtual Teams: A Meta-Analysis," www.shrm.org/foundation/findings.asp.

[18] Stacie A. Furst, Martha Reeves, Benson Rosen, and Richard S. Blackburn, "Managing the Life Cycle of Virtual Teams," *Academy of Management Executive* 18.2 (2004), pp. 6–11; ibid.; Duarte and Schneider, op. cit.; Lipnack and Stamps, op. cit.; and J. Richard Hackman by Diane Coutu, "Why Teams Don't Work," *Harvard Business Review* (May 2009), pp. 99–105.

[19] See, for example, Paul S. Goodman, Rukmini Devadas, and Terri L. Griffith Hughson, "Groups and Productivity: Analyzing the Effectiveness of Self-Managing Teams," Chapter 11 in John R. Campbell and Richard J. Campbell, *Productivity in Organizations* (San Francisco: Jossey-Bass, 1988); Jack Orsbrun, Linda Moran, Ed Musslewhite, and John H. Zenger, with Craig Perrin, *Self-Directed Work Teams: The New American Challenge* (Homewood, IL: Business One Irwin, 1990); Dale E. Yeatts and Cloyd Hyten, *High Performing Self-Managed Work Teams* (Thousand Oaks, CA: Sage, 1997).

[20] Marvin E. Shaw, *Group Dynamics: The Psychology of Small Group Behavior*, 2nd ed. (New York: McGraw-Hill, 1976).

[21] Bib Latané, Kipling Williams, and Stephen Harkins, "Many Hands Make Light the Work: The Causes and Consequences of Social Loafing," *Journal of Personality and Social Psychology* 37 (1978), pp. 822–832; E. Weklon and G. M. Gargano, "Cognitive Effort in Additive Task Groups: The Effects of Shared Responsibility on the Quality of Multi-Attribute Judgments," *Organizational Behavior and Human Decision Processes* 36 (1985), pp. 348–361; John M. George, "Extrinsic and Intrinsic Origins of Perceived Social Loafing in Organizations," *Academy of Management Journal* (March 1992), pp. 191–202; W. Jack Duncan, "Why Some People Loaf in Groups While Others Loaf Alone," *Academy of Management Executive* 8 (1994), pp. 79–80.

[22] D. A. Kravitz and B. Martin, "Ringelmann Rediscovered," *Journal of Personality and Social Psychology* 50 (1986), pp. 936–941.

[23] John M. George, "Extrinsic and Intrinsic Origins of Perceived Social Loafing in Organizations," *Academy of Management Journal* (March 1992), pp. 191–202; and W. Jack Duncan, "Why Some People Loaf in Groups While Others Loaf Alone," *Academy of Management Executive*, vol. 8 (1994), pp. 79–80.

[24] A classic article by Richard B. Zajonc, "Social Facilitation," *Science* 149 (1965), pp. 269–274.

[25] See, for example, Leland P. Bradford, *Group Development*, 2nd ed. (San Francisco: Jossey-Bass, 1997).

[26] J. Steven Heinen and Eugene Jacobson, "A Model of Task Group Development in Complex Organization and a Strategy of Implementation," *Academy of Management Review* 1 (October 1976), pp. 98–111; Bruce W. Tuckman, "Developmental Sequence in Small Groups," *Psychological Bulletin* 63 (1965), pp. 384–399; Bruce W. Tuckman and Mary Ann C. Jensen, "Stages of Small Group Development Revisited," *Group & Organization Studies* 2 (1977), pp. 419–427.

[27] Quote from Alex Markels, "Money & Business," *U.S. News online* (October 22, 2006).

[28] Ibid.

[29] Example from "Designed for Interaction," *Fortune* (January 8, 2001), p. 150.

[30] David M. Herold, "The Effectiveness of Work Groups," in Steven Kerr (ed.), *Organizational Behavior* (New York: Wiley, 1979), p. 95; see also the discussion of group tasks in Stewart, Manz, and Sims, op. cit. (1999), pp. 142–143.

[31] F. J. Thomas and C. F. Fink, "Effects of Group Size," in Larry L. Cummings and William E. Scott (eds.), *Readings in Organizational and Human Performance* (Homewood, IL: Irwin, 1969), pp. 394–408.

[32] Robert D. Hof, "Amazon's Risky Bet," *BusinessWeek* (November 13, 2006), p. 52.

[33] Thomas and Fink, op. cit.

[34] Shaw, op. cit.

[35] William C. Schultz, *FIRO: A Three-Dimensional Theory of Interpersonal Behavior* (New York: Rinehart, 1958).

[36] William C. Schultz, "The Interpersonal Underworld," *Harvard Business Review* 36 (July/August 1958), p. 130.

[37] Matt Golosinski, "Teamwork Takes Center Stage," *Northwestern* (Winter 2005), p. 39.

[38] Daniel R. Ilgen, Jeffrey A. LePine, and John R. Hollenbeck, "Effective Decision Making in Multinational Teams," in P. Christopher Earley and Miriam Erez (eds.), *New Perspectives on International Industrial/Organizational Psychology* (San Francisco: New Lexington Press, 1997); Warren Watson, "Cultural Diversity's Impact on Interaction Process and Performance," *Academy of Management Journal* 16 (1993).

[39] Stewart, Manz, and Sims, op. cit.

[40] See Daniel, R Ilgen, Jeffrey A. LePiner, and John R. Hollenbeck, "Effective Decision Making in Multinational Teams," in P. Christopher Earley and Miriam Erez (eds.), *New Perspectives on International Industrial/Organizational Psychology* (San Francisco: New Lexington Press, 1997), pp. 377–409.

[41] L. Argote and J. E. McGrath, "Group Processes in Organizations: Continuity and Change," in C. L. Cooper and I. T. Robertson (eds.), *International Review of Industrial and Organizational Psychology* (New York: Wiley, 1993), pp. 333–389.

[42] See Ilgen, LePiner, and Hollenbeck, op. cit.

[43] Golosinski, op. cit., p. 39.

[44] "Dream Teams," *Northwestern* (Winter 2005), p. 10; and, Matt Golosinski, "Teamwork Takes Center Stage," *Northwestern* (Winter 2005), p. 39.

[45] George C. Homans, *The Human Group* (New York: Harcourt Brace, 1950).

FEATURE NOTES

Opener/Tandberg: Great Place to Work Institute Europe. (2009). 100 Best Workplaces in Europe. *European Great Place to Work Magazine, 2009.*

Mastering Management: Developed from Wayne F. Cascio, "Managing a Virtual Workplace," *Academy of Management Executive* 14 (2000), pp. 81–90; and, Stacie A. Furst, Martha Reeves, Benson Rosen, and Richard S. Blackburn, "Managing the Life Cycle of Virtual Teams," *Academy of Management Executive* 18 (2004), pp. 6–20.

Leaders on Leadership: Information from Kate Klonick, "Pepsi's CEO a Refreshing Change" (August 15, 2006), www.abcnews.go.com; Diane Brady, "Indra Nooyi: Keeping Cool in Hot Water," *BusinessWeek* (June 11, 2007); special report; Indra Nooyi, "The Best Advice I Ever Got," CNNMoney (April 30, 2008), www.cnnnmoney.com; and, "Indra Nooyi," *The Wall Street Journal* (November 10, 2008), p. R3.

Ethics in OB: Information from "MBAs 'Cheat Most,'" *Financial Times* (September 21, 2006), p. 1; "The Devil Made Me Do It," *BusinessWeek* (July 24, 2006), p. 10; Karen Richardson, "Buffett Advises on Scandals: Avoid Temptations," *The Wall Street Journal* (October 10, 2006), p. A9; Alma Acevedo, "Of Fallacies and Curricula: A Case of Business Ethics," *Teaching Business Ethics* 5 (2001), pp. 157–170.

MARGIN PHOTOS

Microsoft—Information from "Two Wasted Days at Work," *CNNMoney.com* (March 16, 2005), www.cnnmoney.com.

Cleveland Clinic—Information from "Getting to No. 1," *Continental.com Magazine* (March 2009), pp. 48–49.

Chapter 8

ENDNOTES

[1] See Owen Linzmeyer and Owen W. Linzmeyer, *Apple Confidential 2.0: The Definitive History of the World's Most Colorful Company* (San Francisco: No Starch Press, 2004); and Jeffrey L. Cruikshank, *The Apple Way* (New York: McGraw-Hill, 2005).

[2] Diane Coutu, "Why Teams Don't Work," *Harvard Business Review* (May 2009), pp. 99–105.

[3] Ibid.

[4] Ibid.

[5] Steven Levy, "Insanely Great," *Wired* (February 1994), www.wired.com.

[6] For an interesting discussion of sports teams, see Ellen Fagenson-Eland, "The National Football League''s Bill Parcells on Winning, Leading, and Turning Around Teams," *Academy of Management Executive* 15 (August 2001), pp. 48–57; and Nancy Katz, "Sport Teams as a Model for

Workplace Teams: Lessons and Liabilities," *Academy of Management Executive* 15 (August 2002), pp. 56–69.

[7] See William D. Dyer, *Team Building*, 3rd ed. (Reading, MA: Addison-Wesley, 1995).

[8] Dennis Berman, "Zap! Pow! Splat!" *BusinessWeek*, Enterprise Issue (February 9, 1998), p. ENT22.

[9] Developed from a discussion by Edgar H. Schein, *Process Consultation* (Reading, MA: Addison-Wesley, 1969), pp. 32–37; Edgar H. Schein, *Process Consultation*, Vol. 1 (Reading, MA: Addison-Wesley, 1988), pp. 40–49.

[10] The classic work is Robert F. Bales, "Task Roles and Social Roles in Problem-Solving Groups," in Eleanor E. Maccoby, Theodore M. Newcomb, and E. L. Hartley (eds.), *Readings in Social Psychology* (New York: Holt, Rinehart & Winston, 1958).

[11] For a good description of task and maintenance functions, see John J. Gabarro and Anne Harlan, "Note on Process Observation," Note 9-477-029 (Harvard Business School, 1976).

[12] Christine Porath and Christine Pearson, "How Toxic Colleagues Corrode Performance," *Harvard Business Review* (April 2009), p. 24.

[13] See Daniel C. Feldman, "The Development and Enforcement of Group Norms," *Academy of Management Review* 9 (1984), pp. 47–53.

[14] See Robert F. Allen and Saul Pilnick, "Confronting the Shadow Organization: How to Select and Defeat Negative Norms," *Organizational Dynamics* (Spring 1973), pp. 13–17; and Alvin Zander, *Making Groups Effective* (San Francisco: Jossey-Bass, 1982), ch. 4; Feldman (1984).

[15] For a summary of research on group cohesiveness, see Marvin E. Shaw, *Group Dynamics* (New York: McGraw-Hill, 1971), pp. 110–112, 192.

[16] See Jay R. Galbraith, *Designing Organizations* (San Francisco: Jossey-Bass, 1998).

[17] Jerry Yoram Wind and Jeremy Main, *Driving Change: How the Best Companies Are Preparing for the 21st Century* (New York: Free Press, 1998), p. 135.

[18] The concept of interacting, coacting, and counteracting groups is presented in Fred E. Fiedler, *A Theory of Leadership Productivity* (New York: McGraw-Hill, 1967).

[19] Research on communication networks is found in Alex Bavelas, "Communication Patterns in Task-Oriented Groups," *Journal of the Acoustical Society of America* 22 (1950), pp. 725–730. See also "Research on Communication Networks," as summarized in Shaw (1976), pp. 137–153.

[20] A classic work on proxemics is Edward T. Hall's book, *The Hidden Dimension* (Garden City, NY: Doubleday, 1986).

[21] Mirand Wewll, "Alternative Spaces Spawning Desk-Free Zones," *Columbus Dispatch* (May 18, 1998), pp. 10–11.

[22] "Tread: Rethinking the Workplace," *BusinessWeek* (September 25, 2006), p. IN.

[23] Amy Saunders, "A Creative Approach to Work," *The Columbus Dispatch* (May 2, 2008), pp. C1, C9.

[24] Michelle Conlin and Douglas MacMillan, "Managing the Tweets," *BusinessWeek* (June 1, 2009), pp. 20–21.

[25] See Wayne F. Cascio, "Managing a Virtual Workplace," *Academy of Management Executive* 14 (2000), pp. 81–90; Sheila Simsarian Webber, "Virtual Teams: A Meta-Analysis," http://www.shrm.org/foundation/findings.asp; and Stacie A. Furst, Martha Reeves, Benson Rosen, and Richard S. Blackburn, "Managing the Life Cycle of Virtual Teams," *Academy of Management Executive* 18 (2004), pp. 6–20.

[26] Adam Bryant, "He Wants Subjects, Verbs and Objects," *The New York Times* (April 26, 2009), www.nytimes.com.

[27] The discussion is developed from Schein (1988), pp. 69–75.

[28] Developed from guidelines presented in the classic article by Jay Hall, "Decisions, Decisions, Decisions," *Psychology Today* (November 1971): 55–56.

[29] Norman R. F. Maier, "Assets and Liabilities in Group Problem Solving," *Psychological Review* 74 (1967): 239–249.

[30] Irving L. Janis, "Groupthink," *Psychology Today* (November 1971): 33–36; Irving L. Janis. *Groupthink*, 2nd ed. (Boston: Houghton Mifflin, 1982). See also J. Longley and D. G. Pruitt, "Groupthink: A Critique of Janis' Theory," in L. Wheeler (ed.), *Review of Personality and Social Psychology* (Beverly Hills, CA: Sage, 1980); Carrie R. Leana, "A Partial Test of Janis's Groupthink Model: The Effects of Group Cohesiveness and Leader Behavior on Decision Processes," *Journal of Management* 1.1 (1985): pp. 5–18. See also Jerry Harvey, "Managing Agreement in Organizations: The Abilene Paradox," *Organizational Dynamics* (Summer 1974): 63–80.

[31] See Janis, op. cit. (1971, 1982).

[32] Gayle W. Hill, "Group Versus Individual Performance: Are Two Leads Better Than One?" *Psychological Bulletin* 91 (1982): 517–539.

[33] Bryant, op, cit.

[34] These techniques are well described in George P. Huber. *Managerial Decision Making* (Glenview, IL: Scott, Foresman, 1980); Andre L. Delbecq, Andrew L. Van de Ven, and David H. Gustafson, *Group Techniques for Program Planning: A Guide to Nominal Groups and Delphi Techniques* (Glenview, IL: Scott, Foresman. 1975); William M. Fox, "Anonymity and Other Keys to Successful Problem-Solving Meeting," *National Productivity Review* 8 (Spring 1989): 145–156.

[35] Delbecq, Van de Ven, and Gustafson, op. cit. (1975): Fox, op. cit. (1989).

[36] Information from Jessi Hempel, "Big Blue Brainstorm," *BusinessWeek* (August 7, 2006), p. 70.

[37] Delbecq et al., op. cit.

FEATURE NOTES

Opener/Toyota: www.toyotainternational.com; Spear, S.J. (2008). Chasing the Rabbit: How Market Leaders Outdistance the Competition.

Ethics in OB: Information from Ken Gordon, "Tressel's Way Transforms OSU into 'Model Program,'" *Columbus Dispatch* (January 5, 2007), pp. A1, A4.

Leaders on Leadership: Information from Jeffrey D. Sachs, *The End of Poverty* (New York: Penguin, 2005); Muhammad Yunus, *Creating a World Without Poverty: Social Business and the Future of Capitalism* (New York Public Affairs, 2008); "Executive MBA Students Learn about Micro-Lending from Its Founder, Nobel Laureate Muhammad Yunus," *Stern Business* (Spring/Summer 2008), p. 41; Steve Hamm, "When the Bottom Line Is Ending Poverty," *BusinessWeek* (March 10, 2008), p. 85; Yunus, op. cit.; Daniel Pimlott, "Bangladeshi's Aid for US Poor," *Financial Times* (February 16/17, 2008), p. 4; and Simon Hobbs, "Big Payback," *CNBC European Business* (January/February 2009), pp. 36–38.

Mastering Management: Developed from guidelines presented in the classic article by Jay Hall, "Decisions, Decisions, Decisions," *Psychology Today* (November 1971), pp. 55–56.

MARGIN PHOTOS

Deadly Meetings—Developed from Eric Matson, "The Seven Sins of Deadly Meetings," *Fast Company* (April/May 1996), p. 122.

Seagate Technologies—Sarah Max, "Seagate's Morale-athon," *BusinessWeek* (April 3, 2006), pp. 110–111.

American Psychological Association—"Stress Survey: Stress a Major Health Problem in the U.S.," APA Health Center, www.apahelpcenter.org.

Chapter 9

ENDNOTES

[1] www.google.com/corporate; Great Place to Work Institute Europe. (2009). 100 Best Workplaces in *Europe*. *European Great Place to Work Magazine, 2009*.

[2] For concise overviews, see Susan J. Miller, David J. Hickson, and David C. Wilson, "Decision-Making in Organizations" in Steward R. Clegg, Cynthia Hardy, and Walter Nord, *Handbook of Organizational Studies* (London: Sage, 1996); George P. Huber, *Managerial Decision Making* (Glenview, IL: Scott Foresman, 1980), pp. 293–312.

[3] This figure and the related discussion are developed from conversations with Dr. Alma Acevedo of the University of Puerto Rico at Rio Piedras and from her articles "Of Fallacies and Curricula: A Case of Business Ethics," *Teaching Business Ethics* 5 (2001), pp. 157–170; and "Business Ethics: An Introduction," working paper (2009).

[4] Acevedo, op. cit. (2009).

[5] Based on Gerald F. Cavanagh, *American Business Values*, 4th ed. (Upper Saddle River, NJ: Prentice-Hall, 1998).

[6] www.josephsoninstitute.org.

[7] Stephen Fineman, "Emotion and Organizing," in Clegg, Hardy, and Nord (eds.), op. cit., pp. 542–580.

8 For discussion of ethical frameworks for decision making, see Joseph R. Desjardins, *Business, Ethics and the Environment* (Upper Saddle River, NJ: Pearson Education, 2007); Linda A. Trevino and Katherine A. Nelson, *Managing Business Ethics* (New York: Wiley, 1995); Saul W. Gellerman, "Why 'Good' Managers Make Bad Ethical Choices," *Harvard Business Review* 64 (July/August 1986), pp. 85–90; and Barbara Ley Toffler, *Tough Choices: Managers Talk Ethics* (New York: Wiley, 1986).

9 For scholarly reviews, see Dean Tjosvold, "Effects of Crisis Orientation on Managers" Approach to Controversy in Decision Making," *Academy of Management Journal* 27 (1984), pp. 130–138; and Ian I. Mitroff, Paul Shrivastava, and Firdaus E. Udwadia, "Effective Crisis Management," *Academy of Management Executive* 1 (1987), pp. 283–292.

10 Quote from Chesley Sullenberger III in photo feature from Robert I. Sutton, "In Praise of Simple Competence," *BusinessWeek* (April 13, 2009), p. 67.

11 This section stems from the classic work on decision making found in Michael D. Cohen, James G. March, and Johan P Olsen, "The Garbage Can Model of Organizational Choice," *Administrative Science Quarterly* 17 (1972), pp. 1–25; and James G. March and Herbert A. Simon, *Organizations* (New York: John Wiley, 1958), pp. 137–142.

12 See, for example, Jonathan Rosenoer and William Scherlis, "Risk Gone Wild," *Harvard Business Review* (May 2009), p. 26.

13 See KPMG, Enterprise Risk Management Services, www.kpmg.com.

14 This traditional distinction is often attributed to Herbert Simon, *Administrative Behavior* (New York: Free Press, 1945); see also Herbert Simon, *The New Science of Management Decision* (New York: Harper and Row, 1960).

15 For a historical review, see Leight Buchanan and Andrew O'Connell, "Thinking Machines," *Harvard Business Review* 84.1 (2006), pp. 38–49. For recent applications, see Jiju Antony, Raj Anand, Maneesh Kumar, and M. K. Tiwari, "Multiple Response Optimization Using Taguchi Methodology and Nero-Fuzzy Based Model," *Journal of Manufacturing Technology Management* 17.7 (2006), pp. 908–112; and Craig Boutilier, "The Influence of Influence Diagrams on Artificial Intelligence," *Decision Analysis* 2.4 (2005), pp. 229–232.

16 Also see Mary Zey (ed.), *Decision Making: Alternatives to Rational Choice Models* (Thousand Oaks, CA: Sage Publications, 1992).

17 Simon, *Organizations* (1958).

18 For discussions, see Cohen, March, and Olsen (1972); Miller, Hickson, and Wilson (1996); and Michael Masuch and Perry LaPontin; "Beyond Garbage Cans: An AI Model of Organizational Choice," *Administrative Science Quarterly* 34 (1989), pp. 38–67.

19 For a good discussion, see Watson H. Agor, *Intuition in Organizations: Leading and Managing Productively* (Newbury Park, CA: Sage, 1989); Herbert A. Simon, "Making Management Decisions: The Role of Intuition and Emotion," *Academy of Management Executive,* vol. 1 (1987), pp. 57–64; Orlando Behling and Norman L. Eckel, "Making Sense Out of Intuition," *Academy of Management Executive,* vol. 1 (1987), pp. 57–64; Orlando Behling and Norman L. Eckel, "Making Sense Out of Intuition," *Academy of Management Executive,* vol. 5 (1991), pp. 46–54.

20 Agor, op cit. (1989).

21 Alan Deutschman, "Inside the Mind of Jeff Bezos," *Fast Company* 85 (August 2004), www.fastcompany.com.

22 The classic work in this area is found in a series of articles by D. Kahneman and A. Tversky, "Subjective Probability: A Judgment of Representativeness," *Cognitive Psychology* 3 (1972), pp. 430–454; "On the Psychology of Prediction," *Psychological Review* 80 (1973), pp. 237–251; "Prospect Theory: An Analysis of Decision under Risk," *Econometrica* 47 (1979), pp. 263–291; "Psychology of Preferences," *Scientific American* (1982), pp. 161–173; and "Choices, Values, Frames," *American Psychologist* 39 (1984), pp. 341–350.

23 See Max H. Bazerman, *Judgement in Managerial Decision Making,* 6th ed. (New York: John Wiley, 2005).

24 See discussion by James A. F. Stoner, *Management,* 2nd ed. (Englewood Cliffs, NJ: Prentice Hall, 1982), pp. 167–168.

25 Quote from Susan Carey, "Pilot 'in Shock' as He landed Jet in River," *The Wall Street Journal* (February 9, 2009), p. A6.

26 They may also try and include too many others as shown by Phillip G. Clampitt and M. Lee Williams, "Decision Downsizing," *MIT Sloan Management Review* 48.2 (2007), pp. 77–89.

27 Victor H. Vroom and Arthur G. Jago, *The New Leadership: Managing Participation in Organizations* (Englewood Cliffs, NJ: Prentice-Hall, 1988). This is based on earlier work by Victor H. Vroom, "A New Look in Managerial Decision-Making," *Organizational Dynamics* (Spring 1973), pp. 66–80; and Victor H. Vroom and Phillip Yetton, *Leadership and Decision-Making* (Pittsburgh: University of Pittsburgh Press, 1973).

28 Vroom and Yetton, op. cit. (1973); and Vroom and Jago, op. cit. (1988).

29 See the discussion by Victor H. Vroom, "Leadership and the Decision Making Process," *Organizational Dynamics* 28 (2000), pp. 82–94.

30 Barry M. Staw, "The Escalation of Commitment to a Course of Action," *Academy of Management Review* 6 (1981), pp. 577–587; Barry M. Staw and Jerry Ross, "Knowing When to Pull the Plug," *Harvard Business Review* 65 (March/April 1987), pp. 68–74. See also Glen Whyte, "Escalating Commitment to a Course of Action: A Reinterpretation," *Academy of Management Review* 11 (1986), pp. 311–321.

[31] Joel Brockner, "The Escalation of Commitment to a Failing Course of Action: Toward Theoretical Progress," *Academy of Management Review* 17 (1992), pp. 39–61; and J. Ross and B. M. Staw, "Organizational Escalation and Exit: Lessons from the Shoreham Nuclear Power Plant," *Academy of Management Journal* 36 (1993), pp. 701–732.

[32] See, for example, Roger von Oech's books, *A Whack on the Side of the Head* (New York: Warner Books, 1983); and *A Kick in the Seat of the Pants* (New York: Harper & Row, 1986).

[33] See Cameron M. Ford and Dennis A. Gioia, *Creative Action in Organizations* (Thousand Oaks, CA: Sage, 1995).

[34] G. Wallas, *The Art of Thought* (New York: Harcourt, 1926), cited in Bazerman (1994).

[35] E. Glassman, "Creative Problem Solving," *Supervisory Management* (January 1989), pp. 21–26; and B. Kabanoff and J. R. Rossiter, "Recent Developments in Applied Creativity," *International Review of Industrial and Organizational Psychology* 9 (1994), pp. 283–324.

[36] Teresa M. Amabile, "Motivating Creativity in Organizations," *California Management Review* 40 (Fall 1997), pp. 39–58.

[37] Developed from discussions by Edward DeBono, *Lateral Thinking: Creativity Step-by-Step* (New York: Harper-Collins, 1970); John S. Dacey and Kathleen H. Lennon, *Understanding Creativity* (San Francisco: Jossey-Bass, 1998); and Bettina von Stamm, *Managing Innovation, Design & Creativity* (Chichester, England: John Wiley & Sons, 2003).

[38] R. Drazen, M. Glenn, and R. Kazanijan, "Multilevel Theorizing about Creativity in Organizations: A Sensemaking Perspective," *Academy of Management Review* 21 (1999), pp. 286–307.

[39] Developed from discussions by DeBono, *Lateral Thinking;* Dacey and Lennon, *Understanding Creativity;* and Von Stamm, *Managing Innovation.*

[40] See "Mosh Pits for Creativity," *BusinessWeek* (November 7, 2005), pp. 98–99.

FEATURE NOTES

Opener/Google: www.google.com/corporate; Great Place to Work Institute Europe. (2009). 100 Best Workplaces in Europe. *European Great Place to Work Magazine, 2009.*

Ethics in OB: Information from Ciaran Byrne and Niall Lynch, "Racism Rife As Irish Twice As Likely to Be Given Job," *Irish Independent* (May 7, 2009), p. 8.

Mastering Management: Reported in Eric Schmidt and Hal Varian, "Google: Ten Golden Rules," *Newsweek* (December 2, 2005), msnbc.com (retrieved September 17, 2006).

Leaders on Leadership: Information from Erica Noonan, *Boston Globe* (January 4, 2009), www.boston.com/bostonglobe; "Six Million Users: Nothing to Twitter At," *BusinessWeek* (March 16, 2009), pp. 51–52; and, Michael S. Malone, "The Twitter Revolution," *The Wall Street Journal* (April 18–19, 2009), p. A11.

MARGIN PHOTOS

Ford—Information from Matthew Dolan, "Ford Takes Online Gamble with New Fiesta," *The Wall Sreet Journal* (April 8, 2009), p. B8.

Google—Quotes from Dan Fost, "Keeping it all in the Family," *The New York Times* (November 13, 2008), p. 6.

McDonald's—Janet Adamy, "McDonald's Coffee Strategy is Tough Sell," *The Wall Street Journal* (October 27, 2009), p. B3

Chapter 10

ENDNOTES

[1] See, for example, Henry Mintzberg, *The Nature of Managerial Work* (New York: Harper & Row, 1973); and John R. P. Kotter, *The General Managers* (New York: Free Press, 1982).

[2] One of the classic discussions is by Richard E. Walton, *Interpersonal Peacemaking: Confrontations and Third-Party Consultation* (Reading, MA: Addison-Wesley, 1969).

[3] Kenneth W. Thomas and Warren H. Schmidt, "A Survey of Managerial Interests with Respect to Conflict," *Academy of Management Journal* 19 (1976), pp. 315–318.

[4] For a good overview, see Richard E. Walton, *Managing Conflict: Interpersonal Dialogue and Third Party Roles*, 2nd ed. (Reading, MA: Addison-Wesley, 1987); and Dean Tjosvold, *The Conflict-Positive Organization: Stimulate Diversity and Create Unity* (Reading, MA: Addison-Wesley, 1991).

[5] Walton (1969).

[6] Ibid.

[7] Information from Hal Lancaster, "Performance Reviews: Some Bosses Try a Fresh Approach," *The Wall Street Journal* (December 1, 1998), p. B1.

[8] Richard E. Walton and John M. Dutton, "The Management of Interdepartmental Conflict: A Model and Review," *Administrative Science Quarterly* 14 (1969), pp. 73–84.

[9] Geert Hofstede, *Culture's Consequences: International Differences in Work-Related Values* (Beverly Hills, CA: Sage Publications, 1980); and Geert Hofstede, "Cultural Constraints in Management Theories," *Academy of Management Executive* 7 (1993), pp. 81–94.

[10] Information from "Capitalizing on Diversity: Navigating the Seas of the Multicultural Workforce and Workplace," *BusinessWeek*, Special Advertising Section (December 4, 1998).

[11] These stages are consistent with the conflict models described by Alan C. Filley, *Interpersonal Conflict Resolution* (Glenview, IL: Scott Foresman, 1975); and Louis R. Pondy, "Organizational Conflict: Concepts and Models," *Administrative Science Quarterly* (September 1967), pp. 269–320.

[12] Information from Ken Brown and Gee L. Lee. "Lucent Fires Top China Executives," *The Wall Street Journal* (April 7, 2004), p. A8.

[13] Walton and Dutton (1969).

[14] Rensis Likert and Jane B. Likert, *New Ways of Managing Conflict* (New York: McGraw-Hill, 1976).

[15] See Jay Galbraith, *Designing Complex Organizations* (Reading, MA: Addison-Wesley, 1973); and David Nadler and Michael Tushman, *Strategic Organizational Design* (Glenview, IL: Scott Foresman, 1988).

[16] E. M. Eisenberg and M. G. Witten, "Reconsidering Openness in Organizational Communication," *Academy of Management Review* 12 (1987), pp. 418–426.

[17] R. G. Lord and M. C. Kernan, "Scripts as Determinants of Purposeful Behavior in Organizations," *Academy of Management Review* 12 (1987), pp. 265–277.

[18] See Filley (1975); and L. David Brown, *Managing Conflict at Organizational Interfaces* (Reading, MA: Addison-Wesley, 1983).

[19] Ibid., pp. 27, 29.

[20] For discussions, see Robert R. Blake and Jane Strygley Mouton, "The Fifth Achievement," *Journal of Applied Behavioral Science* 6 (1970), pp. 413–427; Kenneth Thomas, "Conflict and Conflict Management," in M. D. Dunnett (ed.), *Handbook of Industrial and Organizational Behavior* (Chicago: Rand McNally, 1976), pp. 889–935; and Kenneth W. Thomas, "Toward Multi-Dimensional Values in Teaching: The Examples of Conflict Behaviors," *Academy of Management Review* 2 (1977), pp. 484–490.

[21] See Roger Fisher and William Ury, *Getting to Yes: Negotiating Agreement Without Giving In* (New York: Penguin, 1983). See also James A. Wall Jr., *Negotiation: Theory and Practice* (Glenview, IL: Scott Foresman, 1985).

[22] Roy J. Lewicki and Joseph A. Litterer, *Negotiation* (Homewood, IL: Irwin, 1985), pp. 315–319.

[23] Ibid., pp. 328–329.

[24] For a good discussion, see Michael H. Bond, *Behind the Chinese Face* (London: Oxford University Press, 1991); and Richard D. Lewis, *When Cultures Collide* (London: Nicholas Brealey Publishing, 1996), ch. 23.

[25] The following discussion is based on Fisher and Ury (1983); and Lewicki and Litterer (1985).

[26] This example is developed from Max H. Bazerman, *Judgment in Managerial Decision Making*, 2nd ed. (New York: Wiley, 1991), pp. 106–108.

[27] For a detailed discussion, see Fisher and Ury (1983); and Lewicki and Litterer (1985).

[28] Developed from Bazerman (1991), pp. 127–141.

[29] Fisher and Ury (1983), p. 33.

[30] Lewicki and Litterer (1985), pp. 177–181.

FEATURE NOTES

Opener/Alan Mulally: Information and quotes from David Kiley, "Ford's Savior?" *BusinessWeek* (March 16, 2009), pp. 31–34; and Alex Taylor III, "Fixing Up Ford," *Fortune* (May 14, 2009).

Ethics in OB: Information and quotes from Dana Mattioli, "With Jobs Scarce, Age Becomes an Issue," *The Wall Street Journal* (May 19, 2009), p. D4.

Leaders on Leadership: Information and quotes from "Secretary General—My Priorities for a Better World," www.un.org/sg/priority.

Mastering Management: Information from Robert Moskowitz, "How to Negotiate Increase," www.worktree.com (retrieved March 8, 2007); Mark Gordon, "Negotiating What You're Worth," *Harvard Management Communication Letter* 2.1 (Winter 2005); and Dona DeZube, "Salary Negotiation Know-How," www.monster.com (retrieved March 8, 2007).

MARGIN PHOTOS

Twitter—Douglas MacMillan, "A Twitter Code of Conduct," *BusinessWeek* (May 8, 2009), www.businessweek.com.

Workplace Bullying Institute—Mickey Meece, "Backlash: Women Bullying Women at Work," *The New York Times* (May 10, 2009), www.nytimes.com.

Caterpillar in France—David Gauthier-Villars and Leila Abboud, "In France, CEOs Can Become Hostages," *The Wall Street Journal* (April 3, 2009), pp. B1, B4; "Bossnapping of Executives Wins 45% Backing in Poll," *The Wall Street Journal* (April 8, 2009), p. A8.

Chapter 11

ENDNOTES

[1] See Richard L. Birdwhistell, *Kinesics and Context* (Philadelphia: University of Pennsylvania Press, 1970).

[2] Edward T. Hall, *The Hidden Dimension* (Garden City, NY: Doubleday, 1966).

[3] See D. E. Campbell, "Interior Office Design and Visitor Response," *Journal of Applied Psychology* 64 (1979), pp. 648–653; P. C. Morrow and J. C. McElroy, "Interior Office Design and Visitor Response: A Constructive Replication," *Journal of Applied Psychology* 66 (1981), pp. 646–650.

[4] Variation on quote by Ralph Waldo Emerson, http://www.quotationspage.com/quotes/Ralph_Waldo_Emerson/. Feb 15, 2009.

[5] Information from "Chapter 2.2," *Kellogg* (Winter 2004), p. 6; "Room to Read," *Northwestern* (Spring 2007), pp. 32–33.

[6] The statements are from *BusinessWeek* (July 6, 1981), p. 107.

[7] Epictetus quote found at http://thinkexist.com/quotation/we_have_two_ears_and_one_mouth_so_that_we_can/765 0.html. Feb 15, 2009.

[8] M. P. Rowe and M. Baker, "Are You Hearing Enough Employee Concerns?" *Harvard Business Review* 62 (May/June 1984), pp. 127–135.

9 This discussion is based on Carl R. Rogers and Richard E. Farson, "Active Listening" (Chicago: Relations Center of the University of Chicago).

10 Modified from an example in ibid.

11 N. Shivapriya, "Accenture All Set to Venture into Corporate Training," *Economic Times* (February 17, 2007), p. 5.

12 See C. Bamum and N. Woliansky, "Taking Cues from Body Language," *Management Review* 78 (1989), p. 59; S. Bochner (ed.), *Cultures in Contact: Studies in Cross-Cultural Interaction* (London: Pergamon, 1982); A. Furnham and S. Bochner, *Culture Shock: Psychological Reactions to Unfamiliar Environments* (London: Methuen, 1986); "How Not to Do International Business," *BusinessWeek* (April 12, 1999); Yon Kagegama, "Tokyo Auto Show Highlights," *Associated Press* (October 24, 2001).

13 Edward T. Hall, *Beyond Culture* (New York: Doubleday, 1976).

14 Quotes from "Lost in Translation," *The Wall Street Journal* (May 18, 2004), pp. B1, B6.

15 See Gary P. Ferraro. "The Need for Linguistic Proficiency in Global Business," *Business Horizons* 39 (May/June 1966), pp. 39–46.

16 Networking is considered an essential managerial activity by Kotter (1982).

17 Thomas J. Peters and Robert H. Waterman Jr., *In Search of Excellence* (New York: Harper & Row, 1983).

18 Patricia Kitchen, "Businesses Beginning to See Benefits of Employee Wikis," *The Columbus Dispatch* (March 26, 2007), pp. C1, C2.

19 Diane Brady, "*#!@the E-Mail. Can We Talk?" *BusinessWeek* (December 4, 2006), pp. 109–110.

20 See Daniel Goleman, *Social Intelligence: The New Science of Human Relationships* (New York: Bantam Books, 2006).

21 Katherine Reynolds Lewis, "Digital Debris," *Columbus Dispatch* (February 26, 2007), p. B1.

22 "Four presence potholes to avoid," *Network World* 24 (1) (January 8, 2007), p. 28.

23 This research is reviewed by John C. Athanassiades, "The Distortion of Upward Communication in Hierarchical Organizations," *Academy of Management Journal* 16 (June 1973), pp. 207–226.

24 F. Lee, "Being Polite and Keeping Mum. How Bad News Is Communicated in Organizational Hierarchies," *Journal of Applied Social Psychology* 23 (1993), pp. 1124–1149.

25 *The Wiki Workplace,* by Don Tapscott and Anthony D. Williams, BusinessWeek Online, 00077135, accessed March 26, 2007.

26 Andre Martin, *The President's Challenge: Creating the Space for Transformation,* internal company document, copyright Mars Inc., 2008.

27 C. Crossley and G. Vogelsang, "Measuring interactional transparency and testing its impact on trust and psychological capital," working paper, University of Nebraska, 2009.

28 D. A. Whetten and K. S. Cameron, *Developing Management Skills* (New York: Prentice Hall, 2006).

FEATURE NOTES

Opener/IDEO: Description of design thinking found on IDEO Web page at www.ideo.com. Feb 22, 2009; Information taken from Web site at http://www. ideo.com/culture/careers/. Feb 22, 2009; Harvard Business School case 9-600-143 titled "IDEO Product Development," April 26, 2007, written by Stefan Thomke and Ashok Nimgade, p. 5; See www.ideo.com; All quotes in this paragraph can be found in Harvard Business School case 9-600-143 titled "IDEO Product Development," April 26, 2007, written by Stefan Thomke and Ashok Nimgade, pp. 5–6. See also T. Peters, "The Peters Principles," *Forbes ASAP*, September 13, 1993, p. 180.

Leaders on Leadership/Anita Roddick: Information from www.treehugger.com/files/2007/10/anita_roddick

Ethics in OB: Randall Stross, "How to Lose Your Job on Your Own Time," *The New York Times*, December 30, 2007 (late ed., sec. 3, col. 0, Money and Business/Financial Desk; Digital Domain, p. 3).

MARGIN PHOTOS

The Wiki Workplace—Don Tapscott and Anthony D. Williams, BusinessWeek Online, 00077135, accessed March 26, 2007.

Chapter 12

ENDNOTES

1 Several scholars emphasize interdependence, such as W. Richard Scott and Gereal F. Davis, *Organizations and Organizing: Rational, Natural and Open Systems Perspectives* (Upper Saddle River, NJ: Pearson-Prentice Hall, 2007).

2 The most extensive early work was done by Jeffrey Pfeffer, *Organizations and Organization Theory* (Boston: Pitman, 1983); Jeffrey Pfeffer and Gerald R. Salancik, *The External Control of Organizations* (Englewood Cliffs, NJ: Prentice Hall, 1978).

3 Rosabeth Moss Kanter, "Power Failure in Management Circuit," *Harvard Business Review* (July–August 1979), pp. 65–75.

4 John R. P. French and Bertram Raven, "The Bases of Social Power," in Dorwin Cartwright, ed., *Group Dynamics: Research and Theory* (Evanston, IL: Row, Peterson, 1962), pp. 607–623.

5 Pfeffer (1983); Pfeffer and Salancik (1978).

6 Stanley Milgram, "Behavioral Study of Obedience," in Dennis W. Organ, ed., *The Applied Psychology of Work Behavior* (Dallas: Business Publications, Inc., 1978), pp. 384–398. Also see Stanley Milgram, "Behavioral Study of Obedience," *Journal of Abnormal and Social Psychology* 67 (1963), pp. 371–378; Stanley Milgram, "Group Pressure

and Action Against a Person," *Journal of Abnormal and Social Psychology* 69 (1964), pp. 137–143; "Some Conditions of Obedience and Disobedience to Authority," *Human Relations* 1 (1965), pp. 57–76; *Obedience to Authority* (New York: Harper and Row, 1974).

7 Randal Morck, "Behavioral Finance in Corporate Governance: Economics and the Ethics of the Devil's Advocate," *Journal of Management & Governance* 12.2 (2008), pp. 179–191; N. Craig Smith, Sally S. Simpson, and Chun-Yao Huang, "Why Managers Fail to do the Right Thing: A Empirical Study of Ethical and Illegal Conduct," *Business Ethics Quarterly* 17.4 (2007), pp. 633–649.

8 Chester Barnard, *The Functions of the Executive* (Cambridge, MA: Harvard University Press, 1938).

9 For recent studies, see Karin A. Orvis, Nicole M. Dudley, and Jose M Corlina, "Conscientiousness and Reactions to Psychological Contract Breach: A Longitudinal Field Study," *Journal of Applied Psychology* 93.5 (2008), pp. 1183–1195; Prashant Bordia, Simion Lyod D. Restubog, and Robert L. Tang, " When Employees Strike Back: Investigating Mediating Mechanisms between Psychological Contract Breach and Work Place Deviance, "*Journal of Applied Psychology* 93.5 (2008), pp. 1004–1010. For a review, see Neil Conway and Rob B. Briner, *Understanding Psychological Contracts at Work: Critical Evaluation of Theory and Research* (Oxford, UK: Oxford University Press, 2005).

10 Barnard (1938).

11 See Joseph R. DesJardins, *Business Ethics and the Environment: Imagining a Sustainable Future* (Upper Saddle River, NJ: Pearson-Prentice Hall, 2007); Steven N. Brenner and Earl A. Mollander, "Is the Ethics of Business Changing?" *Harvard Business Review* 55 (February 1977), pp. 57–71; Barry Z. Posner and Warren H. Schmidt, "Values and the American Manager: An Update," *California Management Review* XXVI (Spring 1984), pp. 202–216.

12 French and Raven, 1962.

13 We have added process, information, and representative power to the French and Raven list.

14 We have added coalition power to the French and Raven list.

15 See Jean-Jacques Herings, Gerald Van Der Lean and Doif Tallman, "Social Structured Games," *Theory and Decision* 62.1 (2007), pp. 1–30; and William Matthew Bowler, "Organizational Goals Versus the Dominant Coalition: A Critical View of the Value of Organizational Citizenship Behavior," *Journal of Behavior and Applied Management* 7.3 (2006), pp. 258–277.

16 For an interesting but different take on power, networks, and visibility, see Calvin Morrill, Mayer N. Zold, and H. Roa, "Covert Political Conflict in Organizations: Challenges from Below," *American Sociological Review* 29 (2003), pp. 391–416.

17 David Kipinis, Stuart M. Schmidt, Chris Swaffin-Smith, and Ian Wilkinson, "Patterns of Managerial Influence:

Shotgun Managers, Tacticians, and Bystanders," *Organizational Dynamics* 12 (1984), pp. 60–69.

18 Ibid. David Kipinis, Stuart M. Schmidt, and Ian Wilkinson, "Intraorganizational Influence Tactics: Explorations in Getting One's Way," *Journal of Applied Psychology* 65 (1980), pp. 440–452.

19 See Conway and Briner (2005).

20 Warren Schilit and Edwin A. Locke, "A Study of Upward Influence in Organizations," *Administrative Science Quarterly* 27 (1982), pp. 301–316.

21 Ibid. and see Amil Somech and Anat Drach-Zahavy, "Relative Power and Influence Strategy: The Effect of Agent-target Organizational Power on Superiors' Choices of Influence Strategies," *Journal of Organizational Behavior* 23.2 (2002), pp. 167–194.

22 For discussion of empowerment, see Scott E. Seibert, Seth R. Silver, and W. Allan Randolph, "Taking Empowerment to the Next Level: A Multiple-level Model of Empowerment, Performance and Satisfaction," *Academy of Management Journal* 47.3 (2004), pp. 37–53; John E. Mathieu, Lucky L. Gibson, and Thomas M. Ruddy, "Empowerment and Team Effectiveness: An Empirical Test of an Integrated Model," *Journal of Applied Psychology* 91.1 (2006), pp. 1–10; Jean M Bartunek and Gretchen M. Spreitzer, "The Interdisciplinary Career of a Popular Construct Used in Management: Empowerment in the Late 20th Century," *Journal of Management Inquiry* 15.3 (2006), pp. 255–274.

23 M. Anita, M. Liu, W. M. Chiu, and R. Fellows, "Enhancing Commitment Through Work Empowerment," *Engineering, Construction and Architectural Management* 14.6 (2007), pp. 568–574.

24 M. S. Logan and D. Ganster, "The Effects of Empowerment on Attitudes and Performance: The Role of Social Support and Empowerment Beliefs," *Journal of Management Studies* 44 (2007), pp. 1523–1531.

25 J. Pfeffer, "Producing Sustainable Competitive Advantage Through the Effective Management of People," *Academy of Management Executive* 19.4 (2005), pp. 85–115.

26 Useful reviews include a chapter in Robert H. Miles, *Macro Organizational Behavior* (Santa Monica, CA: Goodyear, 1980); Bronston T. Mayes and Robert W. Allen, "Toward a Definition of Organizational Politics," *Academy of Management Review* 2 (1977), pp. 672–677; Dan Farrell and James C. Petersen, "Patterns of Political Behavior in Organizations," *Academy of Management Review* 7 (1982), pp. 403–412; D. L. Madison, R. W. Allen, L. W. Porter, and B. T. Mayes, "Organizational Politics: An Exploration of Managers' Perceptions," *Human Relations* 33 (1980), pp. 92–107.

27 Pheffer (1981).

28 For a discussion, see Christopher Gresov and Carroll Stephen, "Context of Interunit Influence Attempts, "*Administrative Science Quarterly* 38.2 (1993), pp. 252–304.

[29] Warren K. Schilit and Edwin A. Locke, "A Study of Upward Influence in Organizations," *Administrative Science Quarterly* 27 (1982), pp. 304–316.

[30] Mayes and Allen (1977), p. 675; James L. Hall and Joel L. Leldecker, "A Review of Vertical and Lateral Relations: A New Perspective for Managers," pp. 138–146 in Patrick Connor, ed., *Dimensions in Modern Management*, 3rd ed. (Boston: Houghton Mifflin, 1982); John P. Kotter, "Power, Success, and Organizational Effectiveness," *Organizational Dynamics* 6 (1978), pp. 27–43.

[31] See Susan William and Rick Wilson, "Group Support Systems, Power, and Influence in an Organization: A Field Study," *Decision Sciences* 28.4 (1997), pp. 911–938.

[32] B. Ashforth and R. T. Lee, "Defensive Behavior in Organizations: A Preliminary Model," *Human Relations* (July 1990), pp. 621–648; personal communication with Blake Ashforth, March 2006; Pfeffer (1983).

[33] For discussion of attribution theory, see Simon Tagger and Michell Neubert, "The Impact of Poor Performers on Team Outcomes: An Empirical Examination of Attribution Theory," *Personnel Psychology* 57.4 (2004), pp. 935–979; Robert G. Lord and Karen Maher, "Alternative Information-Processing Models and Their Implications," *Academy of Management Review* 15.1 (1990), pp. 9–29.

[34] For more extensive discussions, see Richard Ritte and Steven Levy, *The Ropes to Skip and the Ropes to Know: Studies in Organizational Behavior*, 7th Ed. (Hoboken, NJ: John Wiley and Sons, 2006); Gerry Griffin and Ciaran Parker, *Games Companies Play: An Insider's Guide to Surviving Politics* (Hoboken, NJ: John Wiley and Sons, 2004).

[35] See J. M. Ivancevich, T. N. Deuning, J. A. Gilbert, and R. Konopaske, "Deterring White-Collar Crime," *Academy of Management Executive* 17.2 (2003), pp. 114–128.

[36] See J. P. O'Connor Jr., R. Priem, and K. M. Gilly, "Do CEO Stock Options Prevent or Promote Fraudulent Financial Reporting," *Academy of Management Journal* 49.3 (2006), pp. 483–500; D. Dalton, C. Daily, A. E. Ellstrand, and J. L. Johnson, "Meta-Analysis of Financial Performance and Quality: Fusion or Confusion, "*Academy of Management Journal* 46.1 (1998), pp. 13–26.

[37] Ibid.

[38] Gerard Sanders and Donald Hambrick, "Swinging for the Fences: The Effects of CEO Stock Options on Company Risk Taking and Performance," *Academy of Management Journal* 50.5 (2007), pp. 1055–1078; Xiaomeng Zhang, Kathryn Bartol, Ken Smith, Michael Pfarrer, and Dmitry Khanin, "CEOS on the Edge: Earnings Manipulation and Stock-Based Incentive Misalignment," *Academy of Management Journal* 51.2 (2008), pp. 241–258.

[39] See David Henry, "Worker vs. CEO Pay: Room to Run," *BusinessWeek* (October 30, 2006), pp. 13–14; Takao Kato and Katsuyuii Kubo, "CEO Compensation and Firm Performance in Japan, Evidence from New Panel Data on Individual CEO Pay," *Journal of the Japanese and International Economics* 20.1 (2006), pp. 1–31; Jeffery Moriarty, "Do CEOs Get Paid Too Much," *Business Ethics Quarterly* 15.15 (2005), pp. 257–266; O'Connor, Priem, and Gilly (2006); C. Daily, D. Dalton, and A. A. Cannella, Jr., "Corporate Governance: Decades of Dialog and Data," *Academy of Management Review* 28 (2003), pp. 114–128.

[40] See Pfeffer (1983).

[41] Richard N. Osborn, "Strategic Leadership and Alliances in a Global Economy," Working Paper, Department of Business, Wayne State University (2007).

[42] The notion of a dominant coalition was a key concept in James D. Thompson, *Organizations in Action* (New York: McGraw-Hill, 1967). Also see Rony Simons and Randall S. Peterson, "When to Let Them Duke It Out," *Harvard Business Review* 84.6 (2006), pp. 23–49; M. Firth, P. M. Y. Fund, and O. M. Rui, "Firm Performance, Governance Structure, and Top Management Turnover in a Transition Economy," *Journal of Management Studies* 43.6 (2006), pp. 1289–1299; John A. Pearce, "A Structural Analysis of Dominant Coalitions in Small Banks," *Journal of Management* 21.6 (1995), pp. 1075–1096.

FEATURE NOTES

Opener/Wikipedia: Jimmy Wales/Vivan Schiller: CBC News, "Errors are Human, Says Wikipedia Found," CBC News Comments. January 15, 2009 www.cbc.ca/technology/ story/2009/01/15/jimmy-wales. Katherine Mangu-Ward, "Wikipedia and Beyond," Reasononline, (2007) June. www.reason.com/news/show/1989, 1–21 Chriirs Anderson, "Jimmy Wales," *Time*. April 30, 2006. Farhad Manjoo, "Where Wikipedia Ends" *Time*. September 28, 2009, pp. 50–51.

Research Insight: Amy J. Hillman, Christine Shropshire, and Albert Cannella, "Organizational Predictors of Women on Corporate Boards," *Academy of Management Journal* 5 (2007), pp. 941–968; http://www.catalyst.org/file/241/08_Census_ COTE_JAN.pdf.

Leaders on Leadership/Jose Mourinho: Information from Cowley, J. (2005).NS Man of the Year — Jose Mourinho. *New Statesman* www.newstatesman.com

Ethics in OB: Based on Ruth W. Grant, "Ethics and Incentives: A Political Approach," *The American Political Science Review* 100.1 (2006), pp. 29–40.

Mastering Management: Gerald Ferris, Sherry Davidson, and Pamela Perrewe, *Political Skill at Work* (Mountain View, CA: Davies-Black Publishing, 2005).

MARGIN PHOTOS

Mellody Hobson—Information from "New Xerox Leader Marks a Milestone for Diversity," *The Irish Times* (June 26, 2009), p. 12.

A.D. Marble—A. D. Marble & Company.com

Empowerment—www.jcempowerment.org

Cisco Systems—www.cisco.com

Chapter 13

ENDNOTES

[1] For more information on Andrea Jung see www.avon.com.

[2] Arthur G. Bedeian and James G. Hunt, "Academic Amnesia and Vestigial Assumptions of Our Forefathers," *The Leadership Quarterly* 17 (2006), pp. 190–205.

[3] See J. P. Kotter, *A Force for Change: How Leadership Differs from Management* (New York: Free Press, 1990).

[4] Gary Yukl, *Leadership in Organizations*, 6th ed. (Upper Saddle River, NJ: Prentice Hall, 2006), p. 8.

[5] Ibid.

[6] See Bernard M. Bass, *Bass and Stogdill's Handbook of Leadership*, 3rd ed. (New York: Free Press, 1990).

[7] See Alan Bryman, *Charisma and Leadership in Organizations* (London: Sage, 1992), ch. 5; Ralph M. Stogdill, *Handbook of Leadership* (New York: Free Press, 1974).

[8] Based on information from Robert J. House and Ram Aditya, "The Social Scientific Study of Leadership: Quo-Vadis?" *Journal of Management* 23 (1997), pp. 409–474; Shelley A. Kirkpatrick and Edwin A. Locke, "Leadership: Do Traits Matter?" *The Executive* 5.2 (1991), pp. 48–60; Gary Yukl, *Leadership in Organizations*, 3rd ed. (Upper Saddle River, NJ: Prentice-Hall, 1998), ch. 10.

[9] Rensis Likert, *New Patterns of Management* (New York: McGraw-Hill, 1961).

[10] Bass (1990), ch. 24.

[11] Robert R. Blake and Jane S. Mouton, *The Managerial Grid* (Houston: Gulf Publishing Co., 1991), p. 29.

[12] See M. F. Peterson, "PM Theory in Japan and China: What's in It for the United States?" *Organizational Dynamic,* 16 (Spring 1988), pp. 22–39; J. Misumi and M. F. Peterson, "The Performance-Maintenance Theory of Leadership: Review of a Japanese Research Program," *Administrative Science Quarterly* 30 (1985), pp. 198–223; P. B. Smith, J. Misumi, M. Tayeb, M. F. Peterson, and M. Bond, "On the Generality of Leadership Style Measures Across Cultures," paper presented at the International Congress of Applied Psychology, Jerusalem, July 1986.

[13] Gretchen Spreitzer, "Giving Peace a Chance: Organizational Leadership, Empowerment, and Peace," *Journal of Organizational Behavior* 28 (2007), pp. 1077–1095.

[14] House and Aditya (1997).

[15] Kirkpatrick and Locke (1991); Yukl (1998), ch. 10; J. G. Hunt and G. E. Dodge, "Management in Organizations," *Handbook of Psychology* (Washington, DC: American Psychological Association, 2000).

[16] This section is based on Fred E. Fiedler and Martin M. Chemers, *Leadership* (Glenview, IL: Scott, Foresman, 1974).

[17] This discussion of cognitive resource theory is based on Fred E. Fiedler and Joseph E. Garcia, *New Approaches in Effective Leadership* (New York: Wiley, 1987).

[18] See L. H. Peters, D. D. Harke, and J. T. Pohlmann, "Fiedler's Contingency Theory of Leadership: An Application of the Meta-Analysis Procedures of Schmidt and Hunter," *Psychological Bulletin* 97 (1985), pp. 274–285.

[19] Yukl (2006).

[20] F. E. Fiedler, Martin Chemers, and Linda Mahar, *Improving Leadership Effectiveness: The Leader Match Concept*, 2nd ed. (New York: Wiley, 1985).

[21] For documentation, see Fred E. Fiedler and Linda Mahar, "The Effectiveness of Contingency Model Training: A Review of the Validation of Leader Match," *Personnel Psychology* 32 (Spring 1979); 45–62; Fred E. Garcia, Cecil H. Bell, Martin M. Chemers, and Dennis Patrick, "Increasing Mine Productivity and Safety Through Management Training and Organization Development: A Comparative Study," *Basic and Applied Social Psychology* 5.1 (March 1984), pp. 1–18; Arthur G. Jago and James W. Ragan, "The Trouble with Leader Match Is That It Doesn't Match Fiedler's Contingency Model," *Journal of Applied Psychology* 71 (November 1986), pp. 555–559; Yukl (1998); R. Ayman, M. M. Chemers, and F. E. Fiedler, "The Contingency Model of Leadership Effectiveness: Its Levels of Analysis," *The Leadership Quarterly* 6.2 (Summer 1995), pp. 147–168.

[22] See Yukl (1998); R. Ayman, M. M. Chemers, and F. E. Fiedler, "The Contingency Model of Leadership Effectiveness: Its Levels of Analysis," *The Leadership Quarterly* 6.2 (Summer 1995), pp. 141–188.

[23] This section is based on Robert J. House and Terence R. Mitchell, "Path-Goal Theory of Leadership," *Journal of Contemporary Business* 3 (Autumn 1977), pp. 81–97.

[24] House and Mitchell (1977).

[25] C. A. Schriesheim and L. L. Neider, "Path-Goal Theory: The Long and Winding Road," *The Leadership Quarterly* 7 (1996), pp. 317–321; M. G. Evans, "Commentary on R. J. House's Path-Goal Theory of Leadership Effectiveness," *The Leadership Quarterly* 7 (1996), pp. 305–309.

[26] R. J. House, "Path-Goal Theory of Leadership: Lessons, Legacy, and a Reformulated Theory," *The Leadership Quarterly* 7 (1996), pp. 323–352.

[27] See the discussion of this approach in Paul Hersey and Kenneth H. Blanchard, *Management of Organizational Behavior* (Englewood Cliffs, NJ: Prentice Hall, 1988); Paul Hersey, Kenneth Blanchard, and Dewey E. Johnson, *Management of Organizational Behavior*, 8th ed. (Upper Saddle River, NJ: Prentice Hall, 2001).

[28] R. P. Vecchio and C. Fernandez, "Situational Leadership Theory Revisited," in M. Schnake (ed.), *1995 Southern Management Association Proceedings* (Valdosta, GA: Georgia Southern University, 1995), pp. 137–139; Claude L. Graeff, "Evolution of Situational Leadership Theory: A Critical Review," *The Leadership Quarterly* 8 (1997), pp. 153–170.

[29] Yukl (1998); George Graen, "Leader-Member Exchange Theory Development: Discussant's Comments," paper

presented at the Academy of Management meeting, San Diego, August 1998; Peter G. Northouse, *Leadership Theory and Practice* (Thousand Oaks, CA: Sage, 1997), ch. 7.

[30] Based on Gary Yukl, "Leader-Member Exchange Theory," *Leadership in Organizations* (Upper Saddle River, NJ: Prentice Hall, 2006), pp. 117–120.

[31] G. B. Graen and M. Uhl-Bien, "Relationship-Based Approach to Leadership: Development of Leader-Member Exchange (LMX) Theory of Leadership over 25 Years: Applying a Multi-Level Multi-Domain Perspective," *The Leadership Quarterly* 6 (1995), pp. 219–247.

[32] The discussion in this section is based on Steven Kerr and John Jermier, "Substitutes for Leadership: Their Meaning and Measurement," *Organizational Behavior and Human Performance* 22 (1978), pp. 375–403; Jon P. Howell, David E. Bowen, Peter W. Dorfman, Steven Kerr, and Phillip M. Podsakoff, "Substitutes for Leadership: Effective Alternatives to Ineffective Leadership," *Organizational Dynamics* 19.1 (Summer 1990), pp. 21–38.

[33] Phillip M. Podsakoff, Peter W. Dorfman, Jon P. Howell, and William D. Todor, "Leader Reward and Punishment Behaviors: A Preliminary Test of a Culture-Free Style of Leadership Effectiveness," *Advances in Comparative Management* 2 (1989), pp. 95–138; T. K. Peng, "Substitutes for Leadership in an International Setting," unpublished manuscript, College of Business Administration, Texas Tech University (1990); P. M. Podsakoff and S. B. MacKenzie, "Kerr and Jermier's Substitutes for Leadership Model: Background, Empirical Assessment, and Suggestions for Future Research," *The Leadership Quarterly* 8.2 (1997), pp. 117–132.

[34] See J. Pfeffer, "Management as Symbolic Action: The Creation and Maintenance of Organizational Paradigms," in Cummings and Staw, *Research in Organizational Behavior*, vol. 3 (Greenwich, CT: JAI Press, 1981), pp. 1–52.

[35] James R. Meindl, "On Leadership: An Alternative to the Conventional Wisdom," in Staw and Cummings, *Researching Organizational Behavior*, vol. 3 (Greenwich, CT: JAI Press, 1981), pp. 159–203; compare with Bryman (1992); also see James G. Hunt and Jay A. Conger (eds.), *The Leadership Quarterly* 10.2 (1999), special issue.

[36] D. Eden and U. Leviatan. "Implicit Leadership Theory as a Determinant of the Factor Structure Underlying Supervisory Behavior Scales," *Journal of Applied Psychology* 60 (1975), pp. 736–741.

[37] See T. R. Mitchell, S. G. Green, and R. E. Wood, "An Attribution Model of Leadership and the Poor Performing Subordinate: Development and Validation," in L. L. Cummings and B. M. Staw (eds.), *Research in Organizational Behavior*, vol. 3 (Greenwich, CT: JAI Press, 1981), pp. 197–234.

[38] Robert Lord and Karen Maher, *Leadership and Information Processing* (Boston: Unwin Hyman); Jun Yan and James G. Hunt, "A Cross-Cultural Perspective on Perceived Leadership Effectiveness," *International Journal of Cross Cultural Management* (in press, 2006).

[39] Yan and Hunt (in press, 2006).

[40] V. R. Carter, "Lincoln's Legacy," *Associations Now* (January 2008), pp. 60–66.

[41] James G. Hunt, Kimberly B. Boal, and Ritch L. Sorenson, "Top Management Leadership: Inside the Black Box," *The Leadership Quarterly* 1 (1990), pp. 41–65.

[42] C. R. Gerstner and D. B. Day, "Cross-Cultural Comparison of Leadership Prototypes," *The Leadership Quarterly* 5 (1994), pp. 122–134.

[43] Jun Yan and James G. Hunt (in press, 2006).

[44] Olga Epitropaki and Robin Martin, "Implicit Leadership Theories in Applied Settings: Factor Structure, Generalizability, and Stability Over Time," *Journal of Applied Psychology* 89 (2004), pp. 293–310.

[45] See R. J. House, "A 1976 Theory of Charismatic Leadership," in J. G. Hunt and L. L. Larson (eds.), *Leadership: The Cutting Edge* (Carbondale: Southern Illinois University Press, 1977), pp. 189–207.

[46] R. J. House, W. D. Spangler, and J. Woycke, "Personality and Charisma in the U.S. Presidency," *Administrative Science Quarterly* 36 (1991), pp. 364–396.

[47] Pillai and E. A. Williams, "Does Leadership Matter in the Political Arena? Voter Perceptions of Candidates' Transformational and Charismatic Leadership and the 1996 U.S. Presidential Vote," *The Leadership Quarterly* 9 (1998), pp. 397–416.

[48] Adapted from Jeffery S. Mio, Ronald E. Riggio, Shana Levin, and Renford Reese, "Presidential Leadership Charisma: The Effects of Metaphor," *The Leadership Quarterly* 16 (2005), pp. 287–294.

[49] See Jane M. Howell and Bruce J. Avolio, "The Ethics of Charismatic Leadership: Submission or Liberation," *Academy of Management Executive* 6 (May 1992), pp. 43–54.

[50] T. L. Stanley, "Ethical Decision Making in Tough Times," *Supervision* 70.3 (2009), pp. 3–5.

[51] Jay Conger and Rabindra N. Kanungo, *Charismatic Leadership in Organizations* (San Francisco: Jossey-Bass, 1998).

[52] Conger and Kanungo (1998).

[53] J. Conger and R. Kanungo, "Training Charismatic Leadership, A Risky and Critical Task," in J. Conger and R. Kanungo (eds.), *Charismatic Leadership: The Elusive Factor in Organizational Effectiveness* (San Francisco: Jossey-Bass, 1988), ch. 11.

[54] Boas Shamir, "Social Distance and Charisma: Theoretical Notes and an Exploratory Study," *The Leadership Quarterly* 6 (Spring 1995), pp. 19–48.

[55] See B. M. Bass, *Leadership and Performance Beyond Expectations* (New York: Free Press, 1985); Bryman (1992), pp. 98–99.

[56] B. M. Bass, *A New Paradigm of Leadership* (Alexandria, VA: U.S. Army Research Institute for the Behavioral and Social Sciences, 1996).

[57] Bryman (1992), ch. 6; B. M. Bass and B. J. Avolio, "Transformational Leadership: A Response to Critics," in M. M.

Chemers and R. Ayman (eds.), *Leadership Theory and Practice: Perspectives and Directions* (San Diego, CA: Academic Press, 1993), pp. 49–80; Kevin B. Lowe, K. Galen Kroeck, and Nagaraj Sivasubramanium, "Effectiveness Correlates of Transformational and Transactional Leadership: A Meta-Analytic Review of the MLQ Literature," *Leadership Quarterly* 7 (1996), pp. 385–426.

[58] Bass (1996); Bass and Avolio (1993).

[59] See J. R. Kouzas and B. F. Posner, *The Leadership Challenge: How to Get Extraordinary Things Done in Organizations* (San Francisco: Jossey-Bass, 1991).

[60] Marshall Sashkin and Molly G. Sashkin, *Leadership That Matters* (San Francisco: Berrett-Koehler, 2003), ch. 10.

FEATURE NOTES

Opener/Andrea Jung: www.avon.com.

Fiedler model based on F. E. Fiedler and M. M. Chemers, *Leadership and Effective Management* (Glenview, IL: Scott, Foresman, 1974).

Path-goal information adapted from Richard N. Osborn, James G. Hunt, and Lawrence R. Jauch, *Organizational Theory: An Integrated Approach* (New York: Wiley, 1980), p. 464.

From Paul Hersey and Kenneth H. Blanchard, *Management of Organizational Behavior* (Englewood Cliffs, NJ: Prentice Hall, 1988), p. 171. Used by permission.

Mastering Management: Based on Steven Kerr and John Jermier, "Substitutes for Leadership: Their Meaning and Measurement," *Organizational Behavior and Human Performance* 22 (1978), pp. 387; Fred Luthans, *Organizational Behavior*, 6th ed. (New York: McGraw-Hill, 1992), ch. 10.

Close and distant based on Boas Shamir, "Social Distance and Charisma: Theoretical Notes and an Exploratory Study," *The Leadership Quarterly* 6 (1995), pp. 19–48.

Leaders on Leadership/Angela Merkel: Information from *Forbes Magazine* "100 Most Powerful Women in the World" list 2006–2009; Boege, J., & Kletzing, U. (n.d.). A manager at home and a leader abroad? Insights into Angela Merkel's career, personality and leadership style. Hertie School of Governance Graduate student paper.

Ethics in OB: Adapted from T. L. Stanley, "Ethical Decision Making in Tough Times," *Supervision* 70.3 (2009), pp. 3–5.

OB Savvy: J. Conger and R. Kanungo, "Training Charismatic Leadership, A Risky and Critical Task," in J. Conger and R. Kanungo (eds.), *Charismatic Leadership: The Elusive Factor in Organizational Effectiveness* (San Francisco: Jossey-Bass, 1988), ch. 11.

OB Savvy: V.R. Carter, "Lincolin's Legacy," *Associations Now* (January 2008), pp. 60–66.

Based on Gary Yukl, "Leader-Member Exchange Theory," *Leadership in Organizations* Upper Saddle River, N. 5. Prentice-Hall 2006) pp. 117–120.

www.avon.com.

goldsea.com/ww/jungandrea

Bill George, "Andrea Jung Corporate Executive: A new Makeover for an old retail face." *U.S. News and World Report* November 12, 2007 p. 37.

MARGIN PHOTOS

Tiger Woods—Information from "Accenture: High Performance Delivered," *BusinessWeek* (June 22, 2009), p. 58.

Janet Napolitano—R. G. Edmonson, "DHSS New Boss," *Journal of Commerce* (March 9, 2009).

Lynn Willenbring—Anonymous, "CIO Profiles," *InformationWeek* (March 23, 2009), p. 12.

Chapter 14

ENDNOTES

[1] Based on Bruce J. Avolio and William L. Gardner, "Authentic Leadership Development: Getting to the Root of Positive Forms of Leadership," *The Leadership Quarterly* 16 (2005), pp. 315–338; William L. Gardner, Bruce J. Avolio, Fred Luthans, Douglas R. May, and Fred O. Walumba, "'Can You See the Real Me?' A Self-Based Model of Authentic Leader and Follower Development," *The Leadership Quarterly* 16 (2005), pp. 343–372; Bill George, Peter Sims, Andrew N. McLean, and Diana Mayer, "Discovering Your Authentic Leadership," *Harvard Business Review* (February, 2007), pp. 1–9.

[2] For a more extended discussion based on positive psychology, see Avolio and Gardner, 2005.

[3] Judith A. Ross, "Making Every Leadership Moment Matter," *Harvard Management Update* (September, 2006), pp. 3–5.

[4] James K. Dittmar, "An Interview with Larry Spears," *Journal of Leadership & Organizational Studies* 13 (2006), pp. 108–118.

[5] Based on Lewis W. Fry, "Toward a Paradigm of Spiritual Leadership," *The Leadership Quarterly* 16 (2005), pp. 619–622; Lewis W. Fry, Steve Vitucci, and Marie Cedillo, "Spiritual Leadership and Army Transformation: Theory, Measurement, and Establishing a Baseline," *The Leadership Quarterly* 16.5 (2005), pp. 835–862.

[6] For a discussion, see Michael E. Brown and Linda K. Trevino, "Ethical Leadership: A Review and Future Directions," *The Leadership Quarterly* 17.6 (2006), pp. 579–609.

[7] Michael E. Brown and Linda K. Trevino, "Ethical Leadership: A Review and Future Directions," *The Leadership Quarterly* 17 (2006), pp. 595–616.

[8] L. Jon Wertheim, "Do College Athletics Corrupt?" *Sports Illustrated* (March 5, 2007), p. 67.

[9] This discussion relies heavily on that of Katrina A. Zalatan and Gary Yukl, "Team Leadership," in George R. Goethals, Georgia J. Sorenson, and James McGregor Burns, *Encyclopedia of Leadership*, vol. A (Great Barrington, MA, Berkshire/Sage, 2004), pp. 1529–1552.

[10] See Mary Uhl-Bien, Russ Marion, and Bill McKelvey, "Complexity Leadership Theory: Shifting Leadership from the Industrial Age to the Knowledge Era," *The Leadership Quarterly* 18(4) (2007), pp. 298–318.

[11] For specific aspects of self leadership, see Jeffery D. Houghton, Christopher P. Neck, and Charles C. Manz, "Self Leadership and Super Leadership," in Craig L. Pearce and Jay A. Conger (eds.), *Shared Leadership* (Thousand Oaks, CA: Sage Publications, 2003), pp. 123–140.

[12] This discussion is built primarily upon Robert J. House, Paul J. Hanges, Mansour Javidan, Peter W. Dorfman, and Vipin Gupta (eds.), *Culture, Leadership, and Organizations* (Thousand Oaks, CA: Sage Publications, 2004); Mansour Javidan, Peter W. Dorfman, Mary Sully de Luque, and Robert J. House, "In the Eye of the Beholder: Cross Cultural Lessons in Leadership from Project GLOBE," *Academy of Management Perspectives* 20.1 (2006), pp. 67–90.

[13] For a discussion of top-management teams, see Amy C. Edmonson, Michael A. Roberto, and Michael D. Watkins, "A Dynamic Model of Top Management Team Effectiveness: Matching Unstructured Task Streams," *The Leadership Quarterly* 14 (2003), pp. 297–325.

[14] See Michael D. Mumford, Alison Lantes, Jay J. Caughron, and Tamara L Friedrich, "Charismatic, Ideological and Pragmatic Leadership: Mult-level Influences on Emergence and Performance," *The Leadership Quarterly* 19.2 (2008), pp. 144–160.

[15] D. C. Hambrick, "Top Management Teams," in Nigel Nicholson (ed.), *Blackwell Encyclopedic Dictionary of Organizational Behavior* (Oxford, U.K.: Blackwell Publishers, 1995), pp. 567–568.

[16] This discussion of top management teams draws heavily upon A. C. Edmonson, Michael A. Roberto, and Michael D. Watkins, "A Dynamic Model of Top Management Team Effectiveness: Matching Unstructured Task Streams," *The Leadership Quarterly* 14 (2003), pp. 297–325.

[17] For a discussion of top management teams, see D. C. Hambrick, T. S. Cho, and M. J. Chen, "The Influence of Top Management Team Hetrogenity on Firm's Competitive Moves," *Administrative Science Quarterly* 41 (1996), pp. 659–684; T. Simons, L. H. Pelled, and K. A. Smith, "Making Use of Difference, Diversity, Debate and Decision Comprehensiveness in Top Management Teams," *Academy of Management Journal* 42 (1999), pp. 662–673.

[18] R. N. Osborn, J. G. Hunt, and L. R. Jauch, "Toward a Contextual Theory of Leadership. *The Leadership Quarterly* 13 (2002), pp. 797–837.

[19] Ibid.

[20] This discussion of the multiple-level perspective is based primarily on James G. Hunt, *Leadership: A New Synthesis* (Thousand Oaks, CA: Sage Publications, 1991), Ken Shepard, Jerry L. Gray, James G. (Jerry) Hunt, and Sarah McArthur (eds.), *Organization Design, Levels of Work and Human Capability* (Ontario, Canada: Global Organization Design Society, 2007), p. 534.

[21] Gerry Larsson, Thorvald Haerem, Misa Sjöberg, Aida Alvinius, and Björn Bakken, "Indirect Leadership Under Severe Stress: a Qualitative Inquiry into the 2004 Kosovo Riots," *International Journal of Organizational Analysis* 15.1 (2007), pp. 23–35.

[22] Yair Berson, Shaul Oreg, and Taly Dvir, "CEO Values, Organizational Culture and Firm Outcomes." *Journal of Organizational Behavior* 29 (2008), pp. 615–633.

[23] See R. Marion and M. Uhl-Bien, "Leadership in Complex Organizations," *The Leadership Quarterly* 12.4 (2001), pp. 389–418.

[24] This discussion of Boal and Hooijberg's strategic leadership perspective is based primarily on Kimberly B. Boal and Robert Hooijberg, "Strategic Leadership Research: Moving On," *The Leadership Quarterly* 1 (2000), pp. 515–550.

[25] Robert E. Quinn, Sue R. Faerman, Michael P. Thompson, and Michael R. McGrath, *Becoming a Master Manager,* 4th ed. (Hoboken, NJ: Wiley, 2006).

[26] Boal and Hooijberg (2000).

[27] Ibid.

[28] L. W. Porter and G. B. McLaughlin, "Leadership and the Organizational Context: Like the Weather," *The Leadership Quarterly* 17 (2006), pp. 559–573.

[29] Osborn, Hunt, and Jauch, 2002.

[30] Gary Johns, "The Essential Impact of Context on Organizations Behavior," *Academy of Management Review* 31.2 (2006), pp. 386–408.

[31] Based on Osborn, Hunt, and Jauch (2002).

[32] R. Marion, *The Edge of Organization: Chaos and Complexity Theories of Formal Social Systems* (Thousand Oaks, CA: Sage, 1999).

[33] Osborn, Hunt, and Jauch (2002).

[34] R. N. Osborn and R. Marion, "Contextual leadership, Transformational Leadership and the Performance of Innovation Seeking Alliances." *The Leadership Quarterly* (in press).

[35] Osborn, Hunt, and Jauch (2002).

[36] Adopted from Karlene Grabner, "Giving circles bring people together for the sake of charity." *Lubbock Avalarche Journal* (November 12, 2006), p. 6.

[37] Michael Beer and Nitin Mitra, "Cracking the Code of Change," *Harvard Business Review* (May–June 2000), p. 133.

[38] See David Nadler and Michael Tushman, *Strategic Organizational Design* (Glenview, IL: Scott, Foresman, 1988); Noel M. Tichy, "Revolutionize Your Company," *Fortune* (December 13, 1993), pp. 114–118.

[39] Jerry I. Porras and Robert C. Silvers, "Organization Development and Transformation," *Annual Review of Psychology* 42 (1991), pp. 51–78.

[40] Ibid.

[41] The classic description of organizations on these terms is by Harold J. Leavitt, "Applied Organizational Change in Industry: Structural, Technological and Humanistic

Approaches," in James G. March (ed.), *Handbook of Organizations* (Chicago: Rand McNally, 1965). This application is developed from Robert A. Cooke, "Managing Change in Organizations," in Gerald Zaltman (ed.), *Management Principles for Nonprofit Organizations* (New York: American Management Association, 1979). See also David A. Nadler, "The Effective Management of Organizational Change," pp. 358–369, in Jay W. Lorsch (ed.), *Handbook of Organizational Behavior* (Englewood Cliffs, NJ: Prentice-Hall, 1987).

[42] Beer and Mitra, 2000, p. 133.

[43] Kurt Lewin, "Group Decision and Social Change," pp. 459–473, in G. E. Swanson, T. M. Newcomb, and E. L. Hartley (eds.), *Readings in Social Psychology* (New York: Holt, Rinehart & Winston, 1952).

[44] Noel M. Tichy and Mary Anne Devanna, *The Transformational Leader* (New York: John Wiley & Sons, 1986), p. 44.

[45] The change strategies are described in Robert Chin and Kenneth D. Benne, "General Strategies for Effecting Changes in Human Systems," pp. 22–45, in Warren G. Bennis, Kenneth D. Benne, Robert Chin, and Kenneth E. Corey *The Planning of Change,* 3rd ed. (New York: Holt, Rinehart & Winston, 1969).

[46] Example developed from an exercise reported in J. William Pfeffer and John E. Jones, *A Handbook of Structural Experiences for Human Relations Training,* vol. II (La Jolla, CA: University Associates, 1973).

[47] Pfeffer and Jones, 1973.

[48] Pfeffer and Jones, 1973.

[49] Donald Klein, "Some Notes on the Dynamics of Resistance to Change: The Defender Role," in Bennis et al., 1969, pp. 117–124.

[50] See Everett M. Roberts, *Communication of Innovations,* 3rd ed. (New York: Free Press, 1993).

[51] Everett M. Roberts, 1993.

[52] John P. Kotter and Leonard A. Schlesinger, "Choosing Strategies for Change," *Harvard Business Review* 57 (March–April 1979), pp. 109–112.

FEATURE NOTES

Opener/Oxfam GB: www.oxfam.org.uk/oxfam_in_action/history

Leaders on Leadership: Information from Miguel Helft, "Yahoo's New Chief Makes Decisive Appearance," *The New York Times* (January 16, 2009): www.nytimes.com; Jessica E. Vascellaro, "Yahoo CEO Set to Install Top-Down Management," *The Wall Street Journal* (February 23, 2009), p. Bl; and, "A Question of Management," *The Wall Street Journal* (June 2, 2009), p. R4.

Adapted from Karlene Grabner, "Giving Circles Bring People Together for Sake of Charity," *Lubbock Avalanche Journal* (November 12, 2006), p. D6.

Based on John P. Kotter, "Why Transformation Efforts Fail," *Harvard Business Review* (March–April 1995), pp. 59–67.

Ethics in OB: L. Jon Wertheim, "Do College Athletics Corrupt?" *Sports Illustrated* (March 5, 2007), p.67.

MARGIN PHOTOS

John C. Lechleiter and Carol Bartz—Quote from "An Old Pro's Wisdom: it Begins with a Belief in People," New York Times (September 10, 1989), p. F2. Max DePree's books include *Leadership Jazz* (New York: Dell, 1993) and *Leadership is an Art* (New York: Broadway Business, 2004), and *Leading Without Power: Finding Hope in Serving Community* (San Francisco: Jossey-Bass, 2003).

Fred Smith—Fred Smith of FedEx on Change- Ellen Florian, "I have a Cast-Iron Stomach," *Fortune* (August 1, 2006).

Gene Smith and Oprah Winfrey—Information and quotes from the Associated Press, "Oprah Opens School for Girls in S. Africa Lavish Leadership Academy Aims to Give Impoverished Chance to Succeed," www.MSNBC.com (January 2, 2007); "Oprah Winfrey Leadership Academy for Girls–South Africa Celebrates Its Official Opening," www.oprah.com/about; and, Jed Dreben, "Oprah Winfrey: 'I Don't Regret' Opening School," www.people.com (December 12, 2007).

Chapter 15

ENDNOTES

[1] This and many analyses of corporate culture are based on Edgar Schein, "Organizational Culture," *American Psychologist* 45 (1990), pp. 109–119; and E. Schein, *Organizational Culture and Leadership* (San Francisco: Jossey-Bass, 1985).

[2] For a recent treatment, see Ali Danisman, C. R. Hinnings, and Trevor Slack, "Integration and Differentiation in Institutional Values: An Empirical Investigation in the Field of Canadian National Sport Organizations," *Canadian Journal of Administrative Sciences* 23.4 (2006), pp. 301–315.

[3] Schein (1990).

[4] See www.dellapp.us.dell.com.

[5] This example was reported in an interview with Edgar Schein, "Corporate Culture Is the Real Key to Creativity," *Business Month* (May 1989), pp. 73–74.

[6] www.Sherwinwilliams.com.

[7] Schein (1990).

[8] Ibid.

[9] Jeffery Pfeffer, *The Human Equation: Building Profits by Putting People First* (Boston: Harvard Business School Press, 1998).

[10] For an extended discussion, see J. M. Beyer and H. M. Trice, "How an Organization's Rites Reveal Its Culture," *Organizational Dynamics* (Spring 1987), pp. 27–41.

[11] A. Cooke and D. M. Rousseau, "Behavioral Norms and Expectations: A Quantitative Approach to the Assessment of Organizational Culture," *Group and Organizational Studies* 13 (1988), pp. 245–273.

[12] Mary Trefry, "A Double-edged Sword: Organizational Culture in Multicultural Organizations," *International Journal of Management* 23 (2006), pp. 563–576; J. Martin

and C. Siehl, "Organization Culture and Counterculture," *Organizational Dynamics* 12 (1983), pp. 52–64.

[13] www.apple-history.com.

[14] For a recent discussion of the clash of corporate cultures, see George Lodorfos and Agyenim Boateng, "The Role of Culture in the Merger and Acquisition Process: Evidence from the European Chemical Industry," *Management Decision* 44 (2006) pp. 1405–1410.

[15] See R. N. Osborn, "The Aftermath of Daimler and Detroit," Working Paper, Department of Management, Wayne State University 2008.

[16] Ibid.

[17] www.flowserve.com.

[18] Osborn (2008).

[19] Taylor Cox Jr., "The Multicultural Organization," *Academy of Management Executive* 2.2 (May 1991), pp. 34–47.

[20] See Schein (1985), pp. 52–57, and Schein, (1990).

[21] For a discussion from a different perspective, see Anat Rafaeli and Michael G. Pratt (eds.), *Artifacts and Organizations: Beyond Mere Symbols* (Mahwah, NJ: Lawrence Erlbaum Associates, 2006).

[22] For early work, see T. Deal and A. Kennedy, *Corporate Culture* (Reading, MA: Addison-Wesley, 1982); and T. Peters and R. Waterman, *In Search of Excellence* (New York: Harper & Row, 1982), while more recent studies are summarized in Joanne Martin and Peter Frost, "The Organizational Culture War Games: The Struggle for Intellectual Dominance," in Stewart R. Clegg, Cynthia Hardy, and Walter R. Nord (eds.), *Handbook of Organization Studies* (London: Sage Publications, 1996), pp. 599–621.

[23] Schein (1990).

[24] www.montereypasta.com.

[25] H. Gertz, *The Interpretation of Culture* (New York: Basic Books, 1973).

[26] See Rafaeli and Pratt (2006) and Beyer and Trice (1987).

[27] H. M. Trice and J. M. Beyer, "Studying Organizational Cultures Through Rites and Ceremonials," *Academy of Management Review* 3 (1984), pp. 633–669.

[28] This description was provided by Marcus B. Osborn.

[29] www.lamre.com.

[30] J. Martin, M. S. Feldman, M. J. Hatch, and S. B. Sitkin, "The Uniqueness Paradox in Organizational Stories," *Administrative Science Quarterly* 28 (1983), pp. 438–453; *BusinessWeek* (November 23, 1992), p. 117.

[31] For a recent study, see John Barnes, Donald W. Jackson, Michael D. Hutt, and Ajith Kumar, "The Role of Culture Strength in Shaping Sales Force Outcomes," *Journal of Personal Setting and Sales Management* 26.3 (2006), pp. 255–269. This tradition of strong cultures goes back to work by Deal and Kennedy (1982) and Peters and Waterman (1982).

[32] Trice and Beyer (1984).

[33] R. N. Osborn and D. Jackson, "Leaders, River Boat Gamblers or Purposeful Unintended Consequences," *Academy of Management Journal* 31 (1988), pp. 924–947.

[34] For an interesting twist, see John Connolly, "High Performance Cultures," *Business Strategy Review* 17 (2006), pp. 19–32; a more conventional treatment may be found in Martin, Feldman, Hatch, and Sitkin (1983).

[35] Osborn and Jackson (1988).

[36] R. N. Osborn, "Purposeful Unintended Consequences and Systemic Financial Risk," Working Paper, Department of Management, Wayne State University (2009).

[37] www.generalmills.com.

[38] For the classic popular work see, Peter F. Drucker, *Innovation and Entrepreneurship* (New York: Harper, 1985); Edward B. Roberts, "Managing Invention and Innovation," *Research Technology Management* (January/February 1989), pp. 1–19 provides a practitioner perspective, whereas an interesting extended case study is provided by John Clark, *Managing Innovation and Change* (Thousand Oaks, CA: Sage, 1995).

[39] Miller (2008).

[40] P. Berrone, L. Gelabert, A. Fosfuri, and L. Gomez-Mejia, "Can Institutional Forces Create Competitive Advantage? An Empirical Examination of Environmental Innovation. *2008 Academy of Management Proceedings* (2008).

[41] D. Dougherty, "Organizing for Innovation," in S. Clegg, C. Hardy and W. Nord (eds.), *Handbook of Organization Studies* (Thousand Oaks, CA: Sage, 1996), pp. 424–439.

[42] For a discussion of product cannibalization, see S. Netessie and T. Taylor, "Product Line Design and Production Technology," *Marketing Science* 26.1 (2007), pp. 101–118.

[43] Gerard J. Tellis, Jaideep, C. Prabhu, and Rajesh K. Chandy, "Radical Innovation Across Nations: The Preeminence of Corporate Culture," *Journal of Marketing* 73.1 (2009), pp. 3–23.

[44] N. Clymer and S. Asaba, " A new approach for understanding dominant design: The case of the ink-jet printer," *Journal of Engineering and Technology Management* 25.3 (2008), pp. 137–152.

[45] V. Acha, "Open by Design: The Role of Design in Open Innovation," *2008 Academy of Management Proceedings* (2008), pp. 1–6.

[46] The first to emphasize the role of lead uses was E. von Hipple, *The Sources of Innovation* (New York: Oxford University Press, 1988).

[47] See J. Birkinshaw, G. Hamel, and M. Mol, "Management Innovation," *Academy of Management Review* 33 (2008), pp. 825–845.

[48] The terms exploration and exploitation were popularized by James G. March. See James G. March, "Exploration and Exploitation in Organizational Learning," *Organization Science* 2.1 (1991), pp. 71–87.

[49] For a recent review, see Sung-Choon Kang, Shad S. Morris, and Scot A. Shell, " Relational Archetypes, Organizational Learning, and Value Creation: Extending the Human Resource Architecture," *Academy of Management Review* 32 (2007), pp. 236–256.

[50] Tellis, Prabhu, and Chandy, (2009). For an extended discussion of radical innovation, see R. N. Osborn and C. C. Baughn, *An Assessment of the State of the Field of Organizational Design* (Alexandria, VA: U.S. Army Research Institute, 1994).

[51] See M. Tushman and P. Anderson, "Technological discontinuities and organizational environments," *Administrative Science Quarterly* 31 (1986), pp. 439–465.

[52] M. Tushman and C. O, Reilly, "Ambidextrous organizations: Managing evolutionary and revolutionary change," *California Management Review* 38.4 (1996), pp. 8–30.

[53] M. Tokman, R. G. Richey, L. Marino, and K. M. Weaver, "Exploration, Exploitation and Satisfaction in Supply Chain Portfolio Strategy," *Journal of Business Logistics* 28 (2007), pp. 25–48.

[54] See C. Mirow, K. Hoelzle, and H. Gemueden, "The Ambidextrous Organization in Practice: Barriers to Innovation Within Research and Development," *2008 Academy of Management Proceedings* (2008), pp. 1–6.

[55] This section was originally based on Osborn and Baughn (1994).

[56] Y. Berson, S. Oreg, and T. Dvir, "CEO Values, Organizational Culture and Firm Outcomes," *Journal of Organizational Behavior* 29 (2008), pp. 615–633.

[57] www.cisco.com.

[58] J. Kerr and J. Slocum, "Managing Corporate Culture Through Reward Systems," *Academy of Management Executive* 19.4 (2005), pp. 130–138.

[59] J. Karpoff, D. S. Lee, and Gerald Martin, "A company's reputation is what gets fried when its books are cooked," uwnews.org (2007).

[60] Martin and Frost (1996).

[61] For example, see Tellis, Prabhu, and Chandy (2009).

[62] For an excellent review, see C. Miller, *Formalization and Innovation: An Ethnographic Study of Process Formalization* (Ann Arbor, MI: Proquest Company 2008).

[63] Ibid, p. 391.

[64] See K. Boal and P. Schultz, "Storytelling, time and evolution: The role of strategic leadership in complex adaptive systems," *The Leadership Quarterly* 18 (2007), pp. 411–428; and A. Grove, *Only the paranoid survive* (New York: Double Day, 1996).

FEATURE NOTES

Opener: Information and quotes from Chick-fill-A.com; Daniel Yee, "Chick-Fill-A Recipe Winning Customers," The Columbus Dispatch (September 9, 2006), p. D1; and, Tom Murphy, "Chick-fil-A plans aggressive product rollout initiatives," Rocky Mount Telegram (May 28, 2008), retrieved from: http://www.rockymounttelegram.com.

Leaders on Leadership/Ulrich Schwanengel: Information from http://www.greatplacetowork-europe.com/gptw/GPTW-Magazine-EU.pdf; http://www.consol.com/fileadmin/pdf/presse/2009-02-13_Consol_BestEmployer.pdf; http://www.businessawardseurope.com/?p=762

Ethics in OB: http://ethics.flowserve.com.

MARGIN PHOTOS

Aetna—www.aetna.com.

Microsoft—www.microsoft.com.

LAM Research—www.lamrc.com.

Hope Labs—Information from "HopeLab Video Games for Health," *Fast Company* (December 2008/January 2009), p. 116; www.hopelab.org.

Cousins Subs—www.cousinssubs.com. Carloyn Wlakup, "Having words with Christine Specht," *Nations Restaurant News* 42.49 (2008), p. 78.

Chapter 16

ENDNOTES

[1] www.nytimes.com/2009/08/01/world/europe/01oleary.html

[2] The bulk of this chapter was originally based on Richard N. Osborn, James G. Hunt, and Lawrence R. Jauch, *Organization Theory: Integrated Text and Cases* (Melbourne, FL: Krieger, 1985). For a more recent but consistent view, see Lex Donaldson, "The Normal Science of Structural Contingency Theory," in Stewart R. Clegg, Cynthia Hardy, and Walter R. Nord (eds.), *Handbook of Organizational Studies* (London: Sage Publications, 1996), pp. 57–76. For a more advanced treatment, see: W. Richard Scott and Gerald F. Davis, *Organizations and Organizing: Rational and Open Systems* (Englewood Cliffs, NJ: Prentice-Hall. 2007)

[3] Osborn, Hunt, and Jauch (1985).

[4] H. Talcott Parsons, *Structure and Processes in Modern Societies* (New York: Free Press, 1960).

[5] See B. Bartkus, M. Glassman, and B. McAfee, "Mission Statement Quality and Financial Performance," *European Management Journal* 24.1 (2006), pp. 66–79; J. Peyrefitte and F. R. David, "A Content Analysis of the Mission Statements of United States Firms in Four Industries," *International Journal of Managemen* 23.2 (2006), pp. 296–305; Terri Lammers, "The Effective and Indispensable Mission Statement," *Inc.* 7.1 (August 1992), p. 23; and I. C. MacMillan and A. Meshulack, "Replacement versus Expansion: Dilemma for Mature U.S. Businesses," *Academy of Management Journal* 26 (1983), pp. 708–726.

[6] www.cummins.com.

[7] Anonymous, "Making Vision Statements Meaningful," *The British Journal of Administrative Management* (April/May 2006), p. 17; and L. Larwood, C. M. Falbe, M. Kriger, and P. M. Miesing, "Structure and Meaning of Organizational Vision," *Academy of Management Journal* 38 (1995), pp. 740–770.

[8] See Scott and Davis (2007); Stewart R. Clegg and Cynthia Hardy, "Organizations, Organization and Organizing," in Clegg, Hardy, and Nord (eds.), *Handbook of Organizational*

Studies (1996), pp. 1–28; and William H. Starbuck and Paul C. Nystrom, "Designing and Understanding Organizations," in P. C. Nystrom and W. H. Starbuck (eds.), *Handbook of Organizational Design: Adapting Organizations to Their Environments* (New York: Oxford University Press, 1981).

[9] See Jeffery Pfeffer, "Barriers to the Advance of Organization Science," *Academy of Management Review* 18.4 (1994), pp. 599–620; Richard M. Cyert and James G. March, *A Behavioral Theory of the Firm* (Englewood Cliffs, NJ: Prentice-Hall, 1963). A historical view of organizational goals is also found in Charles Perrow, *Organizational Analysis: A Sociological View* (Belmont, CA: Wadsworth, 1970) and in Richard H. Hall, "Organizational Behavior: A Sociological Perspective," in Jay W. Lorsch (ed.), *Handbook of Organizational Behavior* (Englewood Cliffs, NJ: Prentice-Hall, 1987), pp. 84–95.

[10] See Osborn, Hunt, and Jauch (1985) for the historical rates, and for differences in survival rates by time of formation in the development of a technology, see R. Agarwal, M. Sarkar, and R. Echambadi, "The conditioning effect of time on firm survival: An industry life cycle approach," *Academy of Management Journal* 25 (2002), pp. 971–985.

[11] Janice Beyer, Danta P. Ashmos, and R. N. Osborn, "Contrasts in Enacting TQM: Mechanistic vs. Organic Ideology and Implementation," *Journal of Quality Management* 1 (1997), pp. 13–29; and for an early treatment, see Paul R. Lawrence and Jay W. Lorsch, *Organization and Environment* (Homewood, IL: Irwin, 1969).

[12] Kate Klonick, "Pepsi's CEO a Refreshing Change" (August 15, 2006): www.abcnews. go.com; Diane Brady, "Indra Nooyi: Keeping Cool in Hot Water," *BusinessWeek* (June 11, 2007), special report; Indra Nooyi, "The Best Advice I Ever Got," *CNNMoney* (April 30, 2008), www. cnnmony.com; and, "Indra Nooyi," *The Wall Street Journal* (November 10, 2008), p. R3.

[13] Osborn, Hunt, and Jauch (1985).

[14] For reviews, see Scott and Davis (2007); Osborn, Hunt, and Jauch (1985); Clegg, Hardy, and Nord (1996).

[15] See www.nucor.com.

[16] For instance, J. Gao, R. Kishore, K. Nam, H. R. Rao, and H. Song, "An Investigation of the Factors that Influence the Duration of IT Outsourcing Relationships," *Decision Support Systems* 42.4 (2007), pp. 21–37; J. E. M. McGee, M. J. Dowling, and W. L. Megginson, "Cooperative Strategy and New Venture Performance: The Role of Business Strategy and Management Experience," *Strategic Management Journal* 16 (1995), pp. 565–580; and James B. Quinn, *Intelligent Enterprise: A Knowledge and Service Based Paradigm for Industry* (New York: Free Press, 1992).

[17] F. T. Rothaemel, M. A. Hitt, and L. A. Jobe, "Balancing Vertical Integration and Strategic Outsourcing: Effects on Product Portfolio, Product Success, and Firm Performance*,*"

Strategic Management Journal 27.11 (2006), pp. 1033–1049. Also see L. F. Cranor and S. Greenstein (eds.), *Communications Policy and Information Technology: Promises, Problems and Prospects* (Cambridge, MA: MIT Press, 2002); P. Candace Deans, *Global Information Systems and Technology: Focus on the Organization and Its Functional Areas* (Harrisburg, PA: Ideal Group Publishing, 1994); and Osborn, Hunt, and Jauch (1985).

[18] Haim Levy and Deborah Gunthorpe, *Introduction to Investments,* 2nd ed. (Cincinatti, OH: South-Western, 1999); and L. F. Cranor and S Greenstein (eds.), *Communications Policy and Information Technology: Promises, Problems and Prospects* (Cambridge, MA: MIT Press, 2002).

[19] William G. Ouchi and M. A. McGuire, "Organization Control: Two Functions," *Administrative Science Quarterly* 20 (1977), pp. 559–569.

[20] This discussion is adapted from W. Edwards Deming, "Improvement of Quality and Productivity Through Action by Management," *Productivity Review* (Winter 1982): pp. 12–22; Edwards Deming, *Quality, Productivity and Competitive Position* (Cambridge, MA: MIT Center for Advanced Engineering, 1982).

[21] For related reviews, see Scott and Davis (2007); Osborn, Hunt, and Jauch (1985); Clegg, Hardy, and Nord (1996).

[22] Rhys Andrews, George A. Boyne, Jennifer Law, and Richard M Walker, "Centralization, Organization Strategy, and Public Service Performance," *Journal of Public Administration Research and Theory* 19.1 (2009), pp. 57–81.

[23] See C. Bradley, "Succeeding by (Organizational) Design," *Decision: Irelands Business Review* 11.1 (2006), pp. 24–29; Osborn, Hunt, and Jauch (1985), pp. 273–303, for a discussion of centralization/decentralization.

[24] Rhys et al. (2009).

[25] For reviews of structural tendencies and their influence on outcomes, also see Scott and Davis (2007); Clegg, Hardy, and Nord (1996).

[26] Ibid.

[27] For a good discussion of the early use of matrix structures, see Stanley Davis, Paul Lawrence, Harvey Kolodny, and Michael Beer, *Matrix* (Reading, MA: Addison-Wesley, 1977).

[28] www.NBBJ.com.

[29] See P. R. Lawrence and J. W. Lorsch, *Organization and Environment: Managing Differentiation and Integration* (Homewood, IL: Richard D. Irwin, 1967).

[30] See Osborn, Hunt, and Jauch (1985); Scott and Davis (2007).

[31] Chris P. Long, Corinee Bendersky, and Calvin Morrill, "Fair Control: Complementarities Between Types of Managerial Controls and Employees' Fairness Evaluations," *2008 Academy of Management Proceedings* (2008), pp. 362–368.

[32] Max Weber, *The Theory of Social and Economic Organization,* translated by A. M. Henderson and H. T. Parsons (New York: Free Press, 1947).

[33] Stephen Cummings and Todd Bridgman, "The Strawman: The Reconfiguration of Max Weber in Management Textbooks and Why it Matters," *2008 Academy of Management Proceedings* (2008), pp. 243–249.

[34] Ibid.

[35] These relationships were initially outlined by Tom Burns and G. M. Stalker, *The Management of Innovation* (London: Tavistock, 1961).

[36] See Henry Mintzberg, *Structure in Fives: Designing Effective Organizations* (Englewood Cliffs, NJ: Prentice-Hall, 1983).

[37] Ibid.

[38] Ibid.

[39] See Osborn, Hunt, and Jauch (1984) for an extended discussion.

[40] See Peter Clark and Ken Starkey, *Organization Transitions and Innovation—Design* (London: Pinter Publications, 1988).

FEATURE NOTES

Opener/Ryanair: www.nytimes.com/2009/08/01/world/europe/01oleary.html

Mastering Management: www.lobar.com.

Leaders on Leadership—Information from Kate Klonick, "Pepsi's CEO a Refreshing Change" (August 15, 2006): www.abcnews.go.com; Diane Brady, "Indra Nooyi: Keeping Cool in Hot Water," *BusinessWeek* (June 11, 2007), special report; Indra Nooyi, "The Best Advice I Ever Got," CNNMoney (April 30, 2008), www.cnnmony.com; and, "Indra Nooyi," *The Wall Street Journal* (November 10, 2008), p. R3.

Ethics in OB: Anne L. Davis and Hannah R. Rothstein, "The effects of the perceived behavioral integrity of managers on employee attitudes: A meta analysis," *Journal of Business Ethic* 67.4 (2006), pp. 407–426.

Research Insight in OB: Beth A. Bechky, "Gaffers, gofers, and grips: Role-based coordination in temporary organizations," *Organization Science* 17.1 (2006), pp. 3–23.

Jerry Brewer, "Storm Begin Life of Independence," *Seattle Times,* 2009 May 20, p. C3. Greg Bishop, "Karen Bryant is Building a Foundation for the Storm," Seattle Times (2004) July 29 pC1. www.wnba.com/storm/ news/bry and Allison Espiritu, "Seattle Storm Ownership Group Awarded Business of the Year," Ballard New-Tribune (2009) March 26, p. B1.

MARGIN PHOTOS

HopeLab—Information from "HopeLab Video Games for Health," Fast Company (December, 2008/January, 2009), p. 116; and www.hopelab.org.

Bear Workshop—Information from "Build-A-Bear Workshop, Inc., Funding Universe: www.fundinguniverse.com/company-histories/BuildABear-Workshop-Inc (accessed March 9, 2009); and, www.buildabear.com. See also Maxine Clark and Amy Joyner, The Bear Necessities of Business: Building a Company with Heart (Hoboken, NJ: John Wiley & Sons, 2007).

ATA Engineering—Information from "Top Small Workplaces 2008," *The Wall Street Journal* (October 13, 2008), p. R4.

Shiseido—www.shiseido.com/2008annual report.

Land O' Lakes—www.landolakes.com.

Chapter 17

ENDNOTES

[1] www.hubpages.com/Apple_and_Nintendo_Innovation; www.nintendo.com

[2] This view of strategy was drawn from several sources, including David Simon, Michael Hitt, and Duane Ireland, "Managing Firm Resources in Dynamic Environments to Create Value: Looking Inside the Black Box," *Academy of Management Review* 32 (2007), pp. 273–292; Alfred D. Chandler, *The Visible Hand: The Managerial Revolution in America* (Cambridge, MA: Belnap, 1977); Michael E. Porter, *Competitive Strategy* (New York: Free Press, 1980); L. R. Jauch and R. N. Osborn, "Toward an Integrated Theory of Strategy," *Academy of Management Review* 6 (1981), pp. 491–498; B. Wernefelt, "A Resource-based View of the Firm," *Strategic Management Journal* 5 (1984), pp. 171–180; J. B. Barney, "Firm Resources and Sustained Competitive Advantage," *J. Management* 17 (1991), pp. 99–120; Russ Marion, *The Edge of Organization: Chaos and Complexity Theories of Formal Social Systems* (London, Sage, 1999); Arie Lewin, Chris Long, and Timothy Caroll, "The Coevolution of New Organizational Forms," *Organization Science* 10 (1999), pp. 535–550; Michael A. Hitt, R. Duane Ireland, and Robert E. Hoskisson, *Strategic Management: Competition and Globalization* (Cincinnati, OH: Southwestern, 2001).

[3] G. Huber, "Organizational Learning: The Contributing Process and the Literature," *Organization Science* 2.1 (1991), pp. 88–115.

[4] J. W. Myer and B. Rowan, "Institutionalized Organizations: Formal Structure as Myth and Ceremony," *American Journal of Sociology* 83 (1977), pp. 340–363.

[5] M. Mumford, "The Leadership Quarterly Special Issue on Leading Innovation," *Leadership Quarterly* 14 (2003), pp. 385–387; and M. Mumford, G. Scott, B. Gaddis, B. Strange, and J. Strange, "Leading Creative People: Orchestrating Expertise and Relationships," *Leadership Quarterly* 13 (2002), pp. 705–750.

[6] See Bjame Espedal, "Do Organization Routines Change as Experience Changes," *The Journal of Applied Behavior Science* 42.4 (2006), pp. 468–491.

[7] See Raji Srinivasan, Pamela Haunschild, and Rajdeep Grewal, "Vicarious Learning in Product Development

Introductions in the Early Years of a Converging Market," *Management Science* 53.1 (2007), pp. 16–29.

[8] James G. March, *Decisions and Organizations* (Oxford: Basil Blackwell, 1988).

[9] For an illustration with dire consequences, see R. N. Osborn and D. H. Jackson, "Leaders, Riverboat Gamblers, or Purposeful Unintended Consequences in the Management of Complex Technologies," *Academy of Management Journal* 31 (1988), pp. 924–947.

[10] O. P. Walsch and G. R. Ungson, "Organization Memory," *Academy of Management Review* 16.1 (1991), pp. 57–91.

[11] Jansen, Van Bosh, and Volberda (2006).

[12] Simon, Hitt, and Ireland (2007).

[13] This discussion of organizational design was initially based on R. N. Osborn, J. G. Hunt, and L. Jauch, *Organization Theory Integrated Text and Cases* (Melbourne, FL: Krieger, 1984), pp. 123–215. For a more advanced treatment, see W. Richard Scott and Gerald F. Davis, *Organizations and Organizing: Rational and Open Systems* (Englewood Cliffs, NJ: Prentice-Hall, 2007).

[14] http://domino.research.ibm.com/comm/research_people. nsf/pages/nabe.index.html.

[15] Simon, Hitt, and Ireland (2007); Marion (1999); Jauch and Osborn (1981).

[16] Porter (1980).

[17] For example, Simon, Hitt, and Ireland (2007).

[18] Jeffery Pfeffer, "Producing Sustainable Competitive Advantage Through the Effective Management of People," *Academy of Management Executive* 19.4 (2005), pp. 85–115.

[19] Marion (1999).

[20] Samuel J. Palmisano, "The New CIO: Setting the Innovation Agenda," speech for the first IBM CIO Leadership Forum, Monte Carlo, www.IBM.com.

[21] See Henry Mintzberg, *Structure in Fives: Designing Effective Organizations* (Englewood Cliffs, NJ: Prentice-Hall, 1983).

[22] www.g24i.com. Carla Power, "Green Contrarian," *Fortune Small Business* 19.1 (2009), p. 76.

[23] This inertia may be due to both fixed routines and resources; Gilbert Clark, "Unbundling the Structure of Inertia: Resource Versus Routine Rigidity," *Academy of Management Journal* 48.6 (2005), pp. 741–763.

[24] See R. Lord and M. Kernan, "Scripts as Determinants of Purposeful Behavior in Organizations," *Academy of Management Review* 12 (1987), pp. 265–278; A. L. Stinchcombe, *Economic Sociology* (New York: Academic Press, 1983).

[25] This treatment of the boundaryless organization is based on R. Ashkenas, D. Ulrich, T. Jick, and S. Kerr, *The Boundaryless Organization: Breaking the Chains of Organizational Structure* (San Francisco, CA: Jossey-Bass, 1995). For earlier discussion, also see R. Golembiewski, *Men, Management and Morality* (New Brunswick, NJ: Transaction, 1989). For a critical review, see R. Golembiewski, "The Boundaryless Organization: Breaking the Chains of Organizational Structure, A Review," *International Journal of Organizational Analysis* 6 (1998), pp. 267–270.

[26] S. Kerr and D. Ulrich, "Creating the Boundaryless Organization: The Radical Reconstruction of Organization Capabilities," *Planning Review* 23 (1995), pp. 41–46.

[27] See Scott and Davis (2007); David A. Nadler and Michael L. Tushman, *Competing by Design: The Power of Organizational Architecture* (New York: Oxford University Press, 1997); Jack Veiga and Kathleen Dechant, "Wired World Woes: www.help," *Academy of Management Executive* 11.3 (1997), pp. 73–79.

[28] A. A. Marcus, *Business and Society: Ethics Government and the World of Economy* (Homewood, IL: Richard D. Irwin, 1993).

[29] See Scott and Davis (2007); Osborn, Hunt, and Jauch (1984).

[30] Ibid.

[31] See Peter M. Blau and Richard A. Schoenner, *The Structure of Organizations* (New York: Basic Books, 1971); Joan Woodward, *Industrial Organization: Theory and Practice* (London: Oxford University Press, 1965).

[32] Gerardine DeSanctis, "Information Technology," in Nigel Nicholson (ed.), *Blackwell Encyclopedic Dictionary of Organizational Behavior* (Cambridge, MA: Blackwell Publishers Ltd., 1995), pp. 232–233.

[33] James D. Thompson, *Organization in Action* (New York: McGraw-Hill, 1967).

[34] Woodward (1965).

[35] For an updated review, see Scott and Davis (2007). This discussion also incorporates Osborn, Hunt, and Jauch (1984); and Louis Fry, "Technology-Structure Research: Three Critical Issues," *Academy of Management Journal* 25 (1982), pp. 532–552.

[36] Mintzberg (1983).

[37] See Henry Mintzberg and Alexandra McHugh, "Strategy Formulation in an Adhocracy," *Administrative Science Quarterly* 30.2 (1985), pp. 160–193.

[38] Halit Keskis, Ali E. Akgun, Ayse Gunsel, and Salih Imamoglu, "The Relationship Between Adhocracy and Clan Cultures and Tacit Oriented KM Strategy," *Journal of Transnational Management* 10.3 (2005), pp. 39–51.

[39] DeSanctis (1995).

[40] Prashant C. Palvia, Shailendra C. Palvia, and Edward M. Roche, *Global Information Technology and Systems Management: Key Issues and Trends* (Nashua, NH: Ivy League Publishing, 1996).

[41] DeSanctis (1995).

[42] Osborn, Hunt, and Jauch (1984).

[43] Jaana Woiceshyn, "The Role of Management in the Adoption of Technology: A Longitudinal Investigation," *Technology Studies* 4.1 (1997), pp. 62–99; Melissa A. Schilling, "Technological Lockout: An Integrative Model of the Economic and Strategic Factors Driving Technological Success and Failure," *Academy of Management Review* 23.2 (1998), pp. 267–284.

[44] David Lei, Michael Hitt, and Richard A. Bettis, "Dynamic Capabilities and Strategic Management," *Journal of Management* 22 (1996), pp. 547–567.

[45] www.moen.com.

[46] Veiga and Dechant (1997).

[47] Michael A. Hitt, R. Duane Ireland, and Robert E. Hoskisson, *Strategic Management: Competitiveness and Globalization* (Cincinnati, OH: South-Western College Publishing, 2007).

[48] www.amazon.com.

[49] While this form is known under a variety of names, we emphasize the information technology base that makes it possible. See Peter Senge, Benyamin B. Lichtenstein, Katrin Kaeufer, Hilary Bradbury, and John S. Carol, " Collaborating for Systematic Change," *MIT Sloan Management Review* 48.2 (2007), pp. 44–59; Josh Hyatt, "The Soul of a New Team," *Fortune* 153.11 (2006), pp. 134–145; M. L. Markus, B. Manville, and C. E. Agres, "What Makes a Virtual Organization Work," *MIT Sloan Management Review* 42 (2002), pp. 13–27; B. Hedberg, G. Hahlgren, J. Hansson, and N. Olve, *Virtual Organizations and Beyond* (New York: John Wiley and Sons, 2001); and Janice Beyer, Danti P. Ashmos, and R. N. Osborn, "Contrasts in Enacting TQM: Mechanistic vs Organic Ideology and Implementation," *Journal of Quality Management* 1 (1997), pp. 13–29.

[50] M. L. Markus, B. Manville, and C. E. Agres, "What Makes a Virtual Organization Work," *MIT Sloan Management Review* 42 (2002), pp. 13–27.

[51] Ibid.

[52] This section is based on R. N. Osborn, "The Evolution of Strategic Alliances in High Technology," working paper, Detroit: Department of Business, Wayne State University (2007); R. N. Osborn and J. G. Hunt, "The Environment and Organization Effectiveness," *Administrative Science Quarterly* 19 (1974), pp. 231–246; and Osborn, Hunt, and Jauch (1984). For a more extended discussion, see P. Kenis and D. Knoke, "How Organizational Field Networks Shape Interorganizational Tieformation Rates," *Academy of Management Journal* 27 (2002), pp. 275–294.

[53] Michael Skapinker, "Why Corporate Responsibility is a Survivor," *Financial Times* (April 21, 2009), p. 11.

[54] See R. N. Osborn and C. C. Baughn, "New Patterns in the Formation of U.S. Japanese Cooperative Ventures," *Columbia Journal of World Business* 22 (1988), pp. 57–65.

[55] This section is based on R. N. Osborn, "International Alliances: Going Beyond the Hype," *Mt Eliza Business Review* 6 (2003), pp. 37–44; S. Reddy, J. F. Hennart, and R. Osborn, "The Prevalence of Equity and Non-equity Cross-boarder Linkages: Japanese Investments in the U.S.," *Organization Studies* 23 (2002), pp. 759–780.

[56] Wepin Tsai, "Knowledge Transfer in Interorganizational Networks: Effects of Network Position and Absorptive Capacity on Business Unit Innovation and Performance," *Academy of Management Journal* 44.5 (2001), pp. 996–1004.

[57] Osborn (2007).

[58] Osborn (2003).

[59] Osborn (2007).

[60] Thomas Keil, Markku Maula, Henri Schildt, and Shaker Zahra, "The Effect of Governance Modes and Relatedness of External Business Development Activities on Innovative Performance," *Strategic Management Journal* 29 (2008), pp. 895–907.

FEATURE NOTES

Opener/Nintendo: www.hubpages.com/Apple_and_Nintendo_Innovation; www.nintendo.com

Leaders on Leadership: www.g24i.com. Carla Power, "Green Contrarian," Fortune Small Business. (2009) VI.19 #1 p. 76.

Ethics in OB: www.millenniumchem.com/.

Mastering Management: M. L. Markus, B. Manville, and C. E. Agres, "What Makes a Virtual Organization Work." *MIT Sloan Management Review* 42 (2002), pp. 13–27.

Research Insight: Thomas Keil, Markku Maula, Henri Schildt, and Shaker Zahra, "The effect of Governance Modes and Relatedness of External Business Development Activities on Innovative Performance," *Strategic Management Journal* 29 (2008). pp. 895–907.

MARGIN PHOTOS

Innocent—Information from Aaron O. Patrick and Valerie Bauerlein, "Coke Teams Up with Socially Responsible Smoothie," *The Wall Street Journal* (April 8, 2009), p. B6.

IBM's Watson Research Center—http://domino.research.ibm.com/comm/research_people.nsf/pages/nabe.index.html.

Fab India—Information from Manjeet Kripalani, "Weaving a New Kind of Company," *BusinessWeek* (March 23 & 30, 2009), pp. 64–65.

Fairtrade—http://www.tradingvisions.org/. Michael Skapinker, "Why Corporate Responsibility is a Survivor," *Financial Times* (2009), April 21, p. 11.

Jim Collins—Information from Jim Collins, "How the Mighty fall," *BusinessWeek* (May 25, 2009), pp. 26–38. See also Jim Collins, *How the Mighty Fall: And Why Some Companies Never Give In* (New York: HarperCollins, 2009).

Corning—www.corning.com.

M. L. Markus, B. Manville, and C. E. Agres, "What Makes a Virtual Organization Work," *MIT Sloan Management Review* 42 (2002), pp. 13–27.

Photo Credits

Chapter 9

Page 208: Mario Tama/Getty Images, Inc. **Page 212:** Courtesy Ford Motor Company. **Page 214:** Peter DaSilva/The New York Times/Redux Pictures. **Page 215:** Jacob Wackerhauser/iStockphoto. **Page 217:** Tim Boyle/Getty Images, Inc. **Page 225:** Peter DaSilva/Redux Pictures.

Chapter 10

Page 231: STAN HONDA/AFP/Getty Images, Inc. **Page 233:** Comstock Images/Getty Images, Inc. **Page 236:** Jessica Peterson/Getty Images, Inc. **Page 239:** iStockphoto. **Page 243:** CHIP EAST/ Reuters/Landov LLC. **Page 244:** Francois Henry/ REA/Redux Pictures.

Chapter 11

Page 255: Courtesy of IDEO. **Page 256:** NewsCom. **Page 258:** iStockphoto. **Page 263:** arabianEye/Getty Images, Inc. **Page 270:** Golden Pixels/Alamy.

Chapter 12

Page 277: Photographed by Lane Hartwell (http:// fetching.net/) on behalf of the Wikimedia Foundation. **Page 280:** Key Wilde/Getty Images, Inc. **Page 284:** REUTERS/Molly Riley/Landov LLC. **Page 289:** Photodisc Green/Getty. **Page 291:** Photo by Bill Whittacker from Wikipedia. **Page 292:** INDRANIL MUKHERJEE/AFP/Getty Images, Inc. **Page 296 (top):** CHUCK CROW/The Plain Dealer /Landov LLC. **Page 296 (bottom):** Eric Francis/©AP/Wide World Photos.

Chapter 13

Page 306: Marty Lederhandler/©AP/Wide World Photos. **Page 308:** Chris Carlson/©AP/Wide World Photos. **Page 312:** Alex Brandon/©AP/Wide World Photos. **Page 325:** Photo by Bernard Photography. Courtesy Lynn C. Willenbring, City of Minneapolis.

Chapter 14

Page 335: Kevork Djansezian/©AP/Wide World Photos. **Page 336:** Michael L. Abramson/Time Life Pictures/Getty Images, Inc. **Page 343:** Thinkstock/ Getty Images, Inc. **Page 344:** iStockphoto. **Page 347:** Rajesh Jantilal/AFP/Getty Images, Inc. **Page 350:** NewsCom. **Page 353:** Rogelio Solis/©AP/Wide World Photos.

Chapter 15

Page 365: Dima Gavrysh/©AP/Wide World Photos. **Page 368:** Bob Child/©AP/Wide World Photos. **Page 370:** Courtesy Flowserve. **Page 372:** Dan Levine/AFP/Getty Images, Inc. **Page 373:** Thomas Barwick/Getty Images, Inc. **Page 374:** Courtesy Lam Research Corporation. **Page 382:** Courtesy of Cousins Submarines, Inc.

Chapter 16

Page 390: Photo by Eric Millette, courtesy HopeLab, www.hopelab.org. **Page 394:** Thibault Camus/ ©AP/Wide World Photos. **Page 396:** NewsCom. **Page 398:** David Sherman/NBAE/Getty Images, Inc. **Page 400:** Al Behrman/©AP/Wide World Photos. **Page 406 (top):** Photo courtesy of ATA Engineering, Inc., www.ata-e.com. **Page 406 (bottom):** TORU YAMANAKA/AFP/Getty Images, Inc.

Chapter 17

Page 420: Photo courtesy Naoki Abe, IBM Corporation. **Page 421:** India Today Group/ Getty Images, Inc. **Page 423:** Richard Harbus/ The New York Times/Redux Pictures. **Page 425:** Edmond Terakopian/©AP/Wide World Photos. **Page 431:** Kyodo/Landov LLC. **Page 432:** Carrie Devorah/WENN/NewsCom. **Page 434:** Courtesy Corning, Inc.

Organizations Index

Name Index

Subject Index